INTERPRE[TING]

MOZAR[T]

Frontispiece Unfinished oil of W. A. Mozart by his brother-in-law Joseph Lange Ca. 1782/3 (and 1789?). (Mozarteum Salzburg).

INTERPRETING MOZART

The Performance of His Piano Pieces and Other Compositions

SECOND EDITION

EVA & PAUL BADURA-SKODA

Routledge
Taylor & Francis Group
New York   London

Routledge
Taylor & Francis Group
711 Third Avenue New
York, NY 10017

Routledge
Taylor & Francis Group
2 Park Square
Milton Park, Abingdon
Oxon OX14 4RN

© 2008 by Taylor & Francis Group, LLC
Routledge is an imprint of Taylor & Francis Group, an Informa business

International Standard Book Number-13: 978-0-415-97750-0 (Hardcover)

Library of Congress Cataloging-in-Publication Data

Badura-Skoda, Eva.
     [Mozart-Interpretation. English]
     Interpreting Mozart : the performance of his piano pieces and other compositions / Eva and Paul Badura-Skoda. -- 2nd ed.
          p. cm.
          Includes bibliographical references (p.) and index.
     ISBN 978-0-415-97750-0
     1. Mozart, Wolfgang Amadeus, 1756-1791. Instrumental music. 2. Piano music--Interpretation (Phrasing, dynamics, etc.) 3. Performance practice (Music)--History--18th century. I. Badura-Skoda, Paul. II. Title.

ML410.M9B1413 2008
786.2092--dc22   2007015171

Visit the Taylor & Francis Web site at
http://www.taylorandfrancis.com

and the Routledge Web site at
http://www.routledge.com

Contents

Preface to the First Edition ix

Preface to the Second Edition xi

List of Abbreviations xiii

List of Illustrations xv

Key to Music Sources, Editions, Documents,
   and Most Frequently Mentioned Treatises xvii

Introduction 1

1 Mozart's World of Sound **7**
Keyboard Instruments of Mozart's Time 7
Mozart's Training on All Kinds of Keyboard Instruments . 10
The Sound of Mozart's Own Fortepiano by Anton Walter .. 19
Knee Levers for Lifting the Dampers on Mozart's Pianos . 22
Necessary Use of the Damper-Lifting Device or Pedal ... 24
Mozart's Fortepiano Pedal Instrument 33
The Range of Mozart's Fortepiano 35
A Word about Piano Mechanics 40

2 Dynamics **43**
Basic Dynamic Signs Customary during the Eighteenth Century . 43
Dynamic Signs in Mozart's Piano Works 45
The Indications *Sotto Voce* and *Dolce* 48
Static and Dynamic Markings 50
Crescendo and *Decrescendo* 51
Mozart's Accent Signs 53
Supplementing Incomplete or Missing Dynamics 60
The Echo Syndrome 65

3 Problems of Tempo and Rhythm **71**
Tempo Problems 71
A List of the Most Important Tempo Markings 77
Alla breve Time 82
Playing "In Time" 84
Agogics 85
Rubato 88

Some Peculiarities of Rhythmic Notation	93
Tripletization	97
Hemiolas	98

4 Articulation — **103**

Legato	105
Legato Slurs and *Articulation Slurs*	107
Mixed Articulation	121
Portato	123
Staccato	123
Unmarked Passages	129

5 Ornaments — **135**

Appoggiaturas	138
Arpeggios	174
Turns	176
Trills	188
Endings of Trills	203
The Half-Shake *(Pralltriller)*	205

6 Improvised Embellishments — **213**

The Old Rules for Placing Embellishments	215
Necessary Additions of Notes	216
Embellishment Models by Mozart	227
When Additions Are a Matter of Taste	233
When Additions Are Definitely Out of Style	243

7 Cadenzas and Lead-Ins *(Eingänge)* — **251**

Are Cadenzas Improvisations or Premeditated Compositions?	252
Structural Differences between Cadenzas and Free Improvisations	253
Composing Cadenzas for Mozart's Concertos	254
Lead-ins and Other Fermata Embellishments	275
Proper Places for Fermata Embellishments	279
Where Fermata Embellishments Are Questionable and Where No Lead-ins Should Be Played	284
The Various Meanings of Fermata Signs	285

8 "Expression and Gusto" — **289**

Expression with the Help of Dynamic Shadings	292
Expression with the Help of Articulation	295
Expressive Rhythmic Shadings	300
Harmonic Expression	301
Proper Accompaniment Helps Expression	303
Expression of Comic or Tragic Moods	307
Keep Smiling!	313
Are Repeats Compulsory?	315

9 In Search of the Best Text   **319**
The *Neue Mozart Ausgabe* (*NMA*)   320
Other Recommendable Editions   322
Text Problems in Piano Sonatas   322
Text Problems in Piano Concertos   328
What Comes after the *Neue Mozart Ausgabe*?   337
A Recent New Edition of the Piano Concerto in E-flat Major,
    K. 271 (Breitkopf & Härtel N° 5300)   338
About Page Turning   342

10 Playing with Orchestra   **343**
How Pianists Should Study Piano Concertos   343
Orchestra Sizes and Ripieno Parts   350
Continuo Playing   352
Playing the Final Chords of a Concerto Movement Together
    with the Orchestra   367

11 Some Technical Questions in the Piano Works   **369**
Finger Action   370
Scales and Arpeggios   373
Trills   375
Octaves   375
Technical Problems of the Use of the Damper-Lifting
    Pedal (Knee Lever)   378

12 Remarks on the Interpretation of Selected Piano Works   **383**
Concerto in D Minor, K. 466   384
Concerto in A Major, K. 488   396
Concerto in C Minor, K. 491   406
Piano Sonata in A Minor, K. 310   432
Sonata in A Major, K. 331   441

Appendix 1: Mozart's Reported Tempo for Pamina's G-minor Aria   449

Appendix 2: A List of the Best Presently Available Editions
  of Mozart's Piano Music   451

Appendix 3: An Example for *basso continuo* Realisation (K. 449/I)   453

Selected Bibliography   455

Subject Index   463

Index of Works Cited   471

Preface to the First Edition

This book has been written after long, affectionate study of Mozart. The discoveries and insights granted us during this study daily increased not only our love for his music but also our admiration for this unique man and artist. We now find it hard to realize that some people, not only music lovers, but also professional musicians, see nothing in Mozart's music. Simple and uncomplicated as it seems to the layman, every musician realizes its underlying complexity, its balance of content and form, so hard to recreate; truly, to play Mozart is the acid test of musical taste.

As everybody realizes, good Bach playing needs stylistic awareness—acquaintance with the style of the time and of the composer—and this is just as true of Mozart. Without a knowledge of Mozart's style, such as the present book aims at providing, one cannot fill out the sketchy passages in many of his compositions in roughly the way he might have done himself; nor can one produce stylistically accurate cadenzas for his concertos, amplify his sparing dynamic markings, play his ornaments correctly, and so on. (Incidentally, if our musical examples differ from the texts of the best-known printed editions, this is because wherever possible we have quoted from Mozart's manuscripts or from the next most reliable source.)

Naturally, there are certain limits to any knowledge of Mozart's style. So in treating various problems, some purely personal views are bound to be expressed. Nor have we even tried to make all our conclusions wholly acceptable—rather, our main aim has been to bring to light problems of Mozart interpretation and to help solve them.

Although we have often chosen the piano works as a starting point, this book is by no means directed merely to pianists. We have also examined many compositions for other instruments, and violinists, singers, and conductors will find here much that concerns them.

We are glad for this opportunity to sincerely thank our revered teachers, the late pianist, Dr. h. c. Edwin Fischer, Professor Dr. Wilhelm Fischer, and Professor Viola Thern, for everything they taught us. It is also our pleasant duty to thank very warmly all those who helped us in our work on the German edition, above all Professor Dr. Alfred Orel, Professor Dr. Hellmut Federhofer, Dr. Oswald Jonas, and the conductor George Szell. We are also indebted for assistance to the directors and staff of various libraries: New York Public Library, Music Department (Dr. J. Braunstein); German National Library, Berlin (Dr. Virneisl); the West German Library, Marburg/L. (Director Cremer); the University Library of Tübingen (Dr. von Reibnitz); the Library of the Gesellschaft der Musikfreunde, Vienna (Dr. Hedwig Kraus); and the Music Department of the Austrian National Library in Vienna (Professor Dr. L. Nowak). As for the translation into English, we should like to express our thanks to publisher and translator for their kind cooperation; to H. C. Robbins Landon, Paul Hamburger, and Fritz Spiegel for their help and good advice; and to Emily Anderson for the kind permission to use her translation of Mozart's letters. We also wish to thank those publishers referred to in the translator's note. We are much obliged to Alfred Brendel, Maurits Sillem, Christa Landon, and Renée LaRoche for helping us with reading and correcting the proofs.

We would like to thank the following publishers for the use of quotations from books published by them:

Cassell & Co. for *C. P. E. Bach: Essay on the True Art of Playing Keyboard Instruments* (1949), translated by W. J. Mitchell.

Oxford University Press for *Leopold Mozart: Treatise on the Fundamental Principles of Violin Playing* (1948), translated by Editha Knocker.

T. Schirmer & Co. for *Busoni: Sketch of a New Aesthetic of Music* (1911), translated by T. Baker.

Preface to the Second Edition

Every genuine artist wants to preserve and keep alive sacred heritage. But every century tries in its own way to secularize what is sacred and to drive at profanation, to simplify the complexities and to turn earnestness into fun, against which one would not object if not every earnestness and fun would go awry in the process...[1]

Johann Wolfgang v. Goethe

One reason for us to think about revising and enlarging our book *Interpreting Mozart on the Keyboard* was the discovery of lost or missing Mozart autographs and of other hitherto unknown sources that had come to light in the last fifty years and were available for inspection, either in Krakow or elsewhere. The new complete edition *Neue Mozart Ausgabe (NMA)* edited by the **Zentralinstitut für Mozartforschung** of the **Mozarteum** in Salzburg/Austria (now **Akademie für Mozartforschung**) appeared in the meanwhile, and the members of the institute were a motor behind the intensive research needed for its publication. The increasing quantity of excellent books on Mozart as well as the articles that have appeared in the *Mozart Jahrbuch*, the *Mozarteums Mitteilungen*, and in other periodicals were often a result of new insights by the editors of the *NMA* and not only by knowledgeable Mozart scholars and period connoisseurs. Today we can profit from the wealth of many good books and articles on Mozart topics, often also dealing with performance questions. From these publications and from our own experience we gained additional insights. We saw with delight that various authors used our book as the basis for some of their discussions of performance problems. All this was a welcome inducement for further thoughts and insights. Many friendly debates with musicians and musicologists helped to convince us that an enlargement of the old book was most desirable. Besides, some questionable new concepts and trends in Mozart research were in need of commentaries. The possibility to discuss these opinions was an additional reason to start working on this enlarged second edition.

Another and probably the most important reason to consider a new enlarged and revised version of our Mozart book has to do with the technical development of electronic means during the last decades, which now easily allows an author–performer such as Paul Badura-Skoda, with the help of a CD enclosed in the cover of the book, to demonstrate the execution of ornaments, articulation problems, *rubato*, and subtleties of dynamics and suggestions for slight (!) tempo changes (agogics).

The revision of the chapter on instruments of Mozart's time was necessary insofar as in the meanwhile our old *desideratum* regarding the interpretation of Mozart's piano works on original fortepianos has been fulfilled: many fine replicas of grand pianos of Mozart's time are now available and are often used for private and public performances. Fifty years ago it was still an outstanding event if a pianist decided to give a recital on a period instrument (if he could find one properly restored—a rare possibility). In the meanwhile, many restorers and piano builders

---

[1] *[Jeder echte Künstler ist als einer anzusehen, der ein Heiliges bewahren und mit Ernst und Bedacht fortpflanzen will. Jedes Jahrhundert aber strebt nach seiner Art ins Saeculum und sucht das Heilige gemein, das Schwere leicht und das Ernste lustig zu machen; wogegen gar nichts zu sagen wäre, wenn darüber nicht Ernst und Spaß zugrunde gingen ...]*

have been at work to make valuable old instruments playable again and—more importantly—to construct good replicas. They are used by many fine artists not only in museums but also in concert halls. Malcolm Bilson was probably the first artist who started concertizing exclusively on period instruments and thus became an important pioneer as a so-called "fortepianist." A large group of younger pianists, many of them his students, followed in his footsteps, and many CDs appeared with Mozart's sonatas and concertos played on original or replica instruments of Mozart's time. More music schools all over the world acquire replica fortepianos, which help young musicians to learn and understand better what it means to play in Mozart's style, not only on period instruments but also on modern pianos. Fine Urtext editions are available, and many old bad editions of Mozart's music with their often corrupted and altered articulation signs disappeared from the market and are far less often used by young pianists. All these fortunate developments required an updating of our old book.

When preparing this new enlarged edition we suddenly realized that it had become partly a new book. Therefore, we decided to give it a slightly different title.

During the preparation of this new text we were greatly helped with numerous most valuable suggestions and critical commentaries by the excellent composer–pianist, Professor Dr. h. c. mult. Robert Levin, not only a profound connoisseur of Mozart's works and an all-around musician, pianist, and musicologist, but also a wonderful friend with a lot of wit and humor. We cannot thank him enough for the time and the effort he spent with our typescript in spite of his many concert engagements all over the world and his teaching duties at Harvard University. He managed to read nearly all the chapters and detected many omissions, errors, and printing mistakes. Another wonderful friend, Professor Malcolm Bilson, also helped us with his valuable commentaries. Even if we do not share all the opinions of these friends, notably in matters of improvised embellishments, the discussions with them were always inspiring and often resulted in finding additional arguments for our standpoints. Thanks are due also to the young pianist Albert Frantz for typesetting all the music examples, not a small task as everybody will notice, and for helping in computer and language matters. For the latter we are also very much indebted to Bruce Cooper Clarke, whose knowledge of Mozart research led to the discovery of some inaccuracies, mainly in the translations of Mozart's letters but also elsewhere.

Thanks are also due to our editor Constance Ditzel, to Denny Tek, and to Robert Sims of our publisher Routledge, a division of Taylor & Francis.

Eva and Paul Badura-Skoda

List of Abbreviations

AMA   *Alte Mozart Ausgabe* (old complete edition): *Wolfgang Amadeus Mozarts Werke. Kritisch durchgesehene Gesamtausgabe,* 67 volumes in 24 Serien, Leipzig 1876–1905 (Breitkopf & Härtel).

ca   Circa

Fg.   Bassoon (Fagott)

K.   Köchel-Catalogue: *Chronologisch-thematisches Verzeichnis sämmtlicher Tonwerke W.A.Mozarts,* Leipzig 1862. All numbers quoted are the original ones, used among musicians. No additional numbers according to the 3rd, 4th and 5th Edition of the Koechel Catalogue, prepared by Alfred Einstein, (Wiesbaden 1937–1947), are quoted in parenthesis, because in the meanwhile they are partly outdated and re-numbered. A new 7th edition of the Koechel Catalogue, this time edited by Neal Zaslaw, is in preparation.

Letters   *Mozart. Briefe und Aufzeichnungen* (Complete Edition), ed. and with commentary by W.A. Bauer und O.E. Deutsch im Auftrag der Internationalen Stiftung Mozarteum, 6 vols., Kassel 1962–2005 (Bärenreiter); with an index by J.H.Eibl, (= vol.7) and a supplement volume, ed. by Ulrich Konrad (= vol.8).
Letters of Mozart and his Family, Chronologically Arranged, translated and edited by Emily Anderson, 3 vols., London 1938.

LH, l.h.,   Left hand

mvt.   Movement

NMA   *Neue Mozart Ausgabe: W.A.Mozart. Neue Ausgabe sämtlicher Werke,* in *Verbindung mit den Mozart-Städten Augsburg, Salzburg und Wien herausgegeben von der Internationalen Stiftung Mozarteum,* Kassel 1955–2007.

Ob.   Oboe

p. pp.   page(s)

RH, r.h.   Right hand

Vla   Viola

Vln.   Violin

Identification of Pitch

In those cases where it seemed necessary to denote specific pitches, we did this according to the following European system:

FF   C   B   c   b   c¹   b¹   c²   b²   c³   f³

List of Illustrations

The cover portrait of Mozart is a reproduction of a painting by Joseph Grassi, preserved as part of a portrait collection kept until 1917 in a Ukrainian castle. It is now in the possession of the *Glinka Museum* in Moscow.

The painter Joseph Grassi (brother of the sculptor Anton Grassi who portrayed Joseph Haydn) and his wife were indeed friends of Wolfgang and Constanze Mozart and Joseph and Aloysia Lange, all of whom participated in the Pantomime K 446 (416d), a little carnival masque performance described by Mozart in his letter to his father of February 15, 1783. This may have been the year from which the painting (or at least a sketch for it) probably stems. The question of the dating and whether it was depicted on the basis of an earlier painting or drawing is presently still a matter of dispute among art experts, and even the question has been raised whether it is indeed a portrait of Mozart as indicated on the backside. The painting has been evaluated and discussed in a *Round Table Session* at a Mozart Congress in Salzburg (see *Bericht über den Internationalen Mozart-Kongress, Mozart-Jahrbuch 1991, vol. 2*, pp. 1067–1095). A claim for its authenticity as a Mozart portrait has been recently supported by new analysis methods by the art historian Elmar Worgull, who will present them in an article to appear in a forthcoming *Mozart-Jahrbuch*.

Frontispiece Unfinished oil painting of W.A. Mozart by his brother-in-law Joseph Lange, ca 1782/3 (and 1789?). (Mozarteum Salzburg). (See p. ii)

Figure 1.1 The Mozart Family portrait. Wolfgang and Nannerl play four-hands, apparently on Friderici's two-manual harpsichord, the R.H. (for melody parts) on the lower (invisible) keyboard, the L.H. on the upper manual. Oil painting by J. N. della Croce (?), ca 1780/81. (Mozarteum Salzburg). (See p. 13)

Figure 1.2 Mozart's fortepiano made by Anton Walter. (Mozarteum Salzburg). (See p. 20)

Figure 1.3 Wilhelm Rück's copy of Mozart's fortepiano made by Anton Walter and a reconstruction of Mozart's *fortepiano pedale* likewise by Walter (lost). The depicted pedal piano was built by Matthias Arens in 1990. (Collection Badura-Skoda). (See p. 34)

Key to Music Sources, Editions, Documents, and Most Frequently Mentioned Treatises

Our study of Mozart's autographs and first editions was based on microfilms and photocopies from our personal archive as well as some few facsimile editions.

If not pointed out otherwise, our music examples follow the text of the NMA (= W.A.Mozart. Neue Ausgabe sämtlicher Werke, in Verbindung mit den Mozart-Städten Augsburg, Salzburg und Wien herausgegeben von der Internationalen Stiftung Mozarteum, Kassel 1955–2007).

Mozart's Works are identified by K. numbers

Köchel, L. Ritter von. *Chronologisch-thematisches Verzeichnis sämtlicher Tonwerke Wolfgang Amadeus Mozarts.* Third ed. Edited by Alfred Einstein, with a supplement. *Berichtigungen und Zusätze* [Addenda and Corrigenda], by Alfred Einstein. Ann Arbor, MI: 1947; abbreviation: K.

We used only the original Köchel numbers, best known to musicians, and we decided not to add the additional numbers of this Köchel-Einstein edition, because of the fact that many of these additional numbers are outdated by now and have to be revised.

Mozart's letters are often quoted after

Anderson, Emily, ed. and trans. *The Letters of Mozart and His Family,* Third ed. London: Macmillan, 1985.

Some were translated by us after:

Bauer, W., Deutsch, O. E., and Eibl, J., eds., *Mozart: Briefe und Aufzeichnungen, Gesamtausgabe* (7 vols.). Kassel: Bärenreiter, 1962–75; vol. 8 (addenda) BVK 2005.

Documents are quoted after

Deutsch, Otto Erich. *Mozart: Die Dokumente seines Lebens.* Kassel: Bärenreiter, 1961; Translated by Eric Blom, Peter Branscombe, and Jeremy Noble under the title *Mozart: A Documentary Biography* (Stanford: 1965).

Eisen, Cliff. *New Mozart Documents: A Supplement to O. E. Deutsch's Documentary Biography.* London: Stanford University Press, 1991.

Most frequently used Eighteenth Century Treatises

Bach, C. P. E. *Versuch über die wahre Art das Clavier zu spielen.* Berlin: 1753 (first part); Berlin: 1762 (second part). Quotations in English are taken from the translation by William J. Mitchell, *Essay on the True Art of Playing Keyboard Instruments.* London: Cassell, 1949; abbreviated: *Essay . . .*

Mozart, Leopold. *Versuch einer gründlichen Violinschule. Augsburg*: 1756. Translated by Editha Knocker under the title *A Treatise on the Fundamental Principles of Violin Playing* (Oxford University Press, 1951); abbreviated: *Violinschule.*

Quantz, J. J. *Versuch einer Anweisung die flute traversière zu spielen.* Facsimile reprint of the third edition, 1789. Edited by Hans-Peter Schmitz, Kassel: Bärenreiter, 1953. Quotations in English are taken from the translation by Edward R. Reilly, *On Playing the Flute* (New York: Schirmer, 1966).

Türk, G. D. Fr. *Klavierschule.* Halle: 1789; second edition, Halle: 1802.

Introduction

The problem of musical interpretation must be as old as music itself. Put at its simplest, it is the problem of leaving the listener with the most powerful, direct, deep, and lasting impression possible. This is expressed in the classical legend of Orpheus, whose songs have such a miraculous effect, whose playing is so moving and enchanting that it overcomes the gods and even death itself. The ultimate goal of all musical activity is to make an impression on the soul of the listener. That is the goal, but the way to it is a long and uncertain one. There are indeed a few favorites of Fortune for whom at first everything seems automatically to go right; but in the long run they, too, find that art is the result of hard work and often of suffering—or even, quite often, of a process of destruction (illness, sin) that blights the soul and lays it bare. The essence of artistry lies in the power to create, to love, and the desperate need to communicate—the path is "infinite pains." The careers of these "favored" artists are no reflection on their degree of vocation. Nor can the essence of greatness, of creativity, be wholly communicated or passed on, and ultimate perfection in playing remains a secret reserved for the moment of performance.

But one thing is common to artists of all ages: they were not born as finished artists—their path was that of effort and endurance. Disappointment lies in store for anyone who thinks that all he has to do is to wait passively for the moment of enlightenment. Favored or not, he who wishes to achieve anything must seek to exploit his talents to the full and to increase his knowledge. This means that the musician, the interpreter, must come to grips with the essential problems of musical interpretation.

Of course, musicians have always been concerned with the basic questions of interpretation, and much has already been said and written on the subject. However, great interpreters have held contradictory views, and it often seems hard to reconcile various principles. Take, for instance, those laid down by two such authorities as C. P. E. Bach and Busoni. Bach said:

A musician cannot move others unless he, too, is moved: He must of necessity feel all of the effects that he hopes to arouse in his audience …[1]

whereas Busoni wrote:

If an artist is to move others, he must not be moved himself—otherwise he will lose control of his technique at the vital moment.[2]

It may sound a paradox, but the ideal interpretation should fulfill both these conditions. One plays with absolute conviction, yet somewhere inside there is a controlling function that must remain unmoved; otherwise, one's feelings overflow the banks laid down by the intellect and the result is amateurish. The following quotation, also from Busoni's *Sketch of a New Aesthetic of Music*, shows incidentally that he was by no means hostile to feeling; his words were originally written in reply to the criticism that he played without feeling:

---

[1] C. P. E. Bach, *Essay* …, I, III, 13. Leopold Mozart writes to the same effect in his *Violinschule* (XII, §7): "Finally, in practising every care must be taken to find and to render the effect which the composer wished to have brought out; and as sadness often alternates with joy, each must be carefully depicted according to its kind. In a word, all must be so played that the player himself be moved thereby."

[2] Frederico Busoni, *Sketch of a New Aesthetic of Music*, p. 21.

Feeling, like honesty, is a moral necessity, a quality nobody may renounce ... even though in everyday life one can forgive lack of feeling if it is compensated by some more brilliant quality of character ... in art it [feeling] is the ultimate moral quality.[3]

Every musical phrase can be regarded as the symbol of a certain expressive content. The true artist is privileged not merely to recognize this content but to fix it so firmly in his consciousness that his intellectual and spiritual qualities are set free for other tasks. Thus, even when the artist knows that a phrase expresses sorrow, he cannot afford to feel miserable every time he plays the passage, particularly when practicing or rehearsing. The vital thing is that he knows what the phrase means—and what sorrow means; and that he is able to portray it without losing control of himself. Unless he can objectify the waves of feeling conjured up by the music—i.e., subordinate them to a higher level of consciousness—he will be incapable of the intellectual effort needed to mold a large-scale musical form as an organism; he will be too concerned with the succeeding emotions and will lose sight of the horizon. He must view the work as a whole if he is to fill every part of it with the appropriate expression of feeling and give the listener the impression of a coherent, harmonious whole.

The relationship between composer and interpreter is another problem that has been much discussed. Should the interpreter use a composer's work to express himself and his "emotions," or should he stand out of the way, hide behind the work, force his own personality into the background? The answer must depend not only on the temperament of particular interpreters but on the taste of the time. The Romantics demanded that the interpreter, too, should be allowed free scope for his imagination and for interpretation. Franz Liszt wrote in one of his letters:

The virtuoso is not a mason, chiseling his stone conscientiously according to the sketches of the architect. He is not a passive tool for reproducing feelings and thoughts, without adding anything of his own. He is not a more or less experienced "interpreter" of works which leave him no scope for his own comments. ... For the virtuoso, musical works are in fact nothing but tragic and moving materializations of his emotions; he is called upon to make them speak, weep, sing and sigh, to recreate them in accordance with his own consciousness. In this way he, like the composer, is a creator, for he must have within himself those passions that he wishes to bring so intensely to life. ...[4]

Many modern composers go to the opposite extreme in their views; they demand that the interpreter shall simply play the notes put before him, with no comments of his own, as impersonally as a soldier carries out the orders of his superior officer. Ravel is believed to have said, "I do not want to be interpreted!" and Stravinsky has made similar remarks. Ravel's words are obviously a protest against a too subjective, romantic interpretation of his works, against the fact that many performers take too little trouble to find out what the composer really wants and to express it. His deliberately wrong use of the word *interpretation* does not affect the basic idea.

Liszt's words are no surprise, coming from a romantic and, moreover, from an improviser of genius; his ideas reflect the interpretative style of an age that has finally passed away. But it must not be forgotten that now, as always, romantic works demand a freer, more personal interpretation than do the works of other periods. The interpreter of romantic music will always stand

---

[3] Ibid., p. 26. See also the ensuing pages.
[4] Josef Huneker, *Franz Liszt*, p. 303.

especially in need of improvisation, the magic of the moment, if he is to express the moods intended by the composer.

It is, however, harder to understand the views of the various modern composers who tend toward the opposite extreme. It is quite impossible to perform a piece of music impersonally, for even the coldest, most matter-of-fact musician interprets; i.e., he expounds, communicates, translates, whether or not he realizes that he is doing so. If a composer wished to ensure a slavishly impersonal performance of his work, he could never be content with merely writing his music down but would always have to simultaneously make a recording of his work, which the performer (for one could hardly go on calling him the interpreter) would simply have to imitate as best he could. But there is no need to emphasize that such soulless imitation would be the death of all musical performance.

On the other hand, once the performer is recognized as an interpreter, not an imitator, then a record of the composer's performance can naturally assist him very much, particularly as he is glad of any help in understanding what the composer is trying to say. Incidentally, composers' recorded performances of their works are the best proof that even those among them who stand out for objective performance can rarely remain at all objective or impersonal when they themselves perform. Above all, they can rarely play a work the same way twice. Quite the opposite; composers tend to play their own works not merely with more life, less constraint, and more naturally, but also often with more imagination than do the fanatical advocates of literal exactness.

All the same, most composers nowadays tend to undervalue the function of the interpreter and to allow him less freedom than is in fact his due. Since their own psychological worlds and processes of thought are naturally clear and obvious, they are often under the illusion that they have expressed their thoughts quite clearly in musical notation. But there is a great difference between a musical text's relation to actual music and the way the plan of a house is related to the finished building. Given a good plan, even an untalented but conscientious builder can erect a building that answers its purpose, whereas in performing a work even the most gifted interpreter can at times go so appallingly wrong that the composer's intentions are completely distorted. This is often the case in our concert halls and not only in performances of modern music. Even if two interpreters adhere as strictly as possible to the given markings, they will never reproduce the work in the same way, whereas it is a fact of daily experience that machines, council flats, etc., are as alike as two peas. Although musical notation is becoming constantly subtler, our way of notating acoustic processes with optical symbols must remain an imprecise transcription. The sequence of tension and relaxation and the wide scale of sensory values can never be exactly pinned down by graphic means. Printed music replaces a continuum by points, and only the intuition and skill of the interpreter can link these up and bring them to life.

There have been many attempts to demonstrate the great changes that take place, during the course of generations, in the current picture of some great composer of the past. It almost looks as if any period's idea of Bach, Beethoven, or Mozart told us more about the period than about the composer. If we now imagine that we appreciate Mozart's greatness more completely and deeply than our grandfathers did, there is only one thing that may entitle us to do so: the ever more prevalent conviction that we must respect composers' intentions, and that it is impossible to study too fully the text of their music and the customs of their time. In other words, we must do everything possible to ensure that our playing is faithful to the work and to its style.

What does this involve? First, it must be made clear that faithfulness to a work is not to be confused with what we may call *literal exactness*.[5] In the history of interpretation there is a contrast between a period before 1900, which tended to allow great freedom—indeed, arbitrariness—in interpretation, and one after 1900 in which the tendency has been developed to remain faithful to the text, and still another one toward the end of the twentieth century when the respect for adhering rigidly to the printed score is in danger of disappearing and certain inhibitions to alter great masterworks is diminishing. The demand for adherence to the text was a welcome and most important development but, unfortunately, this often resulted in academic adherence to the printed text. Nowadays we have learned, from our efforts to understand genius and the historical situation in which it flourished, that literal exactness alone cannot ensure faithful and stylish interpretation—that classical composers' works not merely permit but demand of the performer a degree of freedom. The one thing we can be absolutely sure of is, that they did not want inexpressive, dry performance.

Let us return to our basic demand in interpretation—to achieve the deepest and most lasting effect possible[6]—and proceed from there. From this standpoint, the question of exact or free interpretation at first seems a subsidiary one. For if we insist on exact interpretation, we do so not for its own sake but in the conviction that Mozart's works are most effective when reproduced in a *Mozartean* style (as far as this is possible; by *style* we mean the totality of the psychological phenomena to which a creative artist is subject, by which he is formed and which, for his part, he influences). If a particular performer were able to play Mozart, producing a stronger and deeper effect than anyone else, we should willingly be converted to playing Mozart in his style from then on.[7] But this is not very likely to happen. Mozart's works, of all music, possess such incomparable organic unity, so complete a balance between content and form, that any interpolation of foreign elements, even on the part of a genius, would ruin their harmony—that harmony that seems to lift his music above mere human frailty.

Although faithfulness to a particular work and to the style as a whole is necessary, it carries with it a danger of attaching too much importance to the intellect. An excessively intellectual approach blocks the paths to the unconscious, to the earth, where all musical performance has its roots. For when all is said and done, art can only be grasped intuitively. No amount of historical research alone can make a performance truly stylish; the work must sound as if it had never been played before. Historical discoveries resulting in new perceptions can often increase the liveliness of a performance; one has only to think of our rediscovery of Baroque music's rhythmic subtleties, which the nineteenth century completely failed to appreciate. The intellect must support intuition and often guide it, too; it organizes, divides, analyzes. But these particles, separated by the intellect, can only be molded into a living entity through a long experience of feeling and intuition. Throughout history, the living breath of music has been great men's instinct for grasping melody, tension and relaxation, extension and contraction.

---

[5] It has nothing to do with the above-mentioned refusal to reproduce a composer's performance by mere imitation; imitation can lack style just as creative interpretation can be stylish.

[6] Incidentally, one must beware the fallacy that composers are not interested in effectiveness, or even in superficial effects. Many composers have delighted in effects, and Mozart was no exception. In his letters he justifies many an idea in his works with the words "It makes a good effect." See E. Reeser, *Ein Augsburger Musiker in Paris: Johann Gottfried Eckard 1735–1809*, p. 74.

[7] Composers' minds, too, can work this way: "I wish you could have been at Liszt's this morning. He is quite extraordinary. I was absolutely spellbound by the way he played some of the Novelettes, the Fantasia and the Sonata. *Often not at all as I had intended*, but with genius, so tenderly and boldly as even he can not always play. Only Becker was there — with tears in his eyes …" (italics added). Letter from Robert to Clara Schumann, Leipzig, 20 March 1840, quoted after: Clara Schumann, *Jugendbriefe Robert Schumanns*.

This is why there must be a little of the gypsy in every musician. Theoretical study is only the preparation—a necessary preparation, like practice at an instrument. But the artistic experience depends solely on the life that imbues one's playing. Edwin Fischer always used to impress on his pupils:

> Do not destroy this world of artistic visions that come up from your unconscious—make room for it; dream dreams, see visions, don't listen to records till you in turn become a record, forever repeating yourself: suffer, rejoice, love and live a life that constantly renews itself.[8]

---

[8] Lecture given at the opening of the 1953 Summer Course, Lucerne Conservatoire.

1
Mozart's World of Sound

It is nearly impossible to reconstruct the actual sound of Mozart's compositions at the time of their first performance. Even if one were to produce the same acoustical conditions—using original eighteenth-century instruments in a Rococo hall—this would be not enough to achieve a 100 percent historically faithful presentation. Other criteria, too, would have to be the same as in Mozart's day; for instance, the aesthetic standards of performers and audiences as well as social conditions. As we all know, however, the general lifestyle and the aesthetic attitudes of musicians and their audiences have altered greatly since the eighteenth century, even if we ignore the complete change in the structure of society and of the musical life in larger cities since Mozart's time.

Still, we usually play music not because we are interested in history, but, firstly from a delight in playing and in sound itself, and, secondly because we have fallen in love with a great masterpiece or we are interested in a particular work. On the other hand, we cannot do full justice to a composition from another period unless we perform and hear it in a way similar to that of its creator. The attempt to reproduce it, as far as possible, in the style and with the resources of the relevant period of its composition has to be based on historical studies. Around 1956, when the first version of our book was printed, a statement saying that Mozart should be played in his personal style and the style appropriate to his time and surroundings was never called into question. Toward the end of the twentieth century, however, some musicians seemed to arrive at a different view. They considered it acceptable to use (and abuse) Mozart's music for various purposes. Such musicians either had lost their respect for the art of great composers altogether or their respect had greatly lessened; in any event, they seemed satisfied with an interpretation that revealed only a rather limited part of Mozart's art. Today Mozart's compositions are often altered in various ways, sometimes arranged into jazz or film music, sometimes used tastelessly as models for rock or trivial background music; there are many ways to diminish or spoil their value and impact as great art.

We shall not deal here with any kind of exploitation of Mozart's works for modern adaptations of this kind. Instead, we shall try to show how one can approach an understanding of Mozart's intentions and grasp his personal style when interpreting his masterpieces.

Keyboard Instruments of Mozart's Time

Today's frequent use of historical keyboard instruments is a most welcome achievement that many music lovers find eminently satisfying, and the use of the "fortepiano" (as old pianos are nowadays named) from Mozart's time is greatly appreciated not only by Mozart connoisseurs. Half a century ago, it was a most unusual enterprise when Paul Badura-Skoda decided to play a Mozart recital on a piano made by Anton Walter, the builder of Mozart's own piano; and it was even more adventurous when, afterwards, he succeeded in persuading the president of the Westminster Recording Company to issue an LP of such a recorded recital. "Nobody will buy that!" was the claim of the company's spokesman. (He was wrong—the record sold quite well.) At that time, many critics voiced their dissatisfaction with Walter's fortepiano and took the view that period instruments had no future because they were "so obviously inferior to modern pianos."

During the Mozart anniversary year 1956, there were perhaps grounds for a certain dissatisfaction with the pianos of Mozart's time—the lack of experience in making old instruments playable still hindered satisfactory restorations. Very few restorers in museums dared to try making valuable old pianos playable again. It took several years before a new generation of piano builders, specializing as restorers, emerged—persons who had developed the knowledge and had the enthusiasm necessary for careful restoration work. In 1956, the main problems included the lack of special parts, such as proper strings, and the necessary tools. Today, these problems have been solved, and we enjoy the existence of satisfying replicas in many cities and countries. The replicas often are of a quality that can compete easily with that of old master instruments. This fortunate development we owe to the pioneers among pianists, of whom Malcolm Bilson needs to be singled out. He not only learned to play well on period instruments and soon specialized as a fortepianist, giving many concerts on good replicas, but he also became an excellent and rightly famous teacher of many gifted young musicians who are now following his example.

Nevertheless, performing on original fortepianos, which often are the property of a museum, still poses a number of problems. To begin with, really good original keyboard instruments of Mozart's time that can be used for concerts or serve as models for replicas are not always available. It is only natural that the sound of the few genuine old pianos that can be played and heard today would differ slightly from that of replicas; due to the aging of the wood, their sound may also differ from what it had been in Mozart's time. This is one reason why there are limits to the extent to which we can carry the demand for an authentic re-creation of the original sound. It is a problem known to violinists as well—excellent modern violins have been built in the last century, but their sound differs slightly from that of a Stradivari or Guarnieri. Although we must avoid the nineteenth century's mistakes of regarding all later technical and instrumental achievements as the *non plus ultra*, we must have a critical regard for the instruments and the acoustical conditions of ages past. To look at everything old as beautiful simply because it is old would be just as much a mistake as to apply present-day aesthetic standards uncritically to the art of past ages. In re-creating a work in performance, we often face the need to find a compromise between our historical knowledge, the existing possibilities, and the world of present-day perception.

Around the middle of the eighteenth century, several square pianos were built without any dampers, or without a damper-lifting device or other stops. These pianos were usually cheap instruments and were seldom used by professional pianists like Georg Christoph Wagenseil or Mozart. In southern Germany we may assume that more wing-shaped fortepianos were in use in Mozart's time than those north German, large, square pianos, for which various sound modifications had been invented. The damper-lifting device (the same as the modern right pedal, which will be discussed in detail below), was for a long time called *forte stop* and was considered a sound-mutation stop like the lute or bassoon stops. And, indeed, as with those stops, when in action, it creates a modification of sound. Though it was perhaps already the most common stop in Mozart's time, it was far from being the only one. Besides hand or knee lever(s) to lift dampers and those levers or knobs for *sordino* or *moderato* effects (often corresponding to the *una corda* pedal in modern pianos), it seems that initially at least one other stop, namely a device imitating the harpsichord sound, was often added. Throughout the eighteenth century, documents inform us that apparently many compound harpsichord-pianos were built, and they also show that musicians still liked the sound of the quilled harpsichord and wanted the choice between different sound possibilities. Besides, devices for the imitation of wind instruments, especially flutes and bassoon stops, were also desired, leading to an increase in the number of stops. In 1770, the piano builder Franz Jakob Späth proudly announced that his compound instruments allowed a change of sound more than 50 times, and in 1783, another builder (Milchmeyer) claimed that on his instruments the sound could be changed 250 times. Late Viennese eighteenth-century and early nineteenth-century pianos often had various hand and knee levers or pedals to activate devices for altering the sound. After 1800, practically all pianos were built with pedals instead of knee levers, and those pianos that did not get four, five, or six pedals for sound modifications had at least two pedals for lifting the dampers and for a piano stop (*sordino*, *moderato*, or *una corda*). After circa 1830 most playful sound modifications lost their attraction and pianos were built usually with two pedals only.

If we consider the fact that only very few original eighteenth-century instruments have survived—probably far less than 1 percent of those that were made and played in Mozart's time—it is hard to ascertain exactly when a newly invented stop became fashionable and when musicians and piano builders lost interest in these devices. Nearly all of the few extant original Hammerflügel from the time before and after 1800 have one or more of those stops mentioned in old documents: forte, trumpet, bassoon, lute, sordino (moderator), harp, and drums, or what had been called the *Janissary* or *Turkish music* stop. The earliest known document describing a piano with a Turkish music stop dates from 1796. We have no such descriptions from earlier years, but this does not say much. It may have been mere coincidence that no piano with a Turkish music stop from the 1780s has been preserved. There are reasons to assume that the centennial of the Turkish siege of 1683, which created an unusual fashion for references to Turkish topics, gave piano builders the idea to invent the Turkish music stop, necessary for the interpretation of *alla Turca*—impressions and their imitation in compositions for the piano. Did Mozart perhaps employ and enjoy such a Turkish music stop when playing the *ritornellos* of his Turkish March from his A major Sonata K. 331, composed during the early 1780s as we now know? If this was indeed the case, it would probably have been exceptional; there are reasons to believe that Mozart was otherwise not fond of such modifications of sound. Unlike Haydn or Beethoven, who sometimes—though rarely—took advantage of the "gimmicks," Mozart's means of wit were more subtle.

TRACK 80 On the accompanying CD for this book, the sound of this device is demonstrated in a recording of the Turkish March movement of the Sonata K. 331 as the very last example No. 80; it is played on a Viennese fortepiano of Mozart's time. Having no Janissary stop on modern pianos, we now use different means to imitate the typically Turkish music quality of the movement with the help of subtleties of touch such as pointed rhythm, etc. In fact, the modern piano is particularly well suited to a play of tone color, since the tone of the present-day piano, as compared to old fortepianos and to that of other instruments—e.g., the oboe or cello—is intrinsically indifferent, characterless, and needs to be given color through touch. It is wrong to say that on the piano one can merely play loud, soft, *legato*, *staccato*, etc., and that it is impossible to achieve an imitation of tone colors, say, of a woodwind instrument or something like a cello pizzicato. From the standpoint of physics, the piano's tone cannot be altered, of course. But it is one of the inexplicable secrets of interpretation that the pianist can communicate to the listener not only moods, but also particular sound images. How else could one understand the artistry with which pianists such as Alfred Cortot, Wilhelm Kempff, Edwin Fischer, or András Schiff created piano tone images? Mozart achieved amazing sound effects by changes of register, frequent opposition of high and low notes (e.g., in the Variations for Piano—Four Hands in G Major, K. 501), hand crossings, alternations of *legato* and *staccato*, as well as full textures and two-part writing, trills in the bass, etc. Indeed, Mozart's piano writing imitates trumpet flourishes, the gently melting tones of the flute, the *lamento* sounds of the oboe, and the consoling clarinet sounds, the veiled sound of the basset horn, noisy orchestral *tutti*, just as it contains utterly magical sounds that could belong only to the piano. But the most intimate and inward expression of all can be achieved by using a fortepiano's *una corda* stop: it may sound "as if the player were breathing the music into the listener's ear." To play Mozart without the magic of a richly varied tonal palette is not only inartistic, it is stylistically unidiomatic.

The musician interested in gaining a clear idea of the sound of fortepiano instruments in Mozart's time should examine the changes that have been taking place during the past 250 years. The tonal picture has altered in many respects as the developments have aimed at a greater volume of tone, greater compass, better intonation possibilities, and perhaps a greater technical virtuosity of performance. The reasons for these changes are easy to understand. For example, one reason for the increased volume of sound in present-day piano performances is that concerts in private rooms are becoming rarer and rarer, while it is now quite common for audiences of two or three thousand to hear solo and chamber music recitals. Another reason lies, of course, in the development of the music itself. Beethoven's ideal of sound clearly differed from Mozart's, and it is partly because of his influence (and Liszt's, too) that piano makers ever since Mozart's time have aimed at a fuller, rounder tone, with fewer overtones and less contrast of pitch registers and, above all, more power. But in achieving greater volume, the sound character (timbre) of the piano tone has been steadily transformed.

It seems that today the average human ear reacts favorably to very bright sounds rich in overtones only if the music is played relatively softly. When the sounds of older pianos, originally not very loud, are amplified in loudspeakers to a modern "normal" *forte*, these forced sounds tend to make a sharp, shrill effect; and when they are played *fortissimo*, they are almost unbearably strident. Those who own records of old instruments (clavichord, eighteenth-century fortepiano) will be able to confirm this statement: these delicate instruments sound attractive only if the loudspeaker's volume is not allowed to exceed the original level of the recording.

So it is not at all surprising that, in comparison with Mozart's piano, even Beethoven's and, *a fortiori*, the pianos of the twentieth century, not only have a fuller, louder tone but one that has become increasingly darker and usually duller, an inevitable development in the manufacture of pianos. Compared with the modern piano, Mozart's piano produces an extraordinarily translucent, sharply defined, silvery sound effect. The instruments were much more delicately built; the strings and the soundboard were thinner, which produced a relatively soft yet beautiful tone due to the richness of overtones. The levels of volume that we are accustomed to were impossible to achieve prior to the introduction of steel frames for pianos (invented around 1825, but generally applied only from ca. 1850 on); only then did the necessary increase in string tension become possible. Moreover, the eighteenth-century piano had leather-covered hammers, not the felt covers now customary, and the hammers were slimmer in shape and considerably lighter in weight. To demonstrate the difference between a grand piano of Mozart's time and a modern grand piano, one need only compare their weights: a Walter fortepiano weighs about 140 pounds, whereas a Steinway concert grand far more than 1,000. On 12 March 1785, Mozart's father wrote Nannerl: "Since my arrival [in Vienna], your brother's fortepiano has been carried at least a dozen times to the theatre or to some other house." One wonders whether Mozart nowadays could have had his piano carried through various streets twelve times in three weeks!

Hardly any instrument of the modern orchestra is unchanged since Mozart's time. Often technical difficulties and imperfections stimulated mechanical improvements, which in turn altered the volume and timbre of the instruments. But no other instrument was so strongly affected and has been so fundamentally altered as the piano.

Mozart's Training on All Kinds of Keyboard Instruments

Leopold Mozart can certainly be regarded as a well-educated, enlightened teacher, aware of the modern trends and remarkable changes in music during his lifetime. On 17 September 1755, he wrote to Pater Meinrad Spieß (a member of Mizler's *musikalischer Sozietät* and author of a musical treatise):[1]

> *Within [only a] few years, music making has really changed a great deal: everything that stirs the feelings of listeners is [now] based on a good, a beautiful and natural way of performing. The soft and the strong (dynamics) must now be applied not only to entire passages, but also to individual notes; the different way that sometimes equal and at other times unequal notes are slurred together or separated contrary to the normal manner, and similarly many other such things in an otherwise well-made composition properly reveal the expression [affect] and show [what we] therefore must do.*[2]

The expressive device of gradually increasing and decreasing dynamics (in German called *Übergangsdynamik*) as well as the *singing Allegro* originated in Italy. According to contemporary reports, in the German-speaking countries this manner of expression was brought to perfection by the court orchestra in Mannheim and of course, by individual musicians as well. It could be achieved best on fortepianos, better than on normal harpsichords with quills. The clavichord usually allowed the new expression only within a limited volume range. Quantz (p. 175) pointed this out in his treatise from 1752:

> *Everything required* [for proper accompaniment] *can be executed most conveniently on a pianoforte, for this instrument, more than any others that are called "clavier", has in itself most of the attributes that are necessary for proper accompaniment; and this depends exclusively on the player and his judgement. The same is true indeed of a good clavichord as regards playing, but not as regards effect, as fortissimo is lacking.*

For this revised edition of our book we would like to include some words about recent research results regarding the keyboard instruments on which Mozart played and was trained as a child. The instruments in Leopold Mozart's home definitely included a valuable two-manual harpsichord made by Christian Ernst Friderici (Friederici), which Leopold Mozart acquired second-hand around 1760 for the training of his children, and he owned also at least one if not two clavichords, one of which was probably also made by Friderici. In 1763 he bought a clavichord (*Reiseclavierl*) from Stein in Augsburg for use as a practice instrument for his children during their extensive tour from 1763 to 1766.

Until recently, Leopold Mozart's double-manual Friderici harpsichord, which he had bought from Count Pranck, who had to leave Salzburg, was generally assumed to have been a harpsichord with quills only. However, new research suggests that this Friderici cembalo probably was a compound instrument with quills and a built-in hammer action as well (today referred to as *harpsichord-piano*). These instruments have two keyboards, one of which activates the harpsichord with quills, while the other is linked to a hammer action. During the eighteenth century, such compound harpsichords were apparently rather *en vogue* among Italian and

[1] The letter is reproduced in facsimile in *Acta Mozartiana*, 34, no. 4, pp. 78–82. Chr. L. Mizler's *Korrespondierende Sozietät der Musikalischen Wissenschaften* was a society of men of learning, founded in Leipzig in 1738. Limited to 20 members, such names as Handel, J. S. Bach, Graun, and Telemann are found among them. Mizler died highly respected as physician, mathematician, musician, and philosopher in 1778.

[2] In German, this text, reflecting Leopold Mozart's awareness of trends in music, reads: "*Es hat sich die Practische Musik in wenig Jahren wirklich sehr verändert: und alles, was immer die Gemüter der Zuhörer rühren solle, beruhet auf der Art eines guten schönen und natürlichen Vortrages. Das Schwache und Starke, welches man itzt nicht nur in ganzen Passagen, sondern auch bey einzelnen Noten anbringen muß; die verschiedene Art, die theils gleichen, theils ungleichen Noten zu verbinden und zusammenzuhängen oder auch wider die sonst gewöhnliche Art, zu trennen, und derley viele andere Dinge sind es, die in der sonst wohlgesetzten Composition den Affect recht anzeigen und [die wir] ergo machen müssen.*"

German instrument builders and performers. The assumption that Leopold's instrument was a compound harpsichord receives strong support by various passages in his letters to his friend Lorenz Hagenauer. If it was indeed a harpsichord with an additional hammer action, it may have enabled Nannerl und Wolfgang to learn playing on a fortepiano at an early age.

The organ and instrument builder Christian Ernst Friderici probably began his professional life as an apprentice to Gottfried Silbermann. Afterwards he worked the necessary term of three years as a journeyman for the organ builder Trost in Altenburg, and then he opened his own workshop in Gera in 1737 and employed his brother Gottlieb as his helper. An innovative builder of stringed keyboard instruments with hammers, he soon became famous. An advertisement from 1745 presents a picture of an upright instrument with a hammer action built by him, a kind of Pyramidenflügel. The Friderici brothers probably made all kinds of keyboard instruments: clavichords, harpsichords, compound harpsichords, and wing-shaped pianofortes as well as probably those in rectangular or square form. (The latter were not yet called *Tafelclavier* but usually named *clavier* or *pantalone* or "fortbien.") Compound harpsichords with quills and hammer actions had been offered for sale in Leipzig as early as 1731, and it seems likely that many more harpsichords with an additional hammer action were built in the following decades than has hitherto been assumed. They seem to have been fashionable. For instance, during the 1760s, Franz Jakob Späth as well as Johann Andreas Stein repeatedly advertised such instruments in Leipzig. This is but one reason to believe that the Mozart family owned such a compound instrument.[3] If the harpsichord that Leopold Mozart bought for his children was indeed a compound instrument, light is thrown on the interesting question: for which clavier did young Mozart compose his earliest keyboard works?

The Friderici harpsichord (Figure 1.1) was still in Leopold's possession when he died, and after his death an announcement of the auction of his belongings appeared in the *Salzburger Intelligenzblatt*, dated 15 September 1787, in which the following description was given:

> *Fourth a harpsichord of the famous Friderizi from Gera with two manuals and a range of five full octaves besides a cornet stop and a lute stop. [... viertens eine Flüg [Flügel] von dem berühmten Friderizi aus Gera in zwey Manualen von Ebenholz, und Elfenbein durch fünf ganze Oktaven, dann [mit] einem besonderen Kornet, und Lautenzug.]*

Thus, the harpsichord had a range of five octaves and, in addition, not only the usual lute stop, but apparently also a stop imitating the sound of a high-pitched trumpet. The presence of a *cornet* stop (high-pitched horn or *Trompetenzug*) is somehow strange in a harpsichord built as late as the middle of the eighteenth century; stops imitating wind instruments were built by then more often into hammer-harpsichords than harpsichords with quills.[4] This suggests again that the Friderici harpsichord may have been indeed a compound instrument. The *cornet* stop, by the way, may also explain a report (Schachtner) that as a child Wolfgang was fearful of high trumpet sounds; and, indeed, Mozart had a life-long aversion against high-pitched sounds of solo trumpets.

Though little Wolfgang may have disliked this stop, he nevertheless seems to have been very fond of this Friderici instrument. In November 1762, after the Mozart family had spent their

---

[3] The evidence and an analysis in support of this judgment will be presented in detail in the forthcoming book by Eva Badura-Skoda, *The History of the Fortepiano from Scarlatti to Chopin*.

[4] See Edward L. Kottick, *A History of the Harpsichord*, p. 494n.36; Christian Ahrens, *Hammerklaviere mit Wiener Mechanik*, p.59.

Figure 1.1 The Mozart Family portrait. Wolfgang and Nannerl play four-hands, apparently on Friderici's two-manual harpsichord, the R.H. (for melody parts) on the lower (invisible) keyboard, the L.H. on the upper manual. Oil painting by J.N. della Croce (?), ca 1780/81. (Mozarteum Salzburg).

first weeks in Vienna, Leopold Mozart told Hagenauer (10 November 1762) that Wolfgang often was thinking of his *Flügel* at home in Salzburg:

> He wants to know how the harpsichord is doing?—and thinks of it quite often, because here we have not found one like it.

What is said with this sentence? Is it possible to believe that no ordinary harpsichord with two manuals could be found in Vienna? Hardly true. It seems much more likely that the Friderici harpsichord of the Mozart family was a compound instrument, less often found than common harpsichords and perhaps not generally available in Vienna.

It seems likely that his proud father made sure that Wolfgang became acquainted with all kinds of keyboard instruments. This includes the organ, which Wolfgang obviously learned to play at an early age, too. When the family went to Vienna in October 1762, Leopold wrote about his travel experiences to Hagenauer:

> On noon on the following day, Tuesday, we arrived at Ips [Ybbs], where two Minorites and a Benedictine [monk], who were with us on the boat, read masses, during which Wolferl strummed on the organ and played so well that the Franciscan monks, who happened to be entertaining guests at their midday meal, left the table and with their company rushed to the choir and were almost struck dead with amazement. ...

Young Mozart's interest in the organ seems to have been extraordinary, and the sound of low organ registers especially impressed him. One year later, during travels to Munich, Leopold Mozart wrote to Hagenauer on 11 June 1763:

> The latest news is that in order to amuse ourselves we went to the organ and I explained to Wolferl the use of the pedal. Whereupon he tried it stante pede, shoved the stool away and played standing at the organ, at the same time working the pedal, and doing it all as if he had been practising it for several months. Everyone was amazed. Indeed this is a fresh act of God's grace, which many only receive after much labor. ...

In October 1777, when Mozart met Johann Andreas Stein in Augsburg, he asked him whether he might play on his organ in the *Barfüßerkirche* because organ-playing was his passion. In a letter to his father (17 October 1777), Mozart reported Stein's great surprise:

> What? A man like you, such a fine clavier-player, wants to play on an instrument which has no douceur, no expression, no piano, no forte, but is always the same? "That does not matter", I replied. "In my eyes and ears the organ is the king of instruments."

When Stein heard Mozart perform on his organ, he apparently understood why Mozart was fond of playing the organ. Thus it seems obvious that Mozart became accustomed to playing well on all available keyboard instruments and that he always delighted in discovering new sounds and techniques.

It was the fortepiano, however, that became Mozart's preferred instrument. He knew, of course, that music lovers lacking a good piano instrument would play his works on other keyboard instruments such as a normal harpsichord or a clavichord, or even a spinet. But we may reasonably assume that Wolfgang soon thought of these instruments only as substitutes for the more expressive fortepianos. For a while he may have accepted Späth's tangent pianos (wing-shaped instruments, comparable in sound and expression to pianos, but with less dynamic range than fortepianos). After trying out Stein's pianos in 1777, Mozart certainly preferred pianos with hammers. Mozart's mature piano works, his sonatas, concertos, and fantasies, were certainly all composed with the fortepiano in mind and not intended for any other keyboard instrument, a fact hardly ever doubted by serious musicians.

The name *pianoforte* for keyboard instruments with hammer actions (*Hammerflügel*) was coined around 1731 by Gottfried Silbermann, and it came into use first and foremost in Saxony, Prussia, and other north German Protestant countries. In the Catholic south German regions, however, musicians often followed Italian habit and kept using the word *cembalo* for the new instruments with a hammer action. Cristofori had always named his instruments with a hammer action *cembalo*, and from Cristofori's time on and during the whole eighteenth century, the term *cembalo* continued to be used for hammer-harpsichords in Italy. Italians clearly preferred this term for the new instrument to Silbermann's "pianofort." This explains why whenever they were using the Italian language, Mozart, Beethoven, and other composers wrote "Cembalo," meaning a *cembalo con martelli* or piano. The fact that in the autographs of Mozart's piano concertos (with the exception of the last ones) we find "Cembalo" written before the first accolade only means that Mozart was following Italian usage. (Would anybody want to hear, say, the C minor Concerto K. 491 played on a harpsichord with quills? Hardly.)

In north German writings of the second half of the eighteenth century, the name *Pianoforte* (or, in two words, *Piano-Forte*) was generally used, whereas in the German-speaking south and in Vienna the piano was more often named *cembalo* than *Fortepiano*. Today, *Fortepiano* has come to be the name of period instruments of Mozart's time.

It has been proven by now that the terms *cembalo*, *clavecin*, or *harpsichord* had different meanings in Mozart's time than in the twentieth century.[5] This is still misunderstood by many musicians and some musicologists. During most of the eighteenth century, the terms *cembalo*, *harpsichord*, and *clavecin* only meant that these keyboard instruments were wing shaped or harp shaped in form (wing in German = *Flügel*; hence also the later terms *Kielflügel* and *Hammerflügel*). Cristofori had built his hammer mechanism into a cembalo and called his newly invented piano a *gravecimbalo che fa il piano e il forte*. For him it remained always a cembalo. The eighteenth-century terms *hammer-harpsichord*, *clavecin à maillet*, or the Italian designations *cimbalo con martellini*, *di martellati*, etc., tell us the broader meaning of the eighteenth-century terms: a cembalo could be both a *cembalo con penne* (quills) and a *cembalo con martelli* (hammers). The English term *hammer-harpsichord* and the later German term *Hammerflügel* would make little sense if we did not know that a harpsichord could have either quills or hammers, or both quills and hammers, and still was named usually only *harpsichord*. And there would be no explanation for why Mozart wrote "cembalo" when he undoubtedly meant a piano.

The Italians preferred anyway their old term *cimbalo* or *cembalo* instead of the new name *pianoforte*, which was invented by a German with little feeling for their language. They obviously had a hearty dislike for this name pianoforte: after all, it was both grammatically wrong, combining two adjectives, and created an odd noun. Would any English musician have accepted readily a name *soft-loud* for a new musical instrument?

Mozart himself told us what he meant with the term *Cembalo* when he wrote in his letter of 16 January 1782, about the rival fortepianist Clementi:

> *Now a word about Clementi. He is an excellent cembalo-player but that is all. He has great facility with his right hand, his best passages are thirds. Apart from this he does not have a penny's worth of taste or feeling; he is a mere mechanicus.*

Doubtless the competition took place on two fortepianos, as Mozart explained a few lines later in his letter, and this proves that Mozart did not hear him playing a harpsichord with quills.

---

[5] This terminology fact was pointed out in 1980 by E. Badura-Skoda in *Prolegomena to a History of the Viennese Fortepiano*; though at the beginning still doubted or discussed, by now there is nearly general agreement in this matter among colleagues.

It could be asked whether Mozart's earliest keyboard compositions were meant for a fortepiano. Of course, these works could have easily been played on any kind of keyboard instrument—whatever "clavier" was available; Wolfgang had learned to play them all. We believe, however, that Mozart clearly intended already his six "difficult" Sonatas K. 279–284 for a fortepiano. The mere fact that Mozart notated many dynamic signs in these works, as well as their inherent and often dramatic musical expression (especially in the slow movements), and the already demanding virtuosity (especially of K. 284), speak for their interpretation on an instrument capable of more dynamic shadings and brilliance than was possible on a harpsichord or a commonly found clavichord with its limited capability of true "forte" sounds. We have every reason to believe that in southern Germany, most available clavichords were usually small and rather cheap instruments with a very soft sound; unlike the exceptionally large and loud clavichords built in the Protestant part of Germany and Scandinavia, they were not loud enough for use as concert instruments. Had the Mozarts owned such an extraordinarily well-built silbermann clavichord as C. P. E. Bach possessed, it would have hardly remained unnoticed and without commentary. The fact that Mozart's famous letter from Augsburg about the Stein pianos, in which he referred to his former great esteem for Späth's and other builders' wing-shape fortepianos, makes it more than likely that he had favored pianos well before coming to Augsburg in 1777. We are therefore on safe ground when we assume that he composed his six sonatas for an instrument on which he also could perform for larger audiences—as he did in Munich before arriving in Augsburg and also later often on his tour to Paris. He spoke of these sonatas as difficult pieces (*"meine schweren Sonaten"*), and they were indeed virtuoso pieces, more difficult than usual, especially the last one in D major, K. 284, of which he told his father (17 October 1777) that "it sounds exquisite on Stein's pianoforte."

If the piano concertos K. 175, K. 238, and K. 246 may have been played first on harpsichords in the modern sense of the word and not on eighteenth-century fortepianos (a claim for which there exists no proof), it may have been so because no proper fortepiano was available. But it is questionable whether Mozart welcomed such an instrument. Though common harpsichords with quills were loud enough to be partners of an orchestra and may have been so used, their limited expressiveness excludes them as an ideal instrument. Particularly in the case of the Concerto K. 271, it is hardly imaginable that Mozart considered a *Kielflügel* as an ideal instrument.

With regard to Mozart's earliest published compositions K. 6–9, it is usually assumed that Mozart played them in Paris on a harpsichord and not on a pianoforte. Leopold took care to publish them in 1763 as "Sonates Pour le Clavecin qui peuvent se jouer avec l'Accompagnement de Violon" in the year of their composition in Paris, but as explained above, this word *clavecin* does not necessarily exclude the fortepiano. Soon after their arrival in Paris, the Mozarts had met the German immigrant composers Johann Schobert and Johann Gottfried Eckard (Eckardt). Schobert had become well known for his preference of the pianoforte and for his new style connected with the use of this instrument. Eckard, who arrived in Paris together with the piano builder Stein in 1759, obviously also preferred a fortepiano to a normal clavecin. In Eckard's *Six Sonates pour le clavecin, op. I* (published in 1763), he wrote in the preface:

> I have tried to adjust this work for being played on the harpsichord, the clavichord and the pianoforte. For this reason I felt obliged to mark often soft and strong; these signs would be superfluous if I had had only the harpsichord in my mind.[6]

---

[6] *"J'ai tâché de rendre cet ouvrage d'un utilité commune au Clavecin, au Clavicorde, et au forté et piano. C'est pas cette raison que je me suis cru obligé de marquer aussi souvent les doux, et les fort, ce qui eut été inutile si je n'avais eu que le Clavecin en vue."*

Still during the same year 1763, Eckard published his op. II, and this time already with the title *Deux Sonates pour le Clavecin ou le Piano Forte*. Leopold Mozart thought highly of Eckard, and Wolfgang later arranged one of his sonata movements as the middle movement for his Concerto K. 40. The other German refugee immigrants, Hermann Friedrich Raupach and Leontzi Honauer, of whom young Wolfgang arranged likewise movements, may also have favored the fortepiano. Did Wolfgang follow their example? The many *Alberti* bass figures and the simple melodic lines in Wolfgang's Sonatas K. 6–8 speak for the use of a fortepiano—unlike, for example, the later composed (Trio) Sonata K. 12 with its more sophisticated texture, published in London in 1764.

Although there are still few musicians who insist that not only Mozart's Sonatas K. 279–284 but also various concertos, among them the Concerto in E-flat Major, K. 271, should be played on a harpsichord with quills, their arguments do not have any validity. It is probably true that in the decades prior to 1760 fortepianos were still relatively rare instruments, and thus not always easily available, but they were certainly well known enough and in use, especially among professional musicians and composers. Because of their delicately built action often with tiny, light hammers, most early fortepianos may not have been durable instruments. The action and strings required constant care and the replacement of parts may have been difficult. If the Mozarts' Friderici harpsichord was indeed a harpsichord-piano, it might well have been that the hammer action in this compound instrument was not functioning well after a decade or so. Späth's piano, which Mozart had probably come across in Salzburg (see below), was also perhaps in not very good condition. This would explain a remark in a letter from Mozart's mother, written to her husband from Mannheim on 28 December 1777, about Wolfgang's sonata performances in München, Augsburg, and Mannheim:

> *Indeed he* [Wolfgang] *plays quite differently from what he used to in Salzburg—for there are* [good] *pianofortes everywhere here, on which he plays so extraordinarily well that people say they have never heard the like.*

It could have been this remark that caused some musicologists to believe that Mozart had no piano at his disposal in Salzburg—a contention contradicted *inter alia* by the beginning of Mozart's famous letter to his father from 17 October 1777, about Stein's pianos:

> *This time I shall begin at once with Stein's pianofortes. Before I had seen any of his make, Späth's instruments had always been my favorites. But now I much prefer Stein's...*

Who was Späth (often wrongly spelt Spath),[7] and where did Mozart play on a Späth pianoforte? We know little about the oldest member of the south German organ-building family Johann Jakob Späth (1672–1760), who had settled in Regensburg prior to 1700. It was his son Franz Jakob (1714–1786) who became famous. He had apparently traveled through Saxony as a journeyman, perhaps working briefly for Gottfried Silbermann; later he became known for the invention of various stringed keyboard instruments, among them the so-called *Tangentenflügel*, and for new stops. An article—published in the *Leipziger Zeitung* on 10 September 1765—recommended "Franz Jacob Späth of Regenburg" as builder of so-called *Pantaleons* or *Forte-piano-clavecins*. According to this article, compound instruments by other builders were usually defective, hard to play, made a lot of unwanted noise, and did not always permit the intended *forte*, *piano*, and *pianissimo*. But

---

[7] Though various documents spell Späth's name as "Spath," it becomes clear through all later spellings and pronunciations of this family name that the omission of dots was caused by the ignorance of the meaning of still rarely used dots as well as the usual neglect of proper spelling in eighteenth-century archive material.

> *... all these deficiencies were remedied by the famous artist and organ-builder, Hr. Franz Jacob Spath from Regensburg in such a way that all the tones of his Pandaleons-Clavecins are not only completely even [in sound] but can also be played as easily and delicately as a clavichord, and all passages can be tenderly expressed; besides the instruments are so durable that they do not require constant repair. Herr Spath, who is also known for the silvery and majestic sound of his clavecins and their accurate construction, combined the Forte-Piano-Clavecin [sic.] with the quilled Flügel, and the two manuals allow a pleasant diversion* [change of dynamics and timbres]. ...

Another advertisement of Späth's compound instruments, this time announcing many more possibilities for sound mutations (more stops), appeared in 1770 in Hiller's "Wöchentliche Nachrichten," featuring again a combination of a harpsichord with quills and a hammer action. Interestingly, according to his diary, Johann Andreas Stein had worked for several months in 1749 as a journeyman for Späth in Regensburg before founding his own workshop in Augsburg in 1750.

In Salzburg, the Mozart family was acquainted with the merchant Franz Xaver Anton Späth, who may have been a distant relation of the Regensburg instrument builder and could have been the owner of a Späth pianoforte. (F. X. A. Späth married Elisabeth Haffner, the daughter of the mayor of Salzburg, on 22 July 1776, for which event Mozart composed the so-called Haffner Serenade K. 250.)

When playing for an audience as a grown-up, a professional performer, Mozart would certainly have considered wing-shaped fortepianos as the best instruments rather than square pianos or clavichords. Only they could be used for the interpretation of concertos, and they were best also for the performance of piano sonatas. Earlier square pianos (usually called *Tafelklaviere* after ca. 1780) sometimes did not even have dampers; if they did they had often only hand levers for lifting the dampers. That the piano was doubtless Mozart's favorite instrument can be gathered from the simple fact that Mozart wrote such a great number of wonderful masterworks for this instrument. The piano concertos in particular reflect his most personal thoughts, and it was in these works that he attained the highest peaks of instrumental art.

Everywhere that Mozart performed on the piano, for example, in Munich in 1775, he was admired and usually favorably compared with other virtuoso pianists. Once, however, it seems that he did not win a contest, as one can see from the following excerpt of an article printed in the *Deutsche Chronik* on 27 April 1775:

> *In Munich last Winter I heard two of the greatest clavier players, Herr Mozart and Captain von Beecke; my host, Herr Albert, who is enthusiastic about all that is great and beautiful, has an excellent fortepiano in his house. It was there that I heard these two giants in contest on the clavier. Mozart's playing had great weight, and he reads at sight everything that was put before him. But no more than that; Beecke surpasses him by a long way.* ...[8]

But two years later, in Augsburg in 1777, Mozart had more success than Beecke. His piano playing was received with adulation, as a contemporary critic wrote in a newspaper report:

> *Everything was extraordinary, tasteful and powerful, so unexpected, so elevating; the melody so agreeable, so playful and all so original; his performance on the fortepiano so pleasing, so pure, so full of expression, yet at the same time so extraordinarily fluent that one hardly knew what to listen to first, and the whole audience was moved to ecstasy.* ...[9]

---

[8] Quoted from R. Marshall, *Mozart Speaks*, p. 10.
[9] Quoted from E. Mueller von Asow, who issued these reports in his edition of Mozart's letters, *Briefe W. A. Mozarts*, vol. 1, p. 271.

Many years later, a critic of the *Musikalische Real-Zeitung* in Dresden/Saxony (where the beautiful grand clavichords of the northern and central regions of Germany could be found in private homes) was equally enthusiastic and described his playing with these words:

> *On the 14th of April the famous composer W. A. Mozart from Vienna played on the fortepiano before His Eminence, and he has also performed here in Dresden in many aristocratic and private houses, with limitless success. His abilities at the clavichord and fortepiano are quite indescribable: one should add also his extraordinary ability to read at sight, which is truly incredible—for even he is hardly able to play a piece better after practice than he does at a first reading.*[10]

Mozart has often been called the first great pianist (a title for which he had for a long time only one possible rival as virtuoso performer: Muzio Clementi). His piano style clearly shows that he was a born pianist who had an amazing gift of exploiting his favorite instrument's technical and acoustical possibilities, at times reaching their utmost limits. After moving to Vienna, his preference for Stein pianos was soon superseded by that for the fortepianos of Anton Walter, from whom he bought two instruments (the second was a fortepiano pedal; Figure 1.2). Walter seems to have been successful in giving the instrument greater power.

The Sound of Mozart's Own Fortepiano by Anton Walter

Around 1780, the fortepianos of Anton Walter became known among Viennese musicians for allowing more dynamic gradations from **pp** to **ff** and permitting more varied modes of touch than other pianos. The development of piano building between 1777 (when Mozart visited Stein) and 1782 (the year Mozart probably acquired his Walter piano) was most remarkable, both for the quality of sound as well as the quantity. Even though the action of Walter's fortepianos is in many ways different from that of today's pianos, it should not be assumed that our modern instruments are capable of subtler nuances. Stein's and Walter's pianos both had a clear and bright sound in the upper register, which made it easier to play *cantabile* and with full tone colors. The lower notes had a peculiar round fullness, but none of the dull, stodgy sound of the low notes of a modern piano. Whereas the tone becomes somewhat thinner toward the top, the full sound of the bass is probably the most satisfying register of Mozart's own piano made by Anton Walter. The strings are so thin that chords in the bass can be played with perfect clarity even when they are very closely spaced. On a modern piano, chords in the bass register usually sound sodden and earthy, so stodgy that one can hardly pick out the individual notes. This is why such chords as the following one,

Ex. I/1:

which often occur in Mozart's piano works, are enough to challenge a modern pianist's taste and feeling of style when he is playing on a Steinway or Bösendorfer grand. We shall show in chapter 11 (p. 377) how to overcome this technical problem.

---

[10] *Musikalische Realzeitung* from the year 1789, p. 191; Quoted after E. Mueller von Asow, *Briefe W. A. Mozarts*, vol. 2, p. 259.

Figure 1.2 Mozart's fortepiano made by Anton Walter. (Mozarteum Salzburg).

It has been assumed that Mozart, like most of the musicians of his time, tuned his instruments himself. Whether he found time for this necessary but time-consuming work we do not know—he may have occasionally commissioned also a piano builder or tuner. But we may take it for granted that his sensitive ear disliked tuning in the old-fashioned, non-tempered style because it would have limited the possibilities of modulations to more distant keys. Though it is a proven fact that various tuning systems were still in use during the entire eighteenth century, Mozart—like J. S. Bach—was certainly among the advocates of a more modern well-tempered tuning. C. P. E. Bach's treatise recommends this system in the "Introduction to Part One" (p. 377) with the following words:

> Both types of instrument [harpsichord and clavichord] must be tempered as follows: In tuning the fifths and fourths, testing minor and major thirds and chords, take away from most of the fifths a barely noticeable amount of their absolute purity. All twenty-four tonalities will thus become usable. ... In practice, a keyboard so tuned is the purest of all instruments, for others may be more purely tuned but they cannot be purely played. The keyboard plays equally in tune in all twenty-four tonalities, and, mark well, with full chords, notwithstanding that these, because of their ratios, reveal a very slight impurity. The new method of tuning marks a great advantage over the old [system], even though the latter was of such a nature that a few tonalities were purer. ... [underline added by authors]

This statement by C. P. E. Bach should tell all harpsichordists what probably also Johann Sebastian Bach meant by "well-tempered" in the title of his famous forty-eight preludes and fugues.

It is understandable that, even if many contemporary musicians—especially of Italian origin—still tuned their instruments in an old-fashioned way, Mozart was certainly glad to use the modern system of equal temperament, perhaps following the advice of Johann Christian Bach, a pupil of his father and C. P. E. Bach. A proof for this assumption is found in a literal translation of a paragraph from Giuseppe Sarti's pamphlet "Esame acustico fatto sopra due frammenti di Mozart"[11] in which Sarti harshly criticized Mozart's String Quartet K. 465 ("Dissonanzen-Quartett") and then wrote:

> From these ... one can judge that the author [Mozart] ... is nothing more than a mere piano player with spoiled ears [orrecchie guaste]. ... He is a proponent of the false system of dividing the octave into twelve equal semitones, a system that has long been considered as demonstrably false by all sensible artists [sensati artisti].

But because Mozart certainly came across and also had to play on instruments tuned in a more traditional way, he obviously chose for his early Piano Sonatas K. 279–284 basic keys with no more than two flats or two sharps. The Sonata K. 282 in E-flat major with its three flat signs is rather an exception, more so the Piano Trio in E major, K. 542; apart from these works, he avoided basic keys with many flat or sharp signs.

It is not so easy to recreate on a modern piano the full differentiation of tone colors of a Mozart piano, and perhaps this is one reason why some pianists recommend the avoidance of the damper-lifting device, activated on modern pianos by the right pedal. Originally built as a stop and activated by hand, it was in Mozart's time used with the help of knee levers, which had the same function as a pedal on nearly all pianos built after 1800.

---

[11] This article was translated into German and summarized by an unknown correspondent of the *Allgemeine Musikalische Zeitung* and published in vol. xxxiv/1832 on June 6, 1832.

Knee Levers for Lifting the Dampers on Mozart's Pianos

We know from Mozart's letter of 17 October 1777, of which we have quoted the beginning and in which he praised the Stein pianos so vividly, that he used and appreciated the mechanism of lifting the dampers with the knees. He was also impressed by the fact that the damper-lifting device responded so perfectly on Stein's pianoforte. The same letter continues thus:

> Previously ... Späth's pianos had always been my favorites. But now I much prefer Stein's, for they damp ever so much better than the Regensburg instruments. When I strike hard, I can keep my finger on the note or raise it, but the sound ceases the moment I have produced it. In whatever way I touch the keys, the tone is always even. It never jars, it is never stronger or weaker or entirely absent; in a word, it is always even. It is true that he does not sell a pianoforte of this kind for less than three hundred gulden, but the trouble and the labour which Stein puts into the building of it cannot be paid for. His instruments have this special advantage over others that they are made with an escapement action. Only one maker in a hundred bothers about this. But without an escapement it is impossible to avoid jangling and vibration after the note is struck. When you touch the keys, the hammers fall back again the moment after they have struck the strings, whether you hold down the keys or release them. ... Here and in Munich I have played all my six sonatas by heart again several times. ... The last one, in D [K. 284], sounds exquisite on Stein's pianoforte. The device too which you work with your knee is better on his than on other instruments. I have only to touch it and it works; and when you shift your knee the slightest bit, you do not hear the least reverberation.

From these statements, two facts emerge clearly: Mozart was familiar with knee levers and apparently had used this damper-lifting mechanism on other pianos before he visited Stein's workshop and thus could praise Stein's mechanism as "better than on other instruments." There can and should be no question that Mozart welcomed the knee levers for the damper-lifting effect.[12] His own Walter piano, which was bought by him most probably in 1782, is preserved and exhibited in Mozart's birthplace (Geburtshaus) in Salzburg. Like Stein's fortepianos on which Mozart had played in 1777, it has knee levers.

However, Walter's piano originally had hand levers for lifting dampers, which suggests that the knee levers were added after the instrument had been initially finished.[13] This possibility gave rise to a controversial discussion in the 1990s. The question of when these knee levers were added has been the subject of much debate. Michael Latcham[14] considered it possible that Mozart bought and used his own concert grand piano without knee levers and advanced the curious notion that long after Mozart's death, his widow Constance asked Walter to add knee levers before sending the instrument to her son in Milan in 1811. However, this idea is absurd for various reasons. In the years after 1800, pedals were already replacing the then old-fashioned knee levers. Besides, Mozart's enthusiasm in 1777 for the well-functioning damper-lifting device in Stein's pianos is reason enough to regard Latcham's hypothesis as highly unlikely.

---

[12] See Joseph Banowetz, *The Pianist's Guide to Pedaling*. Banowetz correctly points out (p. 136) that *not* using the damper-lifting mechanism for Mozart is "not historically accurate." See also David Rowland, *The History of Pianoforte Pedalling*, p. 14ff.

[13] See Alfons Huber and Rudolf Hopfner, "Instrumentenkundlicher Befund des Mozart-Flügels," in *Mitteilungen der Internat. Stiftung Mozarteum* 48, p. 146ff.

[14] Michael Latcham, "Mozart and the Pianos of Anton Gabriel Walter," p. 382ff. Eva Badura-Skoda, "The Anton Walter Fortepiano—Mozart's Beloved Concert Instrument," p. 469ff. See also Paul Badura-Skoda, "Mozart without 'Pedal?'" p. 332ff.

Recent research by Ingrid Fuchs[15] confirms our assumption that Walter had several pianos ready for sale in 1782, the time when Mozart could afford to buy one. Thus, Mozart was able to choose among several available grand pianos, some of which may have been built a decade earlier. Because these instruments were relatively expensive, Mozart would have known the importance of his choice. Why should he have settled for an already antiquated instrument without knee levers for his intended concert activities in Vienna? Much more likely is that when he found the tone of one of Walter's available fortepianos especially beautiful and to his liking, but noticed that it only had a hand lever, he almost certainly requested that Walter build knee levers before he bought the piano. To add knee levers to a piano was only a matter of one or two hours' work for a builder.

The theory that Mozart bought a piano without knee levers and used it as such for all his concerts is simply not credible. In short, we believe that the knee levers were added at the time of purchase, and not after Mozart's death in 1791 or even after 1800. And so the answer to the question of whether it is historically correct to use the damper-lifting device (in modern language: *pedal*) when playing Mozart's piano works should never be a matter of yes or no but only one of when and how often.

Strangely enough, during this entire published controversy, one important feature of the knee levers in Mozart's own Walter piano has not been mentioned in the *Early Music Journal* discussion. Unlike in his other grand pianos, Walter installed here not one but two knee levers for raising the dampers. The right knee lever raises the dampers on the right side only; the left knee lever, however, operates all the dampers. (The *moderato* or celeste stop in the middle is hand operated.) The right knee lever is well suited to play a sequence of chords *legato* or to make a melody "sing" while the notes in the bass are played detached. On the other hand, the left knee lever (which corresponds to the modern pedal) is ideally suited for arpeggios and broken chords in *legato* context. Since 1956, Paul Badura-Skoda has played concerts on Mozart's own instrument as well as recorded repeatedly on this and many other Walter pianos. Only one other grand piano by Walter has damper-lifting devices similar to Mozart's piano and is found in the private collection of Signora Fernanda Giulini (Briosco/Italy).

We firmly believe that these different functions of the two knee levers were not the result of a later builder's whim but reflect a genuine idea of Anton Walter or Mozart. For a modern player, it is at first rather inconvenient to raise the dampers only with the left knee. The hand-operated levers on both sides of the keyboard also lifted once the dampers but would not be used by any performer today due to the fact that knee levers are much more convenient.

It is perhaps worth noting that the device of not only one but two damper-lifting possibilities (namely, either half or all of the dampers lifted), invented already by Gottfried Silbermann around 1730, was abandoned in Continental Europe around 1800. It was "reinvented" by Broadwood around 1815, when he introduced the split pedal which is found, e.g., on Beethoven's Broadwood concert grand (now preserved in Budapest) and on a Broadwood piano from 1817 in the Badura-Skoda Collection (now housed in the Musical Instrument Museum in Schloss Kremsegg, Kremsmünster, Austria). On all other known Walter pianos as well as on those fortepianos from the same period by Schantz, Hoffmann, Jakesch, etc., all the dampers are raised with only one knee lever, often located on the right side, while a second lever usually raises a piano or moderator stop. Another Walter piano from a slightly later time than Mozart's had an additional bassoon stop.

Why did Mozart select a piano in 1782 made by Anton Walter and not one made by Stein, whose pianos he had still recommended in 1781 to the Countess Thun? Obviously, because by

---

[15] Ingrid Fuchs, "Nachrichten zu Anton Walter in der Korrespondenz einer seiner Kunden," *Mitteilungen der Internat. Stiftung Mozarteum* 48, p. 107.

1782 he preferred Walter's grand pianos to Stein's pianos and considered them superior to all others. (He was not alone with this opinion in Vienna: other pianists including Beethoven shared his belief.) Even today the Walter pianos are most highly valued, though Stein's pianos and those of Schanz have their own merits and advantages. Walter's grand pianos are triple strung from the middle register to the treble and produce a much larger volume than Stein's double-strung instruments, and—what was probably even more important to Mozart—they had and still have an extraordinarily good singing quality.

Necessary Use of the Damper-Lifting Device or Pedal

The view has been advanced that Mozart regarded the employment of knee levers as a special effect to be used only on rare occasions. For this, however, we have no proper evidence, let alone proof; still, there might be a grain of truth in such an assumption. We know, for instance, from contemporary Viennese reports that Beethoven used pedal effects much more often than Mozart had done. An often quoted remark of Johann Nepomuk Hummel, who as a nine-year-old child had been Mozart's pupil, should not be taken too seriously. He complained in later years only about the then already fashionable abuse of the pedal, which he called a *Sündendecker* or *sin-coverer*. That led to the assumption that he (and perhaps Mozart as well) rarely needed the damper-lifting effect or pedal. Thus, Hummel may have unintentionally contributed to a mere misunderstanding of the facts that could support the above-mentioned claim that Mozart's piano did not have knee levers for the damper-lifting device on his own Walter piano and that he was satisfied with a hand-operated lever.

It is certainly possible to play Mozart's piano works without any pedal or damper-lifting device, granted a few exceptions, which we shall quote below. But is it appropriate historically? And is it right aesthetically? We hope to demonstrate that it is neither, and we shall now give a number of musical reasons to validate our belief. Because Mozart's left knee lever is identical in function to our modern right pedal, from now on—for the convenience of modern readers—we shall use the term *pedal* in the modern sense, instead of the clumsy expression *damper-lifting device*.

Let us first deal with the most obvious places to use our right pedal. In the second movement of the Sonata in D Major, K. 311, mm. 86–89, Mozart's notation makes it obvious that he expects pedaling and counts on its use by others. His autograph quarter note stems would otherwise make no sense at all:

Ex. I/2:

Does the way Mozart notated the quarter notes in the bass allow any other explanation than that he wanted them to sound longer than the sixteenth of the accompaniment? In his *Violinschule*, Mozart's father Leopold repeatedly expressed warnings against the shortening of notes, starting in the first chapter of his book (see section III, p. 45, and also later on p. 46). Therefore, it is hard to imagine that the left-hand quarter notes in K. 311 should be played shortened. But without the use of the pedal, they cannot sound as quarter notes.

But let us assume, for the sake of argument, that Mozart, ignoring his father's advice, was following another old tradition—namely, keeping only half the note values—and that he may have considered a performance of this passage without pedal. Alas, not even half of the note value can be sustained by the fingers alone, because the fifth finger has to leave the lower key as soon as the second or third crosses over:

Ex. I/3:

would become

Thus, the bass notes, if played without pedal, would get not half but only a quarter of their value—an absurdity.

Even worse: imagine what would happen to many of Mozart's accompaniments if the bass notes were so shortened; for instance, in a *cantabile* passage such as found in K. 570/I, mm. 23–26 (and in the many similar passages):

Ex.I/4:

There are other examples where the sound of lifted dampers is necessary; for instance, in the many *arpeggio* passages.

Arpeggios

As the very name suggests, the word *arpeggio* is derived from *arpa* (harp). We all know that the harp has no damper mechanism, and the harpist has to damp the vibration of the strings with his hands. Broken chords can be played on the harp over the full tonal range and are usually not damped, except afterwards with the hands. Few eighteenth-century composers did not write this sort of harp imitation when composing works for stringed keyboard instruments.

Because the normal harpsichord with quills, the *Kielflügel*, has no pedal and no knee levers for damper lifting, arpeggios have to be sustained by the fingers only. The most meticulous notation for meeting this necessity was given by Johann Sebastian Bach; e.g., in his Chromatic

Fantasy BWV 903 (mm. 18–31). Bach wrote the first of those chords that have to be performed as arpeggios, in the same way in which he wished all of these harmonies to be arpeggiated:

Ex. I/5:

When we look at similar arpeggios in Mozart's piano writing, we can notice that he wrote the harmonies out in full, and naturally their sound should be harp-like and the sound intermingled. Examples of this kind are numerous; e.g., in the D minor Fantasia K. 397:

Ex. I/6:

In the opening of the C minor Fantasy K. 396, the first arpeggio could theoretically still be played with hand levers, though the damping afterwards would be difficult and noisy. Mozart certainly welcomed his knee levers in this case:

Ex. I/7:

And from m. 8 on in this fantasy, hand levers are certainly insufficient and knee levers essential:

Ex. I/8:

In the Fantasy in C major, K. 394, m. 46, the use of the pedal is advisable. To play all these arpeggios without any damper lifting would sound odd not only to modern ears and standards.

Ex. I/9:

In the Menuetto cantabile section of the third movement of the Concerto in E-flat Major, K. 271, Mozart had notated in mm. 270–271 two *arpeggios*:

Ex. I/10:

When this passage occurs a second time in mm. 287 and 288, the *arpeggios* are written out and slurred—another indication that Mozart intended a harp-like effect and counted on the damper-lifting device of his knee levers:

Ex. I/11:

Notes That Can Be Properly Sustained Only with Pedal

In the same concerto movement (K. 271/III) from which the last *arpeggio* examples were taken, we find in the presto part a passage in which the left hand has to play *Alberti* figures and the melodic notes are given to the right hand, playing them alternately in the bass and treble:

Ex. I/12:

If played on a fortepiano with hand levers only or on a harpsichord, the two high half notes in mm. 67–68 would definitely sound too short and unpleasantly sharp.

In the following example from Mozart's Piano Sonata in A minor, K. 310/II, m. 83, only an incredibly large hand can sustain the sound of the low note C beneath the second trill without the help of the pedal:

Ex. I/13:

It is significant that at the parallel passage in m. 49 Mozart notated the low note as an *appoggiatura*, apparently with the pedal in mind in order to sustain the lower note.

Ex. I/14:

The Sound of Repeated Portato *Notes Gain from Pedaling*

In a certain type of *portato* passage, the piano strings should not be struck by the hammers but put into gentle continuing vibration; e.g., in the Sonata in A minor, K. 310, second movement, m. 64, a demand for which the pedal is of great help:

Ex. I/15:

A similar example is found in the Variation VIII (Adagio), m. 3, of the so-called Duport Variations, K. 573:

Ex. I/16:

(Naturally, one has to change pedal before the third beat of this measure.)

Such *portato* notes are also found in the second movement of the A minor Sonata K. 310. Even on a modern piano with its double escapement action, it is difficult to render them well without pedal and more so on a fortepiano. These softly repeated notes (*tenuto*) must be well distinguished from the "real" *staccato*, where use of the pedal is forbidden:

Ex. I/17:

Not Only Arpeggios—Broken Chords Also Need Pedaling

The difference between arpeggios and broken chords (*Dreiklangs-Zerlegungen*) lies in the speed of the note succession. A fine example demonstrating the useful help of the pedal for making these chords sing is found in the second movement of the Concerto in D Minor, K. 466.

Ex. I/18:

Here the use or non-use of the pedal makes a remarkable difference in sound volume (apart from the sound quality). This passage, of course, seems to invite free ornamentation. Robert Levin suggested this tasteful embellishment:

Ex. I/19:

For many years, Paul Badura-Skoda played a similar embellishment. In 1992 he recorded the following embellished version (on an Auvidis-Valois CD Nr. 4664):

Ex. I/20:

Presently, however, Paul Badura-Skoda, who was never quite satisfied with the result, shares the opinion of his coauthor that Mozart's unembellished version sounds best (with the necessary damper lifting, of course. Even in the case of embellishing these notes, a performance without

pedal sounds rather dry.). In contrast to other themes in the Romance with a more lively character and faster notes, we believe today that the whole passage from m. 40 onwards is based on
calm sustained notes, and we find an unembellished performance more satisfying. In the last
analysis, however, this is a matter of taste and not of historical knowledge.

If this concerto is played with an orchestra on an eighteenth-century piano, experience
confirms that this movement is even more in need of maximum resonance than when a modern piano is used; thus, this passage needs pedaling, whether it is played with or without
embellishments.

Hand Crossing in Lyrical Movements

In the course of the discussion about the use of the damper-lifting device mentioned above, issue
was taken with the example of the Variation IV of the first movement of the Piano Sonata in A
Major, K. 331. The argument, that a lifting of the dampers helps to render this passage satisfactorily, apparently did not convince every reader:

Ex. I/21:

However, this hand-crossing passage is found in a movement marked by Mozart Andante
grazioso, and, in addition, this variation features throughout a *legato* touch. Here the high
notes (especially in the third measure) sound more gracious, with a bell-like quality when
produced by lifting the dampers. The same is true for similar passages in Mozart's fast movements, such as those from the third movement of his Piano Concerto K. 450, or in various
variation works for piano solo such as K. 352, K. 455, and K. 460. But in all these cases, the
use of the damper-lifting device is not as compulsory as, for instance, in the Sonata K. 311/II,
mm. 86–89 (Ex. I/2).

Singing Quality of Sustained High Notes

This important aspect of piano playing is often overlooked, yet *cantabile* playing is of vital
importance in performance in "the new style," as described by Leopold Mozart (see p. 11 of this
chapter). A single note played with pedal has much more resonance than without it. This is due
to the sympathetic vibrations of other strings: not only more resonance, but a longer duration
of sound is thus achieved, especially needed when one is playing on period instruments. A few
examples may suffice; e.g., the following passage, once more taken from the Romance of K. 466
(which we again would like to hear without embellishments):

Ex. I/22:

Another example of a passage from the second movement of the last Piano Concerto K. 595 (which Mozart prepared for publication and therefore would have probably ornamented had he wanted it to be played embellished), mm. 17 and 90 needs pedaling:

Ex. I/23:

On any piano, whether modern or a period instrument, pedaling can increase the singing quality of this beautiful passage when unembellished.

To another kind of long notes that get more resonance through pedaling belongs the very first entry of the solo piano in Mozart's C minor Concerto K. 491, where the dotted half notes g^2 and aflat^2 need a special emphasis and duration if the phrase should properly sing:

Ex. I/24:

TRACK
56

To sum up the discussion of pedaling: Mozart's keyboard textures present ample evidence that he counted on the use of the damper-lifting device. As shown in Mozart's manner of notation in Ex.I/2, pedaling is indeed at times essentially required; at other times, the effects gained with the help of pedaling are musically desirable. Mozart was an unchallenged master of exploiting the timbres and tonal possibilities of his instruments—one may recall the wonderful soft trumpet solo in the first finale of *Don Giovanni*, or the treatment of the clarinet in the Trio K. 498, the Clarinet Concerto K. 622, or the Wind Serenade K. 361—again why should he not have used a mechanism about which he wrote so enthusiastically in his letter? In addition, an occasional use of the pedal when playing Mozart's piano works is fully justified historically.

That Beethoven used the pedal more often than Mozart does not imply that Mozart did not use it when necessary or desirable. Even with the dampers raised, the pianos of Mozart's time sounded much more translucent than those of the present day.

However, if we would have to choose between two extremes of no pedal or too much pedal, a performance of Mozart's music would be more tolerable when played without a lifting of dampers than with too much use of that effect. Naturally, the modern use of the pedal must in no way be allowed to mar the clarity of performance, and we should expressly warn against excessive pedaling on modern pianos with their muddier timbre. On the pianos of Mozart's time, with their clearer and more distinct tone, the careful use of the pedal seems not only less dangerous but often a welcome enrichment of sound and, in some cases, a necessity.

Mozart's Fortepiano Pedal Instrument

We mentioned above that Mozart was a trained organist and that, when he first tried out the pedal board of an organ, he was immediately taken by the sound of it.

In later years, the possibility of enlarging the range of his piano may have induced him to order a pedal-piano instrument, a separate bass instrument with a hammer action. Mozart's pedal fortepiano presumably had a range of two bass octaves, and it was placed underneath his fortepiano and played similarly to an organ pedal board. In March 1785, Mozart announced a concert with the help of printed handout flyers in which he promised to perform not only a new fortepiano concerto but also to employ an especially large fortepiano pedal for his improvised fantasy. The text of the original "Handbillett," preserved in the Theatersammlung of the Austrian National Library is the following:

> *Announcement: / On Thursday, the 10th of March 1785 / Maestro di Capella Mozart will have the honor / of presenting / a grand musical academy / for his benefit /in the National Imperial Court Theatre, in which he will not only play a newly / finished Fortepiano concert / but will also perform on an especially large / Forte piano Pedal in his Fantasy improvisation. The remaining pieces will be announced on a poster on the day of the performance.*[16]

With this flyer Mozart informed his admirers that he intended to use his pedal piano. It was also built by Anton Walter, the builder of his beloved concert grand, as we know from a sale of it after Mozart's death (see footnote 22). An interesting correspondence (in Latin) of an amateur violinist, physician, and great admirer of Mozart named Amand Wilhelm Smith, with his patron in east Hungary, has been recently discovered.[17] Smith wrote that he had heard Mozart playing on his piano with the pedal piano. This correspondence also contains a letter from an agent, Johann Samuel Liedemann, mentioning Anton Walter as the builder of the pedal piano. Liedemann's report confirms our old assumption that Mozart already used the pedal piano publicly on 11 February 1785 for the first performance of his Piano Concerto K. 466.[18] Leopold Mozart, visiting his son in Vienna at this time (February 1785), saw and heard the new pedal piano and reported on 12 March 1785 to his daughter in St. Gilgen:

---

[16] The German original text reads: "Nachricht / Donnerstag den 10. März 1785 wird / Herr Kapellmeister Mozart die Ehre haben / in dem / k. k. National= Hof =Theater / eine / grosse musikalische Akademie / zu seinem Vortheile / zu geben, wobey er nicht nur ein neues erst /verfertigtes Fortepiano = Konzert / spielen, sondern auch ein besonders grosses / Fortepiano Pedal beym Phantasieren gebraucht wird. Die übrigen Stücke wird der große Anschlagzettel am Tage selbst zeigen."

[17] See Ingrid Fuchs, "W. A. Mozart in Wien. Unbekannte Nachrichten in einer zeitgenössischen Korrespondenz aus seinem persönlichen Umfeld," *Festschrift Otto Biba zum 60.*

[18] See I. Fuchs, "Mozarts Klavierkonzert d-moll KV 466. Bemerkungen zum Autograph und zum Instrument der Uraufführung," in *Mozartiana. Festschrift for the 70. Birthday of Professor Ebisawa Bin.*

Figure 1.3 Wilhelm Rück's copy of Mozart's fortepiano made by Anton Walter and a reconstruction of Mozart's *fortepiano pedale* likewise by Walter (lost). The depicted pedal piano was built by Matthias Arens in 1990 (Collection Badura-Skoda).

> *He has had a large Fortepiano pedal made, which is under the instrument and is about two feet longer and extremely heavy.*

During the Baroque period, keyboard instruments with pedal boards, whether harpsichords or clavichords, were usually built as practice instruments for organists. They were mostly connected with the main instrument using the same strings but sometimes were built as separate pedal harpsichords. Pedal instruments for fortepianos, however, seem to have been rarely commissioned—certainly a reason for Mozart, after the initial entry of some notes for the pedal board in his autograph of the Concerto K. 466—to stop writing notes for it.

The Danish actor and musician, Joachim Daniel Preisler, who visited Mozart in 1788, mentioned the pedal piano in his diary:

Sunday the 24th August. In the afternoon Jünger, Lange and Werner came for us to go to Kapellmeister Mozart's. The hour of music I heard there was the happiest ever granted me. This little man and great master improvised twice on a pedal piano, so wonderfully! so wonderfully! that I did not know where I was. Weaving together the most difficult passages and the most ingratiating themes.[19]

And Michael Rosing, who also was accompanying J. D. Preisler and the other admirers to hear Mozart play, confirmed the report:

... for myself; particularly his pedal in the second fantasy made the greatest impression on us.[20]

Another visitor, a doctor named Frank, also spoke enthusiastically about this pedal piano after a visit at Mozart's home:

I played him a fantasia he had composed. "Not bad", he said to my great astonishment. "Now listen to me play it." Wonder of wonders! Under his fingers the piano became quite another instrument. He had reinforced it with a second keyboard instrument that served as a pedal.[21]

Such an additional pedal instrument with a hammer action, similar to the one Mozart possessed, can now be found only rarely in museums and collections of musical instruments, and none from the eighteenth century is known to us; only a few from the early nineteenth century seem to be extant. Close to the appearance of the original might be the picture of our reconstructed pedal piano (see Figure 1.3), and the sound of it can be heard on the enclosed CD as example 5.

TRACK
5

Mozart's own instrument has been lost, because after Mozart's death, his widow Constance, when moving into new quarters, apparently sold the pedal piano; it eventually came into the possession of the amateur composer and pianist Ignaz Werner Raphael, a known music lover, who died in 1799.[22] An advertisement in the *Posttäglichen Anzeigen aus dem k. k. Frag-und Kundschaftsamte in Wien*, a supplement of the *Wiener Zeitung*, tells us that in 1799 the assets of the late Raphael's property were offered publicly for sale. It is not known who acquired the pedal piano *"gegen baare Bezahlung licitando"* (for cash) at that time or its subsequent whereabouts.

The Range of Mozart's Fortepiano

Mozart would hardly have acquired a pedal piano without some special reason. The fortepiano of Mozart's time had a compass of only five octaves. The lowest note of his pedal piano was probably the low CC of the modern piano, and its compass was about two octaves. Apparently, Mozart did not regard his piano's bottom F as a desirable lower limit and wanted to be able to play the lower EE, EE flat, DD, or even CC when performing. As a trained organist he obviously

---

[19] Quoted after O. E. Deutsch, *Dänische Schauspieler zu Besuch bei Mozart*, *Österreichische Musikzeitschrift*, *11*, p. 406 et seq.

[20] Ibid., p. 410.

[21] See Hermann Abert, *W. A. Mozart*, vol. 2, note to p. 1007.

[22] See W. Brauneis, "...eines der besten Forte Piano von Herrn Wallter, mit einem Pedal von dem sel. Herrn Mozart," in *Mitteilungen der Internationalen Stiftung Mozarteum* 48. Jg., pp. 200–209.

could play the pedal board without problems. From the wording of his flyer announcing a concert, and also from the reports of his visitors, we know that he certainly used the pedal piano for his free fantasies. It allowed him to extend the compass in the bass, to double important bass notes and motives, and thus increase the sound volume.

When ordering his pedal piano, Mozart may indeed have thought primarily of his free fantasies, a very popular offering on concert programs of pianists in his and Beethoven's day. But he may also have felt a need for such a pedal piano for his piano concertos, which he conducted from the keyboard, not only to emphasize the bass part in the *col basso* passages of the *tutti* sections but also to enlarge the compass in the sections where the piano had to play a "solo." This assumption is substantiated by his notation of the first solo in his Concerto in D minor, K. 466, where it is shown in his autograph how he employed the pedal board. The passage in mm. 88–90 was notated by Mozart in such a way that a pianist cannot play all notes without a pedal board. Regrettably, the editor of this concerto in the NMA did not understand the reason why Mozart wrote down this passage as he did. He was convinced that the passage simply contained, an error and he left out the low notes and altered these measures so that they could be played without a pedal board.

Unfortunately, a normal facsimile reproduction does not show as clearly as the autograph the different colors of the ink that point to Mozart's two stages of writing this passage:

Ex. I/25:

It had been argued in the preface to the *NMA* volume of this concerto movement that Mozart was revising an original notation and in M. 88 made "a mistake." A careful study of the autograph, however, reveals that Mozart wrote (as he usually did) the notes in these measures at different times, writing first the piano part in a version for two hands with a simple bass part in light brown ink. At a later time he notated (in dark brown ink) above the simple bass notes the organ-like accompaniment, with low notes for the pedal board and with chords for the left hand in the middle of the keyboard. For these added notes there was no real correction necessary and, indeed, no visible erase or smear signs can be discovered at this spot in the autograph.

Until recently, most publishers of Mozart's D minor Concerto, including the *NMA*—realizing the impossibility of playing this passage on a piano without a pedal board—decided to alter the passage in print so that the two hands alone can play these measures. In the Eulenburg score, however, the notes are reproduced as written in Mozart's autograph:

Ex. I/26:

Naturally, on a fortepiano without a pedal board, these measures cannot be played as written. Apparently, Mozart became aware of this, too, and, realizing by then that only very few people were in the possession of a fortepiano pedal and could render the text as written, he decided not to continue the organ-like notation. It was probably for this reason that in the next solo passage for the piano he did not notate notes for his pedal instrument. But he himself certainly used his newly acquired pedal piano more extensively than is fixed in notation, and certainly not only in this Concerto K. 466.

Thus it is not out of style to remember the pedal piano in certain cases where this is particularly justifiable. A good example for such a possibility is the augmentation of the fugue subject from the Fantasy and Fugue K. 394, where one could double the bass notes an octave lower to enrich the sound:

Ex. I/27:

One could also play the chromatic bass line in the development of the first movement of the E-flat major Concerto K. 482 an octave lower on the modern piano; when a pedal piano from Mozart's time is used by the soloist, the additional pedal notes could be played instead of the notated ones:

Ex. I/28:

(Sustained notes on the analogy of the orchestral basses)

In Mozart's cadenza for the A major Concerto K. 488, Mozart may also have used the low pedal notes:

Ex. I/29:

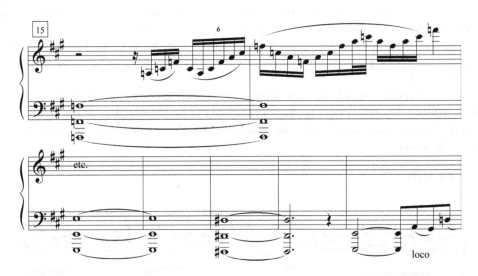

But all those passages mentioned are probably exceptional cases. In general, one would be better advised to adhere to the traditional text written down by Mozart, particularly if one is playing on modern instruments, as there is the danger of making the tone of the modern grand piano too thick and unclear by using its deep bass notes.

The highest key in the upper range of Mozart's Walter piano was f³. Mozart always kept to this range of five octaves in his piano compositions with only one exception: in the Duet Sonata in D Major, K. 448/III, m. 98, he demands an f-sharp³. The apparent ease with which Mozart otherwise observed the upper limits of this compass is indeed astounding. He always found an elegant way to keep the melodic line sounding "natural." Most fortepianos of Mozart's time had the f³ as its highest tone, but exceptions existed. Indeed, the dating of extant fortepianos according to their compass turns out to be a rather dangerous matter. Domenico Scarlatti, for instance, sometimes wrote higher notes than Mozart—we find g³ and a³ in his sonatas, so one of the pianos or harpsichords at the Spanish court must have had this compass. The range of an extant fortepiano by Anton Walter also includes g³. Regarding the Sonata K. 448, in which the performer of the first piano has to play that unusual f-sharp³, Mozart composed this sonata for a performance with his student Barbara Ployer and probably knew that the Ployer family owned a piano with a compass reaching to g³. (Tuning the f³ to f-sharp³—a so-called *scordatura*—would not have been possible for K. 448 because the f³ is also needed in this sonata.)

To reiterate: Mozart's ability to restrict himself when composing to the compass offered by his own Walter piano is astonishing. If it should happen that in the recapitulation of a second subject the theme threatened to go above the top f³ because of its transposition into the tonic key, then Mozart would alter the motive, and he succeeded in doing this in a so subtle and elegant way that "necessity became a virtue." Often this change is done in the simplest possible way with the most convincing results. Such an example is found in the Concerto in B-flat Major, K. 595, third movement, mm. 112–113:

Ex. I/30:

Here, at the recapitulation (mm. 251–252), the original diatonicism is altered into chromaticism.

Ex. I/31:

A literal transposition would have required the high g³:

Ex. I/32:

In Beethoven's works, one often comes across passages in which the compass of the contemporary piano seems to have imposed unwelcome limitations on the composer's fantasy (e.g., his G major Piano Concerto, first movement, m. 318, or the Sonata op.10, no. 3, first movement, mm. 20ff.). In Mozart's piano works, on the other hand, it is hardly ever necessary, and in most cases not possible, to make alterations such as many present-day pianists make in these particular passages from Beethoven. One can point to only two possible exceptions to this rule in

Mozart's works: in the G major Piano Concerto K. 453, third movement, m. 56, retaining the original upward motion (as in mm. 40), would mean reaching g^3:

Ex. I/33:

Suggested adaptation in bar 56:

The other exception is found in the Concerto for Three Pianos K. 242/III, where a literal transposition of the figuration from mm. 34ff. at mm. 155ff. would result in having the top a^3 found as highest note, which would hardly disturb today's listener if played as such:

Ex. I/34:

But all these alterations are by no means really necessary, let alone compulsory.

A Word about Piano Mechanics

Mozart was well aware of possible shortcomings in the mechanism of contemporary pianos. Throughout the first paragraph of his letter from 1777 about Stein's pianos, Mozart was referring to its action. The sentences

> *In whatever way I touch the keys, the tone is always even. It never jars, it is never stronger or weaker or entirely absent; in a word, it is always even. … When you touch the keys, the hammers fall back again the moment after they have struck the strings, whether you hold down the keys or release them. …*

imply that he often had encountered mechanical problems on other pianos. It can happen even nowadays that, with a bad or badly restored fortepiano, the hammer does not fall back into place when one plays *legato* (i.e., keeping the finger on the key) but stays pressed against the string.

Because modern hammers are felt covered, in today's pianos this merely results in an undesired damping of the string. But the narrow leather hammers of Mozart's pianos would have given a disagreeable buzzing tone, like the noise produced by touching a vibrating string on a present-day piano with a metallic object, such as a screwdriver. Fortunately, in the last fifty years a number of excellent piano builders have concentrated on learning the art of restoring fortepiano actions while retaining (not replacing) as many parts of old instruments as possible, so that the action works properly, the original sound is better preserved, and a new tone color is not created.

Everyone knows that a tender touch produces a soft sound and that forceful attacks produce a loud one. If too much force is used, the sound of the fortepiano can become harsh and metallic, ugly to our ears—indeed, the strings might not survive the attacks; the amplitude of string vibration is thus increased, sometimes even up to the breaking point. Yet few pianists really know what happens inside the piano. It is solely the speed with which the hammer strikes that determines the intensity of sound (i.e., the amplitude of string vibration)—the faster the speed of the hammer, the louder the result. On modern pianos, the ratio between key depression and hammer speed is 1:5—that is, the hammer moves five times faster than the speed with which the key is depressed; on Mozart period pianos, the ratio is larger, 1:7 or 1:8.

Why is so much more strength needed to play a fortepiano very loud? This has something to do with physics. Kinetic energy, and therefore the resistance, increases with the square of the speed with which a key is struck. If a key is struck so that it moves twice as fast, it will produce four times more energy; if it is struck so that the key moves three times faster, then the energy, and with it the resistance, will be increased ninefold. In other words, with increased speed, those light hammers come to exert pressure measured in pounds.

To play loudly requires quick depression and strength of muscles. This is a matter of practice (and exercise) and, as such, does not pose specific problems. The real problem for the pianist comes in playing a controlled *p*. As we have said elsewhere (see p. 369), in playing eighteenth-century music, the fingers are more involved than either the wrists or the arms. Obviously, in slow tempos, soft, delicate sounds are achieved by depressing the keys slowly, right down to the bottom. Of course, if this motion is too slow, the escape mechanism will keep the hammer from touching the string and no sound at all will be produced. But most passages demanding *p* playing are in a fast tempo, making slow key motion impossible. To move a hammer relatively slowly while playing fast may seem like a contradiction in terms—and yet, we know it can be done. If the key is depressed rapidly, but only two to three millimeters deep without going to the bottom, the hammers will receive only a very short initial impulse and will continue by their own momentum toward the string, relatively slowly. This type of playing requires great finger and wrist control and is not easy to achieve.

This difficulty might offer one explanation for the fact that many pianists are actually "forteists," unable to play a controlled piano with their fingers. To compensate for their lack of this ability, they resort to using their feet. Repeatedly we have made the observation that many pianists (even good ones) automatically press the left pedal down whenever they see the indication *p* in the score.[23] It is true that with the shifting of the action on grand pianos (*una corda*), the lesser used softer surface of the hammer will indeed produce a more delicate sound. However, due to the concomitant reduction of overtones, the result will not only be a softer but a duller sound as well. Instead of the singing piano called for by the composer, the result will be

---

[23] This is particularly true of the Russian school of pianists. One reason for this might lie in the fact that for decades good pianos were rarely found in Russian conservatories and private homes, and good piano technicians were even more scarce. Because in time the overused, worn-out hammers came to produce ghastly metallic sounds, pianists would often try to remedy this shortcoming by pressing the left pedal. Unfortunately, after a while the shifted part of the hammer's surface became as hard as the original part, sometimes even harder.

a lifeless, muddy sonority. Think of it this way: It is as if a violinist, whenever he wanted to play a soft passage or *cantilena*, put on the mute (*sordino*); obviously, no intelligent violinist would do that. In other words, the *una corda* effect, produced by pressing down the left pedal is a register comparable to the stop of an organ that produces a distant, muffled sound. Furthermore, the indication *una corda* (one string only) is often a misnomer. On most pianos, the hammers still strike all three strings but with their softer part not hardened by normal use. On period pianos, only two of the three strings are struck when the left pedal is used. (In our experience, we have found but one or two English fortepianos where only one string was touched. And many old pianos have a moderator [*sordino*] instead of an *una corda* stop.)

As it is, the modern piano is already lacking in overtones in comparison with the silvery, bright sound of pianos of Mozart's time, and using the shifting pedal *una corda* or a moderator only widens this gap, doing injustice to the lively character of Mozart's music. Only on those rare occasions when a change of tone color is desirable—for example, with *pianissimo* or *sotto voce* indications—is its use appropriate. As we have noted elsewhere, Mozart's piano did have a moderator stop whose effect was to make the sound softer and reduce the overtones. It is important to know, however, that this stop was operated by hand with a knob above the center of the keyboard and not by a knee lever or a pedal, as found in later fortepianos. This means that one of the pianist's hands had to leave the keys for a second or two to actuate the stop, obviously making it impossible for him to change the tone color in the middle of a passage. This stop later came to be replaced in Vienna by the shifting pedal that had already been built into early English and French fortepianos.

In short, the moral of the story is this: We pianists must learn to play *piano* with our fingers and not with our left foot!

Everyone who plays Mozart nowadays could profit immensely from occasionally playing a period instrument of Mozart's time. Eighteenth-century pianos were wholly suited to be played with varied tone colors. Practice at an old fortepiano is the most direct way to gain an idea of the sound that must have been in Mozart's ear and mind. This kind of personal study cannot be replaced by merely listening to recordings of the old instrument and certainly not by even the most exhaustive description of the Mozart piano. Today, many good replicas exist and many music schools have acquired one; therefore, young pianists *can* find opportunities to play a Mozart fortepiano and discover which sounds are possible and what Mozart's intentions may have been.

2
Dynamics

Intensity and volume of sound are marked by dynamic signs in musical notation. In acoustics, the amplitude of sound waves is measured in decibels (dB), ranging from 1 dB (just audible) to 120 dB (pain level) and higher. In music, loudness and softness have been expressed up to the present by the well-known symbols for *forte*, *f*, and *piano*, *p*, and their more refined gradations (*mf*, *pp*, *ff*, etc.). Dynamics define not only the general basic degree of loudness or softness in music, but the changes of intensity as well: accents, *crescendo*, *decrescendo*, and verbal indications such as *sotto voce*, *marcato*, *dolce*, etc., form part of our musical vocabulary.

Dynamic variation is so natural in speech as well as in music that normally its presence in at least small degrees can be assumed. What we call a *dynamic performance* implies many changing levels of intensity, whereas a *flat* performance tires the listener by its relatively monotonous sound volume. (In this respect, the almost unchanging loudness of some rock music may be considered "undynamic.") We shall see later that Mozart's music is full of inner dynamics and requires constant subtle changes and a sensitive rendering of the sound level, even when we regretfully have to state that Mozart's dynamic indications are sometimes much too scarce or even missing altogether.

Basic Dynamic Signs Customary during the Eighteenth Century

It is generally known that the signs *f* and *p* are already found in a few compositions from the time around 1600, but only from the beginning of the eighteenth century did dynamic notation become increasingly more refined. In seventeenth-century keyboard music, most works had no dynamic indications at all. Some of the lesser known composers wrote one or the other sign around 1700, but in the works of, say, Domenico Scarlatti,[1] Handel, and many others, we find no or very few dynamic markings. The lack of those hints for musicians was hardly felt as an impediment by the performers: the various genres of music were so well defined that there was no doubt that an *ouverture*, a *sinfonia*, or the best known dance movements such as the *menuet* or the *sarabande* had to be played rather *forte*; all lyrical *cantabile* movements, however, demanded a *piano*. Only a fool would play, for instance, Scarlatti's most famous Sonata in E major, Kirkpatrick 380 (Fadini 326, Longo 23) in a voluminous *forte*. Likewise, it must have been rather obvious for an eighteenth-century player that the E major prelude in the second book of J. S. Bach's *Well-Tempered Clavier* would require a less loud delicate *cantabile* singing style, while the ensuing fugue in the antique style suggested a full *pleno organo* sound on any given instrument of the time, including the fortepiano.[2] Bach was one of the first composers who realized that inherent dynamics were not always obvious and self-understood. He introduced carefully designed dynamic indications into his published keyboard works starting with the second

---

[1] Emilia Fadini, the notable Scarlatti scholar, observed that of the six hundred–odd Scarlatti sonatas only one has several dynamic indications in one of the two main sources.

[2] Regarding Sebastian Bach's use of the fortepiano, see Eva Badura-Skoda, "Komponierte J. S. Bach Hammerklavier-Konzerte?" *Bach Jahrbuch 1991*, p. 159ff. In the course of the nineteenth century the "Romantic" notion did gain observation that a fugue has to start like a kitten and finish like a roaring lion.

part of his "Clavier-Übung," the *Italian Concerto*. It is important to realize that in large portions of this special work the melody is marked *forte* and the accompaniment *piano*. Though this is a logical hint for a two-manual harpsichord or a compound harpsichord-piano (a clavichord is hardly the proper instrument for the performance of this work), it is nevertheless a milestone, a futuristic, modern approach. In his fifth *Brandenburg Concerto*, Bach went even further, giving different dynamic marks for simultaneous passages,[3] a departure from the uniform *f* or *p* signs, often found in orchestral scores of the nineteenth and the beginning of the twentieth centuries.

One of the most refined composers in matters of dynamics was C. P. E. Bach, who composed many of his keyboard works for his rather special, large, sensitive Silbermann clavichord and also for the fortepiano. Although his compositional matrix[4] has little bearing on Mozart or even Haydn, his sensitivity with regard to rendering music as "a language of the heart" must have produced a deep impact on both Viennese classical masters. His well-known demand that "one must play from the soul and not like a trained bird"[5] found open ears. Similarly, he declared his preference for sensitive, soft, and expressively varied dynamics:

> I believe that first of all music must move the heart, and a pianist will never achieve that by simply banging, drumming, arpeggiating [durch bloßes Poltern, Trommeln und Harpeggiren]—not with me, at least![6]

Gradually, more and more works, solo and chamber music, as well as orchestral compositions, were provided with dynamic markings during the Rococo period. For the composers of galant music, it became essential that the melodies were like speeches full of slight dynamic variation and prominently heard in the foreground; thus, they should be played considerably louder than the accompaniment, which, according to Rousseau, should be heard only as a background sound, comparable to the "rushing of a brooklet" (Rousseau). In homophonic music in all styles, the accompaniment had to be softer than the main melody. Great pianists of all periods distinguished themselves by simply giving more weight to all singing melodies—a hundred years of recording history have confirmed this observation.

Mozart's use of dynamic signs places him in the middle between the Baroque tendency toward few or nonexistent dynamic indications (J. S. Bach is an exception) and the thoroughness of the Romantic period—not to mention the overly refined dynamics of the post-Romantic or Impressionistic period (Tchaikovsky, for example, uses a sextuple *pppppp* in the first movement of the *Symphonie Pathétique* in m. 160, and *crescendo* and *diminuendo* signs from *pppp* to *pp* shortly before, in mm. 154–157.)[7] Beethoven usually notated many more dynamic markings than Mozart, with a frequent use of *pp*. Schubert likewise often wrote *pp* and altogether more signs from *fff* to *ppp*. Yet, even these subtle differentiations fall short of hundreds of audible changes between the softest and the loudest. In this respect, musical notation is still rather crude and imperfect.

Mozart's frequent use of the word *cantabile* makes more sense if the accompaniment is played softer. So-called *Alberti* basses, which occur often in a varied form in Mozart's piano works, should be subdued and played much softer than the melodic part. Good examples for

---

[3] See Paul Badura-Skoda, *Interpreting Bach at the Keyboard* (Oxford 1993, Clarendon Press), p. 133.

[4] See Dominique Patier, "La dynamique musicale au XVIIéme siécle," pp. 446–520; John Irving, *Mozart's Piano Sonatas, Contexts, Sources, Style* pp. 29–31.

[5] C. P. E. Bach, *Essay ...*, p. 83.

[6] C. P. E.Bach, "Autobiography," published in Ebeling's translation into German of *Carl Burney's der Musik Doctors Tagebuch seiner Musikalischen Reisen ... Aus dem Englischen übersetzt von C.D.Ebeling* (1773; reprint, Kassel: 1959), p. 209. (Not contained in Burney's English book!)

[7] An excellent account of the history of dynamics is given in Hermann Dechant, *Dirigieren*, pp. 147–175, including a discussion of the size of orchestras from the Baroque period to modern times.

this kind of accompaniment include the main subject of the first movement and the Andante of the *Sonata facile* K. 545/II, or the Adagio section of the D minor Fantasy K. 397. The problem of distinguishing between leading voices and accompanying parts also exists naturally in chamber music and orchestra works.

In Mozart's time, dynamic indications in his piano music were usually written and printed separately for the upper and the lower staves, as can be noticed at, for example, the opening of the C minor Fantasy K. 475 or throughout its companion, the first movement of the C minor Sonata K. 457 (mm. 9–12).

Ex. II/1:

Since in most cases these signs were synchronized, modern editors preferred to print one sign in the middle only. This system was altered in cases where the dynamics are different, as in the Sonata K. 457/I, end of exposition where the *p* is meant for the left hand only.

Dynamic Signs in Mozart's Piano Works

While it can be said that in his earliest works Mozart is still sparing in his dynamic notation,[8] this is certainly no longer the case in his six piano sonatas K. 279–284, which are already mature works that Mozart performed in private concerts. The profusion of dynamic signs in the autographs and the (most obviously authentic) original edition of K. 284, culminating in the Variation XI (Adagio) of the final movement of this Sonata in its printed version (published nearly nine years after its composition), bears witness to that. As one can see in Ex. VI/17 on p. 228, in the first eight measures of this Adagio variation alone Mozart added twenty-seven dynamic signs, certainly an unusually high number and something that neither Torricella (whom Mozart apparently knew personally and to whom he gave the Sonata for publication) nor his engraver would have dared to add without Mozart's authorization. Strangely enough, at the same time Mozart also gave Torricella the Piano Sonata K. 333 for which he added only a few dynamic markings. Was this perhaps because he suddenly was in too great a hurry and simply ran out of time? We shall discuss this case below. If we exclude the A minor Sonata K. 310, which was composed under exceptional circumstances, in later years the notation of dynamic markings in Mozart's piano works became more and more sparse and nearly disappeared altogether in his last three piano sonatas, which were not printed during his lifetime. In fact, Mozart's evolution of dynamic notation is the opposite of Haydn's, whose early sonatas are devoid of dynamic signs, whereas his last ones contain the subtlest indications of

---

[8] Patier, pp. 500–501.

dynamics, culminating in the subito *ff* of his last Piano Sonata in E-flat major, Hob. XVI/52, second movement, m. 10.[9]

In Mozart's case, the contrary seems to be true: His last piano sonatas contain hardly any dynamic signs. Nonetheless, those piano works that he was able to sell to publishers for printing during his lifetime nearly always show far more dynamic indications than his autographs. They are in most cases fully consistent with those indications found in the earlier group of sonatas K. 279–284, published by Artaria, and later in the remarkable Rondo in A Minor, K. 511, certainly a unique piece in which Mozart took pains to write a particularly large number of dynamic markings—far more than usual—maybe for teaching purposes or perhaps with the intention of providing a model for how to play the less fully marked works.

Why do the editions of works he authorized for publication contain more *forte* and *piano* indications than do his manuscripts? The most probable answer is quite simple: notating dynamics is in most cases the last step in fixing the compositional matrix. Obviously, the most important task for a composer is to write down the notes and their rhythms. Indications of articulation and dynamic signs, even tempo markings, normally come at a later or at the final stage of the writing process, when reviewing the composition perhaps the next day or on a performance day. When a work is prepared for publication, a composer generally provides more clues for its proper interpretation. This fact has been observed in the working process of all great composers through our own time.

Yet, in the case of Mozart, something strange happened: Modern editors, sanctioned by the dubious conviction of some scholars, claimed that Mozart probably never personally prepared his works for publication. Unfortunately, in this respect the editors made no distinction between authentic and pirated prints: in the latter (unauthorized) editions it seems possible to assume that somebody else may have added a dynamic marking or perhaps a tempo indication here or there, though normally only a few signs were then added. But why should any of the Viennese publishers, who were in personal contact with Mozart, have added anything without Mozart's consent in the authentic original editions? In his letters to his father in 1784 (9 and 12 June), Mozart reported that he not only gave three sonatas to Artaria for publication (K. 330–332) but that he had decided to give (probably personally) another three sonatas to Torricella, among them the Dürnitz Sonata K. 284 and the Sonata K. 333. Nearly all modern editors of Mozart's works give priority to the readings of the autograph over those of the printed edition. For instance, the Henle edition printed the signs *f, p, cresc.,* etc., found in original authentic editions, in small print only, thus neglecting the importance of Mozart's apparent own alterations and additions as he prepared the works for publication. In the *NMA* the dynamic signs of the authentic print of the Duet Sonata K. 497 are found only in the critical report.

Since 1991 we have had documentation of Mozart's involvement of additions and alterations in printed versions of Viennese publishers, provided by the rediscovered autograph of the Fantasy and Sonata in C minor, K. 475 and K. 457. For the first time we now know all the sources for these great works: the newly discovered autograph supplies the missing link for evaluating the manuscript copy for Therese von Trattner and the printed version. This is most enlightening in the Sonata's Adagio movement (in rondo form). In the original manuscript as well as in the dedication copy for Therese von Trattner, the return of the theme (the *ritornello*) was unmarked and was therefore identical with the beginning. In two successive attempts Mozart created embellished versions for the returns of the opening theme, also adding more elaborate versions in other places. The rediscovery of the autograph provides for the first time unshakable proof

---

[9] Unfortunately, this *fortissimo* is often spoiled due to a preceding, non-notated *crescendo* in many unconvincing performances of this sonata, thus destroying the effect of an explosion of energy.

that the differences between Mozart's autographs and the versions printed in Vienna during his lifetime originated with him and were not the whims of an arrogant publisher or engraver. This fact has far-reaching consequences: In the great Piano Sonata in F major for Four Hands K. 497, for example, nearly all modern editions print the end of the last movement after the autograph and not in the printed version, thus condemning the wonderful four-part canon of the original edition to an appendix or a critical report.

It is nearly certain that in the case of other works such as K. 330, K. 331, or K. 332, Mozart followed the same procedure of adding and altering when reviewing his works for publication, in this case by Artaria. Indeed, in these sonatas all his added notes and dynamic indications ought to be presented in large print. It is most regrettable, even shameful, that in some modern editions they are sometimes left out altogether, while in others they are offered only in small print, as if they were less important. Editors never made this mistake of neglecting authentic alterations in original editions when editing the works of Beethoven, Chopin, or Brahms, to name but a few. With regard to Mozart's added dynamic indications in the authentic editions of Artaria and Torricella, however, they were either presented in small print above the autograph texts (*NMA*, Henle-Verlag) or omitted altogether (Wiener Urtext Edition). Inevitably, this distinction gives the player the wrong impression that these signs are of secondary importance or even only the editor's suggestions. But they are not; and they should be presented the same way as in the authentic editions of other great composers, namely, in large print. The argument of modern editors—that, in the case of Mozart (only), differences between autograph and print could have been the result of a pupil's or an engraver's fancy—has no proper substantiation. One might well raise similar doubts in the case of Beethoven, Chopin, or Brahms, where many differences of the same kind can be found. If a conscientious editor feels compelled to point out the differences, he should do so in a critical report but not in the main music text.

In view of the fact that Mozart added dynamic signs as a last step before a work was going to be printed, we can understand why late piano works such as the *Sonata facile* K. 545 have no dynamic indications: Mozart saw no immediate necessity to write them down because he had not yet had (and as it turned out would not later have) an opportunity to prepare them for publication. Thus, the Sonata K. 545 is not preserved in a finished state but only incomplete in its notation—dynamic indications are missing.

Mozart's basic dynamic range runs from *pp* to *ff* via *p*, *mf*, and *f*.[10] While *pp* is fairly frequent, *mf* and *ff* are rather rare signs: a *mf* is found in the introduction to his Violin Sonata in B-flat major K. 454 and in the first movement of the C major Piano Sonata K. 330 (mm. 21 and 108); in works with keyboard instruments an *ff* occurs only in the Piano Sonata in A minor, K. 310 (first movement, mm. 58, 64); in the cadenza of the last movement of the Violin Sonata in D major, K. 306; in the Sonata for Two Pianos K. 448 (first movement, m. 90); in the *tutti* of the first movement of the Concerto in E-flat major, K. 271 (mm. 45, 139, 377); and once in the finale of the G major Concerto K. 453.

TRACK 7

Usually Mozart wrote his dynamic signs with more than one letter, something like *for:* and *pia:*, and placed them often four to six millimeters to the left of the respective note. (While he haphazardly changed from writing three letters [*for:*, *pia:*] to writing one letter [*f*, *p*], in modern editions only the single letters *f* and *p* are used). However, in several cases, when Mozart was writing in a hurry, these indications were written nearly under the note or even slightly to the right. Most Mozart scholars agree that the exact placing of dynamic signs in modern prints at

---

[10] A very rare indication is *poco forte*, found, for example, in the second movement of the G major Symphony K. 199, where the horns have four times the indication *un poco forte*, while the rest of the orchestra has only *forte*.

times presents a problem that cannot be resolved on philological grounds alone but requires musical judgment as well.

It is simply amazing how Mozart could limit himself in many of his works to only three basic levels of volume, namely, *f* and *p* and the occasional *pianissimo* (the latter often spelled out), without losing the dynamic impact. Even in the highly expressive and nearly *"romantic"* Fantasy and Sonata in C minor, K. 475 and K. 457 we do not find a single *fortissimo*. This does not mean, of course, that this most monumental work for solo piano is less dramatic, less dynamic, less intense than the A minor Sonata K. 310 or any of Beethoven's sonatas where *fortissimo* signs are found in abundance. It simply means that Mozart's *forte* covers a wide range between very loud and moderately loud, and likewise that his *piano* vacillates between a full singing *mezzo piano* and the very softest *piano*. The *forte* at the beginning of the development section in the first movement of the C minor Sonata certainly equals a Beethoven *ff*. Needless to say, dynamics must of course be understood in context, not least of all because late eighteenth-century fortepianos can hardly compete with a modern concert grand's dynamic capabilities. It would be foolish to attempt to match Mozart's *fortissimo* to that of Rachmaninoff, for example. But it would also be a mistake to play only *mf* on a modern grand where Mozart wrote *ff*. The impact of a climax must be maintained, regardless of which instrument one plays. When teaching his young son, Leopold Mozart surely conveyed the advice that he gave his readers in his *Violinschule* (p. 261):

> *Everywhere a forte is written one has to carefully consider the strength of the forte, and not exaggerate it. This is especially the case when accompanying a concerto part. Some musicians either do nothing upon seeing a forte sign, or if they play forte it is exaggerated.*

Instead of a *p* sign, Mozart also frequently used word indications such as *sotto voce* (literally, "subdued voice," soft), *mezza voce* (literally, "middle voice"), or *dolce* ("sweet"). The indication *dolce* is particularly worthy of discussion.

The Indications *Sotto Voce* and *Dolce*

Sotto voce, frequently demanded in violin sonatas, string quartets, and sometimes in the orchestral part of piano concertos—e.g., K. 414/II and K. 413/II—is found only twice in the piano sonatas, namely in the C major Sonata K. 330/III, m. 96 (perhaps two measures too late?) and at the beginning of the Adagio from the C minor Sonata K. 457. It could mean: "with the moderator stop" (somewhat equivalent to the modern left pedal), but then Mozart probably meant it only for the theme and its returns. The instruction *sotto voce* demands not only a delicate, quiet sound level, something between *p* and *pp*, but also an emotional quality as well, somehow similar to *dolce*, the meaning of which needs certainly more attention.

Is Dolce *a Dynamic Indication?*

The Italian word *dolce* has several connotations, such as sweet, soft, delicate, tender, pleasing, agreeable, amiable, engaging, serene, sensitive. It seems obvious that in language as well as in music, *dolce* belongs to the realm of sweetness and softness (as opposed to harshness and crudeness). Mozart uses the word *dolce* often as a substitute for *piano*, in contrast to a previous or subsequent *forte*. Good examples for this use may be found in all three movements of the Piano Trio in E major, K. 542, at the beginning of the Andante movement of the C major Sonata K. 330, or at the start of the concluding D major Allegretto in the Fantasy in D minor, K. 397. There is an element of tenderness in all these places that goes beyond the mere indication *piano* one might expect there.

In an interesting essay, Robert Levin claims that Mozart's *dolce* is a dynamic marking of its own and not a mere indication of character, meaning simply "more intense than piano."[11] At first sight, this interpretation appears to be a baffling departure from the traditional meaning. But Professor Levin supports his thesis with arguments that seem to confirm his assumptions, namely:

> *Given Mozart's consistent use of dolce without a dynamic sign, the addition of p in modern editions seems not merely superfluous but incorrect.* (p. 34)

for the first movement of the Sonata for Two Pianos in D major, K. 448, Levin states (p. 34):

> *[T]he second theme [m. 34], which follows a* forte *cadence, is marked* dolce. ... *Fifteen measures later, at measure 49 (m. 48 in the first piano), the dolce is countermanded by a piano marking. ... Unable to explain Mozart's piano at measure 49, [Ernst Fritz] Schmid [the editor of the relevant NMA volume] then fabricated a dynamic of **mf** ... at measure 42 in an attempt to justify the subsequent piano.*
>
> *In the opening of the first movement of the String Quintet in C major, K. 515, the four lower instruments are marked* piano *(in the cello, **f** yields immediately to **p**); the first violin is marked* dolce. *The absence of a **p** marking for the first violin and its melodic dominance appear to confirm that* dolce *mandates an intensity greater than that of the accompanying voices, and thus that its dynamic be stronger than the ambient* piano.

Robert Levin's observations are—as always—interesting and deserve a serious discussion. With regard to point 1, we observed that **p** *dolce* does occur in Mozart's works, e.g., in the E major section of the Tempo di Menuetto of the Violin Sonata in E minor, K. 304/I, m. 101[12] or at the beginning of the String Quintet in D major, K. 593, entrance of the first violin, as well as in the recapitulation, m. 233. Also, in the Wind Serenade in C minor, K. 388, one can find repeatedly the indication **p** *dolce* or (second movement, horns) *piano e dolce* (here it is interesting to note that in his transcription of this Serenade for String Quintet K. 406 Mozart wrote only **p**, without dolce). In a personal communication, Professor Levin confirmed that *dolce* alone is more frequently found in Mozart than **p** *dolce*. He also pointed out that in the *Largo* Introduction to the Piano Quintet with Winds K. 452, in mm. 4–6, the leading voices of oboe, clarinet, and horn are marked consecutively *dolce*, whereas the other wind instruments have only **p**. Since performers played here from parts without knowledge of the full score, this was apparently the best way to tell them to play with more expression and possibly more volume of sound.

In discussing point 2, it should be noted that at the recapitulation of that *dolce* theme (in m. 36) of K. 448/I, a *crescendo* follows at m. 146 leading to an **f** (mm. 148–149), which is subsequently countermanded by a **p** in both parts. Although there is no such *crescendo* in the parallel place of the exposition, the increase of voices from one part in m. 34 to eight parts in m. 47 implies a similar *Spannungscrescendo* and leads to such an increase of sound that the ensuing **p** in m. 150 seems to be a necessary indication. But does this really mean that the entire theme was meant to be played louder than *piano*? Perhaps.

Levin's most convincing example, however, is the one taken from the opening of the String Quintet in C major, K. 515, mentioned under point 3). But this is an exact parallel to the opening of the Quintet K. 593, where Mozart himself wrote **p** and *dolce*. Certainly there can be no doubt that in K. 515 the first violin entering three measures after the lower strings should play the

---

[11] Robert D. Levin, "The Devil's in the Details: Neglected Aspects of Mozart's Piano Concertos," pp. 32–35.

[12] When Robert Levin performed this sonata at a concert in 1991 in memory of the unforgettable great pianist Malcolm Frager, he did play the **p** *dolce* indication there and performed it beautifully, adding his own embellishments.

theme with more intensity than the rest, naturally. Also, in the many chamber music works where all instruments are marked *piano*, the first violin (or first oboe) has to assume a leading role. Even the famous horn solo in the *Dorfmusikanten-Sextett* K. 522 is marked *dolce*.

A case that contradicts Levin's thesis is probably the beginning of the Larghetto of the B-flat major Quartet K. 589: While the middle strings (second violin and viola) have the indication *piano*, the violoncello enters with *sotto voce* followed by the same indication for the first violin in m. 9. No sensible musician would claim that *sotto voce* means "louder than *piano*"; yet "softer than *piano*" makes even less sense here in view of the thematic matrix. It probably indicates that the leading voices should be played in a more personal way. Thus, we suggest to modify Robert Levin's call for an increase in *dynamic* intensity to an increase in *emotional* intensity. According to the context, *dolce* can be either louder or softer than a simple *p*. (Let us remind ourselves that the word *piano* does not only mean "soft" but "flat" as well.) While at the beginning of the C major Quintet K. 515, or in the Largo introduction of the Piano Quintet K. 452, *dolce* can mean indeed "more sound" for the part or parts of an ensemble where it is placed, we cannot possibly imagine that the beginning of the Andante in the C major Sonata K. 330 should be played something like *mf*. No, here *dolce* clearly belongs to the realm of emotional indicators such as *grazioso*, *affetuoso*, *amoroso*, *agitato*, *cantabile*, *espressivo*, etc.

Static and Dynamic Markings

In Mozart's time, such indications as *forte* and *piano*, if they occur at the beginning of a movement or before a new subject, may be called *static* signs; for some musicians they are relics of Baroque terrace dynamics. They usually indicate a dynamic level that remains more or less permanent until recalled by another sign. But in Mozart's music, a change of intensity is often needed within static *forte* or *piano* passages, whereby either stronger or weaker notes within a given level demand a subtle difference in dynamics; small gradual changes from loud to soft or vice versa may usually be needed to enhance the expression. On the other hand, there are also greater changes of volume level or intensity, which we might call *dynamic* in the stricter sense as opposed to static signs. They are often expressed by verbal descriptions like *crescendo* ("augmenting, growing") or its contrary *decrescendo* ("diminishing"). It is interesting to note that these dynamic signs for changing the intensity of single notes and for the volume level of longer passages occur more frequently in lyrical middle movements, while in opening and in final movements a juxtaposition of *forte* and *piano* sections is more predominant. In his valuable study of Mozart's violin sonatas,[13] Karl Marguerre makes a distinction between *register dynamics*, when a piece requires an outspoken, sometimes sudden contrast between *forte* and *piano*, and *expression dynamics*, with shades and nuances and with transitions between both levels. Marguerre, quoting mainly from string quartets and violin sonatas, gives valuable hints as to how to distinguish between both principles in performance. A good example for registral dynamics is found in the opening of the C minor Sonata K. 457:

Ex. II/2:

---

[13] Karl Marguerre, "Forte und Piano bei Mozart," pp. 153–160.

No transition is possible between the bold first unison motive (a "Mannheim rocket") and the plaintive *piano* answer in mm. 3–4 (which one could imagine played by an oboe). A similar juxtaposition between "white and black" is found in the unmarked opening of the D major Sonata K. 576, where the delicate answer in mm. 3–4 is not of a complaining nature but rather affectionate or teasingly *grazioso*.

As stated earlier, many of Mozart's works are sparse or entirely lacking in dynamic indications. It is the duty of a good performer to supply them in a Mozartian way. Most helpful for decisions in this respect is, of course, the study of Mozart's own signs for *forte* and *piano* and for dynamic gradations and transitions in his well-marked works. Works such as the Rondo for Piano in A minor, K. 511, can and must serve as models for those with fewer or no indications. Yet, before we begin to examine this shining example, we have to establish a catalogue of Mozart's vocabulary for changes of dynamic levels.

Crescendo **and** *Decrescendo*

It is generally known that *crescendo* ("growing") indicates a gradual increase of volume. Yet even experienced performers sometimes commit the mistake of becoming immediately (or at least too rapidly) louder, starting even before the indication *crescendo*. Thus, von Bülow's witticism, "crescendo means piano, diminuendo means forte," is still valid today.

In Mozart's works, short *crescendo* indications are found rather frequently, while long ones are comparatively rare. Was this perhaps Mozart's critical reaction toward the then famous long *crescendo*s of the "Mannheim school," still found one generation later in the works of Beethoven and Rossini? Mozart's father warned his son not to copy the mannered "Mannheim goût," and Mozart obviously took this advice to heart. About the Sonata K. 309 Leopold could thus write to his son on 11 December 1777:

> *Your sonata is a strange composition. It has something in it of the rather artificial Mannheim style, but so very little, that your own good style is not spoilt thereby.*

A few "Mannheimerisms" do indeed still appear in Mozart's works even afterwards, though they are rare exceptions: Long *crescendo*s can be found in the first movement of the Posthorn Serenade K. 320, in the opening *tutti* of the Sinfonia Concertante K. 364, and in the Concerto for Two Pianos K. 365, as well as (very much later) in the overture to the opera seria *La Clemenza di Tito*.

But there exists another method of building an extensive *crescendo*, namely by raising the pitch or by accumulating more and more instruments repeating the same phrase. Such unmarked *crescendo*s gradually alter the intensity of sound. They can be found in the opening of the Symphony in F Major, K. 43, later in the opening *tutti* of the C major Piano Concerto K. 467 (mm. 36–43), or in the opening and concluding *tutti* in the other famous C major Concerto K. 503 (mm. 82–89, m. 423 to end). In solo piano works, the need for an unwritten *crescendo* can be felt in the first movement of the Piano Sonata in D major, K. 576, where at the pedal point that in mm. 92–98 leads back to the recapitulation, an increased intensity is appropriate.

For the diminishing effect, Mozart used different terms besides the word *decrescendo*; namely, *calando*, *mancando* (e.g., in Sonata K. 457/II, mm. 15, 55; also in the Minuet K. 355 [576b], m. 28), and, very rarely, *diminuendo* (Rondo in A minor, K. 511, m. 127). *Calando* does not yet have the modern meaning of "decreasing and slowing down"; there is never an *a tempo* following Mozart's *calando* indications. A *calando* Mozart prescribed, for instance, in his Sonata K. 284/III, Adagio Var. XI, m. 4.

A remarkable fact has been noted by several authors: Mozart's *crescendo* markings are by far more frequent than their opposite, the indication *decrescendo*. In a lecture held in Salzburg in

1927, published only in 1997, Stefan Strasser[14] noted that *diminuendo* or *decrescendo* is found, for instance, only three times in *Le Nozze di Figaro*, only once as **poco a poco p** in *Don Giovanni*, and never in *The Magic Flute*. David Boyden[15] reported a similar observation after searching for these signs in the autographs of Mozart's ten famous string quartets. Commenting on this fact, he concludes: "How does it happen, then, that in a body of music occupying over 300 pages in modern score that there is but a single short decresc. marked?" (he referred to K. 428/IV, m. 161).

Boyden forgot to note, by the way, that there are a few passages marked *calando*, also meaning *decrescendo*. Boyden comes to the same concluding result as Strasser:

> *The reason is that Mozart has a notational method of indicating a short decrescendo by [writing] f p, so that only under the most exceptional circumstances is the word decresc. necessary for a short diminuendo of less than a measure. That f p must mean a short diminuendo and not a forte followed by subito p can be inferred from above, and its intent is clarified in explanations given in Leopold Mozart's Violinschule, Chapter XII particularly.*

With this opinion we do not fully agree. While it is true that in Mozart's works *decrescendo* markings are rare, this is not a reason to interpret all *f p* markings as *diminuendo*. Particularly where the *f* and *p* letters appear directly adjacent to one another as *fp*, this interpretation becomes less plausible. In Mozart's A minor Rondo K. 511, we can observe that in contrast to many *crescendo* markings there exists only one *diminuendo*, namely in m. 127.[16] However, there can be no intermediate *diminuendo* between the end of the *crescendo* in m. 3 and the following *piano*, which symbolizes a sudden contrast. Nor can there be a gradual dynamic decrease after *fp* in certain passages of other works, as in the Concerto in E-flat, K. 449/I, mm. 219–222 (see below). In certain cases, for example in the Sonata in D Major, K. 311/II (mm. 73–74) or in the Andante of K. 330 (mm. 17 and 19), however, a gradual decrease in volume could well be intended by the marking *f p*. We shall soon return to this sometimes problematic indication of Mozart.

Unlike the late operas or the string quartets, the piano sonatas do contain quite a few *diminuendos*, though under different names as previously mentioned. A *decrescendo* (following a previous *cresc.–forte*) is found in the Andante amoroso from the B-flat major Sonata K. 281 (mm. 4–5 and 62–63). *Calando* occurs three times in the A minor Sonata K. 310, namely in the first movement (mm. 14 and 94) and in the second (m. 50). Yet even here, where the intimate expression calls for more dynamic subtlety than elsewhere, the number of *crescendos* far exceeds that of *decrescendos*.

A word about so-called hairpins, marking *crescendo* and *diminuendo* (in German: Gabeln; literally, "forks") ⊂═══ ═══⊃ : They are absent in Mozart's piano music for a simple reason: He reserved this symbol nearly exclusively for the *messa di voce* (swelling and eventual ebbing) of single long notes, something that keyboard instruments are incapable of doing. This famous vocal effect is used by Mozart a few times in order to express a special state or stress of emotion. In the aria "O wie ängstlich, o wie feurig" from the *Abduction from the Seraglio*, the hairpins express the swelling of Belmonte's heart. Neal Zaslaw pointed out that Mozart also used swell signs twice in his orchestral music. They occur in the dénouement of Idomeneo K. 366 (for brass instruments) and in the opening measures of the Masonic Funeral Music K. 477, where the swell was meant to evoke the supernatural.[17] In the D minor String

[14] Stefan Strasser, "Mozarts Orchesterdynamik," Mozart-Jahrbuch 1997, pp. 38–40.
[15] David D. Boyden, "Dynamics in Seventeenth- and Eighteenth-Century Music," pp. 185–193.
[16] See Paul Badura-Skoda, "Mozart's Rondo in A Minor," pp. 29–32.
[17] See Neal Zaslaw, *Mozart's Symphonies*, pp. 474–475 and 478. But Zaslaw is mistaken when he says, "Only twice did Mozart notate the swell in his orchestral music." More instances could be quoted.

Quartet K. 421/I, following extreme dynamic contrasts, the swell in m. 51 is followed by a *subito piano*; it certainly expresses emotional distress. Similarly, the swell of oboes and horns in the "little" G minor Symphony K. 183/I, mm. 115–116, points to the same expression. But there exist two examples of hairpins where neither the supernatural nor any anguish is evoked and that are meaningful also for pianists: The first example (already mentioned by Strasser) is to be found at the opening of the Andante moderato movement of the Symphony in B-flat Major, K. 319.

Ex. II/3:

Here the *decrescendo* and the *crescendo* hairpins comprise more than one note. But when the theme returns at the end of the movement, m. 80, the *decrescendo* sign is missing: There the first violin and viola have an ***fp*** mark on the first beat, while the second violin and the bass have a *forte*, followed by *piano* on the fourth beat. And in mm. 92 and 94, only the first violins have ***fp*** markings, whereas all other instruments have ⎯⎯⎯⎯⎯>. Clearly a *diminuendo* is also meant there for the first violins.

The only hairpin in a work with *pianoforte* is found in the second measure of the Andante movement of the C major Piano Concerto K. 503, where the orchestra plays:

Ex. II/4:

Why did Mozart write the *diminuendo* hairpin here? Probably because the *sforzato* would perhaps otherwise have been sustained through the whole bar. Later, when the piano enters, the accompanying instruments have no *sf*, but instead an ***mfp*** without the hairpin. There can hardly be a doubt that a similar decrease, but on a lower dynamic level, was intended, "just as the sound of a bell, when struck sharply, by degrees dies away" (Leopold Mozart, *Violinschule*, I/3, §19).

Mozart's Accent Signs

It is well known that in Mozart's time the common accent sign > was not yet in use. Mozart's accent signs, listed in gradually increasing intensity, were these:

mfp	*mezza-fortepiano*	relatively light accent
fp	*fortepiano*	wide range between moderate and strong accents

	vertical stroke (or wedge)	on long or on tied notes this sign indicates an accent of various degrees; see p. 128
rf	*rinforzando*	"reinforcing"; stress on longer notes or passages; similar to *poco forte*
sfp	*sforzato-piano*	stronger than *fp*
sf	*sforzato*	strongest form of accent, sometimes on top of a *forte*

Any of these accent signs can relate either to one single note or to a group of notes. Good examples for both types can be found in the third movement of the String Quartet in B-flat major, K. 458, mm. 43–45: while the first violin has *sf* and later *cresc.*, the middle strings have *sf* and *p* valid for several notes. As Robert Levin correctly states in his already cited article (see footnote 11): "an audible intensity of sound must continue beyond the initial attack."

Ex. II/5:

Mozart frequently made a distinction between *mfp*, *fp*, *sfp* (written close together) and a notation where the *p* sign is put more to the right and noted separately, such as *sf: p:* or *for: pia:* (see facsimile Ex. II/6). Obviously the duration of the accents has to be longer in the latter case; e.g., in the third movement of the D major Concerto K. 451, mm. 9 and 11, where most editions print an *fp* instead of separated letters *f p*.

Ex. II/6:

Mozart's *fp* markings when written with one stroke of the pen should be attacked abruptly and then suddenly decrease in loudness, so that there is no gradual *decrescendo*, such as one so often hears nowadays. An example of this kind of interpretation is necessary in the D minor Concerto K. 466, first movement, mm. 341 et seq.:

Ex. II/7:

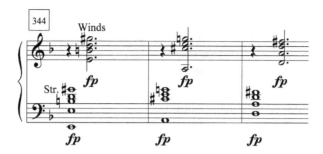

In the next example (E-flat major Concerto K. 449/I mm. 219–220), the *p* should already have been reached by the second eighth notes f² and g², respectively:

Ex. II/8:

Naturally, the *fp* accent should not be exaggerated. For instance, the countless *fp* markings in the middle movements of the sonatas K. 309 in C major and K. 310 in A minor are never to be taken as more than indications of a more or less slight accent for expressive purposes.

One can find an explanation of the *fp* markings in Quantz (XVII/VII, § 24, p. 252):

> *If a Forte is indicated beneath a long note, and immediately after it a Piano, and no change of bow-stroke is possible, you must produce this note with the greatest possible force, using pressure on the bow, and immediately diminish the tone without breaking the movement of the bow, and through a diminuendo transform it into a Pianissimo.*

And Leopold Mozart, too, explained it in his *Violinschule* (XII, §8):

> *It is customary always to accent a half note strongly when mixed with short notes, and to relax the tone again. … And this is in reality the expression which the composer desires when he sets f and p, namely forte and piano, against a note. But when accenting a note strongly the bow must not be lifted from the string as some very clumsy people do, but must be continued in the stroke so that the tone may still be heard continuously, although it gradually dies away.*

Whether written in one stroke of the pen or with two or three separate letters, Mozart's accents *fp* and *sfp* appear often on off beats (see Ex. II/11) on syncopations or on dissonances. Off-beat accents are found, for instance, in the second movement of the E major Piano Trio K. 542 (mm. 40ff.) onward. Autograph version:

Ex. II/9:

Incorrectly printed version in many editions:

Ex. II/10:

The Andante cantabile movement from the A minor Sonata K. 310 also contains in m. 11 such off-beat accents:

Ex. II/11:

It is this latter example that helped us half a century ago to discover a printing error in the Adagio of the C minor Sonata K. 457 that had remained undetected until then (and is still not observed by many pianists). In the second movement of this sonata, m. 48, all editors following the first edition put the accent sign on the strong beats. Here is the incorrect version, the one usually found in prints:

Ex. II/12:

These two *fp*, which appear in the first edition only, were apparently added by Mozart in the proofs and misunderstood by the engraver. Most likely his intended version is this one:

Ex. II/13:

As in the case of K. 310, they almost certainly belong to the ensuing thirty-second notes of the right-hand g^2 and e-flat^2, for throughout the rest of this Adagio there are no single isolated accents in the accompaniment, but there are several off-beat accents for the melody, namely in mm. 21, 31, and 44. (In this context, it should be mentioned that in m. 50 another problem presents itself: the *forte* is not found in the autograph, but the *p* sign is there and is placed more to the right than in the first edition.)

In the 1950s, we started a prolonged discussion about the correct interpretation of these *fp* signs in the C minor Fantasy K. 475, mm. 19, 169 (174), and 172 (176); we claimed that these accents ought also to be played on the off-beat; namely, on the second note of each group. Most editors, however (including the *NMA*), in our opinion still printed them one sixteenth note too early. It was this off-beat principle that led us to believe, for instance, that the *fp* in the C minor Fantasy K. 475, m. 19, must have been wrongly aligned in most editions, as in the following example:

Ex. II/14:

Correct reading:

Ex. II/15:

Unfortunately, the editors of the *NMA* at a time before the autograph was rediscovered did not follow our reasoning and placed the signs—erroneously in our opinion—on strong beats in the print. Fortunately, the rediscovery of the autograph (July 1990) seems to prove the correctness of our assumption beyond any doubt:

Ex. II/16:

It cannot be emphasized enough that the *fp* does not mean a really loud *forte* followed by a really soft *piano*. It is more of an inflection sign than an accent and means a strong note followed by one or more weaker ones. This can be inferred from the fact that Mozart frequently added a *p* shortly after the *fp*, as, e.g., in the Andante cantabile of the A minor Sonata K. 310:

Ex. II/17:

Suggested execution

Thus, it is the expressive context only that should lead a musician to decide how strong or weak an accent should be and how soft the following notes ought to be played. The mistake of too harsh and too loud accents had been criticized already by Leopold Mozart, who wrote in his *Violinschule* (XII §17, p. 261):

> *One has to consider the affect to see whether a note needs a strong attack. Others need only a moderate attack, and often only a hardly noticeable one. The former is necessary if the forte is written as an accent for all instruments, and this is usually shown through f. p.*

If a *piano* sign appears at a larger distance from the previous *f*, *sf*, or *mf*, the question naturally arises: What happens in between? Here the musical taste of each individual performer has to find the right answer. It would be simply presumptuous to decree dogmatic solutions for every single case. Sometimes a gradual decrease of volume might be the most musical interpretation; sometimes a rather abrupt change from loud to soft might sound more convincing. Only in cases where *f* and *p* are more than a few notes apart can one assume that this really is no more a prolonged written *fp* but that it means a sudden change from loud to soft, a kind of registral dynamics, as described above. This seems to be the case in mm. 11–12 of the Adagio in B minor, K. 540:

Ex. II/18:

A particular case in question is the Andante from the C major Sonata K. 309. As mentioned earlier, even Mozart's father and sister had difficulty adjusting to its frequent *fp* and other markings that threatened to destroy the overall line, *il filo*, as Leopold used to call it. They thought that it was Mozart's homage to the somewhat mannered Mannheim "goût" (taste). Yet, Mozart liked this movement very much and reported to Salzburg on 6 December 1777 that young Rosa Cannabich played it to his liking. She was the daughter of Christian Cannabich with whom Mozart was on friendly terms:

> His daughter who is fifteen, his eldest child, is a very pretty and charming girl. She is very intelligent and steady for her age. She is serious, does not say much, but when she does speak, she is pleasant and amiable. Yesterday she again gave me indescribable pleasure; she played the whole of my sonata—excellently. The Andante (which must not be taken too quickly) she plays with the utmost expression. Moreover she likes playing it. I had already finished the Allegro, as you know, on the day after my arrival, and thus had only seen Mlle Cannabich once. Young Danner asked me how I thought of composing the Andante. I said that I would make it fit closely the character of Mlle Rosa. When I played it, it was an extraordinary success. … She is exactly like the Andante.

For us it is probably less easy to see a parallel between the movement and the character of a young girl or to picture her when interpreting the sonata.

Sforzato

Thomas Busby's book, *A Musical Manual—A Technical Directory*, offers as a definition of *sforzato*: "An expression apprizing the performer that the note or passage to which it refers is to be emphatically played." Though this book appeared some time after Mozart's death, this understanding of the sign might still be considered relevant.

Rinforzando

Contrary to widespread opinion, *rinforzando* (*rf*) is not entirely absent in Mozart's works, but he used it only on a few occasions. It appears, for instance, in the *finale* of the Violin Sonata in F major, K. 377, mm. 102, 104, and in Belmonte's aria "O wie ängstlich, o wie feurig" from *The Abduction from the Seraglio*, m. 9. From mozart's piano works, this sign seems otherwise to be absent, with one probable exception, hitherto unobserved: In the B-flat major Sonata K. 333/II, the authorized original edition has sixteen *sf* or *sfp* signs printed in the normal way. But in four places there appear accent signs in the left-hand part where the letter *f* is preceded by a reversed *s*, namely in mm. 21, 25, 71, 75. If the other sixteen *sfp* had been printed the same way, one could surmise that the engraver's tools had gone awry. But in these four parallel places such an error is most improbable. It is more likely that Mozart had written in the proofs *rf:*, a sign with which the engraver was not familiar and which he printed as an enigmatic symbol *ℓf*:

Ex. II/19:

Musically speaking, these *rinforzandi* would be much better fitting here than the two *sforzati* found in all modern editions (without any commentary about the strange distinctive signs).

Another example where a *rinforzando* seems appropriate and could be placed is found in the same movement of the Sonata K. 333/II, m. 25:

Ex. II/20:

Supplementing Incomplete or Missing Dynamics

Among Mozart's compositions there are a few that are carefully marked, but the bulk of them are either scarcely marked or not marked at all. This is not surprising—a composer with such an immense creative output simply may not always have had the time to attend to every detail;

he also may have felt after finishing writing the notes that articulation signs and dynamics could be added at a later time when publication was planned.

When trying to provide dynamics for works that Mozart did not complete in this respect, and in trying to emulate what he likely would have done, our attention has to be focused on those few works where Mozart's notation is probably completed and contains a large number of performance indications (*Vortragsbezeichnungen*) or expression marks. They deserve careful study and should serve as paradigms for the insufficiently marked works in a similar style. Fortunately, we pianists are lucky in this respect: more piano solo works are full of expression marks and more completed. They contain many more articulation and dynamic indications than concertos, symphonies, or chamber music works.

Though Mozart was familiar with all the dynamic gradations between *pp* and *ff* he, unfortunately, was often content, in accordance with tradition, to give mere hints about dynamics. To complete these in the way required by the music is a difficult problem in interpretation. Nineteenth-century editors of Mozart's works almost always went too far in this direction—editors suggested too many dynamic nuances that destroyed the line, Leopold's *filo*. But the other extreme—renunciation of all additions to the often hasty dynamic indications—can lead to results that are at least equally misguided. Quantz's demands in his famous textbook (XVII, VII, §30, p. 254) still apply:

> From all that has so far been said, one can now see that it is by no means enough merely to observe piano and forte at those points where they are written; but that an accompanist must also know how to introduce them judiciously in many places where they are not indicated. To achieve this, a good education and great experience are necessary.

The older and more mature Mozart became, and the greater the independence with which he went his way as man and artist, the more obviously he tended to avoid ambiguity in his notation. Among the works of his maturity we find a few in which the dynamic indications are beautifully worked out in full. The wonderful A minor Rondo K. 511 is a good example of the wealth of nuance that Mozart desired in performances of his works. Here, for once, the manuscript contains exact and frequent performing indications, so that in matters of dynamics and articulation this piece serves as an excellent starting point for a study of Mozart's style.

It is quite clear that in Mozart's works, *p* and *f* are merely basic types. Thus, a *p* in Mozart can mean *p* or *pp*, but also *mp* in present-day notation, while *f* takes in all the gradations from *mf* to *ff*. We must reconcile ourselves to the fact that a performer, wishing to create what to us will sound like a *forte*, will produce a dynamic that is acoustically louder than that of Mozart's time. For a *forte* is not only an acoustical but also a psychological effect. Naturally, one can only decide in each individual case the degree of loudness to be chosen, and one often needs to know a work very well indeed if one is to decide correctly in any particular case. As an obvious example, not every *forte* requires maximum dynamic intensity, but some do. It is difficult to draw up general rules for this, but it may be pointed out once more that *ff* is often indicated by Mozart's marking *f*, not only in a final orchestra *tutti* with trumpets, timpani, and string tremolo, but also in the emotional outbursts that occur in the development sections of many of his mature solo sonata movements.

It is in the instrumental concertos, above all, that we see the full importance of the division of *p* and *f* into several degrees of loudness. During the solo sections of his piano concertos, Mozart mostly prescribed a uniform *p* for the orchestra, whether they are given important motivic material or mere accompanying figures (sustained or reiterated chords). In purely accompanying harmonies, the powerful modern orchestra should be particularly careful to remain close to *pp*, whereas it is not merely permissible but necessary to enhance the melodic climaxes, especially in the *tutti*, by allowing the orchestra a higher dynamic level. In performances with modern grand pianos, the orchestra, and especially the wind instruments, which so often have a leading melody, should also have a broader dynamic spectrum.

As we have said, Mozart was often extraordinarily sparing with his dynamic indications. In particular, the solo parts of the piano concertos only rarely contain any markings at all. For all that, it is usually not difficult to recognize the right dynamics by examining the musical structure. As an aid, one could give the following rules:

In works for the pianoforte, a *forte* is appropriate in the following cases:

1. Octave passages and full chords (e.g., Sonata in F Major, K. 533/II, development; Piano Concerto in C Major, K. 503/I, mm. 298ff.)
2. Passages in broken chords over several octaves (C minor Concerto K. 491/I, mm. 332ff.)
3. Cadential trills in allegro movements, and virtuoso scales in development sections (e.g., almost always before a cadenza or lead-in)
4. Tremolo and quasi-tremolo figures such as broken octaves (C minor Fantasia K. 475, first Allegro, m. 3; Piano Concerto in E-flat major, K. 482/I, mm. 345ff.)
5. Often in left-hand runs (C minor Concerto K. 491/III, mm. 41ff.; A minor Sonata/I, mm 70ff.; D major Sonata K. 576/III, mm. 9ff.)

There is some dispute as to the interpretation of chords written in the following way:

Ex. II/21:

which occur frequently in the piano works where *f* chords are to be especially well marked and full in sound (e.g., Concerto K. 503/I, mm. 298ff.). We believe this notation should generally be regarded as a marking for accentuation. As Robert Levin has pointed out, an example of this kind that is found in the third movement of the Piano Quartet in G minor, K. 478 is similarly notated:

Ex. II/22:

It may only occasionally be correct to play the shorter middle or lower parts with literal exactness. In many cases, a sharply broken-off *arpeggio* may also be intended (as, e.g., in K. 310/II, m. 82), but for that we have no proof (Mozart's customary *arpeggiando* marking is a transverse stroke through the chord: see p. 175). According to Türk (*Klavierschule*, 2nd edition, p. 329), however, such chords are to be played exactly as written.

Naturally, there are exceptions to these rules. In the finale of the A minor Sonata K. 310, the principal theme occurs in octaves in the left hand, in mm. 64 and 203. Both times Mozart expressly demands *p* for these *legato* octaves.

As a good example for the necessity to supplementing Mozart's missing dynamics we shall now discuss in detail the Piano Sonata in B-flat major, K. 333.

This sonata, composed in 1783, was published in 1784 together with the Sonata K. 284 and the Violin Sonata in B-flat major, K. 454 (composed for Regina Strinasacchi). While the Sonata K. 284 and the Violin Sonata leave little to be desired in matters of dynamics, the Sonata K. 333 is sadly deficient in dynamic indications, particularly in the first two movements. Only a handful of markings and a few ornaments and slurs were added by Mozart for publication. This is odd, for the preceding sonatas for Artaria, K. 330–332, were supplied with sufficient dynamic markings. Whatever reasons account for this absence in the Sonata K. 333, it is our task as interpreters to try ourselves to complete the sparse indications found here. Fortunately, there are many similarities with the preceding sonatas, particularly with the F major Sonata K. 332, that may help us to solve our task.

The lyrical opening of K. 333 calls for a *p* start and a *crescendo* in m. 8, leading to the highest note (f³ on Mozart's piano) of the opening theme in mm. 9/10. A *forte* statement from the beginning would be out of the question here. The mood is not unlike the *p* beginning of the preceding F major Sonata K. 332 or the last Piano Concerto K. 595 in B-flat Major. Analogously, this *crescendo* is felt to lead to the affirmative ending of the opening phrase in mm. 9–10, ending like an orchestral *tutti*. The following restatement of the opening motive in the lower octave (m. 10ff.) ought to revert again to *p*. All this seems to be so obvious that practically all performers agree in this respect. Already the half cadence before the second theme should be *f* (starting probably in m. 18) without banging the last octave C in m. 22. The full chord at the start of the second theme in m. 23 would gain from an accent, a crisp *fp* or *sfp* that would enhance the phrase. A quick arpeggio for the right hand would be in style. (In a similar place at the beginning of the second movement of the Piano Trio in G major, K. 496, there is a written-out *f* followed by a *p*.)

In m. 24 and its repetition in m. 32, the four-part chord on the second beat should get an *fp* accent. Such accents on the off beat are found in many other works (e.g., in the Piano Trio in B-flat major, K. 502/I, mm. 52–53). The first notes in mm. 26 and 29 need emphasis; mm. 35–37 should be played *f*. For mm. 39–43 and for the recapitulation (mm. 135–139) we observe that these are the only measures with dynamic markings by Mozart. While together with the exception of the cadenza-like insert at the end in mm. 148–150, the *fp* signs indicate only smaller accents within a *p* section, the *f* in mm. 40 and 42 should be truly *forte* and sustained over the last four eighth notes. In mm. 46–48 (and mm. 142–146), many young pianists commit the error of shortening the second of each pair of half notes, thus creating a dynamic vacuum. The passage leading to the trill in m. 58 has to be raised to a *forte* somewhere, preferably in m. 55; the last five measures (which recall the end of the exposition in the D major Sonata K. 311/I) should, of course, be played *piano*.

In the development section, starting with the opening *piano* statement, the passionate agitating passage in F minor (mm. 71ff.) certainly deserves an *f* rendering, until the dominant of G minor is reached in mm. 85–86. The ensuing section, leading back to the recapitulation, calls for a freedom of expression and dynamics but should not become too loud in mm. 89–91. Why do nearly all pianists make a *ritardando* in m. 93? Mozart wrote a connecting bridge, not a "spasm."

The dynamics of the second movement, an Andante cantabile, are incomplete as well. This movement has a noble, elegiac character, contrasting well with the two outer movements. There is a prevalence of parallel thirds in the right hand. *Cantabile* means, of course, that the upper notes of these thirds need more finger pressure than the lower ones in order to make the *p* dynamic sing. But it also means that phrases of four measures are to be sung in one breath (which implies a somewhat fluid tempo of about ♩ = 55). For most of the time, this movement is written in three parts, like a string trio. The main theme consists of two beautiful arches of four measures each. Although the first notes of the two opening measures are identical, the principle of the rising arch requires more emphasis in the second measure, where the bass starts to be set in motion toward its climax in m. 3. In both these opening bars, the second note needs to be weaker than the first in conformity with ternary rhythm. The thirty-second notes in the fourth measure have the function of a bridge, which has to start very softly (with the alternating notes of these "miniature sighs" to be unaccented). Measure five is a highly charged variation of the first measure and has to increase in volume like a soprano voice leaping by a tenth (from e-flat[1] to g[2]). The tension relaxes, and the ensuing six measures form a calm epilogue to the opening theme. The last three notes in mm. 13, 15, and 17 are like connecting links typical of lower strings or horns in symphonic movements and should be played without weight, whereas the first notes in these same measures need to be sung with emphasis. The last two eighth notes in mm. 14 and 16 (and mm. 64 and 66) are probably meant to be played detached and light. (It seems that—due to a writing slip—Mozart's slur was written too far to the right in m. 64.)

A harmonic ambiguity, typical of Mozart, occurs in m. 19 of this movement K. 333/II, as can be seen in the following example (mm. 18 and 19):

Ex. II/23:

Inevitably, the first note, F-sharp of m. 19, will be perceived as G-flat, namely the minor third of E-flat minor, until it is resolved into G. (We recommend placing a light accent on this F-sharp.)

If the repeat is played (and here it should indeed be played), the last three notes of m. 31 lead to the perfect consonance of the beginning. But after the repeat: what a shock, when the same three notes of m. 31 lead into the "Schoenbergian" dissonance of E–F-sharp—a natural in m. 32! Dissonances always need to be accented, but this painful dissonance needs an especially strong accent, after which the tension subsides gradually until m. 35. The following passage—an abyss of sadness—might start *pp* and gradually increase with the rising bass line. The sighs in mm. 44–47 are marked *sf p* in the first print. What could not be marked, though, is the increase of those painful accents with the rising notes and the modulation into the far-away tonality of D-flat minor—a challenge for the interpreter. Afterwards, by a stroke of genius, Mozart reaches the redeeming dominant of the basic key E-flat in m. 48 simply by continuing the descent of the bass line started earlier. The recapitulation of this great movement ends peacefully with the only *pp* found in this sonata. It is perhaps more than a coincidence that the Andante of the Violin Sonata K. 454 published simultaneously finishes with the identical kind of *pianissimo*.

Fortunately, the third movement of the Sonata K. 333 is far more explicitly marked dynamically than are the previous movements and therefore does not require urgently supplementary

TRACK 63

signs, with the possible exception of mm. 62–64, where a crescendo, an increase of loudness, is recommended.

Less problematic in supplementing dynamics is the opening of Mozart's last Piano Sonata in D Major, K. 576, for here we have a typical case of "registral dynamics." The energetic rising unison of mm. 1–2 is answered by a delicate phrase with a feminine ending. Therefore, like in the C minor sonata or the "Jupiter" Symphony, it seems appropriate that the first motive starts *forte* and that the second answering phrase (starting with the mini-trill D–C-sharp–B–C-sharp) is *piano*. This contrast should be maintained throughout this movement.

Naturally, "static dynamics" are seldom enough, certainly not here, where we also have to consider the inner dynamics that are part of our musical heritage and language. To play the first ten notes of the opening equally loud (like a bad harpsichordist or a computer) would deprive this phrase of its sense. No, strong and weak notes have to be properly arranged, and the Mannheim rocket calls for a considerable increase of energy (loudness). One can only hint at the correct execution, which defies correct notation:

Ex. II/24:

Nor does this suffice: The left hand (second horn) has to play a shade softer than the right hand. The ensuing witty canonic imitation gains in clarity by this articulation:

Ex. II/25:

(For more hints about inner dynamics and motivic directions, see chapter 8, "Expression and Gusto.")

The Echo Syndrome

Not long after serving as a juror in the Yehudi Menuhin Competition for Young Violinists in London, coauthor Paul Badura-Skoda complained in a letter:

42 violinists played a movement of a Mozart concerto. Not one of them failed to play an echo at every repeat of a phrase of one or two measures. The effect was ridiculous, to say the least. It was like chopping up a coherent movement into little fragments. The same happens with most contemporary pianists. Sometimes I even hear an echo in the fifth bar of the "percussion section" of Mozart's Turkish March. Why do young artists feel compelled to leave no repeat unaltered and why does it have, in most cases, a negative effect?

Undoubtedly, the echo effect is a "nicety," a mannerism, inherited from Rococo music of the mid-eighteenth century, a period when keyboard players obviously delighted in echo effects, for there is no lack of such effects, not only in galant works by the musicians of the second quarter of the eighteenth century but also in works by composers of the succeeding generation.

In his *Treatise*, Quantz (XVIII/VII, §26, p. 277) gave the following instruction:

In the repetition of the same or of similar ideas consisting of half or whole bars, whether at the same level or in transposition, the repetition of the idea may be played somewhat more softly than the first statement.

It is noteworthy that Quantz wrote "may be played somewhat more softly," rather than "must be played [much] more softly." The fact that in Türk's *Klavierschule* of 1789 the use of echo dynamics is similarly recommended, without any mention of particular composers, does not necessarily mean that such an echo effect is everywhere appropriate and tasteful.

In the music of a classicist such as Mozart, one should be careful in introducing this effect. Although repetitions of motives occur frequently in his works, such repetitions nearly always have a structural justification. There is indeed nothing more wearisome than the constant stereotyped recurrence of echo effects, which can often hopelessly break up the overall line. They are only appropriate in markedly galant melodies, playful tunes or phrases, as, e.g., in the E-flat major Concerto K. 482/III (mm. 120–121, 173–174, 180–181), but certainly not in codettas, in which one of the hallmarks of Mozart's style is the strengthening effect of a movement-ending repetition. From the few works for which Mozart did provide scrupulously exact dynamic markings one can see that he only very rarely asked that the echo effect to be used. In the final movement of the "Haffner" Symphony, for example, Mozart expressly denies himself any echo effect when motives are repeated (Presto, mm. 11–12, 17–19, etc.); although here the effect could well be applied, he uses it only once (mm. 102–103).[18] On the other hand, there are countless examples of passages in which Mozart wished a repetition to be louder. If, for example, a two- or four-bar idea is first played by the solo piano in a piano concerto and is repeated then with orchestral accompaniment, this kind of scoring naturally precludes any echo effect.

Why is the echo effect at repeated phrases or patterns less welcome in the classical style? Because in classical music repeats of the same motives or phrases have become an element of structure, a principle necessary for building large, coherent forms. Often such repeated patterns have the function of columns supporting a gate, an archway, a dome. It is obvious that in architecture a building would probably collapse if the columns on the right were shorter than those on the left.

A well-known musical example calling for an intended unvaried repeat and certainly not an echo may be taken from the Presto agitato movement of Beethoven's "Moonlight" Sonata, op. 27/II, mm. 9–14:

---

[18] Cf. H. Kroyer's Foreword to the Eulenburg miniature score of this symphony.

Ex. II/26:

To play the third and fourth measures of this example *piano*—indicated here by signs with question marks—would be utterly ridiculous and would destroy the effect of passionate agitation. Alas, in the case of Mozart, pianists are less respectful.

In the first movement of the C major Sonata K. 330, the following *forte* passage occurs four times, clearly marked in the original authentic edition:

Ex. II/27:

There is no dynamic sign to demand an echo. Why do "echoists" (mostly younger pianists) disregard the text and arbitrarily add *p* in mm. 43, 49, etc.? This is not at all necessary.

Another typical case of a structurally unjustified echo sometimes is heard in the third movement of the D major Sonata K. 576 (mm. 18 and 82):

Ex. II/28:

Yet it is evident that the entire passage starting in m. 9 has the character of a *tutti* in a concerto, thus needing an uninterrupted *forte*.

Similarly, the *f* at the end of the exposition of the opening movement of this Sonata K. 576 (one of the very rare dynamic indications found in this work) should be more or less maintained until the entrance of the authentic *p* in m. 59 (see p. 65).

If we take a look at Mozart's piano sonatas in order to find authentic echo indications, we discover only two of them; namely, in the A minor Sonata K. 310/I (mm. 18 and 99) and in the Adagio of the C minor Sonata K. 457/II (m. 38; there, unlike in a true echo, the *piano* is continued); in addition, there is, of course, the unique double echo in the finale of the Piano Concerto in E-flat major, K. 271 (mm. 196ff. and 324ff.). The scarcity of these indications provides food for thought. Even in works with an abundance of dynamic signs, markings for echo effects are largely absent.

These observations do not suggest, however, that the application of echo effects should be completely banned; but, as said before, it should be used with discretion. In works of Mozart's youth or in those later works where charm is most prevailing, there is no harm if a repeated phrase is played somewhat softer before a return to the previous volume level, thus signifying to the listener a kind of echo. On the other hand, Mozart's orchestration of repeated passages in his piano and violin concertos often indicated clearly that he wanted the repeated passages performed intensified rather than diminished in volume.

According to Walter Gerstenberg,[19] keyboard musicians of the Baroque period preferred the echo only as the "voice of nature," and the galant musicians followed their example with some frequency; however, a repetition with increased intensities is a welcome confirmation of a statement. Gerstenberg raised the question of whether the frequent repetitions of passages, e.g., in Haydn's early Sonatas Hob. XVI/22 and XVI/31, are still imitations of echo in nature (Baroque approach) or of human speech ("logos") when the repeat of a phrase means intensification and thus an affirmation of the previous statement.[20] He concedes that both interpretations are feasible as a sign of the inherent dialectic ambiguity of the "*Vorklassik*." To answer this question, we should like to add that Mozart and Haydn, in his mature years, had already removed themselves more from Baroque practices than the young galant Haydn in his earliest sonatas.

In case of doubt, it is advisable to play the repeated phrases at approximately the same dynamic level.

---

[19] See Walter Gerstenberg, "Die Krise der Barockmusik," pp. 81–84.

[20] Marianne Danckwart recently came to a similar conclusion in her essay on Mozart's dynamics: "Muss accurat mit dem Gusto, Forte und Piano, wie es steht, gespielt werden," pp. 293–316. Several echo pieces of the Baroque period (pp. 296–297) are "imitazione della natura," while in the second half of the eighteenth century, music was compared with human rhetoric. She cites Jean Jacques Rousseau, *Dictionnaire de la Musique*, p. 150: "*Cet usage* [the *p* 'echo'] *ne subsiste plus* [is not in vogue anymore]."

Mozart's use of a repetition as a confirmation and an intensification of a motive or phrase is often obvious, especially in his concertos. Examples include the first movements of the Concerto for Two Pianos K. 265, the Concerto in D major, K. 451, as well as the Violin Concerto in A major, K. 219. Also in the Piano Concerto in B-flat major, K. 595, third movement, mm. 94–97, an intensification of the repetition is far more appropriate than the contrary, a soft echo:

Ex. II/29:

What distinguishes the sound of a top orchestra from that of a mediocre one? In a great orchestra the main melody comes out in a natural flow while the accompanying instruments give support without killing it by being too loud. This right balance—this is what the old treatises have in mind when they speak of the "ripieno players," those who fill in or replenish the harmony, warning them to be aware of the soloists who have to be heard clearly.

Not only in Mozart's time but well into the nineteenth century in works for orchestra, *f* or *p* was uniformly marked for every instrument in the score. Yet orchestra players knew and know up to this day that the sound has to be balanced. Instruments playing only sustaining harmonies must simply play less loudly than instruments carrying the thematic discourse. In some of Beethoven's works, this balancing of forces poses serious problems. Mozart, and Haydn in particular, had more experience with orchestral scoring. Yet their symphonies still need adjustment of the ripieno in order to sound good.

A well-defined compilation of the various meanings of dynamic signs is given by Patier:

> *The dynamic in music constitutes a complex notion, the important principles of which need to be stated [with precision]: In fact, respecting the dynamics of a work cannot be limited to observing [only] the indications found in the score, indications which in the eighteenth century often leave something to be desired. Other elements have to be accounted for: These are, for example, the melodic line [guidance] on which depend the phrasing, the harmony, the rhythm, the tempo, the structure. Also, the musical genre as well as the choice of instruments (solo or ensemble) are not indifferent and exercise an influence on the nuances. ... Therefore, dynamics are not an aesthetic refinement added to the text ... but are an integral part of the musical language.*[21]

---

[21] Patier, p. 541 (translation into English by Paul Badura-Skoda).

3
Problems of Tempo and Rhythm

Tempo Problems

One must also be able to divine from the piece itself whether it requires a slow or a somewhat quicker speed. It is true that at the beginning of every piece special words are written which are designed to characterize it, such as "Allegro" (merry), "Adagio" (slow) and so on. But both slow and quick have their degrees. … So one has to deduce it (the tempo) from the piece itself, and it is this by which the true worth of a musician can be recognized without fail. Every melodious piece has at least one phrase from which one can recognize quite surely what sort of speed the piece demands. Often, if other points be carefully observed, the phrase is forced into its natural speed. Remember this, but know also that for such perception long experience and good judgment are required. Who will contradict me if I count this among the chiefest perfections in the art of music?

These words were written by Leopold Mozart and printed in his *Violinschule* (I/2, §7, p. 33). Note his statement requiring "long experience and good judgment" in order to find the right tempo; in addition, a feeling for style is essential. No one tempo is right to the exclusion of all others. The individual musician retains a certain freedom that should not be undervalued—within a certain range, any tempo *can* be artistically valid. Here we will try to show the limits of this freedom.

It is often said that the old masters would have been horrified at the tempo of present-day performances—surely they can't have played so fast in the old days! In response to this claim, it is a tempting assumption that in an age of speed we have also increased the tempo of musical performance; but this seems doubtful. To say "the older, the slower" is certainly wrong. If we go back through history, we find that in the mid-eighteenth century J. J. Quantz, Frederick the Great's famous flute teacher, worked out mathematically derived tempos with the aid of the human pulse, which he took as beating at eighty to the minute. However, physicians have recently assured us that a normal pulse is rather between sixty-eight and seventy-two rather than eighty, at least nowadays. Did Quantz suffer from a flu fever or was he just not able to count his pulse correctly? For an Allegro assai tempo in 4/4, he prescribes "a half note to one pulse beat," i.e., MM. $\it{d}$ = 80, but for an Allegro assai in *alla breve* time he demanded a tempo twice as fast, and this indeed yields astonishingly fast tempos for the works of his generation. According to the normal pulse of ca. seventy per minute, however, all his tempos seem just right.

In the second half of the eighteenth century it seems that basic tempos were, if anything, quicker than ours, not slower. Besides, Quantz did expressly declare that his tempo indications should not be taken too literally, and that in choosing a tempo one should bear in mind various other factors, particularly "the quickest notes that occur in a passage" of the work. Apart from the pulse, there are other inborn "pacemakers" in the human constitution (for example, normal walking speed), and these seem so deeply ingrained that they would hardly be influenced by the passage of time or a changing world.

Mozart left neither metronome markings nor tempo calculations based on the pulse. As regards his tempos, we have to rely on the few imprecise indications found, for example, in his letters, where he complained about the excessively fast tempos of some performers or warned against playing certain movements too slowly. These remarks are refreshingly direct; they were part of his everyday musical activities and were certainly not written with an eye toward posterity. Although it would be hard to base any general principles on these remarks, we should mention the most important of them, if only because one has to be thankful for any remarks of Mozart's that cast light on this "most difficult and chief requisite in music," as Mozart once called it when writing about young Nannette Stein's playing in a letter to his father (from 14 October 1777).

About the "Haffner" Symphony Mozart wrote (7 August 1782): "The first Allegro must be played with great fire, the last—as fast as possible." In the famous letter of 26 September 1781, he refers to the end of the first act of *The Abduction of the Seraglio* where "the major key begins at once pianissimo—it must go very quickly—and wind up with a great deal of noise." Regarding the "Osmin" aria from the third act he tells his father:

> The passage "Drum beym Barte des Propheten" is indeed in the same tempo, but with quick notes; but as Osmin's rage gradually increases, there comes (just when the aria seems to be at an end) the Allegro assai, which is in a totally different meter and in a different key; this is bound to be very effective. For just as a man in such a towering rage oversteps all the bounds of order, moderation and propriety, and completely forgets himself, so must the music too forget itself.

In the same letter he says about the Overture to the *Abduction of the Seraglio*: "and I doubt whether anyone, even if his previous night has been a sleepless one, could go to sleep over it."

On the other hand, there is no lack of remarks showing clearly how much Mozart opposed excessively quick performances of his works. In a letter from 17 January 1778, quoted more completely elsewhere (see p. 250), he wrote:

> … before dinner he [the Abbé Vogler] scrambled through my concerto. … He took the first movement prestissimo, the Andante Allegro and the Rondo even more prestissimo. … Well, you may easily imagine that it was unendurable. At the same time I could not bring myself to say to him, "Far too quick!"

If Mozart stated shortly afterwards in a letter (4 February 1778) that he preferred the playing of the sixteen-year-old Aloysia Weber to that of the celebrated Abbé Vogler, he probably sincerely meant this. We do not think that his assessment of Aloysia's musical abilities was affected by the fact that he was in love with her. Mozart's judgment in musical matters was at all times incorruptible—one should compare what he wrote to his father about this time on the subject of Aloysia's singing—it is by no means purely laudatory.

> Mlle. Weber … played the clavier twice, for she does not play at all badly. What surprises me most is her excellent sight-reading. Would you believe it, she played my difficult sonatas at sight, slowly but without missing a single note! On my honor, I would rather hear my sonatas played by her than by Vogler!

The composer and pianist F. X. Sterkel also aroused Mozart's disapproval. Sterkel played five pieces "so quickly that it was hard to follow them, and not at all clearly, and not in time," he wrote to his father on 26 November 1777. Thus, Mozart was constantly raising objections when clarity and rhythmic exactness suffered through overly fast tempos. Here he was at one with his father, for Leopold also often found tempos too fast. In a letter to his son from 29 January 1778, he wrote:

> Indeed, I am no lover of excessively rapid passages, where you have to produce the notes with the half tone of the violin and, so to speak, only touch the fiddle with the bow and almost play in the air.

In the letters from Mozart's last years, after the death of his father, he does not discuss tempos, but his contemporaries' remarks are some guide. Rochlitz's recollections of Mozart in the *Leipzig Allgemeine Musikalische Zeitung* of 7 November 1798 seem to reflect some truth,[1] even though he has often been described as a rather "overly imaginative" writer:

> *Nothing roused Mozart to livelier protest than did the botching of his compositions when performed in public, mainly through excessively fast tempos. "They think that will add fire to it," he would say, "The fire has got to be in the piece itself—it won't come from galloping away with it."*

Hardly twenty years after Mozart's death there were clear differences of opinion about the tempos in Mozart's works. In the *Allgemeine Musikalische Zeitung* (Leipzig, 5 May 1813), one could read:

> *One need only remark, for example, the widely differing tempos adopted in differing places for some pieces, even very famous and characteristic ones. To mention only one, I heard Mozart's Overture to* Don Giovanni *played under the great man himself, by the Guardasonic Society [as it then was] of Prague, and I also heard it in various other places, including Paris, Vienna and Berlin. The Adagio[2] was taken a shade slower in Paris, in Vienna quite noticeably faster and in Berlin almost as lively again as under Mozart, and in all three places the Allegro was played either faster or slower than he played it.*

It is interesting that many reports suggest that Mozart tended to take his allegro movements at a moderate speed. Nowadays, movements simply marked *Allegro* are often played too fast. If Mozart wanted a movement played really quickly, then he marked it *Presto* or *Allegro assai*. An unadorned *Allegro* carries the original meaning of the word: merry, joyful, cheerful. The well-known D major Rondo K. 485, for example, is wonderfully effective when played cheerfully, graciously, even if in a moderate tempo—and how much does it lack grace and sounds uninteresting when played merely fast!

As regards andante and adagio movements, Mozart's remarks and those of his contemporaries rather suggest that he preferred a flowing tempo. Of course, one does sometimes hear a grave, stately Adagio played at a very ungrave, overly fast tempo; but the opposite, an Andante movement played with excessively slow pathos, is a much more common mistake. In a letter to his father, Mozart (9 June 1784) advised his sister about the piano concertos K. 413–415: "Please tell my sister that there is no Adagio in any of these concertos—only Andantes."

We should remember that in Mozart's time "andante" was not really a slow tempo—that was a nineteenth-century development. For Mozart it was a fairly flowing tempo, still in accordance with the word's original meaning of "moving," and it lay roughly halfway between slow and fast. He indicated the tempo in the autograph of the F major Rondo K. 494 as *Andante*, but two years later he used it as the finale of the F major Sonata K. 533, marking it *Allegretto* and expanding it by twenty-seven measures. Since the music remained the same in those measures, there cannot have been any significant difference between the tempos *Andante* and *Allegretto*, though the *Allegretto* of the sonata will likely be played slightly faster than the Rondo (suggested tempos ♩ = ca. 72–79 *versus* ♩ = 66–69 for the Rondo).

Another example demonstrating that some themes can be played in more than a single correct tempo can be found in the final movement of the Sonata for Piano and Violin in G major, K. 379. The contemplative theme (♩ = ca. 66) in the *Andante cantabile* of this variation form piece appears unchanged at the end of the movement as a cheerful return to the *Allegretto* tempo (♩ = ca. 80).

---

[1] See Maynard Solomon, "The Rochlitz Anecdotes …," p. 23f.
[2] Mozart did not mark "Adagio" but "Andante"—an interesting error of Rochlitz.

Naturally, not all of Mozart's andante movements require the same tempo, and there are a number where one should take care not to play too rapidly. There must always be a clear distinction between the lighter *"grazioso"* Andantes[3] and those more intimate and deeply felt, such as those in the C major Concerto K. 503 or in the A minor Sonata K. 310. The Andante of the Violin Sonata in B-flat Major, K. 454, is another piece not to be taken too quickly; Mozart originally marked this movement *Adagio*, then crossed this out and replaced it with *Andante*. The reason will be clear to those who know the sonata. The unusual content of this movement is itself enough to necessitate a more flowing tempo that will hold the form together. On the other hand, mm. 30–33 show that this Andante, which Mozart himself thought resembled an *Adagio*, must be played relatively calmly; if the initial tempo is too quick, these measures will be difficult to play with the appropriate expressiveness. We propose a tempo of ♩ = ca. 52.

The Andante of the C major Concerto K. 503 should be also taken more slowly. Alfred Einstein rightly once remarked that this movement is certainly very akin to an *Adagio* in character. Similarly, Mozart marked the second movement of the Sonata K. 309 *Andante un poco Adagio*. On 6 December 1777, he wrote to his father that this particular Andante movement "must not be taken too quickly."

In an Adagio in a 3/4 meter, the tempo should flow so that one can still feel the rhythm in whole bars. In this way, figurations in small note values can be played melodically and evenly without superfluous accents, yet lose none of their expressiveness.

Pamina's famous G minor aria from *The Magic Flute* "*Ach, ich fühl's, es ist verschwunden ...*" is marked "Andante":

Ex. III/1:

This aria is usually sung as if Mozart had indicated the tempo marking *Adagio* or even *Lento* and not prescribed *Andante*; with other words, its interpretation is far to slow. Some voices already protested against too slow a tempo during the early nineteenth century. (For more remarks on this question and for another similar view, see Appendix 1.)

In considering this vital problem of tempos, one should bear in mind that a full tone tends to stretch the tempo, whereas the more slender the tone, the more mobile it is. This is a decisive factor in Mozart's music. If one takes the trouble to secure a tone that is free from thickness, it is astonishing how much room there is for expression, even in a flowing *Andante* movement. The individual notes may perhaps lose a little, but the coherence of complete phrases more than makes up for this.

In general, composers imagine their slow movements as going faster than interpreters in fact play them. Recordings and live performances by present-day composers have shown us, on the other hand, that in performing their own works they often choose slightly slower tempos than those they have indicated by their metronome markings. This is mainly explained by the fact

---

[3] A fine example of the light, floating *Andante* is the *Andante grazioso* middle movement of the E major Trio K. 542, proposed tempo ♩ = c. 58. Nor should the *Andante grazioso* of the A major Sonata K. 331 be taken too slowly, ♪ = c. 138–144, but "gazioso," i.e., with charm and an undulating rhythm; a very slight *ritardando* in mm. 12 and 18 seems appropriate.

that all sound has to be realized and is bound to move more easily in the composer's mind than when played or sung, with all the various factors of inertia (mechanical and acoustical) that are involved. All the same, the tempo should not be allowed to slow down too much in performance, as is unfortunately often the case.

We should not be surprised that Mozart's music has given rise to more differences of opinion about tempos than have the works of later composers, who often provided metronome markings as a basis for interpretation. There are many musicians who hold that Mozart's music must be played as weightlessly as possible, lightly and quickly; the justification for this opinion is sought in Mozart's childlike temperament, his effortless way of overcoming even the greatest technical difficulties when composing, or in the inherent grace of his idiom, which is indeed far less weighty than that of Beethoven or Brahms. Other musicians hold the opposite view, seeing the tragic, demonic elements in Mozart as the most striking. In their determination to reject the idea of Mozart as a euphoric Olympian who poured out melody after melody throughout his life, they often run the risk of reading tragic qualities into works that really are playful and less tense and whose charm is easily destroyed by an overly serious, too weighty approach.

Naturally, both views contain an element of truth: Mozart's music contains both galant charm and tragedy. This is one of the qualities that mark his unique place in the history of music. In even his most galant works there is a trace of deep seriousness, and the reverse is also true. The predominant character of any particular work is very important in choosing its tempos. For example, the first movement of the tragic C minor Concerto K. 491 would lose much of its expressive depth if taken too quickly, as would the second movement of the E-flat major Concerto K. 271. (For the latter we would suggest a tempo of ♪ = ca. 80–84. Here it is best not to try to be too precise metrically, since the movement contains *recitative* passages, and a certain freedom is thus in order.) Brilliant movements, with less spiritual depth, demand quick tempos if they are to make the maximum effect; for example, the first movement of the Piano Concerto in D major, K. 537; the first movements of the piano sonatas K. 284 in D major, K. 309 in C major and K. 311 in D major; as well as the Sonata for Four Hands in D major, K. 381; and the first movement of the Sonata for Two Pianos K. 448 (♩ = ca. 152). It is interesting to note that nearly all these movements are in D Major.

Mozart's articulation marks often hint at the appropriate tempo. In the outer movements of the Concerto in B-flat major, K. 595, there are subtleties of articulation that are impossible to convey if the tempo is too quick; e.g., in the first movement, m. 106 (suggested tempo ♩ = ca. 129–132):

Ex. III/2:

(The words in brackets are suggestions from the authors.)

Likewise, in the third movement of the Concerto in B-flat major, K. 595, the articulation provides a pointer to the correct tempo in mm. 1–8:

Ex. III/3:

or mm. 102ff.:

Ex. III/4:

and also in mm. 150ff. (suggested tempo = ca. 150–108):

Ex. III/5:

and in mm. 163ff., too:

Ex. III/6:

Another movement in which a fairly moderate tempo matches best the character of the music is the finale of the Piano Concerto in E-flat major, K. 449; this is why Mozart marked it *Allegro*

ma non troppo. At an excessively fast tempo it loses its incomparable magic (suggested tempo ♩ = ca. 108–116).

In his tempo markings Mozart was a good deal more exact than is often assumed. Since even nowadays there is still a good deal of confusion about the meaning of Mozart's tempo markings, we shall try to arrange them in a scale. (On this matter the valuable study by Jean-Pierre Marty deserves mention,[4] as Marty researched all of Mozart's tempo markings and attempted to systematize them with metronome values.) According to our practical experience, we find that on average his tempos are sometimes too slow. For example, a 4/4 Allegro as in the opening movements of the Piano Concertos K. 466 and K. 467, he suggests ♩ = 126. However, it can hardly be only a coincidence that nearly all recordings by significant interpreters of the past seventy years have ♩ = ca. 132–138 (in other concertos even faster) as their basic pulse.

A List of the Most Important Tempo Markings

Largo

This is Mozart's slowest tempo, since, as far as we know, he does not use the marking *lento* in his piano works or anywhere else. An example of the rarely used marking *Largo* is found in the introduction to the first movement of the Violin Sonata in B-flat Major, K. 454; there we would suggest a tempo of ♪ = ca. 69–72.

Grave

This tempo marking was, apparently, in Mozart's mind the slowest possible tempo, and he used it only once, namely in the introduction to an unfortunately unfinished Sonata for Two Pianos K. 375b.[5]

Adagio

Although this is definitely a marking for a slow tempo, it should be realized that an eighteenth-century adagio is faster than a nineteenth-century one. Even Italian musicians have sometimes to be reminded that it derives from *a[d']]agio*—at ease, relaxed. In playing Mozart one should as a rule adopt a rather more flowing tempo for the Adagio movements of the galant works (e.g., Concerto for Three Pianos in F Major, K. 242/II, suggested tempo: ♩ = ca. 40–42) than for the markedly lyrical Adagio movements in his late works such as the Piano Sonata K. 457/II: ♪ = ca. 72–76 or (♪ = 76–80 in the A-flat major section in the middle). Fantasia in C Minor K. 475, opening, ♪ = ca. 72–80; mm. 11 onward, ♪ = ca. 80–88; the D major section, ♩ = ca. 84–88. Adagio in B Minor, K. 540, ♪ = ca. 76.

The festive *Adagio* at the beginning of the C major Fantasia K. 394 is a special case and should be taken at ♪ = ca. 92; we also feel the Adagio movement of the D major Sonata K. 576 in a rather more flowing tempo, ♩ = ca. 92–96. In our opinion, the second movement of the Sonata in F major, K. 332, is often played in too slow a tempo: here the continuity of the four-bar periods should be maintained.

TRACK
61

Larghetto

It is unfortunate that a Larghetto should widely and wrongly be regarded as slower than an Adagio.[6] (See the discussion in chapter 12, Concerto K. 491.) Türk defines *Larghetto* as "ein wenig langsam," which can be translated as "somewhat slow." Often a Larghetto movement is

---

[4] J.-P. Marty, *The Tempo Indications of Mozart.*

[5] Ibid., p. 108.

[6] Chopin was very exact about his tempo markings, and in the Nocturne, op. 27, no. 1 ('Larghetto') he writes a final long *Ritardando,* which ends "Adagio"; this shows clearly that *Larghetto* in his time was still considered to be played quicker than *Adagio.*

combined with an *alla breve* sign; for instance, in the Piano Concerto in b-flat Major, K. 595 (suggested tempo ♩ = ca. 84–88).

Andante

As already stated, *Andante* is the most problematical tempo marking in Mozart's music. Mozart often qualifies it with additional words to show whether he intends a slower or more flowing tempo. He indicates a steady tempo with *Andante un poco adagio*—e.g., Piano Sonata K. 309/II or Piano Concerto K. 238/II (♩ = ca. 56),—or with *Andante con espressione*—e.g., Piano Sonata K. 311/II. The indication *Andante cantabile con espressione* allows some agogic freedom; e.g., in the Piano Sonata K. 310/II (♪ = ca. 84–88, the middle section rather quicker, to ca. 96). The marking *Andante sostenuto* is found in the second movement of the Violin Sonata K. 296. A flowing *Andante* is most often marked *Andante grazioso*, as, e.g., in the Piano Sonata K. 331 (suggested tempo ♪ = ca. 138–144). Altogether it seems that these tempo indications of *Andante* with additional word(s) usually do not suggest a slower tempo. For instance, the *Andante cantabile* of the second movement of the Sonata K. 333 should not be taken too slow—a singer should be able to sing each four-measure period in one breath.

TRACK
62

Most *Andante* markings, however, are not qualified through additional words, and a great deal of investigation is then often necessary to find the right tempo. Particularly difficult in our opinion is the choice of tempo for the *Andante* of the F major Sonata K. 533, which has to be played with solemnity and yet must flow (♩ = ca. 58–60); a slight quickening in the more excitable development section seems appropriate. A definitely stormy *Andante* occurs in the C major Fantasia K. 394 (♩ = ca. 66).

Andantino

Already during Mozart's lifetime musicians disagreed as to the meaning of *Andantino*: "little *andante*" or "less *andante*"? This fact may be due to the literal meaning of the root word *andante*, or "walking." If one walks quickly, then "less *andante*" would indicate a calmer tempo; however, if one walks slowly, *Andantino* would mean "less slowly" (i.e., faster). Haydn appears to have been of this opinion when he marked the second movement of his D major Trio for Flute, Cello and Piano (Hob. XV/16) with *Andantino più tosto* [= rather] *Allegretto*. And two generations later Schubert reversed the phrase (but intended the same idea) when marking the second movement of his A minor Piano Sonata (D 537): *Allegretto quasi Andantino*. On the other hand, *Andantino* for Mozart appears to have had the meaning "slower than *andante*." Mozart's student Hummel, who during his childhood lived with the Mozart family, states this emphatically in his *Klavierschule* and warns against the contrary opinion that appears to have been widespread.[7] *Andantino* is also explained as "slower" in Friedrich von Starke's *Wiener Klavierschule* (1819–29).

Above all, however, it is the internal evidence found in Mozart's music that often supports a slower Andantino tempo: In the recitative and aria "Ch'io mi scordi di te? Non so, d'onde viene" K. 505), an Andantino section (suggested tempo ♪ = ca. 96–100) with a pronounced Adagio character is followed by an Andante in rondo form (₵, ♩ = ca. 96–100, twice as fast, indeed!). Yet the edges sometimes blur themselves: the second movement of the Piano Concerto in E-flat Major, K. 271, is an *Andantino*, but the big cadenza to this movement Mozart marked *ferma nell' Andante*. In the *Andantino* of the E-flat major Concerto K. 449, the ornamentation, where many notes are to be played in the space of short note values, also suggests a moderate tempo but one that does not drag (♩ = ca. 48–52).

---

[7] Hummel, *Ausführliche Theoretisch-Praktische Anweisung zum Pianoforte-Spiel*. p. 66, footnote.

Tempo di menuetto

This is a frequent marking, which, like the simpler label *Menuett*, should be defined more exactly. Just as in the later *Ländler*, German dances (*Deutsche*) and waltzes, there is a broad range between the calm, leisurely minuet and the fast minuet that can sometimes assume the character of the later *scherzo*. What all minuets have in common, however, and which unfortunately can almost never be determined from the notation, is a genuine dance character: The strong first beat must decidedly be more emphasized than the second and third beats, which are generally played light and short, especially in the accompaniment.[8] Not only minuets, but rather nearly all fast movements in 3/4 time have this dance character. Figaro's Cavatina, no. 3, from *The Marriage of Figaro*, offers an excellent example, where the emphasis of the first beat is clearly determined from the declamation of the text:

Ex. III/7:

The aristocratic minuet from *Don Giovanni* is interesting in that it belongs to the slower variety (♩ = ca. 84–96). Note that in the ball scene this minuet is combined with a fast German dance—three eighths to every quarter of the minuet:

Ex. III/8:

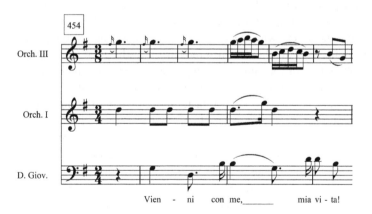

In the *Allgemeine Musikalische Zeitung* of 1839, the editor Fink cited the evidence of W. Tomaschek, who had heard the early performances of *Don Giovanni* conducted by Mozart in Prague. Tomaschek recalled a tempo of approximately ♩ = 96; despite the long period of time that had passed, such recollections are often quite accurate. In this case, the tempo can essentially be considered authentic.

---

[8] Unfortunately, most present-day performances miss this point and lack the distinction between a strong first beat and lighter afterbeats.

Among the more moderate Tempo di Menuetto movements can be counted the finales of the Concerto for Three Pianos in F Major, K. 242, and the A major Violin Concerto K. 219.

It is another matter if one must choose a tempo for minuets that are indeed meant to be danced. As part of the International Haydn Congress in Vienna in 1982, the Danze Antiche ensemble under the direction of Professor Eva Campianu planned to present a performance of Haydn's Redoutenball minuets based on old dance treatises and in historical costumes. Along with other Viennese classical composers, Haydn had composed for Redouten; these festivities were held in the emperor's castle. Initially, the budget for the congress did not accommodate a hired orchestra for the performance. Responsible for the planning of the congress, Eva Badura-Skoda therefore obtained all available recordings of those minuets that were to be danced. However, she found out during the dress rehearsal that none of these recordings could be used, since in each case the tempos on the records were too fast for a performance of *menuetti ballabili* in costumes. The female dancers were all professional ballet dancers and could of course execute the dances perfectly in leotards, but in Rococo costumes with crinolines they were simply unable to turn as fast as the tempos on the recordings would require. Therefore, a small orchestra had to be engaged for the performance of the dances (Hob. IX:11 and Hob. IX:16/5, 12, and 16), which could be executed at the most in $\quarternote = 100$.

Could a costume problem have been one of the reasons for Mozart's observation that minuets were performed slower in Italy? The Viennese minuet was obviously taken a good deal quicker than the Italian type. On 24 March 1770, Mozart wrote from Bologna to his sister about a ball in Milan:

> *The minuet itself is very beautiful. It comes, of course, from Vienna and was most certainly composed by Deller or Starzer. ... The minuets in Milan, in fact the Italian minuets generally, have plenty of notes, are played slowly and have many measures. ...*

Recent research by other musicologist has confirmed that most minuet movements from symphonies were probably played in Vienna at a significantly faster speed than *menuetti ballabile*, namely with only a single beat conducted per measure.[9] Later transcriptions and arrangements by Hummel and others, who specified metronome markings, also support this conclusion. One such fast minuet may well be the third movement of the great G minor Symphony K. 550, ($\dottedhalfnote = 140$), as well as that of the "Jupiter" Symphony K. 551 (for which $\dottedhalfnote$ ca. 60–69, is recommended; Hummel and Czerny have $\dottedhalfnote = 88$ which is certainly too fast).[10]

Mozart often indicated *Allegretto* for his faster movement with minuet character. This would lead one to conclude that these tempos should not be too fast.

The rare indication *Menuetto cantabile* is the slowest form of a minuet tempo. The intermezzo in the last movement of the Piano Concerto in E-flat major, K. 482, can hardly be played faster than $\quarternote = $ ca. 86.

Interestingly, in the *Menuetti* of the String Quartet in G major, K. 387, Mozart first wrote *Allegretto* in the sketch, *Allegro* in the final autograph, and afterwards changed it back again to *Allegretto* when it was published by Artaria in 1785 (Czerny suggests $\quarternote = 60$). Thus, we can conclude that Mozart intended many minuets to be played between *Allegretto* and *Allegro*. Examples for these faster movements are the second movement of the Piano Sonata in G major, K. 283, and the E-flat major Symphony K. 543 ($\dottedhalfnote = $ ca. 58–66; Czerny suggests $\dottedhalfnote = 72$, which is probably too fast for a minuet marked *Allegretto*).

---

9 See Max Rudolf, letter to Frederick Neumann, 27 January 1991 in Max Rudolf, *A Musical Life: Writings and Letters* (Hillsdale, NY: Pendragon Press, 2001), 411 ff. The letter comments on a critique of William Malloch; see W. Malloch, *The Minuets of Haydn and Mozart: Goblins or Elephants?* Early Music (August 1993), 437–445.

10 Interestingly, Schubert indicated *Menuetto* for dance movements with an unmistakable *scherzo* character in his early sonatas and symphonies. But in Schubert's days nobody was dancing any more with crinolines.

Maestoso

In Mozart's time *maestoso* was a byword that means to slow down a tempo slightly; it not only means "majestic" but also "magnificent" or "played with grandeur." On 20 April 1782, Mozart sent his sister the Fantasy and Fugue in C Major K. 394 and wrote about the fugue:

> *I have purposely written above it Andante maestoso, as it must not be played too fast. For if a fugue is not played slowly, the ear cannot distinguish the theme when it comes in and consequently the effect is entirely missed.*

Türk defines *maestoso* as "majestic and lofty" and adds: "With regard to the movement [tempo] it means rather slower than faster as *Andante*" (or *Allegro*).

Allegretto

Allegretto is very similar to *Andante* and only moderately fast. In outer movements it can be more like an *Allegro*, whereas as a marking for a slow middle movement it should be taken as a very flowing *Andante*. An example is the second movement of the F major Concerto K. 459. In the third movement of the D major Sonata K. 576, marked *Allegretto* and often unfortunately taken too fast, we recommend ♩ = ca. 92–96.

Allegretto grazioso

Whereas the suffix grazioso in an Andante movement may sometimes indicate a more flowing tempo, in Allegretto movements the opposite holds true. Here, grace goes with leisure. Typical of this kind of movement are the final movements of the G major Trio K. 496 and (above all) the Concert Rondo in D major, K. 382 (ca. ♩ = 56–60).

Allegro

This is Mozart's most frequently used tempo indication. *Allegro* takes in everything that comes under the heading "lively," "vividly," "cheerful," "quick." Suffixes for a steady Allegro movement are *Allegro ma non troppo* or *Allegro maestoso*. The first movement of the A minor Sonata K. 310 is the only Allegro maestoso in Mozart's piano sonatas; and among the piano concertos we also find this tempo marking only twice, namely in the first movements of the Piano Concertos in C major, K. 467 and K. 503, the last of the great series of concertos of 1784–86. But even among other Allegro movements where there is no additional word specifying the tempo, one must make a clear distinction between lyrical *cantabile* movements (Piano Concerto in A major, K. 488/I) and the fiery, virtuoso ones (e.g., the first movement of the "Haffner" Symphony). In the autograph of the C minor Piano Sonata K. 457, the first movement Mozart marked *Allegro*, whereas in the first edition it is headed *Allegro molto*; one naturally will choose a fairly brisk *Allegro* tempo here (♩ = ca. 88–92). Less frequent markings for a likely faster *Allegro* are *Allegro aperto* (Piano Concerto in C Major, K. 246) and *Allegro con spirito* (Sonata for Two Pianos K. 448/I). Mozart used the indication *Allegro aperto* only in his early Salzburg years. Later he wrote more frequently *Allegro molto* and *Molto allegro*, presumably meaning the same. These indications meant "lively and somehow faster" than *Allegro*.

Allegro vivace/Allegro assai

Allegro vivace (Concerto K. 449, first movement) means that the *Allegro* is to be lively, but not necessarily quicker, whereas *Allegro assai* movements are more akin to Mozart's quickest tempo: *Presto*. The proper tempo for the *Allegro assai* in the finale of the Sonata K. 457 is around ♩ = ca. 76–84.

Presto/Prestissimo

Presto should be played "as fast as possible" according to Mozart (letter of 7 August 1782), that is, while still allowing every note and every articulation mark to be observed to come through clearly and without obscuring the translucency of the texture. It is interesting that in a copy of the Concerto in E-flat Major, K. 271, which Mozart's sister made for herself, the *presto* finale has the designation *Allegro assai* instead of *Presto*, perhaps on Mozart's insistence (♩ = ca. 138–144). Thus, it could be meant to be played slightly slower than most *presto* movements. A really fast *Presto* is found in the last movement of the A minor Sonata K. 310 (suggested tempo ♩ = ca. 96–102). *Prestissimo* does not occur in Mozart's piano works.

All in all, we may say that Mozart was very exact about indicating his tempo intentions. This we can gather indirectly from a well-known passage in one of his letters about Clementi (from 7 June 1783):

> *Clementi is a ciarlatano, like all Italians. He writes "Presto" over a sonata or even "Prestissimo" and "Alla-breve", and plays it himself Allegro in 4/4 time. I know that this is the case, for I have heard him do so.*

Alla breve Time

This remark about Clementi reveals that Mozart felt there were clear differences between *Allegro* ¢, Allegro 4/4, *presto* ¢, and Presto 4/4, etc.; that when he wrote "*Allegro* 4/4," he did not mean *Allegro alla breve*, and vice versa. How seldom is this fact taken into account in performance, and what a difference it makes if observed! Genuine *alla breve* movements with half the number of beats include, for instance, the first movement of the Piano Sonata in F major, K. 533 (♩ = ca. 92) and the final movements of the piano concertos K. 466 and K. 488. In these movements the eighth notes are the smallest units (excluding ornaments) and should be played in approximately the same tempo as sixteenths in a lively *Allegro* (♩ = ca. 138–144⁺). According to Mozart's letter to his father from 7 August 1782, the finale of the "Haffner" Symphony is an example of a *presto* ¢ that—as Marty rightly pointed out—should be taken "as fast as possible."

It is remarkable that the Piano Concerto in F major, K. 459, is the only concerto with an opening movement in *alla breve* time. As in the C minor Sonata K. 457, the justification for the ¢ in K. 459/I lies probably in the fact that instead of sixteenth notes, eighth-note triplets form the smallest unit of pulse (suggested tempo ♩ = 76–84). It is interesting to note that in his own thematic catalogue Mozart wrote *Allegro vivace* as this movement's tempo indication.

Mozart also deliberately demanded *alla breve* for certain slow concerto movements. In these cases, there are again only two instead of the customary four beats per measure. This is not only entirely possible at a slow tempo but also musically necessary, and it is most regrettable that the old Breitkopf Complete Edition (*AMA*), still used by many orchestras today omitted the *alla breve* signs in innumerable Andante and Larghetto movements; for example, in the Andante of the Concerto K. 467 and in the Larghetto of the Piano Concerto K. 595, where the ¢ is of decisive importance. That Mozart indeed intended the *alla breve* here can be seen by the fact that—with the singular exception of the closing measures—there are no passages in thirty-second notes, as is the case with his other Larghetto movements in *alla breve* meter (suggested tempo for K. 595/II ♩ = ca. 42).

Alla breve time is also a telling feature in the slow movement of the D minor Concerto K. 466, which combines the song of a nocturne with serenade-like grace (as in the *staccato* accompaniment of mm. 11–12). Here the test of the correct tempo is whether one can make the transition to the stormy middle section without any noticeable acceleration. Leopold Mozart, who heard the first performance of this Concerto, wrote to Nannerl on 9 June 1784:

I am sending you herewith a concerto. The Adagio is a Romance, the tempo is to be taken at the speed in which the noisy passage with the fast triplets … can be executed.

More than all other *alla breve* movements, the gracious second movement of the C major Concerto K. 467 often suffers from an excessively slow tempo of roughly ♩ = 54–56. If performed in Mozart's prescribed *alla breve* tempo (we suggest ♩ = ca. 80), one gets the impression of hearing a different piece of music.

Nonetheless, we wonder if even Mozart may have once inadvertently omitted an *alla breve* sign. In the first movement of the C minor Sonata K. 457 such a sign seems appropriate. In our opinion, this movement needs only two beats per measure to be shaped properly; otherwise, the excited *Molto allegro* character would be lost. One naturally perceives the eighth-note triplets as the smallest note values apart from the ornaments. Perhaps the ornaments (turns in mm. 23, 25, 79, 81, and 139) prevented Mozart from writing *alla breve*? Or did he really want the heavier execution with four beats (Malcolm Bilson's opinion)?

A special case include sicilianos and other pieces in a 6/8 meter. We can distinguish between those movements with only two accented beats per measure and those with more, analogous to the 4/4, and *alla breve* indications, though these are sometimes only subtle differences. The theme of the finale of the Piano Concerto in E-flat major, K. 482, shows a clear duple division of each measure (♩ = ca. 108). Likewise, the first movement of Mozart's last Piano Sonata in D major, K. 576, has more than two melodically important beats per measure and therefore must not be taken too quickly (♩ = ca. 92–96).

As we mentioned at the beginning of this chapter, every interpreter is left a certain freedom in choosing his or her proper tempo, within the bounds of the artistically valid. It would be pointless to try to tie all artists down to particular metronome markings, for there are too many purely personal variations involved. Over a number of years the radio station RIAS in Berlin observed that all conductors adopted slower tempos in morning concerts than in the evening, so that the same program would be several minutes shorter in the evening than when broadcast live before lunch. Even more than the time of day, the personal condition of the artist plays a part—whether he is tired or exuberant, placid or excited; and obviously much depends on his or her temperament. Age, too, has a great effect on the way one feels tempos. As the ninth of his ten "golden rules," Richard Strauss wrote in a young conductor's album, "When you think you have reached the ultimate prestissimo, then double the tempo!"[11] Twenty-three years later, in 1948, Strauss added the remark, "Nowadays I would alter it to 'then halve the tempo'" to conductors of Mozart!

Furtwängler, too, became famous for the relatively slow tempos he preferred toward the end of his life. Nonetheless, at that time he took the first movement of the G minor Symphony K. 550 nearly as fast as Toscanini, who was well known for his extremely fast tempos. More than anyone else, Furtwängler demonstrated that a feeling of absolute rightness depends less on the tempo itself than on the maintenance of tension and psychological interest. When Karajan conducted the first movement (marked in common time) of the Jupiter Symphony K. 551 in a very fast *alla breve* tempo, we were not convinced that it reflected Mozart's intentions.

Interestingly, during the second half of the twentieth century, a strange discrepancy developed regarding tempo: Traditional orchestras often played slower and s°ometimes even boringly slow, while performances on period instruments were often fast but sometimes at the expense of expression. Perhaps it is as well that Mozart could not leave behind any metronome markings; the current passion for faithfulness to the text might lead musicians to follow such markings against their own inner conviction, and nothing leads to such lifeless rigidity as this kind of

---

[11] See Marty, *The Tempo Indications of Mozart*, p. 108.

violation of one's instincts. An appropriate tempo played with utter conviction is the lesser evil. Metronome markings should show neither more nor less than the correct average tempo within a particular range, and where we have suggested figures, this is how they should be regarded.

Playing "In Time"

Time makes melody ["Takt macht die Melodie"]; *therefore time is the soul of music. It does not only animate the same, but retains all the component parts in their proper order. Time decides the moment when the various notes must be played, and is often what is lacking in many who have otherwise advanced fairly far in music and have a good opinion of themselves. This defect is the result of their having neglected time in the first instance.* (Leopold Mozart, Violinschule, I, II, §1, p. 30)

Musical performance that fails to keep time will always sound amateurish, apart from the fact that it makes the syntax unrecognizable. Unfortunately, there have always been musicians who played every measure at a different tempo, and usually they were proud of it. Schumann, in his "Musikalische Haus-und Lebensregeln," compared their playing with the walking of drunkards, and Mozart expressed himself still more strongly in his famous letter from 24 October 1777 on the subject of what is possibly the most serious of all musical defects:

Further, she [Nannette Stein] *will never acquire the most essential, the most difficult and the chief requisite in music, that is time, because from her earliest years she has done her utmost not to play in time. Herr Stein and I discussed this point for two hours at least and I have almost converted him, for he now asks my advice on everything. He used to be quite crazy about Beecké; but now he sees and hears that I am the better player, that I do not make grimaces, and yet play with such expression that, as he himself confesses, no one up to the present has been able to get such good results out of his pianofortes. Everyone is amazed that I always keep strict time.*

Rhythmically exact playing, the alpha and omega of all good interpretation, costs much labor; even pianists with a natural feeling for rhythm must work very hard at the outset if they are to achieve absolute rhythmic steadiness, which is a superlative musical quality. Even experienced musicians sometimes run away with difficult passages and never notice it. Leopold Mozart, too, has something to say on the subject:

These running notes are the stumbling-block. … Many a violinist, who plays not too badly otherwise, falls into hurrying when playing such continuously running equal notes, so that if they continue for several bars he is at least a quarter note in advance of the time.[12]

The only remedy for this persistent error is constant self-education, by counting or by practice with the metronome. Even though the usefulness of the metronome is disputed as an aid to practice (and naturally it should never be more than this), we have found that as a means of checking it is indispensable. Another excellent way to develop rhythmic steadiness is to play chamber music. Piano duet playing, in particular, is of incalculable educational value. Only those who are able to play in time should allow themselves to make conscious deviations in tempo known as *agogics* and *rubatos* (see the following sections). Of course, playing in time does not mean

---

[12] *Violinschule*, IV, §38 (p. 87). This paragraph continues: "Such an evil must therefore be avoided and such pieces be played at first slowly … not pressing forward but holding back, and in particular, not shortening the last two of four equal notes." This has lost none of its validity; in passage work, particular attention should be paid to the notes at the end of a group.

rattling off a piece with the precision of a metronome any more than it means automatically accenting every first beat. Compare Liszt's words:

I may perhaps be allowed to remark that I wish to see an end to mechanical, fragmented, up and down playing, tied to the barline, which is still the rule in many cases; I can only concede real value to playing that is periodic, that allows important accents to stand out and brings out the melodic and rhythmic nuances.[13]

In many cases the bar line as such must not be felt. One could compare bar lines with the pillars of a bridge and the melody with a road that runs over the bridge. If at each pillar one had the sensation of passing over a humpback bridge, this would be a fairly sure sign that the architect was incompetent. Nothing of the kind should disturb the form and inner flow of a piece—Leopold Mozart's *filo* (thread)—that runs through any composition and must not be allowed to snap.

However, it is also very important to be clear about the way Mozart constructs his periods. The norm is a symmetrically subdivided 8- or 16-bar period (song strophe) the construction of which is straightforward. But deviations from this norm are much more common than many musicians assume. In the development section of the first movement of the D major Sonata K. 576 (mm. 81ff.) there is the grouping 2 + 3 + 3 + 3 + 5 = 16. It is amazing that even in a dance movement (the Menuetto of the A major Sonata K. 331) there are asymmetrical formations such as 2 + 3 + 3 + 2. The subject of the menuetto of the String Quartet K. 590 is built on 7 + 7 measures, the Trio on 5 + 5 (Levin). Consciously correct interpretation is impossible unless one appreciates and communicates these asymmetrical groupings of measures within higher order formal principles that are regular. Just as at the microcosmic level, in a, 4/4 bar, the first and third quarter notes must be felt to be stronger than the second and fourth, or in a 3/4 bar the first and third are stronger than the second, and in a group of three measures, the accent lies on the first bar and the least weight will, as a rule, be given to the second.

Agogics

Audible tempo deviations within a movement will usually be unnecessary and disturbing in Mozart. Most of his movements have such structural unity that the filigree details can be played at the same tempo as the most excited passage work. If this sometimes seems impossible, the trouble is usually an excessively quick tempo, which Mozart repeatedly stigmatized as a crude offense against good taste. Yet there are places, mostly in the nature of elisions, where even a very steady and musical performer will press unobtrusively onward or else hold back the tempo a little. We would describe those adjustments of tempo as "imperceptible"—they amount to not more than one degree of the metronomic scale (e.g., from $\downarrow$ = 132–138). We call these subtle variations in tempo *agogics*. The use of agogics is what distinguishes a steady player from an arhythmical one; a rhythmical player will only vary the tempo to match the sense of the music; an unsteady player varies the tempo indiscriminately.

A good musician will hardly ever vary the tempo within a theme or a self-contained section; the most he will do is use *rubato*. The principal use of agogics is to give a natural feeling for the transitions that occur in multithematic musical forms (sonata or rondo, as against earlier monothematic forms). We see from C. P. E. Bach (*Essay ...*, II/6, p. 375) that this sort of slight agogic deviation is wholly in accordance with eighteenth-century musical practice:

---

[13] Liszt, Preface to his symphonic poems. Quoted by Wilhelm Furtwängler in *Ton und Wort*, p. 262.

It is customary to drag a bit and depart somewhat from a strict observance of the bar. ... This applies to fermatas, cadences, etc. as well as caesuras.

But it would be incorrect to introduce this kind of agogic deviation in all such transitions. They depend so much on the actual feel of the music that one cannot draw up hard and fast rules, but we should like to give a few examples in which we feel that a certain freedom of tempo is necessary.

In the great Sonata in C minor, K. 457, the first and third movements sound best if one can do justice to their expressive qualities without altering the basic tempo. (An exception is the *recitative* passage in the finale, mm. 228–243, where Mozart's own marking is *a piacere* and then *a tempo*.) In the second movement, on the other hand, one will make a slight *ritardando* in the second half of m. 40 (41) as a natural preparation for the return of the first subject. (While this measure is marked *calando* in the first edition, we should remember that for Mozart *calando* obviously meant only "get softer" and not "get slower.") Measures 17 and 58 also demand a certain rhythmic freedom. The passage in mm. 35–39, which builds up by painful chromaticism and modulates from the distant key of G-flat to the dominant of C minor, is the climax of the movement. As the excitement grows, the tempo can press forward a little; then at the climax, to match the distressed tension, it can broaden again and effect the return to the basic tempo.

Ex. III/9:

In such a process of intensification, a long buildup is usually followed by a relatively brief release of tension. However, precisely because in this passage the buildup is fairly long, the *accelerando* can take its course quite gradually, so that it will not sound forced or obtrusive.

In Mozart's concertos, clearly audible switches of tempo are equally out of place: this applies particularly to the orchestra. Mozart must surely have agreed with his father, who wrote in his *Violinschule* (XII, §20, pp. 223–224):

Many who have no idea of taste, never retain the evenness of tempo in the accompanying of a concerto part, but endeavor always to follow the solo part. These are accompanists for dilettanti, and not for masters.

In the first movement of the E-flat major Concerto K. 482 there are places where it seems in order for the soloist to make slight *ritardandos*, especially when the orchestra is silent; e.g., in mm. 117–119 and 149–151:

Ex. III/10:

(Prolong the rests slightly)

Note in the first two measures the subtle way in which the transitional notes F–E–E-flat are repeated in the third measure with a composed *accelerando*. In this measure there is room for a technical trick that makes the transition sound more organic: One does not prolong the *ritardando* until the entry of the new subject but resumes the basic tempo just a little earlier. A slight *ritardando* is also advisable in m. 247, so that one does not pass too abruptly into the peaceful A-flat major passage that follows.

The second movement of this concerto is an interesting combination of (free) variation and rondo form. In a variation form it has always been customary—though sometimes questionable—to take particular variations or groups of variations at a tempo different from that of the theme, according to their character. Frequently, last variations of variation cycles are played a bit faster. (One has only to remember Mozart's Adagio variations, or the final Allegro variations in his Andante movements in variation form; e.g., the second movement of the F major Violin Sonata K. 377/II, where Variation IV should doubtless be played *più mosso e energico*, though there is no proper indication of a tempo change at this point.) However, within any one variation, the tempo must, of course, be strictly maintained. Although it is not essential to play the energetic second variation (mm. 93–124) in K. 482/II slightly faster than the basic tempo of $\flat$ = ca. 74, this is quite justifiable. The last measure before the coda (m. 200) is one of the joints at which a *ritardando* seems desirable.

In the finale of K. 482 one must aim at maintaining a constant tempo. Even if in this movement one makes involuntary tempo alterations of the kind already discussed, they must be perceptible only to a listener who is following with a metronome. In m. 181 one can introduce a very slight *ritardando*, since this is a lead-back, and then reintroduce the solo subject in exactly the original tempo. Before the pauses in mm. 217 and 264 one will also broaden out a little, but not before the cadenza (m. 361), where a *ritardando* would in fact be disturbing; significantly, the fermata is in this case not over the 6/4 chord but over the ensuing rest.

It must be expressly emphasized that all musicians, even the steadiest, make slight agogic deviations. It is, in fact, impossible to mold the musical form of a work of art, which is an organic entity, without agogics. Here we are concerned less with justifying agogics than with their extent. This has varied with different generations of composers and interpreters; Mozart differs from Beethoven and Brahms in the degree of agogics required. Similarly, pianists born in the nineteenth century, such as Backhaus, Kempff, Schnabel, and Fischer, allowed themselves many more agogic liberties than those of later generations. Apart from this, individual temperament and personal taste affect the degree to which agogic variations are used.

Though slight agogic deviations are indispensable for free, relaxed and expressive playing, audible changes of tempo are not. One should recall Schnabel's reply to the question, "Do you play in time or with feeling?": "Why should I not feel in time?"

Rubato

Judicious use of *rubato* is one of the most difficult problems in playing Mozart's works. In his letter of 23 October 1777 Mozart wrote from Augsburg:

> *What these people cannot grasp is that in* tempo rubato *in an Adagio, the left hand should go on playing in strict time. With them, the left hand always follows suit.*

This is an unambiguous description of *tempo rubato*, perhaps the very best one can give, which Mozart himself obviously placed frequently as an embellishment in his slow movements: The accompanying parts are to remain steady while the melody makes slight rhythmic alterations for the purpose of expression. With the application of *rubato*, there will be a very slight, hardly noticeable deduction from the length of one note, in order that the next shall be slightly prolonged (or vice versa: a note will be slightly prolonged and the next one shortened). This also produces slight emphases that the composer may have had in mind. An exact notation of a rubato is hardly possible.

Tempo rubato was not invented by Chopin, as many people nowadays believe. The history of this expressive device of "stolen time," as *rubato* has been rightly called, is certainly very old.[14] But descriptions of this device do not surface until the Baroque period, an era that also invented the tempo markings with which we are so familiar today. It is an expressive device that has always been in use (no doubt it is particularly associated with vocal music), though the first descriptions of it dates from the time around 1600; later written-out *rubatos* were composed by Frescobaldi and Froberger and discussed by Tosi. *Rubato* is used mainly in passages of an arioso or declamatory nature. The essence of true *rubato* is that the accompaniment remains steady and is not allowed to follow the slight *accelerando* and *ritardando* of the melody. To quote Leopold Mozart (*Violinschule*, XII, §20, p. 224):

> *But when a true virtuoso who is worthy of the title is to be accompanied, then one must not allow oneself to be beguiled by the postponing or anticipating of the notes, which he knows how to shape so adroitly and touchingly, into hesitating or hurrying, but must continue to play throughout in the same manner; otherwise the effect which the performer desired to build up would be demolished by the accompaniment.*

And he added in a footnote:

> *A clever accompanist must also be able to evaluate a concert performer. To a sound virtuoso he certainly must not yield, for he would then spoil his* tempo rubato.

Today, *rubato* playing has nearly become a lost art. Where is the pianist who is capable of playing strictly in time with his left hand while allowing his right hand rhythmic freedom? The widespread disappearance of this gift is to be regretted, since it was one of the most important elements in lively and expressive performance of early classical works. There are many examples of metric construction

---

[14] See Tosi, *Opinioni de cantori antichi e moderni*, Bologna, 1723. For a book devoted to the earlier and later kinds of *rubato* (including *agogics*), see Richard Hudson, *Stolen Time: The History of Tempo Rubato*. Especially useful is the discussion of Mozart's "*contrametric rubato*" in Sandra Rosenblum, *Performance Practices in Classic Piano Music*, pp. 373–392.

in two-, four-, or eight-bar periods, which strike us as all too simple and which only take on life when one uses *rubato*, loosening the symmetry while not destroying it. Much of the blame for this lies with current teaching methods, which do nothing to encourage the hands to be independent. In teaching beginners, all the attention is directed to absolute simultaneity of the hands, and their independence of movement is neglected, though it is absolutely indispensable for correct *rubato* playing.

Judicious use of *rubato* is one of the most difficult problems in playing Mozart's works. In the slow movement of the C minor Sonata K. 457, Mozart wrote out a *rubato* in the second half of m. 12 (the turns are not found in the autograph, only in the first edition):

Ex. III/11:

Without the written-out *rubato*, this passage would probably read:

Ex. III/12:

The main difficulty in both cases is to get the accentuation right; in Ex. III/11, the rising melodic phrase is shifted forward by a sixteenth, so that the melodic accents coincide with the unaccented notes of the accompaniment, whereas the turns must not be accented even though they coincide with the rhythmic accents of the left hand. The difference between this and a normal syncopation is that the latter is felt as a contradiction of the prevailing beat, whereas in this case one must if possible be aware of two simultaneous systems of beats, which run alongside each other, unconnected and therefore not contradictory. One may at first practice as follows:

Ex. III/13:

In this way, one will gradually grow into the right way of playing the passage.

In m. 19 of the same movement (K. 457/II), Mozart again tried to write out a *rubato*, as can be seen from comparing m. 3 with m. 19:

Ex. III/14:

TRACK 11

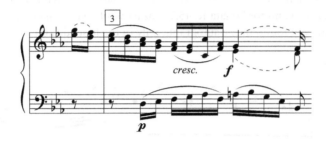

Ex. III/15:

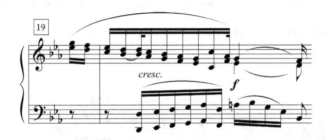

The subtlety of this passage lies in the fact that the syncopation sets in only after the fourth note of the melody. But for real *rubato* the prolongation of the b-flat[1]–d[2] and the shortening of the last note need not be taken literally. One could, for instance, make a slight *accelerando* in the right hand toward the penultimate octave note c[2] and linger on it for a fraction of a second. One essential feature of *rubato* therefore is that very often the notes on the unaccented parts of the measure are prolonged (and thus may get slight accents).

There is another example of a written-out *rubato* in the Piano Sonata in F major, K. 332, second movement. In m. 34 and its upbeat, the first edition (which appeared during Mozart's lifetime) contains a *rubato* (which in this case could also be called a syncopation—a proper *rubato* is very hard to notate):

Ex. III/16:

First edition

Ex. III/17:

The finest example of a written-out *rubato* in all keyboard music is perhaps the slow movement of Bach's Italian Concerto BWV 971. We select two passages to show the way such a composer of genius uses this device, though there are many others. Ten measures before the end, the passage written without a *rubato* would appear like this:

Ex. III/18:

Bach notated:

and four measures before the end of the movement, the text reads:

Ex. III/19:

Without the written-out *rubato* it would have to read:

Ex. III/20:

For the most part, composers only rarely wrote out their *rubato* effects but played them in performance. To figure out the complicated rhythmic notation of *rubato* requires a great deal of time, because this important expressive effect cannot be reproduced exactly by means of existing notation, which is too crude to accurately register the subtle rhythmic displacements involved in true *rubato*. All the same, great composers such as Bach and Mozart, and especially the Romantic composers, have constantly sought to find such a notation. C. P. E. Bach wrote (*Essay*, I/6, §28, p. 160, ex. 4):

> *Fig. 178 contains several examples in which certain notes and rests should be extended beyond their written length for affective reasons. In places, I have written out these broadened values; elsewhere they are indicated by a small cross. … In general, the retard fits slow or more moderate tempos better than very fast ones.*

This is the figure to which C. P. E. Bach referred:

Ex. III/21:

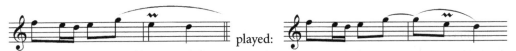

In Mozart's earlier works, in which he rarely ever wrote out a *rubato* but certainly often played one in performance, such passages can be realized in this way. But it should be confined to slow movements, and even there, used only in particular passages. In slow movements from his Viennese period the texture is often too polyphonic, or in homophonic movements the melody too closely bound up with the accompanying parts, for any opportunities for *rubato* to present itself. For instance, a *rubato* would be unthinkable in the first subject of the slow movement of the Piano Sonata K. 533/494 or at the beginning of the chorale-like second movement of the Piano Concerto K. 595.

Even when Mozart wrote out his *rubato* (as in the examples quoted above), his notation is only a cue for the use of the effect, for in fact the *rubato* effect consists not of any constant metrical syncopation but of very uneven prolongations and diminutions (Couperin's notes inégales), which are too subtle to be reproduced by our notation. Thus, Leopold Mozart's words from his *Violinschule* (XII, §20, p. 224, footnote) prove true: "What this 'stolen tempo' is, is more easily shown than described."

Despite other subtleties of our musical notation, our spelling out of rhythms is still rather square or unnatural compared to the infinite variety of rhythms presented in real life. The necessary subdivision of long notes into half, quarter, and eighth notes, etc., suggests a march-like rendering even in lyrical *cantabile* movements that have little in common with military marches. Admittedly, uneven subdivisions such as triplets, quintuplets, septuplets, and the like bring relief, but they still cannot fully remedy a certain weakness of a system that is based on rational and straightforward considerations. Certain rhythms defy precise notation in our system and need to be performed with intuition or acquired by direct teaching through oral tradition. It is in this domain that *rubato* belongs. We are apt to speak of a *rubato* rendering whenever a rhythm is played or sung in such a way that cannot be fully explained by simple mathematical divisions. Take as an example two even eighth notes: On paper, their length is identical to the ratio 1:1. But if the first note is played a trifle longer, the ratio may become 25:22 or so, not enough difference to evoke *notes inégales* and yet perceived as a "living," natural rendering.

Where all theories of *rubato* agree is the fact that no tempo change should occur during *rubato* execution; that the accompanying voice(s) should continue in precisely the same tempo. Of course, subtler tempo changes—*agogics*—are another means of expressing rhythmic freedom but ought not to be confused with *rubato* in the proper sense. (As said earlier [see pp. 85–86], *agogics* are very rare in Mozart; if applied, they should be exercised with utmost discretion.)

Another type of *rubato* occurs often in passages with the even sixteenth or thirty-second notes. They become livelier if the first notes are delayed and the last ones accelerated. For instance, in the Andante of the G major Concerto K. 453, m. 51:

Ex. III/22:

one could play something like:

Some Peculiarities of Rhythmic Notation

On a few occasions Mozart observed traditional Baroque customs in his notation, which we will discuss next.

Overdotting

During the Baroque period, the custom originated in France to sharpen dotted rhythms, often rows upon rows of them, in the performance of solemn overtures, thereby playing the music differently than it was originally notated. This custom spread to Germany, so that frequently music was performed in the French style; even Bachs's and Handel's works were played rhythmically other than written. About this custom Leopold Mozart wrote (*Violinschule* I, III, §2, p. 41; see also the musical examples in the ninth chapter of *Violinschule*, p. 168):

> *There are certain passages in slow pieces where the dot must be held rather longer than the afore-mentioned rule demands if the performance is not to sound too sleepy. For example, if here*

Ex. III/23:

> *the dot were held at its usual length it would sound very languid and sleepy. In such cases dotted notes must be held somewhat longer, but the time taken up by the extended value must be, so to speak, stolen from the note standing after the dot.*

Though Wolfgang, on the other hand, tended to write rhythms the way he wished them played following one of his father's precepts that the composer should be as exact as possible in notating rhythms and that composers should only in certain cases use the double dot (*Violinschule* I, iii, §ii, p. 42). Mozart—in his late years and mainly under the influence of Bach and Handel, whose music he had come to know through van Swieten—obviously wanted to write in the "old style." There is a characteristic example in the first movement of the Andante and Fugue in A major for Violin and Piano, K. 402/I, four measures before the double bar, where he wrote the following passage:

Ex. III/24:

Both the complementary rhythm and the canon between piano and violin mean that the eighth notes in the violin's first measure must be played as if double-dotted, and the sixteenths as thirty-second notes.

Mozart also used another form of notating this Baroque convention; in the "Qui tollis" section of his C minor Mass K. 427 he wrote:

Ex. III/25:

In the music of the ordeals (trials) in Act II of *The Magic Flute*, it again seems advisable on rhythmic grounds to apply a double-dotted rhythm throughout, making all the *anacruses* thirty-seconds:

Ex. III/26:

This view is confirmed by the sketches for *The Magic Flute* (see Preface to the *NMA* edition).

There is a similar example in the well-known introductory Adagio from the Adagio and Fugue K. 546, in which a double-dotted rhythm should be played throughout. Again, the rhythmic figure in m. 97 of the Piano Duet Sonata K. 521/III:

Ex. III/27:

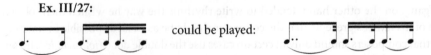

But in our opinion it would be wrong to double-dot all passages, where such a diminution from dotted eighths to dotted sixteenth notes occurs. In the Concerto for Two Pianos K. 365 the motive:

Ex. III/28a:

appears repeatedly in *tutti* and solo passages. The fine spelled-out rhythmic *accelerando* from ♩ to ♪ to ♪ would get lost if the dotted quarter note a-flat² were sharpened; besides, Mozart did in fact use double dots in the second movement.

There are further examples of this shortening of the anacrusis: e.g., in the A major Symphony K. 201/II (opening of the second movement) and in the Duet Sonata K. 497, second movement, upbeat to mm. 29 and 96.

In Mozart's operas there are also numerous passages where rhythms have to be aligned. Here we can mention only a few: In *Don Giovanni*, Act I, Finale, Scene 20 (2/4 G major section) the following rhythm constantly returns in the orchestra (p. 283 of the Eulenburg score):

Ex. III/28b:

But, according to the score, Don Giovanni has to sing the words "Viva la libertà" to the dull rhythm:

Ex. III/28c:

Of course, an adjustment must be made here so that the sixteenths are sung as a dotted rhythm.

In this same finale, Scene 20, Adagio (B-flat major section, *alla breve*), all the parts have a sixteenth-note anacrusis:

Ex. III/29:

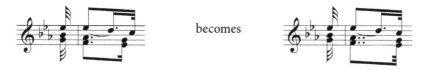

Here again a thirty-second note should, of course, be played at the first anacrusis (upbeat). In eighteenth-century performing practice this went without saying; it was, in fact, so obvious that very few theorists even bothered to mention it. It is reassuring to find it mentioned in Türk's very thorough *Klavierschule* (1802, p. 404):

If in passages with several parts there are simultaneous dotted notes of differing values, then to make them agree better one generally prolongs the longer of the notes by a second dot, thus playing the ensuing note of all the parts simultaneously; i.e.,

Ex. III/30:

becomes

The same applies for Variation IV of the Piano Duet Variations K. 501, m. 2, and corresponding passages:

Ex. III/31:

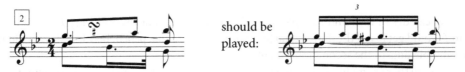

Here only the old edition of K. 501 (by the editor Lebert, published by Cotta) gives the correct version, at least in a footnote (otherwise this edition certainly cannot be recommended). In the coda, shortly before the end (m. 140), the player of the primo part must also double-dot his eighth notes.

Similarly, in Variation IV of the last movement of the Violin Sonata in G major, K. 379, the sixteenth note in the violin and the thirty-second note in the piano should be played together.

Ex. III/32:

In the "Rex Tremendae" section of the Requiem, the rhythm ♪· 𝅘 again has to be performed as if double-dotted; otherwise, there would be constant disturbing collisions between the rhythms of the various vocal parts (e.g., at the end of m. 10). There is even a case where the two rhythms are written simultaneously: in the Larghetto of the Piano Concerto K. 595, mm. 103, and later also 124ff.):

Ex. III/33:

Here the Eulenburg score correctly alters the piano's rhythm to correspond to that of the flute and the other instruments. Many similar cases need similar alignments.

A case of double-dotting that apparently has been overlooked until now is found in the Piano Concerto K. 271/I. In m. 24 of the opening *tutti* Mozart wrote out a double-dotted rhythm in a special way for the violins, and the piano has to shorten the sixteenth note as well; but when the piano plays the same passage in m. 86 and m. 215, Mozart trusted his performers to prolong correctly the first and the third notes:

Ex. III/34:

Tripletization

One very frequent practice of the Baroque, which also occurs occasionally in Mozart, is that one part will have triplet eighths and another normal eighth, in which case the two rhythms often have to correspond.[15] In the ensuing example from the first movement of the Piano Concerto K. 482, the clarinets and bassoons will obviously play their first eighth notes as an upbeat eighth-note triplet:

Ex. III/35:

---

[15] Schubert, too, obviously intended such rhythms to be "ironed out" at times; for instance, in the autograph of the song *"Wasserflut"* from the *Winterreise* his notation suggests this, since in m. 3 (and similar places, e.g., m. 17) he writes the eighths of the dotted figure exactly under the third note of the triplets. This can hardly be an accident, since Schubert was very precise in his notation. Even in Chopin there are still passages of this kind of corresponding rhythms; see the commentary in Paderewski's edition of the B minor Sonata, op. 58, first movement, m. 73.

Clarinet and bassoon

A similar adjustment is recommended when the following rhythm occurs:

Ex. III/36:

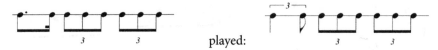

played:

We can see that this supposition is correct if we look at the original notation of m. 76 of the first movement of the B-flat major Concerto K. 450; the right hand of the piano has:

Ex. III/37:

and in the autograph the third of each eighth-note triplet is written exactly under the sixteenth. A similar instance occurs in the third movement of K. 365, a movement in which all dotted rhythms ought to be played as in the above example.

But it would certainly not always be correct to equate triplets and dotted eighths. In the second movement of the Violin Sonata in F major K. 296, for example, a polyrhythm is probably intended. This is obviously suggested by the rhythm of the third and fourth measure:

Ex. III/38:

Hemiolas

To conclude this chapter we would like to say something about the observation and correct performance of so-called hemiolas. The hemiola is an accentual displacement of the meter by which two bars of triple time produce a higher order bar (the *hypermeasure*) containing three accents.

Ex. III/39:

The hemiola is often wrongly believed to be rare in Classical music.[16] However, it is at least as common and as frequently found as in Renaissance choral music or nineteenth-century piano music (Schumann, Brahms), even if not as easily recognizable as in fifteenth- and sixteenth-century notation, when the relevant notes were written in red color.

True hemiola occurs when all the parts undergo this change of accent, as in the second movement of the Piano Sonata K. 281, mm. 24 and 25:

Ex. III/40:

or the second movement of the Piano Concerto K. 482, mm. 58–59:

Ex. III/41:

These two measures are felt as a hemiola:

---

[16] See also K. Ph. Bernet-Kempers, *Hemiolenbildungen bei Mozart*.

Ex. III/42:

(See also the bass part in mm. 25–28.) The same applies to mm. 9–13 of the cadenza of the first movement of the Piano Concerto K. 449, or for some passages in the Requiem ("Hostias," mm. 19–20; "Recordare," mm. 18–19, etc.).

There are, however, many cases in which it is hard to say definitely whether a hemiola is felt as such or rather as a syncopation. There are hybrid passages, a mixture of hemiola and syncopation, in which the accompaniment retains its original accentuation while the melody undergoes the accentual displacement that amounts to a change of barring. The theme of the minuet in the G minor Symphony K. 550 is a case in point:

Ex. III/43:

The attraction of this kind of disguised hemiola is the simultaneous flow of two different rhythms and meters.

There is a wonderful combination of simultaneous barrings, creating a kind of hemiola, in the Act I Finale of *Don Giovanni*, where the stage orchestra plays a contredance in 2/4 meter against the main orchestra's accompaniment written in 3/4 (see the Ex. III/8).

Sometimes Mozart even provided hemiola dynamic markings that emphasize its displacement of accents, as in the first movement of the Piano Sonata K. 332, m. 64:

Ex. III/44:

In playing hemiolas, the shift of the bar line must be clearly audible, for it is this varied distribution of rhythmic accents that gives the figure its particular interest.

4

Articulation

Performers often still confuse *phrasing* and *articulation*. In music, as in language, *articulation* refers to the style of delivery necessary to make clear the meaning of a word or combinations of words; so, too, in music: the projection of a musical motive or phrase with the help of subtle accents and dynamic shadings, right down to the smallest detail. How important it is to articulate properly may be shown with the help of a sentence where the absence of proper voicing of the end of a phrase through lowering the pitch (i.e., correct punctuation) renders the sentence completely nonsensical and incomprehensible: "King Charles walked and talked half an hour after his head was chopped off." Only by adding a semicolon after the word *talked* and a comma following *after* will the sentence make sense.

Since the end of the sixteenth century, many composers have used various notational signs to show the articulation of single notes or motives they wanted—such as *staccato* dots and strokes, accent signs, or *legato* slurs. As for phrasing, we understand by a phrase a melodic section, such as a theme, which is usually self-contained and hangs together as a significant whole. Phrasing (an expression first used in the nineteenth century) should only be applied to longer subjects or thematic figures used in the construction of a melody, and a phrasing mark, usually a longer slur than those used for articulation, is a way of notating the coherence of a musical phrase.

Mozart never used slurs as phrasing marks. They were added only later to his texts by certain editors, who published phrased editions full of these markings. They are open to the common criticism that the inner relationships between melody and rhythm, etc., are far too complicated and intangible to be represented by merely adding a few long slurs, which seriously obscure or even distort Mozart's graphic presentation. The use of phrasing marks is often defended on the grounds that a piano pupil needs help to make out how themes and phrases are laid out; the answer to this is that any pupil who cannot see for himself how music hangs together must be completely unmusical. Moreover, an intelligent teacher can help a child by adding any necessary phrasing slurs into the music. We heartily recommend the reading of Heinrich Schenker's article, "Weg mit den Phrasierungs-Bögen" (pp. 41–46).

The need to mold phrases was obviously recognized in the eighteenth century, too. In his treatise, Quantz (VII, §10, p. 76) wrote:

> One should be just as careful not to separate what belongs together as to avoid linking together things which, because they are ambiguous, ought to be separated; for much of the expressiveness of performance depends on this.

But it was left to interpreters to grasp the more general relationships.

Mozart's use of articulation signs was immensely rich and varied but certainly not complete. This poses problems for modern performers, who are used to a rather uniform approach: either everything should be played *legato* (connected, or "tied") or everything detached. Yet correct articulation is the key to understanding music, as with speech, and this is certainly true not only for music of the eighteenth century. There is a saying, attributed to Chopin, that the playing of many pianists is comparable to the declamation of a speaker who recites a poem in a foreign language without understanding the meaning of the words. Musical articulation, whether vocal or instrumental, is derived from speech. Correct pronunciation is the very basis of communication. Before we can express anything, we need to pronounce it correctly. In the same way, the meaning of music (whatever it may be) needs, first of all, a grammatically correct rendering with regard to pitch and rhythm, long and short, accented or unaccented, slurred or detached, etc.—in other words, a correct execution of all notational signs.

Mozart, like most other composers, uses five ways to indicate articulation:

1. Slurs for *legato*
2. A combination of slurs and dots for *portato* (carried, *appoggiato*), a very slight separation, used mostly for repeated notes, but sometimes also for scales
3. Strokes or dots for *staccato* (detached): this demands a separation and a shortening of the notes to varying degrees
4. Strokes or wedges for accents
5. No articulation signs: During the eighteenth century the absence of signs meant normally *non-legato*, detached, but not as short as *staccato*. However, the absence of specific articulation signs can also be an instruction to continue the previous articulation. For example, if the first measure of a repeated pattern has one or two slurs, *legato* should be continued until a new figuration sets in. On the other hand, the lack of signs can also mean "I had no time to write them down—make your own articulation!"

Türk, in his *Klavierschule* from 1789, made a relevant remark (§9, p. 334):

> When someone reads an unknown poem not yet fully understood by him, he hardly will be in the position to recite it in such a way that an educated listener is content with the declamation. This is certainly also the case in music. Only when a musician has perceived the content of the piece will he be able to render every individual passage with perfection and with its proper expression.

There are more ways to indicate articulation than slurs or dots, such as rests to call for change of breath, or ornaments that nearly always connect notes.

Other important means to express articulation in the notation are the grouping of notes with the help of flags and beams as, for example, in m. 9 of the Piano Sonata in E-flat Major, K. 282/I:

Ex. IV/1:

Obviously, in this example the first note ought to be played clearly detached from the following ones. Strangely enough, this kind of notation is nearly always disregarded by most pianists, who play:

Ex. IV/2:

In the Piano Sonata in F Major, K. 332/I, m. 76, Mozart's way of writing the beams is also telling:

Ex. IV/3:

Legato

Undoubtedly the most frequent articulation sign in Mozart's piano works are *legato* slurs. The slur symbol has also other meanings: Over two or more notes of the same pitch it means a "tie": The next note should then not be struck again. Besides, in vocal notation a slur means that two or more notes should be sung on the same syllable or vowel (or diphthong; other meanings are irrelevant here).

Legato slurs can mean that two or more notes should follow each other in one breath, without any interruption of the sound. Slow movements are the natural place for this singing style, and many of them are marked *cantabile*. But Mozart also wrote numerous *legato* slurs in his fast movements. This alone should dispense with the strange remark, attributed to Beethoven, that Mozart's piano playing was "choppy and smartly detached," a remark apparently conditioned by Beethoven's personal taste; obviously Beethoven did not like the older, *non-legato* sounds and used the damper-lifting device far more often than Viennese pianists did. (That Mozart composed after 1774 already for the pianoforte only was pointed out in chapter 1.) Even his earliest known sonatas are full of dynamic indications that cannot be realized on the harpsichord. But *non-legato* was still a preferred interpretation for scales in his time.

As it is well known, *legato* in Mozart's time was mainly achieved by a delayed raising of a finger, by holding the finger down until the next note is played. Indeed, it is often propitious to raise the finger even later, after the following note has been played. The resulting overlapping of sounds (*legatissimo*) is pleasant because it reduces the hammering effect and enhances the singing quality. In both cases, exact control of the (quick) raising of fingers is necessary. Unfortunately, this type of finger articulation is the most neglected aspect of modern piano playing. The reason for this is our increased use today of a damper-lifting device, the right pedal on modern instruments, which connects sounds more easily. As pointed out in chapter 1, in Mozart's time the lifting of the dampers was a device activated through knee levers and was used more seldom and mainly for special effects.

Pianists are taught today to put their fingers down with energy and precision, but rarely are they trained to raise them with the same amount of control, and many pianists connect sounds with their feet instead. This lack of finger movement is even more acutely felt on the fortepiano of Mozart's time, where the much lighter action does not help to raise the finger automatically when the key rises upon release.

In broken chords, particularly in the accompaniment, more than two notes may be kept down by the fingers, overlapping. This type of *super-legato* is sometimes called *finger pedaling*. This approach to increasing the resonance with a finger *legato* was suggested by Türk (1789, VI/ III, §38, p. 355), among others, more than 200 years ago:

*When a slur is written above slowly arpeggiated harmonies, as in the following examples a),
one allows the fingers to remain on the keys until a new harmony is reached, especially in
pieces of a pleasing character. Thus, the following measures a) can be played as in b).*

Ex. IV/4:

An appropriate application of this principle can be found at the beginning of the Piano Sonata
in B-flat major, K. 333:

Ex. IV/5:

(The two slurs that are here in parentheses are Mozart's obviously later written additions when
preparing the sonata for publication. They are found in the Viennese print of Torricella and
should be considered authentic.)

Nonetheless, finger *legato* alone does not suffice to make the piano sing. To that, the feeling of stress and release, emphasis on a dissonance followed by deemphasis when the latter
resolves into a consonance, has to be added. Just as the vocal chords of a singer are tenser
when higher notes are sung, rising passages on the piano will also call for an increase of
the dynamic level. Long notes need more weight than short ones; besides, the piano cannot
sustain long notes like a violin. But the most important help in playing *legato* is the principle
of heavy–light: Nearly all eighteenth-century treatises agree that the first note under a slur
should be slightly accented or stressed. Deemphasis of the following note is then equally
important:

Ex. IV/6:

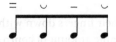

Leopold Mozart wrote (*Violinschule*, VII, 1, §20):

*Now if in a musical composition two, three, four, and even more notes be bound together by
the half-circle [slur], so that one recognizes therefrom that the composer wishes the notes not
to be separated but played singingly in one slur, the first of such united notes must be somewhat more strongly stressed, but the remainder slurred on to it quite smoothly and more and*

more quietly. It will be seen that the stress falls now on the first, now on the second or third quarter note. ...

Türk stated less detailed but more succinctly (*Klavierschule*, 1789, p. 355):

One should remember that the note on which the slur begins has to be very slightly (hardly noticeably) accented.

The most controversial issue among conscientious *Urtext* editors and users concerns the ending of slurs. Should the last note of a two-note slur be shortened, should the finger (or bow) be released before the following note, or should a slur be carried into the next note without separation? Only few pianists or musicologists believe that there should be an interruption after every slur that otherwise would often produce a musical "hiccup" effect. Sequences of two-note figures bound by slurs, however, need to be detached.

Unfortunately, it has to be admitted that Mozart's notation of slurs is often ambiguous, inconsistent, and at times even misleading, as we shall see below.

Legato Slurs and Articulation Slurs

Let us try to disentangle this thorny issue and to find reasonable solutions that might be acceptable to both scholars and musicians. In the first English edition of this book we spoke of *legato slurs* and distinguished them from what we called *articulation slurs*.

In our opinion, Mozart's slurs served two purposes:

1. To indicate a *legato* over a fairly long section, which, however, Mozart usually wrote with slurs lasting only to each bar line if he did not write the word "legato." Thus—in accordance with the established practice of his time—they were written over only one measure; we call them *legato slurs*.
2. To indicate that two (or three or even on occasion four) notes are to be grouped together in instances where it is musically necessary to shorten the last note (by cutting it off), Mozart wrote short slurs that are often placed over very short note values; we call these *articulation slurs*.

Mozart's *legato slurs* do not mean that there is to be a break at the end of each slur; this is only necessary in the case of *articulation slurs*.

It is not always easy to see from the printed page which sort of slur is intended; the musical content is the decisive factor here. This is why many editors have tried to replace Mozart's *legato* notation with long slurs of a more modern kind:

Ex. IV/7:

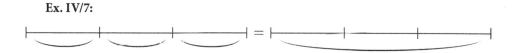

When such long slurs occur in an edition, they are usually not written by Mozart (there are exceptions in Mozart's late works). It is most important to know this: A slur stretching over more than one measure may sometimes concur with Mozart's intentions, but just as often it does not; Mozart may have intended a separation instead.

The so-called *articulation slurs* are mainly found over two-note figures. There exists wide agreement about the execution of these short slurs: The first note needs a slight accent or emphasis, the following one(s) a release, a deemphasis, and the latter is usually shortened, particularly in fast passages, as in Variation XI from the variations on "Ah, vous dirai je Maman," K. 265, m. 14:

Ex. IV/8:

or in the Rondo in A minor, K. 511, m. 4:

Ex. IV/9:

In the following example from the Sonata in A minor, K. 310/II (m. 9), it does not make a difference that all first notes are written as small notes:

Ex. IV/10:

The slurs between *appoggiaturas* and the following notes were not always notated by Mozart. However, as Leopold Mozart remarked in his treatise (*Violinschule*, IX, §1), the *appoggiatura* should never be separated from its main note; this connection is a rule without exception.

It should be noted that in repeated notes marked *portato*, the second note should be played softer but hardly shorter. Leopold Mozart gives an example:

Ex. IV/11:

and then wrote (I, 3, §7):

> In particular one must be at pains not to shorten the second part of the divided note but give it the same value as the first part, for this inequality in division of notes is a common fault which soon causes the tempo to quicken.

(See also §18 of the same chapter.)

In the Sonata in D major, K. 311/I, mm. 40ff., one must be careful to avoid the pitfall of not separating the repeated notes at all, or (worse) linking them by pedal.

On the other hand, many pianists commit the opposite error of shortening the second eighth note of each pair too much, thereby cutting the line into pieces:

Ex. IV/12:

We recommend in this case limiting the execution to accented and unaccented notes:

Ex. IV/13:

We added in this example longer phrasing slurs, thus following a suggestion by Türk in his *Clavierschule* (1789, VI/ 3, §38, p. 355, ex. k), who showed the phrase in order to avoid chopping off after the short slurs:

Ex. IV/14:

If any pedal on a modern piano is taken with this passage (Sonata K. 311/I, mm. 40), it should be on the first note of each two-note sigh. A good way to avoid unwanted accents on the off-beat notes 2, 4, 6, and 8 is to caress these notes by bending the second finger while playing.

Ex. IV/15:

The word *poco* before the $\boldsymbol{f}$ in the second measure should remind the reader that in some cases when f and p were written close to each other $\boldsymbol{fp}$ meant simply an accent on a note (here d-sharp[2]) because the hairpin sign > was not yet in use in Mozart's day.

Very frequently we find two shorter slurred eighth notes by Mozart; it is in connection with motivic anticipation. The best known example for it is the beginning of the G minor Symphony K. 550:

Ex. IV/16:

We find the same motive in the first movement of the C major Concerto K. 467 (downbeat of mm. 111–114). To shorten each second note of the slurred figures would be a grave error. A singer would undoubtedly sing the whole phrase in one breath. For pianists it is strongly recommended not to change fingers on the same repeated note, thus playing 3 2 2.

This type of anticipation can also appear on downbeats, as at the beginning of the Sonata in B-flat major, K. 333 (the slurs in parentheses are found in the first edition):

Ex. IV/17:

Proposed execution:

Ex. IV/18:

It helps to better grasp this *legato* problem if we recognize the upbeat in the first measure as an embellished version of the last two notes in the second and third measures:

Ex. IV/19:

In other cases when Mozart indeed wanted the second of two slurred notes shortened, he notated rests. Telling examples of both kinds of notations can be found in the last movement of the C major Sonata K. 330, mm. 69–76:

Ex. IV/20:

and in the variation theme of the finale of the Violin Sonata in E-flat major, K. 481:

Ex. IV/21:

If *articulation slurs* appear in the company of *staccato* dots or strokes, these dots nearly always cut off the last note, which should be played softer and shorter, as in the following example from the Piano Four-Hand Sonata K. 521/III, m. 7:

Ex. IV/22:

Here the unaccented sixteenth notes g^2 and d^2 at the end of the slurs may be played softly *staccato*.

If an *articulation slur* is over two notes of equal length, it may also indicate an accent on the first of the two notes, as in the next two examples: (a) from the A major Concerto K. 488/III, mm. 300ff.:

Ex. IV/23:

and (b) the C minor Concerto K. 491, finale, m. 28:

Ex. IV/24:

An exception is given if longer sequences of paired notes begin on an upbeat; for example, in the Fantasy in C minor, K. 475, mm. 141–145:

Ex. IV/25:

Here we prefer to put the accent on the second note of the slur because of the rhythmic displacement.

A slur followed by *staccato* dots does not always have to be taken as an *articulation slur*. In mm. 100 and 102 of the first movement of the E-flat major Concerto K. 449, we recommend playing a *legato slur*:

Ex. IV/26:

But such exceptions are infrequent.

Finally, a frequent error of today's performers concerning Mozart's *articulation slurs* needs to be mentioned. Many players change Mozart's preferred downbeat slurring (which starts on the first note) into an upbeat slurring, thus distorting his clear intentions. A few examples may suffice:

Four-Hand Sonata in C major, K. 521, opening:

Ex. IV/27:

(a) as written:

(b) as wrongly
performed:

The solo entry in the second movement of the Concerto in C Major, K. 467/II, should be played:

Ex. IV/28:

(a) as written:

(b) often
wrongly
performed:

In the Sonata in A Minor, K. 310/I, m. 8, one should play:

Ex. IV/29:

(a) as written:

(b) as wrongly
    performed:

or in the cadenza to the first movement of the B-flat major Concerto K. 595, mm. 11f.:

Ex. IV/30:

(a) as written:

(b) as wrongly
    performed:

A similar example of wrongly slurred upbeats one unfortunately can hear too often in the opening variation theme of the A major Sonata K. 331.

Usually one can distinguish *legato slurs* from *articulation slurs* by the fact that a row of slurred figures extend generally over several measures, and the slurs are of the length of a violin bow and always end before the bar line, as, for example, in the theme of the Andante of the Piano Concerto in D major, K. 451/II:

Ex. IV/31:

It would be wrong to interrupt the *legato* flow at the bar line. That this *cantabile* theme did not originally get a long *legato slur* is disconcerting at first, but it is easily explained by the fact that in classical music the use of slurs originated in violin bowing. Interestingly, in his "Thematic

List of Works," Mozart notated the first slur for this theme over two bars instead of writing a slur for each measure. The slurs in the above example following the autograph indicate three changes of bow. Only a very bad violinist makes an audible break at a change of bow (the bow should not leave the string); on the other hand, a completely inaudible change is hardly possible; besides up- and down-bows are different not merely technically but in their psychology. It is understandable, therefore, that toward the end of his life Mozart indicated a *legato* by slurs over half a measure or a whole or even two measures, or in a few rare cases even several bars. But during the Classical period, throughout their music composers in general (and especially Mozart) adopted a notation typical of the violin. The extreme rarity of long slurs is, thus, the obvious consequence of the limited length of the violin bow. (In an exceptional case, Mozart used rather long slurs over several measures in the finale of the "Jupiter" Symphony, in which, according to the autograph, there is a whole series of seven-measure slurs and also one over six measures [mm. 362–367]; another exceptionally long slur is found in the F major Concerto K. 459/I, mm. 358ff., where Mozart wrote in the first violin part a slur over seven measures, anticipating the long slurs of Chopin by half a century.)

In the first movement of the Sonata K. 570, mm. 104–112, Mozart wrote longer slurs:

Ex. IV/32:

As an example of the very common single-measure slurs we show the very first subject of the B-flat major Concerto K. 595/I, played by the orchestra:

Ex. IV/33:

Naturally it would be a grave error to make a separation at the end of the first measure. When the piano enters with the same theme, it has written-out turns following the half notes that connect the first two measures anyway.

At the beginning of the F major Sonata K. 533, the slurs in the first, third, fifth, and sixth measures should certainly extend over the bar line:

Ex. IV/34:

When criticizing the common error of cutting off at the end of every slur (still sometimes heard in today's performances), in an example that resembles Mozart theme Türk quoted the following example (*Klavierschule*, 1789, p. 340):

Ex. IV/35:

and says:

> *If then the pianist, rather than at the end of a period, does not connect the sounds well and separates a phrase [Gedanke] where it should not be separated, he commits the same error as an orator, who in the middle of a word would stop to take a new breath.*

Recently we heard a young pianist play the D major section of Mozart's Fantasy in C minor, K. 475, exactly in the way criticized by Türk:

Ex. IV/36:

This can hardly have been Mozart's intention in such an expressive melody.

Naturally, there are frequently transitional stages between *legato slurs* and articulating slurs. In our opinion, the first subject of the A major Concerto K. 488 contains a *legato slur* in m. 1, whereas in m. 2 those slurs over the third and fourth beats are articulating slurs. We feel that the first slur in m. 2 is a kind of transition from one kind of slur to the other, and it needs a very slight break after it:

Ex. IV/37:

There are two possible ways of playing the common formula:

Ex. IV/38:

either as a *legato slur*:

Ex. IV/39:

or as an *articulation slur*:

Ex. IV/40:

The question of which kind seems more appropriate has to be judged from case to case. Sometimes, it is also a matter of taste.

The best way, of course, to interpret Mozart's works in a true singing or *cantabile* fashion is to look for parallel passages in his vocal works. As mentioned earlier, Mozart rarely notated articulation signs for the singing parts of his operas or songs. It is the meaning of the words on the one hand, and the phrasing of the accompanying parts on the other, that tell the singer how to phrase his or her vocal lines. Thus, in one of the most beautiful of Mozart's arias, the Countess's "Dove sono i bei momenti" (*The Marriage of Figaro*, act 3, scene 8), the only slurs for the singer are those where two notes are sung on one syllable. No singer would separate the notes after these slurs, because the syllables *sono* and *momenti* belong each to one word:

Ex. IV/41:

Besides, every good singer sings the first two measures and the next two in one breath each, and mm. 5 to 8 in a longer breath, all *legato*. It should be noted that the wind instruments connect these phrases while the singer breathes, thus creating the effect of an uninterrupted melody. A good singer will also bridge the gaps between these three phrases, thus creating also the impression of a continuous spoken sentence!

In Figaro's famous Aria "Non più andrai" (from the end of the first act) the violins have detached notes at the beginning that concur with the *parlando* style of that opening. However, from the fifth measure on they have *legato slurs* even over the bar lines, a definite invitation to Figaro to change into an expressive—and here ironically meant—*bel canto* line (the slurs are from the violin part):

Ex. IV/42:

Conversely, *staccato* accompaniment might invite a singer to sing short notes even if he did not understand the sense of the words. A good example is the "Pa-pa-pa-pa" duet in the finale of the second act of *The Magic Flute* (m. 624). Here the accompanying strings play nearly exclusively *staccato*:

Ex. IV/43:

In recent years we have learned that many articulation problems can be resolved by treating Mozart's instrumental (mostly *cantabile*) themes as if they were operatic arias, underlying them with an appropriate text.

When two long notes are connected by a slur ending before the bar line, one is often in doubt as to whether to separate or to connect. This problem arises at the very opening of the F major Sonata K. 332:

Ex. IV/44:

In nearly every language there can be found a text to sing to these notes:

Ex. IV/45:

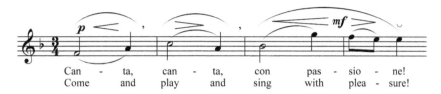

| Can | - | ta, | can | - | ta, | con | pas | - | sio | - | ne! |
| Come | | and | play | | and | sing | with | | plea | - | sure! |

The singing of this theme teaches us a few things:

1. The rising of the melody over more than an octave increases the tension of the vocal chords, leading to a considerable increase of volume between the third and the fourth bars, followed by a slight release to go along with the declamation.
2. The comma after the first and second measures comes quite naturally. It leads to an ever so slight interruption of the air flow; yet no new breath is taken until the end of this melody.
3. Measures 3 and 4 are more closely connected than the two opening bars. They form a two-measure unit. The only admissible interruption between g^2 and f^2 might be caused by the spoken consonants.

Although the opening of the B-flat major Sonata K. 570 is nearly identical in rhythm, its melodic direction is nearly the opposite of the one shown in the previous example. Here Mozart's articulation markings are also less consistent: At the outset the theme has three one-measure slurs, yet later on (e.g., in mm. 101–115) Mozart wrote one simple slur over three measures. To complicate matters, in his own catalogue he wrote a slur over mm. 1 and 2 and a second one above the third measure. Which version is right?

By happy coincidence, there is an Austrian Christmas carol with nearly the same melodic curve:

Ex. IV/46:

| Jo- seph, | lie - ber | Jo - seph | mein, | hilf | mir | wie-gen | mein | Kin - de - lein |

The tenderness of this cradle song speaks for itself: Nobody sings this phrase in a detached way, and nobody separates the last note from the rest of the melody. We hardly can fail to give the theme of K. 570 a similar gently lifting or rocking rendering, opposing it to the more vigorous, lively answer mm. 5–12.

The question of whether one should interrupt a *legato* at the end of a long measure has also been raised in connection with the opening of the great C minor Fantasy K. 475.

Ex. IV/47:

First of all, the difference of slurring between mm. 1 and 3 can hardly be intentional: In the parallel passage (m. 163) Mozart notated different slurs again, omitting the *legato* slur of the first two notes altogether. Yet, we may safely assume that this dark, sinister motive is always meant to be played *legato*, as is clearly written in mm. 5–7. The real question, as stated above, is whether the B natural in m. 2 and the A natural in m. 4 should be connected with the previous motifs. Our answer is a definite "yes" for the following reasons:

1. The first notes of the opening five bars form a chromatic descent, an age-old symbol for death and suffering. Such chromatic sighs were always connected:

Ex. IV/48:

2. A very similar motif appears repeatedly in orchestrated form in the "Maurische Trauermusik" (Masonic Funeral Music) K. 477, where the first violins have one-measure slurs (necessitated by the bowing) but the lower strings and the winds always connect these two bars by a longer slur.

Ex. IV/49:

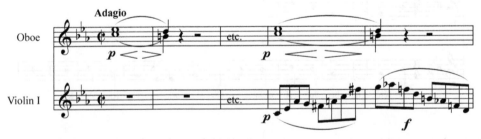

Certainly, the first violins will avoid making an audible separation when changing bows.

The main accent of the opening phrase in the Adagio movement of the Sonata in D major, K. 576, as so often lies clearly on the second measure. It is an important observation, usually not found in textbooks, that in many classical themes the main emphasis should be brought in the second measure, which often needs more weight than the first one. In inventing underplayed words one can take notice of this.

One may sense this more readily by inventing words that fit the theme. Not only are serious themes fit for such texting, but even more lighthearted tunes might benefit from this procedure. In the last movement of the "Coronation" Concerto in D major, K. 537, the exuberance of the theme and the ever so slight hesitation after the downbeat can be well illustrated by the following words:

Ex. IV/50:

Note: In the beginning, the *staccato* markings look like dots; however, later (mm. 301–302) Mozart clearly wrote strokes.

Mixed Articulation

A special problem is given when we encounter mixed articulation; namely, *legato* notes followed by *staccato* dots. What perhaps first appears as an inconsistency in Mozart's writing often turns out to be illuminating.

At the beginning of the Rondo for Piano and Orchestra in D major, K. 382 (the autograph of which is now in Kraków), Mozart clearly finishes the trill motif (flute, violin) before the bar line and starts m. 2 with three *staccato* strokes, just as he does later in Variation II (flute), mm. 41–44. But later, without apparent reason, he continues the slur over the bar line into the following measure (Ex. a) while omitting the first *staccato* stroke after the trill in mm. 54–56 (Ex. b), though not in mm. 97–100) (Ex. c):

Ex. IV/51:

While the flute part has the longer slur (version b), the simultaneous piano part has the shorter version (a), though without the following *staccato* strokes. When the *tutti* theme appears for the third time, the first violins have version (a) in mm. 79–80 while simultaneously Mozart notated version (b) in the flute. The same inconsistency is to be found in the trill variation (mm. 111–112): flute has (a), oboes (b). Finally, the two versions are combined; in mm. 13–14 and 15–16 the first violins have version (c) while the flute has version (a) in mm. 15–16. There can be hardly any doubt that all three notations mean the same execution. On the piano, version (c) corresponds to modern notation, despite the fact that Mozart's notation for the violins must have been a writing slip (compare with the notation a) in mm. 6–7, 7–8.

A similar discrepancy of notation also appears (among other inconsistencies) in the third movement of the Concerto in B-flat major, K. 456, in a passage as notated for the winds and those for the piano, mm. 53–56:

Ex. IV/52:

Piano mm. 139–142:

Ex. IV/53:

These observations lead to the conclusion that in those cases where a slur is followed by a *staccato* note, it is meant to be extended to this note. Therefore, the slur in the oboe 1 should be extended over the bar line, also in the first movement of the B-flat major Sonata K. 333, mm. 15, 16, 111, 112:

Ex. IV/54:

It is clear by nature that the third note in m. 111 and the first note in m. 112 have to be *staccato* (written here in parentheses); otherwise, there could be no separation from the ensuing *legato* notes. (A similar articulation is found in the penultimate measure of the exposition and recapitulation.)

Many pianists make a questionable double separation in such places:

Ex. IV/55:

This sounds awkward. In view of the above observations we recommend the obviously intended execution:

Ex. IV/56:

It sounds much more graceful and certainly is more in line with the gentle character of this movement.

Portato

The combination of dots and slurs is usually called *portato*. It is mostly found on repeated notes (e.g., Rondo in A minor, K. 511, m. 15) or stepwise rising or descending notes, as in the Fantasy in D minor, K. 397, m. 17, or the Sonata in D Major, K. 576/II, m. 16:

Ex. IV/57:

Portato (literally "carried") means "not detached" and is closer to the *legato* than to the *staccato* touch. One should avoid the common mistake of playing such notes too short; rather, they should be caressed, without finger change on repeated notes. The use of the pedal might enhance the *portato* effect.

For the description of *portato* in eighteenth-century treatises the reader may consult Türk's *Klavierschule* (VI, 3, §37), and—even more appropriate—Leopold Mozart's *Violinschule*, who wrote (I, 3, §17):

> *It happens also that under the circle [slur] or, if the circle be under the notes, over the same, dots are written under or over the notes. This signifies that the notes lying within the slur are not only to be played in one bow-stroke, but must be separated from each other by a slight pressure of the bow.*

Staccato

The literal meaning of *staccato* is "separated"; in music it is a direction "to take away from the length," "to detach," but certainly not "to beat the piano."

Before entering into the discussion about its forms of notation (wedges, strokes, dots, or the grey areas in between) we should like to issue a general warning to all performers (not just pianists) against too short and too percussive an execution of *staccatos*. In his valuable treatise, Türk (*Klavierschule*, 1789, VI/3, §36, p. 353) describes *staccato* in the following way:

> *The pushing (Stossen) or detaching is indicated ... by strokes or dots above the notes. If a whole piece or section is to be played in this detached way one writes the word staccato at the beginning. Strokes and dots have the same meaning; yet a few [composers] want to indicate by the stroke a shorter execution than by dots. At staccato notes one raises the finger [!] from the key shortly before half the value of the note has passed and pauses for the rest of the time. It actually needed not to be mentioned that soft notes may also be "pushed" (gestossen). However, a few players perform all staccato in the shortest possible way, without paying attention to the value of the notes—a common mistake—while almost one half of the prescribed note value should be kept. The character and tempo of a piece should also determine the stronger or weaker execution. In a work of serious, tender or sad character the staccato notes ought not to be played as short as in a piece of lively, teasing (scherzhaften) character. ... In general one may play the staccato shorter in forte than in piano sections.*

Türk's statements remain still valid for us today and ought to be better known and observed.

With regard to the execution of *staccato* in tender passages we should go further than Türk: Not a little less than half the value but exactly half of the value seems to yield the best results. This opinion is somehow corroborated by Mozart's own notation. In many cases he writes the same musical idea either with quarter notes marked *staccato* or with eighth notes followed by eighth rests; e.g., in the third movement of the C minor Concerto K. 491:

Ex. IV/58:

Later Mozart notated this motive in the following way:

Ex. IV/59:

In a private conversation Malcolm Bilson remarked that this kind of notation also points to a slightly different touch; namely, a lighter one than the notation with quarter notes. Lighter yes, but hardly shorter—one should compare the corresponding mm. 84/85 (♩) with the ♪ ⁊ in mm. 220/221, where certainly the same length is intended. When the clarinets enter in m. 97, they have quarter notes with dots (not strokes) in Mozart's autograph, as do the strings eight measures later. But from m. 113 onward the same motive is notated in eighthswithout *staccato*. (As usual, Mozart supplied no articulation signs for these same notes in the piano part.)

Mozart was apparently rather fond of the various *staccato* markings, which are a type of articulation sign found very frequently in his works. Their notation employs a scale of markings from very small, scarcely perceptible dots to powerful, wedge-shaped strokes. It is an age-old question discussed among editors and musicians whether these different signs have the same or sometimes different meanings. As we have seen, Türk mentioned two possibilities. The editors of the *NMA* decided to differentiate, whereas other editors working for publishers such as the Henle-Verlag preferred to print only dots. A recent edition (for Breitkopf & Härtel, edited by Robert Levin and Cliff Eisen) printed only strokes. The difference of presentation in print even goes back to Mozart's time: As far as we know, the publisher Artaria printed mainly dots, whereas Hoffmeister printed only strokes (except for *portato*). If Mozart accepted both ways of representation by his publishers, it does not necessarily mean that he did not care about the difference between dots or strokes. But the question must have been of secondary importance to him, because he had enough trouble to get his works on paper and also printed. Most probably he was more concerned that the right notes and the correct rhythms were printed (which was certainly not always the case: an abundance of wrong notes is found in the early editions of Mozart's works). It is worthwhile noting, however, that the first edition of Mozart's Violin Sonata in G Major, K. 379, by Artaria "distinguishes conspicuously between *staccato* dots and strokes in the piano system" as Wolf-Dieter Seiffert writes in the critical report of his new Henle edition of Mozart's violin sonatas.

Strangely enough, the controversy about strokes and dots, which seemed to have been more or less settled in the 1950s,[1] flared up again in the 1990s when the new Mozart edition *NMA* was practically complete. Frederick Neumann concluded in an excellent article[2] that the difference between both notations must often have been intentional. There exist strokes and dots plus a grey area in between where it is hard to decide whether Mozart wrote small strokes or large points. But Neumann's view was contradicted shortly afterwards in an article by Clive Brown[3] in which he comes to the conclusion that all dots in Mozart's writing are but shrunken strokes. He postulates:

> ... I should like to cut this particular Gordian knot by suggesting that the question of whether mid- to late eighteenth-century composers employed dots and strokes over un-slurred notes with distinctly different meanings is essentially a red herring.

More convincing to us is a view expressed in an article by Wolf-Dieter Seiffert,[4] who tries to reconcile both opinions while being closer to Neumann's view than that of Clive Brown. He wrote (p. 136):

> In contrast [to this view], it must be pointed out that many other autograph passages distinguish so strikingly unambiguously between dot and stroke that it would require a high degree of self-deception to dismiss this circumstance as a mere "oversight."
> [Dem steht gegenüber, daß viele andere autographe Stellen so frappant eindeutig und geradezu demonstrativ zwischen Punkt und Strich unterscheiden, daß es eines hohen Grades an Selbstverleugnung bedarf, um diesen Umstand als reines 'Schreibversehen' abzutun.]

Seiffert went back to Leopold Mozart's view of the stroke as a way of bowing. He mentions the important fact that Wolfgang, apart from *portato* notation, wrote thousands of unmistakable dots, namely prolongation dots after notes and abbreviation dots after his usual notation *pia: for:*. Thus, if *staccato* dots have the same shape, they are really meant to be dots. We share Seiffert's opinion and the resulting conclusion that Mozart's signs cannot be blindly followed: A good critical edition should interpret signs not only by their appearance but also by their probable meaning. Were it only an editor's problem how to print Mozart's *staccato* signs, we could simply forget this controversy over dots and strokes. But since we are interested in how to play them, we have to enter into the discussion. To pursue Clive Brown's figurative speech: If we treat this question as a red herring we risk throwing out the baby with the bathwater. We simply found more real dots than mentioned in the just quoted articles, dots that have a definite meaning; namely, a less short, rounder *staccato*, somehow halfway between *portato* and stroke-*staccato*.[5]

---

[1] See Ewald Zimmermann, "Das Mozart-Preisausschreiben der Ges. für Musikforschung."
[2] Frederick Neumann, "Dots and Strokes in Mozart," pp. 429–435.
[3] Clive Brown, "Dots and Strokes in Late 18th- and 19th-Century Music." pp. 593–610.
[4] Wolf-Dieter Seiffert, "Punkt und Strich bei Mozart," pp. 133–143; following quote on p. 136.
[5] One could say it also in a pun: "If we get too excited from this heated controversy, we might even die from a stroke, but never from a dot."

Let us inspect a few autograph passages where the dots are beyond any doubt (and not misread) small strokes: In the Sonata in A minor, K. 310, the second movement is marked *Adagio cantabile con espressione*; there we find dots in mm. 15 and 26:

Ex. IV/60:

Ex. IV/61:

In the second movement of the Concerto in A major, K. 488/II, marked *Adagio*, we find dots in m. 21 (also in m. 97):

Ex. IV/62:

As can be easily observed, these examples resemble those given above for *portato*. Mozart perhaps forgot only to add the slur.

The most beautiful differentiation between dots and strokes can be found in the Rondo for Piano and Orchestra in D major, K. 382, of which the autograph—long hidden in Polish archives—is now accessible again in Kraków. In mm. 1–8 there are *staccato* strokes for nearly all instruments, including (a rarity!) horns, trumpets, and tympani. Admittedly, in some of the wind parts they occasionally become smaller, but at the repeats of the theme from mm. 33 and 73 onward, they are clearly strokes. But then, from mm. 9 to 12, the first violins and the flute have only faintly written dots:

Ex. IV/63:

The artist may wonder what this means. It speaks for the sensitivity of Edwin Fischer that in his recording of this work he let the violins play these four bars much softer and the notes *quasi portato tenuto*. Two facts speak for this differentiation between strokes and dots: When the rondo theme is presented in the Allegro variation, the winds have *staccato* signs in mm. 145–168, but *portato* in mm. 169–172.

Ex. IV/64:

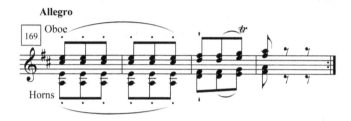

(It should be noted that here—as in many similar phrases—the last note bears no *staccato* sign. This is certainly meaningful.)

An indirect proof that the second part of such a dancing theme could be played softer can be seen in the similarly constructed rondo theme of the Concerto in G major, K. 453/I: There the first violins and flute have *staccato* strokes in mm. 2–3 and 6–7 but no *staccato* at all in mm. 9–12.

The generally accepted sign for *staccato* in most printed editions of the late eighteenth century, however, was the stroke. It was also used exclusively by Leopold Mozart and can be found in the autographs of Haydn (with the exception of occasional dots in late works).[6]

Mozart also wrote strokes most frequently; we often find them in his autographs, especially as single *staccato* signs. As in Haydn's works, the stroke does not necessarily mean a more energetic approach: It is the context that will decide this issue and should influence the performance; one must take into account the length, loudness, and timbre of any particular note, and, equally important, the feeling of the piece, the "affect."

Sometimes, it seems that Mozart used the *staccato* marking as an accent sign, apparently in cases where his contemporary markings for an accent, *sfz* or, *fp* struck him as too strong. Had he been composing during the nineteenth century, he probably would have written a > sign.

We have seen from Mozart's manuscripts that on a purely philological basis it is impossible to make a distinction between dots and strokes or wedges. To attempt to force Mozart's markings into a system based on their appearance and function, and to distinguish *staccato* dots from accentual wedges is to oversimplify the multiplicity of markings in Mozart's manuscripts and to do less than justice to their often contradictory musical meaning. Performers can decide here with greater ease than editors because they easily can change their opinion. When preparing an edition, however, editors are forced to decide for the record as to whether they may take this sort of distinction into account or not.

---

[6] See Seiffert, "Punkt und Strich bei Mozart," p. 138.

Only in rare cases do Mozart's strokes or wedges inevitably indicate accents: In the Trio of the Jupiter Symphony he wrote "accentual strokes" over each of the dotted half notes in the first violins (mm. 68–75 inclusive), and again in the finale, at each *forte* entry of the first subject:

Ex. IV/65:

Here, of course, Mozart cannot have meant a *staccato* in the usual sense but intended accents, probably including a slight separation after each note. Even more interesting are the accent strokes in the following passage (mm. 68–92 of the finale of the "Jupiter Symphony" K. 551):

Ex. IV/66:

Thus, detached execution can be excluded when a note with a stroke is slurred or tied to the following note; this also holds true for the following examples: Piano Concerto in A major, K. 414, second movement, mm. 26–27; third movement, m. 26 (also earlier in mm. 34 and 36):

Ex. IV/67:

The tie does not exclude a slight separation in the second measure of the example. Separation is also demanded in the Piano Concerto in D major, K. 537/III, mm. 42ff.:

Ex. IV/68:

It is hardly surprising that editors from the nineteenth and early twentieth centuries left out such markings, which they (and their clients) found incomprehensible. Yet the stroke as a simple accent sign did exist in the eighteenth century. As shown in chapter 2 on dynamics, it had been already explained as such in Telemann's "Singe-Spiel-und Generalbaßübungen" (1733) and was described in this way also by Leopold Mozart in his *Violinschule* (VII, pp. 126–127), where he used the word *Nachdruck*, meaning "emphasis" or "stress."

A special feature of Wolfgang's style needs still to be mentioned here, because it is often misunderstood by editors and performers: After a series of *staccato* notes the concluding note is normally not marked and apparently not meant *staccato*:

Ex. IV/69:

It happened only occasionally, in very rare cases, that Mozart added one more *staccato* sign to the final note, evidently by mistake due to his enormous writing speed. Instead of eliminating this wrong *staccato* notation in these few cases, several editors felt compelled to add countless *staccato* signs in parallel places (in brackets or small print), thus misleading players into cutting off those ending notes.

Unmarked Passages

Both Mozart's own articulation markings and the testimony of his contemporaries show that *non-legato* and sometimes even *staccato* were the dominant types of touch in his playing. According to the practice of the eighteenth century, absence of any articulation signs therefore meant primarily *non-legato*. Marpurg wrote (1755, p. 29):

> *Normal onward movement is the opposite of both slurring and detaching: it consists of lifting the finger nimbly from the preceding key just before one touches the next note. This normal onward movement was always taken for granted, was never indicated.*

(By the way, in this respect Beethoven is still an eighteenth-century composer. As late as 1818 when writing the fugue of the Hammerklavier Sonata Op. 106, for fast passages he prescribed: *non-legato*. Unfortunately, well-meaning nineteenth-century editors changed it erroneously into *ben legato*.)

In the 1802 edition of his *Klavierschule*, Türk wrote (VIII, 3, §442, p. 400):

> *For notes that are to be played in the usual way, i.e., neither detached nor slurred, one lifts one's finger from the key a little earlier than the value of the note demands.*

It is most important for Mozart interpreters to know this fact. There is a very widespread fallacy that Mozart's passage work requires a constant *legato*. He did indeed often demand a *legato* but usually reserved it for melodic passages in any instrument. Otherwise, he almost always wanted virtuoso passage work played particularly *non-legato*. There is one type of virtuoso passage, however, for which Mozart favored long *legato* slurs: rising chromatic scales in quick tempo of the kind that frequently occur in cadenzas. It will nearly always be right to play all other such passage work *non-legato* or *staccato*, whether in a violin work or a piano work.

Fortunately, we have one interesting proof of *non-legato* being the main articulation in eighteenth-century passage work. In the former Heyer Collection (now Musical Instruments Museum of the University of Leipzig) there exists a Flötenuhr (musical clock) in reasonably good playing condition with an eighteenth-century recording of Mozart's Andante in F major, K. 616, in an abridged version. The many runs in thirty-second notes are played there in a stylish *non-legato*.

After Mozart's death, Czerny (who certainly had much first-hand experience of the Mozart tradition) wrote in his *Pianoforte-Schule* (1839):

> *Mozart's school; notably brilliant playing, more with an eye to staccato than legato; intelligent and lively performance.*[7]

---

[7] Carl Czerny, *Vollständige theoretisch-praktische Pianoforte-Schule*, p. 72.

As mentioned at the beginning of this chapter, absence of articulation signs can also mean that the player has to supplement an appropriate articulation. Leopold Mozart wrote in his *Violinscule* (XII, §11, p. 220):

> *Similarly, from the sixth and seventh chapters is to be seen how greatly the slurring and detaching distinguishes a melody. Therefore, not only must the written and prescribed slurs be observed with the greatest exactitude, but when, as in many a composition, nothing at all is indicated, the player must himself know how to apply the slurring and detaching tastefully and in the right place.*

This also applies to the melodic passages of his son's music.

Correct articulation, over and above Mozart's markings, is not as difficult as it looks at first sight. Mozart gives us a good deal of help. In a piano concerto, intensive study of the orchestral parts is useful, and for this reason alone a pianist should study not merely the piano part very carefully, but the whole score. Time and again the orchestral parts contain carefully written-out performing indications that provide an adequate basis on which to add articulation signs to the same themes and motives in the piano part. As an example of this we would like to quote from the E-flat major Concerto K. 482, second movement, mm. 105ff.:

Ex. IV/70:

In the piano part there are no slurs from each third beat to the ensuing strong one, but the accompanying violins in mm. 106–107 and 108–109 have slurs across the bar line (dotted in our music example). Most likely, the piano should also articulate the phrase in this eloquent way, which is supported by the way the eighths are grouped.

In the next example, from the second movement of the E-flat major Concerto K. 449, we again find Mozart reluctant to slur across the bar line. But the motivic overlapping of piano and violins loses its point unless the piano plays the three notes c²–a¹–b-flat¹ *legato*.

Ex. IV/71:

In the second movement of the Concerto in D major, K. 451, mm. 32–33, the flute slur is interrupted at the bar line while the oboe and bassoon have an uninterrupted *legato* slur, despite the fact that all instruments play the identical line. Obviously the flute was also intended to be played *legato* (as is in fact written two measures later).

Ex. IV/72:

Indeed, one should study Mozart's autographs for one can always learn from scrupulously marked orchestra parts.

The most elaborate articulation in Mozart's piano solo works is found in his first four piano sonatas K. 279–282 as well as in the great A minor Rondo K. 511, which is especially famous in this regard; however, the sonatas K. 310, K. 331, and K. 570, the D major Rondo K. 485, and the B minor Adagio K. 540 also exhibit an extraordinary wealth of articulation signs that is rare in works by other eighteenth-century composers.

In accompaniments, too, Mozart liked to make fine distinctions between *legato, non-legato,* and *staccato.* Observing these signs one can often lend charm to the least interesting *Alberti* bass figures. In the introductory *tutti* of the B-flat major Concerto K. 595, we find them in mm. 16–19:

Ex. IV/73:

When this passage occurs later in the piano part, the *staccato* dots can well be borne in mind. In the first solo, Mozart previously placed *legato* slurs over similar accompanying figures, but here, on the other hand, since there are no slurs one might play a delicate *staccato.* (Why do nearly all pianists play the same theme afterward with a *legato* accompaniment?)

A similar observation could perhaps be made about the opening theme in the G major Concerto K. 453, where the second violins and violas have *staccato,* but the piano has different *Alberti* figures here—food for thought.

There are other instructive examples of the alternation of *legato* and *non-legato* accompanying figures in the C minor Sonata K. 457, first and third movements.

(a) First movement, m. 23:

Ex. IV/74:

(legato)

(b) First movement, m. 59:

Ex. IV/75:

TRACK
49

(non legato)

(c) Third movement, m. 74ff.:

Ex. IV/76:

(non legato)

Noteworthy here is the principle of complementarity: in (a), irregular and broken-up articulation of the melody is opposed by a peaceful accompaniment, whereas in (b) and (c) the symmetrical rhythmic figures in the melody are opposed by an accompaniment that is *non-legato* or *staccato*.

For stylistically proper articulation in playing Mozart's works it is important to remember the old rule that a suspension or dissonance and its resolution must always be smoothly joined, whether the dissonant note is notated as a long *appoggiatura* in a small type or written out in notes of a normal size. Naturally, it is always the dissonant note that receives the accent, and the resolution may be slightly shortened. This rule for playing accented passing notes is found in C. P. E. Bach (*Essay* I, Part II, i, §7):

> With regard to execution we learn from this figure that [accented] *appoggiaturas are louder than the following tone, including any additional embellishments, and that they are joined to it in the absence as well as the presence of a slur. Both of these points are in accord with the purpose of an appoggiatura, which is to connect notes.*

And Leopold said in his *Violinschule* (IX, §1):

> Here now is a rule without an exception: the appoggiatura is never separated from its main note, but is taken at all times in the same [violin] stroke [= slur].

This rule was so obvious for Wolfgang that he often omitted to write a slur connecting his *appoggiaturas* with their following main notes (consonances) as well as his accented passing notes (see p. 107). Knowing this simple but fundamental rule, we can usually work out the articulation of doubtful passages for which the manuscript is lost and early editions are faulty. In the theme of the Finale of the C minor Sonata K. 457, the manuscript of which was lost for over one hundred years but is now available, Mozart notated the following slurs:

Ex. IV/77:

Thus the theme consists of a series of sighing figures. For teaching purposes, it is a good thing to imagine the theme without its shifts of bar line, which are akin to *rubato*:

Ex. IV/78:

Granted a few exceptions, dissonances, whether long or short, are normally slurred to the following consonance, even if Mozart did not bother to write these slurs. A good example can be found in the third movement of the Violin Sonata in A Major, K. 526: When the opening theme appears first in m. 1 with the piano part leading, there are no slurs. However, when this theme reappears later in the violin part, namely in mm. 176, 224, and 376, it has slurs over the dissonances and their suspensions. We believe that Mozart wrote these slurs because the violinist cannot see the bass line, whereas the piano can easily discern the dissonances formed in the upper part in relation to the bass notes. In our opinion, the pianist has to play the same slurs in the RH part, adding also a slight accent to the dissonant notes, in order to give this theme more inner life:

Ex. IV/79:

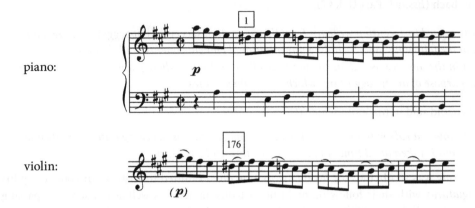

piano:

violin:

What is true for speech is equally true for music and valid not only for Mozart: Only well-articulated phrases can speak to the listener, be understood, and potentially move him as well.

5
Ornaments

Indeed, nobody has ever doubted that ornaments are necessary. This is evident, since one is always coming across large numbers of them. They are, however, indispensable, when one observes their usefulness. They link the notes together, they enliven them, when necessary they give them special emphasis and importance; they lend them charm and thus draw special attention to them; they help to make clear their content—whether this be sad or merry or of any other kind, they always make their contribution; they provide a considerable proportion of the opportunities for true performance, and of the means toward it. A moderate composition can gain by their help; without them, on the other hand, the best melody is empty and monotonous, and its content, however clear, must inevitably appear but indistinctly. (C. P. E. Bach, Essay..., I, II, §1, p. 79)

Mozart's application of ornaments is tasteful and distinguished, detailed but never excessive, and eloquent, refined and yet naïve; it raises even the most banal eighteenth-century formulas to the level of eternal verity. In his notation of ornaments, Mozart again aimed for the maximum of clarity. Even so, many of his embellishments are ambiguous, because as far as ornaments were concerned, he lived in a period of transition, and because basic musical assumptions change over time. Procedures and interpretations that were a matter of common knowledge in his time lapsed into obscurity in the course of the nineteenth century, and these changes are overlooked by all too many musicians today. Moreover, Mozart could count on his contemporaries' taste and artistic sensitivity. We are firmly convinced that he left his interpreters a certain freedom in performing his ornaments. It has always been true that strict, inflexible rules exist only in books of theory; art, being alive, constantly produces exceptions, deviations, and variants.

In rereading the first edition of our book we note to our satisfaction that most of what we said fifty years ago is also valid today. Few sources and textbooks we did not know then have come to light and nearly always confirmed the solutions we had proposed. We still maintain that the purpose of all embellishments is to make music more *belle*, more beautiful. As it turns out, for example, a turn properly played is simply more beautiful and elegant than one played wrongly. Let us remind the modern performer that many ornaments are called *grace notes*. By emphasizing the original meaning of *grace*, one realizes that these notes require a graceful, light execution (the only exception perhaps being accented long *appoggiaturas*).

Of the abundant Mozart literature that has appeared since our first publication, a few books deserve special mention with regard to ornamentation. The most important is Frederick Neumann's substantial volume *Ornamentation and Improvisation in Mozart* (1986). Another important book, also with regard to this topic, is Sandra Rosenblum's *Performance Practices in Classic Piano Music* (1988), which deals (pp. 216ff.) with the interpretation of ornaments in chapter 7.

There exist two basic sources of information concerning the proper performance of Mozart's music in general and his ornamentation in particular; namely, contemporary (or nearly contemporary) treatises and the internal evidence derived from his music. Let us look at contemporary sources first. The most important textbook relevant to Mozart is naturally the *Violinschule* by his father Leopold, who guided Mozart's musical education. Less important for Mozart are the pianoforte schools by Daniel Gottlob Türk (Leipzig and Halle 1789; revised 1802), Johann Peter Milchmeyer (Dresden, 1797), and Muzio Clementi, *Introduction to the Art of Playing on the Piano Forte*, London 1801 (thereafter, *Pianoforte School*, London 1801). Others, like Georg Simon's *Löhlein Clavierschule* (Leipzig 1764, many editions, most elaborate the fourth edition of 1784), Johann Carl Friedrich's *Rellstab's Anleitung für Clavierspieler* (Berlin, 1790), or Johann Samuel Petri's *Anleitung zur praktischen Musik* (second edition, Leipzig, 1782), are sometimes irrelevant but should be taken into account nevertheless.

The *Violinschule* by Mozart's father is refreshing to read because of its common sense. Mozart senior expects the violinist to add embellishments now and then, but he abhors those violinists who add ornaments everywhere and cannot leave a long note unaltered. He wants *appoggiaturas* to be played on the beat, but he admits that there are quite a few to be played before, or in between as it were, a kind of *Zwischenschläge*. This leads to occasional inconsistencies that are perhaps more enlightening than strict, unalterable, rigid rules found elsewhere. While Wolfgang was undoubtedly influenced by his father's teaching, he did not always adhere to his rules, his own approach being more modern. This can be seen, for example, in his different treatment of trill endings (see below).

Türk's *Klavierschule* was probably the most important treatise of the last two decades of the eighteenth century. It is extremely thorough and systematic (408 pages in the first, 460 pages in the second edition). The chapter on *appoggiaturas* alone comprises thirty pages in the first edition. Being deeply indebted to C. P. E. Bach's *Essay...* (originally published in two parts, 1753 and 1762), which he praises repeatedly, Türk's approach reflects the fact that, like Bach, he was fond of those large, beautifully sonorous clavichords, not common in the southern part of Germany, and he treats the clavichord as an most important stringed keyboard instrument; this makes him somewhat old-fashioned by Mozart's standards. With regard to (short) *appoggiaturas*, Türk naturally distinguishes between accented (long) and unaccented *appoggiaturas*. According to him, however, even the shortest, unaccented ones must start on the beat without exception. This approach adheres to typically Prussian rules and does not always fit Mozart. But being a good musician, Türk conceded (1789, p. 200) that there are "debatable cases" and mentioned (p. 223) that there are "passing appoggiaturas" in "the French way" that are not good for the (north) German taste. And following this, he later added a chapter of five and a half pages to *Nachschläge* ("after-beats" or "closing suffix"; or in Rosenblum's translation: "after notes"), of which the majority consists of anticipated *appoggiaturas*.

Milchmeyer, who in his youth lived in Bavaria, is in many ways Türk's southern German counterpart. In 1797 he published his treatise "Die wahre Art, das Pianoforte zu spielen" in Dresden. As a matter of fact, he wrote exclusively for the pianoforte, the clavichord being only briefly mentioned (p. 58) as a substitute for those pianists who cannot afford to buy a pianoforte. His approach to trills is refreshing. There are trills that start on the written (main) note, whereas most trills start with the upper note (p. 42). But his most revolutionary statement concerns his support of the unaccented *appoggiaturas*, which, according to him, have to be principally played as anticipations and thus before the beat. Understandably, he was severely criticized by Türk in the latter's second edition (cf. Türk, *Klavierschule*, pp. 271–272). As we shall see later, neither of the two authors can be applied blindly to Mozart's ornamentation, but Milchmeyer gives us valuable hints.

Clementi's *Pianoforte School* is less ambitious regarding those details. Yet his treatise is, apart from Leopold Mozart's, perhaps the only one relevant for Mozart. Clementi was born four years earlier than Mozart and trained in Italy, and he also used pianofortes most probably from the beginning of his life and traveled widely later as a piano virtuoso. On Christmas Eve of 1781 he met Mozart in Vienna at the invitation of Emperor Joseph II, and together with him he improvised on two pianos. It may be assumed that their playing of ornaments was similar. Clementi stayed afterwards for quite long periods in Vienna. His list of ornaments (Figure 5.1) shows clearly that in certain contexts trills and *pralltriller* ("short shakes") may start on the main note, and for him long trills nearly always need a closing suffix. His short *appoggiaturas*—mentioned not in the list but elsewhere in the treatise are played on the beat.

Figure 5.1 Clementi's list of ornaments

The internal evidence of Mozart's music regarding ornaments is revealing, indeed. It is very fortunate that Mozart, with his immense wealth of creative invention, frequently used different types of notation for the same successions of notes, often in parallel passages within the same movement: Sometimes he wrote large notes, in other places small notes or symbols. Since the notation in large notes is unambiguous, it can help us in many cases to interpret his other notations. Thus, he wrote the turn in various forms: large ♫♫♪ small ♫♫♪ in a combination of both ♫♪ or as a symbol ∞. Here one notation explains the other. Likewise, with *pralltriller*: rather rarely he wrote ∿ or ♫♪, frequently, however, a *tr* sign, which leaves several possibilities open according to context. Different notation occurs also with *appoggiaturas*; e.g., third mvt. of the C major Sonata K. 330 ♪♪♪ m. 54, and ♪ ♪ m. 153. While here a doubt is hardly possible (cf. first mvt., mm. 33 and 120), there might be other instances where a different notation of the same motive may mean different ways of playing.

Mozart's ornaments prescribed by signs consist mainly of *appoggiaturas*, *arpeggios*, turns, and trills. Whereas in playing single *appoggiaturas* the most difficult problem is usually one of accent, in the case of compound *appoggiaturas* we shall be concerned mainly with their place within the meter; i.e., with such questions as anticipation. We shall mention the question of so-called vocal *appoggiaturas*, since these also occur in the piano works. On the other hand, there are few problems in playing the occasional intermediate groups of small notes (*Zwischenschläge*)—scales, etc., so these will not be treated separately. The playing of *arpeggios* and turns is also relatively simple, whereas trills present problems that are often difficult to solve.

Appoggiaturas

Single Appoggiaturas

Appoggiaturas were originally nothing but accented passing notes. If in the course of the eighteenth century they lost some of this meaning, it is still a very good thing to remember their origin.

Mozart's notation of *appoggiaturas* is usually based on their real value: ♩ = half note execution, ♩ = a quarter, and ♪ = an eighth execution (though in this case there are exceptions).

Mozart's use of *appoggiaturas* shorter than an eighth is inconsistent; he often writes a sixteenth note *appoggiatura* when he must have meant a thirty-second or sixty-fourth execution, as, for example, in the Andantino of the E-flat major Concerto K. 271/II, m. 61:

Ex. V/1:

which
should be
played:

and rather not:

Conversely, sixteenth-note *appoggiaturas* can at times call for eighth-note execution.

It must be noted that Mozart (as well as Haydn) always wrote a slashed eighth note for a sixteenth and a doubly slashed eighth always for a thirty-second note, etc.—regardless of whether the note is an *appoggiatura* or not. (We have chosen to follow modern notational practice so as not to confuse today's musicians.)

All the same, the duration of *appoggiaturas* presents only one of several problems; in the interest of terminological clarity we shall classify them as (1) accented versus unaccented, and (2) on the beat versus upbeat (anacrusic, anticipatory) grace notes.

There is little to be gained by referring to long and short *appoggiaturas*, since the difference is only rarely one of length but rather of whether they are accented or unaccented, on the beat or anacrustic. The only possible combinations are as follows:

1. Accented and on the beat
2. Unaccented and on the beat
3. Unaccented and anticipatory

The fourth combination (accented and anticipatory) is ruled out on musical grounds. Therefore, accented *appoggiaturas* can only be played on the beat.

One further general remark that Leopold Mozart mentioned as "a rule without exception" we mentioned earlier (p. 109): All *appoggiaturas* must be slurred to the main note they precede, even when this is not expressly indicated by a slur. Here the editors of Mozart's works have different opinions on whether to add slurs where Mozart had not notated them. The *NMA* added slurs to all *appoggiaturas*. We do not agree with the "postmodern opinion" that where Mozart did not write the slurs the lack of them could mean a detached execution, though there might exist one two exceptions in his complete output.

Accented Single Appoggiaturas. This kind of *appoggiatura* is akin to an accented passing note. For performance purposes this means that the note value of the *appoggiatura* is deducted from that of the ensuing note, which is also played softer, as, for instance, in the opening theme of the Violin Sonata in E minor, K. 304/II:

Ex. V/2:

TRACK 19

or in the Piano Concerto K. 466/I, m. 85 (solo):

Ex. V/3:

or in the Romance of K. 466, m. 35, first and second violins:

Ex. V/4:

played:

Usually, an accented *appoggiatura* lies a second above the main note. But there are cases in which *appoggiaturas* leap through larger intervals (from thirds to sevenths), such as the sixth in the Violin Sonata in B-flat major, K. 454, second movement, m. 104. Both here and in the parallel passage (m. 37) Mozart wrote an eighth-note *appoggiatura* before the third beat, despite the obviously shorter execution:

Ex. V/5:

 played:

Such accented passing tones, resolved by leap, occur in Mozart's works only when they repeat the preceding note (in this case the c³). Regarding the second *appoggiatura* g², one need not be dogmatic. It may also be played as an accented thirty-second note on the beat or unaccented before the beat.

A definite accent is to be given to *appoggiaturas* that are longer than an eighth, as well as in the combinations

Ex. V/6:

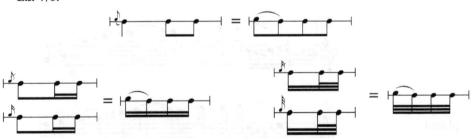

This execution with four even notes is universally accepted nowadays, a practice confirmed by the treatises of Milchmeyer, Friedrich Starke, Mozart's pupil Hummel, and several others. Mozart himself gave us many clues because he often shifted inconsistently between grace note notation with

appoggiatura and written-out large notes. Thus, in the third movement of his C major Concerto K. 467 he notated [symbol] in m. 146, but [symbol] in the parallel passage (m. 396), apparently wanting the same slurred execution in both places. We found only one possible exception, namely in Variation VIII of the Variations for Violin and Piano K. 359, mm. 103–116. Since the basic rhythm here is [symbol] a short *appoggiatura* might be appropriate at the beginning of the variations [symbol] rather than [symbol]).

In the first movement of the A major Symphony K. 201, second subject (mm. 41–43 and 147–149), Mozart wrote [symbol] [symbol], thus avoiding ambiguity.

Sixteenth- and thirty-second-note *appoggiatura*s can be either accented or unaccented. It is especially difficult to decide whether any particular *appoggiatura* is accented or not. For sixteenth-note *appoggiatura*s, Mozart had a habit of using the sign [symbol], regardless of whether he wanted them played long or short. [symbol] is merely the south German form of the single eighth note. Mozart also wrote the *appoggiatura* this way as a normal note (i.e., not as a grace note), as in the song "Ein Veilchen…" K. 476. In this book we have used the word *appoggiatura* to mean all grace notes, with or without a stroke through the stem. It is not generally known that [symbol], and [symbol], [symbol], and [symbol] mean exactly the same, and that it was not until the nineteenth century that the transverse stroke came to be used exclusively for the short, crushed *appoggiatura*. Sixteenth- and thirty-second-note *appoggiatura*s are always accented and on the beat if they are obviously accented passing tones, as in the following examples; e.g., Variations for Piano K. 455, m. 4 (first version):

Ex. V/7:

In the final version, however, Mozart changed the sixteenth *appoggiatura* into a small eighth note in m. 4 as well as in the parallel places.

Also, in the E-flat major Piano Concerto K. 271, second movement, m. 34, we find them:

Ex. V/8:

or in the Concerto for Two Pianos K. 365, first movement, m. 58:

Ex. V/9:

played:

The very common figures of this kind, as found, for instance, in the second movement of the Sonata K. 310, m. 36:

Ex. V/10:

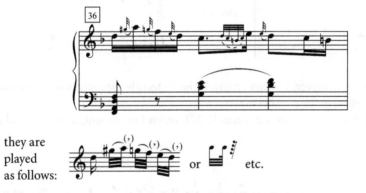

they are
played
as follows:

Here the notes a², f², and d² are slightly cut off at the end; they just have to be shortened a tiny amount.

Other accented thirty-second-note *appoggiatura*s are found in mm. 9, 13, and 62 of the second movement of the A minor Sonata K. 310:

Ex. V/11:

In the Two-Piano Concerto K. 365, second movement, m. 67, the *appoggiatura*s

Ex. V/12:

should probably be played as follows:

Ex. V/13:

but according to C. P. E. Bach and Leopold Mozart, *appoggiaturas* of this kind (filling in a descending third) will sound less dull if given less than half the value of the ensuing note:

Ex. V/14:

However, in the second movement of the C major Sonata K. 330, such a foreshortening of the sixteenth-note *appoggiaturas* in mm. 8 and 11 is hardly advisable (see the written-out sixteenth in m. 15). We recommend, therefore:

Ex. V/15:

Mozart often tried to indicate this by his notation, writing the *appoggiatura* as a smaller note value, as at the opening of the D major Rondo K. 485 (see Ex. V/43 on p. 151). A similar situation pertains to the second subject of the finale of the G minor Piano Quartet.

The autograph of the B-flat major Violin Sonata K. 454 reveals that in the introduction to the first movement Mozart first wrote eighth-note *appoggiaturas* that he later changed into six-teenth-note *appoggiaturas* by adding a transverse stroke in darker ink. This shows two things: first, that Mozart was not indifferent to the duration of *appoggiaturas*, as has been sometimes assumed, and second, that in this passage he preferred the rhythm known to British and other musicians as the *Scottish snap* (also called *Lombardian rhythm*), mm. 5ff.

Ex. V/16:

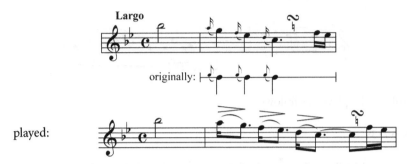

(See also the commentary on Exs. V/12–14).

It is well known that Mozart, like many composers of his time, was fond of these Scottish snaps or Lombardian rhythms. They are produced by rhythmic foreshortening of a pair of (originally) equal note values:

Ex. V/17:

In playing such examples, one must make a clear accent on the short sixteenths, playing the dotted eighths softer. A spelled-out version of this rhythm is found in the opening theme of the Piano Concerto in A major, K. 414:

Ex. V/18:

In the opening of the C major Sonata K. 309, Mozart makes a fine distinction between

in mm. 37–38 and

in mm. 41–42. Did he want to point to a lighter playing in the first case?

A beautiful example of accented *appoggiatura*s occur at the very end of the F major Sonata K. 332/ III in m. 221: here the *appoggiatura* has the value of a sixteenth note. But when in mm. 230–231 the same motive reappears in augmentation, the value of the *appoggiatura* is augmented as well:

Ex. V/19:

In Mozart's earliest works one may still sometimes apply the old rule that *appoggiaturas* in triple time are to be given more than their written value. An example occurs in the Menuets K. 4 and K. 5, where the notation of the concluding measures vacillates between:

Ex. V/20:

in K. 4 and:

Ex. V/21:

in K. 5.

Unaccented Single Appoggiaturas.   *Appoggiaturas* are to be unaccented and short in the following cases (temporarily leaving open the question of anticipation):

(a) *In almost all rising appoggiaturas*, for instance, in m. 29 of the C major Sonata K. 279/I:

Ex. V/22:

or in m. 22 of the first movement of the C major Sonata K. 545:

Ex. V/23:

They should be short also in the B-flat major Concerto K. 595, first movement, m. 31, first violins (also m. 311, piano):

Ex. V/24:

and also in the Sonata K. 331/I, second variation, mm. 7–8, and sixth variation, mm. 15–16. Here again, we believe that if Mozart had wanted long *appoggiaturas*, he would have undoubtedly written them as in mm. 8ff. of the first movement of the C major Trio K. 548. It appears to have been Mozart's habit that, if he wanted this kind of *appoggiatura* played as a long one, to write it out in normal notes, as in mm. 154–155 and 332–333 of the first movement of the Piano Concerto in C major, K. 503:

Ex. V/25:

or in m. 205 of the second movement of the E-flat major Concerto K. 482:

Ex. V/26:

On the other hand, he wrote the descending *appoggiatura* in m. 206 as a grace note, since there was no risk of ambiguity. It should certainly be accented.

For reasons hard to understand, most pianists play the *appoggiaturas* in the second movement of the C major Sonata K. 330, m. 25, as long accented ones:

Ex. V/27:

as written:

as wrongly
performed:

Had Mozart wanted it played this way, he nearly certainly would have written it in large notes, as he did with the E-flat on the first beat or in the previous examples. The same observation applies to the beginning of the third movement of the *Serenata Notturna* K. 239:

Ex. V/28:

In such cases, Türk's rule that *appoggiaturas* before repeated notes are always short may be followed.

(b) *When the main note is itself an accented passing tone*, as is the case with the B minor Adagio K. 540, m. 4:

Ex. V/29:

See also Ex. V/1.

This unaccented execution was recommended by Quantz as early as 1752 in a nearly identical example (*Treatise*, p. 79).

Another example appears in the Sonata in F major, K. 332/I, mm. 207–212:

Ex. V/30:

Recommended execution:

(The *staccato*s correspond to m. 77.) Some pianists play here:

Ex. V/31:

But in view of Mozart's notation in large notes two measures later this could hardly be intended.

(c) *When the main note has a staccato marking (dot or stroke)*, as in m. 4 of the sixth variation of the A major Sonata K. 331, first movement:

Ex. V/32:

or the C major Concerto K. 246/I, mm. 14–15 (first violins; see also Ex. V/41):

Ex. V/33:

This unaccented execution is recommended because in Mozart the *staccato* stroke can be a definite indication of an accent, rather like our marking >.

(d) *Appoggiaturas must be unaccented wherever the main note has a marked accent*; otherwise, the main note would lose its effectiveness if preceded by an accented *appoggiatura,* whereas it will be enhanced by an unaccented one; e.g., the opening of the second movement of the B-flat major Concerto K. 595:

Ex. V/34:

In the String Quartet K. 458/I, m. 3, it is best to play the *appoggiatura* as an upbeat:

Ex. V/35:

This is also always the case when a sixteenth-note *appoggiatura* precedes a half note, as, for example, in the Three-Piano Concerto K. 242/I, mm. 53ff.

It is difficult and often misleading to try at all costs "to lay down the law." In passages similar to those considered here, much can often depend on the character and speed of the piece because, as we have said, Mozart relied not only on contemporary notation, but also always on the taste and understanding of his interpreters.

The common formula

Ex. V/36:

can be played in a number of ways:

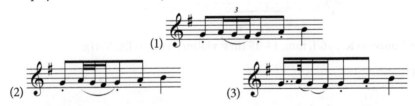

If the sixteenths (or thirty-seconds) after the *appoggiatura* are on an unaccented part of the measure, then version (1) is usually the best. In some works, Mozart also wrote out this figure in triplets, as in the first variation of the second movement of the F major Violin Sonata K. 377:

Ex. V/37:

or in mm. 17, 49, and 101 of the F major Rondo K. 494 (although not in mm. 98–99). However, each particular case should reflect the character of the piece as a whole, an important factor.

In the opening of the F major Sonata K. 533, m. 7, we prefer the execution as anticipated short *appoggiatura*:

Ex V/38:

first edition:

recommended
execution:

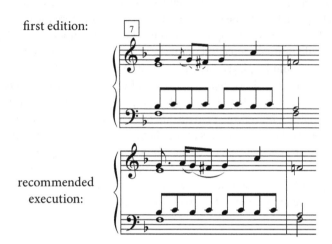

In this case it is a matter of taste. In the Violin Sonata in C Major, K. 296/I, Mozart wrote triplets in mm. 1–2 and *appoggiaturas* in mm. 63 and 65. Again, it is a decision of taste, an open question insofar as Mozart uses both notations, and it is not clear what he meant.

Also, in the second movement of the F major Concerto K. 459, mm. 67ff. (and in the corresponding passage mm. 126ff.) there is a sequence in which all the instruments have sixteenth-note (not thirty-second-note) *appoggiaturas*, and here again one cannot say definitely whether they should be unaccented (short) or accented (long). We tend to prefer the passage played with short *appoggiaturas*; these strike us as more natural and less forced. Moreover, if Mozart had wanted long *appoggiaturas*, he could perfectly well have written them out, in accordance with the rules applying at the time:

Ex. V/39:

But he wrote grace notes instead. Either way, there is a friction with the piano part from m. 71 onward; if the *appoggiaturas* are short, they clash with the right hand, whereas if they are long, they clash with the left. Given this fact, too, it seems more natural if the right hand of the piano has the accented passing tones but the violins unaccented ones.

Finally, according to Leopold Mozart (*Violinschule*, IX, §18), *appoggiaturas* should be short when they occur in descending stepwise motion. Therefore, we suggest in m. 71 for the first violins:

Ex. V/40:

One can summarize the following rule for playing short *appoggiaturas* as listed above under (a) to (d): a short, unaccented *appoggiatura* is to be played lightly and quickly. The accent falls then always on the ensuing main note.

The question, however, as to whether short, unaccented *appoggiaturas* should be played on or before the beat is controversial, and theorists of Mozart's time offered no generally accepted solution. All manner of rules were recommended, according to which unaccented short *appoggiaturas* should be played on the beat (C. P. E. Bach, Türk), or before the beat (J. P. Milchmeyer). As stated above, Leopold Mozart's opinion is somewhere in the middle, holding that most short *appoggiaturas* should be unaccented but on the beat. But he also advocated certain types of short *appoggiaturas* that should be played before the beat. According to him, there are two different ways of playing unaccented short *appoggiaturas*. In his treatise (*IXth Hauptstück*, §9), Leopold says that a short *appoggiatura* is to be played "as rapidly as possible" and that "the stress falls not on the appoggiatura, but on the principal note." He first treats the unaccented on-the-beat *appoggiatura* in §9, and later, in §16–§18 of the chapter (*Hauptstück*), he deals with the necessity of unaccented upbeat *appoggiaturas*, calling them "passing appoggiaturas," and finally gives examples of their use in §17 and explains how to play them; namely, unaccented and before the beat. In §18 Leopold Mozart then states that one can add "passing appoggiaturas ... with notes which ascend or descend by conjunct degrees, e.g.:" and gives the following examples:

Ex. V/41:

In application of this example, the *appoggiaturas* in the first movement of the Concerto K. 246 (mm. 14–15) should indeed be played as anticipations (see Ex. V/33).

After these examples, Leopold Mozart recommended to his readers (and by extension certainly also his son): "He who wishes to express it in print, sets it down in properly distributed notes."

Interestingly, Wolfgang Mozart never wrote the *appoggiaturas* before the bar line, as did his father in his example above. It would therefore be quite wrong to rely blindly on another example in §17 (*appoggiaturas* before descending thirds) and play the *appoggiaturas* in the D major Rondo K. 485 as anticipations. These *appoggiaturas* are certainly to be played on the beat, for a particular characteristic of Mozart's music is its continuity, its rhythmic flow and freedom from jerkiness.

Only the *appoggiaturas* in the Adagio of the Sonata in F major, K. 280, mm. 45 and 49, might have been meant to be played before the beat in the manner of Leopold Mozart:

Ex. V/42:

But then it was an exception to Wolfgang's usual preference for playing these *appoggiaturas* on the beat. The Rondo K. 485 is another case:

Ex. V/43:

mm. 1–2:

played:

It is the variant in m. 54 of this Rondo that is one more sign that Mozart regarded these linking notes as accented, not unaccented, passing tones.

Ex. V/44:

codetta, mm. 54–55:

According to the *Köchel Catalogue*, this famous Rondo theme is a reminiscence of Mozart of a melody used by Johann Christian Bach (the editors of the sixth edition of the *Köchel Catalogue* failed to state from which work of Bach). Marc Pincherle discovered that the initial motive of this theme was originally composed by the French composer M. Alexandre Guénin, who started his Sonata IV of his "Six Duos pour deux Violons," published 1772, alike:

Ex. V/45:

Guénin's motive apparently became well known. His notation of it makes it quite clear that Mozart's *appoggiaturas* were intended to be accented passing tones and have to be played on the beat. Interestingly, Guénin later wrote—like Mozart—the same figure out in eighths notes:

Ex. V/46:

Had Mozart wanted anticipating short *appoggiaturas* in his D major Rondo theme he would have written them in large notes just as he did, for example, in the A major Symphony K. 201, where he made a clear distinction between written-out anticipating *appoggiaturas* and *appoggiaturas* written in small notes and played on the beat:

K. 201, first movement, m. 105, first violins:

Ex. V/47:

(written-out upbeat appoggiaturas)

m. 183, first violins:

Ex. V/48:

(sixteenth-note appoggiaturas on the beat)

If one is to follow Leopold Mozart, the above example from the Concerto K. 246 (Ex. V/33) should be played as an anticipation, whereas the examples from the Sonata K. 545 (Ex. V/23) should be played on the beat and unaccented. However, in the example from the Piano Sonata K. 279 (Ex. V/22), anticipation seems to be the only musically viable way.

Unaccented, Anticipatory Appoggiaturas. As one can see, there are differences of opinion as to the way unaccented short *appoggiaturas* should be played. The question here is simply whether one regards a short, unaccented *appoggiatura* as an accented passing tone that has degenerated (lost its accent) or as an undeveloped (because very short) upbeat. Whereas some theorists have to this day not accepted Leopold Mozart's innovation and insist that *appoggiaturas* should always be played on the beat, practical musicians and theorists with a pragmatic approach have always preferred to play nearly all of them before the beat. A problem of this kind is certainly less interesting to the listener, who in most cases will hardly notice any difference between *appoggiaturas* on and before the beat than to the performer, who even in these minor questions needs to know where he stands if he is to be able to concentrate on artistic form at a higher level. This is probably also the reason why many textbooks and tutors attempt to dispose of all such questions by means of oversimplification and generalization.

This is seen clearly in the table given by J. C. F. Rellstab (*Anleitung für Clavierspieler*, 1790). Rellstab claimed that performers "often play many of the small notes in this distribution before the beat [i.e., anticipatory] without being aware of it," as Sandra Rosenblum rightly stated (*Performance Practices*, pp. 234–235). Therefore, in Rellstab's opinion, example (3) would be the correct execution:

Ex. V/49:

In the second edition of Türk's *Klavierschule* from 1802 (pp. 271–283), Türk also advances an opinion similar to that of Rellstab. This is an understandable preference. If *appoggiaturas* are to be unaccented, then any musician's natural tendency is to play them as an upbeat—it is less trouble, and at first one will almost automatically play them in this way. If an unaccented *appoggiatura* is played on the beat:

Ex. V/50:

there is a danger that the listener will not hear an *appoggiatura* played on the beat but an accompaniment that comes in off the beat (early). It is all too easy to hear not (as intended):

Ex. V/51:

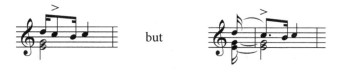

All the same, in this case we cannot share the opinion of these northern German authors or of A. Beyschlag,[1] who regarded this effect as a reason for saying that short *appoggiaturas* should not be played on the beat. On the contrary, much pleasure can be derived, especially in *cantabile* movements, from this delayed accent; the delay is quite slight because the *appoggiatura* is played very quickly, and it results in a true *rubato*—that is to say, an occasional slight veiling of the meter, which prevents the impression of a purely mechanical beat. Melodic feeling is easily weakened by too close a synchronization with meter. If all unaccented *appoggiaturas*, single or compound, were played as anticipations, then the main melodic accents would always coincide with those resulting from the meter, and the result would be often a dry, inexpressive playing, a kind that is unfortunately all too common.

There is no definitive solution to the question "To anticipate or not to anticipate?" nor would one be desirable; but in most examples listed under (a) through (d) above, we advocate anticipation.

The following examples seem to show that Mozart himself often played *appoggiaturas* as anticipations. In the D minor Concerto K. 466/III, he notated the *appoggiaturas* in large notes:

Ex. V/52:

Ex. V/53:

Here, for once, Mozart writes out a typical octave *appoggiatura*, obviously to emphasize its thematic relationship with the first solo in the first movement.

---

[1] A. Beyschlag, *Die Ornamentik der Musik*, p. 168.

Another example of a written-out anticipatory *appoggiatura* is found in the G major Violin Concerto K. 216/II. In m. 16, Mozart wrote a thirty-second-note *appoggiatura* before the D-sharp on the second beat:

Ex. V/54:

But in the recapitulation (m. 39) he notated:

Ex. V/55:

If this *staccato* stroke is not Mozart's error, the second *appoggiatura* in Ex. V/54 is one of the very rare exceptions to the rule that an *appoggiatura* should always be slurred to its main note.

Often discussed are the *appoggiatura*s at the beginning of the A minor Sonata K. 310:

Ex. V/56:

Before the recapitulation of this subject the *appoggiatura* D-sharp is written out in the form of an anacrusic sixteenth:

Ex. V/57:

Here various editors have added the original d-sharp² *appoggiatura*: This seems a crude misunderstanding of Mozart's abbreviation *Da Capo 8 mesues*. If Mozart had written out the eight measures he surely would not have repeated the d-sharp².

Mozart's notation in the third movement of the String Quartet K. 458 (the "Hunt"), on the other hand, seems to indicate a performance on the beat:

Ex. V/58:

A similar example where one must play the *appoggiatura*s on the beat is found in the third movement of the C minor Sonata K. 457, mm. 28–29 and corresponding passages:

Ex. V/59:

Here as well as in Ex. V/58 the *appoggiatura* has to a large extent kept its character of an accented passing tone because the preceding note is repeated. (Some pianists play this *appoggiatura* as an eighth note; however, both autograph and the first edition clearly show a sixteenth note.)

But octave *appoggiatura*s may often be treated as anticipations. In the following example from the C minor Concerto K. 491/I, first solo m. 100, we recommend playing them as follows:

Ex. V/60:

Octave *appoggiatura*s must never be accented. Even in his earliest youth, Mozart made a clear distinction, in works such as the Variations on a Minuet by Fischer K. 179, between written-out broken octaves with the lower note accented (a), as in Variation X, m. 5:

Ex. V/61:

(a)

and octave *appoggiatura* grace notes with the upper note accented (b), as in Variation XI, m. 44:

Ex. V/62:

(b)

We feel it is sometimes more important for the sound to be full and smooth than for the upbeat to be separately perceptible. Thus, m. 40 of the Romance from the D minor Concerto K. 466 may be played on the beat, but lightly:

Ex. V/63:

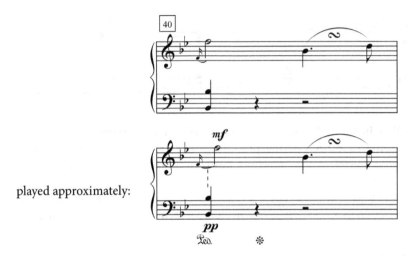

played approximately:

However, there indeed a technical problem arises: most pianists have difficulties playing a note with the thumb unaccented on a strong beat. Paul Badura-Skoda (as a juror at the Queen Elisabeth International Piano Competition in Brussels in May 2003) observed this and wrote in a letter to his coauthor:

To my disliking I heard several young pianists playing the *appoggiaturas* this way:

Ex. V/64:

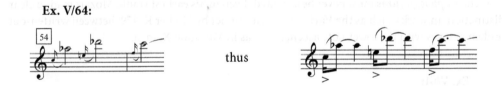

thus

As a result, the *appoggiaturas* "killed" the melody. Afterwards I listened to several recordings: nearly all pianists had anticipated these *appoggiaturas*, myself included, without being aware of it! Nevertheless it sounded good. With more awareness I have studied the problem of the rising appoggiatura in the first movement of this D minor concerto:

Ex. V/65:

No matter how hard I had tried to play it on the beat, it did not sound "natural"! I found two satisfying solutions since then: I either play it before the beat or "in between":

Ex. V/66:

Nobody has criticized me so far!

Maybe Milchmeyer was again right after all. Here is his corresponding table in which he shows his preference for anticipation:

Ex. V/67:

Although an unaccented thirty-second *appoggiatura* can often be played much shorter than an accented anacrustic sixteenth, we must expressly warn against coldly rattling off these grace notes. They still must sound like part of the melody.

We have already mentioned that the duration of *appoggiaturas* offers far fewer problems than their accentuation, given that Mozart mostly wrote down the exact note values he wanted played. Nonetheless, there are cases when he indicated the duration of *appoggiaturas* inaccurately, whether on purpose or by mistake is hard to say. Thus the duration of eighth-note *appoggiaturas* does not seem to always be precisely fixed. We have already mentioned the introduction to the Violin Sonata K. 454, where Mozart (if only after the first performance) made an alteration in dark ink, changing the eighth-note *appoggiaturas* into sixteenths thus showing an interest to be precise. In an older autograph manuscript of the Variations on "Unser Dummer Pöbel meint" K. 455, m. 4 contains a sixteenth-note *appoggiatura* that in the later (final) autograph is written as an eighth note.

The voice part of the song "Ein Veilchen" has eighth-note *appoggiaturas* in mm. 10–11. But are they meant to be eighth notes? To take this literally would produce intolerable clashes with the piano part:

Ex. V/68:

What did Mozart mean here? Apparently he made a mistake. With accented sixteenth-note *appoggiaturas* this passage sounds far more natural:

Ex. V/69:

However, one can hear this song with accented eighth-note *appoggiaturas* (not recommended) sometimes, too:

Ex. V/70:

We believe that the best and probably intended solution is to sing the *appoggiaturas* as sixteenths and to keep the rests as in Ex. V/69. Perhaps Mozart did not think at first of writing sixteenth-note *appoggiaturas* because then, as a result of the clash with the piano part, there would have been a temptation to make the sixteenth-note *appoggiaturas* into anticipations or to perform them as thirty-second notes. But the accentuation of the *appoggiaturas* is more important than their duration.

In the Andante of the C major Sonata K. 279 we would regard the eighth-note *appoggiaturas* in mm. 1 and 43 as coming on the beat, and perhaps a sixteenth note long, for in his youth Mozart was apparently not very exact in indicating the difference of the lengths of his *appoggiaturas* (that Mozart wrote indeed an eighth-note *appoggiatura* one can see on the facsimile page of the autograph reproduced in the *NMA* vol. IX/25/1, p. XVIII. The sixteenth-note *appoggiatura* on p. 7 is an emendation).

Ex. V/71:

played best:

The on-the-beat sixteenth-note *appoggiaturas* in m. 21 may be played shorter or as a sixteenth note on the beat. To play them as eighth-note triplets would make the rhythm of the passage monotonous but would not be incorrect.

In the C minor Fantasy K. 475, mm. 31–32, Mozart wrote an eighth-note *appoggiatura* after the bar line that does not fit well—one would expect a thirty-second note here (and most pianists indeed play a thirty-second *appoggiatura* here). According to the autograph and first edition he wrote:

Ex. V/72:

Perhaps this also was a "slip of the pen."

There is a similar passage in mm. 44–45 of the F major Rondo K. 494, where the *appoggiatura* has the value of the preceding notes:

Ex. V/73:

Either Mozart's notation in the Fantasy K. 475 is a writing slip or Mozart wanted the *appoggiatura* to be expressive and therefore not too short. However, the execution as a real eighth note is hardly advisable as it would damage the all-important melodic flow.

In exceptional cases the duration of a sixteenth-note *appoggiatura* can be played rather longer. This is almost certainly the case in the finale of the B-flat major Concerto K. 238: in mm. 4 and 7 Mozart wrote an eighth-note *appoggiatura* in the piano part,

Ex. V/74:

whereas in the otherwise identical reappearances of the passage in the *tutti* (m. 12) he wrote sixteenth notes:

Ex. V/75:

But from the prevailing eighth notes in this Allegro movement one can take it that Mozart can only have intended eighth-note *appoggiaturas*.[2] A similar case of a probable error occurs in the

---

[2] Since the orchestration in the middle *tutti* is different, Mozart wrote out the return of the *ritornello*: Again, in the *piano* ♪ mm. 103 and 106, and again ♪ in mm. 172 and 175. However, at the last return of the solo theme (m. 264) he wrote (probably by mistake) ♪ in m. 269 and ♪ in m. 267!

last movement of the A major Violin Concerto K. 219. Mozart wrote sixteenth-note *appoggiaturas* for the solo violin (m. 3) and the orchestra (m. 11) here and in all ensuing recurrences, which, unlike in other works, were written out rather than being signaled by *da capo* signs.

Ex. V/76:

(With the exception of m. 112, Mozart forgot to write the slurs between *appoggiaturas* and main notes throughout this movement, probably a sign that he wrote it in a great hurry, and it was clear to every musician that the *appoggiatura* had to be slurred to the main note.) While a literal execution as an accented sixteenth note in this example cannot be ruled out, it speaks for the instinct of most violinists that they prefer the execution of the *appoggiatura* as an eighth note, here as well as in mm. 24, 26, probably also 28–29, and certainly in m. 319 also (where Eulenburg wrongly prints a large sixteenth note). A proper proof for our opinion cannot be given,[3] but in a similar passage in the third movement of the early Piano Concerto in D major, K. 107, m. 3, the notation as sixteenth notes occurs in the beginning, while eight measures later (also in m. 41) there are eighth-note *appoggiaturas* in the piano part—another example of a probable writing slip by Mozart:

Ex. V/77:

(This theme is not by Mozart but by Johann Christian Bach: three piano sonatas from Bach's op. V had served as models for the three K. 107 concertos).

The even rhythm of mm. 265 and m. 23 in the Violin Concerto in A major, K. 219/III, could be an indication that eighth notes might be intended as well. On the other hand, the *appoggiaturas* in mm. 13–15, 20–22, and most likely 32–33 (in contrast to the written-out sixteenth notes of mm. 36–37) should be played as short *appoggiaturas* (see *appoggiaturas* before repeated notes, p. 169).

Violin Concerto in A major, K. 219/III, violin, mm. 13–15:

Ex. V/78:

---

[3] Let us remind ourselves that we are not performing for eighteenth-century audiences but for our own pleasure and that of our listeners: "What pleases, is allowed," said Goethe's Tasso ("Erlaubt ist, was gefällt").

Vocal Appoggiaturas

A particular form of accented passing tone, with which every educated pianist should be familiar, is the one known as the *vocal appoggiatura*, an Italian orthographic habit where a note is sung on a pitch other than written. As it can also occur in instrumental music, it must be discussed here. According to a tradition that lasted well into the nineteenth century, this type of accented passing tone is often obligatory and only sometimes a matter of taste. Bernhard Paumgartner explained it with the following words:

> In Mozart there are many classic passages where failure to use an appoggiatura must be regarded as a crude offence against the style of the music. In Mozart's time, as before and for a long time after, this accented passing-note was used far more than even the most passionate present-day advocates of the appoggiatura might suppose.[4]

Extensive discussions of vocal *appoggiaturas* are found more recently in Friedrich Neumann's book, *Ornamentation and Improvisation in Mozart* (p. 16ff.). Though there will always be some few controversial cases, in principle one can heartily recommend singers to study carefully Neumann's examples.

This type of *appoggiatura* is to be used, above all, when a phrase (or section) ends with two notes of the same pitch in a *recitative* (and also often in an aria); in this case, the first of the two is almost always sung one tone (or a semitone) higher than it is written.

The Marriage of Figaro, act 4, recitative:

Ex. V/79:

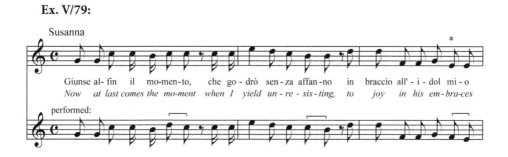

At *momento* it would also be possible, though unusual, to introduce an upward *appoggiatura*, but singers normally prefer the *appoggiatura* from above. At *affano* and *mio*, upper *appoggiaturas* are also appropriate; but the melodic filling-out of the leap of a third, indicated by the asterisk (*), is particularly important and persuasive, and it is hardly possible to excuse a misguided faithfulness to the text that motivates some singers to sing such passages as written.

To demonstrate that in arias, too, this type of *appoggiatura* was clearly to be used (though more rarely than in *recitatives*), we take as an example Fiordiligi's aria from Act 2 of *Così fan*

---

[4] Quoted after Bernhard Paumgartner, "Von der sogenannten Appoggiatur in der älteren Gesangsmusik," p. 229ff.; see also Kurt Wichmann, *Der Ziergesang und die Ausführung der Appoggiatura*, pp.185–203. The following music example is taken from Hans Joachim Moser's *Musiklexikon* and was used also by Wichmann and Neumann.

tutte, No. 25 (Rondo), mm. 3–5, of the Allegro moderato (and their later reprise). Here, according to the autograph, the first violins have to play:

Ex. V/80:

whereas in the vocal part Mozart notated:

Ex. V/81:

If, however, there are two notes of the same pitch following a downward leap of a fourth, then the first of them should be sung a fourth higher than it is written:

Ex. V/82:

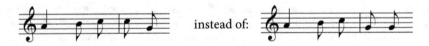

An example from Act 1, no. 1, *Terzetto of Così fan tutte* (mm. 35–36) shows that, even over larger intervals, here the seventh, this kind of *appoggiatura* is still to be employed. Here the oboes play:

Ex. V/83:

whereas the voices have:

Ex. V/84:

Surprisingly, only in this specific case did our late friend Frederick Neumann not concur with our opinion. (We gratefully remember the many fruitful discussions with him in the 1980s about ornamentation problems.)

Quite a number of other publications appeared in the last decades of the twentieth century discussing the problems of improvised and prescribed ornamentation and usually they dealt with the question of prosodic accents present in the Italian music. As is well known, Italian music dominated musical life in Mozart's time, and Mozart followed Italian habits in many respects. There can be no doubt that far more freedom and liberties were customary in Italy and also Vienna than in northern Germany. Therefore, theorists such as Mancini, Manfredini, Salieri, or Corri, but not Marpurg or Schultz, should be consulted concerning Mozart's notational habits.

The vocal *appoggiatura* developed out of the natural melody inherent in the language. If one translates the text of the above example as *O fuori la spada*, it is incomparably more natural to give an accent, a musical emphasis, to the word *spada* ("sword"), just as it is unnatural in our opinion to sing the phrase literally as written, thus giving the main melodic emphasis to the syllables *-ri la*.

Naturally, it would not be a good idea to employ the *vocal appoggiatura* every time notes are repeated in a *recitative*. Sometimes this would have a disturbing effect, and at other places it might be a matter of taste. Yet in most cases comparable to the following:

Ex. V/85:

the *appoggiatura* (a¹ instead of g¹ in the following example) seems necessary on musical grounds.

In the eighteenth century, the *appoggiatura* was often used in conjunction with other arbitrary ornaments, those that could be added at will, the discussion of which will be in chapter 6. A fine example of a decorated *appoggiatura* occurs in Figaro's aria "Non più andrai farfallone amoroso...":

Ex. V/86:

Non più andrai farfal-lo-ne a- mo-ro- so...

Naturally, intelligent singers will follow the first violins:

Ex. V/87:

But often the singer will have to sing a dissonance not supported by the violins or other instruments. This is certainly the case in Donna Anna's aria "Or sai che l'onore" in *Don Giovanni*, act 1:

Ex. V/88:

Or sai chi l'o - no - re   l'o - no - re

Unfortunately, some singers are still reluctant to sing what sounds good, which was certainly done in Mozart's time, and was most probably also Mozart's intention.

Vocal Appoggiaturas in Instrumental Compositions

Vocal *appoggiaturas* are suitable not only in vocal music, but often in instrumental works where there are passages of a recitative-like character. Thus we are firmly convinced that in the G major Violin Concerto K. 216/I, mm. 149–152, where Mozart wrote a typical accompanied recitative, vocal *appoggiaturas* should be played by the solo violin, since most violinists of Mozart's time were familiar with operatic practice.

Ex. V/89:

is to be played as follows, despite the dissonance created in m. 152 (the fermata in m. 154 must of course be slightly embellished):

Ex. V/90:

Unfortunately, this passage is still sometimes incorrectly played as written, because some modern violinists are unfamiliar with conventions of Mozart's time and instead try to be faithful to the text. (That the fermata on g² is an invitation to the soloist to improvise at least a short connection to the following note will be discussed in chapter 7.)

There exists a similar passage in the Minuet of the "Haffner" Symphony K. 385, mm. 13–16, where Mozart wrote out the *appoggiaturas* in the first violin part (presumably because he followed the advice of his father, who did not expect every orchestra player to be equally familiar with this kind of ornamentation):

Ex. V/91:

There exists another form of vocal *appoggiatura*, less obvious and even more difficult to comprehend: when a small note is placed in front of two notes of the same pitch, the small note may absorb the first of these two:

Ex. V/92:

Of course, it would have appeared natural to eighteenth-century musicians just to write the two notes g¹ without the preceding *appoggiatura*; but then a contemporary singer of Mozart's time might have added another arbitrary ornament and might have started this little phrase a third above the g¹. It is also necessary to know that, while the notation of two equal notes left often a (limited) freedom of choice to the singer as to whether or not to sing the first one higher, in this special case the notation with a preceding grace note made this execution compulsary.

An application of this principle (the small note "eats" the first of two repeated ones) can also be seen in the finale of the first act of *Così fan tutte*:

Ex. V/94:

A very instructive example of this second type of vocal *appoggiatura* is found in the "Laudate Dominum" from the *Vesperae Solemnes de Confessore* K. 339. Here nearly all dissonances on the first beat are written as small sixteenth notes. However, in m. 36, Mozart (maybe erroneously) wrote out the motive for the solo soprano thus:

Ex. V/95:

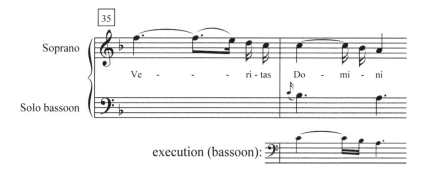

But twenty-one measures later the soprano of the choir has the identical tune notated in this way:

Ex. V/96:

et - - in sae - cu - la

There can hardly be any doubt that the solo soprano, the bassoon, and the choir should perform this passage the same way: the small sixteenth note assumes the length of five sixteenth notes. This passage was pointed out to us by members of an Italian choir. They had been unhappy with the rickety execution:

Ex. V/97:

After being assured that it would be in style to sing a long vocal *appoggiatura*, they were truly delighted.

From a later time there exists a historical proof of this execution of *appoggiaturas*: Schubert's friend, the famous singer Michael Vogl, as well as other friends from Schubert's circle of admirers, told the young music historian Max Friedlaender, the inquiring editor of Schubert's songs, that Schubert's notation

Ex. V/98:

invariably means

Ex. V/99:

and not

Ex. V/100:

thus, ♪♪ means (according to them: "of course"): ♪♪ .

Schubert had been a pupil of Salieri and therefore learned to follow the old Italian practice in the notation of vocal works.

Mozart's notation of this type of *vocal appoggiatura* only occasionally applies to his piano music. In the finale of the F major Piano Sonata K. 332, mm. 15–18, Mozart may have intended this kind of execution:

Ex. V/101:

played:

We base this reading on m. 18, the next measure but one, where Mozart wrote out his *appoggiatura* (in this case resolving upward). One could also perhaps play:

Ex. V/102:

but hardly:

If the first solo subject of the D minor Piano Concerto with its vocal narrative character had appeared in an opera, Mozart would have probably written:

Ex. V/103:

TRACK 24

A similar *vocal appoggiatura* in an instrumental work could be intended in the slow movement of the Piano Concerto in D major, K. 451/II:

Ex. V/104:

RACK 25

One reason for Mozart's different notation might have been the slurred execution in mm. 25–26 versus the detached one in m. 27. To play here according to a *vocal appoggiatura* seems appropriate:

Ex. V/105:

The *appoggiatura* sounds good and avoids too many repeated notes; the different notation two measures later also makes more sense this way.

The form of *vocal appoggiatura*s discussed above might explain the remarkable fact that in his instrumental works Mozart very often wrote sixteenth-note *appoggiatura*s before repeated notes where, from the point of view of musical expression, he must have meant eighths; e.g., in the Violin Sonata in G major, K. 301/I, opening:

Ex. V/106:

If Mozart had written the *appoggiatura*s as eighth notes, many players of the time would have played quarter notes, as was then still the practice.

In the manuscript of the D major Sonata K. 284, Variation XI, we read:

Ex. V/107:

In the first edition, published by Torricella at Mozart's own instigation, most of the *appoggiatura*s are written out normally, and we find:

Ex. V/108:

Again, in Variation XII, the *appoggiatura*s should surely be played as accented eighth notes:

Ex. V/109:

This version at (b) shows how the notes were printed in the first edition.

For the same reason, the *appoggiatura*s in mm. 2 and 4 at the opening of the A minor Sonata K. 310 should be played as eighth notes. And by the same reasoning, the *appoggiatura*s in the first movement of the Serenade *Eine kleine Nachtmusik* K. 525, composed much later, mm. 11 and 12:

Ex. V/110:

might be played:

Ex. V/111:

Here we must confess, however, that we have gotten used to the often heard way of playing these measures with a Lombardian rhythm, and we also find this very attractive:

Ex. V/112:

As far as we can see, there can be no all-purpose solution to the problem of how to play sixteenth-note *appoggiaturas* before repeated quarters. It is indeed true that Mozart usually wrote upward-resolving *appoggiaturas* not as ornaments but in normal notes, and if we examine some of these cases we may conclude that he did in fact often intend a Scottish snap or Lombardian rhythm; i.e., accented sixteenth-note *appoggiaturas*. For example, we find the following rhythm in the G major Concerto K. 453/I, mm. 97ff., where we find the following rhythm notated:

Ex. V/113:

and in the C major Concerto K. 246, first movement, mm. 64ff.:

Ex. V/114:

This seems to allow the assumption that in the G major Violin Concerto K. 216, in the first violin solo, Mozart may have wanted the same rhythm:

Ex. V/115:

Here the first beat of m. 39 is:  and not: ; otherwise, he could have written out the eighths in m. 2 as well as in m. 3. However, one must be careful not to draw overly subtle conclusions. Composers have often written similar ideas in different ways.

Compound Appoggiaturas

Mozart usually treated compound *appoggiaturas* like unaccented single ones. Here again there is no general answer to the question of whether or not they should be anticipations. J. C. F. Rellstab's table, referred to on p. 136, shows that in this respect the second half of the eighteenth century was a time of transition.

As mentioned above, Milchmeyer's *Clavierschule* (1797) advocates anticipation unreservedly:

Ex. V/116:

Milchmeyer's innovation was energetically opposed by Türk in the second edition of his *Klavierschule* of 1802. It is particularly interesting that—to refute Milchmeyer—Türk draws on examples from piano works by Haydn and Mozart. On page 272 he quotes from Mozart's Variations for Piano K. 264, Variation VIII, m. 24:

Ex. V/117:

(left hand originally an octave lower)

In this case, an anticipation would result in consecutive octaves a–g. The F# must therefore be played on the beat and lightly accented. (One may also study the §281 and §282 on pp. 271–272 of Türk's *Klavierschule* from 1802, the examples not quoted here.)

Since theory usually lags a generation behind practice, Milchmeyer's views could in many cases apply to Mozart's music. But in general we would recommend Leopold Mozart's compromise solution; i.e., playing short *appoggiaturas* without an accent but on the beat. This produces a good effect melodically, and a true *rubato* results. We particularly recommend playing the ornament in this way when Mozart consciously writes in an old-fashioned style.

In the second movement of the Concerto K. 453 there is an Anschlag, or so-called Überwurf, an ornament very popular in the generation before Mozart, but one that Mozart used only on few occasions:

Ex. V/118:

Here we advocate playing the ornament on the beat, in accordance with Türk and Clementi:

Ex. V/119:

The Andante of the F major Sonata K. 533, written in three-part polyphony, also has a compound *appoggiatura* on the beat (mm. 3, 13, et alia). Here we especially recommend accenting the main note, so that the ornament is not too clumsy. In the first edition, in the recapitulation (m. 85) this ornament is aligned as follows:

Ex. V/120:

This rhythmic placing seems to support our views. Moreover, the accented passing tone b-natural moving to c¹, only has its full effect if played on the beat. Similarly, the ornament in the last measure of the Andante of the Concerto K. 450 in B-flat major must surely be played on the beat. Leopold Mozart calls all compound *appoggiaturas* of this kind (including the turn when placed above the note) *mordente* (*Violinschule*, XI, §8, p. 206):

> *By mordent is meant the two, three or more little notes which quite quickly and quietly, so to speak, grasp at the principal note and vanish at once, so that the principal note only is heard strongly.*

However, the three-note ornament that starts the A minor Rondo K. 511 may be an exception and needs discussion:

Ex. V/121:

According to the above-mentioned rule, it should be played on the beat, but (as quoted elsewhere above): quickly and quietly (= unaccented):

Ex. V/122:

But a few problems arise here:
 If played too slowly, the dotted *Siciliano* rhythm is lost:

Ex. V/123:

wrong:

And in this case one would have to sharpen the rhythm:

Ex. V/124:

possible execution:

But even when played in a fast tempo this ornament would create an unwanted off-beat accent:

Ex. V/125:

as written:

correct but questionable
execution:

No doubt an anticipation à la Milchmeyer sounds more convincing here (and is easier to play):

Ex. V/126:

Maybe this was the reason why Edwin Fischer played this compound *appoggiatura* throughout in anticipation with very pleasing results. Probably the best solution is a middle road: more or less on the beat at the beginning and at all returns of the main theme, but anticipation in the F major section (mm. 31–54).

In those cases where this ornament, sometimes called an *inverted turn* (Türk, in the second edition of 1802, called it a *Schleifer* or *Coulé*) occurs in the middle of a phrase, it might well be treated like an afternote (*Nachschlag* in Leopold Mozart's treatise and in the Türk's *Klavierschule* of 1789) and anticipated. This is the case in the Andante from the Sonata for Two Pianos K. 448:

Ex. V/127:

played:

(Note the similar placing of the turn in m. 3.)

The same might apply for the *cantilena* starting in m. 21 of the Andante of the F major Four-Hand Sonata K. 497:

Ex. V/128:

Even Türk (second edition of 1802, p. 262) admits that such cases are ambiguous with regard to anticipation or on-the-beat performance.

There is a remarkable ornament in the second movement of the E-flat major Concerto K. 271, mm. 62–63 and 68:

Ex. V/129:

To maintain the sequence, m. 62 would probably have to be played:

Ex. V/130:

With regard to the preceding m. 61, the reader will note that the last two *appoggiatura*s have to be anticipated as discussed earlier (see Ex. V/1 on p. 138). On the other hand—as we shall see later—a grace note before a trill nearly always indicates an accented on-the-beat execution, even though, as in this case, the main notes in both mm. 61 and 62 are dissonances.

The ornament in m. 8 of the Andante from the E-flat major Concerto K. 482 is very reminiscent of the Baroque slide (*Schleifer*). Here again we would recommend playing it on the beat:

Ex. V/131:

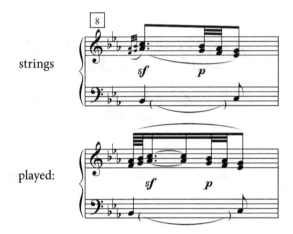

Against the B-flat the c^2 creates a dissonance that is very harsh for Mozart's time, and the effect of the ornament is perhaps meant somehow to ease its passage into the listener's consciousness.

In most of Mozart's earlier works, it will also be right to play such ornaments on the beat; for example, in the C major Sonata K. 279/II, mm. 1, 11, 12, 13. Türk (1802, p. 272) also recommends this execution:

Ex. V/132:

Arpeggios

As Haydn and later also Beethoven did, Mozart indicated *arpeggios* by a transverse stroke and not by the wavy line customary nowadays. This notation is modernized in nearly all present-day editions for a good reason: The transverse stroke can be misunderstood. While in southern Germany, Austria, and Italy it meant a simple *arpeggio*, in northern Germany it meant an *acciaccatura*, where dissonant notes are quickly played between the notes of the written chords. Thus, in Ex. V/131 a pianist in the Bach tradition would play an e^2 between the d^2 and f^2, etc. (In fact such a misunderstanding happened to Wanda Landowska in one of her Mozart recordings.)

If the right hand has an *arpeggio* or an *arpeggio*-like ornament against a chord or held note in the left hand, we believe that the lowest note of the arpeggiated chord should coincide with the left hand, as Türk (1802, VI, 4, §364, p. 272) demanded:

Ex. V/133:

Concerning the notation of the chord in the left hand it could also be interpreted as an *arpeggio*, though in this case it is unlikely that Mozart meant it this way—why use two different notations? One example occurs in the Rondo K. 494, m. 59; another is m. 1 of the minuet from the A major Sonata K. 331:

Ex. V/134:

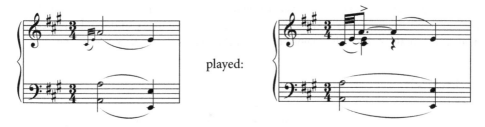

We also recommend this latter reading in m. 11 of the *Menuetto* of K. 331.

On the other hand, left-hand *arpeggios* should often be played as anticipations, as, for example, in the *Rondo alla Turca* of this same Sonata K. 331 (mm. 25ff., et alia). If both hands have *arpeggios* simultaneously, as, e.g., in m. 88 of the first movement of the B-flat major Concerto K. 595, the ornaments should again be anticipations. (The best way to pedal this passage is to start half a measure ahead and to fling the hands at the top of the *arpeggio*, which will go on sounding because the pedal is down.)

But there are a few exceptions. Among the theorists, J. P. Milchmeyer advocates playing *arpeggios* as anticipations, whereas most of the earlier theorists say they should come on the beat. To prove that *arpeggios* should not be anticipated, Türk (1802) quotes instructive examples from Mozart's violin sonatas; for example, the Violin Sonata in G major, K. 379, first movement, mm. 19–20:

Ex. V/135:

Of this passage Türk writes (*Klavierschule*, p. 272):

> *Furthermore it would often not even be possible to play this in the way demanded by Milchmeyer. ... For who could play the broken chord in the time left by the notes immediately before it? The forte added here also shows that the d¹ is to come on the strong beat.*

As a second example, Türk quotes (ibid.) m. 98 from the second movement of the B-flat major Violin Sonata K. 454:

Ex. V/136:

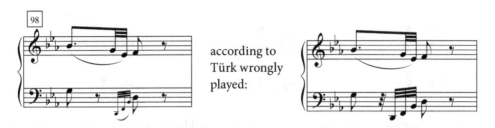

according to
Türk wrongly
played:

We recommend to follow Türk's suggestion and to start the *arpeggio* on the beat.

Turns

The Turn Immediately over a Note

If the turn is written over a note, then, according to an old rule (expressed, e.g., by C. P. E. Bach), it will start with the next note above, thus consisting of three notes, and will be played on the beat, as in the finale of the B-flat major Sonata for Piano and Violin K. 378, opening:

Ex. V/137:

played:

The turn is the favorite ornament in the music from Mozart to Chopin; even Wagner used it (*Liebestod*!). It helps to connect notes in a graceful yet expressive way and starts **always** on the upper note; i.e., one step higher than written:

Ex. V/138:

Starting the turn on the main note was introduced only toward the end of the nineteenth century; it is odd that some musicians play Mozart's turns in the wrong five-note way. These practices persist even into the twenty-first century! Below are a few typical examples with the right and the wrong execution of turns in Mozart's works:

1. The Allegro movement of the G major Violin Sonata K. 379, opening:

Ex. V/139:

2. Romance of the D minor Concerto K. 466, mm. 13–15 (first vln.):

Ex. V/140:

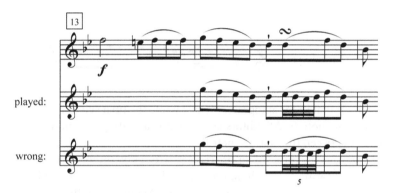

3. Fantasy in C minor, K. 475, m. 115:

Ex. V/141:

Sometimes, in a relatively fast tempo, where a turn is placed between two notes it could easily sound like an ornament starting on the main note. This is the case in the middle solo from the first movement of K. 466, m. 194:

Ex. V/142:

which sometimes could sound like:

Ex. V/143:

But this would be the performer's fault. If played in a musically convincingly way, the turn sounds lighter than the surrounding notes and starts a fraction of a second later:

Ex. V/144:

approximately:

(It must be admitted that in his autograph Mozart wrote the turn symbol a bit too far to the left side, nearly above the note f². All editors consider this a writing slip, because a few measures later, he notated it between the first two notes.)

More often than using the symbol ∾ Mozart wrote out the turn, using either small or large notes, thus indicating the pitch he wanted. Only on one occasion did he write turn-like ornaments in nineteenth-century style, namely in the Andantino of the E-flat major Concerto K. 449, mm. 107–108:

Ex. V/145:

Apparently Mozart used these ornaments here in order to avoid monotony in view of the frequent preceding turns. Leopold Mozart calls this ornament a *Halbtriller* (*Violinschule*, IX, §27; see also the English edition pp. 185 and 233) and, according to him, it should be played before the beat. It is noteworthy that Wolfgang Mozart never used the official contemporary symbol found occasionally in Haydn's sonatas and explained by Türk, Milchmeyer, and others:

Ex. V/146:

Mozart's notation of the theme of the A major Violin Sonata K. 305/II is an exception, unique in his output, and probably meant an execution of this ornament à la Haydn:

Ex. V/147:

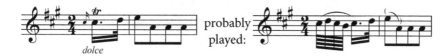

Mozart hardly ever marked any accidentals within a turn. But it is obvious that in major keys the lowest note will be raised (sharpened) when there is a turn on the dominant and (usually) when there is one on the mediant. In minor keys one will raise the lowest note of a turn on the tonic and often also of a turn on the subdominant or dominant.

Sometimes it is better to play the turn as an anticipation, particularly when the rhythm necessitates a clear accent on the main note. This is the case, for instance, in the finale of the Concerto K. 450, mm. 113–117.

Ex. V/148:

played:

The *staccato* markings over the ornamented notes are authentic and occur even in the first measures of the movement. If one were to play the turns on the beat:

Ex. V/149:

this would give the impression of a *legato*, connecting the turn in m. 113 with the following c^3. But as Mozart indicates that the notes should be separated, the turn must be slightly anticipated.

In the Andante movement of the Concerto K. 482, there is a turn in m. 33 written out in small notes:

Ex. V/150:

Here we suggest anticipation:

Ex. V/151:

A good example in which such an anticipated execution is necessary can be found in the Concerto for Two Pianos K. 365/I, mm. 247–248:

Ex. V/152:

But the turn in m. 47 of the Concerto K. 482/II seems more satisfying when played on the beat:

Ex. V/153:

 played:

The different ways of playing the turn in the last two examples result from the fact that the turn comes at different points within the meter.

If a group of three small notes occurs before a strong beat, this is often the equivalent of a turn between two notes, as demonstrated by a passage from the first movement of the Duet Sonata K. 521/I, m. 92:

Ex. V/154:

In the theme of the finale from the G major Trio K. 496 we feel that anticipation is more appropriate:

Ex. V/155:

can be played according
to Milchmeyer:

In Variation VIII of the variations on "Ein Weib ist das herrlichste Ding," K. 613, the turn could theoretically be played on the fourth beat:

Ex. V/156:

but we believe that, if Mozart had wanted this, he would have written out the ornament in normal notes, or in the form of a symbol ∞, instead of notating it with three small notes as in Ex. V/157:

Ex. V/157:

Finally, we should consider another possible way of playing the turn, not mentioned in any textbook and yet often the most elegant solution (also in Beethoven's works): It is a compromise between anticipation and playing on the beat. This is how we recommend playing the very difficult turns in the flute part of the Concerto K. 595/III, mm. 122 and 261. The advantages are obvious; the figure slips lightly over the bar line, and at the same time the dotted rhythm is preserved:

Ex. V/158:

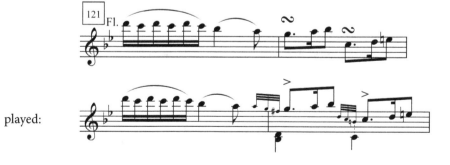

played:

Fitting these figures into the metrical scheme is less crucial than ensuring that they remain unaccented—they should slip gently on to the ensuing main note.

The Turn between Two Notes

It is often impossible to determine exactly whether a turn should be over or after a note. In such doubtful cases we must once again rely on our musical taste. In the *Andante* of the E-flat major Concerto K. 482, m. 154, the turn is probably placed wrongly and meant to be played after the first note.

Ex. V/159:

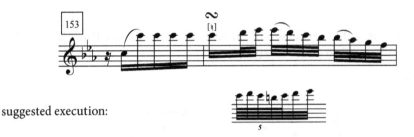

suggested execution:

If a turn is between two notes, then it always consists of four notes instead of three and is usually played as late as possible and with a considerably lighter touch than the surrounding notes. This can be achieved by playing on the surface of the keys, not more than three millimeters deep.

Ex. V/160:

in slow tempi this is played:

(See opening of the second movement of the D major Sonata K. 576, where Mozart wrote out this ornament.) At quicker tempos it is played:

Ex. V/161:

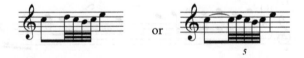

or

And at a very quick tempo:

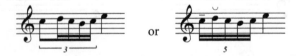

or

The Turn after a Dotted Note

When a turn comes after a dotted note it is played before the dot is reached:

Ex. V/162:

played: or

At quicker tempi:

This rule also applies when Mozart wrote a turn in small notes, as in m. 61 of the first movement of the Two-Piano Concerto K. 365:

Ex. V/163:

played:

or in the Adagio of the F major Sonata K. 332, opening:

Ex. V/164:

played:

or:

This way of playing the turn after a dotted note is supported by rules found in all the contemporary literature; for example, Milchmeyer. The succeeding note e-flat^2 must not be accented, which would inevitably happen if it were immediately preceded by the turn symbol.

One of Mozart's favorite formulas occurs in the C minor Fantasy K. 475, mm. 58 and 62:

Ex. V/165:

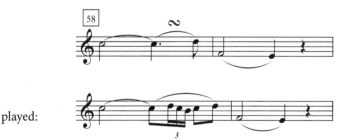

played:

and also in the Concerto in D major, K. 451/II, m. 56, and Concerto in C major, K. 467/II, m. 62.

It has to be noted that in earlier works, Mozart sometimes used the trill symbol where only a turn could be meant; for instance, in the E-flat major Piano Concerto K. 271/III, m. 99:

Ex. V/166:

Here the turn should start before the dotted note. At the beginning of Var. II in the variations on "Ah, vous dirai-je, maman," K. 265, he also wrote a *tr* sign instead of a turn symbol.

In some cases, one can also consider making the dotted rhythm sharper, as Leopold Mozart (pp. 210–211) and Türk (p. 286) suggested:

Ex. V/167:

A good application of this sharpening can be found in the Piano Four-Hand Variations K. 501, where we find the following passage at the beginning of the G minor variation:

Ex. V/168:

Certain problems with the metric placing of Mozart's turns arise when a dotted note is followed not by one but by two short notes. There are two possible solutions, depending on whether these short notes should be accented (a) or unaccented (b).

(a) If they are accented, then the turn should immediately precede them. This is the case in the third movement of the C major Sonata K. 330, m. 21:

Ex. V/169:

or in the coda of the Adagio from the C minor Sonata K. 457, m. 47:

Ex. V/170:

See also Mozart's notation in the third movement of the Concerto in C Major, K. 503, m. 171.

(b) But if these two notes are unaccented, the normal rule of a turn after a dotted note seems to yield the best musical results. Mozart himself wrote it out in the Rondo K. 494, m. 101:

Ex. V/171:

He could have written:

Ex. V/172:

In view of this written-out execution, the turn in m. 50 of the Andante cantabile from the Sonata K. 333 similarly benefits from a smooth *cantabile* execution:

Ex. V/173:

proposed execution:

Ex. V/174:

In the middle section of the Andante from the D major Concerto K. 451 we find:

Ex. V/175:

The embellishment of this passage that Mozart sent his sister includes this turn:

Ex. V/176:

here one should
obviously play:

A similar execution is recommended in the Andantino of the E-flat major Concerto K. 449:

Ex. V/177:

to be played:

In the Romance of the D minor Concerto K. 466, m. 4, we find:

Ex. V/178:

Three different executions are possible:

TRACK
33

(a)

(b)

(c)

One cannot say with certainty that any of these is exclusively correct, but we believe that Mozart may have preferred version (a), because in mm. 101–102 of the F major Rondo K. 494, (quoted in Ex. V/171 above), he wrote out this ornament in normal notes. Of all the versions, this is the more placid and the clearer one. Version (b), which is often preferred by present-day performers, only sounds good when the ornament is played a good deal more lightly than the succeeding notes. Otherwise, the final sixteenth loses clarity and the listener may be given a wrong impression of the rhythm:

Ex. V/179:

Some pianists struggle with the turn after the dotted note in m. 13 of the Variation V (Adagio) from the A major Sonata K. 331:

Ex. V/180:

But undoubtedly, like in the cases cited above (see Ex. V/164 from the Sonata K. 332), the last of the four small notes will become a sixteenth note:

Ex. V/181:

(But one measure later, where the ornament consists of only three notes, it leads into the next notes without delay.)

After a double-dotted note the following version is advisable; for example, in the Adagio movement of the C minor Sonata K. 457, m. 4:

Ex. V/182:

but rather not:

It is interesting to note that in the parallel places, mm. 16, 20, and 41, Mozart wrote only one dot followed by a sixteenth note, probably because he took double dotting for granted here.

In the next example, Mozart's notation clearly shows how the turn should be played (Sonata K. 311/III, m. 159 and m. 161):

Ex. V/183:

In this movement, Mozart took remarkable pains to attain clarity of notation. In mm. 21 and 23 he wrote:

Ex. V/184:

and, clearest of all, in m. 163:

Ex. V/185:

All three ways of notation lead to approximately the same execution.

Finally, we should point out once more the necessity of playing turns with subtlety and liveliness of expression. The performer's fingers must react with lightning speed. The delicacy of the ornament notwithstanding, the first of the four notes normally needs a very light stress.

Trills

Beginnings of Trills

It seems that there are still two distinct schools of thought about how to begin a trill: the unprepared and prepared trill schools. To clarify: One group of performers and their teachers believe that trills should always start with the upper auxiliary note and the other school consists of pianists who are convinced that they should begin every trill on the note that carries the trill sign.[5] So what do these two kinds of trills look like?

A prepared trill would be written according to eighteenth-century practice:

Ex. V/186:

without an initial *appoggiatura*:

according to modern notation:

---

[5] See also Paul Badura-Skoda, "Mozart's Trills"; Frederick Neumann, *Ornamentation and Improvisation in Mozart*, pp. 104–135; and Sandra Rosenblum, *Performance Practices*, pp. 239–259.

usual execution:

This kind of trill is characterized by a certain acuity and brilliance. It satisfies old-fashioned theorists because it can be analyzed as a succession of *appoggiaturas* and their resolutions:

Ex. V/187:

Its disadvantage is that in some cases it can obscure the flow of the melody, since it accents the upper auxiliary note (e² in the example quoted above). For instance, in a rising scale it will anticipate the succeeding note, and this can often rob a line of some of its sense of direction.

Executing the above example as an unprepared trill, that is, starting on the main note,

Ex. V/188:

does, on the other hand, make the main note quite unmistakable. But it doubtless has a duller effect than a prepared trill starting with the upper auxiliary note because one misses the piquant acuity of the accented dissonance.

If one uncritically applies to Mozart the theoretical maxims of the second half of the eighteenth century, there is no problem about how to begin the trill: they are nearly unanimously in favor of starting on the upper auxiliary note. Students are usually told as a general rule that trills starting on the upper auxiliary were customary in the eighteenth century, whereas trills with main note beginning are a matter of the nineteenth century. As we have pointed out elsewhere, during the second half of the eighteenth century a yawning gap existed between theory and practice; indeed, theorists are usually behind the latest practice, and in this case they were also not wholly consistent. Tartini (1692–1770), in a famous letter to a student, advocates beginning the trill on the main note, but in his *Trattato delle appoggiature* he is in favor of the upper auxiliary.[6] J. G. Albrechtsberger, born in 1736, recommended in his piano tutor *Anfangsgründe der Klavierkunst* the beginning on the main note (which was new for his time):

---

[6] On this matter, see also Beyschlag, p. 145.

Ex. V/189:

The trill   is played as follows

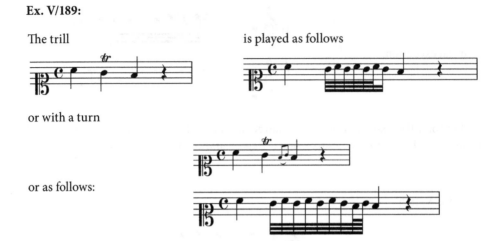

or with a turn

or as follows:

Albrechtsberger, who lived in Vienna as an organist, composer, and teacher and was a friend of Haydn and Mozart, advocated another important convention. In his undated manuscript (Archiv der Gesellschaft der Musikfreunde, Signatur VII 14372), he also wrote:

> ... the long trill  is always to be played with a closing turn whether the two notes are written or not.

This same opinion was expressed also in the treatises of G. S. Löhlein (fourth ed., 1782) and Milchmeyer (1797). According to Leopold Mozart's *Violinschule*, however, the trill in Albrechtsberger's example would have to be played at the end:

Ex. V/190:

Albrechtsberger gives only this single example of a trill, but it is presented as a rule and not as an exception.

The first well-known Viennese *Klavierschule* to make the main-note trill a rule and not an exception is that of Mozart's pupil J. N. Hummel, which appeared in 1828. Though Hummel claims that his rule is completely new, this is doubtless a considerable exaggeration. Both Milchmeyer, in 1797, and Clementi, in 1801, favored starting the trill on the main note in certain contexts, as the reproduction of Clementi's list of ornaments on p. 137 shows.[7] Sandra Rosenblum mentions barrel organs with works by Haydn, where most trills start on the upper note (*Performance Practices*, p. 243). Apparently the habit of beginning trills on the main note did not become widespread until Czerny, the great piano teacher, came out in its favor in his *Klavierschule*, op. 500 (1840). In practice it seems that by that time most if not all pianists—with the notable exception of Chopin—started their trills on the main note.

Turning from theory to Mozart's works, we find many passages where, in our opinion, one can only begin a trill on the main note. But we feel that these examples, which we shall give later, by no means prove clearly that Mozart began all his trills in this way.[8] There are numerous cases

---

[7] See also James H. Dee, "Mozart's Trills, Some Eighteenth-Century Evidence," p. 24.

[8] Nor does the fact that Ernst Pauer, a pupil of W. A. Mozart, Jr. (1791–1844), is said to have begun all trills on the main note (Beyschlag, p. 177). Two generations are too great a lapse of time when the correctness of a tradition is in question. Mozart's son scarcely knew his father!

in which it seems more appropriate to begin on the upper auxiliary. Apart from these, there are many neutral cases where either execution is possible. Much depends, then, on the question of which execution we regard as normative and which as exceptional. So, short of the discovery of contemporary evidence, there seems to be no all-purpose solution to the problem of Mozart's own execution of trills.

We were able to listen to a fascinating piece of contemporary evidence, an eighteenth-century *Flötenuhr* (barrel organ) playing the Andante in F major K. 616, with most of the trills, including the first one, starting with the main note. The fact that this piece was originally composed for a barrel organ indicates that in all probability it reflects Mozart's intention. Since there were also a few trills starting with the upper auxiliary note, our theory—that this was a time of transition and that a certain amount of freedom of execution was allowed—seems to be confirmed. It should be borne in mind that manufacturers of barrel organs obviously intended to reproduce a live performance. This *Flötenuhr*, for instance, follows the text most accurately, playing strictly in time yet adding some delicate *rubato* in the passage work.

Main-Note Trills

Let us present not only some examples but also some "rules of thumb" for cases in which the trill should begin on the main note:

1. When in a legato passage the trill is preceded by the next note above. An example is found in the Two-Piano Concerto K. 365, first movement, m. 154:

Ex. V/191:

Others in the Variations on "Salve tu, Domine" (K. 398), Variation V, mm. 12–13:

Ex. V/192:

or in the Variations on a Minuet by Duport K. 573, coda:

Ex. V/193:

or the B-flat major Concerto K. 595, first movement, m. 114 (and mm. 116, 276, 278):

Ex. V/194:

2. *When the trill is preceded by three rising or falling notes like a slide.* These figures grew out of the Baroque ornaments ⟨ornament symbols⟩ and ⟨ornament symbols⟩. Some examples may show that Mozart used this ornament: Sonata in B-flat Major, K. 333, third movement, m. 198[II]:

Ex. V/195:

D major Rondo (K. 485), m. 52 (and m. 135):

Ex. V/196:

played approximately:

Variations on "Come un' agnello" K. 460, cadenza before the Adagio variation:

Ex. V/197:

TRACK 35

(Note the imitation in the bass part of the initial motive.)

Mozart's ending of the cadenza for the third movement of the B-flat major Concerto K. 450:

Ex. V/198:

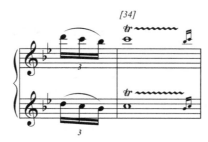

3. When the trill is placed on a dissonant note. E-flat major Concerto K. 482/II, m. 167 (also in mm. 151 and 173 of the same mvt.):

Ex. V/199:

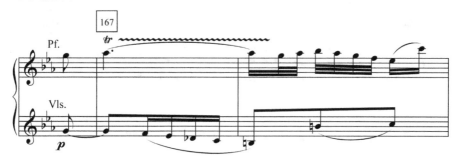

The friction of the a-flat² with the suspended g¹ must, of course, be preserved. To begin this trill on the upper auxiliary (b-flat²) would have exactly the result that eighteenth-century theory wished to avoid: The accented dissonance would thus become an unaccented one.

Similarly, in Mozart's original cadenza for the first movement of the B-flat major Concerto K. 450 a main-note start of the trill is recommended:

Ex. V/200:

4. When the trills are in the bass. The function of the bass as harmonic support might suffer if one would begin the trill on the upper auxiliary.[9]

---

[9] There are organ toccatas by J. S. Bach with written-out trills in the bass; these begin on the main note, probably for the reason given here, namely, that the effect of the harmonic support is more important than the characteristic charm of a trill starting on the upper auxiliary.

E-flat major Concerto K. 482, second movement, m. 149 (also mm. 165, 171). Here the dissonant rule also applies.

Ex. V/201:

Ditto for Variation V of the variations on "Salve tu, Domine" K. 398, mm. 12–23 (see Ex. V/192, p. 192).

Fugue for Two Pianos K. 426, mm. 80–82:

Ex. V/202:

5. In trills at the end of rising and descending scales.

Opening of Mozart's authentic cadenza for the first movement of the Concerto K. 365:

Ex. V/203:

Two-Piano Concerto K. 365, third movement, mm. 139–141:

Ex. V/204:

(fingering by the authors)

Here another factor enters in—Mozart's genius in writing for the piano. To begin the trill on the upper note d³ would be unpianistic and awkward to play.

6. *When the trill is preceded by the same note, as a sharply attacked upbeat* as in the C major Concerto K. 467, first movement, m. 382, likewise in the F major Concerto K. 459, third movement, original cadenza, mm. 41ff.:

Ex. V/205:

If one began this trill on the upper auxiliary note, the impression would be of an unprepared trill starting a sixteenth note too soon. Mozart was fond of these sharply attacked anacruses (see the two b-flats¹ in Ex. V/195, p. 192.

C minor Sonata K. 457/I, mm. 2, 6, et alia. Here, however, we contend that different solutions are possible:

Ex. V/206:

possible execution:

suggested execution:

Comparing the first violin motif from mm. 63–66 of the first movement of the E-flat major Concerto K. 449 and the notation of the same motive in the original cadenza (mm. 14–17), the notation in this cadenza apparently indicates an easier (shorter) version of the trill, which, as it is known, violinists always start with the upper note. Applying this observation to the trill in the C minor Sonata, one could play it either with a start on the main note or on the upper auxiliary (like a violinist) as in the above proposed execution (Ex. V/206) or else as a four-note ornament as found in the original cadenza to the first movement of the E-flat major Concerto K. 449:

Ex. V/207:

First violin:

Piano (in Mozart's cadenza):

Yet, the often heard main-note start of the trill is certainly also acceptable.

7. In chains of trills. An example is found in the second movement of the Concerto K. 482, mm. 151–152 and 173–176. To start on the upper auxiliary would obscure the chromatic progression, since in each case there would be two trills beginning on the same note. The rule concerning dissonant notes (here a-flat²) also applies.

Ex. V/208:

8. In the following Presto or Allegro formula.

Ex. V/209:

In *Allegro molto* and *Allegro* movements it is often not possible to play more than three notes at such points, if the sixteenth notes are played in time, as, for instance, in the second subject of the first movement of the F major Sonata K. 533.

9. Finally, in a number of special cases, difficult to classify. Two-Piano Concerto K. 365, second movement, mm. 47 et seq.

Ex. V/210:

As so often in this concerto, the second piano here (m. 48) hands over the note a-flat² to the first piano. If the first piano were to begin the trill on the a-flat² above, the result would be a dissonance that would sound as if someone had made a mistake.

Variations on "Come un' agnello" K. 460, Variation VII:

Ex. V/211:

Here it would seem plausible to begin the trill on the upper auxiliary but for the fact that there has already been a note repetition (e¹) in the middle of this run. As it is best, the fourteenth (e¹) and twenty-eighth (d-sharp³) notes are given a sharp attack and repeated, whereas the climactic e³ is reserved for the next measure.[10]

Since there are so many examples of this kind, we can at least deduce that Mozart had a certain preference for main-note trills. On the other hand, one should not try to make too much out of the fact that in a very few cases he added a short *appoggiatura* before a trill, as in the second movement of the C major Symphony K. 128, opening, in the G major Symphony K. 129/I, mm. 80–81, or in the A major Symphony K. 201/I, m. 59. The last example mentioned here is informative in this respect: the first and second violins trill in octaves; in the first violins Mozart has added a short *appoggiatura*, but not in the second violins. Nor do the first violins have an *appoggiatura* in any of the subsequent corresponding passages. A reasonable explanation of this fact is that, although it was obvious that the trills were to begin on the upper auxiliary, Mozart wanted to confirm this explicitly on the first occasion when the trills occurred.

In other passages of this kind one must consider, above all, the probability of an accented passing tone (*accento con trillo*), an accented note in front of the trill; as in the first movement of the B-flat major Concerto K. 238, mm. 47–48 (and corresponding passages):

Ex. V/212:

Second movement of the C major Concerto K. 246, mm. 38 and 104:

Ex. V/213:

---

[10] We believe that these Variations are authentic and not spurious, as has been claimed by Kurt von Fischer.

Ex. V/214:

It is remarkable that these accented *appoggiatura*s before trills are found only in works from Mozart's Salzburg youth period (until about 1777). In this connection, the opening of the theme of the variation movement in the A major Violin Sonata K. 305/II is also interesting. In all the old editions there is an *appoggiatura* d^2 before the trill, both here and in Variation I. However, the autograph has a c-sharp^2 in both cases; see Ex. V/147).

It is interesting that the majority of nineteenth-century instruction books for string players do not show this swing toward unprepared trills. This makes us think that pianists could learn much from good string players. Listening keenly to such performers, one notices that usually they do not accent the upper auxiliary note at the beginning of the trill but play it as an anacrusis, which is easier on a violin than on a piano; note the short trills in Var. II of the first movement of the Piano Sonata in A major, K. 331/I. The writing for woodwind instruments may complicate the matter. We have heard good orchestras where the string players started all trills with the (quick) upper note, while clarinets or oboes, for example, started them with the main note. Surprisingly, it sounded good and did not disturb.

Frederick Neumann called this type of smooth beginning with the short *appoggiatura* "upper auxiliary grace note trills." This seems an inspired compromise; the accent can fall on the main note, but the preceding upper auxiliary note allows the trill to begin easily and smoothly. The string players of most orchestras play the first subject of the finale of the Sinfonia Concertante K. 364, written:

Ex. V/215:

played as:

However, a pianist will find it almost impossible to flick off the short *appoggiatura* in this way when the trill is so short because of the greater inertia of his instrument's mechanism. (Compare the identical notation in the first movement of the Sonata K. 457, mm. 63–64.)

Sometimes the trill has to be so short that it consists of only one added note and is actually identical to an *appoggiatura*. We find such a trill in the first Allegro movement of "Eine kleine Nachtmusik" K. 525, m. 18, where practically all orchestra musicians play only one note, a^2:

Ex. V/216:

When a passage of this kind occurs in a piano work, a similar execution is recommended as e.g. at the beginning of the D major Piano Sonata K. 576, mm. 2–3. Trills on short upbeats often mean execution as turns (see p. 207f).

Of the three possible ways to play the closing trill in the next example, from the Concerto in A major, K. 488/I (mm. 283ff.), (b) or (c) will be preferable to (a):

Ex. V/217:

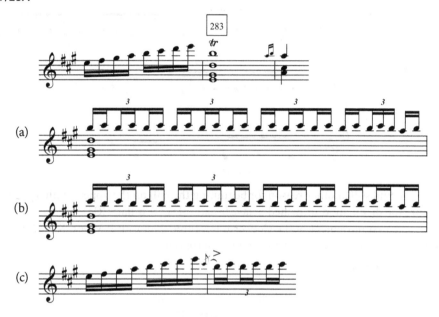

(We simplified the accompaniment harmony in this example.)

But when a trill begins a passage, as in the first piano entry of the Concerto for Two Pianos K. 365/I, it is best to begin it on the main note:

Ex. V/218:

The same principle applies for the very start of the Sonata in B-flat major, K. 281.

Upper Auxiliary Trills.   In the following cases we recommend beginning the trill on the upper auxiliary note:

1. If in a melodic run a trill is preceded by the same note (this should not be confused with the sharply attacked anacrusis mentioned above in Ex. V/205). For instance, in the E-flat major Concerto K. 482/I, mm. 84, such a run occurs in m. 83:

Ex. V/219:

played:

Here we find still another reason for beginning the trill on the upper auxiliary note; namely, to ensure the dissonant diminished octave b-natural (LH)/b-flat[1] (RH).

In the first movement of the Concerto for Three Pianos in F Major, K. 242, m. 237, a beginning with the upper auxiliary note is also appropriate:

Ex. V/220:

and likewise in m. 243:

Ex. V/221:

Also, in the third movement of the G major Concerto K. 453 (m. 169), the beginning of the trill with the upper auxiliary note is recommendable, but not in the fourth measure of the G minor Piano Quartet K. 478/I: here the note repetition across the bar line has a thematic significance; moreover, the trill is on a dissonant note (accented passing tone). It should be noted that Mozart wrote no trill in m. 8, where many modern editions add a trill symbol without justification.

2. In a frequently occurring formula that often appears in quick movements when a trill is marked over an eighth-note upbeat. Concerto for Three Pianos in F Major, K. 242, first movement, mm. 145 et seq.:

Ex. V/222:

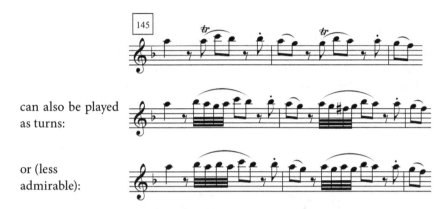

can also be played as turns:

or (less admirable):

Concerto for Two Pianos K. 365, first movement, m. 64 (and m. 281):

Ex. V/223:

should be played:

C major Concerto K. 467, third movement, mm. 120ff.:

Ex. V/224:

played:

In all these cases it would be hard even to fit in quintuplets. If, however, these **tr** markings occur in the course of rising stepwise motion, and are not over isolated upbeat notes, (e.g., in the Concerto K. 456/III, m. 77), then we should instead prefer a main-note trill in order to make the melodic line clearer.

Ex. V/225:

In the Examples V/222–223, the trill is played exactly as if it were a turn. Indeed, the two markings were often interchanged in Mozart's time, particularly in printed editions. For instance, in the finale of the Jupiter Symphony, m. 61, Mozart seemed to have erred in notating ∽ instead of *tr*. This also applies to the notation of m. 98 of the first movement of the Concerto K. 453, where the piano's trill must obviously be played in the same way as the figures on the first violins (and bassoon).

Ex. V/226:

played:

As for how fast to play trills: Naturally, Mozart's trills must usually be played with great sparkle and as rapidly as possible. It is only with long trills in Andante and Adagio movements that one may sometimes begin a little slower, for the sake of expressiveness, and then gradually make the trill quicker, or possibly slow it down a little toward the end. But these two ways of playing trills can all too easily sound affected, and this makes us recommend the greatest caution in varying the speed of one's trills. It is also obvious that trills should be played as clearly and evenly as possible. Speed must on no account mean a loss of precision. Mozart's remarks about the singer Mlle Kaiser in a letter to his father (2 October 1777) bear this out:

She still takes her trills slowly and I am very glad. They will be all the truer and clearer when later on she wants to trill more rapidly, as it is always easier to do them quickly in any case.

In playing longer trills we find it indispensable to make a slight buildup dynamically a slight crescendo or a slight *diminuendo*, according to the character of the passage. As regards touch, there is a subtle but perfectly audible distinction between the virtuoso fluttering *staccato* trill and the expressive *legato* trill. The one is achieved by throwing the fingers from the knuckles, whereas in the other the fingertips never leave the keys. And indeed the mechanism of the modern piano makes it possible to play the same note again before the damper falls back on to the string, so that one can tie a note to itself.

Endings of Trills

We mentioned above the rule noted in Albrechtsberger's treatise that trills should end with a suffix. In the theme of the variations from the G major Violin Sonata K. 379, Mozart did not notate the suffix, but it should be played nevertheless:

Ex. V/227:

In the manuscript score of the B-flat major Concerto K. 238 there is not a single final turn written after any of the numerous trills in the first movement. It would be a breach of style to play all these trills without a final suffix. Also, in the autographs of Mozart's early piano sonatas and the violin concertos, the closing suffix is practically absent after all cadential trills; in all later works, whether sonatas, trios, concertos, etc., every long trill has the closing suffix.

It would be quite wrong to think that this change of notation meant a change of style. What is much more likely is that in early works, Mozart took the execution of trills with a resolution (closing suffix) for granted, which was recommended in virtually every violin or piano textbook of the eighteenth century. But at some point he must have realized that not all his performers knew this rule. Actually, the tradition of performing trills with closing suffix, written or not, continued via Schubert and Beethoven to Brahms, who once said: "Ein Triller ohne Nachschlag ist wie ein Hund ohne Schwanz. [A trill without a suffix is like a dog without a tail]."[11]

But here again there is obviously a limit to the degree of artistic freedom left to the interpreter. According to an old rule, found inter alia in Türk (1789, p. 293), one may omit the final suffix only in descending stepwise motion; for instance, in m. 3 of the second movement of the E minor Violin Sonata K. 304:

Ex. V/228:

played:

Yet it sounds much better with closing suffix:

Ex. V/229:

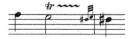

---

[11] Recently we heard Anne Sophie Mutter play the Mozart concertos with such "tailless" trills—it did not give us thrills, though her playing was otherwise impeccable.

In the second movement of the Sonata K. 533, m. 4, we also recommend a suffix:

Ex. V/230:

In a similar passage in the Andante of the Two-Piano Sonata K. 448, m. 4, Mozart wrote such a trill with a closing turn (see Ex. V/127), as well as in the Andante movement of his String Quintet in C Major, K. 515, m. 4.

If a trill without a final turn occurs in an ascending line, then one must cut off the trill in time in order to leave the course of the melody clear, as in m. 152 of the second movement of the E-flat major Concerto K. 482:

Ex. V/231:

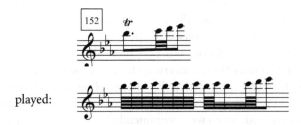

played:

Some artists add a final turn here (suggested by the editor of the *AMA*); this has no justification whatsoever—Mozart never wrote such a closing suffix:

Ex. V/232:

C. P. E. Bach said that in such cases it was a moot point whether the short notes after the trill should be regarded as a kind of final turn, in which case one should refrain from also adding a normal afterbeat (*Versuch*, 2/III, §13).

Thus, there are several possible ways to play the second measure of the C major Sonata K. 330:

Ex. V/233:

played: (a)

(b)

(c)

The execution (c) appeals to us least but cannot be totally excluded. As stated above, is noteworthy, though, that Mozart never added small notes in such a configuration. They were added, however, in some cases by nineteenth-century editors and unfortunately are still sometimes played by pianists.

The Half-Shake *(Pralltriller)*

Mozart's notation does not distinguish between trills and half-shakes. The marking ⌇, is extremely rare in his works. The few exceptions are found in the autographs of the Quintet for Piano and Winds K. 452/I (mm. 65–67 and 120) and the concertos K. 449 and K. 456.

Piano Quintet in E-flat Major, K. 452/I, m. 65:

Ex. V/234:

played as *Schneller* on the beat, à la C. P. E. Bach and Türk (pp. 251 and 273):

or before the beat à la Milchmeyer (p. 38):

Since this ornamentation sign is so rare, one has to decide according to context whether in similar passage the sign *tr* means an ordinary trill or a *pralltriller*. This is not so difficult; a half-shake should be played only whenever there is no time to play a full trill. It can be played in the following ways:

Ex. V/235:

(a) in a slower tempo:

(b) or at a quicker tempo:

(See also Clementi's approach in Figure 5.1, p. 137.)

Often the first note of the half-shake is to be accented, as in m. 8 of the finale of the E major Piano Trio K. 542.

Ex. V/236:

played:

This execution is certainly the correct one. Mozart himself wrote out the ornament in a similar place at the end of his Concerto in E-flat Major, K. 449/III, mm. 302–303 and 306–307, and he wrote similar triplets for the flute in the aria "Voi che sapete" from *The Marriage of Figaro* (mm. 14, 16, et alia).

Ex. V/237:

Yet there are many pianists who follow in the track of those wrongly guided harpsichordists who start Ex. V/235 with a note added on top:

Ex. V/238:

Mozart never wrote such an ornament; it destroys the melodic line. However, it is found in Leopold Mozart's treatise and is called the *trilletto*. Such a repetition of the initial note f-sharp² is easy to play for violinists, but simply unpianistic; it is against the nature of the hammer mechanism.

In the frequent formula:

Ex. V/239:

we recommend making an anticipation (what Türk called the *Schneller*); e.g., in the finale of the Sonata for Two Pianos K. 448; or in the coda of the Variations on a Menuett by Duport, K. 573; or in the original cadenza for the A major Concerto K. 488/I; and also in the first movement of the B-flat major Concerto K. 595, m. 106, and the corresponding place m. 269.

Ex. V/240:

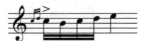

To play this ornament any other way:

Ex. V/241:

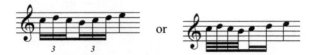

or

would disturb the even flow of the sixteenth-note figure. However, in such cases one can also play only a short *appoggiatura* instead of the half-shake:

Ex. V/242:

To the best of our knowledge, nobody has pointed this out so far. As already stated above, there are various examples to show that Mozart at times wrote *tr* when he obviously meant only an *appoggiatura*, as, for example, in the Variations on a Minuet by Duport K. 573 toward the end of Variation IX, where an *appoggiatura* is written, but in the immediately ensuing coda, where the same motive is sequentially developed, there is a *tr* sign. It is highly unlikely that Mozart wished this same passage to be played in two different ways.

In the A minor Piano Sonata K. 310, second movement (m. 12), the two last *tr* signs are unplayable as trills, even as *Schneller*. But if they are played as *appoggiaturas*, the result is a wholly Mozartean line, identical with the run at the end of the second movement of the Piano-Duet Sonata K. 521, m. 93. In this latter passage, Mozart wrote *appoggiaturas*. In the third movement of the E-flat major Concerto K. 482 he wrote *tr* in m. 23 and an *appoggiatura* at the corresponding measure 376, certainly intending the same execution. Thus, Mozart himself authorized the *appoggiatura* execution.

But for pianists—and only for them—there exists an even a shorter formula for the *pralltriller*, namely to play the two notes together (one should try it—this solution sounds brilliant!), or to play the upper note a fraction of a second later without releasing or repeating the lower one. Such an execution was recommended by Haydn's pupil Ignaz Pleyel (1804).

Ex. V/243:

Die Präcision fordert es bisweilen, daſs man diese Manier auch auf folgende Art ausführen muſs:

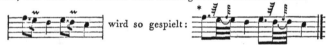

wird so gespielt:

* Die Ausführung dieses präcisen Pralltrillers läſst sich auf dem Papier nicht besser darstellen. Man merke nur dieses, daſs der Hauptton gebunden liegen bleiben muſs.

"Precision demands that one must also execute these ornaments as follows: [Ex. 1] is played thus: [Ex. 2]." Footnote: "The execution of this exact pralltriller *does not permit a better notation on paper. One should simply note that the main note must remain held."*

(Remarkably, as early as 1753, C. P. E. Bach had already recommended a similar execution of the mordent as Pleyel in 1804).

If a *pralltriller* appears on a rather short note, both notes can be struck together. A good application of this unusual execution can be found in the first movement of the F major Sonata K. 332, mm. 7–8:

Ex. V/244:

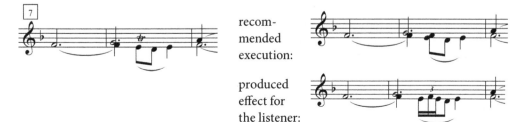

recom-
mended
execution:

produced
effect for
the listener:

Many pianists anticipate this trill, thus reducing the effect of the dissonance G–F, which is not desirable here.

In the formula

Ex. V/245:

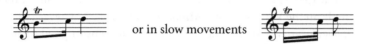

or in slow movements

a *pralltriller* is usually again intended; e.g., in the G major Concerto K. 453/I, m. 1:

Ex. V/246:

best played:

or as an anticipation (but this does not sound as good as playing on the beat):

Ex. V/247:

But many violinists start this ornament on the note above:[12]

Ex. V/248:

This seems to contradict our previous statement that the start on the upper note is wrong for pianists. It requires an explanation: The difference of execution of this ornament is based on the simple fact that pianos and violins are different instruments. Whereas the pianist sets in motion a rather complicated action between his finger and the string, the violinist has his finger on the string, and that, of course, makes it possible for him to play every ornament faster than any keyboard player. Thus, Leopold Mozart's *trilletto* (explained only in the second edition of his *Violinschule*) works well for violinists but not for pianists.

Yet we should avoid being pedantic about such issues. Did indeed every performer in Mozart's time know the rules? And if so, did the musicians follow them? Therefore, three possibilities can

---

[12] In the original cadenza, the Eulenburg and *AMA* editions wrongly give a final suffix. We were able to inspect the autograph of this cadenza and discovered that Mozart did not write a single final turn.

be envisaged as to how to play the delightful passage from the first movement of the Three-Piano Concerto K. 242:

Ex. V/249:

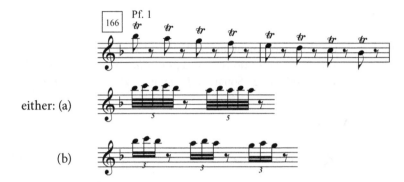

either: (a)

(b)

This corresponds to Leopold Mozart's *trilletto*;

or (c)

However, in the Andante of the C major Sonata K. 330, m. 15, a genuine main-note trill (with or without suffix) seems to be intended:

Ex. V/250:

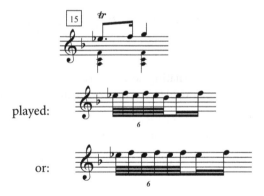

played:

or:

The above-cited motive from the opening of the G major Concerto K. 453 (Ex. V/245) resembles a similar configuration in mm. 34ff. of the first movement of the C major Sonata K. 330:

Ex. V/251:

Misled by bad nineteenth-century editions, some pianists still perform wrongly:

Ex. V/252:

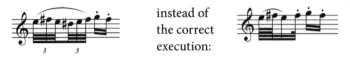

instead of
the correct
execution:

(similarly in the third movement, mm. 39–41 and 42–45).

In *Siciliano*-type configurations, only a *pralltriller* ought to be played; otherwise, the dotted rhythm would be spoiled; e.g., Sonata in F Major, K. 280/II, beginning of the Adagio:

Ex. V/253:

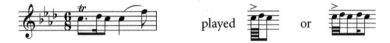

played   or

Sometimes a half-shake is intended even on long notes when the wavy line after the trill symbol is missing. This is the case in the third movement of the B-flat major Sonata K. 281, mm. 18 and 20, and in the last movement of the Concerto in E-flat K. 271, mm. 112–115, 121–123, 385–388, and 394–396 (strings, where older editions printed wavy lines by mistake) as shown in the facsimile from Mozart's autograph: Vln. I in mm. 120–127.

Ex. V/254:

A final word about the higher alternating note in a trill. Leopold Mozart (p. 218) finds harsh words for those musicians who are unable to recognize the underlying harmony:

> *It is a shameful mistake that some players make, who never bother to notice whether they must execute the trill with the major or minor second. …*

Mozart himself gave us beautiful examples in the second movement of his Violin Sonata in B-flat major, K. 454, mm. 65–66:

Ex. V/255:

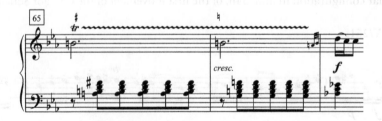

and also in the Variations on a Theme by Gluck K. 455, Var. VI.

When the harmony changes from B minor to the dominant of C minor, the trilled note must change from c-sharp² to c-natural². In many other cases, however, Mozart did not notate the accidentals. Apparently he trusted the performers to find the right upper note of the trill (what a dangerous risk!). A similar harmonic motion occurs in the Andante from the A major Concerto K. 414, mm. 71–73:

Ex. V/256:

If a pianist is not aware that the underlying harmony is D minor, he might trill with a b², yet b-flat² is necessary here. In the third measure, however, the music turns in a subtle way from the minor key to the dominant of D major; therefore, a b² is suggested here as the upper note.

In the development section of the second movement of the A minor Sonata K. 310, the music modulates from C minor to D minor via G minor. Some young pianists, unaware of the G minor harmony, do not trill with the necessary e-flat but with a doubtful e-natural:

Ex. V/257:

But who would dare to start, e.g., Mozart's G minor Symphony K. 550 with an E-natural?

Clearly the problems touched on in this chapter are often very difficult to solve and demand a great deal of musical sensitivity as well as historical knowledge. Textbooks or practical editions of Mozart's works often contain summary tables and rules, devised to give an "infallible" answer to all problems that could arise. It is certainly very convenient for a performer to be able to play ornaments in a standard way, but unfortunately it is often wrong, as we have tried to show. Even if students adhere to these oversimplified rules, a responsible artist will not, must not, find them sufficient.

6
Improvised Embellishments

In his treatise *Essay on the True Art of Playing Keyboard Instruments*, C. P. E. Bach described the *Manieren*, a term then applied to all ornaments and to free ornamentations, and he divided them into two major groups: *wesentliche* and *willkürliche Manieren*, terms that could be translated as "essential" and "optional" (or "arbitrary") ornaments. In the first group, Bach included all ornaments that are indicated by conventional signs or a few small notes; in the second are those that lack signs and consist of many short notes (*Essay ...*, I, 2/1, §6, p. 80).

This division is justified not only logically, but historically. The signs for prescribed essential ornaments (*wesentliche Manieren*) came mostly from the French school of clavecinistes, while Italy, as we know, was generally acknowledged to be the home of optional and often fanciful melodic decoration. It is this second group of *Manieren* that we shall discuss in this chapter, investigating the extent to which these embellishments could or should be added when playing Mozart's music.

During the eighteenth century, vocalists and instrumentalists alike had to learn the secrets and logic of harmonic progressions from the very beginning of their studies. They usually knew, therefore, how to realize a figured bass, how to accompany a melody on a keyboard instrument, how to extemporize a fantasy, and how to embellish a melody in various ways. Many performers thus also became composers.

In a certain sense, performances have always involved an element of improvisation. But eighteenth-century audiences expected more from a performer than just the placing of accents, the more or less tiny rhythmic adjustments or dynamic shadings with which we grew up as musicians in the twentieth century. In Bach's and Mozart's time, the occasional addition of ornaments or more extended embellishments was commonplace, both expected and accepted. Chosen free embellishments of melodic lines were often played where themes or passages appear several times (as in an aria or a concerto) and where an unaltered recurrence of a passage might be boring if played without any decoration. However, these ornamentations should embellish (literally: "beautify," from the Italian *bello*) the melodies, they should show the ability of a performer–composer to invent a variant of a given melodic passage that intensifies its intrinsic character, making it more beautiful (*più bello*) and interesting when the passage appears a second or third time. Such ornamentations, which include alterations in rhythm and dynamics, were usually created ad hoc and ad libitum, extemporized by all gifted performers. Embellishments for repetitions of themes or sections were thus often not written down by composers. Nonetheless, embellishments presented as ad hoc improvisations during a concert may well have been composed in advance and practiced prior to the performance.

In simple compositions, it was certainly not too difficult for a performer to improvise embellishments and ornament a melodic line, to add some runs or alter the rhythm through a syncopation, a *rubato*, or a Scottish snap (Lombardic rhythm). No Italian musician would have hesitated to decorate a simple melody at a recurrence and surely would not have stuck to the text when performing a passage that was obviously a mere sketch, a melodic or harmonic skeleton of the kind so often found in old manuscripts. After all, the *basso continuo* of the Baroque period had been nothing other than a sketchy, or "shorthand," notation, needing completion by every performer. But if in Mozart's time a composition was more complicated than usual, even gifted performers such as Dittersdorf considered it necessary to think about effective embellishments well in advance and prior to public performance and to compose and secretly practice these embellished versions before the concert in order to impress their audience. When admitting to this procedure in his autobiography, Dittersdorf added the warning that only great masters such as Mozart or Clementi could dare to improvise ad hoc—and to do this elegantly and to the delight of all connoisseurs.[1] Too frequently, he complained, improvisations of musicians of only average gifts offered only disappointing, often boring, ornamentations of dubious quality.

When we first wrote on this subject of improvised embellishments shortly after World War II, it seemed to us that it was necessary to deal at length with this custom of improvised embellishments in Mozart's time because the general knowledge of this convention had nearly been lost and often was unknown to younger musicians. Around 1900, composers and conductors such as Maurice Ravel, Ferruccio Busoni, and especially Gustav Mahler had developed a passion for faithfulness to the text, responding to the fact that music had suffered under extreme quantities of arbitrary ornamentations and alterations. Nineteenth-century instrumentalists and opera prima donnas had exaggerated their freedom, taking liberties to such a degree that composers in particular felt misunderstood and misrepresented. Highly disapproving of the then common lack of respect for what composers had written down, Mahler started to strictly forbid any ornaments not prescribed in the notated musical text and any rhythmic alterations by his soloists. His strong reaction to the abuse of an old practice is understandable if we recall that not only were many nineteenth-century virtuoso performers arranging their music, but also that, for instance, the older Franz Liszt, after having been seriously criticized by Berlioz for embellishing Beethoven's "Moonlight Sonata," confessed that as a young pianist he always had performed Beethoven's sonatas with various alterations and additions. Only later did Liszt realize that his additions really did not increase the impact of these great Beethoven works. Also, Giuseppe Tartini, who once created a table for his students containing as many as twenty different embellishment versions for one given melody, learned as an elderly musician that it is a greater art—though more difficult—to play a good composer's Adagio movement the "simple," unaltered way without additional notes.[2] Around 1900, it was probably mainly Gustav Mahler's condemnation of all improvised ornamentations that finally led to a complete break with the old performing traditions. Fifty years later, few artists would dare to add any notes, even necessary ones, to a composition of such great composers as Mozart or Beethoven.

Another shift from one extreme to the other, however, seems to have taken place in the decades since 1950. During the last quarter of the twentieth century, thanks to a newly increased awareness of the old Italian performance conventions, some musicians again started to embellish music of the eighteenth century. They often added far too many notes, however, and not only to works of minor composers, but also to the carefully notated music of such great masters as Haydn and Mozart. Such ornamentations and additions, usually justifiable only in a meager composition of a lesser composer or in a Mozart work that is obviously incompletely notated, are often highly questionable. These performers would be well advised to always ask themselves if their additions or alterations truly enhance the effect and the emotional impact of a work. To alter a melodic passage in an obviously completed sonata by Haydn, Mozart, or Beethoven usually does not beautify the work, and that, after all, is the *conditio sine qua non* for any alteration or addition. On the contrary: instead of being *abbellimenti*, added notes are too

---

[1] The autobiography of Karl von Dittersdorf, p. 44ff.
[2] See Martin Staehelin, "Giuseppe Tartini über seine künstlerische Entwicklung," p. 251ff.

often *abbruttimenti* (literally: "en-ugliments"), degradations and disturbing foreign substances in an otherwise perfect entity.

It is another matter if an obviously not-quite-finished solo part of a Mozart concerto movement—one where necessary accompanying figures are missing or a diatonic or chromatic run is marked only with the end notes—is played without alteration; in such cases, some added notes are indeed necessary and should be tastefully placed. This is only proper, however, if it is done with a melodic beauty and noblesse analogous to Mozart's own embellished versions of originally simpler notated themes or passages. Fortunately, we have wonderful models of Mozart's art of tasteful embellishment (see below), and these models should be studied most carefully.

The Old Rules for Placing Embellishments

It is important to take note of certain eighteenth-century rules, which demanded some embellishment at some points and forbade it at others. Investigations have shown that in practice the following types of embellishment were permitted if they enhanced the effect: in slow movements, all types of small ornaments (the *wesentlichen Manieren*) such as trills or turns; additionally (under certain conditions such as repeated sections), free ornamentations, longer embellishments, or alterations. Runs and figurations could be applied to melodic passages observing certain restrictions. Fast movements, however, were usually expected to be played as written, because there were limits to what one could improvise and embellish at such speed. In all cases, a general rule can be offered for this period: The quicker the movement, the more parts it has, the lower these parts lie, and/or the more instruments are playing, the fewer ornaments are necessary or recommended.

The exceptions are fermatas, which a composer notated as a cue for the insertion of a cadenza or an *Eingang* (lead-in). But misjudgments by performers regarding the meaning of some fermatas are unfortunately frequent (see chapter 7, p. 275, and p. 284).

Thus, it should be emphasized that embellishments apart from cadenzas and other fermata embellishments are appropriate mainly in slow movements; they are hardly ever compulsary and sometimes impossible in a quick tempo. D. G. Türk, discussing the question "When to decorate?" in his *Klavierschule* (1789; V/3, §22), recommended:

> [G]enerally speaking, that one may indeed make occasional alterations in the repeat of an *Allegro*, or in similar cases: but major additions are most often appropriate in an *Adagio*.

Leopold Mozart also says obliquely in his *Violinschule* that *Allegro* movements do not offer opportunities for embellishment. A much quoted paragraph from his treatise (XII, §2, p. 215) tells us:

> Many succeed so far that they play off with uncommon dexterity the most difficult passages in various concertos or solos which they have practiced with great industry. These they know by heart ... so long as they play an Allegro, all goes well: but when it comes to an Adagio, there they betray their great ignorance and bad judgment ... the embellishments are in the wrong place, too overloaded, and mostly played in a confused manner; and often the notes are far too bare and one observes that the player knows not what he does. ...

There is another indication that embellishments are appropriate only in slow movements: most of Leopold Mozart's examples of embellishment contain figurations that can only be played satisfactorily at a slow tempo. Since even Leopold Mozart's and Wolfgang's contemporaries regarded the decoration of quick movements as exceptional, in Mozart's own works—apart from the incomplete notation cases in concertos such as those from K. 482, K. 537, and others (see below)—ornamentations will usually be acceptable only in slow movements, if at all.

We may distinguish three kinds of embellishing ornamentations, i.e., insertions (added or altered notes):

1. Those additions that are required because of Mozart's incomplete or abbreviated notation. This group of note additions falls into two categories; namely, filling-in of runs and passages (where outlines are sketched or otherwise incompletely notated passages) and Mozart's use of well-known shorthand notation signs such as the words *Da capo*, etc.
2. Those additions that are not really necessary but permissible and a matter of taste; and
3. Those additions or alterations that are tasteless, superfluous, or stylistically inappropriate, mostly resulting in *abbruttimenti*.

Necessary Additions of Notes

To the first group belong those necessary insertions at fermata signs (on six-four chords, dominant or dominant-seventh chords) that call for cadenzas and Eingänge. These are the most extensive additions, were more or less compulsory, and in Mozart's time often named *capriccios*; but though they belong to this first group, they are not treated here but separately in chapter 7 (p. 249).

Other needed insertions of notes belonging to this first group include those additions required to fill in Mozart's various kinds of abbreviated notation: indications such as *Da capo* or *col basso* and/or figured bass numbers as well as obviously missing articulation and dynamic markings, already discussed in chapter 2 and chapter 4. Besides, Mozart's incomplete notation also apparently includes intended but not fully written-out passages and runs, mostly found in his late piano concertos, of which he indicated only the lowest and the highest notes (see Ex. VI/6). Such occurrences can be explained. When pressed for time in writing down a new concerto movement for his own upcoming *Akademie* (concert), Mozart of course had to notate all the orchestra parts completely. But if necessary, he could afford to omit parts or even the complete notation of his solo part. (The most famous case of such a reported lack of preparation time is Mozart's concert with the famous violinist Regina Strinasacchi in the Burgtheater in 1784. The artists were performing the new Violin Sonata K. 454 when the emperor discovered that Mozart played his keyboard part from nearly empty sheets, containing probably only the finished violin part.)

It was certainly such lack of time that led Mozart sometimes to notate the solo part of his last concertos incompletely, leaving out some notes or signs with the intention to write them down at a later time. Though he could be rather certain that a contemporary performer would have realized that something was missing, Mozart, on the other hand, could be equally certain that nobody knew how to vary a theme as beautifully as he did; he probably had learned the hard way not to trust the taste of other musicians. Therefore, he most probably always preferred to complete the notation of his works himself.

Support for the view that Mozart was unwilling or at least reluctant to let anyone else embellish his works is given by the fact that—whatever resistance he may have had to writing down his music—he nevertheless composed and notated the cadenzas and lead-ins for many, if not (probably) all, of his concertos. Only once did he write a full cadenza into the score (K. 488/I); usually he wrote the necessary cadenzas down on separate sheets (the probable reason why some of them may have been lost). Besides, in the final movement of the E-flat major Concerto K. 271, he wrote two longer lead-ins as well as a simpler fermata embellishment into the score. Interestingly, he later provided this Concerto K. 271 with four more lead-ins plus four cadenzas, written on extra sheets.

If in hastily notating a work Mozart did not have the time to vary a theme when it was repeated several times, he would later take care to devise some such variant for the publication, as in the second movements of the Piano Sonata in F major, K. 332, and the Piano Sonata in C minor, K. 457. Another case where he delayed writing down an embellishment occurs in the second movement of the Piano Concerto in D major, K. 451. Perhaps in response to an inquiry from his sister (assumed, but lacking documentation), Mozart wrote to his father on 9 June 1784:

… There is something missing in the solo passage in C in the Andante of the concerto in D. I shall supply the deficiency as soon as possible and send it with the cadenzas.

The melody of this slow movement in its unembellished form is as follows (m. 56ff.):

Ex. VI/1:

A decorated version of this passage has been preserved in the Abbey of St. Peter in Salzburg, a monastery with which the Mozart family was in close contact. In the third edition of Köchel's catalog (p. 824), Einstein has called the sheet with this version an authentic manuscript; however, it is not Mozart's handwriting but is a copy, apparently from the hand of Nannerl Mozart, and most probably it is indeed the embellished version of the passage that Mozart had promised in his letter. (The *pralltriller* sign in m. 60 may be a copying error—a turn seems to be more appropriate.) Nannerl or the father might have supplied the monastery with this copy, perhaps for a performance there.

Much can be learned from comparing the plain and the embellished versions:

Ex. VI/2:

(In m. 60, the need for some additional notes seems evident.)

The discovery of this tiny variant is a great stroke of luck; it is the only contemporary evidence in a concerto that this kind of melody ornamentation was regarded by Mozart as needing embellishment.

The string accompaniment to the above passage has repeated chords after an eighth rest on the first and third beat:

Ex. VI/3:

In a personal communication to the authors, Robert Levin expressed the opinion that whenever this kind of accompaniment appears in slow movements, the melody should get an embellishment. As examples, he cites passages from the D minor Concerto K. 466/II (m. 40ff.), the Concerto in D major, K. 537/II (m. 44ff.), and the Concerto in B-flat major, K. 595/II (mm. 17ff. and 49ff.). This generalization strikes us as somewhat problematic, however, because Mozart also uses this type of accompaniment to tunes containing sustained notes in many other contexts, such as arias, symphonies, serenades, and chamber music. What would happen if more than one musician had the idea of embellishing in those works? Moreover, the melody in the D minor Fantasy K. 397, from m. 12 on, does not invite embellishment in our opinion, despite the similar accompaniment:

Ex. VI/4:

If, for example, a melody is played in unison by four instruments including the piano, as, for instance, in m. 124 of the Larghetto of the Concerto in B-flat major, K. 595, it would be odd if the pianist were to add any notes that do not match the unison melody of the flute, bassoon, and the violins. On the other hand, it is necessary for the sake of the unison sound that the pianist sharpens the rhythm in m. 124 and plays thirtyseconds:

Ex. VI/5:

If Mozart intended to give a work to a publisher, we may take it for granted that he always took care to complete the notation, even if (from today's perspective) he did not invariably supply enough dynamics and articulation signs. This care and interest in a completed final version is obviously one more reason why, in general, Mozart's music notation shows a welcome attempt to rely as little as possible on his interpreters' talents for compositional tasks. If one takes a glance at the slow movements of Mozart's piano sonatas and variation cycles, most of which were published during his lifetime, and compares them with similar works by composers such as Steffan, Vanhal, Kozeluch, Paganelli, Platti, Pescetti, or Abbé Vogler, one will find a profusion of notes that leaves little room for doubt: Mozart's published sonatas already contain a full texture and their notation is nearly complete everywhere, meaning that all necessary embellishments have been printed, and only here or there a dynamic or an articulation sign might be missing. A need to add notes is rarely felt; indeed, adding such notes would merely "gild the lily" and greatly increase the likelihood that the impact and musical quality of a theme or passage would be disturbed and/or lessened.

The contrast between Mozart and his contemporaries was comparable to the contrast between Johann Sebastian Bach and his fellow musicians. Almost all of Bach's contemporaries (including Handel) relied a great deal more on their interpreters' talents for embellishments than Bach did; very few of them ever took the trouble to write out a movement with such full ornamentation as Bach did, for example, in the slow movement of the Italian Concerto, or as Mozart did in his published piano sonatas, operas, or symphonies. As a result, Mozart encountered much the same criticism as Bach did in his time: his works were held to be too complicated and too full of notes. "Far too many notes, my dear Mozart," as Emperor Joseph is supposed to have said to him. "Not one more than necessary," Mozart is alleged to have replied. Yet, as we shall discuss later in detail, there are indeed some places with too few notes, wanting enrichment.

There exists nowadays a certain fashion that repeats in works for piano solo, particularly recapitulations in slow movements of sonatas, should be ornamented and that variants of Mozart's text should be played. Alas, we could not find any proof or even disputable confirmation for this practice. Leopold Mozart states simply that the repeat sign means "a repeat," and many other contemporary authors echo this equation. In the rare cases where Mozart (or, for that matter, Haydn) wanted alterations in their solo sonatas at the second hearing, they usually wrote these down. Literal repeats are a basic form of artistic expression; they create a feeling of symmetry comparable to equally constructed wings of a beautiful castle; they help the listener to recognize and to remember themes.

Advocates of many improvised embellishments like Robert Levin and (to a lesser degree) Malcolm Bilson argue at this point in the discussion that the eighteenth-century custom of ornamenting all repeats must also apply to Mozart's works. We do not deny that some contemporary musicians of Mozart's time still felt free to use this old Baroque custom to embellish repeats, including recapitulations in Mozart's sonatas. But there are enough hints telling us that times changed in the second half of the century and that during the Classicism of the 1770s and 1780s Mozart considered only tiny alterations of repeated melodies necessary. Unaltered repetition of melodies to make them indelibly familiar to every listener was an age-old device to create and emphasize catchy tunes (*Ohrwuermer*, "ear worms"). It should be remembered that in art as well as in nature there exist two guiding formative principles: repetition and variation. Common sense tells us that repetition is more frequent than variation.

If we recall that most of the performed music in the eighteenth century was ensemble music, varied repeats would have created serious problems. (In Spohr's autobiography he tells of a shocking experience when he conducted an orchestra in Rome and some woodwind players started to decorate their melodies, resulting in musical chaos.)

Even a superficial look at Mozart's works shows that they abound with literal repeats; one need only think of four-or eight-measure periods that appear everywhere. One of the very few examples of an embellished recapitulation in Mozart's solo sonatas is found in the second movement of the Sonata K. 309; another in the Adagio variation of the third movement of the Sonata K. 284 (see Ex. VI/18 on p. 229) results from the alteration Mozart wanted in the text for a *reprise variée*. In other piano sonatas that he prepared for publication, however, the repeats in the slow movements were left without alterations, as, e.g., Sonata K. 333/II.

Even C. P. E. Bach, who published "*Sonaten mit veränderten Reprisen*" ("with varied repeats") composed those for a special purpose; he probably did not intend that dilettantes should do the same in his other slow sonata movements. In §31 of chapter III of his treatise (p. 165) Bach wrote:

> *The F major Lesson is an illustration of the present practice of varying extemporaneously the two reprises of an Allegro. The concept is excellent but much abused. My feelings are these: Not everything should be varied, for if it is, the reprise will become a new piece. Many things, particularly affettuoso or declamatory passages, cannot be readily varied. Also, galant notation is so replete with new expressions and twists that it is seldom possible even to comprehend it immediately. All variation must relate to the piece's affect, and they must always be at least as good as, if not better than, the original. For example, many variants of melodies, introduced by executants [performers] in the belief that they honor a piece, actually occurred to the composer, who, however, selected and wrote down the original because he considered it the best of its kind.*

Literal repeats of whole phrases are often indicated by Mozart through signs in sonata or symphony movements, as, for instance, in the A minor Sonata K. 310, (first and) second movement, where Mozart wrote "*Dacapo* 7 mesure." If short repeats were intended by Mozart, he used the word *bis* (twice) or wrote repeat signs. When Mozart changed a literal repeat at a later time, abbreviated in his autograph by such a *Da capo* indication, into a varied repeat (this way employing the second formative principle mentioned above: variation), a problem arose for him in indicating this in his manuscript. This change happened rarely, in only a few cases in slow movements or in rondo form movements. Examples of varied reprises can be found in the second movement of the F major Sonata K. 332 or the C minor Sonata K. 457, where the original drafts had *Da capo* signs, later changed into varied reprises. Typical rondos with varied returns of *ritornellos* can be observed in the F major Rondo K. 494, or in the A minor Rondo K. 511. It is noteworthy that in both these rondo movements the variants at the return of the original themes were initially written down by Mozart in the first notation and thus were not afterthoughts.

In recent times, heated discussion has arisen about *Da capo* returns in slow movements or rondos where Mozart did not supply a variation of the repeat. The questions are these: (1) Did Mozart want the repeat (recapitulation) unaltered? (2) Did he expect the performer to improvise a various in some cases? or (3) Did he want a variation every time at repeats? Let us quickly dispense with the third possibility, to which we would like to answer an emphatic "No!" An alteration at every repeat would certainly not have been Mozart's intention. Therefore, the question can be reduced to two possibilities: no alteration at all or variants in a few selected cases. Here the pendulum has swung: Whereas one hundred years ago the general opinion was no alteration at all if not prescribed by Mozart, the other extreme has been reached since the 1980s and 1990s: variants in nearly every case of a return.

While we acknowledge this modern trend, we feel that a warning is necessary against too much variation at repeats. Our warning is based on Mozart's own procedures. Only a few written-out varied repeats were introduced in works published during his lifetime; for instance, in the sonatas K. 332/II and K. 457/II. But in the C major Piano Sonata K. 330/II, the *Da capo* of the repeat of the first twenty measures was printed without embellishments following Mozart's written instruction: "*Da Capo maggiore senza repliche* (*Da capo* of the [section in] major without repeats)." There can be hardly any doubt that this published version was prepared and authorized by Mozart, because only the first edition prints the epilogue of four measures not contained in the original manuscript. Other such literal repeats in works printed during Mozart's lifetime are found in the second and third movements of his Duet Sonata in C Major, K. 521, and in the last movement of his G minor Quartet K. 478. In many other works not printed during his lifetime we cannot imagine that Mozart would have wanted varied repeats; most improbable are such ornamentations in a number of orchestral works; for example, in the Symphony in E-flat Major, K. 543, but also in the A major Rondo for Piano and Orchestra K. 386, and particularly in the Rondo movement of the A major Violin Concerto K. 219, ornamentations added by other musicians would hardly have found his approval. In that particular Concerto K. 219, Mozart took even the trouble of writing out the unvaried returns of the *ritornello* every time instead of using any abbreviations, in this way making it rather clear what he wanted to avoid.

Exceptions to Mozart's ambition to notate all notes are found mainly in the late piano concertos; they contain by far the greatest number of passages where notes can or must be added, apparently because (as he said in a letter to his father) he decided to preserve them for some years for his own use only and not for rival pianists, and also because in his later Viennese years he was extremely busy and often wrote the concertos down in great haste. In those piano concertos composed after 1784 we find passages that obviously have been left incomplete, sometimes only sketched; and here we may also consider embellishing repetitions or filling out thin passages. In his book on Mozart, Einstein says (1946, p. 313):

> Now, we do not know exactly how he played any of his concertos. Only four were published during his lifetime, and while in his autographs he wrote out the orchestral parts with complete care, he did not do the same with the solo parts; indeed it would have been in his interest not to write them out at all, so as not to lead unscrupulous copyists into temptation. For he knew perfectly well what he had to play. The solo parts in the form in which they survive are always only a suggestion of the actual performance, and a constant invitation "to breathe the breath of life into them".

There are fewer opportunities to add to the notated text in the earlier piano concertos. This may have to do with the fact that, in Mozart's Salzburg years, his father probably taught him to notate everything immediately, a habit that Mozart kept alive in his first Viennese years. In addition, several of the early piano concertos were written for other performers or pupils.

In the autograph of the "Coronation" Concerto K. 537, the left-hand accompaniment of the piano part is almost completely missing, although Mozart certainly did not intend to compose a concerto for the right hand alone. In this work, Mozart notated the orchestral score and a large part of the upper system of the piano part with great care; however, he left large sections of the lower system of the piano part blank. He notated the left-hand part carefully only in those few passages where the left hand plays virtuosic runs or has its own motives or opposing contrapuntal lines. Naturally, the missing accompaniment must be supplied here, and most published editions include those suggestions for completing the piano part, which were supplied by Johann André, who published the first edition of this D major Concerto shortly after Mozart's death. By and large, André's efforts deserve some praise, but he obviously failed sometimes to consult the orchestra part sufficiently, and that resulted from time to time in clashes with the orchestra bass. It is certainly possible to remedy this, but it is also possible to imagine alternative accompaniments at various places. The *Neue Mozart Ausgabe* is the first edition to reproduce in smaller print those parts that are not originally by Mozart, thus showing what was left blank in the autograph. In addition, the editors, Wolfgang Plath and Wolfgang Rehm, corrected a few of André's most blatant voice-leading errors (e.g., second movement, mm. 45–46 and 50–51).

It is possible that in the first movement from mm. 265 on Mozart intended a slightly different variant for the right hand in the sequential repetitions of the motive mm. 263–264;[3] he did provide such variants for mm. 271–272 and 275–276. Besides, in the second movement of this concerto, one can imagine that Mozart, if he had found time to review and complete this concerto, would have provided embellished versions for mm. 49–53 and 57–67. For this reason, a new stylistically appropriate and more interesting version of the necessary completion of the piano part of K. 537, composed by coauthor Paul Badura-Skoda, has recently been published.[4] For the missing notes in the left-hand part, several accompaniment passages of other concertos by Mozart were used as models.

Where else is a larger quantity of added notes absolutely necessary? If the prevailing motion in the piano part suddenly disturbingly breaks off during an allegro movement for no apparent reason, such passages must be filled out in such a way as to sound as much like Mozart as possible. Such an elaboration can be regarded as successful only if the listener does not notice that anyone else but Mozart was responsible for the text. We should now like to give a few hints as to the form that these embellishments should take in those few cases where additions seem absolutely necessary.

In the third movement of the E-flat major Concerto K. 482, a whole series of measures are merely sketched out; namely, mm. 164–172. Here, after seventeen bars of written-out sixteenth-notes passage work, Mozart wrote a further nine measures that contain only long notes, obviously intended as a framework:

Ex. VI/6:

---

[3] Carl Reinecke, *Zur Wiederbelebung der Mozart'schen Clavier-Concerte*, offered nice suggestions for embellishments for these and the following measures.

[4] A publication of G. Schirmer Inc. (New York, 2004).

These measures will sound extremely strange unless they are filled out, perhaps as suggested here:

Ex. VI/7:

Other passages where notes are missing are found in the Andantino cantabile section of this final movement of K. 482 in mm. 218–253 as well as mm. 346–347 and 353–356. In the Andantino cantabile, Mozart's notation of the piano part may be insofar incomplete as—with the exception of m. 249—the piano part doubles the first violins. One could conceivably play the piano part as it stands—as is done in most performances—but it seems unlikely that that would have been Mozart's final intention. It is a rare occurrence when the solo instrument in a piano concerto plays in unison with the first violins or other melody instruments (although it happens repeatedly in his violin sonatas, e.g., in Sonata K. 377/III). Yet it is quite out of keeping with Mozart's concerto style to reduce the amount of figuration when a phrase is repeated instead of increasing the density of the texture (see mm. 240 and 248); and whereas in mm. 238–239 the rests in the top part are filled out by eighth-note figures for the first bassoon, literal interpretation of the corresponding passages in mm. 246–247, 250–251 would leave wholly unmotivated rhythmic gaps.

Listing those passages where something is missing is one task; the question: "Just what is missing?" presents another more difficult assignment, one much harder to answer. But here, too, we find guidance in a very informative comparison with the A-flat major section of the Larghetto of the C minor Concerto K. 491/II, which closely resembles the Andantino cantabile of K. 482/III in its construction. In both cases, a clarinet melody in A-flat major is repeated by the piano, accompanied by the strings. In K. 491/II, the piano part is discreetly ornamented when it repeats the theme. How is it done?

We have already seen that at a repetition Mozart seldom likes to start altering at the first two bars of a theme (though he does it in a few cases). We feel that in the first measures of the Andantino cantabile, embellishments before the third measure (and there at the earliest) would not enhance but rather reduce the blissful expression prevailing here. Fifty years ago, Paul Badura-Skoda tried a rather prolific embellishment in K. 482/III, m. 226, something like this:

Ex. VI/8:

In our present view, there are far too many notes in this ornamentation in comparison to Mozart's so impressively sparing additions in his original embellishments (see below); it has a conspicuous resemblance with the multinote versions by J. B. Cramer, J. Ph. Hofmann, and J. N. Hummel. Therefore, we now favor a less disturbing and probably more elegant solution:

Ex. VI/9:

or, to be still more cautious, the upper voice embellishes more elaborately only from the fifth measure onwards:

Ex. VI/10:

Among Mozart's late piano concertos, there are scarcely any movements requiring as much elaboration as those of the Concerto K. 537 and of this third movement of K. 482. Nonetheless, consideration of the questions "What is perhaps missing?" and: "How would Mozart have played this passage?" may be applied to nearly all of the six late concertos. The varied recapitulations, for instance, those of the second and third movements of the C major Concerto K. 415, throw interesting light on Mozart's way of embellishing. It is revealing to compare mm. 49–64 of the finale's first Adagio section, already profusely ornamented, with the even more richly decorated one in mm. 216–231 of the second Adagio. Likewise, the varied recapitulation in the Andante movement of the Violin Sonata in B-flat major, K. 454, should be studied for this purpose. All the works that Mozart prepared for publication at a later time show us the small but telling alterations with which he clearly enhanced the effect of his works in a wonderful way.

We feel today that our suggestions for embellishment from earlier years represent the maximum possible additions; if they err, then it is because there are too many notes, too much rather than too little. Neither the peaceful character of this beautiful Andantino cantabile from K. 482/III nor that of the Larghetto of K. 491 should be jeopardized. If in mm. 242–245 a musician prefers not to start doubling the violins again, he may add a trill, comparable to the first solo section in the E-flat major Concerto for Two Pianos K. 365.

Mozart's Piano Concerto in E-flat major, K. 482, offers more occasions to think about embellishments. From m. 246 onward in the finale, the harmonic and metric construction reminds us again of the second movement of K. 365 (mm. 89–94 and 99–101), which in fact is richly ornamented. Thus, from m. 242 onward one could play a trill (inspired by a passage in the Concert Rondo K. 382):

Ex. VI/11:

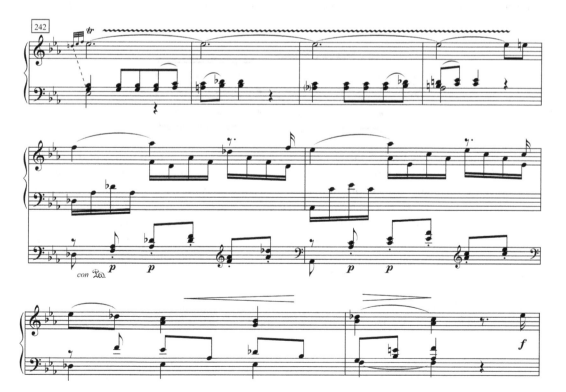

The left-hand doubling of the melody in the first four measures of the above example may appear rather bold, but this kind of doubling is frequently found in Mozart's concertos; for instance, in the *Concert Rondo* K. 382, mm. 97–120.

Also, in the E-flat major Concerto K. 482/III, the measures 346–347 need to be filled out; for instance, as suggested in the *NMA*; or in the following way:

Ex. VI/12:

Likewise, in mm. 353–356 one could play, as suggested in several editions and in the *NMA*:

Ex. VI/13:

On the other hand, the unison passage with the flute and horn at the final return of the rondo theme (mm. 387ff.) does not require completion by passage work, for this kind of farewell often occurs in Mozart's later works; for example, in the second movement of the C minor Concerto K. 491, mm. 74ff. or in the second movement of the Concerto K. 595, mm. 103ff., where an intensification due to the altered instrumentation and harmony is already present (see m. 299).

Embellishment also seems in place where a rhythmic motive appears two or more times in identical form. There is an interesting example of this in the first movement of the C major Concerto K. 503. We know that, starting in m. 96, Mozart made a completely new sketch for the first solo, having rejected his original version as too conventional; he then carefully made a fair copy on a sheet and inserted it into the full score. It is even possible that Mozart used the preserved sketch[5] simply to settle the layout of the form and the number of measures on the extra sheet.

---

[5] See Ulrich Konrad, *Mozarts Schaffensweise*, p. 175; the sketch was first reproduced in facsimile in Georg Schünemann, *Musikerhandschriften von J. S. Bach bis Schumann*, plate 42; cf. also Gerstenberg, "Zum Autograph des Klavierkonzerts C-Dur KV 503," p. 38ff.

In any case, the later, final version is six measures longer than the original one. The first measures in the autograph run as follows:

Ex. VI/14:

transcription:

Mozart then wrote a sketch for an embellishment, which shows the following version:

Ex. VI/15:

In the fair copy, stuck into the autograph above the canceled version, this text is found embellished and completed with articulation markings:

Ex. VI/16:

Such an original embellished completion of a motive is a wonderful model for our own efforts to ornament in a Mozart style. But the most elaborate models of this kind are to be found in Mozart's piano solo works.

Embellishment Models by Mozart

Fortunately, there are a number of works in which Mozart has provided precious illustrations of his rather personal method (manner, style) of embellishment, and these should be studied most carefully by anyone who wishes to add stylistically idiomatic embellishments. For example, much can be learned by comparing the autograph of the Piano Sonata in F major, K. 332, with the decorated text of the authenticated first edition. In the recapitulation of the Adagio movement, the print shows relatively few additions and alterations in comparison to the text of the autograph. This is also true of the Adagio variation (Nr. XI) of the final movement of the D major Sonata K. 284. To make comparisons easier, many editions usefully juxtapose the two versions, printing the later composed version above the original unembellished one; this is done, for instance, in the G. Henle edition and the *NMA*.

Such a "final text" prepared by Mozart for publication, which on the one hand should be respected by us and left unaltered, and, on the other, should serve as a model for stylish embellishment, is given in the second movement of the Sonata in F major, K. 332.

We quote the embellishments from mm. 23–26:

Ex.VI/17:

With the exception of the very fast chromatic scale, Mozart's embellished version shows a noble restraint, which seems to be characteristic: He refrains from altering too much and adding too many notes. Only once, in the last measure of the example reprinted here, does he insert a chromatic run and, thus, many notes. It does not alter the upward movement, however, and thus keeps what is so very important: the contour of the melody, although with a one-octave expansion of the range.

Another example of Mozart's remarkable care in embellishing can be observed in the Sonata in D major, K. 284, third movement, Variation XI:

Ex. VI/18:

Here, too, it is most interesting to see how Mozart preserved the melodic contour when final-izing his notation and preparing the movement for the printer. How little besides the addition of dynamics was actually altered altogether! Continuing on in this Adagio variation, the number of notes hardly increases (with the exception of m. 19); the noble restraint is again surprising. Thus, it can be observed that Mozart's additions consist far more of dynamics and articulation signs than notes (in the autograph we find only one single *p* at the very beginning of the varia-tion). The figurations are never overloaded; the number of extra notes is rather small. Thus, the melodic content of the simple version is not only recognizable but still fully effective when embel-lished—an important observation that should be kept in mind if a modern performer wants to embellish other slow movements. (Regarding modern ways of printing the two differing versions, see p. 46.)

Such comparisons show us how sparingly Mozart used embellishments and how strongly the contours of the original melody emerge in Mozart's decorated versions. In this respect, there is clearly a difference between Mozart's embellishments and those by Hummel, for example, who often introduced turns of a whole phrase that actually invert the rise and fall of the melody.

A discussion at a recent Mozart conference revealed the conviction of some younger musi-cologists that musicians of today should do the same with Mozart's works as was done by musicians in Mozart's time. But there existed good and bad musicians in Mozart's as well as in later or earlier periods. Not everything that was done in Mozart's time was tasteful or pleased Mozart. And, because Mozart once said that whenever he played one of his concertos he played the lead-ins differently each time (see p. 252), it was probably correctly assumed that he him-self may have improvised sometimes more embellishments than he would have written down. Because he did this, the same could and should be done by musicians today. Therefore, these colleagues argue, we never should consider the text of Mozart's piano works as a binding final text, regardless of whether it was completed by him for publication under his supervision or not.

This is a risky view. It was not only Leopold Mozart who complained about tasteless and unnecessary ornamentations by contemporary performers; other composers were also opposed against the addition of too many notes. We believe that it was an entirely different matter if Mozart himself embellished a text differently from the one previously completed by him for a publication of a work; if he ever did so (and there is no proof of this), these alterations would have been perhaps not even an improvement, only another kind of ornamentation. In any case, they would have been a true Mozart embellishment. But if we alter a completed text today, we hardly are able to guarantee an improvement; furthermore, an alteration is certainly not compulsory.

The vital question of whether Mozart liked alterations of his finished works can hardly be answered affirmatively. The likelihood that, when playing a sonata by Mozart, some conceited contemporary musicians altered some of his ornamentations does not at all mean that Mozart would have approved of it! There exist hints that this was not the case; for instance, we should remember Mozart's reaction to the performance of Abbé Vogler (as can be perceived from his letter about Vogler's performance of his sonata in 1778; see p. 250). Leopold Mozart, himself a well-trained composer, when realizing that a passage in his son's Concerto movement K. 451/II needed to be embellished, apparently thought it necessary to request it from Wolfgang. Perhaps he did not dare to ornament the few measures because he knew too well that his son wanted to be responsible himself for every note in his works. Otherwise, it is difficult to explain why he demanded the few "missing notes" from his son, who willingly sent them.

Thus, there are good reasons for our conviction that Mozart did not want other persons to replace his ornaments in the Sonata K. 332/II or the Sonata K. 309/II with different ones or—worse still—to add additional ornamentations to those embellishments written by Mozart. We have to distinguish between the custom of Mozart's time and his approval of it. That some contemporary performers felt free to alter any given text, regardless of whether the work was by Mozart or by, say, Abbé Vogler, certainly did not find Mozart's approval. It is a fact that he took great care to write down all the embellishments he considered appropriate when preparing a publication. In our opinion, it demonstrates his intention to have his works performed without further alterations. Therefore, these texts can be called his final will for posterity rather than just one possibility of ornamentation.

In answer to the other argument that the old custom cannot be revived unless we encourage our students to invent embellishments because they need training and to the view that even bad ornamentations by students are better than none, we would suggest that teachers recommend for this purpose less important works by minor composers. There exists enough second-rate music from the Classical period where even students' ornamentations might indeed provide beautifying embellishment, improving a composition.

The Adagio movement of Mozart's Sonata in C minor, K. 457, offers another good example of Mozart's art of embellishing in such a careful way that the contours of the theme and of all melodic passages are preserved and always recognizable. For a long time, these embellishments were known only through an early handwritten copy of this sonata with embellishments, where, however, the recapitulation is left in an unaltered form. The autograph was discovered as late as 1989 and shows that the additions in the print are indeed by Mozart himself, confirming the view that Mozart prepared his publications carefully himself.

The juxtaposition of Mozart's unembellished version and the subsequently embellished versions (according to the rediscovered autograph, the manuscript copy, and the final print) is telling and certainly worth studying.

Ex. VI/19:

TRACK
56

Certainly the finest example of Wolfgang Mozart's art of thematic ornamentation are the carefully written-out embellishments in the autograph of the A minor Rondo K. 511, in which the theme is repeated ten times, and Mozart varied it every single time. Remarkably, in one case he left the first five bars unaltered, and in another his embellishments start only in the fourth measure.

Perhaps less helpful in connection with ornamentation are specific hints of Mozart's father, but Leopold Mozart's *Violinschule* brings some examples of embellishments that are worth studying (see chapter 11, §19, third and fourth examples; also §20, third through sixth and ninth and tenth examples, p. 211f.).

Although our discussion concentrates on Mozart's piano music, we would like to mention some vocal models of Mozart's art of embellishment. Christian Bach's concert aria "Non so d'onde viene" K. 294, for which Mozart invented and notated an embellished version for his beloved pupil Aloysia Weber, is a good example of Mozart's taste in ornamentation. (It was discovered only after World War II.)[6] Another excellent object for studying Mozart's style is the

---

[6] See the comment in *Acta Mozartiana* IV/1957, p. 66ff.

ornamented version of Bach's aria "Cara la dolce fiamma" from his opera *Adriano in Siria* K. 293e, probably also written down for Aloysia Weber.

All these examples demonstrate a noble reserve with which Mozart used his art of embellishment. In the slow movements of his concertos, there is an even richer mine of information about Mozart's way of embellishing his subjects, when the piano takes over a melody that previously had been given to the strings or wind instruments. The reverse situation should be studied, too; namely, when Mozart first wrote an unadorned melody for the piano that subsequently is repeated in a slightly embellished version by another instrument; e.g., in the violin sonatas or in the Piano Concerto K. 503/III, mm. 163–170, decorated in mm. 171–175 by the oboe. This restraint when ornamenting themes that are repeated by other instruments amounts to a stylistic principle; it must have arisen less from the evanescent tone of the pianoforte than from the natural need for an appeal to the memory of his listeners. It also means an expressive intensification, an observation that justifies a reverse assumption: that wherever, in repeating an orchestral idea, the piano part is definitely more meager, it is likely that "something is missing," as Mozart put it.

When Additions Are a Matter of Taste

We know from a letter written by Leopold Mozart to his daughter that the Concerto in D Minor, K. 466, was one of those works Mozart only finished notating at the very last moment, and that on the day of the performance a copyist was still copying some of the orchestral parts. This makes it even easier than in other cases to understand why Mozart could not spare the time to write out varied repeats of the themes in the solo part. Most probably he improvised variants during the performance, especially since the opening motive of the Romance occurs a total of thirteen times. It is also striking that whereas there is not a single alteration of this motive in the piano part, the orchestral repetitions of the theme show slight variations. It is not until the second entry of the melody that it is doubled an octave lower by the bassoon; on the third repetition of the theme in the orchestra the horn has a new countersubject, and at the end the first violins show a slight embellishment; and on its fourth entry the rhythm of the last measure is varied:

Ex. VI/20:

It is natural that in playing this movement a gifted musician will judicially add some notes to the piano part when the theme is repeated. For example, in m. 119f. of the Romance, one could play in the RH:

Ex. VI/21:

It is obvious, though not equally well documented, that the C minor Concerto K. 491 was written in a particular hurry—in fact, hastily, as we can see from the autograph, full of corrections and in some places illegible. It is not surprising, therefore, if in this work we also find that Mozart only sketched some passages. For example, in K. 491/III, the measures 141–146 in the autograph are notated as follows:

Ex. VI/22:

Obviously, the quarter notes in the left hand in mm. 142–144 should have been written out as scales and should be played in that way. In the best editions of this concerto (*NMA*, Peters, Steingräber, Eulenburg, etc.),[7] this has been done. To be consistent, however, the left hand's eighth notes in m. 145 should be dissolved into sixteenth notes, in such a way as inspired by K. 459/III, mm. 242–243:

Ex. VI/23:

It is interesting to see how Mozart tried to save trouble in writing out a similar passage a few measures later.

We may conclude that in this hastily notated Concerto K. 491, wherever Mozart did not want straightforward scales, he wrote out the sixteenth notes, but elsewhere he used abbreviations; e.g., in the third movement, mm. 155–159:

Ex. VI/24:

Naturally, this passage should be completed in an appropriate way, as is done in fact in most printed editions: The two quarter notes (octave G–g) in m. 156 should be played as a scale of sixteenth notes. The only other open question concerns the eighth notes in mm. 157–158. They may either be embellished in the way suggested for m. 145 (see Ex. VI/22) or played as written.

But already in the first movement of K. 491 we have a similar case in the right-hand part, where the flowing passage work is suddenly interrupted by unmotivated enormous leaps comparable to those of K. 482/III. Playing the notes as written in Mozart's sketchy way would give a rather odd rhythmic structure. These leaps are in mm. 467–470 of the first movement:

---

[7] In the Boosey & Hawkes edition of this concerto K. 491, H. F. Redlich puts forward the wholly incomprehensible view that the text found in the manuscript is to be followed blindly and that the notation of this passage is not an abbreviation on Mozart's part. It would be quite out of the question for Mozart, with no apparent reason, suddenly to break off a continuous sixteenth notes movement—what is more, in a variation! One could explain it if he did so to coincide with the entry of the new motive in the upper part (m. 141). But it is unbelievable that he should have wanted to slow down the movement in the second measure of a motivic chain (m. 142). Redlich alleges that the "logical thematic diminution" of m. 145 proves Mozart's desire for quarter-note movement in the preceding bars; but this is false reasoning, for m. 145 is a cadential figure, in which the right hand drops the phrase it had maintained throughout the previous four measures; moreover, the rhythm of the orchestral parts also changes.

Ex. VI/25:

A suggestion for filling in the leaps in mm. 467–470 can be found in the *NMA*. The completely regular accompaniment in the first six bars (sighing motives on the woodwind, sustained notes for the left hand, quarter notes on the strings) suggests that the sequence should also be continued in the right-hand figurations, perhaps like this:

Ex. VI/26:

The leap in mm. 469–470 is to have pathos and should possibly be played unembellished, according to Edwin Fischer, giving a rise in the emotional level through its contrast with the foregoing passage work, or at least differently due to the altered orchestra accompaniment in these bars.

The solution we consider best for this passage is found below; it is slightly different from that of the *NMA* (though that embellished version is also recommendable):

Ex. VI/27:

A similar necessity to embellish applies to the earlier passage mm. 261–262 of this first movement of K. 491. Here one could fill out these measures in the following way according to Robert Levin:

Ex. VI/28:

(Detailed remarks regarding the performance of the C minor Concerto K. 491 are given in chapter 12.)

In the Andante of the G major Concerto K. 453, the following embellishments in mm. 39–40 are conceivably a proper ornamentation, although perhaps not a necessary one:

Ex. VI/29:

It would be very wrong, however, to fill out all of Mozart's wide leaps. Mozart was particularly fond of directly juxtaposing high and low registers, and these enormous leaps are a stylistic feature that often give his music an incomparable feeling of breadth. We would mention only the opening of the "Haffner" Symphony, with its theme that reaches out through two octaves, or the pathos of the first violins' leap in m. 8ff. of the Andante of the C major Concerto K. 467:

Ex. VI/30:

And Mozart's boldest and widest leaps are those in the finale of the C minor Sonata K. 457, m. 301ff., which certainly were not meant to be filled out:

Ex. VI/31:

(Text according to the autograph. The first edition transposed the bass notes up an octave in mm. 304–308.) Not until the late works of Beethoven does one again find such expressive use of the rapid contrast of notes in the highest and lowest registers of the piano.

In the second movement of the A major Concerto K. 488/II, a beautiful Adagio in F-sharp minor in *siciliano* rhythm, we find a number of passages that suggest that perhaps here something is also missing. Analysis of the passages around m. 80 shows that, from m. 76 on, the piano solo is an (intensified) variation of the preceding *tutti*. In measure 81ff., which corresponds to the melodic climax of the *tutti*, the piano figuration stops for two bars and the piano part contains merely leaps of a fourth and a fifth, such as are otherwise found almost exclusively in the bass:

Ex. VI/32:

TRACK
40

The movement in eighths in the middle parts, so characteristic of the orchestra *tutti*, also breaks off abruptly in m. 80 to give way to a new dialogue between the left hand of the piano and the bassoon. From the point of view of tone color, we might argue that in the second half of each measure the piano is covered up by the first clarinet. Certainly a Mozart piano, with its much weaker tone, would have been quite inaudible in the second half of each measure if the passage is taken at its face value. Here, some added notes seem appropriate when the concerto is played on a period instrument, though it is a matter of taste.

Once more one can find a model in another Mozart work on which to base a completion of this passage: in the *andante* of the C major Concerto K. 467, m. 12ff., in which the first violins have a descending sequence of fourths and fifths that is built very similarly. Unembellished, the passage is as follows:

Ex. VI/33:

The embellished version played later by the solo piano, filling in stepwise the former rising leaps of a fourth, sounds like this:

Ex. VI/34:

Applying this model to the passage from K. 488/II (Ex. VI/32), one might try the following embellishment:

Ex. VI/35:

TRACK
40

But this is perhaps too mechanical an application of the passage of K. 467/II, where long sequences abound. Therefore, we suggest a less regular, more rhetorical embellishment in view of the irregular rhythms found before and afterwards:

Ex. VI/36:

Theoretically, it would be possible to play a two-part version of mm. 81ff. by analogy with the preceding *tutti*:

Ex. VI/37:

but we can take it that in this special case Mozart would probably have written out the variant himself.

The ensuing passage, m. 85ff.:

Ex. VI/38:

is nowadays often embellished; however, this passage has such beauty, pathos, and earnestness if left undecorated (particularly without an embellishment with too many notes) that today we are convinced it is best to play it as notated. The passage is then slightly reminiscent of Pamina's aria "Ach, ich fühl's, es ist verschwunden" from *The Magic Flute*, at the words "So wird Ruh' im Tode sein" (at least when played on a modern piano and not on a Mozart piano, with its less long lasting tones).

In the Concerto in C major, K. 503/II, there are also some passages where a pianist is tempted to add some notes, in mm. 35–42:[8]

Ex. VI/39:

TRACK 41

---

[8] The *NMA* erroneously omits the note a¹ on the third beat of m. 36, clearly visible in the autograph (Berlin, Stiftung Preußischer Kulturbesitz).

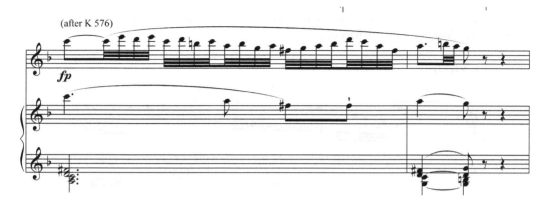

But the more urgent need for filling in large leaps can be felt in mm. 59–62 of the same slow movement of K. 503, where Mozart used an abbreviation very similar to the leaps in the finale of K. 482, discussed above:

Ex. VI/40:

To play these notes as printed makes little sense. We suggest, therefore, an interpretation like the following one (Mozart's original RH part is printed in the middle staff of the example, with our embellishments above):

Ex. VI/41:

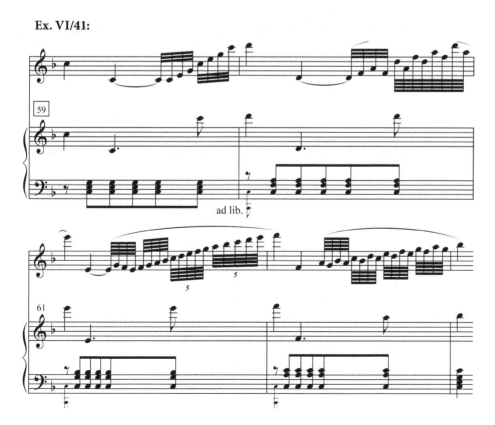

Another passage in the same movement that could be made more brilliant is found in mm. 84–85, though this is a matter of taste:

Ex. VI/42:

In the last movement of this Concerto K. 503, it is again a matter of taste whether one decides to add some notes. Mozart's fermata signs for the orchestra in m. 112 seem to indicate that he intended a more elaborate lead-in than the notated one in the solo part, perhaps something like this:

Ex. VI/43:

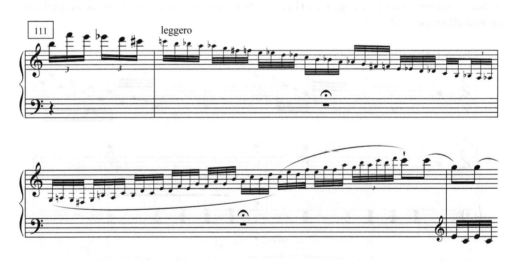

Finally, we should mention a remarkable passage from the first movement of the B-flat major Concerto K. 595. There, in mm. 168–169, we find gaps in the solo part. It is strange that Mozart should have left these gaps of two measures in the score, which otherwise is written out most carefully; moreover, it was printed during his lifetime. At first it seems that something should be added here: Note the steady diminution from m. 164 on, where first in the orchestra is a whole note, in m. 165 two half notes, then quarter notes, then eighth notes, and suddenly in m. 168 nothing substantial for two measures—only a *legato* slur over three octaves, which is unplayable! The only plausible explanation is that here Mozart did not want a performer to be tied to any one version and, in fact, there is a whole series of good ways to fill out this passage; for instance, the one suggested in the *NMA* for K. 595/I, m. 168:

Ex. VI/44:

or perhaps one of these other two elaborations:

Ex. VI/45:

On the other hand, the theme of the Larghetto movement of K. 595 is like a chorale. To embellish the peaceful, even notes of the "chorale" when it is repeated later would be to mistake the character of this movement completely; it is unique among Mozart's concerto movements, and nothing like it was written again until the Adagio of Beethoven's "Emperor" Concerto. Any ornamentation would destroy the beauty of this movement.

This is another reminder that excessive and irresponsible use of embellishment additions must be avoided at all costs. Only in passages that are as obviously sketchy as the ones shown here should one carefully decide to make additions.

When Additions Are Definitely Out of Style

The custom of virtuoso improvised ornamentations was certainly still kept alive in the next generation after Mozart, as we can see from the printed versions (we might prefer to call them arrangements) of Mozart's concertos by such composers as A. E. Müller, P. C. Hoffmann, or J. N. Hummel. If we compare the text of Hummel's editions with Mozart's way of ornamenting his themes, we discover that Hummel embellished Mozart's works much too elaborately. It was said that even Aloys Fuchs, Köchel's precursor as author of a catalogue of Mozart's works, had no reservations or inhibitions about adorning Mozart's themes with too many notes. This was done in spite of the fact that whenever contemporary discussion by outstanding performers touched on the subject of embellishments, there were regular warnings against their frequent overuse.

Leopold Mozart repeatedly had complained about musicians who "embellish and 'befrill' a piece foolishly right out of their own heads." Among a number of relevant passages in his *Violinschule* is this statement (I, III, p. 51, footnote, discussion of *cantabile*):

> *Many imagine themselves to have brought something wonderfully beautiful into the world if they befrill the notes of an Adagio Cantabile thoroughly, and make out of one note at least a dozen. Such note-murderers expose thereby their bad judgement to the light, and tremble when they have to sustain a long note or play only a few notes singingly, without inserting their usual preposterous and laughable frippery.*

Wolfgang also criticized singers who embellished too much. He first praised the singing quality of the famous castrato Raaff in a letter to his father from Paris from 16 June 1778, but then he complained that "Raaff is too much inclined to drop into the cantabile." With these words Mozart was obviously against some unnecessarily added embellishments.

Similar complaints were expressed in Dittersdorf's autobiography (quoted on p. 246) and in C. P. E. Bach's treatise. They were superseded by Beethoven's loud protests against alterations performers allowed themselves in his works.[9] Apparently, the great classical composers disliked foreign elements in their own compositions. And when the next Romantic generation's composition style as well as their performance styles had changed, the alterations became increasingly more estranged and often tended to become questionable arrangements.

Hummel's Embellishments

When Hummel embellished Mozart's concertos, he did not hesitate to alter practically every passage, even in allegro movements. Hummel's embellishments are surpassed in prolixity by those of P. C. Hoffmann (and nowadays perhaps by a few modern performers, some of whom with jazz backgrounds cannot stop inserting foreign elements into Mozart's works). By some modern performers' standards, Hummel's embellishments may be considered interesting hints, because Hummel had been Mozart's pupil as an eight- and nine-year-old child. But when Hummel was ten his father took him on concert tours and he never met Mozart again. Once he had matured in later years, he definitely became a romantic composer. There are some felicitous ideas in those embellishments of Mozart's concertos that he allowed to be published. For example, the ornamentation in the second movement of the D minor Concerto (e.g., mm. 40–67, also mm. 126–134) is nice, but certainly not in the style of Mozart. In our opinion, neither his embellishments nor those of slightly older contemporaries of Mozart's generation give us any guarantee for stylistically proper additions. And although Beethoven's oft-played cadenza to the first movement of this Concerto K. 466 is beautiful in itself, it is not in Mozart's style and does not fit well with the work (in addition to the fact that it exceeds the range of mozart's piano).

In short, Hummel's style belongs more to Beethoven's and Schubert's time than to Mozart's. The incorporation of all his suggested embellishments, as they stand, should be emphatically rejected because they are disturbing foreign elements and thus do not really embellish (i.e., beautify) Mozart's original text. For instance, in the second movement of the Concerto in D minor, Hummel suggests the following embellishment:

Ex. VI/46:

<hr>

[9] This did not hinder him from considering embellishing Mozart's works. Ellwood Derr (1992) discovered recently in Beethoven's sketches virtuoso ornamentations of passages for the Concerto in E-flat Major, K. 271. In our opinion, however, these are "not in style" and therefore hardly recommendable "embellishments."

Apparently, in mm. 40–52 Hummel had a slower tempo in mind than Mozart's *alla breve* (cut time), for which we suggest ♩ = 86. At that tempo, the thirty-second notes in Hummel's m. 50 would sound unduly rushed.

The next example, also from the Romanze of K. 466, (m. 128ff.) shows Hummel's additions, which leave the original contour of the melody behind:

Ex. VI/47:

In the Larghetto of the Concerto in C minor, K. 491, Hummel already embellished the second half of the theme at its first appearance (m. 9ff.):

Ex. VI/48:

The accompaniment is, of course, not following André's text completion but almost entirely new and much too elaborate—far from Mozart's style.

In the Concerto K. 537, Hummel also embellished the slow movement nicely but out of style with his octaves and the overstepping of the range:

Ex. VI/49:

In October 1790, Leopold II was crowned as German emperor in Frankfurt/Main. As court composer, Mozart felt he should be in Frankfurt for the occasion and traveled there on his own expense. A concert that he could give at this occasion included two still unpublished piano concertos (obviously, K. 459 and K. 537). This concert was heard by two young admirers from Mainz, the brothers Heinrich and Philipp Carl Hoffmann, who later claimed that they had heard Mozart embellishing the slow movements of his concertos. Twelve years later, Philipp Carl Hoffmann published *Cadences and Embellishments for 6 Mozart Concertos*, a volume that was reprinted in 1981 by C. F. Peters in Leipzig. It would be wrong to assume that this edition reflects Mozart's own embellishments, for the fact that Hoffmann had heard Mozart perform two concertos appears to have influenced him rather little. The cadenzas are incredibly long (his cadenza to K. 503/I has 100 measures and that to K. 491/I is 133 measures long, whereas Mozart's own cadenzas are usually not longer than ca. 30 measures). In addition, the ornamentations of Mozart's principal themes are much too elaborate. We need only to compare Mozart's own embellishment for the passage of the Concerto K. 451 (see p. 217) with a passage from the second movement of the C major Concerto K. 467 (mm. 58–74), which as originally written happens to be identical with the beginning of this passage: Where Mozart added only a single note, in Hoffmann there are twenty-three![10] "Befrilling" of this kind is surely not what Mozart had in mind.

Facit

Although we must take account of the fact that according to a contemporary report, Mozart himself embellished sometimes when performing his slow concerto movements, it is obvious that neither Hummel nor Hoffmann intended to limit their additions of notes as based on Mozart's models or to show any other interest in copying Mozart's style.

Nowadays it is not easy to get an idea of the extent to which embellishments were used in Mozart's and the next generation's time. The above quotations from Leopold's *Violinschule* clearly point to a general assumption that performers would add embellishments 1.) at places where composers apparently counted on their imagination and left empty spaces for the necessary addition of notes (the first type, discussed on p. 216) and 2.) in passages where taste at least permitted embellishments (the second type): either in repeated sections that otherwise may sound boring or in passages with too thin a texture. But they also added unnecessary or disturbing ornamentation.

In his *Autobiography*, on p. 44, Dittersdorf, regretted that not only "masters such as Mozart and Clementi" but also many less gifted performers ventured to improvise embellishments in such a way that "you never hear the sound of a piano at a concert without knowing that you will be regaled with every sort of twist and twirl and turn."

Thus, although Dittersdorf and Leopold Mozart complained that the interpreters of their time went too far with regard to alterations and additions of ornaments and decorations, they would probably have been also dissatisfied at the intellectually lazy or overly cautious way of some present-day performers, who are afraid to add any notes at those places where they are appropriate and needed. In the words of C. P. E. Bach (*Essay... I/II*, p. 79) without linking notes to bring the music to life, "the best melody...becomes empty and monotonous," and in rare cases this can also be true of Mozart's music. The central question behind this chapter "Where

---

[10] These measures are also reproduced in A. Hyatt King's book *Mozart in Retrospect*, p. 80. See also Paul Badura-Skoda, "Philipp Karl Hoffmanns Kadenzen und Auszierungen zu 6 Klavierkonzerten von Mozart," pp. 658–660; for Hummel, see pp. 97, 98, 100, 103, 140, 153, 157, 159, etc., of the Litolff edition of Mozart's concertos, arranged by J. N. Hummel (plate 2842).

and how is it necessary or recommendable to add embellishments?" does, however, demand of the interpreter a highly developed sense of responsibility. The restraint and caution of Mozart's alterations, for example, at the end of the second movement of the C minor Sonata K. 457 (see p. 231), should be kept in mind.

Unfortunately, instead of a few added or judiciously altered notes, what we sometimes hear today recalls Dittersdorf's lament: The additions are often too numerous, are thus out of style, and are frequently superfluous and seldom tasteful. Mozart's melodies, unadorned, are still utterly Mozartean. The foundation of any addition to them or any modest alteration must be painstaking study and knowledge of his style, needs the necessary respect for and sympathy with his music, and should always reflect on the affect (emotion) of the movement or piece, enhancing its impact.

We have suggested as models for Mozartean embellishments not only passages from his concertos but also from his sonatas. With the possible exception of the very last sonatas, K. 570 and K. 576, all the piano pieces and sonatas seem to us to be completed masterworks; they require hardly any additions except various missing dynamic and articulation signs. Indeed, it is risky to alter anything in this large group of solo piano works. For instance, such a moving piece as the second movement of the Sonata in C Major, K. 330, cannot become more beautiful if some notes are added, even if the ornamentations as such may be quite nice as, e.g., in the following example:

Ex. VI/50:

Many Mozart lovers will agree that the original noblesse of Mozart's passage will not be beautified when these additions are played.

How easy is it to spoil a Mozart theme, sometimes only with the addition of one single note instead of a rest! What would Mozart have thought of such an additional note in his G minor Symphony K. 540:

Ex. VI/51:

Violino I

Taste is and was always a disputable matter, in modern as well as in previous times. We have seen that even good composers such as Hummel could make the mistake of thinking that more is better and added notes to a perfect original composition.

In Donaueschingen, around 1800, a performance of *The Magic Flute* took place and the performance parts are preserved. The famous aria in act 1 of *Tamino* has the following embellishments:

Ex. VI/52:

Dies Bild - niss ist be-zau - bernd___ schön wie
noch kein Au - ge_ je__ge - sehn!

These are most questionable "beautifications," indeed, which should never be copied.

There is not the slightest hint in Mozart's letters that he tolerated other persons making deviations from his written music text. On the contrary: The letter regarding the missing notes in the Concerto K. 451/II quoted at the beginning of this chapter shows that he did not even trust his father to embellish an unembellished passage to his satisfaction. And Mozart's obvious fury not only about wrong tempi but also about alterations to his written music text can be gleaned from a letter to his father (written from Mannheim on 17 January 1778) concerning a performance of one of his concertos by Abbé Vogler:

> I should mention that before dinner he [Vogler] had raced prima vista through my concerto (the one which the daughter of the house plays—written for Countess Lützow) [K. 246]. He took the first movement Prestissimo — the Andante Allegro and the Rondo truly Prestississimo. He played the bass mostly quite different from the way it is written, coming up now and then with other harmonies and melodies. Nothing else is possible, of course, for at that pace the eyes cannot read the notes nor the hands perform them. Well, what good is that? — to me that kind of sight-reading — and shitting are one and the same. The listeners (I mean those who deserve the name) can only say that they have seen music and piano-playing. They hear, think and — feel as little during the performance as the player himself. Well, you can easily imagine that I couldn't bear it, especially because I couldn't say to him, much too fast! Besides, it is so much easier to play something fast than to play it slowly: In difficult passages you can leave out a few notes without anyone noticing it; but is that beautiful? In playing fast the right and left hands can be changed without anyone seeing or hearing it; but is that beautiful? And wherein consists the art of playing prima vista? In this; _in playing the piece in the time in which it ought to be played and in playing all the notes, appoggiaturas and so forth, exactly as they are written and with the appropriate expression and taste, so that you might suppose that the performer had composed it himself_. (Underline by the authors.)

Although today probably few pianists would dare to play a Mozart concerto *prima vista* before an audience and without a rehearsal with the orchestra, it is the underlined sentence that should be kept in mind by all of us.

7

Cadenzas and Lead-Ins (*Eingänge*)

The art of improvisation and free fantasies flourished in the eighteenth century to an extent possible only in centuries of great musical creativity. It was an indispensable part of every virtuoso's equipment if he hoped to satisfy his listeners' artistic expectations. Improvisation was not only a right; it was also a duty that artists occasionally would exercise, even in performing other composers' works.

In the instrumental concertos of this period, there were places where it became customary among composers for the orchestra to stop playing while the soloist was given the opportunity to show off his virtuosic abilities and indulge his fantasy. In other work groups as well, e.g., in some piano sonatas, at certain special fermata points, a performer might be called upon to insert a cadenza or *capriccio*, as these improvisations were occasionally called.

In concertos, these places, which were always marked by a fermata, are a challenge to today's performer to improvise a cadenza or a "lead-in." Cadenzas were an integral part of the concerto form of Mozart's time. If a fermata in a Mozart concerto is placed over a I $^6_4$ chord, the soloist is to play a cadenza; if it is over a half-cadence on the dominant (or—in a few cases—on a fermata over another harmony), he may provide merely an *Eingang*, or lead-in, to the next part of the work. Cadenzas are much longer and more elaborate than lead-ins, and Mozart's own cadenzas almost always develop themes and motives from the concerto movement in which they occur. Lead-ins, on the other hand, are much shorter and usually nonthematic; only a few are related to the preceding motives of the concerto movement, as e.g. in the Concerto in F major, K. 459/III. Though they vary in length, they sometimes consist of only a single scale or, in vocal works, a phrase that can be sung in one breath. Whereas lead-ins are as a rule based on one single harmony (the exception is an *Eingang* in the Concerto in B-flat major, K. 595/III; see below), cadenzas are usually marked by a wider harmonic range.

Mozart—going somewhat against the prevailing custom of his time—liked to write down the cadenzas and sometimes also the lead-ins for his concertos. Many of his cadenzas are preserved, but it is most likely that some of those that he cared to write down have been lost. Often more than one cadenza composed by Mozart for one and the same concerto movement has survived, for instance, for the concertos K. 246, K. 414, K. 453, and K. 456. Some of the cadenzas were obviously written for his pupils, but others may well have been notated for his own use. In any case, we have excellent material at hand on which to base our views on how Mozart treated the harmonic structure of cadenzas.

Mozart probably notated his cadenzas because he wanted them to be balanced compositions, equally perfect in comparison with the movements to which they belong, but apparently also because he did not trust other performers of his works to invent appropriate ones. He did not even trust his father to compose cadenzas for his concertos, as one can see from the following passage of Mozart's letter to him of 15 February 1783:

> Herewith I send my sister the three cadenzas for the concerto in D and the two short cadenzas for the one in E-flat ...

(The concertos in question were obviously K. 175 and K. 271, which Nannerl wanted to perform.) It is most remarkable and should be kept in mind that Mozart did not leave it to his father, who was, after all, an experienced composer, to supply cadenzas for these performances, nor did he trust him to add proper embellishments as we have seen in the previous chapter.

Regarding the shorter lead-ins, however, it appears that in playing his own concertos he often followed the inspiration of the moment, because in another letter to his father (from 22 January 1783), Mozart wrote:

> I shall send the cadenzas and lead-ins to my dear sister at the first opportunity. I have not yet altered [elaborated] the "Eingänge" in the rondo [of K. 271/III], for whenever I play this concerto, I always play whatever occurs to me at the moment....

As for vocal lead-ins, we fortunately also have a few original examples preserved because Mozart notated them for specific singers, mainly for his beloved Aloysia Weber (see K. 293e).

Are Cadenzas Improvisations or Premeditated Compositions?

The title above is misleading, of course, because improvisations are in no way different from other compositions; they simply are compositions "on the spot." Even that view is problematic: Improvisations may be partly the result of premeditation with many or few spontaneous ad hoc alterations.

For a performance of concertos it is, of course, possible that such a creative improviser as Mozart invented ad hoc not only short lead-ins but also long cadenzas. But we assume that, unlike lead-ins, his longer cadenzas usually were, if not at least partly premeditated, fully composed in advance, and therefore often not throughout ad hoc improvisations—at least those cadenzas that have become known to us because Mozart cared to notate them. This is suggested by the perfect balance and the carefully worked out details of many of the surviving cadenzas. We agree with Marius Flothuis that in the case of the E-flat major Concerto K. 271 the two shorter cadenzas for the first and second movement probably are not independent compositions but first drafts for the superb cadenzas in their final form.

It is well known that in his younger years Mozart wrote down many cadenzas to his own piano concertos and sometimes also to concertos by other composers. After 1784, however, Mozart's autographs of cadenzas are conspicuously absent, with the exception of the one cadenza for the Concerto K. 488 (written into the score) and the two cadenzas for the last Concerto K. 595. Mozart's cadenzas were almost always written on separate single sheets. These sheets could later easily have been thrown away, a possibility that cannot be discarded. Due to the fact that only recently a considerable number of hitherto unknown cadenzas were discovered—for instance, those for the Concertos K. 246—there is some hope that more single sheets with cadenzas may still be found. It is fortunate that the cadenza for the A major Concerto K. 488 was written into the score like the cadenzas for Beethoven's "Emperor" Concerto or Schumann's Piano Concerto in A Minor, and are thus preserved. The only other late concerto for which we know original cadenzas are those cadenzas for the B-flat major Concerto K. 595, probably because this concerto was still published during Mozart's lifetime. But, alas, we have no original cadenzas for Mozart's six late concertos K. 466, K. 467, K. 482, K. 491, K. 503, and K. 537.

It is tempting to think that for the late concertos Mozart did not need to write down his cadenzas because when he performed these works himself, he improvised his cadenzas and did not need other pianists to know and study them. As tempting as this view is, it is historically unfounded. Mozart was not an esoteric composer who wanted to hide his output—quite the contrary: He was a man of the theater and he wanted to present himself to his audiences and to have his works staged in public; and he was proud when some passages in his works, calculated for effect, made the intended *furore*. Thus, we are convinced that Mozart did not want to keep his scores to himself for good but only temporarily, in the meanwhile preventing unauthorized copying. He certainly thought of a later publication and a completion of his works for posterity.

The cadenzas for K. 466 and K. 467 must have once existed in a written form because Mozart's father wrote from Vienna in a postscriptum of a letter to Nannerl on 8 April 1785:

> *I shall bring with me 2 new concertos* [K. 466 and 467], *all cadenzas and also various variation cycles. I have got already everything. [Ich habe alles schon in Händen.]*

It is true that many of the surviving written cadenzas were composed by Mozart either for his students or for those patrons who commissioned a concerto, but in quite a number of cases it seems that he notated cadenzas only for himself, because—as far as we know—he was the only performer of a concerto. This was apparently the case for the concertos K. 459 and the two new concertos Leopold Mozart heard in 1785 in Vienna, K. 466 and K. 467. For the last concerto, K. 595, for which he composed the two cadenzas and the unusual lead-in (discussed below), he notated the cadenzas not only for his own performance but certainly also for other performers, the buyers of the print. Thus the question of why Mozart bothered to write down the cadenzas for these works and not, for instance, for the Concerto in E-flat major, K. 482, or the C minor concerto K. 491 may allow more than one answer, but the probability that he actually did write cadenzas for all the late concertos does exist. We consider it rather unlikely that Mozart left so many of his greatest concertos of the Viennese period without any written cadenzas. Many modern scholars concur with our opinion that these cadenzas simply got lost, but other experts believe that Mozart never wrote down anything, thus, referring to the undeniable facts that he reserved the late concertos for his own performances and that, furthermore, he was such a brilliant improviser that he did not need to invent cadenzas in advance and to notate them.

In any event, the architecture of the classical concerto form would be upset by the omission of cadenzas, and we therefore are faced with the difficult task of looking for good cadenzas for these six late concertos by someone else (usually in vain) or of inventing our own cadenzas for these works.

Structural Differences between Cadenzas and Free Improvisations

It has been observed that Mozart's variation cycles for piano can give us an idea how Mozart's free improvisations might have been structured. They probably are nearest to an improvisational style, often more so than his fantasies; and unlike cadenzas, they could last much longer and at will. Mozart's procedures with these at first improvised variation cycles can be helpful for our understanding of his improvised or composed cadenzas.

We know from Mozart's letters that he improvised variations in the presence of Gluck, Sarti, and Duport on themes composed by them in order to please his fellow composers. In a letter (from 12 June 1784) to his father about Sarti, he stated that he had performed the variations "to the delight of the composer," and in this case as well as in all the others he used to write these improvised variations down afterwards, perhaps completing them—if necessary—to a proper cycle at a later time. He could certainly rely on his fabulous memory. In this context, however, two surprising facts emerge: In the case of both the Variations on a Theme by Gluck K. 455 ("Unser dummer Pöbel meint...") and the Variations on a Theme by Sarti K. 460 ("Come un' agnello...") there exist two versions. The Gluck variations are known in a first draft and in a finished version (*Reinschrift*) that was written down one and a half years after he had played them in front of Gluck. It served as a basis for the first edition, which Torricella brought out in 1785, and Artaria in 1786. The case of the Sarti Variations K. 460 is the more intriguing: There exists an unfinished fragment of fifty-six measures containing the theme and only two variations, preserved in his handwriting; in this case, the theme is twenty-four measures long. There also exists a complete set of nine (not eight!) variations where Mozart used a different and more concise part from the same aria "Come un agnello," and here the theme is sixteen measures long and is the same one he quoted in the banquet scene of the opera *Don Giovanni*. Besides, Mozart inserted a cadenza, in this case one that he had also used in the variation set on a theme of Paesiello K. 398.[1] Because it is psychologically impossible to believe that only two variations on his theme would have pleased Sarti "very much," as Mozart reported in his letter, the most likely explanation of this riddle is that Mozart prepared himself for his encounter with Sarti, trying out first the longer variant of the theme and discarded it in favor of the more concise one of sixteen measures. (What we shall never know is whether he wrote them down before or after his meeting with Sarti. He then remembered it when composing the banquet scene.)

Much less is known about the composition of the Duport Variations K. 573, for which Mozart used a minuet from Duport's sixth Sonata for Two Cellos. Again, Mozart's autograph is lost.[2] It is interesting that in his own catalogue, Mozart mentioned only six variations, while the finished version, published also by Artaria, contains nine variations plus an epilogue. The various lead-ins of the Variation cycle K. 613 will be discussed below.

In Mozart's finished and unfinished fantasies one can find many fermatas before and/or after written-out embellishments; e.g., in the D minor Fantasy K. 397 in mm. 11, 28, 34, 53, 54, and 86; or in the C minor Fantasy K. 475 in mm. 35, 82, 85, 160. These fermatas mark the beginning or the end of fully composed and notated lead-ins or virtuoso passages, usually fast runs. It would be absurd to add additional ornamentation notes at those points or replace Mozart's embellishments through new ones. But a study of these fermata embellishments is useful for composing one's own cadenzas and lead-ins for those concerto movements, where an original one is missing.

Composing Cadenzas for Mozart's Concertos

Let us first state that the stylistic characteristics of any particular concerto by Mozart also have to determine the character of its cadenza(s). While it is hardly possible to make up anything that can stand comparison with Mozart's own music, we should still try to come near to his personal style and the quality of his music. Why? We start from the assumption that a cadenza to a Mozart concerto should sound like Mozart. (This view, however, is not universally shared. There exist innumerable cadenzas in styles quite different from Mozart's. Even with cadenzas of great composers like Beethoven, Brahms, Britten, or Frank Martin, who wrote cadenzas to Mozart's concertos in their own style, we adhere to our conviction that these cadenzas are more or less extraneous disturbing entities.)

To write stylistically suitable cadenzas, one must be absolutely familiar with the whole respective scheme of the concerto in question and especially with the harmonic progressions. Mozart's diatonic passages are much easier to imitate than his often very complicated chromatic progressions and enharmonic changes. To imitate the latter while remaining in style

---

[1] As with so many other variation cycles, this set of nine variations is known to us only through an Artaria print; the autograph is lost. In all editions of Mozart's piano variations, these nine variations are printed; sometimes the two variations on the longer theme are also included. The only edition where this set with nine variation is missing is the *NMA* volume because its editor, Kurt von Fischer, doubted Mozart's authorship.

[2] A reconstruction of K. 573's original text, edited by Paul Badura-Skoda, was published in 2007 by Alfred Publications.

is particularly difficult, because even in his boldest chromatic progressions Mozart kept strictly within certain limits, which are sometimes difficult to define. But in his cadenzas, one rule can be observed: Mozart never strays far from the tonic key, never really modulates into other keys using them as a new basis. He rarely employs complicated harmonic alterations. Even when a cadenza seems to modulate strikingly, it always returns after a few measures to the tonic or a related key. Following a short pause, the play of sequences and exploratory harmonies will then start anew. Even Mozart's boldest turns of harmony are achieved only with the aid of major and minor triads, major and minor seventh chords, the dominant seventh, the diminished triad, and the various inversions of the diminished seventh. Augmented triads hardly ever occur in their own right but only as passing harmonies or suspensions. Mozart's harmonic boldness lies mostly in the surprising juxtaposition of chords that are only indirectly related; in other words: it is horizontal (arising from the flow of the music) and not vertical. With his technique in this respect, it is surprising what impressive results he can achieve. (A special well-known example of his great art in this respect is mm. 11ff. of the C minor Fantasia K. 475, where Mozart uses a succession of ordinary dominant sevenths and minor first inversions over a chromatically descending bass and accomplishes an absolutely breathtaking effect without making a single chromatic alteration. Naturally, this cannot be copied. But due to the intended virtuoso element of cadenzas, it is a bit easier to compose cadenzas à la Mozart than to invent a Mozartean fantasy such as K. 475!)

One element of a personal style is the voluntary recognition of certain limits a composer obeys, in which one's fantasy is entirely free. Without such perceived limits, fantasy would lose its sense of direction. Cadenzas in a wholly un-Mozartean style are still a good deal more disturbing than those that, for all their paleness as compared to Mozart's own beautiful cadenzas, do at least keep within the limits of his style. A cadenza in a later style (romantic, impressionistic, atonal, etc.) cannot help but offend the spirit of the work. In the cadenza, the soloist should throw new light on the themes occurring in the piece in an appropriate way; he or she should further extend the content of what has already been said and may give a personal view of it; but one must not go too far in this respect, for this will endanger the external and internal unity of the concerto. Mozart gave the cadenza only a fairly subsidiary place in his concertos. Its function is to delay the final *tutti* and at the same time to enhance its effect. Thus the cadenza must always have a linking character. It is also important that it should not be out of proportion—inappropriate (unstylish) long cadenzas often suggest a tumor in an organism that is otherwise perfect and healthy. A quotation from Daniel Schubart shows that Mozart's contemporaries apparently had a strongly developed sense of the necessity of stylistic unity:

> *If I am to perform a Sonata by Bach* [C. P. E. Bach], *I must sink myself so completely in the spirit of this great man that my identity disappears and becomes Bach's idiom.* (Ideen zur Tonkunst, p. 295)

Mozart's fast concerto movements can usually be classed in a small number of categories: We observed that there are *cantabile* and festive allegro maestoso movements, allegretto grazioso finali, or elegant 6/8 meter final rondos. For almost all of these types there exist appropriate original cadenzas, which one can take as models in writing one's own.

In composing cadenzas, it is useful to begin by selecting from the movement all the motives and passages that may be suited to a development of the kind customary in a cadenza; these should be written out. This makes it much easier to see new ways of combining them. We see no objection to incorporating into one's cadenza whole passages from those by Mozart (transposed if necessary). Thus, mm. 23–30 of the cadenza for the third movement of the

Concerto K. 595 can be used without any great effort in a cadenza for the final movement of K. 482, because these measures are nonthematic and neutral. After all, on more than one occasion Mozart used certain passages repeatedly in his cadenzas—compare, for instance, mm. 23–24 of the second cadenza for K. 414 with the cadenza for K. 488 or the final run in the cadenza for K. 449 with that in K. 453 at the corresponding point. The first twelve bars of the long (second) cadenza for the first movement of K. 414 could thus be used, for example, to open a cadenza for the first movement of the "Coronation" Concerto K. 537, the only necessary alteration being then transpositions to D major and a slight change in the spacing of the *arpeggios*.

One of the most common mistakes of cadenzas composed for Mozart's concertos by performers (today; but not only today!) is that they are often far too long. It seems that the worst offenders in this respect are violinists, who often play intolerable cadenzas of excessive length, which are also available in print and stylistically inept and often lacking in musical originality. (Exceptions to this rule are cadenzas composed by Eduard Melkus, Marius Flothuis, and Robert Levin, which are available in print and heartily recommended to violinists.) In his *Klavierschule* (1789, V/II, §12, p. 309) Türk gave a special warning against excessively long cadenzas:

> *I would be saying nothing new, but merely repeating a complaint already made many times, if I were to speak out against the very great misuse of decorated cadenzas. For it not seldom seems that a concerto, etc., is played solely for the sake of the cadenzas. In them, the performer goes astray not merely with respect to the length that is fitting, but also by introducing all kinds of passage work, etc., that have not the slightest connection with the work that has preceded, so that the impression made by the work upon the listener is to a great extent effaced.*

Mozart's longest cadenza for a 6/8 movement is thirty-nine bars long (for K. 453), for a 4/4 movement forty bars (K. 595), and for a finale in 2/4 meter fifty-four bars (K. 459). The longest cadenza in a 3/4 motion is that for the first movement of K. 413 (thirty-two bars). All his other cadenzas are shorter, some considerably so. Thus, he once composed a cadenza for the first movement of K. 246 that is a mere five measures long and only later wrote longer cadenzas for this same movement. A recently discovered cadenza for the first movement of the Concerto K. 238 also consists merely of a few runs and a final trill. If only we could always hear such short cadenzas, which do not jeopardize the unity of the movement!

Türk was one of the few theorists who formulated rules for constructing cadenzas and lead-ins (*Klavierschule*, p. 387f.). These rules are also valid for Mozart's cadenzas, and we therefore quote them here:

> *1. If I am not mistaken, the cadenza's main effect should be not only to sustain the effect made by the piece, but also to reinforce it as much as possible. This can be most surely done if it presents the main ideas with extreme terseness, or at least recalls them by similar phrases. It must therefore have the most exact connections with the piece that has been played, or rather it should take its material from the latter, on the basis of what is most important.*

And in a note, he added:

> *If this is correct, it follows that much talent, insight, judgment, etc., is necessary to construct a cadenza which will satisfy the demands mentioned.*

2. *The cadenza, like all embellishments introduced at will, should consist not so much of carefully introduced difficulties but should contain phrases which are appropriate to the general character of the piece.*

3. *Cadenzas should not be too long, particularly in pieces whose character is sad, etc. Monstrously long cadenzas lasting several minutes are on no account to be excused.*

4. *One must on no account stray into musical country where the composer has not been in the course of the piece. This rule has its basis, I think, in the law of the unity of a work of art. ...*

And in the same context finally:

9. *Moreover any cadenza, including one that has been sketched and written down beforehand or learned from memory, must be played as if it were a fantasy which has only just been thought of in the course of playing.*

Finally, we should mention two procedures that Mozart avoids in his cadenzas:

1. He avoids introducing one motive or theme after another, without any clear division, as in a potpourri.

2. He never makes the ending of the cadenza identical with the ending of the final solo. In particular, the left hand must have a sustained chord at the end of the cadenza. In concerto movements, the right hand usually ends cadenzas with a trill to facilitate the entry of the orchestra.

We shall now offer some suggestions as to how one can prepare cadenzas for those concertos where none survive from Mozart's pen and how to ensure that they are as faithful as possible to his style. In this respect, his own cadenzas are naturally the ideal models. As might be expected, Mozart's cadenzas vary greatly in form. For purposes of analysis, the most useful models are the cadenzas for first movements, as Mozart was usually freer in laying out the cadenzas for his other movements; moreover, in his late concertos K. 488, K. 491, K. 503, and K. 537, he usually demands a cadenza only in their first movements.

In almost all of Mozart's own cadenzas one can make out a clear division into three parts: (1) an opening, which begins either with one of the themes of the concerto movement or with virtuoso passage work, some of it new and some of it already employed; in either case, the opening passes over into (2) a middle section, which is almost always a sequential development of an important theme or motive from the concerto movement, usually leading to the dominant or a sustained six-four chord, or sometimes a long note in the lower register. This is the starting point for a number of virtuoso runs, *arpeggios*, etc., that leads to (3) the closing section of the cadenza and—with the exception of the cadenza in K. 491/I—always ends on a trill. This stereotypical trill ending made it possible for the orchestra to know when to come in properly, even when there had been no time for rehearsals.

Opening Sections of Cadenzas

Let us first look at the two possible ways of opening a cadenza.

A Thematic Opening. If a Mozart cadenza begins in this way, it tends to use the first subject of the movement (e.g., in the first movement of the Concerto in G major, K. 453, with, however, another harmonization; likewise, in many cadenzas in rondo movements). But it can also be the motive heard in the orchestra immediately before the fermata; this is the case in the cadenzas for the first movement of the E-flat major Concerto K. 271; the *Concert Rondo* in D

Major, K. 382; the first movements of the Concerto K. 415 in C Major; the Concerto in E-flat Major, K. 449; the Concerto in B-flat Major, K. 450; and the Concerto in B-flat Major, K. 238. In this case, it can often happen that the piano takes up for the first time a motive previously heard only in the orchestra. Indeed, this is a very effective way of revealing new strata in the work's materials. It is distinctly rarer for Mozart to use a theme from the middle of a movement at the opening of a cadenza (he does this only in the first cadenza for the first movement of the A major Concerto K. 414 and in the single cadenza for the final movement of the Concerto in F Major, K. 459).

In slow movements, it happens that Mozart sometimes introduces a new theme as in the first cadenza for the slow movement of the G major Concerto K. 453/II and in the cadenza for the slow movement of the B-flat major Concerto K. 238. But this is a liberty that only Mozart could allow himself. We recommend that everybody else should wisely refrain from such audacity.

Almost all these thematic openings do not quote the complete theme; moreover, they often alter the harmonization and soon give way to passage work. This virtuoso continuation is again often taken from motives of the movement concerned. Thus, in the cadenza for the first movement of K. 450, the first eight (thematic) measures are followed by a chain of runs taken from mm. 119ff. of the movement

Ex. VII/1:

transformed into mm. 9ff. of the cadenza:

Ex. VII/2:

In this cadenza, the continuation passes directly into the second subject, the middle section of the cadenza.

But there are many cases in which this virtuoso continuation of the opening reaches a brief point of rest (mostly on a dominant seventh chord), from which there arises further free passage work as a transition to the middle section. One example is the cadenza for the first movement of the B-flat major Concerto K. 595, bars 9–12:

Ex. VII/3:

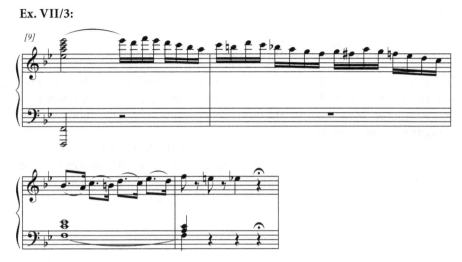

(See also mm. 12–16 of the cadenza for the first movement of K. 271.)

An exception to this rule is the first of the two additional cadenzas (K. 624 [626a], no. 26) for the first movement of the B-flat major Concerto K. 456, in which the middle section is preceded by not one but two fermatas:

Ex. VII/4:

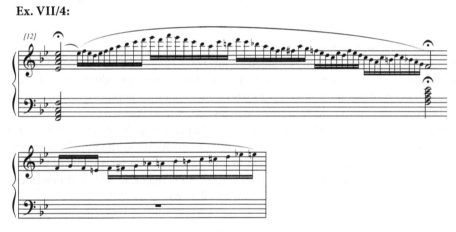

To compensate for this extension, the middle and closing sections of this cadenza are kept unusually short.

A Virtuoso Opening.   The motives of this type of beginning, too, are taken more or less clearly from the preceding movement, as one can see in the cadenzas for the first movements of the piano concertos K. 459 in F Major, K. 488 in A major, and K. 595 in B-flat major; only rarely is it cast in a completely free mold, as in the second cadenza for the first movement of the B-flat major Concerto K. 456 (whose authenticity is not beyond doubt).

From the harmonic point of view, both types of opening, thematic and virtuoso, have the task of facilitating the transition from the six-four chord at the fermata to a motive or theme in the tonic; furthermore, this transition has to be as interesting as possible. Thus most openings of cadenzas are in effect written-out dominants.

Ex. VII/5:

It is noteworthy that the themes quoted in Mozart's cadenzas are, when the opening is thematic, always in the tonic key, in which case the theme is usually heard over the second inversion of the tonic chord. But when the theme does not appear until the middle section, it will have its original harmonization.

One apparent exception to this rule is the cadenza for the first movement of the Concerto in A major, K. 488. In this cadenza, the subsidiary figure enters surprisingly in B minor, but A minor is then reached again after two measures (variant of the tonic A major). The harmonic scheme of the first fourteen bars of this cadenza is the following:

Ex. VII/6:

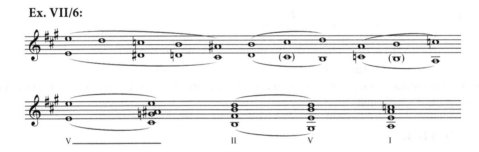

This B minor has a subdominant function.

In his cadenzas, Mozart obviously wanted to confirm the key of the movement rather than call it into question (as is done, for example, by the very widely ranging modulations in Beethoven's cadenzas). It is a pity that most interpreters who compose new cadenzas for Mozart's concertos ignore this important principle: Mozart's cadenzas do not modulate.

Harmonically, Mozart usually makes a link with the preceding chord of the *tutti*. First-movement themes are rarely quoted in their original harmonization (on the tonic) but mostly over a 6/4 chord, usually without any bass in the first two bars, so that for a moment the harmony is only latently heard. This is the case in the Concerto in G major, K. 453, first movement (free continuation with another motive derived from the flute part mm. 311ff.):

Ex. VII/7:

We owe this observation to Robert Levin.

A similar use of motives from the movement is found in the cadenza of the Concerto in B-flat Major, K. 450/I:

Ex. VII/8:

However, in this cadenza, the regular eight-bar period that begins it is a rare exception to the rule that cadenzas usually contain no full periods, which means that themes are never quoted in full but open at the end and continued differently, often sequentially.

One of Mozart's favorite harmonic successions for the opening of a cadenza is built on a descending bass line, as in the Concerto in E-flat major, K. 449, first movement:

Ex. VII/9:

The openings of the cadenzas for the first movement of K. 271/I and the second movement of K. 414/II (second cadenza) are built on the same harmonic scheme. Many cadenzas also begin with a pedal point; e.g., those for the first movements of K. 413 and K. 459 and the Concert Rondo K. 382.

The cadenza for the first movement of the Two-Piano Concerto K. 365 starts on the tonic, after a rising run leading from the 6/4 chord:

Ex. VII/10:

The harmonic scheme in the cadenza for the first movement of the B-flat major Concerto K. 595, with its motive taken from the movement is also very interesting:

Ex. VII/11:

The underlying harmonic scheme is the following:

Ex. VII/12:

$$(\text{latent } I^{6\,5}_{4\,3}) \qquad I \qquad I^6 \quad V^4_2 \quad I^6 \quad I^3 \quad vi^{\;6}\; vi^{\;3} \quad IV^6 \; IV^3 \qquad ii^{\;6}$$

Continuation of the harmonic scheme (mm. 6ff. of the cadenza):

Ex. VII/13:

$$IV \qquad\qquad ii^6 \qquad\qquad V^6 \qquad\qquad I^6 \qquad\qquad IV^6 \; iv^6 \quad V$$

The falling bass line first descends four times through a third, and then, as a harmonic accelerando, three times through a fifth; the upper part moves in contrary motion, three times through a fourth, taking in the intermediate chromatic steps.

One of Mozart's finest cadenza openings is that of the first movement of the F major Concerto K. 459. Mozart starts first with passage work over a pedal point (with chromatic intermediate steps in mm. 3 and 4 of the cadenza), and then he introduces the first subject with a new and, for him, unusual harmonization—the third inversion of the dominant seventh (based on the second note of the scale) at the start of a descending bass progression:

Ex. VII/14:

It is also unusual for Mozart to introduce then the second theme of the cadenza over a 6/4 chord (m. 18), as he does in this movement of K. 459/I. It shows that Mozart liked variety (and sometimes also exceptions to rules).

Here we should mention again that Mozart inserted written-out cadenzas not only in concertos but also in some of his piano sonatas. In one of these sonata cadenzas, the harmonic progression is interesting insofar as at the outset of the cadenza the tonic minor is introduced in the fifth measure. This abrupt change from major to minor is perceived like a "shadow," creating a special emotional effect. (And the change from minor to major is like a "sunlight upshot." Such changes are not only often found in Mozart's works but were typical features of many Viennese composers of the pre-Classical and Classical periods and thus are used in works from Wagenseil to Schubert.) We find an example of this effect in the final movement of the Piano Sonata in B-flat major, K. 333:

Ex. VII/15:

When composing cadenzas for concertos, the use of this major–minor or minor–major change is recommended.

Though the openings of cadenzas vary greatly in length, it is very important to be aware of the fact that they are rarely shorter than six or longer than twelve measures—a length that nowadays too many artists overstep.

Middle Sections of Cadenzas

As shown above, the opening of Mozart's cadenzas often starts with a theme in the tonic or quotes a theme after some introductory runs and figures. For the middle sections of cadenzas, on the other hand, Mozart prefers *cantabile* themes, often second subjects, as in the cadenzas of the first movements of the concertos K. 271, K. 415, K. 450, K. 453, K. 456, and K. 595. In the second cadenza for K. 414, however, the opening of the cadenza is for once followed by the first subject, which Mozart has refrained from using in the introductory passage. An exception is found in the finale of the Concerto K. 450, where the first subject in fact appears twice in the course of the same cadenza: at the beginning in the upper voice, and in the second section in the bass, in the subdominant.

The motivic treatment in the cadenza of the third movement of the B-flat major Concerto K. 595 is particularly skillful and impressive. The first section of this large-scale cadenza develops only the opening bars of the first theme in two waves (mm. 1–10 and 11–27); the middle section then uses mm. 5–6 of the first subject as a kind of new theme (mm. 31–39). This cadenza also furnishes a good example for a nearly uninterrupted succession of sequences.

It is also interesting to study the way Mozart treated the themes in the cadenza of the first movement of his E-flat major Concerto K. 449. The final trill that ends the exposition of this movement appears in the cadenza followed by a striking motive (mm. 169–176). This motive is lacking in the recapitulation but then appears in the cadenza as the second theme. At the close of the movement, he did not give this motive to the orchestra so that, when it appears as the second theme in the cadenza, it would become more effective.

The cadenza for the first movement of the Concerto in A major, K. 488, is a special case. Here Mozart introduced a completely new motive at an important point, an approach he otherwise favored only in cadenzas for slow movements (e.g., in K. 238 and K. 453).

In quoting themes in the middle sections of cadenzas, Mozart generally follows a harmonic scheme. Whereas in the body of the movement these themes are rounded off by means of a cadence in the final bars to form a self-contained whole, in the cadenza Mozart uses a technique that is best described as "continuous development" (*Fortspinnung*).[3] Prior to it, some motive from the theme is unexpectedly treated in sequence, often in rhythmic diminution. This is done in such a way that the motive almost always ends with a sustained chord or note. Often this section leads on to the dominant of the supertonic key; e.g., in the cadenzas for the G major Concerto K. 453, but most often also to the dominant of the dominant, from where it passes back to the dominant or on to the second inversion of the tonic, as in the cadenzas for the first movements of the concertos K. 449, K. 456, K. 459, and K. 595.

We shall quote now four examples of this flow of Mozart's middle sections, and in each case we quote first the theme as it appears in the body of the movement and then as it is used in the cadenza.

1. E-flat major Concerto K. 271, first movement, mm. 225–232:

Ex. VII/16:

Cadenza, mm. 17–29:

Ex. VII/17:

---

[3] The extraordinarily relevant and important concept of *Fortspinnung* (here translated as "continuous development") was first coined by W. Fischer in "Zur Entwicklungsgeschichte des Wiener klassischen Stils"; see also F. Blume, "Fortspinnung und Entwicklung," p. 51ff.

2. E-flat major Concerto K. 449, first movement, mm. 63–70 (orchestra):

Ex. VII/18:

Cadenza, mm. 14–24:

Ex. VII/19:

3. G major Concerto K. 453, first movement, mm. 290–297:

Ex. VII/20:

Cadenza, mm. 19–26:

Ex. VII/21:

The bold harmonies are a result of a succession of first and third inversions, plus accented passing notes, over a chromatically descending bass. This theme is built originally over a diatonically descending bass line, with each entry of the motive a fifth lower than the preceding one. In the cadenza, the bass line's diatonic motion is held up when it reaches the submediant; it remains stationary for a while and then unexpectedly continues downward chromatically.

4. B-flat major Concerto K. 456/I, mm. 299–302:

Ex. VII/22:

Cadenza No. 2, mm. 14–17:

Ex. VII/23:

Another interesting procedure occurs in the cadenza to the first movement of the B-flat major Concerto K. 595, where the sequential treatment culminates not in a sustained note but in a general pause in the twenty-first measure. Mozart thus makes a clear distinction between the way he uses his themes in the body of the movement and in the cadenza: In the concerto itself the themes are linked in a very fluid manner, interwoven with no apparent seams, whereas in his cadenzas he was obviously anxious to show that this network, for all its apparent solidity, could be pulled apart again without difficulty. In contrast, Beethoven had quite a different technique for building up his cadenzas: They became self-contained rounded musical essays, which for dramatic quality could compete with the main body of the movement or even surpass it. An example is the cadenza for the first movement of his B-flat major Concerto, op. 19 (composed much later than the concerto itself); it opens with a *fugato* in the style of the "*Hammerklavier*" Sonata, op. 106.

Closing Sections of Cadenzas

It is in the shaping of final sections of his cadenzas that Mozart allows his imagination its freest play, not tying himself to any scheme. All the same, one can say that, generally speaking, the final section of a cadenza contains a number of virtuoso runs, some of which are written in small notes. These runs occur frequently, not only in the cadenzas of his piano concertos but also in cadenza-like passages in other piano works, such as the finale of the B-flat major Piano Sonata K. 333, the Rondo K. 494 in its version as final movement of Sonata K. 533, and, above all, in his various sets of variations. In these latter works, the cadenzas are usually nonthematic, for the obvious reason that the theme has already been quite sufficiently developed and varied. There is a great deal to be learned from these nonthematic cadenzas; they have a kind of neutral character, and for this reason considerable parts of them can be incorporated in one's own cadenzas for the concertos.

Whereas in the Salzburg concertos, such as K. 271, the closing sections of the cadenzas are distinctly short, Mozart later began to extend this section and to enrich it with thematic material. In those cases where the continuation of the middle section leads to the dominant, the final section almost always leads, after a scale passage, to a new quotation of motives in the tonic, then to the six-four chord again, usually with the aid of the sharpened fourth (dominant of the dominant), as in the first cadenza of the G major Concerto K. 453, from the twenty-sixth bar onward:

Ex. VII/24:

The motive in the left hand marked "NB" stems inter alia from mm. 275ff. of the movement. (By the way, the motive in mm. 28–29 is not only drawn from this concerto but is found also in the Piano Sonata in G major, K. 283.)

In order to delay the end of the cadenza, another harmonic turn toward the subdominant is possible:

Ex. VII/25:

(Compare also the cadenza for the first movement of the Concerto K. 595, mm. 27–31.)

In the final section of the second cadenza for the Concerto K. 456/I (authenticity questioned), we find motives from mm. 95 and 136 of the movement. In the B-flat major Concerto K. 595 we first hear the "call motive" in mm. 5 and 6 of the opening *tutti*, interestingly harmonized, and later, after some runs and *arpeggios*, a slightly varied form of the first subject of the movement, treated in canon (mm. 33ff.):

Ex. VII/26:

(See Ex. IV/33 on p. 115.)

It is a harmonic characteristic of these closing sections that Mozart often introduces the supertonic or subdominant, possibly using secondary dominants (*Zwischendominanten*), to ensure a more definite feeling that the cadenza is reaching its final cadence.

The final trill is usually very simple:

Ex. VII/27:

Double (or even triple) trills in thirds or sixths occur very rarely and only in the concertos for two and three pianos. However, since Mozart sometimes did write these trills, it is clear that he considered them possible and musically admissible and avoided them only on grounds of technical difficulty. In the first movement of the Concerto K. 450, for instance, he wrote an ascending scale of double-thirds triplets leading to a right-hand double trill in thirds over an *Alberti* bass accompaniment. This is one of a number of passages in the two concertos K. 450 and K. 451 that Mozart ultimately simplified, apparently finding those passages too difficult to play. Modern pianists trained on Beethoven and Chopin should consider them less difficult; although there is no real necessity for a use of a double trill in one's own cadenza, it might be introduced occasionally.

As pointed out, one of Mozart's most original cadenzas is that for the third movement of the F major Concerto K. 459. At the end of this cadenza Mozart interchanges the two opening motives from the principal subject, thus deriving at new material:

Ex. VII/28:

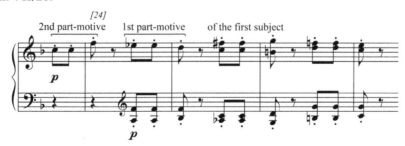

(canonic imitation of the previous measure)

The lowest voice is a canonic imitation (canon in the lower fifth) of the treble voice in the previous measure. There is also a pleasantly Beethovenian effect when Mozart uses the main motive of this movement in the left hand as a counterpoint to an eight-bar-long trill before he finally rounds off the cadenza:

Ex. VII/29:

The texture of Mozart's cadenzas is usually homophonic. There are, however, a few short passages of quite masterful polyphony. The way in which Mozart alters his themes, most of them not very suitable for polyphonic treatment, is extraordinarily interesting. By a great stroke of good fortune, the original cadenzas for the Two-Pianos Concerto in E-flat major, K. 365, were rediscovered after World War I, and the cadenza for the third movement is a good example of this kind.

When Mozart needed a final movement for the two beautiful sonata movements K. 533, he added an extra twenty-seven bars to his Rondo K. 494 and used it as a final movement for this sonata. These extra measures have the character of a cadenza. The interval of a third, so characteristic of the principal theme, is simply altered to a fourth and a fifth, obviously with the intention of using it to facilitate imitation. Mozart then ties the first eighth note of the second bar to the preceding note (mm. 152ff.):

Ex. VII/30:

becomes:

But back to the cadenzas intended for concerto movements: In the twenty-third measure of the cadenza for the third movement of the D major Concerto K. 451, Mozart uses the (unaltered) second subject as the basis of a delightful *fugato*, which starts off with a *stretto*:

Ex. VII/31:

The cadenza for the first movement of this concerto also starts polyphonically, with a canon at a fourth note lower, but this has been already heard in the course of the movement and is therefore not felt to be new when it occurs in the cadenza. The most interesting passage of this type is the "cadenza in tempo" in the finale of the Quintet for Piano and Wind Instruments K. 452, which starts with a four-part *fugato stretto* (*Engführung*).[4]

To compose stylistically proper cadenzas one must be absolutely familiar with the harmonic progressions Mozart used frequently. The so-called "German augmented sixth" chord is an alteration that should not be chosen for cadenzas because Mozart does not use it in his cadenzas. Otherwise, this harmony is found frequently and occurs usually in the form of an augmented sixth chord plus fifth. In his later works, he often makes an enharmonic change in this chord, making it into a dominant seventh, before he finally resolves it; e.g., in K. 491/III. The frequent occurrence of the augmented sixth chord in Mozart's works is matched by his equally decided avoidance of its inversion, the diminished third. Here he adopts a view that survived into many twentieth-century harmony books—that this dissonance is displeasing and therefore forbidden. He usually replaces it by the minor third as though it were produced by an inversion:

Ex. VII/32:

From these observations it follows that in making up one's own cadenzas one should—if possible— avoid harmonies such as the one in the following example marked +, if one wants to keep in style:

Ex. VII/33:

---

[4] Mozart used the same technique for the *Cadenza in tempo* in the aria "Et incarnatus est…" of the C minor Mass K. 427 (Robert Levin).

The diminished seventh chord was apparently still a dissonance for Mozart, whereas in Beethoven's time it had already lost some of its pungent effect. It is the basis of many of Mozart's chromatic harmonies.[5]

In order to create harmonic tension, Mozart had the great composer's ability to exploit passing tones (notes), suspensions, pedal points, and stationary parts (voices). To illustrate the special effect that Mozart achieved by the use of accented passing notes against dominant sevenths and diminished sevenths, we quote here the mm. 31ff. of the B minor Adagio K. 540:

Ex. VII/34:

Harmonic scheme:

Ex. VII/35:

So much for analysis.

To illustrate the practical application of all these ideas, Paul Badura-Skoda composed cadenzas for Mozart's concertos, among them one for the first movement of the E-flat major Concerto K. 482.[6] After improving the alternative ending for this cadenza, which now keeps strictly within Mozartean limits, the closing section sounds like this:

---

[5] There is a typical example of it in the C major Fantasia K. 394, m. 46, where we find a succession of six diminished-seventh chords, which in Mozart's day was probably a bold invention, perhaps without precedence.

[6] Published by Doblinger in 1956 together with cadenzas for the concertos K. 491 and K. 503. For an altered (improved?) version, see Paul Badura-Skoda, *Kadenzen, Eingänge und Auszierungen zu den Klavierkonzerten von W. A. Mozart*, BVK 1967.

Ex. VII/36:

Lead-ins and Other Fermata Embellishments

We have already mentioned that lead-ins, unlike cadenzas, rarely show any motivic connection with the main body of the movement (the *Eingänge* in K. 415, K. 450, and K. 595 are exceptions to this rule) but consist of scales, leaps, ornaments, and various kinds of passage work. They are mostly found at points where two successive but clearly distinct sections of a movement are to be linked by a short solo. Despite this transitional character, they are still introductions and best to be considered literally "as lead-ins" because the preceding section is rarely reflected in them. Marked with a fermata on a dominant seventh chord, they are nearly always built on the dominant of the succeeding section in Mozart's piano concertos. An exception occurs in the third movement of the Concerto in B-flat Major, K. 238; as Robert Levin pointed out, in this movement one of the lead-ins comes after a perfect cadence in D minor preceding the return of the Rondo theme in the tonic key of B-flat, a case also mirrored in several of the violin concertos.

Naturally, lead-ins should be kept much shorter than cadenzas. In other groups of works, such as in the G major Violin Concerto K. 216, there are also half cadences on the dominant of the relative minor. In such cases the lead-in must contain at least two different harmonies to come to a proper continuation, as in K. 216/III, m. 217:

Ex. VII/37:

But usually lead-ins linger on one harmony, as in the sixteen-measure-long lead-in found in the finale of the Piano Concerto K. 450. The following variants are, however, possible:

Transitional harmonies, as in the lead-in of K. 271/III:

Ex. VII/38:

Played (basic harmonic scheme of the lead-in):

Ex. VII/39:

or:

Ex. VII/40:

Another possibility is a detour to the dominant of the dominant as, e.g., the scheme of the lead-in of K. 595/III (transposed into C major):

Ex. VII/41:

This scheme is found, however, only in the lead-in of Mozart's last piano concerto.

One should naturally avoid anticipating the tonic triad in the course of a lead-in. In Ex. VII/39 above, it would be a mistake to play the following bass (the upper parts remaining the same):

Ex. VII/42:

Particularly good examples of model lead-ins composed by Mozart are found in the third movement of the Concerto K. 271 (three different sets) as well as in the piano concertos K. 415, K. 450, and K. 595. For lead-ins in slow movements, one should study the two original examples in the A major Concerto K. 414.

The most instructive examples of original lead-ins, however, are found in the Piano Variations K. 613 on "Ein Weib ist das herrlichste Ding." In this work, the theme already contains a written-out original lead-in, and for each variation Mozart wrote a different version of this lead-in. This is a *locus classicus*; it is immensely informative as to how Mozart regularly reinvented new versions of lead-ins, and they are recommended for special study. The transitional run found in the theme becomes an even eighth-note motion for the right hand in Variation I (Ex. VII/44); in Variation II (Ex. VII/45) the lead-in is given to the bass; in Variation III, triplet motion is used; in Variation V (Ex. VII/46), the motion is in sixteenths throughout; in Variation VII (Ex. VII/47), the lead-in is a particularly interesting and complex adagio passage; and, finally, in Variation VIII (Ex. VII/48), there follows an extended lead-in to the Allegro theme. It is Mozart's longest fermata embellishment in this variation cycle.

The lead-in in m. 32 of the variation theme is relatively short:

Ex. VII/43:

Variation I:

Ex. VII/44:

Variation II:

Ex. VII/45:

Variation V:

Ex. VII/46:

Variation VII:

Ex. VII/47:

Variation VIII:

Ex. VII/48:

Proper Places for Fermata Embellishments

When is a lead-in asked for and when not? Naturally, not every fermata invites or allows the insertion of a lead-in, but fermatas in the piano concertos are usually intended to be interpreted this way. In this connection, we may relate an early experience of the coauthor, pianist Paul Badura-Skoda. Because he felt that the fermata at m. 254 of the finale of the F major Piano Concerto K. 459 needed a lead-in, he invented one and played it in 1956 at a rehearsal for a concert under the direction of Karl Böhm, to the great surprise of the orchestra musicians and the protest of the conductor, famous as a Mozart conductor but still reluctant to add foreign notes to a Mozart work (Mahler's view). Böhm did not consider it proper to embellish this fermata and requested that the young artist leave the fermata unembellished for the concert performance.

To our delight, soon afterwards, Mozart's autograph of a previously unknown original lead-in for exactly this spot was discovered by Hellmut Federhofer and proved that something "was missing" indeed at this fermata. Mozart's original lead-in (it was pasted into a manuscript copy of the concerto formerly owned by one of Mozart's pupils) is now printed in the *NMA* vol. XV/5 on p. 217, and its discovery shows that in rondo movements such as this one Mozart wants a lead-in to be played at fermatas. Besides, Paul Badura-Skoda's lead-in fortunately resembled Mozart's newly discovered one. It was this one:

Ex. VII/49:

More authentic cadenzas and lead-ins would probably have gotten lost and are preserved only because, fortunately, in 1801 the Viennese publisher Artaria decided to print a collection of Mozart's own cadenzas and lead-ins for his piano concertos. In some cases, this print is the only source for authentic Mozart cadenzas and lead-ins. Köchel listed all the cadenzas collected by Artaria together with other authentic cadenzas and lead-ins under the number K. 626a.

Mozart also composed many lead-ins and cadenzas in serenades and in various chamber music works. Thus, lead-ins and short fermata embellishments are not solely a peculiarity of concertos, arias, variation cycles, or sonatas, and sometimes original ones are missing and the performer has to invent one. A typical spot where a lead-in seems necessary is the half cadence in the last movement of the G minor Piano Quartet K. 478, a work in which the piano part has a *concertante* character. In m. 135 we suggest a lively introduction to the return of the main theme, something like this:

Ex. VII/50:

Another lead-in for this fermata, similar to the one Hellmut Federhofer suggested in the relevant *NMA* volume, can also be recommended:

Ex. VII/51:

The fact that Mozart usually notated his fermata embellishments on extra sheets is probably the reason that an original lead-in is missing here. This could be also the reason that we do not have an original fermata embellishment for m. 195 of the first movement of the Concerto K. 414. In this case, however, the editor of the *NMA* volume unfortunately forgot to point out that a lead-in is missing.

We suggest the following embellishment for this fermata in m. 195:

Ex. VII/52:

In the Piano Sonata in B-flat major, K. 281/III, m. 173, a lead-in might have been intended; thus, the following one seems acceptable:

Ex. VII/53:

In the second movement of the Concerto K. 453 in mm. 33–34, this short fermata embellishment is found in the piano part (absent in the *tutti* in m. 4):

Ex. VII/54:

One could leave the fermata as such, but one could also play here the following more elaborate ornamentation:

Ex. VII/55:

Likewise, an embellishment could be played in the same movement of K. 453 in m. 93:

Ex. VII/56:

Also, in the third movement of this Concerto in G major, K. 453, in mm. 169–170, the fermata means perhaps not just a stop but could also be an invitation to play an embellishment (this time not a lead-in), such as the following:

Ex. VII/57:

Fermatas on a half cadence on a six-four chord or dominant seventh chord are always an open invitation to play an embellishment, a lead-in, or a cadenza; for instance, the fermata in m. 254 of the third movement of the Concerto in F major, K. 459:

Ex. VII/58:

There exists another symbol of Mozart's calling for an embellished fermata, found, e.g., in the A major Concerto K. 414/II, m. 73:

Ex. VII/59:

For this fermata Mozart wrote two different versions for a lead-in to the following measure.

It is interesting to know that exactly the same notation is found at the beginning of the Violin Concerto in A major, K. 219, m. 45. Yet every violinist we have heard so far has played the trill literally and without embellishment. In the unlikely event that violinists read this book destined for pianists, we would like to suggest here an embellished version based on Mozart's own notated embellishment in K. 414:

Ex. VII/60:

It has been argued that the second fermata might not invite a lead-in because of the new tempo after the double bar line. This argument has a certain validity, though we feel that the fermata embellishment has a convincing function.

To repeat: Whereas cadenzas have a clearly marked place in concerto movements, it is indeed sometimes difficult to decide where a lead-in should be added and where not. Even musicians well known as Mozart specialists sometimes err; correct answers to questions of placement as well as of style are often difficult to find. These problems can be solved finally only through the discovery of hitherto unknown source material.

Fortunately, unknown sources are still found from time to time. Thanks to the Artaria print of collected cadenzas and lead-ins mentioned above, the cadenzas for the first and the last movements of Mozart's Concerto K. 595 have been known since the year 1800 (when the print was issued). They were listed under the numbers 34, 35, and 36 of K. 626a. Whereas the two cadenzas that are printed in the relevant *NMA* volume XV/8 are based on Artaria's edition, the lead-in K. 626a, no. 35, for the third movement (to be inserted at m. 130) is missing in this *NMA* volume because (as the editor explained in the preface) the editorial board and their advisor Ernst Hess were of the opinion that this special lead-in contained questionable modulations that were viewed as a reason to deny Mozart's authorship. In an article in the *Mozart Jahrbuch 1971*, Paul Badura-Skoda defended the authenticity of this uniquely inventive long fermata embellishment.[7] Fortunately, fifteen years later, in 1986, Mozart's autograph was discovered in Russia (Estonia) among other autographs of cadenzas; but because of the erroneous doubts as to its authorship, this beautiful lead-in could then be printed only in a supplement volume of the *NMA* (vol. X/31/3, p. 112).

Where Fermata Embellishments Are Questionable and Where No Lead-ins Should Be Played

The presence of a fermata is always the *sine qua non* for adding a cadenza or a short lead-in. As a general rule, one can say that the place for a lead-in occurs where two successive sections of a movement in the same tempo suggests that they are to be joined by a brief transition, and a fermata on a dominant chord suggests it. A lead-in seems appropriate here because such a short interlude is the natural way of making the sections join.

This explains why we think that a lead-in would be out of place between the slow introduction to an Allegro movement and its main part. In our opinion, it would diminish the surprise effect if the tempo change were disturbed by some embellishing notes. That would be the case, as stated above, in the first movements of the Quintet K. 452 or the Four-Hand Piano Sonata in F Major, K. 497 and also in the Sonata for Violin and Piano K. 454.

Certainly not to be embellished are the prolongation fermatas toward the end of the final movement of the C minor Sonata K. 457, mm. 231–243, which definitely serve a dramatic function. Because Mozart took pains to notate the embellished versions in the Adagio, it is highly unlikely that in this special sonata he would have simply forgotten to add notes here, had he wanted them. Besides, there is no half cadence in sight there.

To decide which meaning a fermata could have reminds us sometimes of the famous multiple-choice questions students are often confronted with in their exams and where not always a 100 percent correct answer can be given.

As we see from the most recent publications, e.g., in volumes of the *NMA*, it is obvious that the question as to when a fermata may or may not be embellished has not yet been definitely settled and may have to remain open. On the other hand, there are cases in which we feel that fermatas must be embellished; i.e., that stylistically correct interpretation demands a short lead-in as a transition to the next section. In Mozart's instrumental music, this type of fermata occurs almost exclusively in concerto movements. In theory, one could, of course, still consider embellishing a fermata in one or the other movement of the solo piano works. But this is only rarely practical, since Mozart wrote out his piano sonatas and fantasies with scrupulous care unusual for his time (especially when he decided and managed to have the works printed), and he wrote down most of the intended lead-ins himself. (By the way, Mozart's vocal music contains far more places than recognized by performers where lead-ins might be added.)

There exists of course no proof that lead-ins should only be added in concertos (and arias). But it is striking that whereas Mozart left numerous lead-ins for the piano concertos, written

---

[7] Paul Badura-Skoda, "Ein authentischer Eingang zum Klavierkonzert in B Dur KV 595?" p. 76ff.

down on odd sheets of paper, we do not know of a single lead-in for a solo piano work on a separate sheet. This is food for thought, since as a teacher Mozart used his piano sonatas probably even more often than his concertos; and if he had thought a lead-in necessary at any point he would surely have helped his pupils (who probably had little talent for composition) by writing one out for them.

In Mozart's chamber works, too, it is rarely possible or necessary to embellish fermatas and add lead-ins. We, at least, know very few passages in these works where we should welcome the addition of a lead-in; perhaps an exception is the fermata in the third movement of the Piano Trio K. 496 (immediately after the Adagio variation, prior to the *tempo primo*). Another possibility occurs between mm. 108 and 109 in the third movement of the F major Violin Sonata and in mm. 69 and 203 of the Piano Duet Sonata in C major, K. 521. Also, a lead-in might be appropriate in m. 135 of the third movement of the Piano Quartet K. 478; at all these points a lead-in could perhaps be added. For caution demands that we make it our principle to add a lead-in only when we can justify it by pointing to another original lead-in written-out by Mozart himself and at those parallel spots in his works that correspond formally and architecturally. Thus, we find it wrong to introduce lead-ins if there is no parallel passage to be found with an original lead-in to show that our decision is right. Our research has proven, for example, that also in symphonies Mozart never embellished fermatas at the end of slow introductions to following Allegro movements. It would be unsatisfactory on musical grounds to anticipate, for example, the effect of the Allegro in the "Prague" Symphony by adding a virtuoso run by the flute at the end of the short Adagio introduction. The same applies to the fermata at the end of the introduction to the "Linz" Symphony K. 425/I or the Wind Serenade K. 361. But if we feel that embellishment is out of place at these fermatas, then, to be consistent, we must also leave unembellished all other fermatas at similar points of formal construction.

The Various Meanings of Fermata Signs

Naturally, not every fermata found in Mozart's works has to be embellished. On the contrary: The principal function of a fermata sign is to indicate a *tenuto*; i.e., that one is to linger, to pause for a moment. The fermatas inviting players to insert some embellishing notes are rather a kind of exception.

Unlike most other musical symbols, the well-known sign ⌒ is ambiguous and has different meanings according to the context. While musical terminology is for the most part Italian and internationally accepted as such, it is perhaps significant that the word for fermata ("pause" in English) is different in most European languages: *point d'orgue* (French), *calderón* (Spanish), *corona* (originally Italian but often used still in Germany, too), *fermate* (German). In modern Italian, the word *fermata* means "bus stop." And recently, the meaning of a fermata has been compared indeed to a bus stop. Various purposes of these "halt!" indications—other than those demanding cadenzas or lead-ins—will also be dealt in the next chapter. Below, some examples will demonstrate fermatas with a meaning other than an interruption through a *capriccio*.

Regarding the optional meaning of fermatas we may state:

The most common meaning of ⌒ is a prolongation of a note or a rest. The immediate question that comes to mind is, of course: for how long?

Türk (1789, I/6, §84, p. 121) gives an excellent description:

It cannot be told exactly how long one has to stay on a fermata because it depends on various circumstances, e.g. whether one or several persons are playing, whether a piece has a lively or sad character, whether it is embellished or not, etc. If one were to discard these various circumstances, I should advise to double the value of a note or rest in slow movements and to quadruple it in fast tempo.

In our experience, the latter is often too long a hold. In some cases it may suffice to stay for one and a half times of the indicated value.

Only at the end of a cadenza the formula:

Ex. VII/61:

requires exact doubling:

Ex. VII/62:

Thus, even without a rehearsal the accompanying players know where to come in. This rule was so well known that even in case the fermata sign was missing (as, by mistake, in some original Mozart cadenzas), the note value of the final trill had to be doubled.

This happened once in a performance of the Concerto for Two Pianos K. 365: We played the final trill of the first cadenza as printed, namely, as only one measure (without fermata), and the conductor came in a fraction of a second too late. But the opposite mistake could also occur in a Mozart concerto: in the cadenza to the first movement of the Concerto for Three Pianos K. 242, Mozart notated a trill of two measures (as in Ex. VII/61) and added a fermata sign. In this case, however, both here and also later in the second movement, a prolonged trill of two full measures would be interminable.

In slow movements, a fermata sign over a rest may sometimes mean a very short halt or may even be ignored. Our late friend Marius Flothuis pointed out that, for instance, in the D minor Fantasy, K. 397, mm. 11 and 28, a correct observation of the pause would totally disrupt the musical flow, *il filo conduttore*. Here the pause should be shortened.[8]

A fermata can simply indicate an opportunity for taking a breath in between phrases, a "Luftpause." This seems to be the case in the cadenzas to the third movement of the A major Concerto K. 414 (we quote here from the shorter of the two authentic cadenzas):

Ex. VII/63:

---

[8] This advice is given in the performing edition of K. 397, ed. by Paul Badura-Skoda (LeDuc, Paris 1995).

To prolong the notes with every fermata would probably produce, in this case, the effect of approximately a 5/8 meter, rather unusual in Mozart's time, but not entirely to be ruled out.

A fermata could also indicate the end of a movement or a piece. A suggestion was made by Türk (in his *Klavierschule*, 1789, III/2, §146) that composers should be advised to put the word *fine* under those fermatas that signal the piece's end, because a less well-informed musician might misunderstand the fermata otherwise. In pieces with a *Da capo* indication or a *Lied* with several stanzas, the fermata indicating the end is valid only for the last return. If any notes that follow the double bar in a minuet with *Da capo* are there simply to provide continuity to the trio, they ought not to be played at the last return of the minuet.

This applies to the minuet in the Sonata in E-flat Major, K. 282. In the autograph there are two fermata signs in the last measure of the Menuetto I:

Ex. VII/ 64:

(The erroneous fermata signs on the double bar are found in the autograph.)
Here the low B-flat of the left hand is apparently not to be played at the very end of the minuet. (Some modern editions suppress all four fermata signs.)

It is an open question whether this rule also applies to places where the fermata on the first beat is not notated, as is the case in the frequent formula found often in symphonies or serenades.

Ex. VII/65:

But this is not so in the early Menuetto in F major, K. 2, where the left hand must play all three notes because of the right-hand dissonance that is resolved only on the third beat:

Ex. VII/66:

In the Divertimento for Wind instruments in B-flat Major, K. 186, Mozart himself answered this question: In the first menuetto, the last bass notes of the bassoon are an octave lower (B–B-flat) in the first part (m. 8), but at the end (m. 24) there is only one note, B-flat, likewise, in the trio.

For this very reason it seems to be justified to play only one bass note at the end of the menuetto of the Serenade "*Eine kleine Nachtmusik*" K. 525:

Ex. VII/67:

Noteworthy is a remark by Türk (in his *Klavierschule*, 1789, I/6 §85, p. 122), who wrote: "A fermata for indicating the end does not mean holding back (prolongation) in the measure [in time]."

In Mozart's variations on "A vous dirai-je, Maman" K. 265, the repeat of the first eight measures at the end of the theme and of most of the variations (mm. 7–24) is indicated by a *Da capo* sign after m. 16. In other words, the final eight measures are not notated. To make sure that the return ends in the right place, Mozart wrote a fermata sign at the end of m. 8. This fermata is not reproduced in any modern edition for the good reason that nowadays these eight measures are always printed out in full. It would be utterly wrong and disrupt the continuous flow in the succession of the variations if this fermata were to be mistaken for a stop sign before each variation ends.

Most theory books explain that fermatas only mean to hold the time of a deep breath's length (as, e.g., the fermatas in Protestant hymns); but others discuss different meanings. For instance, Leopold Mozart (in his *Violinschule*, I/iii, §19) says:

> *When a half-circle stands alone over a note with a dot in it, it is a sign that the note must be sustained. … It is true that such sustaining is to be made according to fancy, but it must be neither too short nor too long, and made with sound judgement. … Here it must be noticed in particular that the tone of the instrument must be allowed to diminish and die entirely away before beginning to play again. …*

The different meanings of fermatas are also pointed out by Samuel Petri in his *Anleitung zur praktischen Musik* (1782). Unfortunately, however, the theory books of Mozart's day never say just which fermatas are to be embellished and which are not. But, for example, Sulzer, in his *Theory of the Fine Arts* (volume II, p. 226), is clearly referring only to fermatas that should not be embellished when he writes a whole chapter on fermatas:

> *The fermata helps to express powerful emotions at points where they reach their climax, also to enhance the expression of amazement, like an outcry. They interrupt the melody, just as a man strongly moved may hesitate slightly after an outburst, and then go on still more violently.*

It is such a fermata that is, for example, notated in Mozart's C minor Fantasy K. 475 as part of a surprise effect, produced by the ensuing *forte* outburst with its *tremolo* broken chords.

In this fantasy, the fermatas really do serve the dramatic purpose mentioned by Sulzer and others, and such fermatas should certainly not be embellished. Also, once again it should be pointed out that the many fermatas in a movement, such as the third movement of the Sonata in C minor, K. 457, are indeed matching Sulzer's description of drama, and therefore they should never be embellished.

8
"Expression and Gusto"

Leopold Mozart and his son spoke frequently of *Expression und Gusto*, words that are usually translated into English as "feeling and taste." But in the eighteenth century both of these Italian words, *espressione* and *gusto*, had a somewhat broader meaning and evoked more connotations than they do for us today. In music, *taste* referred to a personal style of performing presentation and thus also to the idiomatic style of ornamentation, as Rousseau said about the French equivalent, *goût*.

Every eighteenth-century musician would have probably accepted the proposition that music expresses something and that it is a language in its own right, a language of sentiments, conveying certain feelings and concepts. The idea that a musical performance has much in common with the presentation of a speech is a very old one and experienced a revival during the Baroque period. The eleventh chapter of Quantz's famous flute treatise is titled "Concerning Good Execution in General in Singing and Playing [Vom guten Vortrage im Singen und Spielen überhaupt]" and starts with the following remarks (p. 119ff.):

> *§ 1. A musical performance may be compared with the delivery of an orator. The orator and the musician have, at bottom, the same aim in regard to both the preparation and the final execution of their productions, namely to make themselves masters of the hearts of their listeners, to arouse or still their passions, and to transport them now to this mood (sentiment), now to that. Thus, it is advantageous to both [orator and musician] if each has some knowledge of the duties of the other.*

> *§ 2. We know the effect in a lecture of good delivery upon the minds of the listeners; we also know how poor delivery injures the most beautifully written discourse; and we know again that a lecture delivered with the same words by two different persons will sound much better from one than from the other. The same is true of musical execution.*

The validity of this last statement is certainly not restricted to the time of Quantz. Individual understanding of what it means to perform with the proper expression and taste, however, has always differed considerably among musicians, then as now. During the first half of the eighteenth century, rhetoric was still a compulsory part of the former *trivium* and *humaniora* studies were taught at all Latin schools and universities. Drawing on writings of the classical antiquity, especially those of Quintilian,[1] in 1739 Johann Mattheson wrote *Der vollkommene Capellmeister* and laid out an organized and rational plan of musical composition borrowed from those sections of rhetorical theory concerned with finding and presenting arguments: *inventio* (invention of an idea), *dispositio* (arrangement of the idea into parts of an oration), *decoratio* (the elaboration or decoration of the idea; called *elaboratio* or *elocutio* by other writers), and *pronunciatio* (the delivery or performance of the oration). Around the same time, Sebastian Bach's younger

---

[1] The first scholar in our time to fully perceive the importance of Quintilian's writings on rhetoric for composers during the eighteenth century was Ursula Kirkendale, who proved that the order of J. S. Bach's *Musikalisches Opfer* was built on Quintilian's rules. See Ursula Kirkendale, "Bach's 'Musical Offering': The *Institutio Oratoria* of Quintilian," *Journal of the American Musicological Society*, pp. 88–141.

contemporary Johann Christoph Gottsched was already famous in Germany for his writings on rhetoric, which clearly influenced Quantz as well as Leopold Mozart, who at one point asked his publisher in Augsburg to send him all the available books of Gottsched. The evidence suggests that Leopold instructed his son to rely on the famous rhetoric rules when composing and performing, and he probably shared Quantz's opinion that it was advantageous for a musician to be acquainted with the *Ars rhetorica*. In §7 of the chapter already quoted, Quantz wrote:

> *Now music is nothing but an artificial language through which we seek to acquaint the listeners with our musical ideas. If we execute these ideas in an obscure and bizarre manner that is incomprehensible to the listeners and arouses no feeling, what is the use of our perpetual efforts to be thought learned?*

Although not every poetic text was suitable for musical setting, the presence of a text in vocal music usually rendered the content of musical speech understandable. Precisely because comprehensive sentiments and ideas could not be equally clearly expressed in instrumental works, philosophers and theoreticians had long insisted on the supremacy of vocal music over instrumental music. The validity of this notion diminished toward the end of the eighteenth century in the wake of the Enlightenment and changing aesthetic attitudes. Romantic ideas, for example, favored instrumental music, this time owing to the ambiguity of the sentiments aroused.

In this same chapter, "Concerning Good Execution," Quantz goes on to list the qualities necessary to be a good musician:

> *§ 10. Good execution must be first of all true and distinct. Not only must each note be heard, but each note must be sounded with its true intonation, so that all will be intelligible to the listener. ... You must try to make each sound as beautiful as possible. ...*

In Berlin in the mid-eighteenth century some conservative theorists among the music book writers demanded that an instrumental work be governed by only one basic mood or affection (*Affekt* in German) or passion—a rule that made sense particularly in connection with dance music, but otherwise was soon considered a handicap by composers such as Quantz and Bach's sons (not to mention Haydn, who apparently did not care much about theoretical rules). In general, the eighteenth-century *Affektenlehre* probably had its greatest impact on north and central German musicians and relatively little on those living in the Catholic south or in Italy. As late as 1785, Ernst Wilhelm Wolff (1735–90), Capellmeister to the Duke of Sachsen-Weimar, composed and published "*Vier affectvolle Sonaten fürs Klavier.*" At that time, such a title for a keyboard work was hardly used south of the Danube, where in the realm of music it was mainly the persuasiveness of *opera buffa* and *opera semiseria* that led to a psychologically more realistic understanding of the function of the affections.

In the second half of the century, composers and performers adopted a more natural and subjective attitude toward their creativity; and contrasting emotions were increasingly incorporated in every single piece of music. Quantz, the cosmopolitan mentor of Frederick II, had already demanded in his 1752 treatise that performers carefully observe such changes:

> *§ 15. The performer of a piece must seek to enter into the principal and related affections that he is to express. And since in the majority of pieces one passion constantly alternates with another, the performer must know how to judge the nature of the passion that each idea contains, and constantly make his execution conform to it. ... (p. 124)*

Mozart initially gained his reputation and fame as a surprisingly gifted child, but later he was an outstanding pianist and enjoyed great success with the public as a composer, and his unique expression as a performer on the piano was praised. At an early age he had already learned how to overcome every technical difficulty and could therefore devote all his attention to problems of interpretation. Mozart often missed this ability when listening to other pianists. In a letter of 28 April 1784, he told his father:

> He [the Dutch pianist Georg Friedrich Richter] *plays well as far as execution goes but as you will see when you hear him, he is too coarse and laboured and entirely lacking in taste and feeling* [Expression und Gusto]. *Otherwise he is the best fellow in the world and not the least bit conceited. When I played to him he stared all the time at my fingers and blurted out, "Good God! How hard I work till I sweat—and still I get no applause—and for you, my friend, it's all child's play". "Yes," I replied, "I too had to work hard, so I don't have to work hard any more." Enfin, he is a fellow who will always be counted among our good clavier-players ...*

This is one of the many passages in Mozart's letters in which he discusses good performance, constantly using the words *expression* (feeling), *gusto* (taste). These words he had also used in his previous letter from 24 April 1784, in which he had praised the Italian violinist Regina Strinasacchi as "a very good violinist. She has a great deal of taste and feeling in her playing ..."

And in a letter written on 13 November 1777, he gave his sister the following advice:

> I should advise my sister to play them [Myslivecek's sonatas] *with plenty of expression, taste and fire and to learn them by heart. For they are sonatas which are bound to please everyone, which are easy to memorize and very effective when played with the proper precision.*

Let us recall Mozart's not very flattering (and probably also unjust) opinion of Clementi. About this rival pianist, with whom he had to compete before the emperor on 24 December 1781, he wrote in a letter to his father (on 7 June 1783):

> Clementi is a Ciarlattano *like all Italians ... what he plays well are his passages in thirds, but he sweated over them in London day and night. Apart from them he has nothing, neither taste nor expression.*

And in another letter from 7 June 1783, he repeated this judgment.

Clementi, on the other hand, greatly admired Mozart: "I had never before heard anyone play with such spirit and grace."[2]

Clementi's praise of Mozart's playing is in line with the general opinion of other contemporaries. Dittersdorf reports the following conversation with the emperor in his autobiography:

Emperor:	Have you heard Mozart play?
Dittersdorf:	Three times already.
Emperor:	Do you like him?
Dittersdorf:	Yes; all musicians do.
Emperor:	You have heard Clementi, too?
Dittersdorf:	Yes.
Emperor:	Some prefer him to Mozart, and Greybig is at the head of them. What do you think? Out with it!

---

[2] See E. Mueller von Asow, *Briefe*, vol. 2, p. 152.

Dittersdorf: Clementi's playing is art simply and solely; Mozart's playing combines art and taste.

Emperor: I said the same.[3]

Leopold Mozart said in his treatise about *rubato* that it is "more easily shown than described," and this can also be said—even more so—of *expression* (*Ausdruck*) or *feeling*, a very broad term that defies rational formulation. All the same, we shall try to say a few words about the art of expressive playing, an art that Mozart must have possessed to the highest degree.

Expression with the Help of Dynamic Shadings

As has already been frequently mentioned, Mozart's notation only hints at how the music is to be performed. For example, his dynamic markings are only general indications; both thought and feeling are needed to judge how loud a *forte* or soft a *piano* should be. But loud and soft are usually less important than a feeling for melody and for tension and relaxation. In a melodic curve, not one note must be stiff or lacking in life—each note must stand in a correctly judged relationship to the whole. Every note in a graded dynamic process has its own degree of intensity. What follows is a rather bold attempt to make a graph of this dynamic oscillation, so important in the presentation of all melody: here from the C minor Concerto K. 491/I, first solo entry:

Ex. VIII/1:

TRACK 47

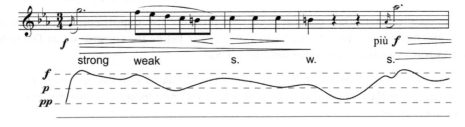

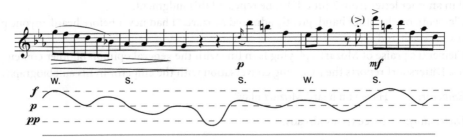

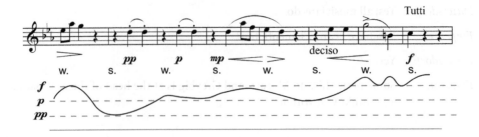

---

[3] Dittersdorf, *Autobiography*, p. 251.

When harmonic, rhythmic, and melodic accents coincide, there is a risk that the meter may become overly emphasized: The music may seem to lumber from one group of bars to the next, or even from one bar to the next—and this is definitely something to be avoided. But all great composers have had a masterly way of displacing the melodic accents in relation to the harmonic and rhythmic ones. This sort of displacement is difficult to determine rationally. There are countless harmony textbooks and numerous essays on rhythm, but a good textbook on melody is lacking, since both in creating and in reproducing melodies we depend to a great extent on our artistic instinct (which can, of course, be astonishingly sound). The few rational and really applicable rules—such as the rule that a suspension must be accented and its resolution unaccented—depend not only on melodic principles but also on those of harmony and rhythm.

In the following example (theme of the D major Rondo K. 485), we find a period of two groups of eight measures:

Ex. VIII/2:

It is obvious that from the rhythmic and metric point of view that bars 1, 3, and 5 are strong, while bars 2, 4, and 6 are weak. Examination of the harmony gives a similar scheme:

Ex. VIII/3:

But it would be rather ungraceful to play the first and third bars as melodically strong, i.e., accented. Here our artistic instinct demands that m. 2 and especially m. 4 should not be played weaker but, on the contrary, a shade stronger:

Ex. VIII/4:

If the accents come on the metric strong points (mm. 1 and 3), this theme loses its charm and even sounds banal. Yet, if one considers the dominant to be domineering, one could treat mm. 2 and 3 as the strong ones. From m. 5 onward, the melodic accents fall into line with the harmonic–metric scheme, so that two melodically strong bars (4 and 5) are adjacent.

This tendency for melodic tension to increase in the second and fourth bars is a common feature of Mozart's *cantabile* themes. Examples of themes built on this principle occur in the Piano Concertos K. 453, first movement, first and second subjects; K. 459, first movement, first subject; K. 467, all themes; K. 482, first movement, all themes; and so on. One could almost call this a stylistic principle.

It is difficult to bridge the gap between instinctive feeling for melody and conscious, rational observation; but there have been continual and often successful attempts to do so. Eighteenth-century textbooks, which are indeed particularly concerned with melodic expression, contain a few rules (most of them rather primitive) for giving form to melodic lines. Quantz (*Treatise*, p. 226), for example, requires harpsichordists to play "the various notes that require emphasis…with more liveliness and force. This applies to long notes that occur amid shorter ones, as well as to the notes at the opening of a principal subject, and above all to dissonances."

And in his *Violinschule* (XII, §9, p. 219, and §13, p. 221), Leopold Mozart says:

> Generally the accent of the expression or the stress of tone falls on the ruling or strong beat, which the Italians call nota buona … if the composer has indicated no other expression (e.g. syncopations). … In lively pieces the accent is mostly used on the highest note, in order to make the performance very merry. So it may happen here that the stress falls on the last note of the second and fourth quarter note in common time, but on the end of the second quarter in 2/4 time; especially when the piece begins with the upbow. For example:

Ex. VIII/5:

> But in slow, sad pieces this cannot be done, for there the upbow must not be detached, but sustained singingly.

In performing Mozart, one should pay particular attention to the very frequent accented passing notes and suspensions. The rule that the resolution is to be sung or played softer than the dissonance (which should be slightly emphasized) must be strictly observed. Mozart often adds an extra expression mark to show the correct accentuation in passages of this kind; for instance, in the B-flat major Piano Trio K. 502/I, mm. 52–53:

Ex. VIII/6:

No good musician is likely to make the mistake of cutting off the final eighth notes with the result that they are unintentionally accented.

A parallel can be drawn between the resolution of accented passing notes and a fundamental rule of rhetoric: In English, as in German and Italian, the accent on two-syllable words falls as a rule on the last syllable but one: *móther, mútter, mádre,* etc. This accent on the next-to-last syllable automatically means that the unaccented one must be pronounced as a light, short sound. The same applies to the resolution of accented dissonances; the rule of tension (dissonance) and relaxation (consonance) demands that the dissonance should receive an accent, and the resolution the opposite of an accent, represented in prosody by a sign that is unfortunately unknown to musical notation, but which could do good service to indicate weak syllables: the sign ⌣.

There are exceptions to this rule, and we find such an exception in the finale of the Concerto K. 466, m. 103:

Ex. VIII/7:

Here the resolution e¹ in m. 104 must be accented; otherwise, because it is so much shorter than the accented passing notes, it will not be heard at all.

Expression with the Help of Articulation

As a general rule one can say that, when two notes are joined by a slur, the first of the two should be played louder, even if it is not an accented dissonance or suspension note (see Ex. IV/58 on p. 124). Again there is an exception to this rule; in upward leaps of more than a third, the second note is often to be played louder than the first, as in the following passage from the E-flat Concerto K. 482/III, second *tutti*:

Ex. VIII/8:

Unless there is a slight accent on the top e-flat^3, the passage sounds dull and colorless.

There is a simple and well-tested device for clarifying the articulation of a theme: one adds a text, ideally one that seems to express the feeling of the music. Just as a speaker respects the rise and fall of the language, making appropriate gradations, so the notes of a theme must always be in the right rhetorical relationship to one another. In the opening movement of the A major Piano Sonata K. 331, for example, the articulation of the *Andante grazioso* theme is printed inconsistently in the first edition (the autograph is lost), and one cannot decide on purely philological grounds whether Mozart wanted the slurs to be over the first two or the first three notes. If we try to imagine this tune with words added, we may think something like this:

Ex. VIII/9:

Lasst ver - trau - te Weis' er - klin - gen,
Sing and play, don't care who hears us?

Lasst uns froehlich Mozart singen!
Mozart's music always cheers us!

In this case it is clear that we can only slur the first two notes of the first measure. Mozart put similar slurs over two notes in the A major section of the Rondo in A minor, K. 511. Anyone trying to invent a good text for the version with a slur over the first three notes would find it rather difficult and would stop trying after a little while. Adding a text brings to light a number of important points, and these lessons can then be consciously applied, with a good effect on one's playing. One realizes that the first four bars hang together and that the eighth notes on the third and sixth beats must be played a good deal more lightly than the strong beats. Moreover, it follows that the fourth bar (specifically on the words *always*) obviously contains the dynamic climax of the phrase. Correct declamation will prevent the carelessness that causes many pianists to play the (feminine) ending of this phrase too loudly. Thus, the addition of words can be a useful pointer to correct interpretation.

In a letter to a young colleague,[4] the late pianist Dinu Lipatti cogently remarked that a good musician will concentrate on the weak beats, since the strong ones have a favored position within the measure anyway and can look after themselves. For this reason, many composers have used accent signs to ensure that notes on weak beats receive the right degree of emphasis. Mozart, too, often wrote expressive accents over notes on weak beats, as in m. 7 of this same theme from K. 331/I:

---

[4] Printed in *Hommage à Dinu Lipatti*, Geneva 1950.

Ex. VIII/10:

or in the C minor Fantasia K. 475, mm. 153–155.

A striking example are the off-beat accents in mm. 25 and 26, which Mozart himself notated in a copy of the slow movement of the Concerto in B-flat major, K. 456, which has been preserved since World War II in a library in Moscow:

Ex. VIII/11:

But even where Mozart did not mark an accent for notes on a weak beat, they are still often the ones the player has to emphasize. See, for example, the finale of the A major Concerto K. 488, mm. 129ff. and mm. 151ff.:

Ex. VIII/12:

In such passages, where the tempo is quick, the short notes must definitely be accented; otherwise, they will not be heard at all.

One has to take care that some special upbeats are heard clearly enough. In the second subject of the first movement of the Piano Concerto in E-flat, K. 482, the eighths are usually "thrown away" and cannot be heard clearly enough:

Ex. VIII/13:

For the same reason, in quick rhythms such as in the C minor Concerto K. 491/III:

Ex. VIII/14:

the sixteenth notes from m. 106 on, despite being partly resolutions of dissonances, might require the hint of an accent if they are not to be inaudible. The same applies to accompanimental rhythms, such as mm. 21 and 29 of the same movement:

Ex. VIII/15:

The accent should be not on the dotted quarter notes but rather on the eighths. The above example from the D major Rondo K. 485 (Ex. VIII/2) is another theme in which the eighth notes in mm. 2 and 4 should not be "swallowed."

Repeated notes often occur in Mozart's music, and there is a very great risk that they will be played lifelessly. Here one must perceive what kind of emotion (*affekt*) they are intended to express. In *cantabile* passages, one should follow the principle that two successive notes of the same pitch are hardly ever to be played in exactly the same way. For instance, our added dynamic signs in the theme of the second movement of the "Coronation" Concerto in D major, K. 537, show how this theme could be played:

Ex. VIII/16:

In this case, the note repetition has some particular expressive purpose, and the notes must be made to speak, which means that they should be given a dynamic shading and, above all, should not be unduly shortened. The first note could be *p*, the second a little softer, the third rather louder than the second, but not quite as loud as the first, the fourth about as loud as the first and the fifth somewhat louder—all this with discretion. The note repetitions in the first movement of the D minor Concerto K. 466 should also be played *con expressione*, though in this case with passionate expression and possibly a slight *crescendo* to build up tension.

Another common mistake is to make repeated notes too short. Pianists are particularly liable to fall into this trap. There is a dramatic passage in the Praeludium of the C major *Prelude and Fugue* K. 394 that should rightly be played as follows:

Ex. VIII/17:

and not as if there were *staccato* dots over the right hand octaves and a *legato* in the left hand, a common misunderstanding found in nineteenth-century editions of Mozart:

Ex. VIII/18:

wrong:

In contrast to these expressive note repetitions, there are playful ones whose whole charm lies in their lack of accents, their complete evenness, with no dynamic gradation. We would number the Allegro theme of the overture of *The Magic Flute* among these subjects or the second episode of the final movement of the Sonata in B-flat Major, K. 570, mm. 45–46:

Ex. VIII/19:

Here the notes should be played short and quick, with considerable inner tension.

One can also refer to the first eight bars of the D major Concert Rondo K. 382 (see also Ex. IV/51 on p. 121), and much the same applies for the repeated notes in mm. 5ff. of the Piano Trio in C Major, K. 548/I:

Ex. VIII/20:

This theme, however, depends not only on its rhythm, but also on a specifically melodic element, which suggests that the interpreter should not play these notes absolutely metrically, but rather slightly irregular in rhythm. The last note of the phrase (downbeat in m. 6 plus upbeat) has the effect of a bow or reverence, an ironical courtesy; it is as if one were transported to the world of *The Marriage of Figaro*. This crop of G's must always be savored to the utmost. The rests between them are very important and must on no account be shortened. Indeed, throughout all of Mozart's music, the rests must never be neglected! To underline the humor of this passage, one can make the Gs slightly shorter than their written length and delay the beginning of mm. 6 and 8 by a fraction:

Ex. VIII/21:

The breathing space before the bar line to m. 2, as suggested, must be so short that there is no question of holding up the even flow of the meter. Such hesitation, such pausing for breath, is very important throughout Mozart's music, that is so strongly influenced by vocal writing.

Naturally, feeling is not limited to the shaping of melodies: Rhythm and harmony serve expressive ends too. In Mozart's works, melody, harmony, and rhythm interpenetrate in a unique way.

Expressive Rhythmic Shadings

A kind of expressive breathing space, a slight *caesura*, is often in place before the entry of a new subject. For instance, in the second movement of the E-flat major Concerto K. 482, such a breathing space is appropriate in m. 124, before the flute motive enters. Without such a *caesura*, the succeeding C major section would lack the necessary feeling of restfulness at its very outset.

It would be a great mistake, however, to make this kind of *caesura* in the middle of a *cantabile* theme, thus breaking up a melody that should be felt as a unit, an extended curve. Great interpreters have always known how to spin a smoothly curving thread, to mold the alternations of musical tension and relaxation so perfectly that formal sections can make their full effect as self-contained units. To make an unmotivated *ritardando* in such places is one of the worst offenses against good taste. We have heard a well-known violinist play the first solo in the *Adagio* movement of the G major Violin Concerto K. 216 as follows:

Ex. VIII/22:

Naturally, Mozart did not conceive notating such a wrong fermata! Our violinist, however, did not halt merely once on the f-sharp[3] but every time the theme appeared! If one were to set words to this phrase, to match the rhythm—for example, "My comfort and my treasure"—the result, if the above phrasing were followed, would be like this: "My comfort and maaaaaa … ii treasure." Even a tenor in a village operetta could not get away with that!

It is sad to see that such offenses against healthy musical sensitivity and taste are seldom noticed either by the public or by the critics. Mozart would have said about such a performer, that he did not "have a penny's worth of taste or feeling." But in this case, the daily press was almost unanimous in their praise of the violinist's expressive playing. As we have said before, the development of a healthy natural feeling for melody can be greatly assisted by adding words to clarify passages where the flow of musical tension is obscure.

Harmonic Expression

A few suggestions on the subject of harmonic expression also seem appropriate. There are—especially in Mozart's piano concertos—bold harmonic progressions, romantic passages in which the expressive effect results less from the melodic lines of the individual parts than from the harmonies, the sound they make together. This is the case, for example, in m. 57 (end of first *tutti*) and again in the *codetta* (epilogue) of the first movement of the G major Concerto K. 453:

Ex. VIII/23:

At first every listener hears the g-sharp[1] in the second measure as an (enharmonic) a-flat[1]. Thus, one somehow expects a progression such as:

Ex. VIII/24:

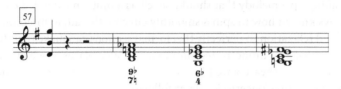

and is surprised when the supposed a-flat[1] remains a g-sharp[1] and unexpectedly resolves to an a[1]. In the ensuing continuation (m. 62), the effect of this passage is enhanced by a counterpoint in the wind section, starting with an f-natural.

The second movement of this concerto, which has an unprecedented range of modulation, also produces some unexpected turns of harmony. The return in mm. 86ff. from G-sharp major (dominant of C-sharp minor) to C major within four bars is one of the boldest and finest modulation passages Mozart ever wrote. Here the C major has the effect of a true revelation, such as: "and there was light."

Ex. VIII/25:

To mark this in performance it is best to broaden the tempo to allow the harmonic intensification its full effect.

The finale of the C minor Concerto K. 491 is another place where Mozart achieves most powerful harmonic effects by enharmonic twists:

Ex. VIII/26:

Any string player would adjust the intonation of the f-sharp[1] in m. 234 (left hand) to make it a little higher than the g-flat[1] in the previous bar. Naturally, pianists cannot adjust their intonation to emphasize this kind of expressiveness. They have to be content with accenting the f-sharp[1] in its function as a leading note to the ensuing g[1].

In m. 6 of the Adagio movement of the A major Concerto K. 488, the right hand has a b-sharp[1] as an accented dissonance before a c-sharp[2]; here again the ear may be enharmonically misled into thinking this is a C (minor third on A). Though one cannot entirely prevent this aural illusion, it would again be in order to accent this b-sharp. At the moment of resolution, the wide-awake listener will correct his mistake retrospectively.

Proper Accompaniment Helps Expression

The accompaniment also has an expressive function. For example, the hammering chordal accompaniment of the first subject of the A minor Sonata K. 310 (first movement) is vitally important in giving the theme its passionate character. The chords must be played absolutely evenly, with firm rhythm and dynamics and an emphasis on the first chord.

Accompaniments with so-called *Alberti* figures, favored by Mozart often with quickly changing harmonies, may underline the lyrical character of a theme and require evidently to be played *legato* or *legatissimo*. This is the case, for instance, in the second movement of the *Sonata facile* K. 545:

Ex. VIII/27:

or in the Andante movement of the Sonata in C major, K. 279:

Ex. VIII/28:

In the first opening solo of the Concerto K. 488/I, the accompanying *Alberti* figures will likewise have to be played gently and *legato* due to the lyrical character of the melody:

Ex. VIII/29:

Alberti bass accompaniment, however, can equally well delight the listener by the special way it brings out the piano's ability to sparkle (as in the Concerto for Three Pianos in F major, K. 242, third movement, mm. 145ff.):

Ex. VIII/30:

In this example the *Alberti* figures need a rather *non-legato* or *staccato* interpretation because of their sparkling leading part.

A typical Mozartean feature can be observed in the second subject of the first movement of the E-flat major Concerto K. 271. Here it is the right hand that accompanies the tune played by the orchestra. This lively figuration requires *staccato* touch in the right hand.

Ex. VIII/31:

When lyrical themes are played *legato*, the first note of each *Alberti bass* figure often can be sustained on the key or tied, which means that the key of each first note of a figure should be pressed down longer than is indicated in the score. This is recommended, for example, in the B-flat major Concerto K. 595/I in mm. 86–87:

Ex. VIII/32:

written:

played:

or for the opening of the C major *Sonata facile* K. 545, first movement. This way of tying certain notes, also recommended by Türk (p. 355), surely accords with Mozart's intentions, as we can see by passages from chamber music works with piano and from piano concertos where this kind of *Alberti bass* figure is supported by sustained chords on other instruments. It is also documented by a passage in the finale of the A minor Sonata K. 310, where Mozart notated the accompaniment in m. 21 as follows,

Ex. VIII/33:

although later, at the corresponding point of the movement, from m. 195 onward, he omitted indicating that the bass part is to be prolonged:

Ex. VIII/34:

This figure should clearly be played in just the same way as the earlier one (Ex. VIII/33).

Many piano accompaniments are a sort of transcription of an imaginary string quartet in which the cello plays the first (bass) note and the viola and second violin the two or three other eighth notes of an *Alberti bass* figure.

A study of the orchestral parts of piano concertos or the settings of harmonies in symphonies and serenades tells us that, in fast movements, accompanying figures were quite frequently marked detached or in mixed articulation (combination of *legato* and *staccato*), while in slow movements, *legato* accompaniment is more often the prevailing one. A beautiful example of a nearly symphonic *legato* accompaniment in a piano sonata is found in the Adagio movement from the F major Sonata K. 332. Particularly from m. 5 onwards, the descending bass line ought to be played *legatissimo*, the bass notes played as eighths or even quarter notes, as if played by a cellist, making a noticeable *crescendo* in m. 6 toward the climax in m. 7, the chord of the ninth in F minor marked *sforzato*:

Ex. VIII/35:

If the accompaniment is written in quiet chords, as in the theme of the variations from the A major Sonata K. 331, one must make sure that they are noticeably softer than the melodic line. The overall impression of a certain degree of loudness is the result of the combined dynamic levels of the various parts. The bass line should sometimes be slightly emphasized and should be louder than the middle voices, which must be kept in the background.

The secret of a singing piano tone lies not least in the fact that the melody is always played one degree louder than the other parts, perhaps *p*, or perhaps *mf*, with the accompaniment a degree softer *pp* or *p* respectively, without becoming inaudible, of course. Most Italian keyboard music from the middle of the eighteenth century was characterized by a homophonic texture, consisting of a *cantabile* melody in the upper part and an accompanying bass part with *Alberti* figures or murky basses (broken octaves). In his *Klavierschule* (1797) Milchmeyer (p. 4) concurred to what Italians had proclaimed that the melody "as the most noble part" should always be heard more prominently in order

> to show its true glamour [proper importance]. Here is the best place where I can say some few words about the relationship of the bass part and the singing part. One should always remember that in all musical pieces we find a singing [Singstimme] and an accompanying part. The singing part I would like to call the master, and the accompaniment the servant. As it is known and accepted that the master should be in the foreground being of greater prominence and the servant remain in the background, this should be also so in music. Therefore, in every piece one performs, the singing voice should prove its ruling eminence and the accompanying part should apply all art [should try hard] to let the former have the star part.

Music is, of course, not a play of absolute forms, and proper expression needs more than can be suggested by pointing out some rules and recommendations. A musically satisfying performance needs more: it should express the whole world of human experience. Mozart, above all in his operas and vocal music, leaves us in no doubt that he is concerned with human expression. In a letter from Paris to Aloysia Weber (in Italian, from 30 July 1778) he wrote:

I advise you to watch the expression marks—to think carefully of the meaning and the force of the words—to put yourself in all seriousness into Andromeda's situation and position!—and to imagine that you really are that very person. With your beautiful voice and your fine method of producing it you will undoubtedly soon become an excellent singer, if you continue to work in this way.

Expression of Comic or Tragic Moods

For Mozart, the instrumental accompaniment and not only the vocal line had a role in depicting extramusical moods. This is how he expressed it in a letter to his father on 26 September 1781:

Now for Bellmonte's aria in A major "0 wie ängstlich, o wie feurig" [from Die Entführung aus dem Serail]. *Do you know how I put it—even showed the throbbing, loving heart—with two violins in octaves. This is the favorite aria of all who have heard it—of mine too—and is perfectly written for Adamberger's voice. You see how he trembles—wavers—you see how his breast swells—which is expressed through a crescendo—you hear whispering and sighing—which is expressed by the first violins with mutes in unison with a solo flute.*

There are countless examples of this kind in Mozart's operas. One need only think of the trio from the act 1 of *Così fan tutte* ("*Soave sia il vento*") in which the violins unmistakably depict the gentle undulation of the waves.

In Mozart's piano music, this direct relationship with an experience expressible in words is not immediately apparent. But throughout his piano music one finds motifs and figurations from his operas, similar moods and experiences. Studying Mozart's operas will lead to these discoveries. In Mozart's letters to his father from Munich during the period from September 1780 to January 1781, when he was occupied with composing and conducting *Idomeneo*, and also in those letters from Vienna during the composition of the *Entführung aus dem Serail* (September/October 1781 and from 21 June 1783), he makes it quite clear that for him opera stood at the very center of his creative life. He composed, for instance, an excited figuration in the C minor Fantasy K. 475 (mm. 43ff.), which returns almost literally in Act 2 of *Così fan tutte*:

Ex. VIII/36:

It occurs also in the orchestra accompaniment of Ferrando's recitative (*Così fan tutte*, Act 2, no. 26):

Ex. VIII/37:

The orchestra plays this motive at Ferrando's words, "In qual fiero contrasto, in qual disordine di pensieri e di affetti io mi ritrovo" ["What an awful predicament, and what a tormented state my heart and soul are in"]. The wholly similar measures in the Fantasy K. 475 are probably intended to express the same mood: helpless despair on the part of an individual faced by an unexpected turn of fate.

One could draw countless further parallels between Mozart's vocal and instrumental music. In this connection, it is interesting and worth pointing out again that Mozart took over many emotional symbols from Baroque music without altering them. The best known example of this kind must be the song of the "Armed Men" ("Geharnischte Männer") in the act 2 of *The Magic Flute*; Mozart wrote this after the manner of Joh. Seb. Bach, not only as regards its technique, but also its spirit, which is akin to that of Bach's chorale preludes. It is too little appreciated that Mozart always gives the dotted rhythm of the old French overture the meaning it had in the seventeenth century: as a symbol of majesty and solemnity; for example, in the *Qui tollis* of the great C minor Mass and in the *Rex tremendae majestatis* of the Requiem or the introductory chords of *The Magic Flute* overture.[5] The Phrygian cadence:

Ex. VIII/38:

was regarded as a symbol of the deepest tragic expression long before Mozart. He also used it frequently, usually intensifying the harmony by sharpening the sixth (i.e., augmented sixth chord) when he intended it to have this effect. An example is the aria "Ach, ich fühl's, es ist verschwunden" from *The Magic Flute*, where this harmony occurs twice at the words "ewig hin der Liebe Glück [Happy dream, 'twill ne'er come true]," the second time as an augmented sixth with the fourth added:

---

[5] This kind of dotted rhythm also occurs at the beginning of the second act of *The Magic Flute* after the March of the Priests. These anacrusic sixteenths are unfortunately almost always played too slowly and heavily. The tempo is *Adagio alla breve*, which means: not too slow an *Adagio*. If the pulse is quietly moving half-notes are beaten, the upbeats are fairly short.

Ex. VIII/39:

This augmented sixth chord has a similarly tragic impact in instrumental works, where it frequently occurs, as in the E-flat Concerto K. 482, first movement, m. 138:

Ex. VIII/40:

or in the finale of the C minor Concerto K. 491, m. 219. Deryck Cooke, in his book *The Language of Music*, a thorough and most valuable investigation into the meaning of certain formulas, discuss the function of this chord admirably.

Many musical symbols can have a number of different, if related meanings. Triadic fanfares, for example, are a symbol of both *joie de vivre* and vitality, and of heroism and triumph. In Figaro's aria "Non più andrai," all these meanings are combined. A similar mood is expressed in the first subject of the Sonata for Two Pianos K. 448 (first movement) or the Piano Concerto in C major, K. 503, and perhaps even more so in the Concerto in D major, K. 451.

Like all great creators, Mozart knew how to exploit every expressive resource available in his time. But in his day, feelings were expressed far more subtly than nowadays, and men's reactions to emotional stimuli were far stronger. To draw an analogy: Whereas once a smart tap was enough to let loose a flood of feeling, nowadays one often needs a hammer stroke. One generation will be moved to tears; the next will give an appreciative smile, and the third generation may say, "A bit too pretty, don't you think?" There were passages where Mozart could "make an effect" so that all his listeners were carried away, as he described in a letter from Paris to his father (from 3 July 1778):

> … just in the middle of the first Allegro there was a passage that I knew would please. The audience was quite carried away—and there was a tremendous burst of applause. But because I knew when I wrote it what good effect it would have, I introduced the passage again at the close—and when it came there were shouts of "Da capo".

Nowadays, similar means tend to produce in us only a pale reflection of their original effect. Nobody would dare to applaud in the middle of a movement. In our present society, it is even strictly forbidden to applaud between movements. Why? Conventions have changed. Mozartean harmonic strokes of genius, such as chromatically descending diminished sevenths or augmented sixth chords and certain other bold modulations, usually have little effect today on ears that have been accustomed to *Tristan harmonies* and later to *tone clusters*, etc. Instead, people often talk today about Mozart's beautiful harmonies, even when they have been listening to a rugged, eerie work such as the Concerto in C minor, K. 491, or the String Quartet in C Major, K. 465, which his contemporary fellow composers found far too daring harmonically, too full of unusual difficulties and too dramatic. Italian composers in general were shocked in Mozart's days when hearing a work like this unique C minor Concerto or the so-called *Dissonance Quartet* K. 465, considered by many to be an impossible mistake, a real blunder on Mozart's part (as Sarti said openly to the acclaim of other Italian composers). And later, did not even Schumann refer to the G minor Symphony's "floating Grecian grace"?

This alteration in the public's aesthetic reaction must necessarily have an effect on the way Mozart's works are played. One has, it seems, to emphasize emotional effects for modern listeners, who are thicker skinned, and to draw the important psychological outlines with broad strokes, particularly in the serious, confessional works. How far can or may the performer go in doing this? The question is one as much of personality as of good taste. It will do Mozart's music no harm to play it forcefully, just as long as one respects its innate limits, as long as one brings out its clarity and beauty, its pure architectonic qualities, and above all its moral stature. Mozart is a great composer, and one must not be afraid to play his works accordingly, on a large scale; to present him as a "gracious little man," a kind of Rococo marionette, is a misinterpretation of history that will never do him justice. The simplicity that later generations have sometimes held against Mozart is an outright fallacy. Publishers such as Artaria or well-disposed contemporary composers such as Dittersdorf were far from finding his music too simple—on the contrary, they found it too complex, too rich and varied. As Dittersdorf wrote about Mozart in his *Autobiography* (p. 251):

> He is unquestionably one of the greatest original geniuses, and I have never yet met with any composer who had such an amazing wealth of ideas; I could almost wish he were not so lavish in using them. He leaves his listener out of breath; for hardly has he grasped one beautiful thought, when another of greater fascination dispels the first, so that in the end it is impossible to retain any of these beautiful melodies. ...

And in a letter to Artaria from 18 August 1788, Dittersdorf promised the publisher that—if he would publish his six string quartets—he could regain all the money he had lost through publishing Mozart's six string quartets dedicated to Haydn:

> [T]hough these works [Mozart's string quartets] *are valued highly by me, also by still greater theoreticians, and which deserve all admiration; but because of the constant high level of art they are nothing for the average buyer.*[6]

Apparently Dittersdorf had learned that Mozart's works did not sell well. Indeed, Mozart often disconcerted his hearers by his unheard-of boldness. Rochlitz published an often repeated anecdote in the *Allgemeine Musikalische Zeitung Leipzig* (November 1798) to the effect that shortly after the first Viennese performance of *Don Giovanni*, a "society of music connoisseurs," the *Musikkenner der Kaiserstadt*, found the work overloaded, chaotic, and unmelodic. And the Swiss

---

[6] Quoted after E. Badura-Skoda, "Dittersdorf über Mozart's und Haydn's Quartette," p. 48.

composer and music critic Hans-Georg Nägeli wrote about Mozart that his most genial and rich works contain "traits of an unpleasant lack of style [Züge einer widerwärtigen Styllosigkeit]."

A hero of feeling as well as of fantasy, full of zeal and power, he [Mozart] seems in many of his compositions, figuratively speaking, to be simultaneously shepherd and warrior, flattering and storming; soft melodies alter with sharp, strident tones, elegance of movement with vehemence. Great was his genius, but equally great was his fault of seeking to make an effect through contrasts. The fault was all the greater because ... it constantly put his singing style in conflict with his free fantasy style.[7]

We have mentioned the need for performers to avoid small-scale interpretation, a certain Rococo lightness, but this must not be confused with coldness or stiffness. Nowhere are these imperfections less in place than in Mozart's music, which has more grace and natural charm than anyone else's. The gift of being able "to smile under tears," even when the situation is at its most hopeless, is reflected in some of Mozarts works. This is a gift that is very difficult to communicate, particularly by means of written words. It is quite distinct from pathos, but also from mere superficiality. An anecdote has been transmitted that may typify one side of Mozart's personality: the way he could free himself from daily problems (not only when concentrating on composing but also occasionally through suppression). He could counter the lack of money and the awareness of his debts that oppressed him through other means:

Mozart and his wife were dancing energetically about the room. When Deiner asked whether Mozart was teaching his wife to dance, Mozart laughed and said, "We are simply keeping warm, because it is freezing and we cannot afford to buy wood." Deiner at once hurried out and brought some of his own wood. Mozart took it and promised to pay well for it when he had some money.[8]

Even Mozart's tragic or melancholy works should not be played completely without charm, though grace and charm will naturally be less prominent in the C minor Concerto or the two G minor Symphonies (K. 183 and K. 550) than in the Divertimento *Eine kleine Nachtmusik* K. 525 or the Concert Rondo in D major, K. 382. It is obvious that charm is indispensable in all his works where grace and high spirits predominate, such as in these famous works where an interpretation will stand or fall mainly by its charm (or lack of it). These hints, like those given earlier, will only be useful if they are really understood and applied with discretion. One of the things that distinguishes a good artist from a bad one is the ability to walk the line between too much and too little. Mozart, a born enemy of all exaggeration, was without parallel in this art of striking a balance in every respect, also in form and expression, and the interpretation of his works is therefore the acid test of good taste.

This balance is indeed one of the main reasons why the interpretation of Mozart's works presents so many difficulties, despite the simplicity of his musical language for those performers, who were mainly playing works of later periods; for instance, Schumann or Liszt. Mozart had a keen sense of the natural; he not only rejected all bombast, he in fact got a good deal of ironic amusement from it. Somehow, this is a bond between him and our present-day, more rational

---

[7] "Gefühlsheld und Phantasieheld in gleichem Maaße, voll Drang und Kraft, erscheint er in vielen seiner Compositionen augenblicklich—um mich bildlich auszudrücken—als Schäfer und Krieger, als Schmeichler und Stürmer; weiche Melodien wechseln häufig mit scharfem, schneidendem Tonspiel, Anmut der Bewegung mit Ungestüm. Groß war sein Genie, aber eben so groß sein Geniefehler, durch Contrast zu wirken. Fehlerhaft war dies um so mehr, als er.... die Cantabilität mit dem freyen Tonspiel in steten Contrast setzte." Quoted after Marie-Agnes Dietrich, "Die Klaviermusik," p. 484ff.

[8] Quoted after O. E. Deutsch, *Mozart, Die Dokumente seines Lebens*, p. 478.

humanity. The nineteenth century, with its plush curtains, its prudishness, and love of often hollow pathos, found Mozart's directness and naturalness hard to appreciate. His humor aroused indignation, as when he wrote canons on indecent texts, and people seriously considered destroying his compromising letters to his young cousin, the Bäsle! In Mozart's time, the letters were far less shocking than they would seem in later times; e.g., around 1900.

Greatness in music manifests itself in a twofold universality, on the humanity level in truthful and tasteful expression, understood independently of time and place over centuries; and in a technically sophisticated musical language, capable of being understood everywhere—as Haydn once said: "throughout the world." The perception and reception of Mozart's music may be different in every century; one generation might celebrate him because he was a highly dramatic, impressive composer, whereas the next generation prizes his music primarily for its charm and looks at on him more as a delightful, harmless entertainer. One generation places his operas in the foreground and enjoys them as a *ne plus ultra* achievement; for the next one, the instrumental concertos, chamber music, and symphonies are the more important works. The wonderful thing about great men such as Shakespeare, Michelangelo, Bach, and Mozart is that their work holds meaning for all generations and in all ages. Even in the course of one's life, one may choose to focus on the different aspects of these geniuses—there are enough sides of them deserving to be admired. After hearing an opera like *Don Giovanni* or *Figaro* even ten or twenty times one can still discover something beautiful that one had not really noticed before: a harmonic progression, a passage—it is never boring to listen again and again to such a masterwork—there is always something new to be discovered.

Mozart himself tried to ensure that he would be readily understood; he explained in a letter to his father (27 November 1777) that he always tried to avoid unnecessary complexity and ostentatious expenditure of energy:

> You know that I am no great lover of difficulties. He [the violinist, Fränzl] plays difficult things, but his hearers are not aware that they are difficult; they think that they could easily do it themselves. That is real playing.

In fact, he was proud if he succeeded in making his own compositions appear easy, as he stated in a letter from 28 December 1782:

> These concertos are a happy medium between what is too easy and too difficult; they are very brilliant, pleasing to the ear, and natural, without becoming empty. Here and there are passages satisfying solely to connoisseurs, but written in such a way that the less learned cannot fail to be pleased, without knowing why.

In the same letter he explained how, when choosing texts to set to music, he particularly looked for simplicity and naturalness:

> The ode is sublime, beautiful, anything you like, but too exaggerated and pompous for my fastidious ears.

And Mozart's amusing remarks about the affected playing of Nannette Stein are well known: for his taste, she pulled too many faces and made too many unnecessary movements.

Mozart was especially averse to exaggerated, unnatural voice trembling. On 12 June 1778 he wrote to his father:

> Meisner, as you know, has the bad habit of deliberately making his voice tremble at times, turning a note that should be sustained into distinct quarter notes or even eighths—and this I never could endure in him. And, really, it is a detestable habit and one quite contrary to nature. The human voice trembles naturally by itself—but in its own way—and only to

such a degree that the effect is beautiful. Such is the nature of the voice; and people imitate it not only on wind-instruments, but on stringed instruments, too and even on the clavier. But the moment the proper limit is overstepped, it is no longer beautiful, because it is contrary to nature. It reminds me then of the organ when the bellows are puffing.

A natural way of singing was one of the main requirements he demanded of his interpreters, as he said repeatedly; it meant the capability to sing or play in a truly natural and not in an artificial style.

In his *Violinschule* (V, §14, p. 101ff.) Leopold Mozart had said:

And who is not aware that singing is at all times the aim of every instrumentalist; because one must always approximate nature as nearly as possible. ...

And Wolfgang wrote on 7 February 1778, to his father from Mannheim:

In my last letter I forgot to mention Mlle. Weber's greatest merit, which is her superb cantabile singing. ...

These words are no surprise, coming from a great composer whose music is so essentially song, for whom "melody is the essence of music."[9] In his essay on Mozart, Edwin Fischer also admonished us: "Let every note sound and be free within the framework of the law which, unwritten, lives in every true musician." In his relentless opposition to mechanical and lifeless playing, Fischer was in agreement also with one of Mozart's contemporaries, Christian Friedrich Daniel Schubart, who wrote in 1789 in his *Ideen zu einer Ästhetik der Tonkunst* (p. 295):

Quite apart from any mechanical ability—the ear, the winged fist, dexterous fingers, steady rhythm, feeling for the instrument, sight-reading, and all the rest of it; no soloist should dare to come before the public unless he has creative energy; unless he knows how to transform the notes into so many balls of fire; unless he can inspire the accompanying players as well as his listeners, and—in fact, unless he can summon up the spirit to burn in all ten of his fingers.

Keep Smiling!

When a person has to convey sad news he automatically puts on a serious face. But when you have good news, you smile. Mozart's music is good news, very good news, indeed; it is a source of happiness; in most of his works it expresses pleasing feelings, well-being, and love. As with acting, the performer on the stage ought to follow the poetic expression and the true inner meaning of a text with his body language, in particular with his facial expression (Laurence Olivier was unique in this respect.) But musicians? Many pianists seem to ignore this principle: even while playing serene works full of happiness and well-being, they put on a deadly serious face.

How often can one observe this in piano competitions or in concerts! Acting as juror, coauthor Paul Badura-Skoda recalls that in the Queen Elisabeth Competition in Brussels there was only one candidate in a hundred who smiled while playing Mozart, a young lady from India. It brightened the day of the jurors, and she passed the first round even though her technique was perhaps less polished than that of other candidates. One of the reasons for a too serious facial expression while playing is the apparent effort and concentration of the other performers. To let it appear is not bad in itself; yet, to perform, for instance, Mozart's *Sonata facile* or the "Turkish March" with a frozen expression is comparable to playing a funeral march with a smile. It is perhaps the highest achievement in art not to let the listeners see any effort when mastering a complicated technical problem. Mozart achieved that clearly in composition and probably also

[9] Edwin Fischer, *Reflections on Music*, p. 44ff.

in performance. One is reminded of his answer to the Dutch pianist Richter (see above), who complained that he had to work so very hard, whereas for Mozart everything seemed to be so easy.

In modern life, Chinese circus artists are models of great facial control. They often perform balancing acts requiring the utmost concentration and seemingly impossible for normal human beings as if it were child's play, and finish with a genuine smile. Yes, the smile of an artist has to be genuine; it has to come from the inside. To put on a stereotypical smile like a receptionist at an insurance company would be worse than showing genuine effort.[10]

Even in serene works of Mozart, there are, of course, also moments of sadness, sorrow, or anguish, where a smile by the performer would be utterly inappropriate. Especially in Mozart's late works, which contain more melancholic moments than his early works, a smile would often be out of place. To these late works belong, for instance, the first movement of the Piano Sonata in F major, K. 533, especially the passage at mm. 35–41:

Ex. VIII/41:

or the Concerto in B-flat major, K. 595/I, 107–116:

Ex. VIII/42:

---

[10] The latter was the case with the unforgettable Russian pianist Sviatoslav Richter, who had suffered a lot in the course of his life. He certainly did not hide his enormous engagement, his effort, his suffering—even when playing Mozart (which he admittedly did seldom. Notwithstanding our great admiration for him, he was not a true Mozartean).

Our observation about corresponding facial expressions is not new. Türk devoted a whole chapter in his *Klavierschule* (1789, VI/4, §56, p. 365ff.) to "the heavy and the light rendering" and to "certain other means ... which contribute to a certain extent to a good performance."

After devoting three paragraphs to the necessity of a beautiful sound, he wrote:

> [A] *beautiful tone must be* clear, round, supple, bright, *yet above all also* pleasant *[ein schöner Ton muß deutlich, voll, geschmeidig, hell, vorzüglich aber auch angenehm seyn].* (Italics in original.)

Türk also speaks at length about a free, unmannered way of playing. On p. 366, he then writes (§56):

> *A very beautiful passage where the player lets us see that he is fighting difficulties and that it could go wrong, will give less pleasure to the sympathetic listener than a somewhat less good passage presented with a certain calm and seeming ease.*

In the following paragraph (§57), Türk, after having warned once more against making grimaces, continues:

> *[H]owever, where the facial expression corresponds to the character of the piece in an honest proper way [auf anständige Art], letting feeling to be imbued with the corresponding mood [Affekt], it will at least not be to the disadvantage of a good performance. ... I doubt that one could seriously object when a player shows a serene expression at lively affects, a pleasing expression at affectionate passages, or a composed one at serious pieces—in short, shows his personal engagement ...*

And in smaller letter types, Türk concluded:

> *... but certainly not a peevish grimace at a technical difficulty or a pursed mouth movement with every difficulty.*

Are Repeats Compulsory?

We have said elsewhere that often the repetition of passages or phrases is an integral part of musical language. We observe symmetry everywhere, in nature or art, in a small flower as well as in a large cathedral. Symmetry, the repetition of the same pattern, is an essential part of life. No wonder that in art, poetry, and especially in music, symmetry is found everywhere: It is a reflection of organic life. There exists hardly a piece of music without repeated motives, patterns, phrases, or whole sections.

No one doubts that repeats of shorter or longer motives or phrases must be observed. To deprive music of this sort of symmetry would be like taking an eye or a hand away from a living creature. As with most great composers, Mozart used different methods to indicate shorter or longer repeats, namely either by writing a passage twice (or thrice) or by using abbreviations of all kinds, either in words or symbols. The most frequent words to indicate repeats are *bis* (twice) or *Da capo* (from the beginning). The well-known symbol for requiring a section to be played twice is: ⫶|

When speaking about echo effects (see p. 66), we quoted two passages where no abbreviation was used but that were written (or printed) out by Mozart. In those cases, there can be no doubt that they have to be played as notated; namely, twice. Whether or not to change their dynamic level or their expression the second time is of no concern in this connection. What matters is that no cuts must be made in such cases.

The problem of whether to repeat whole sections or not starts only when the repeat symbol ⫶| is used. A case in question is the D major section of the C minor Fantasy K. 475. Here Mozart indicated the repeats of mm. 26–29 and mm. 30–33 by the repeat symbol. Yet many editions did not reproduce the second repeat as he had written it but instead printed these four measures twice (for instance, the Henle edition). There is no harm in this procedure since, in this special work, the repeated playing of those measures 30–33 is taken for granted. The only problem here concerns the counting of measure numbers: In those editions where the repetition of these four measures are indicated through a repeat sign, as Mozart wrote them (e.g., *NMA*), the repeated measures are not counted separately and thus miraculously the Fantasy becomes four measures shorter—but without being one second shorter in actual performance time.

This question of numbering is a minor problem, indeed. A greater problem is the notated repetition of long sections, particularly in sonata or symphony movements. Traditionally, the choice is left to the performer of whether or not to observe the repeat signs literally. Some performers play every repeat; others choose to play some while ignoring others. Several reasons may cause a decision for either playing or neglecting the second repeat signs in sonatas. If the artist has to catch a train after the concert, or if he is eager to get to a reception afterwards, he might drop repeats. Seriously speaking: What should one do? Is it historically legitimate to dump repeated sections? Was it done in Mozart's time? The answer is clearly "yes."

Heinrich Christoph Koch stated (in his *Versuch einer Anleitung zur Komposition*, vol. II, Leipzig, 1787, pp. 101, 102, and 108):

> … *the first Allegro of the symphony … has two sections which may be performed with or without repetition.*[11]

Especially in dance music there was a good reason for repetitions—dances needed a certain length! André Grétry, however, loathed repeats:

> *I see almost all instrumental music chained to worn-out forms that are repeated for us without end.*[12]

Nicolas-Joseph Hüllmandel, one of the many German composers living in France during the German midcentury succession wars, became famous for his comparatively precise notation. He was

> … *the first to connect the two parts of his sonatas so that they do not repeat slavishly. … A sonata is a discourse. What would we think of a man who, cutting his discourse in two, repeated each half?*[13]

---

[11] Quoted after John Irving, *Mozart's Piano Sonatas*, p. 100.
[12] Quoted after S. Rosenblum, *Performing Practices*, p. 72.
[13] Ibid.

Also Clementi stated in his *Introduction...* (1801, p. 8), which appeared, however, shortly after the turn of the century:

> *The DOTTED bars [repeat signs] denote the repeat of the foregoing, and following strain. N.B. The second part of a piece, if VERY LONG, is seldom repeated; notwithstanding the DOTS.*

In this context it is interesting to note that alone among Mozart's piano sonatas the second part of the opening Allegro of K. 576 has no repeat sign. In other sonatas we are in favor of a free choice of whether or not to make repeats; our main argument for this attitude lies in the fact that the hearing conditions and the listening habits have drastically changed since Mozart's times. In most cases, contemporary audiences of Mozart could hear a symphony or a serenade only once in their lifetime. In presenting a new composition, it was essential that repeats were made in order to give the listener an opportunity to become familiar with the unfolding of the themes and to appreciate the emotional and formal qualities of a work. But in our day, with countless possibilities of hearing great works many times in concerts or in mechanical reproductions, our audiences know Mozart's sonatas and symphonies usually quite well, in many cases by heart, and they concentrate more on the quality of a performance or recording than on the architecture of a work. Thus, repeats can become cumbersome, at times even annoying.

The only works that were performed more than once in the eighteenth century and sometimes even frequently were operas. It is interesting to note that the overture to *The Magic Flute*, a work in typical sonata form, has no repeat signs.

Let us end this discussion of repeats on a light-hearted note, a joking anecdote: Martin Krause, a student of Franz Liszt who became the teacher of Edwin Fischer, gave the young Edwin the following advice:

> *When you have managed to get through the first part* [of the sonata] *without major calamity, give thanks to God and go on [Wenn Sie durch den ersten Teil ohne Schwierigkeiten gekommen sind, danken Sie Gott und spielen Sie weiter]!*

9
In Search of the Best Text

After World War II and during the following decades in the second half of the twentieth century, there was a remarkable awareness—noticeable all over Europe—of the European continent's great musical heritage. The unfortunate losses of the war also included the destruction of such cultural institutions as libraries and museums, and with them many manuscripts of composers were lost, some of which were destroyed forever; others simply disappeared. This awareness inspired not only the wish to save what could still be saved for posterity by filming the manuscripts and to issue facsimile editions of the most valuable and still available autographs, but it also created a boom of new editions trying to print only what a composer had written down himself. Such editions were called *Urtext editions*, because they were to be cleared of later (unauthentic) additions, and every good music publisher in Germany and Austria as well as in England and the United States tried to follow the trend.

In this endeavor to present the composer's work as finally intended by him, the term *Urtext* refers not exclusively to the oldest text source—usually an autograph—but also encompasses later authentic sources that may offer the most authoritative text. Autographs of Beethoven's works, for instance, contain a number of slips of the pen and are often considered not to reflect Beethoven's corrected final intentions; and in evaluating sources, good editors of his works are right to turn to later sources, such as original prints, which at times may supersede the autograph's text by authentic alterations and those corrections found in Beethoven's letters to publishers. The principle (proclaimed by philologists publishing German literature) that an editor should never mix sources but should decide which source he considers the best text, reflecting most reliably the author's intention, sounds fine in theory. In music, however, it is not always possible to stick to one best source, regardless of whether this is an autograph or a copy with corrections and additions by the author or an authenticated print. Walther Dürr, editor-in-chief of the *Neue Schubert Ausgabe* (*New Complete Edition of Schubert Works*), discussed these problems and came to the conviction that the traditional view that Schubert usually did not receive, read, and correct proofs when his works were printed is wrong.[1] A skeptical attitude toward the text of the original editions is often asserted for Mozart as well, and original prints and authentic copies of his works are still frequently considered of secondary importance in comparison to existing autographs because editors could not believe that Mozart was interested in or found time to consider additions or alterations or that he read proofs when he gave his works for publication to such Viennese publishers as Artaria or Torricella. The fact that today we cannot prove that he received proofs is not a valid reason for assuming that he had no interest in overseeing the copying and printing of his sonatas. We shall challenge this traditional view in the course of this chapter.

In no other realm of Mozart research has more remarkable progress been made since 1956 as in the field of editions. Whereas up to World War II very few editions offered a more or less

---

[1] W. Dürr, "Autograph—autorisierte Abschrift—Originalausgabe," in Festschrift for G.v.Dadelsen (Stuttgart 1978). On p. 93 we read: "Die Originalausgaben Schubert'scher Kompositionen hat man häufig nur mit Skepsis zu Rate gezogen. Man vermutete, dass Verlegerwillkür vielfach den Inhalt, die Wahl der Tonart und oft auch Einzelheiten des Notentextes bestimmt hätten."

reliable text without many disturbing additions not marked as such, we now have a wide choice of *Urtext* editions. Only the better ones among those clearly indicate what Mozart wrote down and what he did not because even if editors supply fingerings or what they consider necessary explanations or missing dynamic signs and other missing indications in Mozart's notation, they always must take care to have those additions marked differently in print—with the exception of fingerings (these are clearly by the editors, because Mozart never supplied fingering notations).

Every musician ultimately reaches the point when he starts to feel uneasy about the text of an edition that he has previously accepted uncritically; perhaps an articulation marking will strike him as odd, or a *forte* in a passage where he feels he should play softly disturbs him and he questions whether it may have been added by an editor or whether it might be a printer's error. The natural thing for him to do is to resolve his doubts by consulting other editions; and now he soon makes a depressing discovery: even *Urtext* editions of the same work often contradict each other in important questions. If one is to go at all deeply into interpretative problems, one obvious precondition is an indisputable musical text, which is or should be a "matter of course" for every musician. Therefore, it can be imagined that after the discovery of discrepancies when comparing editions, we fling ourselves voraciously upon *Urtext* editions that promise to reproduce the composer's text conscientiously. And it is true that many passages that formerly seemed problematical now make sense, as if by magic. We continuously discover during the process of comparing texts that—though great composers were more sparing with performing indications than the editors of their works—the few indications they do give us fit far more naturally and organically into the overall form than do other people's often well-meaning additions and alterations.

Today, good publishers compete with each other for the best Mozart edition as well as the one that is most easily accessible. Some of them supply the edition with a preface and a critical report, a welcome offering for every conscientious Mozart performer, not least because it gives us the opportunity, as we compare different editions and find discrepancies among them to think about the reasons, to understand certain editorial problems and to make our own choice in such a case.

Every editor must ask himself three questions:

1. "What did the composer write?" (Source criticism)
2. "What did the composer mean to write?" (Textual criticism)
3. "How ought the composer to have notated his music in order to be generally understood today?" (Elucidation of the text)

Of these questions, the third can be answered with the least difficulty. True, the purely external difference between the various available editions of the same work, of which some are *Urtext* editions, lies primarily in the quantity of their additions and interpolations—dynamics, indications of articulation, written-out ornaments, and fingerings. But in this area there is agreement in principle among editors: in editions for practicing musicians (as opposed to scholarly editions), elucidations and explanations are welcome provided that they are in a form that does not obscure the appearance of the original text and that clearly identifies all editorial interpolations.

The two questions on source and textual criticism usually present weightier problems for editors and can hardly be analyzed in general terms, much less solved, for each composer had his particular writing habits, and nearly every work presents its own difficulties.

The *Neue Mozart Ausgabe* (NMA)

The most important event in the field of Mozart editions after World War II has been the preparation and the completion of the main corpus of the *Neue Mozart Ausgabe* (*NMA*), the new complete edition of Mozart's works, published by Bärenreiter-Verlag (Kassel). Under the auspices of the Mozarteum in Salzburg, the best known Mozart scholars and musicologists joined forces in this monumental undertaking of more than 120 volumes. An editorial board of high integrity saw to it that certain rules were observed by all the individual editors of single volumes in order to secure uniformity in the printed representation while leaving a margin of freedom to each editor. As stated in the preliminary remarks of each volume, the purpose of this great enterprise was to present a scholarly and practical edition that would also serve performers. More than ever before, the aim of the *Neue Mozart Ausgabe* was to come as close as possible to Mozart's music text and his musical intentions. The editorial board of the *NMA* was diligent and in many respects most successful in collecting known and hitherto unknown source material for this new complete edition. The biggest problem turned out to be the disappearance of those of Mozart's autographs that formerly were in the possession of the Preussische Staatsbibliothek (Prussian State Library) and were brought to Silesia during World War II. For about three decades it was unclear and a matter of speculation what had happened to this invaluable musical heritage. *NMA* editors often had to get along with their work without being in the position to consult these most valuable sources—certainly a handicap for many of them. Fortunately, it is not only known now where nearly all of those missing Mozart autographs and the other invaluable manuscripts of the former Prussian State Library are kept presently, namely, in the University Jagellonian Library of Kraków/Poland; every serious Mozart scholar and interested musician since the 1980s has had the chance to see and consult them. If in some cases the text in the *NMA* gives reason for criticism, this has mainly to do with the postwar dilemma: the lack of accessibility of Mozart's autographs between the years 1945 and 1980.

To a certain extent, those notational habits of Mozart and his time that are not common knowledge today, were modernized in the *NMA* in order to make them comprehensible to the modern performer and to avoid misunderstandings. This was explained in a general preface and also in the various critical reports issued for each volume. Facsimile reproductions at the beginning of each volume show Mozart's handwriting in those cases where an autograph has been preserved, reproducing the most intriguing reading problems or interesting passages. Informative prefaces to each volume discuss the various works included in the volume; all problematic passages of each work are debated and the discussion throws light on the creation of each work and on the history of its composition. Most welcome for every Mozart lover is the fact that (usually for the first time) sketches and unfinished and later abandoned drafts for single movements or passages are also printed and can be found in the appendix of each volume. Some *NMA* editors also offer suggestions for the proper performance of ornaments and for occasional free embellishments and lead-ins (*Eingänge*) in Mozart's concertos. Finally—and this fact deserves special mentioning—for the first time in 150 years, the piano's *continuo* function during most *tutti* sections of Mozart's piano concertos has been presented in the way it appears in his manuscripts and in the original editions.[2] The critical report *(Kritischer Bericht)* for each volume, published separately, gives detailed information concerning discrepancies between the various sources such as authorized copies and first prints and explains the reasons why the editor chose a certain reading that he felt concurred with Mozart's intention.

It is understandable that in such a gigantic enterprise a small number of errors should remain. Fortunately, the publisher plans to correct them in future reprints. In some cases, the late rediscovery of the autographs in Kraków are responsible for certain shortcomings, but the few questionable readings and the very few misprints can be corrected in future reprints of the *NMA*.

---

[2] It is most regrettable that the recent complete edition of Beethoven's piano concertos follows nineteenth-century practice and simply eliminates his *continuo* notations, giving rather flimsy explanations for their disappearance.

Other Recommendable Editions

A few recent Mozart editions from other publishing firms, published after the *NMA*, were able to take advantage of the reappearance of Mozart's manuscripts in Kraków. Among good and recommendable editions are the ones for piano solo works and chamber music with piano by the publisher G. Henle, the *Wiener Urtext Edition* (Universal-Edition and Schott) for the piano sonatas and piano pieces and also the small yellow *Eulenburg* pocket scores for the piano concertos. We should also mention the slightly older print of the Theodore Presser Company, carefully edited by the late Nathan Broder. Most recently, Breitkopf & Härtel (Wiesbaden) issued Mozart's Piano Concerto in E-flat major K. 271, excellently edited by Cliff Eisen and Robert Levin, which will be discussed in detail toward the end of this chapter.

Naturally, it is impossible to cite all the errors and problematic passages, some of them still found in these modern editions but most of them in older editions. In comparing these available good editions, everyone may come across a number of discrepancies. We have selected a few instances where in our opinion Mozart's final intentions were not fully realized.

Without claiming that our solutions of problematic passages are infallible, we think that a discussion of various problems, found mainly in the piano sonatas as well as the piano concertos, could eventually lead to a deeper understanding of Mozart.

Text Problems in Piano Sonatas

Sonata in D major, K. 284

This sonata is a special case because it is the only one of Mozart's early sonatas to be published during his lifetime—albeit with a delay of nine years—in August 1784 by Torricella in Vienna, together with the Piano Sonata K. 333 and the Sonata for Violin and Piano K. 454, both in B-flat major. For this occasion, Mozart revised the Sonata K. 284 and composed a new and more elaborate version of the eleventh Adagio variation in the final movement. For reasons based on the traditional belief discussed above but hard to understand, every modern editor gives preference to the earlier autograph version, thus condemning the changes in Mozart's final revision for Torricella's original edition to small print or leaving them out altogether. Even the editors of the excellent *NMA* volume, Wolfgang Plath and Wolfgang Rehm, committed this error, adding, however, several variants in small print. This method creates confusion. For example, in m. 67 of the second movement, there is a *p* printed in the center, surrounded by two small *pp* signs above and below: Which one should be observed? Worse, in Var. VII, mm. 13–14 (in the Henle edition, where the whole variation movement is numbered continuously: mm. 129–130) the same notes have an *f* underneath and a smaller *p* above as shown in this example:

Ex. IX/1:

Following are a few other points deserving discussion.

First Movement: Allegro.   In m. 23 and at the recapitulation m. 94, Mozart had written a *tr* sign above the first sixteenth note:

Ex. IX/2:

In m. 94 he replaced it with an *appoggiatura* but apparently forgot to cancel the earlier trill symbol. All modern editions print a trill preceded by an *appoggiatura*—an absurdity! (Even with the shortest trill execution one would have to play four notes in a fraction of a second.) The first edition omits the trill in both places and prints the *appoggiatura* only in m. 94, a truly Mozartean solution that ought to be applied to m. 23 also.

Second Movement: Rondeau en Polonaise, Andante.   Confusion could be avoided if the editors were to print the final version only (dynamic signs in large print, of course) and mention the earlier version in footnotes or in the editor's report. This procedure has been successfully applied in the works of later composers; e.g., Beethoven and Brahms.

We reproduce here the last page of the first print this *Rondeau*, containing subtle differences of the text not found in modern editions; for instance, the correct placing of the turn in m. 74 (RH, beat 2) and different dynamics on the repeated notes a (bass clef, in mm. 90ff.).

Ex. IX/3:

(Facsimile of the last page of the authentic first print (Torricella 1784) of the *Rondeau en Polonaise* of the Sonata in D Major, K. 284, mm. 71–92.)

Third Movement: Theme with 12 Variations.   It is in this last movement where differences occur. We list only a few of the most important ones.

Var. 1:   Different articulation in mm. 3 and 10, four times ⌐⌐⌐; also in mm. 7 and 16 from second group onwards.

Var. 2:   Triplets in the left hand with slurs, probably over all six notes, possibly over five notes only.

Var. 4:   mm. 3, 7: first and third group of sixteenth notes in both hands: ⌐⌐⌐⌐. In m. 16, similar including also fourth group, *staccato* in left hand only, not in the right hand.

Var. 5:   m. 5: *cresc.*; m. 7: *f*.

Var. 6:   m. 6, LH, octaves: last three notes in the bass part are B–E–B and not B–E–D.

Var. 7:   m. 6: first sixteenth note after trill has a double sharp, otherwise rarely found in Mozart; m. 12 *f* instead of *p*; mm. 13–14 *piano*; m. 14 *cresc.*; m. 15 *f*; m. 16 *sf* on second beat, both hands, followed by a *p*. This is certainly an improvement over the simpler dynamics of the manuscript.

Var. 8:   RH octaves mm. 1–3 *staccato* (only the g¹–g² in the second half of m. 2 lack strokes).

Var. 9:   from *f* onward, mm. 4–6, all octaves *staccato*; quarter notes in mm. 7 and 16 RH *legato*.

Var. 10: mm. 11–13, first note: no *p* and *pp*, but instead in m. 12: *decresc.* leading to a *p* in m. 13.

Var. 11: Here the editor of the Henle edition had the good idea to print Mozart's final (published) version in the main text (but why only here?); however, *NMA* and Wiener Urtext editors put it in small print above the earlier version. In m. 30 (Henle: m. 217) the first *tr* on the highest note is certainly an engraver's error: the trilled note would demand the only f-sharp³ in all of Mozart's solo piano works.

Var. 12: mm. 1, 5, 22 (Henle 212, 216, 243): The *appoggiatura* [♪ notation] has been replaced by [♪ notation]. In the Henle edition the slur is missing in the footnote. The slurs in mm. 7 and 30 were eliminated in the original edition (because they were probably writing slips).

Sonata in C major, K. 309

There are no problematic readings in the first and third movements.

Second Movement: Andante un poco adagio.   Near the end of the movement, the second bass note on beat two of the penultimate measure is A (see Ex. IX/3) according to the copy in Leopold Mozart's hand. However, in a nearly identical passage at the end of the Andante of the Concerto for Two Pianos K. 365, written one year later, this second bass note is the subdominant. If transposed to the key of the second movement from K. 309, this note would be an octave B-flat, which certainly sounds more convincing.

End of the second movement of the C major Sonata K. 309:

Ex. IX/4:

Compare the alternative version with the close of the Andante movement of the Concerto for Two Pianos K. 365 (originally in B-flat major), transposed into the key of the above example:

Ex. IX/5:

What a pity that the autograph of the Sonata K. 309 is lost!

Sonata in B-flat major, K. 333

First Movement: Allegro. The question as to which upbeat to m. 1 —,

— is the better execution has to remain open because the original edition has the longer slur only over the upbeat to mm. 64 and 66. The dotted slurs in mm. 1, 2, and 9 are to be found in the original edition. The slurs for the upper part in mm. 5, 29, and 98 are one note longer (see m. 125 of the autograph), which seems to be an improvement worth mentioning.

In m. 150, the trill signs might mean turns. (Often *tr* signs have the function of a turn or a *pralltrill*; e.g., in the beginning of the cadenza to the first movement of the Concerto in B-flat Major, K. 456, a motive for which the orchestra had turns earlier. But here the execution as *pralltrill* is equally recommendable.

orchestral motive: compared with the cadenza:

Second Movement: Andante cantabile. Measures 21, 25, 71, 75: As previously discussed, the *sf* here in the left hand could mean *rinforzando*.

Third Movement: Allegretto grazioso. Measure 6: The isolated slur for the left hand in m. 6 (c¹–e¹) is certainly a writing slip of Mozart's and ought to be eliminated, following the original edition. Instead, all modern editors added it also to mm. 2, 42, 46, etc.—nonsense, in our opinion.

Measure 197: only the Henle edition reproduces the correct rhythm found in the original print (sixteenth notes with dots, followed by sixty-fourth notes).

In mm. 203–204 it is hard to understand why all modern editors ignore the fine articulation of the left-hand part in the original edition. We reproduce here this line from m. 199 on in facsimile:

Ex. IX/6:

Measure 199

A mistake in this original print is the first quarter note e-flat¹ in the accompaniment in m. 201 (marked with NB). It should be d¹—a typical printing error.

Sonata in B-flat major, K. 570

First Movement: Allegro. In mm. 57 and 59 (also 187 and 189), there has been some question about the ninth note in the RH part.

Ex. IX/7:

The (posthumous) first edition corrected Mozart's version, replacing a¹ and d¹ by b¹ and e-flat¹, respectively. Since the pattern in mm. 57 and 59 is a varied inversion of the mm. 51 and 53, with a¹ on the third beat (and by analogy 187 and 189 an inversion of 181 and 183), there can be no doubt that the autograph is correct.

Second Movement: Adagio.   Unfortunately, the autograph of the last two movements is lost; we can only surmise a few possible errors in the early editions.

In mm. 3–4, a tie in the middle voice e-flat would be appropriate here and in all subsequent repeats.

It is very likely that—as in m. 24/1—the middle voice in m. 16/1 should start one note earlier with g^1, imitating the upper voice:

Ex. IX/8:

The first edition was rather careless with accidentals. For instance, in the third movement, m. 74, a sharp sign (for C-sharp) is missing. Thus, it is most likely that in the LH part a flat sign before g^1 on the fourth beat of m. 40 is missing.

The facsimile of the first edition starts with the second beat of m. 39:

Ex. IX/9:

If the last beat in m. 40 (marked NB) is played with g-flat^1, thus producing E-flat minor, the harmonic progression would be identical with the same modulation in the C minor Concerto K. 491, second movement, mm. 59–60. (It is noteworthy that the form of the entire *Adagio* movement from K. 570 is modeled upon the Larghetto movement from the C minor Concerto.)

Four-Hand Piano Sonata in F major, K. 497

As stated at the beginning of this chapter, we find it regrettable that many modern editors, when evaluating the sources of a Mozart composition, traditionally give preference to an autograph if there is one extant and thus often suppress better variants found in the original editions published in Vienna during Mozart's lifetime. In the following case, this seems to us a nearly criminal decision; namely, in this great Four-Hand Sonata in F Major, K. 497, where at the very end of the third movement, mm. 315–317, the imitation in the upper voices was changed for the first print into a perfect four-part canon including the bass voice. Obviously, only Mozart himself could have invented this wonderful canon—it is the afterthought of a genius!

Unfortunately, the editor of the *NMA* also blindly followed the autograph, and the text of the original edition is found only in the most recent *Wiener Urtext Ausgabe* (edited by Ulrich Leisinger, with a foreword on interpretation problems by Robert Levin). We reproduce it here in full score.

Ex. IX/10:

This example is a hint also for future editors of those three sonatas K. 332, K. 457, and K. 284, where we find obviously authentic embellishments in the slow movements and in the *Adagio* variation resp. in the original editions. Editors should respect these variants as afterthoughts of Mozart that deserve to be printed in the main text, and older variants of the autographs should be printed as *ossia* versions above, and not vice versa.

Text Problems in Piano Concertos

In practically all editions, including the *NMA*, several errors have remained undetected, mainly because several autographs (now in Kraków, Poland) were not accessible to the editors for so long. Fortunately, they are now available for researchers. Of those undetected errors, we will mention here of course only a few problematic passages, found in the *NMA*.

Concerto for Two Pianos K. 365

First Movement: Allegro

mm. 104, 108, 112, 14, 233, 237, 241, 243	The slurs (RH) should start on the first note
mm. 116–119:	The slurs starting on the first eighth note should continue until the fourth note

Second Movement: Andante

mm. 24, 26, 78, 80	no staccato on last note
m. 38	no trill sign there
m. 49	wrong trill suffix in *NMA* (correct: F–E-natural–F–G)
m. 87	

wrong: correct:

(This correct version is from the autograph.)

In general, the text of the Eulenburg score (No. 741) is more reliable here. But one mistake remained undetected both there and in the *NMA*: in m. 52, fifth note in the left hand, Mozart wrote a G and not an F, as in the similar progression in m. 56 (bass notes there are E-flat–F–F).

It should be noted that in a recent reprint of the *NMA* text (in an edition for two pianos), these errors were corrected after we had pointed them out in a letter to the editors.

Third Movement: Allegro. All dotted rhythmic figures ♪. ♪ are probably meant to be played as triplets: ♪ ♪ in order to match the last note of the LH triplets.

Cadenza: (m. 17) a natural sign is missing before the suffix.

(Measure 44) First piano, LH lowest note should be G and not E-flat (Mozart wrote the chord in first inversion).

Concerto in A major, K. 414

First Movement: Allegro
- Measures 19, 23, viola: half note b is still *forte*; *piano* starts in the following measure.
- Measure 162, viola: after a correction in the autograph, the first note is f-sharp and not a.
- Measures 180–188: upper strings *sfp* instead of *sf*, followed by a *p* on the next note.
- In m. 195, a lead-in should be inserted, or at least a footnote should point this out. A suggestion for such a fermata embellishment has been proposed in chapter 7.
- Measures 249–250, piano, RH: These two bars are connected by a short slur d-sharp^2–e^2.

Second Movement: Andante
- Measure 23, RH: The middle voice e^1–d^1 should be cancelled here but not in mm. 74–77.
- Measure 113, RH: 2nd eighth note d^2 and not f-sharp^2
- Measure 123, LH: Penultimate note e^1 and not g^1
- Measure 64: All sources have c-sharp as the fourth note (f-sharp should be replaced by it).
- Measures 17, 52, 54, 102: In all these measures, the slur on the first beat should be cancelled.

Mozart wrote consistently: ♪ ♪♪ without any slurs.

Strangely enough, the recent Peters Urtext edition (Zacharias and Wolff) prints the same unauthentic slurs as the *NMA*. Also, without any commentary in mm. 21–24, this edition follows the *NMA* and prints the different version for mm. 74–77.

Third Movement, Rondeau: Allegretto
- Measures 18 and 205, first oboe: first note a^2 is an eighth followed by a dotted quarter note e^2.
- Measure 113, RH: 2nd eighth note d^2 and not f-sharp^2.
- Measure 123, LH: penultimate note e^1 and not g^1.
- Measure 129, piano. LH: Cancel the half note A and replace it by rest (according to the autograph).
- Measure 193, RH: In Mozart's first notation, the last two notes are b-flat^1–a^1. But he wrote this passage twice, the second time as printed in *NMA*.
- Measures 196–197, piano, LH: In the autograph score, the octave notes F–E–F–E are one octave lower than in the *NMA*. However, in view of the first octave e–e^1 of the authentic lead-in starting in m. 197, the version of *NMA* is acceptable.

Concerto in D major, K. 451

Second Movement: Andante ¢

m. 11, RH	add slur from notes 5 through 7
mm. 17–18, LH	cancel the lowest notes C-sharp
m. 29, LH	replace the upper note D with E
m. 31, RH	first two notes: add staccato dots under the slur

mm. 32–33 and middle of 34	no ties there, but in the varied repeat in mm. 92–94 Mozart did write ties G–G'
m. 52, RH	slur over whole measure
m. 65, LH	cancel the F-sharp
m. 98, RH	triplet not *staccato*

Concerto in A major, K. 488

First Movement: Allegro

m. 2	both first and second violins have the same notes a–g-sharp¹; this is, of course, a writing slip—the first vlns. have to play a third higher: c-sharp²–b¹

This assumption is based on the later recurrence of the theme in the solo part (m. 236). However, in the initial draft Mozart had notated a¹–g#¹ in the first violins, leaving out all other parts save the bass. In that earlier version, the second violins would have had the lower sixth c#¹–b.

Though writing mistakes are in fact rarer in Mozart's manuscripts than in those of other composers, they are not wholly absent.

Concerto in C minor, K. 491

It is well known that Mozart wrote down the C minor Concerto K. 491 in great haste. It is Beethovenian, not only in character, but in its graphic appearance, which is unusually untidy for Mozart. Some passages are nearly illegible, because three, and on one occasion four, different versions have been written over one another. Thus, it is understandable that there are more problematic passages in this concerto than in any other of Mozart's works. In one case, there must certainly have been a mistake on Mozart's part; in the second movement, a Larghetto, there is an obviously unintentional clash of two different harmonic ideas, which, strangely enough, has never been altered or mentioned as problematic in any editions we have come across. Here the wind instruments have a most beautiful harmonic variant, which was not yet present when the piano part was—obviously earlier—written.

Ex. IX/11:

The bassoon part proves this error, since it is impossible to interpret it as a tenor part (if it were, it would produce parallel fourths with the piano bass on the second and third notes). Thus, it was obviously intended as a bass line. To take this passage at its face value would mean a quite un-Mozartean part writing (e.g., an ugly doubling of the F on the second eighth note and parallel sevenths between bassoon and piano). Here the piano part must be altered to fit the orchestral parts.

A proper execution of the piano part of m. 40 could be:

Ex. IX/12:

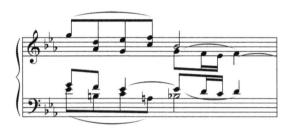

First Movement: Allegro.   In m. 319 of the first movement, the piano part has a d-flat², whereas the second oboe has a d² in the autograph (the flat sign is missing). Three bars later, a natural sign is missing before the first oboe's a². Both the (necessary) flat sign in m. 319 and the forgotten natural in m. 322 have been added to the manuscript by someone else (André) in red ink, but only in the first oboe, and not in the piano part.[3]

There is another problematic passage in the first movement of the C minor Concerto: In m. 332, the authentic notes G in trumpets and timpani are missing in all editions due to a misunderstanding. Here and in the following measures Mozart had written into the piano part a first draft of the *arpeggios*. But since this draft had filled the space of the piano part, due to lack of room Mozart had to use the two staves above for the final version where he had already written the notes G for trumpets and timpani. Since the piano must not play these notes G at the beginning, Mozart crossed them out, but this was most probably meant for the piano only. For the trumpets and timpani they are a musical necessity in view of the previous bars and should certainly be played by these musicians. (We owe this observation to the eminent Mozart conductor Otto Werner Müller.)[4]

---

[3] We mentioned these corrections in our first edition of this book, about fifty years ago. Recently, Robert Levin came independently to the same conclusion in his article "The Devil's in the Details," p. 41.

[4] A facsimile of this page (erroneously printed standing on its head) is found in the essay by Paul Badura-Skoda, "Problematische Textstellen in Mozarts Klavierwerken und ihre fragwürdige Übertragung in die Neue Mozart Ausgabe," p. 128.

A facsimile reproduction shows this page:

Ex. IX/13:

It is odd that trumpets and timpani are silent in the autograph in mm. 334–336; apparently another writing slip by Mozart.

Third Movement: Allegretto.   A small oversight of the *NMA* editor in m. 44 of K. 491/III may also be mentioned here: The four sixteenth notes on the third beat are G–F-sharp–E–D. Certainly not Mozart but a later editor wrote a natural sign before the F-sharp in red ink into the autograph score, which in photocopies comes out in black and therefore can be mistaken to be Mozart's correction.

Another obvious writing error by Mozart was detected by Hans Bischoff in his excellent edition (Steingraeber No. 563) as early as 1887 but never found its way into subsequent editions. Five measures before the end of this movement, in m. 283, the first two notes of the first bassoon should be one third higher, namely F–F instead of D–D.

In his article "The Devil's in the Details," Robert Levin offered interesting suggestions for enriching the texture of this concerto. Only twice do we find ourselves not in agreement. In mm. 175–177 of the first movement, Levin believes that the first bassoon should play in unison with the left thumb of the pianist. In our opinion, however, it is a stroke of genius that both the piano and the lower strings take the bass line over from the bassoon. Mozart might well have simply forgotten to write *col basso* into the bassoon part following m. 174. With this in mind, it appears more likely to us that the first bassoon should play in unison with the cellos rather than the basses. The other instance where we are of a different opinion is found in the third movement: Levin suggests that the thirds in mm. 245–247 and 262–264 should be broken as in the preceding measures. But while the *tremolando* figuration in C minor in mm. 241–244 poses no major technical difficulty, the ascending alternating thirds as suggested by Levin would add an element of difficulty, of nearly Lisztian virtuosity not to be found elsewhere in Mozart, to this concerto:

Ex. IX/14:

As it happens, the chromatic rising chords from m. 245 onwards bring a new element of agitation into the score, which motivates a different figuration in the piano part.

Concerto in C major, K. 503

An error similar to the one mentioned above in K. 491/II can be found in the final movement of the C major Concerto K. 503. In the autograph there are two different harmonies superimposed in this third movement in m. 60, obviously due to a later correction made by Mozart. When Mozart first wrote down the piano part he put the dominant chord of G major as accompaniment to the triplet figuration of the right hand. But when writing the orchestration later, he improved the harmonic progression by introducing the supertonic into the strings, thus creating a perfect cadence II–V–I. It was George Szell who first discovered that the resulting strange harmony was not a bold predecessor of the *Meistersinger* chord (with all the notes of the major key sounding together at once) but a simple oversight of Mozart's.

Ex. IX/15:

TRACK
50

This mistake was also mentioned in an old essay by Walter Gerstenberg.[5] There can be hardly any doubt that the left-hand part ought to be changed like this:

Ex. IX/16:

---

[5] See W. Gerstenberg, "Zum Autograph des Klavierkonzerts KV 503(C-Dur)," p. 38ff.

Two bars earlier, the lowest note G in the piano part has to be eliminated in order to avoid wrong voice leading.

Another harmonic discrepancy between the piano and the orchestra in the Concerto K. 503, this time in the second movement, hitherto unnoticed, has been uncovered recently by Robert Levin. In m. 41 (LH), the piano part has the chord a–c¹–d¹–f-sharp¹, whereas the accompanying strings have the A minor harmony and the half note e¹ in the first violins. All editions changed that half note e¹ in d¹, mostly without comment. But the opposite procedure would have been far more appropriate; Mozart certainly wrote the piano part first, and when he wrote the orchestra part later, he introduced there a more elaborate and interesting harmony. Therefore, it is the piano chord that should be altered from:

Ex. IX/17:

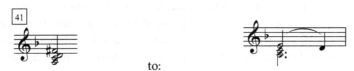

to:

Unfortunately, another mistake in voice leading in the third movement went nearly undetected so far: in mm. 247–248 there are no less than five parallel fifths between the piano and the second bassoon. Were they really intended by Mozart?

Autograph version:

Ex. IX/18:

The critical report of the *NMA* for this volume mentions an old set of parts owned by the monastery Melk, which offers here a corrected version that in our opinion could very well go back to Mozart himself.

Corrected version:

Ex. IX/19:

A small error by the *NMA* in this second movement of this Concerto K. 503 in m. 36 is still worth mentioning: Here the melody note on the third beat should be A and not F sharp, a fact for which we found confirmation when consulting the autograph once more.

Concerto in B-flat major, K. 595

First Movement: Allegro.   One of Mozart's few probable compositional errors was already discussed in 1991 at the Mozart Anniversary Conference in Leipzig by coauthor Paul Badura-Skoda: in this movement of Mozart's last piano concerto, there are parallel fifths between piano and oboe in mm. 212–213; still worse, there are six parallel seconds between piano and flute, which sound almost like Bartók. Two measures later, we find three parallel fifths between the piano and the first bassoon.

After the Leipzig session, the composer Marius Flothuis, referring to these issues, pleaded in a letter for a literal execution of these passages, notwithstanding the dissonances—otherwise, too many alterations would be the result. In spite of our great respect for this eminent Mozart scholar, we still think that something ought to be done here to make the passage smoother. For instance, placing a few notes of flute and oboe in mm. 212–213 one step higher and making a subtle change of the piano part in m. 214 would transform the parallel fifths into pleasant-sounding sixths.

The following example shows the original version with parallel fifths in m. 214:

Ex. IX/20:

Specifically problematic is the parallel fifth in m. 214:

Ex. IX/21:

Suggested correction in the piano part:

Ex. IX/22:

Third Movement: Allegro. On the other hand, we believe that the missing flat signs before the E's in the third movement's cadenza in mm. 28–29 are not an oversight by Mozart but are his intention:

Ex. IX/23:

Such a small alteration into a minor third can be observed in many similar passages; they show that Mozart disliked the interval of the diminished third (according to the *NMA* editor, one should play here c-sharp–e-flat). But other examples of such minor thirds can be found in the first movement of the Concerto in C major, K. 467, mm. 160/I; the Concerto in E-flat major, K. 482/ I, m. 92, note 12, and m. 192, note 4; as well as in the variations on a theme by Gluck "Unser dummer Pöbel meint" K. 455, Var. X, mm. 46/47 (Henle edition numbering: mm. 262–263). In all these cases mentioned here, modern editors have become "additors," adding not authentic flat or natural signs.

The real artist does not merely play for the public, which nowadays rarely appreciates the extreme subtleties of interpretation and usually has only an intuitive feeling whether something has or has not been played correctly. Editing the works of a great master composer such as Mozart, conscientiously working musicologists and editors should try to find out his intentions in even the minutest details. Aware of their responsibility to the composer and to the whole of our musical culture, the performers are prompted to observe with the utmost exactness the text handed down to them, regardless of whether anyone praises them for it or not. This sense of responsibility is, in the last analysis, what distinguishes a true artist from a mere showman concerned only with success.

Despite the problematic passages mentioned above, the *NMA*, the new complete edition of Mozart's works with its critical reports, remains a monumental enterprise worthy of consultation, a needed reference edition for years to come for every devoted Mozart player.

What Comes after the *Neue Mozart Ausgabe?*

Is there now still a need for new editions of Mozart's piano works after the relevant volumes of the *NMA*? Unhesitatingly, we say "yes!" The scholars who edited the *NMA* refrained, for instance, from helping performers with fingering suggestions, and often they did not provide enough editorial explanations for those works where we miss Mozart's detailed indications for performers, such as dynamics or articulation retrained signs or tempo indications.

There are two kinds of new editions to be envisioned:

1. Editions that—while respecting the authentic text clearly visible as such in the print— offer performance suggestions by experts for the inexperienced player. Among these we count our own editions of the D minor Fantasy K. 397 (Leduc, Paris, 1987, N° AL 27300), or of the "Coronation" Concerto K. 537 (G. Schirmer, New York, 2005, N° 2045), where the performance suggestions appear in light blue or light grey print and can be easily distinguished from the authentic text.

2. Editions that are even more scholarly orientated than the *NMA*: These editions try to represent Mozart's text as closely as possible, abstaining as much as possible from editorial

additions (but making the text more easily readable than facsimile editions). Attention should be drawn to the increased number of facsimile editions available today. For the enlightened musician, they always provide additional insights into the composer's creative process and are valuable as a source to find the usually most reliable text.

There also exist editions that fall in between these two categories, such as the excellent new edition of Mozart's violin and piano sonatas edited by Wolfgang Seiffert (Henle). It scrupulously follows Mozart's text but adds fingerings in the piano and violin parts as well as suggested bowings for the violinist.

Below we would like to discuss another recommendable edition of this kind in more detail.

A Recent New Edition of the Piano Concerto in E-flat Major, K. 271 (Breitkopf & Härtel N° 5300)

This excellent print, edited by Cliff Eisen and Robert Levin, is based mainly on Mozart's autograph score of this concerto (now in Kraków), which was not available to the editors of the *NMA* volume. It merits special discussion because this edition could serve as a model for the future. The three most disturbing mistakes of the *NMA* are corrected here, all occurring in the third movement:

1. In m. 142, the first note of the second oboe is a D, not an E-flat. This mistake can already be found in the old complete edition (*AMA*) and had been carried over inadvertently into subsequent editions, including Eulenburg score no. 742 and the *NMA*. Praise to Eisen and Levin for finally printing the proper note D!

2. Likewise, at long last, a grave mistake found in the *AMA* as well as in the *NMA* has been corrected in this edition: Just before the end of the third movement, in mm. 464 and 465, the third eighth note of the piano in the left hand and also in the violins should be g instead of a-flat. Previously, only the old Peters edition (Fischer-Soldan) had printed the correct text.

3. Another mistake occurred in the *Menuetto cantabile* section of the same movement: In m. 253, the *appoggiatura* a-flat[1] of the *NMA* is wrong—it certainly ought to be c[2], repeating the previous note from m. 252.[6] (Strangely, these major differences that are real improvements are not mentioned in the critical report of the Breitkopf & Härtel edition, although the editors had promised: "Given the *NMA*'s exceptional importance and prestige, the present edition takes pains to identify readings that diverge from it" (p. 96).

Even in such an excellent edition as the one from Eisen and Levin, a few errors did occur. The following listing of those is not meant as a Beckmesserian attack but as a helpful criticism; no doubt, the mistakes shall be eliminated in the next reprint of the edition. It should simply show that we are all human and that nobody is perfect.

Eisen's and Levin's editorial policy of this edition has been explained in the well-written preface and in the introduction to the critical report. In the preface we read:

> *In order to give as clear an indication as possible of Mozartian practice, the characteristic notation of the authentic sources—closer to the essence of the work than the normative limitations of modernized notation—has as a rule been preserved. This is especially*

---

[6] There is a similar probable error in the E minor Concerto by Chopin, second movement, m. 54: the original edition shows *appoggiatura* G-sharp with an octave leap upward instead of the more convincing B. Since the autograph of Chopin's work is lost, we cannot ascertain whether this G-sharp is an error or not.

the case in those instances where the peculiarities of Mozart's notation carry performance implications:

> *dual-stemming to indicate not only divisi in the orchestral parts but also the polyphonic basis of much of the piano writing;*
> *Mozart's beaming, which frequently separates individual notes from groups of similar notes to articulate phrase structure and accentuation; and*
> *combinations of ties and slurs in succession, rather than ties subsumed under lengthy slurs.*

Slurs have not been added automatically to connect grace notes with main notes. Although Leopold Mozart prescribed the universal execution of such slurs, even in cases where they are not notated, the evidence of Wolfgang's autographs and performing parts, as well as the musical contexts, suggest that for him this may not always have been the case, at least from the 1770s on.

The preface also states:

> *While some of the numerous corrections in the autographs can be understood as straight-forward improvements, many simply offer alternative, sometimes technically simplified readings. In such cases we have printed both versions, permitting the performer to make a choice.*

Finally (on p. 99 of this Breitkopf & Härtel edition), the critical report tells us:

> *The goal of the present edition is to allow access to the different states of the work through its creative and performance history. In explicating the readings of both sources and common editions we hope to provide the user with the tools to evaluate them and to reach independent judgments on both philosophical and practical issues.*

Unfortunately, we could not find a single instance in this score where two different versions were printed, "permitting the performer to make a choice!" (We learned in the meanwhile from the editors that this sentence was aimed at projected editions of other Mozart concertos K. 449, K. 450, and K. 451, a project that was, alas, later canceled.)

Following are some observations.

Abbreviations and Symbols

Piano, LH: Whenever Mozart wrote the bass notes of the *continuo* during the orchestra *tutti*, they were printed with large note heads. But when he used the abbreviation *Col B* (*col Basso*) they appear in small print; e.g., first movement, mm. 9–54. This distinction creates the impression that the small notes are less important, which is misleading. If all abbreviated notes in the orchestral parts (marked *col B* or *unis. B*, etc.) were distinguished in a similar way, the score would be filled with notes in small print.

The Eisen–Levin edition is the only modern edition that reproduces Mozart's *arpeggio* sign in its original form: a diagonal stroke through a chord. At its first appearance (in m. 80 of the first movement), a note refers to the preface. However, no explanation is given (one is found, though, in the edition of this Concerto for Two Pianos K. 365, no. 8640). This *arpeggio* notation (also found in Haydn's and Beethoven's works) has the disadvantage of being identical to the north German sign for the *acciaccatura*, which has a different meaning: It is an *arpeggio* with nonharmonic notes in between; for example, a C major chord with D, F, A, and/or B. Even a well-informed musician like Wanda Landowska misunderstood Mozart's *arpeggio* notation and played *acciaccaturas* instead of *arpeggios* in one of her recordings. An explanation about the differences of understanding these signs in north and south Germany is therefore indispensable.

Articulation

In m. 12 of the second movement of K. 271, the three repeated notes f in the cello/bass part have an odd articulation: first note *staccato*, second and third notes *portato*—most likely a simple writing slip by Mozart. The Salzburg copy (source B) has *portato* over all three notes, which corresponds to most of the other repeated eighth notes in the strings. Strangely enough, the editors put the same odd articulation in brackets into the parallel m. 110. Should not all three notes be *portato*?

In the piano part in m. 31, the slur in the middle voice e-flat^1–d^1, clearly visible in the autograph, is missing (no mention of this is found in the critical report). Also, in our opinion, in the second movement, m. 128, the editors misunderstood Mozart's writing process: He had first written a slur over the second and third notes f^3–e-flat^3. As an afterthought, Mozart then changed the articulation into:

Ex. IX/24:

The initial articulation had been a slur over the figure on the second beat of the measure. Mozart did not eliminate this slur; it is still visible in the autograph (in m. 128):

Ex. IX/25:

Measure 126–130

(Note: By mistake in the edition for two pianos of K. 271, these measures are numbered one number too high.)

Because the *staccato* strokes or wedges in mm. 128–130 can hardly mean accents, and because the f^2 in m. 128 cannot be played *staccato* and *legato* simultaneously, it becomes obvious that Mozart forgot to eliminate the second slur in m. 128.

Dynamics

In the first movement in m. 115, the editors put a *forte* sign in brackets. This *f* is indeed missing in the autograph but is found in the Salzburg copy written by Mozart's sister. But in mm. 325–326 and 333–338 of the last movement, in a similar editorial situation, the two editors printed the *staccato* strokes found only in the Salzburg copy not with but without brackets. This is inconsistent.

Therefore, we suggest the following correction: Either no brackets should be printed in m. 115 of the first movement but only in the parallel passage 244 (where no source has an *f*) or the *staccato* strokes in the finale should be put in brackets.

After the cadenza to the second movement, the Eisen–Levin edition prints the *p* sign under the fourth note of the right hand. It is true that Mozart wrote the piano indication more to the right than usual, yet musical logic dictates that the *p* belongs to the second note (b-natural). In such cases, musical logic must prevail, and it is significant that Mozart's sister (and all other editors) placed it under the b-natural.

Another case of wrong editorial brackets can be observed in the first *Eingang* (lead-in) on p. 68: At the entrance of the Presto, Mozart wrote a clear *f*, albeit in the left-hand system only. No explanation is given regarding why the editors decided to put brackets around the *f*.

Ornamentation

The editors tried to follow Mozart's distinction between the trill symbol with or without a wavy line, whatever the difference might mean in performance. It has indeed little bearing anyway, because only the context decides whether a short or a long trill was meant in case no wavy line was written. (In two cases they printed such lines that were *not* notated by Mozart, namely, in the first movement in m. 231—inconsistent with the notation in m. 102—and in the second movement in m. 115.)

Unlike the *NMA*, the Eisen–Levin edition offers no suggestions for the execution of ornaments, with only one exception; namely, in m. 181 of the first movement, in the part of the first violins. At least once in the second movement, mm. 62 and 68, where Mozart wrote a compound *appoggiatura* not found elsewhere in this work, similar advice for the presumed execution would have been most welcome. (We supplied a suggestion on p. 173, Ex V/129.)

The brackets in m. 67 of the same movement are a clear mistake and give the impression that the *appoggiatura* G is an editorial addition. It is not; this *appoggiatura* is found in both main sources A and B. (No explanation is found in the critical report.)

Since this edition—according to the preface—claims to be designed for practical use, at least one piece of advice regarding an old rhythmic convention would have been most desirable: In the first movement in m. 24, Mozart took pains to notate the double-dotted rhythm in an unambiguous way. When the same motive reappears in the solo part in mm. 86 and 215, however, the second dot is missing—apparently Mozart was counting on the general knowledge of this eighteenth-century practice. Today, even experienced pianists miss the point and need a hint that double-dotting is meant. A literal single-dotted execution would sound lame, not as lively as the passage sounds in the *tutti*. (Other examples for necessary or possible double-dotting in Mozart's works are given in chapter 3, "Problems of Tempo and Rhythm," p. 93f.)

Critical Report

At the end of the paragraph following the subheading "Individual readings" on p. 99, the editors wrote: "Particularly important observations, above all those relevant questions of performance practice, are printed in **bold type**." An excellent idea! But we cannot agree that the observation about measures mm. 70–71, 163–164 of the first movement qualifies for this treatment. Unlike in measures 72–74, 165, 167, 186, and 189, the first oboe has no slurs here into the following measures. But given the subsequent repetitions of the same motive, this can hardly be intentional. Besides, even if performed literally, the listener will not hear the difference because of the simultaneously sounding trill of the piano, which finishes on the same note. The critical report, meticulous though it is, could have dealt with more relevant questions.

To sum up: Despite the inaccuracies and inconsistencies discussed above, the new Breitkopf & Härtel edition is now the best edition available and can be considered ideally suited for the historically orientated and scholarly interested musician. Editions of this kind should be valued as an alternative to the *NMA* and as a model for future editions, with the aim to come as close as possible to Mozart's intentions. (Professor Levin has assured us that all inaccuracies mentioned above will be corrected in the next reprint.)

About Page Turning

Even the best edition is useless if a pianist cannot read the text. Many modern books and scores are bound in such a way that they refuse to remain open. The pianist tries to open them—they close themselves again. He tries to turn a page—it stubbornly turns back by itself. He tries once more to force the volume open, but to no avail: The binding and the paper are inflexible, they do not yield even a millimeter. After weeks and months of fighting, the fingers ache but the score remains unmoved. If one just reads a novel or a score, one can hold it open with the hands. But what should be done if the music is placed on the music desk? Alas, a pianist does not play with his feet alone; besides, he wants to write notes and fingerings—but not on the previous page! The only remedy is to tear the score apart (provided one is strong enough) and to rearrange it with spirals. No wonder that most musicians prefer to play from photocopies! Instead of complaining, publishers should provide us with decently bound scores. It was possible in the nineteenth and early twentieth centuries. Why this regression of technology in recent times?

Above we quoted the well-known saying: Nobody is perfect. Even Mozart could not avoid making some few (admirably few!) writing mistakes. Editors, publishers, and pianists are all human, and they may forgive us the listings of wrong notes, minor shortcomings, and some inaccuracies, some of which they will certainly find in our book (hopefully not too many!): We are human, too.

10
Playing with Orchestra

Not only have pianos altered a great deal in timbre and in their capacity of sound volume since Mozart's time, the sound of string instruments—above all of the violins—as well as horns and woodwind instruments has changed; and the orchestras of the last two centuries have become increasingly larger and much louder altogether. Compared with the Viennese orchestras of Mozart's day, the present-day orchestra hardly ever allows the wind instruments (including the horns) to sound comparatively loud enough, whereas the strings are dominating.

The sound of wind instruments was very much loved in the eighteenth century in southern Germany and especially by Mozart, and at the time great importance was attached to a clear overall sound. Certainly gaining in this desired clarity are today's so-called period orchestras, using old instruments and performing with a smaller sized string section. Most of Mozart's works gain from performance by a small body of strings; but, of course, in deciding the size of the orchestra, one must be guided not only by the character of the work concerned but also by the acoustics of the hall. We favor smaller sized orchestras even in large halls, although we know that Mozart did come across very large orchestras, too, as is seen from his letter of 24 March 1781, in which he writes about the orchestra of the Vienna Tonkünstlersozietat: "The orchestra consists of 180 players." And on 11 April 1781 he reported to his father:

> *I forgot to tell you the other day that at the concert the Symphony* [probably K. 338] *went magnificently and had the greatest success. There were 40 violins, the wind-instruments were all doubled, there were 10 violas, 10 double-basses, 8 violoncellos and 6 bassoons.*

Such enormous forces seem, however, to have been very much the exception at the time. In his studies of orchestra sizes in European musical centers, Neal Zaslaw came to the same conclusion.[1] Usually Mozart could only count on, say 6 + 6 violins, 4 violas, 3 'celli, and 3 basses.[2]

Mozart's ideal seems to have corresponded to the size of the Mannheim orchestra. In his letter to his father of 4 November 1777 he wrote:

> *Now I must tell you about the music here. … The orchestra is excellent and very strong. On either side 10 or 11 violins, 4 violas, 2 oboes, 2 flutes and 2 clarinets, 2 horns, 4 violoncellos, 4 bassoons and 4 double basses, also trumpets and drums. They can produce fine music. …*

The astonishing shortage of violas is typical of practically all eighteenth-century orchestras. Haydn often complained about this, and Mozart, who frequently divided his viola parts, must also have wished for a larger number of violas for performances of his works.

How Pianists Should Study Piano Concertos

It goes without saying that first the solo part has to be studied carefully in order to achieve the greatest perfection in performance. As we have pointed out repeatedly, beautifully played notes and smooth

---

[1] See Neal Zaslaw, *Mozart's Symphonies, Context, Performance Practice, Reception*, p. 451ff.
[2] The following two works contain tables giving details of the constitution of orchestras in various European cities in Mozart's lifetime: Robert Haas, "Aufführungspraxis der Musik," p. 217ff.; Neal Zaslaw, *Mozart's Symphonies*, p. 449ff.

virtuoso passages alone will not suffice: The coherence of motives and the meaning of phrases, serene or serious, have to be understood and rendered with simplicity according to the context. It is well known that, unlike many solo works, the concertos in general lack in dynamic and articulation markings. In most cases, Mozart was his own interpreter and knew how to articulate well. Only six of his own twenty-three concertos were published during his lifetime: K. 175 + 382, K. 413–415, K. 453, and K. 595. The other concertos Mozart deliberately did not give to publishers, because he wanted to use them for himself, as he reported in a letter to his father from 15 May 1784:

> *I gave to-day to the mail coach the symphony ... and also four concertos* [K. 449, 450, 451, and 453]. *I am not particular about the symphony, but I do ask you to have the four concertos copied at home, for the Salzburg copyists are as little to be trusted as the Viennese. I know for a positive fact that Hofstetter made two copies of Haydn's music. ... And as no one but myself possesses these new concertos in B-flat and D, and no one but myself and Fräulein von Ployer (for whom I composed them) those in E-flat and G, the only way in which they could fall into other hands is by that kind of cheating.*

Eleven days later Mozart wrote to his father:

> *Your last letter tells me that you have received my letter and the music. ... I am quite willing to wait patiently until I get them back, so long as no one else is allowed to get hold of them. Only to-day I could have gotten twenty-four ducats for one of them, but I think it will be more profitable to me to keep them by me for a few years more and then have them engraved and published.*

It is understandable then that Mozart would have allowed himself the luxury of not completing the notation in every detail immediately but postpone this task for a later time. As a consequence of Mozart's attitude it becomes necessary for us to supply those missing articulation signs and dynamic markings that Mozart did not need to notate for himself. As suggested earlier, the early Sonata in B-flat major, K. 281, or the late Rondo in A minor, K. 511, are works rich in authentic articulation and expression marks that might serve as models for relevant completions.

But even more is required from a good soloist: Mozart's concertos are full of dialogues between the soloist and the orchestral instruments. There are questions and answers, antecedent and consequent phrases that have to be discovered. While the solo piano is mostly *primus inter pares* (first among equals) there are phrases where the roles are exchanged, and the piano subtly accompanies the leading voices of the orchestra. This can be observed in the Concerto in E-flat major, K. 271, first movement, mm. 104–107 (and also in mm. 233–236).

Ex. X/1:

This occasional role of the piano as accompanimental instrument occurs even more often in later piano concertos, especially those from K. 449 on.

For the full understanding of Mozart's concerto compositions, it is absolutely necessary for the soloist to carefully study the *tutti* sections; in particular, the opening and closing *tutti* and the central orchestral *ritornello*. From childhood on, coauthor Paul Badura-Skoda was required by his teachers to play the *tutti* in a good piano reduction to accompany other students. Thus, he could perform a concerto on the piano from beginning to end without assistance, in a similar way to Schumann's *Concert sans Orchestre*, op. 14 (or Chopin's Allegro in A major, op. 46, a work that had been conceived originally as Chopin's third piano concerto). Students would gain much insight into their solo part if they observed how the same motives are supplied with articulation and dynamic signs during the *tutti* sections. Thus, it is interesting to note that in Mozart's last Piano Concerto K. 595, for instance, the opening subject is accompanied *legato* by the second violin and violas, but the continuation, from m. 16 onwards, has *staccato* eighths in the accompanying figures of the second violin. This observation is helpful later in an identical solo passage (mm. 292–297) where the piano has no articulation signs in the left hand. Many pianists play these *Alberti* figures *legato*, though more observant ones might more properly follow Mozart's example.

In order to play the orchestral reduction (placed in the second piano part of a two-piano score) skillfully, one should use an edition where the reduction has been made playable and not too complicated. Models of fine orchestral transcriptions for that purpose are the old Peters editions edited by Kurt Soldan (ca. 1935). Alas, some modern scores try to squeeze too much into the piano reduction and make it hard to read or play. Two examples from the Concerto K. 466/I, mm. 285–287, may illustrate this point. In the Peters edition these bars read:

Ex. X/2:

The two-piano edition of this concerto issued by Bärenreiter Verlag tries to squeeze more rhythmic variety into these measures:

Ex. X/3:

For the sight-reader, the version of this Bärenreiter edition is much harder to grasp fully in the necessary quick tempo.

Those great Mozart players we know from the past, Edwin Fischer, Wilhelm Kempff, Artur Schnabel, Rudolf Serkin, and others, always studied concertos from the full score. Nothing can replace a full score: Here you have the evidence and learn everything the composer had in mind for this work. Needless to say, when Mozart and Beethoven conducted from the keyboard, they must have used their (handwritten) full scores, because two-piano scores came into existence only much later.

It is unfortunate that in modern performances of Mozart's piano concertos the collaboration between soloist and orchestra often leaves much to be desired. One reason for this may be that many musicians do not have enough feeling for Mozart's style, and another that the relative forces involved are often of the wrong size; moreover, orchestras still frequently play from parts that have been poorly edited. For reasons of economy, many orchestras frequently still play from old parts, often published more than hundred years ago by Breitkopf & Härtel (and in the United States, the reprint of those by Kalmus)—parts that contain innumerable nonsensical phrasing and expression marks added by unknown arrangers. Not only the *NMA* scores but also the parts published by Bärenreiter as well as the more recently printed Breitkopf & Härtel parts are more recommendable and much closer to the original text. Unfortunately, many conductors accept the discrepancies between score and old parts with stoical indifference, although almost every bar contains some inaccuracy in the orchestral parts. In the *finale* of the D minor Concerto K. 466, mm. 20ff. offer a particularly crass example of arbitrary alterations of the original articulation by the editor of the orchestral parts. Mozart's autograph has the following articulation:

Ex. X/4:

In the old Breitkopf & Härtel (and Kalmus) edition, however, we find in the orchestral parts:

Ex. X/5:

The editor, overly keen on consistency, obviously did not realize the difference between an accented passing note resolving downward by step and a leap of an octave from a harmony note.

We find the same situation in other orchestral parts for Mozart's concertos. If the pianist wants to have a satisfactory accompaniment, there is scarcely anything else he can do but go through every single part, making corrections with a red pencil, unless he prefers to take his own corrected set of parts with him on his travels.

But the unreliability of orchestral parts is not the only reason that orchestra and soloist so rarely play well together. Many deficiencies are simply the result of bad habits ingrained over many generations. Present-day conductors and orchestral players often show terrifying ignorance of the simplest facts about the instruments Mozart used. They often do not know that, for instance, "Horns in B-flat" might mean in present-day language "Horns in B-flat alto," since there is no real proof that Mozart always used horns in B-flat basso in his concertos. (We find the very rare B-flat basso horn in the Serenade for 13 Wind instruments K. 361 [actually twelve wind instruments and double bass]. In that work Mozart placed them under the horns in F, but he did not mark them B-flat basso, since that was apparently taken for granted through the placement.) In his early works, Mozart (like Haydn) probably took the high crooking of horns so much for granted that he never bothered to specify "alto."[3] In the second movement of the D minor Concerto K. 466, it is in our opinion no pleasure to hear the horn parts played an octave too low.

With Mozart's division of the 'cello/bass parts, the upper part is to be played automatically by the double basses, since they always play an octave lower than written. This often leads to misunderstandings, as in the second movement of the E-flat major Concerto K. 482.

Many orchestras are in the bad habit of playing too much of the accompaniment in *staccato* when accompanying Mozart's concertos. Mozart's notation makes a clear distinction between *staccato* and *non-staccato*, as one can see by examining, for instance, mm. 11ff. of the Romanze from the D minor Concerto:

Ex. X/6:

---

[3] See. H. C. Robbins Landon, *The Symphonies of Joseph Haydn*, p. 125. The issue is controversial. See also Hans Pizka, *Das hohe Horn bei Mozart-oder Die situation des hohen Horns zu Mozarts Zeit*, in *Mozart-Jahrbuch* (1987/88): 139–146.

It is not right to make the first violin eighth notes sound as short as those in the second violins and violas.

Mozart's accompaniments always have something to say, and not one note of them should sound empty or inexpressive. In the first movement of the same Concerto K. 466 it is very important to play the string chords in mm. 348–349 fairly weightily and *non-staccato*:

Ex. X/7:

The same applies to the accompaniment in mm. 104–106 and 323–326 of this movement. In general:

Ex. X/8:

Mozart liked to write:

Nowadays, this is often incorrectly taken for an ordinary short *staccato* and played with insufficient expression. It is in fact nothing but another way of writing a soft *staccato* in quarter notes:

Ex. X/9:

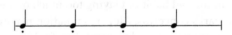

Chordal accompaniments in repeated eighth notes, as in mm. 40–60 of the Romanze from this Concerto, are sometimes even played *spiccato* by violinists; as a result one is usually unlucky enough to hear forty bows hitting the strings but the notes do not sound …

Even simple accompaniment figures, such as those in m. 63, should be made to sing and not be unduly shortened:

Ex. X/10:

The next example shows a contrapuntal variant of the first subject of K. 595/I from mm. 225 onward:

Ex. X/11:

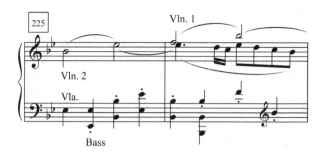

Thus, it is not only in playing eighth notes that one must beware of cutting off the notes too soon; this also applies to quarter notes, especially to single quarter notes at the ends of phrases; for example, in K. 466/I, mm. 112–114, where the orchestra players should be careful not to cut off the quarter notes too abruptly. The last one in particular should not be shortened but firmly held (*tenuto*):

Ex. X/12:

Excessive use of *staccato* is probably the result of an awareness (admirable in itself) that Mozart is usually made to sound too thick, so that the accompaniment often drowns the solo instrument. This is indeed a constant danger, but playing *staccato* is not the right solution. Mozart chose a much more natural way out. At one time, it was the norm to use fewer string players, a quintet or quartet of strings, to accompany the piano's solos. This was absolutely necessary, because the Mozart fortepiano had such a small tone in comparison to our concert grands. Wind solos were also sometimes accompanied only by solo strings, as in mm. 205–207[4] of the first movement of the B-flat major Concerto K. 595, where Mozart first wrote *solo* against all the strings, later crossing this out in the bass part and leaving it only in the violins and violas. This example also shows clearly that Mozart's marking *solo* refers to the accompaniment, which is then to be played by single instruments.

In a letter from 26 April 1783 to the publisher Sieber in Paris, Mozart offered the Concertos K. 413, K. 414, and K. 415 for publication and added the remark:

> … *This letter is to inform you that I have three piano concertos ready, which can be performed with full orchestra, or with oboes and horns, or merely a quattro [string quartet].*

In the case of the Concerto K. 449, Mozart again emphasized that it could be played *a quattro*; i.e., as a piano quintet (he used the *a quattro* phrase both in entering the work in his thematic catalogue and in a letter to his father on 15 May 1785). Even though the louder tone of the modern piano and the increased size of concert halls usually rules out a performance with single strings, a conductor should decide to use between two and four desks of first violins (five at the most), and the other strings in proportion—this is quite enough even for New York's Carnegie Hall. It is sheer nonsense to use fifty or more musicians to play repeated chords as an

---

[4] In older editions: mm. 198–200 (due to the absence of seven bars that Mozart added later).

accompaniment to the piano's cantilenas. One only has to try giving the accompaniment to a few string players who are capable of a smooth, pleasing soft tone and one will see that the effect is incomparably better and more natural.

On the other hand, the modern piano's increased volume of tone is a very distinct advantage from the point of view of collaboration with a modern orchestra. The Mozart piano's *forte* sound was just loud enough to be audible if the accompanying orchestra played *piano*, and its *fortissimo* was about as loud as an *mf* on the modern piano. This explains why Mozart marked the orchestral accompaniment *p* even in passages whose character is clearly that of an *f*. Although one should try to avoid tampering with Mozart's expression marks, in these cases there is not the slightest objection to letting the orchestra play the *forte* (or *poco forte*) demanded by the music; there is no longer any danger of drowning the solo instrument. Obviously, one must consider carefully any alteration of this kind and may only turn a *piano* into a *forte* when this is really in keeping with the character of the music. This is, for instance, the case in the first movement of the festive C major Concerto K. 503: The full orchestral entry in m. 9 clearly demands a *forte*, and this is what Mozart wrote here. But at the corresponding points in mm. 120 and 298, the orchestra has a *p* because the soloist is playing at these times; if this *p* is taken literally, the powerful chords of the modern piano make the orchestra sound rather feeble. There are also a number of passages of this type in the first movement of the D minor Concerto (mm. 110–111, 169–171, 283–284), also in the first movement of the E-flat major Concerto K. 482 (mm. 345/6) and the first movement of the B-flat major Concerto K. 595 (mm. 218–231). Here again the orchestra should play the climax of the melody at least *mf*, as against the prescribed *p* (which is a relic of the concerto style of Vivaldi's time, where at the beginning of every solo the orchestra automatically had to play *p*).

Occasionally, though extremely rarely, it is possible to make slight alterations in the scoring. Although Mozart's instrumentation is for the most part masterly, he sometimes asks too much of certain instruments, particularly the flute and the bassoons; moreover, our modern orchestra has become so much louder that there are passages in which solo wind instruments cannot penetrate. In mm. 362–364 (plus upbeat) of the first movement of K. 482, the flute has to play an important countermelody against the entire orchestra, and in most modern performances one can never hear this melody properly. The best solution to the problem is to double the flutes at this point. But since most orchestral managers will be unable to afford this extra player, another possibility is to let the first clarinet play the part instead of the second flute. The modern clarinet has a much more powerful tone than the flute; this solution has been tried out several times and found always satisfactory. A similar problem arises in the A major Concerto K. 488. In the first movement, mm. 19–20, 83, 214, and 310, the flute can never be heard properly, but here no change of instrument is possible, except in m. 310. A good conductor will—above all—prevent the orchestra from accompanying the soloist with a monotonous *p* devoid of nuances, for this means the end of all effective artistic partnership.

Orchestra Sizes and Ripieno Parts

In Mozart's time, concertos were performed not only in large halls but also in private homes, and thus sometimes in relatively small rooms. Mozart's own fortepiano made by Anton Walter was certainly a comparatively loud instrument; Stein's or other builders instruments would have often been less easily to be heard—certainly a reason to keep the size of the accompanying orchestras relatively small, perhaps smaller than in the preceding symphony. As noted earlier, this may have been the reason why Mozart demanded from the orchestra parts either *p* or *pp*, indicated through signs, at nearly all solo passages in concertos. This way, the soloist was in a position to be heard when playing with expressive dynamic shadings. Only in rare cases did Mozart mark *mf* or *f* for an orchestra part with a leading melody. It was also certainly one of the reasons for the custom of solo and ripieno players among the string orchestras to not always let all string players accompany the soloists solo passages in a concerto.

The reduction of the accompanying string players to a chamber music size is marked in some manuscript copies of Mozart's concertos in the monastery of Melk. We have pointed this out in our preface of the *NMA* volume V/15/5; and Cliff Eisen found further evidence for this custom in Salzburg's monastery archive of St. Peter (where today those manuscript parts are kept that belonged once to Leopold and Nannerl Mozart) and reported about the parts of the D minor Concerto K. 466:[5]

> *The authentic Salzburg copy … confirms apparently Mozart's practice of reducing the orchestra. For alone among authentic copies of Mozart's concertos, it includes additional parts for first and second ripieno violins (Violino Primo Rip.ⁿᵒ and Violino Secondo Rip.ⁿᵒ).*

The breakdown of *tutti* and solo (according to Eisen) is as follows:

- First Movement

1–77	full orchestra (ritornello)
78–111	reduced orchestra (beginning of solo)
112–114	full orchestra (cadence on dominant)
115–172	reduced orchestra (solo)
173–192	full orchestra (medial ritornello)
193–253	reduced orchestra (development)
254–287	full orchestra (beginning of recapitulation)
288–355	reduced orchestra (recapitulation of dominant material)
356–end	full orchestra (final ritornello).

- Second Movement

1–39	full orchestra (ritornello)
40–75	reduced orchestra (solo)
76–83	full orchestra (ritornello)
84–134	reduced orchestra (central episode and return of main theme)
135–141	full orchestra (ritornello; cf. m. 25)
142–end	reduced orchestra (recapitulation of dominant material).

- Third Movement

1–62	full orchestra (ritornello)
63–179	reduced orchestra (solo, including return of rondo theme)
180–195	full orchestra (ritornello; cf. m. 13)
196–336	reduced orchestra (solo)
337–388	full orchestra (ritornello, including cadenza and beginning of the D major coda)
389–411	reduced orchestra (beginning in mid-phrase)
412–end	full orchestra (beginning in mid-phrase).

---

[5] See Cliff Eisen, "The Mozarts' Salzburg Copyists," p. 297ff.

Continuo Playing

Nowadays, hardly anybody doubts that in performing his piano concertos Mozart sometimes used the piano as a *continuo* instrument. Time and again, in *tutti* sections, he scrupulously wrote out the bass part in the piano or he marked it *col basso* on every page. This *col basso* marking is indeed not in itself enough to prove that Mozart wanted a complete *basso continuo* part played, meaning that the piano was to play chords to fill out the harmony, for it is well known that Mozart also used this *col basso* abbreviation on countless occasions for other instruments, such as the violas or bassoons, that could certainly not play full harmonies similar to keyboards in the *continuo* part. And we imagine that Mozart sometimes needed one hand to conduct his orchestra from the keyboard. But there is a whole series of markings that show that—at least in his early concertos until 1783 and including the Concerto K. 415—Mozart expected to play a *continuo* part in the *tutti* sections. This is proven by the following facts:

1. The four early concertos K. 37, K. 39, K. 40, and K. 41 contain a number of passages in Mozart's own hand with a written-out *continuo*. In this connection, it is very interesting to study the way his notation of the *continuo* developed during the composition of these concertos. In the first movement of the first Concerto K. 37, the bass part of the orchestra is carefully entered in small notes in the piano part, and Mozart added detailed b.c. figures. In the second movement, too, there are figures, and the piano part even contains indications of the chords that are to be played before the pause in the *tutti*. By the end of the finale, however, Mozart already uses the indication *col basso*, as in his later concertos, and omits the figures. In the next three concertos, he often wrote *col basso* and added only a few figures here and there.

2. The manuscripts of the three Concertos K. 238, K. 246, and K. 271, which form a group stylistically (though the last Concerto K. 271 became something very special), contain a carefully figured bass throughout, which, however, is not in Mozart's own hand. It has often been assumed (but also sometimes challenged) that this figured bass is by Leopold Mozart. Whether or not this is right it is certain that only an expert could have written the figures and the many *tasto solo* markings.

   We were able to examine all the figures in K. 238, K. 246 and K. 271 for ourselves (those for K. 271 are reproduced in an edition published by Peters). The scrupulously written figures in these three concertos appear to have something to do with the fact that Mozart intended to publish the concertos in Paris: In his letter of 11 September 1778, Mozart wrote to his father that he is prepared to have these three concertos engraved (although in the end they were not published).

3. The three concertos K. 413–15, which were published in Vienna by Artaria in 1785, are also carefully figured in the original edition. It is quite possible that Mozart supervised their publication. The main reason why concertos were always published with a figured bass in those years must have been connected with the fact that concertos were not published in score—only the parts were engraved. Naturally, the solo piano part would not be enough to show the pianist the orchestral harmonies.

4. The most important direct information about Mozart's *continuo* playing we doubtless can get from the Salzburg copy of the Concerto K. 246. This copy, which for a long time was unknown and was only rediscovered around 1920, contains a complete *continuo* part for all *tutti* sections and chords for the right hand written by Mozart himself. This is a valuable source that tells us not only that Mozart played a *continuo* part but also how he played it.

There is less extant documentary material to throw any light on *continuo* playing in the concertos after the composition of the Concerto K. 415. The reason for this deficiency is certainly related to the fact that nearly all of Mozart's later concertos remained deliberately unpublished, so that there was no reason to add figures to the bass.

In a letter from Leopold Mozart to his daughter of 4 January 1786, we read:

> *When I send off the other Concerto [K. 467], you can return this one [K. 466] so that I can write the figures in it.*

Leopold Mozart apparently was convinced that for a Salzburg performance with Nannerl playing the solo part, the bass figures were needed. This, however, would have been superfluous if no chords were played during the *tutti*. Only Wolfgang himself did not need figures to know the harmonies he had prescribed for the orchestra.

In a number of theory books from the Classical period where thorough bass realization was discussed, the authors stressed time and again that a soloist should not be doubling the melody line of an orchestra instrument. This rule was normally observed by Mozart, but we find an exception in the realization of the *basso continuo* of the Concerto K. 246: in mm. 9–12 of the second movement, the short motive of the two oboes is doubled two times:

Ex. X/13:

Why did Mozart fail here to observe a valid rule he otherwise kept? Various explanations have been offered. Charles Rosen, who was the first to point to these measures, concluded that "Mozart had prepared the realization not for one of his own performances with a full orchestra but rather for a performance by some member of his immediate circle (Nannerl or a pupil or friend) who intended to play the concerto with the accompaniment of strings only." Against this view, Faye Ferguson rightly argued: "If Rosen's model of a soloist playing with strings only is correct, we should expect to find that the realization incorporates the more prominent wind parts of the score. Yet it does not."[6] Therefore, Ferguson suggests, Mozart may have thought of something else, perhaps of an arrangement of the concerto for two pianos (rather improbable, because two-piano arrangements became fashionable only in the nineteenth century).

We know of documents from a slightly later time that describe the convention of playing a *basso continuo* in piano concertos. Late in 1791, the publisher Bossler (Speyer, Germany) edited the Concerto in D major, K. 451 (copying an apparently unauthorized edition that had appeared in Paris around 1785). This edition of parts (no score, as usual) was reviewed in the *Musical*

---

[6] Charles Rosen, *The Classical Style: Haydn, Mozart, Beethoven*, p. 193; Faye Ferguson, "Mozart's Keyboard Concertos: Tutti Notation and Performance Models," p. 32ff.; see also P. Badura-Skoda, "Über das Generalbass-Spiel in den Klavierkonzerten Mozarts," p. 99ff.

Correspondence of the German Philharmonic Society, a journal also published by Bossler (dated 16 May 1792), where we read:

> To every friend and admirer of the Mozartean muse this composition ... can be nothing but very precious. The original style of composition, which is unmistakable here, the fullness of the harmony, the striking turns of phrase, the skilled distribution of shade and light, and many other excellent qualities, all give us cause to feel very deeply the loss of Mozart, a paragon of his era. The Concerto under review is in D major, and is one of the most beautiful and most brilliant that we have from this master, in the ritornellos as well as in the solos. The opening Allegro takes up the first twelve pages [of the piano part], and we miss nothing in it but the figuring of the bass line in the tuttis.[7]

In 1799, Rochlitz published an article in the second volume of the *Allgemeine Musikalische Zeitung* (Leipzig) in which he emphasized the necessity of a *continuo* instrument in Mozart's symphonies and then remarked that it would be better to use a pianoforte and not a harpsichord. Though this statement does not directly have something to do with performing a *basso continuo* in concertos, it speaks for the fact that the sound of pianofortes for *continuo* playing was considered appropriate for blending in properly with the orchestral sound.

The third document worth mentioning in this connection concerns the performance of *tutti* sections in concertos. It stems from Nannette Stein-Streicher's booklet from 1801 titled "Playing, Tuning, and Proper Care of Fortepianos."[8] There she mockingly says about bad performers:

> Already the first chords are played with such a force that one asks oneself whether the player is deaf, or whether he thinks his audience is deaf? Through the movements of his body, his arms and hands, it seems that he wants to show us what troublesome hard work it is to perform. He becomes passionate and now treats his instrument as though it were his arch enemy whom he wants to kill slowly with cruel fury. ... Now he plays with the accompaniment of the orchestra and undertakes every effort to drown out all other instruments even in the loudest tutti.

Thus, it is obvious that Nannette Streicher took it for granted that a soloist also played during the orchestra *tutti* of a concerto.

Beginning with the D minor Concerto K. 466, Mozart was almost certainly the sole interpreter of his late concertos and therefore often content to leave the piano part incomplete (especially obvious in the so-called "Coronation" Concerto K. 537). Among those late works, only the last Piano Concerto K. 595 was printed during Mozart's lifetime, in the year of his death. In the first edition of this concerto, *col basso* is written on each page, but there are no figures. It would, however, be premature (to say the least) to conclude that the lack of figures in this last concerto proves anything about Mozart's ideas on *continuo* playing in his late concertos. It is more than likely that, when the work went to print in summer 1791, Mozart was too taken up with composing *La Clemenza di Tito*, *The Magic Flute*, and the *Requiem* to be able to attend to the publication of this concerto. If he had had more time, he would probably also have filled in the obviously incomplete passages in the first movement (mm. 161–162 and 322–324, see Ex. VI/44 on p. 242), as he did in the many other works where the printed edition contains numerous additions not found in the autographs. Early editions of these concertos, published soon after Mozart's death,

---

[7] Quoted after Zaslaw, booklet accompanying the CD of Mozart's Piano Concerto K. 451 (DGG).

[8] Nannette Streicher, *Kurze Bemerkungen über das Spielen, Stimmen und Erhalten der Fortepianos* (Wien, 1801), p. 20.

again contain figured piano parts. Yet it has to be said that only in this Concerto K. 595 are the orchestral harmonies always complete and do not need extra filling notes. Here it might be sufficient to play along with the 'cellos; only occasionally might some chords be added, e.g., in the first *tutti* of the third movement.

The historical reason that *continuo* playing came into use around 1600 was the lack of written-out middle parts in most of the seventeenth- and early eighteenth-century music. As a result, these middle parts had to be improvised on certain bass instruments such as chamber organs, harpsichords, theorbes (lutes), etc., in order to give the performed pieces a harmonic substance. In works with complicated harmonies that could not be guessed, the composers indicated the harmonies by numbers (the system known as *figured bass*) for the desired intervals, a very practical kind of "shorthand" writing. Apart from filling in the harmonies, the *continuo* instruments added tone color, much in the same way as, say, harp and organ still do in orchestral works of the Romantic period (e.g., Richard Strauss in *Also sprach Zarathustra*). With the development of the notation of the inner parts in the pre-Classical and Classical period, particularly as the viola became an instrument in its own right in string quartets or in orchestral pieces instead of merely doubling the bass line, there was no further need to provide the harmonies through a keyboard instrument. Thus, the *basso continuo* had lost its *raison d'être*.

Yet, as is well known, the *basso continuo* was retained alive for many decades. One reason for this was the tradition of conducting the orchestra from a keyboard instrument while playing *continuo* for tone color purposes. That Mozart wanted to do this (and did so by the time he moved to Vienna) is clearly proven by his letter to his father from 11 September 1778, in which he wrote:

> … But there is one thing more I must settle about Salzburg and that is that I shall not be kept to the violin, as I used to be. I will no longer be a fiddler. I want to conduct at the clavier and accompany arias.

Even Haydn conducted his symphonies in London from the harpsichord or fortepiano, although his orchestral harmonies are never incomplete and the sound of the keyboard instrument was not really needed there. In the early nineteenth century, *continuo* playing died out, and the *AMA* unfortunately omitted all the *continuo* indications when publishing Mozart's concertos. This has done a great deal of harm. Even in concertos of the Romantic period there are chords written in the piano part that are a continuation of the *basso continuo* tradition. (The well-known opening of Tchaikovsky's First Piano Concerto furnishes an excellent example: The pompous chords of the piano are nothing less than a glorified written-out *continuo*.) In view of present-day knowledge, it is astonishing that in concerto performances nearly all pianists sit still during Mozart's or Beethoven's *tutti* sections, without playing even one note. Since we began advocating *basso continuo* playing in Mozart's piano concertos in the 1950s, we have known only few pianists who gave the orchestra additional color by playing chords or even occasional contrapuntal lines during the *tutti* sections. All the others played in the late nineteenth-century tradition and many probably from scores where the *continuo* part and all *col basso* indications had been left out. Was it mere ignorance or unwillingness to deviate from a nineteenth-century pattern that was followed by famous pianists? Perhaps the incapacity to play the right harmonies might have been and often still is the reason for this historically wrong approach.

However, *continuo* or *col basso* playing is not appropriate everywhere. Authentic silences are required when the bass line is not given to the string basses (cello/double bass) but to the violas or woodwind instruments instead. Otherwise, proper *continuo* playing could be simple.

In any two-piano score, the right harmonies are printed, and students have only to learn to avoid doubling the melody of the first violins. (Why that? Because filling-in means to provide something that is missing!) One of the reasons for this frequent abstinence of *continuo* playing lies perhaps in the fact that modern piano training neglects the creative aspect of teaching the addition of harmonies; and many young pianists are simply afraid of improvising harmonies.

To help overcome this common inhibition, so often found among students, appendix 3 includes as a model our *continuo* realization of the opening of the A major Concerto K. 414/I, mm. 1–64, which we have based on Mozart's own *continuo* writing elsewhere.

Another reason why *continuo* playing was gradually abandoned in the early nineteenth century may have had to do with the fact that virtuoso pianists became more and more concerned with developing fast fingers, often at the expense of using their time for studying the proper musical understanding of style traditions. Besides, larger orchestras didn't need any sound support.

There are indeed a few objections to using the modern piano as a *continuo* instrument in performances: Orchestral standards have improved, and the piano no longer needs to add support. A few particularly sensitive listeners will be disturbed by the clash between the piano's tempered tuning and the often still pure intonation of the orchestra. Above all, the modern piano has come to sound thicker and is far less able to blend with the orchestra than was the case with Mozart's piano, with its slender, silvery tone. Since the large modern orchestras (and even the so-called period orchestras) have a fuller sound than orchestras of 180 years ago, it is understandable that most musicians are reluctant to make the sound still thicker by adding a *continuo* part on a modern piano. On the other hand, it is wrong to object to a *continuo* on the grounds that in Mozart's concertos the orchestral harmonies are always so sonorously laid out that the composer cannot even have wanted the piano to play a *continuo* part. After all, there are many orchestral works by Bach and Handel in which the harmonies are equally complete and sonorous, but everybody agrees that a *basso continuo* playing is appropriate in performances of their works.

Despite certain objections to *continuo* playing in performances of Mozart's concertos, there are naturally a number of thinly scored passages in the concertos (such as those in which the texture is limited to two parts, a melody and a bass), and in some of these it is not only possible but very desirable to fill out the harmonies discreetly on the piano. Here are some examples: first a passage from the B-flat major Concerto K. 456, second movement, mm. 196ff.

Ex. X/14:

This passage could be played:

Ex. X/15:

Also, in the A major Concerto K. 488, third movement, mm. 50–52, an enrichment of the texture through *continuo* playing in the first *tutti* may be welcome:

Ex. X/16:

Possible *continuo* part:

Ex. X/17:

The fact that Mozart filled out the harmony with a decorative piano part at the end of the movement (bars 506ff.) seems to prove that he did not want merely an empty two-part orchestral texture in this passage. One could, of course, say that these two empty bars give a correspondingly stronger effect to the ensuing *tutti* outburst, but this is not a very convincing argument, for in m. 52 the only instrument playing the very important dominant seventh note b^1 is the second clarinet; so here, too, the piano has to reinforce the harmony. In mm. 250–261 the piano should again play at least the bass line.

We would like to mention also the thin passage in the Piano Concerto K. 450, first movement, mm. 26ff. as a problematic case. In former years, we found the orchestral texture of this passage too empty: no winds, only strings:

Ex. X/18:

One would hardly find such a meager two-part passage of this kind in one of Mozart's earlier concertos. Perhaps the main reason that a feeling of emptiness is felt here is the markedly homophonic character. In contrapuntal passages such as one finds in the opening of the finale of the Concerto in E-flat major, K. 449, the two-part writing is not in the least disturbing for a short time. Here in K. 450, however, the effect could be improved by adding the harmonies of a *continuo* part:

Ex. X/19:

Today, however, we are less sure whether it may not be one of those passages where Mozart intended a literal rendering.

The most convincing case for playing a *basso continuo* can be supported by an incomplete harmony in the A major Concerto K. 414: In the first movement, there is a half cadence on E major with only an empty fifth E–B; namely, in mm. 31–32 and 151–152. It is well known that the bare perfect fifth served as the main closing interval for centuries up to the Renaissance, a symbol of divine perfection. But in the Baroque period, it gave way to the complete triad. During the Classical and Romantic periods it was considered a mistake to write a harmony without the third. There was only one exception: if a composer wanted to evoke through the pure *stile antico* reminiscents of the supernatural or spiritual spheres in music. This happens in a most gripping way at the end of the "Kyrie" in Mozart's *Requiem*.

But in that gentle passage in K. 414 there is nothing supernatural to be found:

Ex. X/20:

Thus, there can be hardly any doubt that the pianist who performs the *basso continuo obbligato* with the *tutti* should supply the missing g-sharp[1] and play thus:

Ex. X/21:

It is odd that we have as yet heard no performance with the proper completion of this harmony.

Among the few artists who are always playing the necessary *basso continuo* is Robert Levin, who also likes to compose or improvise cadenzas (and to embellish sometimes too generously for our taste). Malcolm Bilson also plays the *basso continuo* in Mozart's concertos. When recording these concertos on period instruments (DGG, Archiv production), however, though he played the *basso continuo* as usual, it cannot really be heard. The explanation is that Bilson and his conductor John E. Gardiner listened in the booth after the recording session and decided "to tone it down a good bit—it simply seemed obtrusive." The sound of the piano during the *tutti* was reduced then too much—it is hardly ever audible on the CDs. Asked for the reason why he agreed to this, Bilson told us in a letter:

For me continuo playing is much more a psychological affair than an acoustical one: everyone plays together, then the solo parts begin.

It also has to do with the fact that since Mozart's instrument was not very loud, he put the loud parts all in the tutti. *There is no question that* continuo *is an integral part of the action in the Mozart and Beethoven piano concertos. Indeed, when* continuo *playing went out of fashion (around 1820–1830), the long* ritornellos *tend to disappear. From a practical point of view, in public concerts I have always played it very strongly; in recordings, however, where the microphone is much closer than a listener would be, I play rather quietly. The sound of the fortepiano should always blend in with that of the orchestra and not be prominent in the* tutti.

This seems plausible explanation for why we have not heard much of the *continuo* playing.

The better the orchestra, the less *continuo* playing is necessary. Paul Badura-Skoda has tried different approaches and made many practical experiments in this matter of *continuo* playing and he has performed the concertos both with and without *basso continuo*. From his considerable experience he also would advocate a discreet but always audible addition of *continuo* playing during the *tutti* sections. However, the piano should certainly never play continuously from the first note to the last in a concerto, as we already pointed out.

According to contemporary practice, the orchestra was conducted either by the first violinist (leader) or by the solo pianist—in this case, Mozart. In Mozart's letter of 11 September 1778, he said: "I want to conduct at the fortepiano," but even he can scarcely have played a *continuo* part all the time, because his hands sometimes must have been occupied with conducting motions. According to Schönfeld's *Jahrbuch der Tonkunst* of 1796 (p. 175):

A conductor at the piano must make still more energetic movements (than a violinist leader conducting the orchestra), so that he often has to work with his head, hands and feet for the sake of the tempo and the beat, and it is not seldom that he is obliged to interrupt the piano part altogether, in order to cleave the air with both arms.

Mozart certainly also considered the size of the orchestra accompanying him when deciding how much *continuo* playing seemed necessary. When the orchestra was small, it would have been more in need of harmonic support from the piano, and it could also be controlled more easily by movements of the head, without stopping playing with both hands, so that the pianist could concentrate on the piano part.

As we have said above, nowadays it is usually less necessary to strengthen the bass line than it was in Mozart's day. There is no need to reinforce a bass part that is purely an accompaniment, and in many cases this is not even possible (e.g., the quick repeated notes in the first *tutti* during the finale of the D minor Concerto K. 466). It is only in the *forte* entries that the bass may be doubled, even in octaves (as, e.g., in bars 302–305, 362–365 of the first movement of the C minor Concerto K. 491). There are, however, numerous passages in Mozart's concertos that perplex even the most fervent advocates of *continuo* playing, passages where it is quite impossible to find any chords for the right hand that will not mar the musical structure. The opening *tutti* of the D minor Concerto K. 466 offers a good example of this type. Chords played on the first beat would break up the strings' syncopations in a very unsatisfactory way, and there is no question of doubling the syncopated chords, since this would obscure the contrast between solo and *tutti*—a contrast that is most important to this particular concerto movement. Another case is the opening of the A major Concerto K. 488, which is so much like chamber music that a *continuo* part would merely sound clumsy. In m. 4 it would be quite impossible to find a chord to go over the D in the bass. The same applies to the third subject of this movement. Wherever the orchestra has a suspension (as, e.g., in the Concerto K. 488/II, mm. 14–19 and 51–52) there is again nothing the pianist can do with his right hand except to add pointless doublings. In all such passages Mozart certainly played the bass line only with his left hand and probably used his right hand for conducting. Since there are usually more violoncellos and double basses playing nowadays, one can often do without this doubling of the bass line.

The second movement of the E-flat major Concerto K. 449 begins with an open fifth in the orchestra followed immediately by the third played by the second violins. Thus, at the very outset one can play a soft chord on the piano, as in the later recapitulation of this theme. In the ensuing eight measures, however, it is neither necessary nor desirable to supplement the harmony. Not until m. 10 should one start playing a *continuo* part again, to match the exactly similar passage from m. 89 onward, where Mozart himself wrote out the chords:

Ex. X/22:

In the opening of the first movement of the F major Concerto K. 459, the piano may well add the third of the harmony, as later in m. 9 (first horn and first bassoon); but in this latter case, it is not advisable to play a whole chord on the first beat. The third has such a delightful effect when it enters in the second half of the measure that it should not be anticipated. On the other hand, in the development and at the end of this movement just before the cadenza, it is not only desirable but indispensable to fill out the texture on the piano. Starting in m. 196, the woodwind and strings alternate with chords over a bass that move in descending fifths. Whereas the woodwind chords are complete, the strings are in two parts only, since Mozart uses the violas to strengthen the bass. There can hardly be any doubt that in such a case the right hand of the *basso continuo* must complete the harmony in a manner such as this:

Ex. X/23:

Similarly, the piano must complete the harmony in mm. 246–248 of the third movement of the E-flat major Concerto K. 482, where Mozart himself filled out the incomplete harmony of the strings with two five-part chords on the piano in the following m. 249.

If only wind instruments are playing in the orchestra, the piano should *never* play a *basso continuo*. In the two-piano concertos in minor keys, and also in some other concertos, the relationship of piano and orchestra is markedly dualistic: There is a strong contrast between the sections of wind instruments alone and the string or full orchestra sections.

In the following example from the development section of the first movement of the C minor Concerto K. 491, the piano—if it plays at all—must blend well with the orchestral *tutti* so that the listener does not even notice it as an independent element in the overall sound:

Ex. X/24:

In a similar passage in the first movement of the Concerto in E-flat major, K. 449 (mm. 188–203), Mozart wrote rests for the piano during the two-bar *tutti* passages, and we therefore recommend a similar solution to the one in Ex. X/25.

In Mozart's piano concertos, then, the piano has two quite distinct and contrasting functions: that of a solo instrument, which opposes the orchestra in a concertante way, and that of a versatile orchestral instrument, which here and there has to support and enrich texture and sound. In his *continuo* playing, Mozart adhered to the following rule: The piano should only play when the lowest strings play the bass line; thus, whenever the violas (or in wind passages the bassoon) take over the bass line, there ought to be no *continuo* part. There are, however, occasional odd bars where the left hand of the piano must stop playing, even though the lower strings play the bass (for instance, K. 456, first movement, mm. 129ff., or K. 595, second movement, mm. 127–129).

After final trills, Mozart wants the piano bass to switch immediately to playing the orchestral bass, as in the first movement of the Concerto K. 459, mm. 188ff., where the autograph shows the following:

Ex. X/25:

In polyphonic string passages, such as mm. 143–148 of the first movement of the A major Concerto K. 488, one should not play a *basso continuo*, since it would only adulterate the sound of the strings. In such cases, too little is better than too much. Sometimes it is appropriate to simply double the bass in octaves, as in mm. 185 et seq. of the second movement of the Concerto K. 482 and in the examples quoted (Ex. X/24) from the C minor Concerto 491. Wherever one plays chords, one should try to make them sound as bright and slender as possible; for instance, one can play *staccato* without any pedal, as in the A major Concerto K. 488, third movement, mm. 210–229:

Ex. X/26:

Finally: in realizing the *continuo* harmonies, it is better not to double any of the orchestral parts, particularly the woodwind parts. The orchestral harmonies are to be enriched but not made excessively thick by unnecessary doublings.

Even in solo passages Mozart occasionally added chords that fill out the harmony like a *continuo*; for instance, in mm. 88–90 of the first movement of the D minor Concerto K. 466:

Ex. X/27:

Since these lowest bass notes are unplayable on a piano without a pedal board, for which they obviously were written (see chapter 1, p. 35f), one could perhaps play the chords with the left hand and the figuration with the right hand. In this passage, as it is, one is forced to leave out either the bass notes or the chords. It is a pity that these very important notes have to be omitted nowadays since normally no pedal piano, similar to the one Mozart owned, is available. In recordings or broadcasts when the listener does not see what is happening and no replica of a pedal piano can be organized, one can have these important notes played by the violinist who sits nearest to the bass keys of the piano.

There is another important guide for *continuo* playing in Mozart's concertos; in two of them (K. 414 and K. 449) Mozart wrote *ad libitum* wind parts, indicating that these concertos could be played with strings only (or even with a solo quartet). In these cases, the wind parts are for the most part merely a written-out *continuo*, and one may safely assume that when the works are played without wind instruments the piano must take over this function, at least in all the passages where the wind instruments would complete the harmony. The fact that the wind instruments in these works are used sparingly and the part-writing for them is very skillful suggests once again that filling-in harmonies should not be used too often. If these concertos are played with wind instruments, the piano will only need to add to the harmony where Mozart would have written a fuller texture for the wind instruments, if more players had been available, as, for example, in the first movement of the E-flat major Concerto K. 449, mm. 16ff., which can be played like this (naturally in the same rhythm as the oboe):

Ex. X/28:

Very similar guiding principles can be deduced from a study of Mozart's two-piano quartets and the Quintet for Piano and Wind Instruments K. 452, which are laid out in a very concertante style. In the piano quartets, the strings play the part of a miniature *tutti*, and it is clearly seen that Mozart almost always makes the piano play where the *tutti* is marked *forte*, whereas it does not play where *piano* is demanded for the *tutti*. In the dialogue at the opening of the G minor Piano Quartet, it is striking that the piano takes part on both sides. Could one possibly deduce from this to mean that Mozart also wanted the piano to play at the opening of the E-flat major Concerto K. 271, since the two passages are constructed in exactly the same way? Again, since Mozart lets the piano play in the noisy final *tutti* of this quartet, he may have wanted something similar in the closing passages of his concertos.

The figured bass of the concertos K. 238 and K. 271 provides useful indications that Mozart wanted the *continuo* used only sparingly, playing often *tasto solo* (the cello part only); and, finally, Mozart's original cadenzas allow us to draw a few conclusions, since habit sometimes led him to write out the right hand's *continuo* chord in the introductory measure with the fermata preceding the cadenza. This occurs in the authentic cadenza to the first movement of the B-flat major Concerto K. 456.

The autograph shows the full 6/4 chord; in the score we find no half note d^1 but four fermatas:

Ex. X/29:

This naturally suggests that in the preceding measure the pianist has to double the first and second violins an octave lower:

Ex. X/30:

Mozart very often introduces his cadenza not with a 6/4 chord, but with octave doublings of the bass note (e.g., in the concertos K. 382, K. 414, K. 488, etc.), and this again suggests that in the preceding *tutti* he would only have played a few chords, confining himself for the most part to doubling the bass. The most natural way to play the two measures before the cadenza of the first movement of K. 488 is:

Ex. X/31:

One special case remains to be dealt with: There are many passages in which there is a bass note on the first beat followed by repeated accompanying chords, usually in eighth notes. Whether such passages occur in solo or *tutti* sections, we would strongly dissuade pianists from adding a chord over the bass note on the first beat. To do so would thicken the texture unnecessarily and would produce an effect not unlike the way a waltz is often played on a barroom piano:

Ex. X/32:

In fact, it is hardly ever necessary to add chords to fill in the harmony in solo passages. They are superfluous because Mozart entrusted the harmonic support of solo passages to the orchestra. The mm. 85–87 of the first solo in the Concerto K. 482 are often filled out in this way (added notes are written smaller here), a completion not to be recommended:

Ex. X/33:

These additional notes rob the passage of all its lightness and gaiety.

Finally, we shall attempt to draw up a few generally valid rules for playing the *basso continuo* in Mozart's concertos, taking as our guide his own realization of the *continuo* in the C major Concerto K. 246:

1. Obviously, any *continuo* playing must stop when Mozart wrote rests in the left-hand part. However, there is no need to be bound by rests in the right hand, which Mozart habitually notated at the beginning of a movement. This is how Mozart wrote out his realization of K. 246/II, ignoring the rests added by the copyist:

Ex. X/34:

2. In passages of chamber music or of contrapuntal character, one should play *tasto solo*.
3. Single accented dissonances or suspensions in orchestral parts marked *f* are better not doubled (e.g., Concerto K. 246/I, mm. 7–8, where the piano plays the resolution chord). In chains of accented dissonances or suspensions, above all those marked *p*, one should, however, play *tasto solo*, perhaps adding an occasional octave doubling as in K. 246/II, mm. 1–3; there are also suspensions of this kind at the opening of the second movement of K. 449.
4. The top part should as far as possible not be doubled. Nor should middle parts be doubled for more than a short space. Measure 17 of the second movement of K. 246 is very informative in this respect: Mozart thought out a new middle part for the *continuo*.
5. The *continuo* should only be in three or four parts and should never be ornamented or quote thematic material. (Themes and figures in the bass are the only exception.)
6. In unison passages, the right hand must obviously not play chords but should double the bass if it plays at all (see K. 246/I, m. 36). This rule also applies when the wind instruments have sustained pedal notes (e.g., opening of K. 449).
7. In *forte* passages where the whole orchestra is used, a *continuo* is only necessary if important harmony notes lie very deep or are weakly scored (e.g., K. 449, first movement, mm. 12 and 13). Practical application of this principle leads us to advocate the

addition of chords in m. 52 of the finale of K. 488, where the second clarinet is the only instrument playing the seventh of the important dominant seventh chord.

8. Solo passages should on principle never be filled out. There is not a scrap of proof that Mozart ever added chords in solo passages. (This has nothing to do with embellishment of the melody; the solos in the slow movements lend themselves particularly well to embellishment, as we have pointed out in chapter 6.)

9. Mozart's *continuo* is never *strict* in the Baroque sense. For example, in the second movement of K. 246, the *continuo* in the first *tutti* contains off-beat chords, whereas there are rests over the notes in the bass (m. 3):

Ex. X/35:

(By the way, all good *continuo* players do the same.)

10. In the concertos composed after K. 449, there is increasingly less opportunity to introduce *continuo* chords. In these late concertos one should be rather sparing and careful in making this kind of addition. This does not, however, concern the mere *col basso* playing.

Appendix 3 supplies an example of *basso continuo* playing during the opening *tutti* of the Piano Concerto in A major K. 414, first movement.

A good performer "accompanies with discretion," as C. P. E. Bach remarked in his chapter on "Some Refinements of Accompaniment" (*Essay* ... II, 6, pp. 386–387). This applies particularly in *continuo* playing in Mozart's concertos. One cannot give a strong enough warning against making too frequent and loud additions. Better no *continuo* playing than one that spoils the texture by making the sound too thick or too loud.

In his *Violinschule* (XII, §17), Leopold Mozart wrote:

... Wherever a forte is written down, the tone is to be used with moderation, without foolish scrapings, especially in the accompaniment of a solo part. Many either omit to do a thing altogether, or if they do it, are certain to exaggerate.

And Leopold Mozart then rightly also added the warning, that one should not neglect the affect of a piece or subject or section.

Playing the Final Chords of a Concerto Movement Together with the Orchestra

In all his piano concertos Mozart wrote the concluding bass notes of the orchestra into the piano part as well, apparently taking it for granted that the right hand of the pianist should play chords. All editions of the late nineteenth and early twentieth century eliminated—along with the rest of the *continuo*—these bass notes, thus creating the wrong impression that the pianist has to fall silent during the last five or ten seconds of a concerto performance. In three concertos Mozart even wrote full chords into the piano part; namely, in the concertos K. 271 and K. 456 and in K. 246 in his realization of the figured bass. It is significant that these three concertos were written for other pianists, who might not have been familiar with this practice. Besides, in the B-flat major Concerto K. 456, the notation of the final chords was a necessity because they are higher than the first violins—rather an exception. It is also worth noting that in his two piano quartets (K. 478 and K. 493) or in the Wind Quintet K. 452, where the piano's partners form a miniature *tutti*, the piano also joins into the final chords.

As a suggestion for how this rule may be applied, we shall quote the very end of the C minor Concerto K. 491:

Ex. X/36:

This practice of joining the orchestral forces at the end of a concerto was carried over well into the nineteenth century. We have little doubt that, for instance, in the concertos by Chopin, Moscheles, or Liszt, among others, the solo piano ought to also play the last chords together with the orchestra. Even in Brahms' First Concerto in D minor, Edwin Fischer (born still as a contemporary musician of Brahms) played these chords with most convincing effect. In his Second Piano Concerto, Brahms himself wrote these chords into the piano part, thus providing an answer to any possible doubts.

11
Some Technical Questions in the Piano Works

"When I play Mozart," a well-known pianist once said, "I have a pleasant tingling feeling in my fingers, as if they too, were delighted by his music." This is no accident; Mozart was a born pianist and composer for the piano, and his piano works lie well under the fingers. He was, however, not attracted by virtuosity for its own sake—he tended to avoid unnecessary technical difficulties. Mozart was amused by Clementi's passage work in thirds (see p. 291), which at that time were unusual and difficult to play: "but he sweated over them day and night in London," he wrote. While Mozart's piano works contain no trills in thirds, it has to be admitted that he invented other difficult passages that are hardly easier to play than Clementi's passages, e.g., in the Variation VI of the variations on "Salve tu Domine" K. 398. Certainly, the great simplicity (or simple greatness) often found in subjects (*cantilenas*) in his piano writing creates more and thus major problems, paradoxical though it may sound, and these often defeat even the greatest pianists. "The hardest thing is to be simple—and meaningful" is a saying among artists, particularly applicable to Mozart's music.

A pianist must be in control and command of his fingers if he is to play Mozart's single melodic lines *cantabile* and expressively and give a really even flow ("like oil") to his *legato* passage work as, e.g., in K. 281/I, K. 533/I, and K. 414/I. In a letter to his father from Augsburg 25–27 October 1777), Mozart described rather ironically the piano playing of Stein's eight-year-old daughter:

> … *But the best joke of all is that when she comes to a passage* which ought to flow *like* oil *[italics added] and which necessitates a change of finger, she does not bother her head about it …*

Certain phrases should sound like a melodic line played quickly, like tingling *con brio* passages. For *non-legato* passages, which are found so frequently, the fingers should be kept as curved as possible. The pianist's touch should be clear and sparkling (*jeu perlé*); this is best achieved by slightly drawing in the fingers, so that they tap the keys like little hammers. But here the wrist should always be kept pliable; it should follow the play of the fingers, so that in phrasing it should be quite free to take part, just as it would follow the movement of a violin bow. It is particularly important to keep the whole body free of tension, relaxed, shoulders free of strain, the neck muscles relaxed.

Mozart's finely developed sense for every kind of naturalness often made him criticize a player's posture. As he wrote to his father on 17 October 1777 about a young lady in Munich:

> *All that I can say about the daughter of Hamm, the Secretary of War, is that she undoubtedly must have a gift for music, as she has only been studying [Anderson: learning] for three years and yet can play several pieces really well. But I find it difficult to give you an idea of the impression she makes on me when she is playing. She seems to me so curiously affected. She stalks over the clavier with her long, bony fingers in such an odd way. …*

In the following ironical report to his father a week later about the playing of the aforementioned child Nannette Stein, Mozart criticizes the unnaturalness of her playing even more sharply:

Anyone who sees and hears her play and can keep from laughing must, like her father, be made of stone [a pun on the family name Stein, which means stone]. For instead of sitting in the middle of the clavier, she sits right up opposite the treble, as it gives her more chance of flopping about and making grimaces. She rolls her eyes and smirks. When a passage is repeated, she plays it more slowly the second time. If it has to be played a third time, then she plays it even more slowly. When a passage is being played, the arm must be raised as high as possible, and according as the notes in the passage are stressed, the arm, not the fingers must do this, and that too with great emphasis in a heavy and clumsy manner. … She just leaves out the notes, raises her hand and starts off again quite comfortably—a method by which she is much more likely to strike a wrong note, which often produces a curious effect. She may succeed, for she has great talent for music. But she will not make progress by this method—for she will never acquire great rapidity, since she definitely does all she can to make her hands heavy.

Without elasticity, one's tone will not carry. Only a relaxed singing tone can penetrate to the heart of the listener.

Lightness of touch is indeed very important, especially because present-day pianos, as we have mentioned, have a tone that is basically too full for Mozart's music. To make *legato* scales as clear on a modern instrument as on a Mozart piano, one must often play *non-legato*, particularly in the low register; and a *non-legato* on the old fortepiano must sometimes be played *staccato* on the modern instrument due to the echo effect of large halls. There are, incidentally, endless possible nuances in *staccato* playing, all the degrees in a scale from a gentle separation of unmarked successive notes (a "soft" *staccato*):

Ex. XI/1:

to a sharply cutoff, very short attack. For instance, in the Piano Concerto in A major K. 488, second movement, mm. 10 and 21, a very soft *staccato* is appropriate.

One should also aim at a bright timbre, without, however, trying to force the brightness by hard, glassy playing. A hard touch does indeed make the tone of a modern piano brighter (richer in overtones), but it also makes it uglier, since at a certain level many non-harmonic overtones take part in the vibration process. To list the physical reasons for this would take us too far afield. In any case, an excessively hard touch gives the impression of a certain brutality, which is quite out of place in Mozart.

Naturally, the various kinds of touch should be practiced separately. Exercises such as those given in Alfred Cortot's *Principes rationnels de la Technique pianistique* and *Editions de Travail* can be strongly recommended (available in English editions). Their use is most effective, of course, when supervised by a teacher.

Piano technique is based on a small number of constantly recurring principles, such as finger action (*staccato, legato*), the passing under of the thumb, trills, octaves, chords, etc. We will try to provide a few hints on each of these points.

Finger Action

For a sparkling, *non-legato* touch, the fingers should be kept as curved as possible, as has already been mentioned. To develop the concentrated force that is often needed, the best exercises are those where repeated notes are played (the remaining fingers may perhaps rest on the keyboard):

Ex. XI/2:

and similarly for the left hand, gradually increasing the speed. In doing these exercises it is important to keep the wrist loose. The natural tendency to let it become stiff and cramped in doing this kind of finger exercise must be resisted from the outset. It is best to move the wrist up and down in smooth waves while doing these exercises.

Whereas *staccato* playing is based on distinct finger attack, *legato* playing should rely above all on finger pressure. *Legato* playing is often made easier by keeping the fingers flat, sometimes almost stretched out, as if the fingertips wanted to stroke the keys. But with flat fingers it is not easy to avoid unevenness. One very useful device is to tie the notes; one note is not released as the next one is struck (or rather pushed down or depressed, since a full piano tone results from pressure and not from sudden force) but is prolonged a little; e.g.,

Ex. XI/3:

played:

At the rest sign, the respective finger ought to be raised quickly from the knuckles without being stretched:

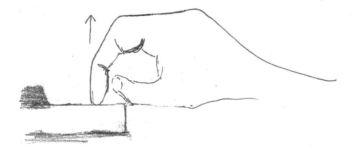

Raised position:

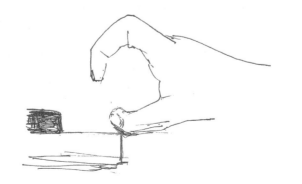

Stretched position (not so good):

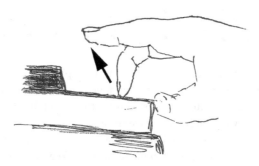

In quicker *legato* passages it is also possible to make a double tie:

Ex. XI/4:

True *legato* playing requires not merely the kind of tie shown in this example but also conscious support by dynamic gradations, as for example, in the theme of the Concerto in B-flat Major, K. 595, first movement, mm. 81ff.:

Ex. XI/5:

Fingers flat! Tie the notes in mm. 82 and 83.

It is particularly important to play the sixteenth notes in mm. 2 and 3 smoothly and not too quickly.

The vocal principle requires here and elsewhere that the longer notes are played with more weight (expression), while the faster ones should flow more lightly. Not every note should be underlined. Singing always helps to find the proper expression. This is also recommended for mm. 107–109 of the same movement K. 595/I:

Ex. XI/6:

Only if the second note of each descending fourth (g², e-natural², b-natural¹, etc.) is played noticeably softer than the others will the impression of a *legato* be given. Good *legato* playing depends on the ability to properly imagine the sound that is to be produced. A player who can feel a melodic line will invariably have a better *legato* than one who regards *legato* playing as a mere task to be carried out mechanically.

Scales and *Arpeggios*

To play scales and *arpeggios* without "bumpiness," elasticity of the wrist and quick lightning reactions in passing the thumb under are essential. The best position for the hand in playing scales is a diagonal one, in which the arm is held at a horizontal or obtuse angle to the keyboard (ground); the third finger reaches furthest inward, and the elbow should move ahead of the fingers. This also applies to extended *arpeggios*.

Exercises such as the following have been found useful for lightning preparation of the next note:

Ex. XI/7:

Other exercises concern the thumb:

Ex. XI/8:

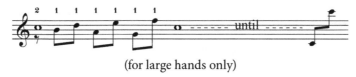

(for large hands only)

Scales for the two hands together should also be practiced with dynamic gradations:

Ex. XI/9:

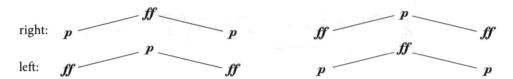

Fingering is a special problem in Mozart; one should avoid wherever possible having to call upon the weaker fourth and little fingers:

Ex. XI/10:

In playing Mozart, it is better not to apply the old teaching rule that the thumb and fifth finger are to avoid the black keys. There are many passages that can only be played evenly if one uses unorthodox fingering; for example, as in the E-flat major Concerto K. 482/I, m. 176 (modern fingering above the stave, orthodox fingering below):

Ex. XI/11:

or in m. 258:

Ex. XI/12:

The orthodox fingering makes the hand more unsteady because the thumb is passed under more often.

In the Concerto K. 488, first movement, mm. 281ff., we suggest the following fingering:

Ex. XI/13:

or K. 488/III, mm. 151ff.:

Ex. XI/14:

Trills

Some pianists are born with a powerful trill; others have to practice for years before they can trill properly. The latter may find the following hints useful.

Above all, trills must be even; a slower, steady trill is preferable to an uneven, quick and bumpy one.

There are a number of exercises that have been proven useful (to be played without accents, quite evenly):

Ex. XI/15:

Ex. XI/16:

These exercises are admittedly only for preparatory use. For the trills in Mozart's works we recommend the following fingerings: 1/2, 1/3, 2/3, 2/4, 3/5. But here there is certainly a good deal of room for individual preference.

To make a trill vibrate with the desired speed, it is a good idea to let the whole of the hand shake slightly to and fro, from the elbow, at the same time carrying out the necessary quick finger movements. Thus, the weight of the arm may help to add power to a *forte* trill.

Octaves

So-called "broken octaves," which are found frequently in Mozart's works:

Ex. XI/17:

must rotate from the elbow and often from the shoulders. The fingers are kept in a fixed position and hardly move. (It is a pity that many teachers pay too little attention to this movement.)

The following exercise is very useful:

Ex. XI/18:

During the rests, one should lift the arm high (at least eight inches above the keys). The wrist must be able to vibrate from the elbow, lightly, loosely, and quickly. The exercise can also be played in sevenths:

Ex. XI/19:

One should not try the exercise in octaves until these examples can be managed without any trouble.

A tendency to reach the upper notes too soon can often be observed. It can be countered by such exercises as this:

Ex. XI/20:

We also often find *legato* octaves in Mozart's piano works. These cause a lot of trouble; for example, in the Sonata in A major, K. 331, first movement, Var. III:

Ex. XI/21:

To play the upper part smoothly is not enough. There will only be a true *legato* feeling if the thumb, too, plays smoothly. The thumb has to be very mobile to play tied to itself in this way. It is very important that the bottom joint of the thumb becomes active. The thumb should leave each individual key as late as possible and then take hold of the next with lightning speed, but without making an accent. The gap between each pair of notes must be kept as short as possible.

As an exercise, complete melodies should be played with the thumb only!

As a curiosity, it should be mentioned that double *glissando*s also occur in Mozart. They are quite exceptional (*glissando* in sixths at the close of the Variations K. 264 and in octaves in the second perhaps authentic cadenza for the Concerto in G major, K. 453, second movement), since Mozart obviously had little use for this type of virtuosity.

As we have already pointed out in chapter 1, Mozart's music often contains closely spaced chords in the lowest register of the piano; these sound full and round on a Mozart piano but distinctly unpleasant on a modern instrument. When playing on a modern concert grand or a smaller *Flügel*, we would recommend occasional alteration of such chords or passages. To make the sound at least bearable, in the second movement of the C minor Sonata K. 457, m. 52, the fifth could be omitted from this dominant seventh chord:

Ex. XI/22:

Moreover, the D (third) should be played softer than the other notes. Better still, one can omit the third, which makes the resulting sound even more agreeable:

Ex. XI/23:

At the opening of the development section of the slow movement of the Sonata in A minor, K. 310, mm. 32ff., the following accompanying chords occur:

Ex. XI/24:

Here Mozart obviously had in mind a full, warm accompaniment sound (like the sound of low strings); but on most modern pianos this passage sometimes sounds ugly rather than full.

In this respect, piano building has changed since the 1950s—most modern pianos have harder hammers than before. Therefore, the literal execution of Ex. XI/24 sounds good on a recently built Bösendorfer. If in the first measure the third is transposed to the octave above, the result will certainly be much more like the sound Mozart intended. But in this case, one must be able to span a tenth with the right hand:

Ex. XI/25:

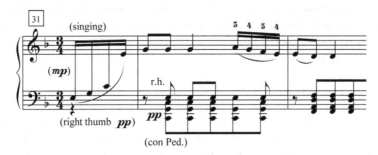

The original version sounds good only on those concert grand pianos that have been voiced to produce a particularly bright, clear sound. Unison passages such as the opening of the C minor Fantasia K. 475 often sound much too thick on the modern piano. It is usually a help to play the left hand a good deal softer than the right. At the opening of the C minor Sonata K. 457 we favor a powerful *forte* in the right hand, with a *mezzo piano* in the left.

The soft pedal (moderator, *una corda*) should not be used too much. The bad habit of depressing this pedal automatically for all soft passages is far too widespread. The moderator pedal does not simply make the instrument softer but alters its timbre, usually in such a way that it hinders the production of a good tone. A good pianist should be able to play even **ppp** without using the soft pedal.

Technical Problems of the Use of the Damper-Lifting Pedal (Knee Lever)

In chapter 1 we could prove that Mozart not only appreciated but also used the so-called *forte* stop of old pianos. His Walter piano had two kinds of damper-lifting possibilities linked to the two knee levers built into his piano, and Mozart sometimes notated passages in such a way that they can be played correctly only with their use. They have the same function as the right pedal of modern pianos; therefore, our convenient use of the word *pedal* for the knee levers.

As long as the damper-lifting device was a hand-operated stop on pianos of Mozart's time, it could not be used while both hands were playing. Thus, a rest for at least one hand was needed to work or stop working the hand levers. Perhaps, a performer who had to play on an instrument with hand levers only would use them for *sotto voce* passages such as K. 457/II, mm. 1–8.

The question of how much the pedal should be used in Mozart's piano works has been raised repeatedly. While we believe that Mozart used his damper-lifting mechanism less often than, for example, Beethoven, we acknowledge that the use or non-use of the right pedal is not only a historical question but a matter of taste and aesthetic outlook as well. With only those few exceptions mentioned in chapter 1, it is indeed possible to play Mozart's sonatas without pedal. The great pianist Walter Gieseking, who recorded Mozart's complete piano solo works on a modern piano, abstained completely from the use of the pedal, which in his opinion thickened the piano sound and blurred the clear lines of Mozart's texture. It has to be admitted that with his sensitive singing touch and his agile fingers he still could produce beautiful results, so much so that his fundamental objection against the pedal use was rarely felt to be a real impediment.

We certainly do not share Gieseking's opinion regarding pedaling. With discrete and tasteful use, pedaling can indeed enhance the effect of the piano sound, not only in *arpeggios* but also in *cantabile* passages. In practicing Mozart's works, however, we agree with Gieseking's goals; only after the fingers alone can produce a beautiful sound should one start to add a discreet use of the pedal to bring even more beauty and color to the piano tone. Even a single note played with pedal produces more resonance due to the sympathetic vibrations of other strings, comparable to the vibrato of a violinist.

There are frequent pedaling problems in playing Mozart. It is an art to use the pedal with discretion and taste. There is something to be said for using the pedal in *cantabile* passages with frequent changes of the pedal. A fine example of such a passage occurs in the G major Piano Sonata K. 283, second movement, m. 11 (also mm. 12 and 34–35):

Ex. XI/26:

Here the articulation indicated (RH slur from g^1 to g^2) is hardly possible without the aid of the pedal. But since the pedal thickens the sound, it should at other times be avoided. Too much pedal is also a hindrance in articulation. Above all, rests in the course of a melody should on no account be covered up because the pianist has neglected to take his foot off the pedal—we would particularly warn against this frequent mistake. If pedaling is to be used at all, the correct one for the following *arpeggio* is:

Ex. XI/27:

and not:

Ex. XI/28:

Here, incorrect pedaling makes all the notes sound as if they were marked *tenuto*.

In a typical *minuet* ending such as in the Duport Variations K. 573, m. 8, no pedaling is needed. Pianists of the older tradition might have sparingly used the pedal in the following way:

Ex. XI/29:

It also is obvious that as a rule in *staccato* or *non-legato* passages the pedal should not be used; for instance, in the opening theme of the Sonata in C minor, K. 457, the eighth notes marked *staccato* must on no account be blurred by the pedal.

Interesting problems of pedaling are raised by the *arpeggios* common to Mozart's works. It would be absolutely wrong to play all *arpeggios* with the pedal down; in many cases, this would make the sound far too thick. But there are *forte* passages in Mozart's works where the piano should be "let off the leash" and should be allowed to make a noise; here the pedal will obviously be needed. The dramatic climax of the first movement of the C minor Concerto, where the piano opposes the entire orchestra (from mm. 332 onward), is such a passage. Others include the stormy *arpeggios* in the Fantasy in C major, K. 394, m. 46 (see Ex. I/9, p.27), which sound even more exciting on a Mozart fortepiano than on the modern instrument, and the *arpeggio* (m. 82) from the Fantasy K. 475, where the sound shoots like a rocket from the lowest notes of Mozart's piano up to the highest register:

Ex. XI/30:

Four measures earlier there must be four changes of pedal in each measure, so that the articulation is not obscured:

Ex. XI/31:

But here, the pedal is not really necessary; this passage can be played as well without pedal.

Only occasionally can different harmonies be played under one unchanged pedal. Haydn, in his Sonata in C Major, Hob. XVI/50, used the term *open pedal* for this type of pedaling. When playing on period instruments, Robert Levin and Malcolm Bilson play the coda of the first movement of the C minor Piano Concerto K. 491 in this fashion. Edwin Fischer did the very contrary and used no pedal at all when playing this coda. Both ways are legitimate and may come to impressive results; it is a matter of taste.

When playing *arpeggios*, the main aim is usually to create a pleasant sound; e.g., in the E-flat major Concerto K. 449, second movement, mm. 103ff.:

Ex. XI/32:

In passages of this kind, the combination of *staccato* or *non-legato* touch with pedal produces magical effects of sound. Frequent changes of pedal prevent the sound from becoming too thick.

One can also introduce some very pleasing pedal effects, which Mozart doubtless intended, for example, at the end of the original cadenza for the A major Concerto K. 488/I:

Ex. XI/33:

However, there are many *arpeggios* that sound best when played with hardly any pedal, since they occur in passages where a slender sound is most appropriate. Examples of such passages are found in the Concert Rondo in D major, K. 382, mm. 41–56 (according to the autograph, many older editions have here printed *legato* slurs):

Ex. XI/ 34:

or the Piano Sonata in F major, K. 533/494, first movement, codetta:

Ex. XI/ 35:

Ex. XI/ 36:

The sparkling quality of these figures can only be properly brought out if the pedal is not used. So that the sound may not become too thick, the left hand must again be a good deal softer than the right. Furthermore, it is the beautiful interplay of the parts that rules out the use of the pedal in the passage that immediately follows the last example:

Playing Mozart demands a pedal technique that uses very exact and frequent changes of pedal. To ensure the slenderness of tone that is its most important prerequisite, it is certainly better to use too little pedal than too much. In playing Mozart, one must above all avoid anything that would mar the clarity, translucency, and evenness of one's playing, the quality that contemporary aesthetics called the "clarity of musical language."

Thus, we would like to end this discussion with a quotation from Daniel Schubart's *Ideen zu einer Äesthetik der Tonkunst* (p. 373):

> *The second quality of good musical performance is: clarity. What one cannot understand cannot go to one's heart. Thus one must give a sharp contour to every musical comma, indeed to every single note; practice detaching the notes (for nothing is clearer than staccato playing): never murmur when one ought to speak out; and in playing, be particularly diligent in attaining a rounded tone.*

12

Remarks on the Interpretation
of Selected Piano Works

No interpretation of a great work can claim more than a certain limited degree of objective validity; we have constantly tried to emphasize this.

There are, of course, many single problems for which one must discover and pass on an objectively correct solution—this has been the principal aim of the present book. On the other hand, being really thorough and treating every interpretation detail, as an analysis demands, often involves decisions that can only be subjective; but these are usually based on careful study and it seems therefore justified and of general interest to report the results of some thorough investigations.

In the ensuing analyses for pianists who are also conducting the orchestra, there is much that is subjective—even the choice of particular works and the extent of the treatment accorded them. We have chosen Mozart's three best known piano concertos for interpretative analysis. In doing so, however, we would emphasize strongly that we believe the less well-known concertos are often unjustly neglected. Some of them are fully comparable with their better known companions. We mention in particular the enchanting Concerto in D major, K. 175, first composed in Salzburg in 1773, with the Concert Rondo K. 382 from 1782 as its new final movement; even in his mature years Mozart was still playing this concerto with great success. He wrote proudly to his father on 12 March 1783, after a performance: "… but the audience would not stop clapping and so I had to repeat the rondo, upon which there was a regular torrent of applause."

Other concertos deserving much more attention are the fine work in E-flat Major, K. 449, with a slow movement of Schubertian intimacy and a graceful contrapuntal finale; the brilliant B-flat major Concerto K. 450; the tender and reflective G major Concerto K. 453, full of romantically bold turns of harmony; the wonderful F major Concerto K. 459; and the grandiose, noble work in C major, K. 503, whose first movement has a dramatic power comparable to that of Beethoven's "Emperor" Concerto; and above all, the beautiful Concerto in E-flat Major, K. 482. The superb concertos K. 414, K. 451, K. 456, and K. 467 also bear limitless repetition. Indeed, if one were to select for a performance an unusual work, it is better to look for the weaker and less well-known concertos—but there is hardly a single one, apart from the four youthful ones K. 37–40 that he modeled on works by other composers.

Mozart followed an old tradition in marking the solo part of his concertos *cembalo* on the first page before the first accolade; the only exceptions are the last two concertos, K. 537 and K. 595. But there should not be the slightest doubt that these concertos, like all his keyboard works, with the possible exception of some compositions written during his early childhood, were composed for the fortepiano (see chapter 1).

The ensuing interpretative analyses are intended to provide suggestions for studying the specific works. As long as the suggestions do not refer to a recorded example on the enclosed CD, the reader should take them with a grain of salt; that is, with allowance, for it is so that the subtle musical nuances of tempo, dynamics, or touch can never be described in words more than approximately.

Concerto in D minor, K. 466

- Best editions
    - *NMA*, V/15/6 (ed. by Hans Engel and Horst Heusner)
    - Eulenburg score 721 (ed. by Paul Badura-Skoda)
    - For a two-piano reduction: Peters edition (ed. by Kurt Soldan and Edwin Fischer)
    - Steingräber (ed. by F. Kullak; out of print); reprinted by Schirmer, New York
- Cadenzas

    Although Mozart obviously did compose cadenzas (see p. 253), no original ones are extant. The best known cadenzas by other composers are those by Beethoven, published separately by Doblinger, Vienna, and also reprinted in the Kullak edition (Steingraeber, Schirmer); they are also contained in the *Complete Edition of Beethoven's Works*, Series IX, No. 70A. Also recommended are cadenzas by Alfred Brendel and Paul Badura-Skoda, both at Doblinger, Vienna.
- Suggested basic tempos
    - First movement, Allegro ₵ ♩ = c. 138–144
    - Second movement, Romance ₵ ♩ = c. 84–88 middle section in G minor, somewhat quicker, ♩ = c. 96. (In view of the ₵ time signature, ♩ = 42–44 would be perhaps more correct, but it is our experience that some metronomes are inaccurate and uneven when beating as slowly as this.)
    - Third movement, presto ₵ ♩ = c. 144

Mozart's works in minor keys contain some of his most intimate self-expression; they show him coming to terms with disappointments and suffering—from the failure of his concert tour to Paris, the death of his mother, and his rejection by Aloysia Weber ("… it has been impossible for me to write to you…today I can only weep.")[1] to the deaths of four of his children and his financial difficulties in later years and, finally, his tears on his deathbed as he realized that he would be unable to finish the *Requiem*. His works in minor keys all explore the wide territory between passionate revolt and ultimate resignation and exhaustion. He was finally inclined to let resignation have the last word. In the works of his last years, his smile returns; but it is often a heart-breaking melancholy smile, stemming from the conquest of his despair, from a region of the mind where neither joy nor sorrow seem to exist any longer[2] but only a composure that resembles a "weightless state"; the only desire left is for ultimate rest, release from everything mortal, a feeling Mozart expressed in a letter to his wife from 7 July 1791.

First Movement: Allegro

But in the D minor Concerto Mozart is still a long way from this divine resignation. The very first measures open up a somber, tragic abyss:

Ex. XII/1:

---

[1] Letter from Mozart to his father, 29 December 1778.

[2] See letter from Mozart to his wife, 30 September 1790. See also Alfred Einstein, *Mozart, His Character and Work*, pp. 80–81.

So let us try to offer solutions for all the detailed problems that arise in performing this concerto.

It is very difficult to catch the mood of the first movement from the outset. The syncopations are often too strongly accented, and thus sound like a hammering rhythm instead of creating an atmosphere of a sustained and yet excited D minor harmony. The syncopated chords should be separated as little as possible. This is best done by allowing each of the syncopations to materialize from nowhere and accenting them quite evenly. On no account should one make the sort of an overly strong accent usually associated with syncopation. Besides, the **p** marking at the beginning is often overlooked. If the opening is played at a thick *mezzo piano* level, any trace of a somber atmosphere disappears. The rising motives in the bass have something mysterious and disturbing about them. They must not be played too quickly and should not make a *crescendo* up to the final note; the reverse approach will help make the triplets clearer. Not until the third measure should the violin line take on a more expressively melodic quality, still within the limits of a somber **p**. From the ninth bar onward, a note of anxiety creeps in; then the music dies down again before the *f* outburst.

In this ensuing *forte*, the horns have upbeat A's, which should be played with the utmost emphasis. On the other hand, the high notes of the first violins in mm. 18 and 20 are usually played too short and with too sharp an attack, whereas the three lower quarter notes are insufficiently accented; the dominant cadence in m. 32 is often broken off too abruptly. It does no harm to prolong the rest in this bar a little, for the F major entry in the succeeding measure should enter as if from another world, quite softly, the wind instruments speaking without any audible stress. The renewed *forte* outburst (begun in m. 44) should leave room for a further *crescendo*. It is best to start the second note of this measure **mf** and let the dynamic level follow the pitch:

Ex. XII/2:

The strings should make a deliberate *diminuendo* just before the bar line; otherwise, together with the *sforzati* of the wind instruments on the first beat, they will unduly emphasize the barring and obscure the overall line. The same applies to the identical figures of the celli and basses from m. 58 on. In the following mm. 66–67, the orchestra must on no account get softer. Measure 68 must then have a completely different feeling and be played very reflectively. An excess of outward expressiveness would also be wrong in the two succeeding bars. In the codetta, only the half notes on the violins (and violas) should be given a slight expressive accent:

Ex. XII/3:

This passage tells of spiritual collapse after a passionate protest. Unfortunately, it is often played too loudly and superficially.

In most of his concertos, Mozart begins the first solo entry with either a kind of free *intrada*, a lead-in (as in K. 450, K. 467, K. 482, K. 503), or immediately gives the piano the first subject (K. 449, K. 453, K. 456, K. 488, K. 595); in the two concertos in minor keys—K. 466 and K. 491— he gives the piano its own introductory narrative, story-telling subject, which, by its pronounced subjectivity contrasts with the impersonal, fatalistic first orchestra subject. This contrast is further underlined by the fact that in the course of the movement the solo theme is never given to the orchestra and the first four bars of the orchestral first subject are never given to the solo instrument.

The expressive solo subject of K. 466 has a recitative-like character, and it may well be played a little slower than the basic tempo ($\quarternote = 132$). It should have a directness that tugs at the heartstrings, but this is incredibly difficult to achieve and can hardly be taught. The melody should sing—too soft a *piano* would thus be inappropriate. In the first full bar (m. 78), the right hand should make a slight *diminuendo* while the left—which should play in an expressive *pp*—makes a slight *crescendo*; the half note should be only slightly detached from the preceding eighth note and given as little accent as possible.

Ex. XII/4:

In the last four bars before the entry of the first orchestra subject (m. 91), the conductor (perhaps the soloist) should unobtrusively return to the basic tempo of the movement (not making a sudden change). This is made a good deal easier by the changing figurations and the unusual instrumentation (bass part in the trumpets and timpani!) in mm. 88–90. Here the eighth notes should not sound like passage work but should be played as if they were a melody, continuing the previous *cantilena*:

Ex. XII/5:

In the next solo entry, a long *crescendo* should be built up after m. 99; first in a pair of two-bar sections (99–100 and 101–102, with their upbeats), then continuously until the *forte* at m. 108. This *crescendo* is also orchestrated—the basses are added at m. 104 and the accompanying string parts condense from broken-up quarter notes to slurred eighths. Obviously, the entire passage should be played *non-legato*.

The following fingering is recommended for those with small or medium-size hands:

Ex. XII/6:

In m. 110 (unless period instruments are used), the wind instruments should play at least *mf* to match the incomparably greater power of the modern piano. In m. 121, the strings are usually too loud, one reason being that most orchestras play the passage *legato* instead of in a gentle, melodious *non-legato* (as Mozart certainly would have wanted). Again, in mm. 124–127, and in the Scottish snap figures in mm. 129–135, the string accompaniment is often too heavy. One must ensure that the final eighths in mm. 131 and 135 are not accented. Naturally, the sixteenths of the second subject should be duly brought out

Ex. XII/7:

without dragging them. The *appoggiatura* c² sounds best if played before the beat. (In mm. 148–149, the only editions that reproduce Mozart's own articulation marks are Eulenburg and the Peters editions, but there are no musical objections to the readings found in the *NMA*.) After m. 153, the musical texture becomes ever denser and one should make sure that the musical line is not interrupted before the *tutti* at m. 174. The *tremolos* from mm. 153 and 159ff. must sound very excited and be given a good deal of dynamic nuance. In mm. 162–164, the contrast of *f* and *p* must not be obscured (no *diminuendo* in the first half of the measure).

The three entries of the solo subject after the F major *tutti* should be molded and varied to differ as much as possible in character. The F major entry can be played a little more gently than at the start of the movement, and the one in G minor rather more dramatically. All the turns need to be played softer than the quarter notes. In mm. 213–214, one should make a *crescendo*, in m. 215 a *diminuendo*; on the other hand, the *crescendo* in mm. 227–228 should culminate in a *forte* at m. 229. The development section that follows can be molded as a triple wave; E-flat major (with the very low E-flat added in m. 230), at a dynamic level around *mp* (*subito*), then F minor *mf* or *f*, and finally G minor *f* or *ff*. The orchestra should also observe these three dynamic grada-tions, being altogether softer within certain limits (perhaps between *p* and *mf*). In mm. 234 and 238, we recommend a modern fingering: 123, 5212, 312, etc. The climax of the development is reached in m. 242 (arrival on the dominant). From around mm. 249ff., there should be a slight *diminuendo* to about *mf* in m. 252 (first quarter note)—the bass *tremolos*, mm. 250–251, suggest thunder rumbling in the distance; and in the two ensuing transitional measures, the eighth rests should be unobtrusively prolonged in order to underline the contrast of *p* and *f*. These two measures should not be rushed; the chromatic rise from A to D rather requires *legato* touch. There should be something uncanny about the next octave *tremolos* (mm. 261ff.); here there should be no *crescendo* to act as a transition to the *tutti* (in contrast to the exposition). Measures 278–280 should be played *non-legato*, so as not to obscure the orchestra's play of motives; m. 281 should be played *f subito*.

The way Mozart alters the second theme of the second subject group in the recapitulation is most interesting (mm. 302ff.). In the third bar there is a complete surprise—an upward leap of an octave (instead of the sixth that is expected). This effect is stronger since the harmony (Neapolitan sixth) is also unexpected. The theme should start very quietly and then give a noticeable accent to this high B-flat; the change enhances its expressive quality in the recapitulation.

The left hand's accompanying eighth notes (mm. 323ff.) should be played *non-legato*. Here it is important that the wind chords in mm. 327–328 should be played *tenuto*; if possible, each chord should be played with a slight *crescendo*. Bars 333–335 should be played *staccato*, with a very slight accent on the second and tenth sixteenth notes. The final *crescendo* should be as dramatic as possible. The last quarter note of m. 343 should be emphasized a little despite its *piano* marking because of the change of harmony; the string and wind chords should be clearly accented *fp* (and *tenuto*). There must be room for a further *crescendo* from these bars to the climax in m. 348. The bass octaves, G–G-sharp should have a full sound!

Now we arrive at the cadenza. Although Beethoven's cadenza for this movement is beautiful and poetic, there is much about it that is un-Mozartean; for example, its modulation to a key as distant from D minor as B major, the *martellato* repeated notes after B major has been reached, its use of sequences:

Ex. XII/8:

and the way the bass motive is angrily tossed about toward the end of the cadenza. The triplet accompaniment of the piano's main theme and the ending (in itself a stroke of genius) are purest Beethoven. But this cadenza has the great virtue of dramatic conciseness, and this makes it well suited to the movement, despite the faults mentioned.

The orchestral postlude is uniquely beautiful. There is probably no need to say that the closing bars should be played without any trace of a *ritardando*. In the words of Alfred Einstein: "The pianissimo conclusion of the movement is as if the furies had simply become tired out and had lain down to rest, still grumbling, and ready at any instant to take up the fight again" (Einstein, 1946, p. 306).

Second Movement: Romance, alla breve

The second movement, the superb Romance, is not in the relative key of F major, as is usual, but in the darker key of B-flat major. In this movement of the D minor Concerto, the horns must at all costs be in B-flat alto, not B-flat basso. Some conductors do not know that Mozart was accustomed to using alto horns without indicating it,[3] and in this movement it is essential.

---

[3] See Hans Pizka, *Das hohe Horn bei Mozart—oder die Situation des hohen Horns zu Mozarts Zeit*, p. 139ff.

The theme has a warm, intimate quality and a light, graceful touch, and it is very difficult to mold correctly. Nonetheless, the listener must not be made aware of the difficulties. This is why the movement (expressly marked ¢ in Mozart's manuscript, as we were able to verify for ourselves) should on no account be played too slowly; to do so destroys its hovering quality, its ecstatically spanned melodic curves.

Ex. XII/9:

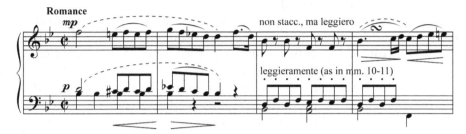

Every note is important. For example, the five B-flat quarter notes in the bass are decidedly reminiscent of a horn and should be separated as little as possible; this can be ensured by keeping the key depressed after each attack, only allowing it to rise halfway before it is again gently pressed down.

The last three eighth notes (including the octave grace notes) before the *tutti* should naturally be played *crescendo* (to prepare the way for the octaves in the *tutti*). But in making this *crescendo* one must take care not to give an unintentional accent to the preceding chord in m. 8, which resolves the dissonance occurring on the first beat. The main problem in the second half of the theme (mm. 17ff.) is to let the sixteenth-note triplets unfurl lightly and evenly, without blurring them. The slurs over the last three notes in mm. 17 to 19 must be extended over the bar line.

Ex. XII/10:

By analogy with the ensuing *tutti*, mm. 18 and 19 could be played *più piano*; but it may be better here not to match the orchestra because of the danger that the theme may become monotonous in the course of its numerous repetitions. The last three high f²'s that close m. 20 must become an expressive lead-back to the opening motive, whether played *diminuendo* or (as is perhaps better) with a slight *crescendo*. It is also good to pedal them so that the individual notes merge into one another to some extent.

In the ensuing *cantabile* passage, mm. 40ff., Mozart shows that the piano can be a wonderfully melodic instrument. Here one must sing from the heart. ("Open wide the shutters of your heart," as Edwin Fischer once remarked to his pupils about a similar passage.) This expressive *cantilena* can also be played a shade quicker than the basic tempo. This eases the pianist's (and the listener's) task of grouping the bars, four at a time, to produce extended phrases. Measures

56ff. should be rather more dramatic (*mf* or *f*), but calm, drawn-out phrasing should return at m. 60 (with its upbeat). There should be nothing feeble or toneless in this kind of song. As mentioned in chapter 5, all rising *appoggiaturas* are unaccented, quasi anticipatory. The long notes should be played like bell tones, the arm being held loose. After each attack, the hand should instantly leave the key and let the pedal prolong the note. Conductors should not overlook the fine subsidiary part for the violas during this section from bar 60 onward. The written-out lead-in m. 67 may be played, of course, with some degree of freedom; we recommend a *sf* on the high E-flat, then a *diminuendo* and *poco ritenuto*.

When the main theme returns, it certainly may be treated to some slight variation. There is good reason to believe that in the later appearances of this theme Mozart himself probably added embellishments, perhaps in the fourth and sixth bars. (One should compare the thematic recurrences in the second movement of the Sonata in C minor, K. 457.) Leopold Mozart's report to Nannerl is evidence that Mozart finished writing out parts for this Concerto K. 466 only at the very last moment before the performance—in his haste, he must surely have omitted to write down the various variations. We feel that the following slight alteration is quite justifiable:

Ex. XII/11:

The *tutti* in mm. 76–83 is more richly orchestrated than on its first appearance. The horn solo must be allowed to make its full effect.

In the G minor section, the first movement's excitement flares up again, and syncopations occur (in m. 87). Nearly everybody plays this part a bit faster, but one should try to avoid a real tempo change. The right hand's sixteenth-note triplets should be played *legato* when they contain a melodic element (mm. 84–85) but *staccato* when they are merely a means of maintaining the excitement (mm. 86–90, first half). In m. 92, the chord written on the upper stave can be played with the LH, to avoid a tiresome leap. In mm. 93 and 94, the G-flats should be slightly accented (within the prevailing *piano*). In the next few bars, one should modify one's touch to minimize the thickening of tone that occurs as the lowest register of the piano is approached:

Ex. XII/12:

Throughout this middle section, the flute must maintain its *espressivo*, particularly in m. 99; on the other hand, the sustained chords of the wind instruments in mm. 86, 93–98, and 102 should not sound too thick.

A dynamic climax comes at mm. 111–114. Here, Mozart marked the strings and wind instruments **p** undoubtedly because the fortepiano of his time had a weak tone and would not have been heard otherwise. These chords must, of course, be softer than the *forte* chords in the preceding bars, but when a modern piano is used, a reasonable **mf** for the orchestra is best. In mm. 113–114, the pedal should be kept down, and the succeeding measures should be played *diminuendo*, with changes of pedal. In the last bar before the recapitulation, a *ritardando* is quite in place. Mozart has molded this return home very convincingly and organically.

The ensuing return of the theme should be played very simply and at a very gentle *pianissimo*, after the preceding storm: there should be a joyful sense of release. The effect of this calm is enhanced by the fact that the piano no longer alternates with the *tutti*, as in the exposition, and that Mozart writes in only a single embellishment. When the orchestra reenters at m. 135, it should not disrupt the romantic mood but should continue it. In view of the increased size and volume of tone of the modern orchestra, Mozart's intentions would probably be better served by a careful **mf** and (a bar and a half later) **pp** than by taking his **f** and **p** too literally. In bars 142–144, the Breitkopf & Härtel parts contain a "*crescendo-forte*" that is not Mozart's and should certainly be ignored. The mood here is still more dreamy and abstracted than at the beginning, and an orchestral *crescendo* would oblige the pianist to force the tenderly hovering *arpeggios* in these bars quite unnecessarily. Nor should one overlook the subtlety of articulation in m. 145, where Mozart omits a slur over the first half of the bar: this is surely deliberate.

The coda must be played intimately and intensely, particularly in mm. 148 and 152, the latter even with a *ritardando*. One should be careful with the pedal in mm. 154–157, so as not to blur the *staccato*. In the penultimate measure, not more than a *pochissimo ritardando* should be made in order to safeguard the subtle effects of the syncopations with which this movement reaches its weightless end.

Third Movement: Rondo, Allegro assai (or Presto)

No tempo marking for the finale is described by Mozart. Different editors mark it *Allegro assai*, *presto*, or even *prestissimo*, but, whichever of them one follows, this movement is one of the stormiest, most elemental pieces that Mozart ever wrote—a movement matched perhaps only by the finale of the G minor Symphony K. 550.

The first five eighth notes are a problem for the soloist and everybody in the orchestra. Although it is usually a good idea to make things easier, here one should not distribute the figure between the two hands, since this would make the upbeat phrase all too easy, all too comfortable. Only by playing these eighths with one hand can one underline their unique momentum, using the arm and the entire body in sympathetic movement with the motive. We find that Edwin Fischer's suggested fingering is the best of many possibilities:

Ex. XII/13:

Within this extended upbeat, the first note should be felt and played as an upbeat to the upbeat, if the listener is not to be misled into hearing a group of quintuplets. Another vital issue here is great rhythmic discipline. An important difference between the piano and the stringed instruments must be compensated for by adaptation of touch and attack when the theme passes from one to the other: The keyboard instrument has a nearly built-in *diminuendo* toward the upper register, where the piano strings are shorter and the sounding board smaller. The very opposite is true of the violin; i.e., the lower strings are always a little weak in comparison with the sparkling E string. If a violinist were to play a *crescendo* in this passage such as is necessary on the piano, the first three notes would inevitably be too soft and get swallowed up. This also applies to the flute and most of the other orchestral instruments. The violins must therefore play this theme in an unnatural way, if it is to be clearly heard:

Ex. XII/14:

TRACK
53

While the listener will still hear a *crescendo* rather than a *diminuendo*, he will at the same time be able to make out the lower notes clearly.

In the old Eulenburg score and in the *AMA* edition, in mm. 4 and 171, the accidentals are missing before the g-sharp[1] half note in the LH; it is a printing error that fortunately is corrected in the *NMA* and the newest Eulenburg score), but at the corresponding points (mm. 76, 209, 349) this augmented sixth is given correctly, as in the autograph.

This theme should be played *molto energicamente* and the accompanying harmonies *espressivo* and *legato*, except for the hammered quarter notes in m. 1 and in m. 5. In mm. 8 and 11, the slur

Ex. XII/15:

TRACK
53

must be emphasized by an energetic accent on the upper note, and in m. 9 the articulation must be clearly audible:

Ex. XII/16:

The *tutti* should be stormy throughout; on no account should there be a drop in intensity in mm. 31 and 41. In mm. 53, 55, and 57, the low notes of the strings should be accented (the higher ones will penetrate in any case); here again it is the last eighth e-flat[1] that needs special accentuation in order to be heard clearly:

Ex. XII/17:

The solo (mm. 63ff.) should be played with great excitement, so as not to become an anti-climax after this *tutti*. The thematic relationship of this theme with the solo subject of the first movement has often been discussed. Whereas the Allegro theme was lyrically expressive, this one is a pugnacious, energetic transformation of it. Rarely are the rests in this theme given exactly their right length, nor is m. 70 often played rhythmically correct. Special care must be taken with the very short upbeat notes. The triplets in m. 66 must be played very quickly but clearly. In the passage work from m. 84 on, all the eighth notes must be played separately (*non-legato* or *staccato*).

Even with the entry of the second subject (F minor, mm. 92ff.), there is no relaxation. Ever since the music of the so-called Netherlandish school in the fifteenth and early sixteenth centuries, there has been an especially expressive poignancy about figures that juxtapose the fifth and the minor sixth (in this case the octave d-flat[2-3] following the octave c[2-3]); unfortunately, this passage is usually played in a gently melancholy, or even lachrymose way—surely the wrong treatment for a figure that, besides being intrinsically eloquent, is doubled in octaves with an energetic, drum-like accompanying rhythm:

Ex. XII/18:

Obviously, the half note should be slurred, and the octave D-flat should be louder than the following C.

From m. 98 onward, the flute should play very expressively. In the figure

Ex. XII/19:

the e[2] is likely to be inaudible unless it is given a slight accent. The change from minor to major must be deeply felt by the pianist and should bring with it a noticeable lightening of the gloom. As of m. 111, the accompanying string parts should be played *detaché* but not *staccato*. Not until m. 123 does Mozart divide up these accompanying parts into alternating *staccato* and *legato*. In mm. 130ff., the flute's *forte* must be loud and clear so that it is not drowned out by the piano's flood of tones (it needs pedal!).

The codetta theme, mm. 139ff., is very light and dance-like but does not endanger the unity of this dramatic movement. On each of its appearances it has a different significance. Here, at its first entry, it is like a slender silver lining behind the clouds. Its bright F major dies away, and after three bold modulations Mozart is back in D minor. The buildup of tension on the dominant in m. 166 definitely needs some form of release, such as can be provided by a short lead-in. An immediate entry of the theme in the tonic would be a much too abrupt resolution of this dominant harmony, which has been reached so dramatically. Note, too, how long Mozart stays on the dominant before the next D minor entry (mm. 271ff.). The one and a half bars of rests and the two fermatas are further evidence that a lead-in is necessary here. If a general pause were all that were intended, a single fermata would have been sufficient.

The question of which lead-in to play at this point seems to us to be easily answered. One possibility here is to take over the second lead-in from the D minor Fantasia K. 397 (m. 44): it hardly needs any alteration at all and has simply to be rounded off with its final e².

Another possibility is the following lead-in, inspired in part by a run (m. 34) occurring at a similar point and fulfilling the same function—release of dominant tension—in K. 397:

Ex. XII/20:

The ensuing entry of the rondo theme leads to a development section that is unusually long for Mozart. The section begins with a ghostly play with the main motive. From m. 212 on, Mozart adds a slur over the last three eighths notes of the theme—this is a softer variant that lets the motivic play of the piano, flute, and bassoon emerge more clearly. When the solo subject reappears in m. 230, it must not burst out energetically as it did on its first appearance but should be played quietly and sadly. This seems to fit the character of the development section, which deliberately avoids anything passionate or stormy. If all the instruments play strictly in time, the redoubtable passage at mm. 246ff. is not so very difficult to play, provided that the upbeat quarter notes are not taken too slowly. The eighth-notes movement should flow from one instrument to another like a *perpetuum mobile*.

In the recapitulation, Mozart does not use the main theme and is content to recall it by twice quoting its initial soaring upbeat phrase (mm. 268ff.). A little earlier (starting in m. 258), one should make a slight *crescendo* to smooth over the change in atmosphere.

The codetta theme occurs a bit sooner than in the exposition, partly to give it greater separation from its subsequent appearance in the coda but mainly because Mozart needed more room to manage the transition from this theme's light mood to the stormy atmosphere of the opening. In the recapitulation of this theme, Mozart's rapid shifts from major to minor harmonies and vice versa are a stroke of genius. The minor third F is replaced in the very next bar by F-sharp, and the next measure introduces the major sixth B. In this way, Mozart hints already at a close in D major. What a contrast to the despairing second subject in the recapitulation of the first movement, where the collapse that occurs in the coda is already beginning to emerge; but what a contrast, too, to the second subjects of most of Beethoven's movements in minor keys, which keep the same bright character unaltered in the recapitulation. This web of iridescence and subtle gradations is Mozart's most personal world; the only other great composer who set foot in it was Schubert.

The lead-back to the *tutti* (mm. 329ff.) is one of the finest passages of its kind. The enormous leaps in mm. 332–334 should not be divided between the two hands, for the same reasons that applied in the opening measure. In a violin concerto, there would be no question of dividing such a passage between two violins. "Better an enthusiastic near miss than lifeless accuracy!" was Edwin Fischer's advice. (Yet, "playing for safety" with two hands is no deadly sin.)

After the *tutti*, Mozart indicated a cadenza. Beethoven's cadenza for this movement is often played, though it certainly is not one of his best ideas; it lacks conciseness, perhaps because it indulges in too many new moods and illuminations, having a retarding effect at a point where an enormous pileup of tension makes a fierce, concentrated release indispensable. For example, what is the point of the switch to F major as early as the third measure to a key that this movement has long since exhausted? One can take it as almost certain that in his own cadenza for this movement (unfortunately lost), Mozart did not quit the key of D minor, and that here, at the culmination of the movement, he had no time to spare for mere virtuoso effects and chains of trills. So near the end, there is only one question: major or minor? And Mozart probably confirmed the feeling of a minor key in a short dramatic cadenza, so that the ensuing major would emerge all the more gloriously.

We have attempted to compose a cadenza to this concerto that might correspond to what Mozart wanted. It is available in the Bärenreiter edition mentioned in chapter 7 (see p. 274).

We are firmly convinced that in m. 353 there should be a long general pause (*Luftpause*). Mozart did not write a fermata over the rest, perhaps because, according to contemporary practice, this would have implied that a lead-in was to be played. But it is quite out of the question that one should plunge straight into the D major coda, thus breaking off the theme on a diminished seventh chord, which at this point has all the shattering effect of a natural cataclysm. A long, eloquent silence is absolutely essential here, during which the pendulum can swing from minor to major—the turning point before the final apotheosis.

In this final movement of Mozart's D minor Concerto, the major tonality does not burst straight in with trumpets and drums, as in a work such as Beethoven's Fifth Symphony—it appears almost hesitantly, first in the oboe, after its way has been prepared by the neutral dominant in m. 353. This oboe entry should sound as gentle as possible; the whole mood will be destroyed if there is any trace of abruptness. But the theme rapidly gains confidence, and in m. 358 it has already become almost exultant. (In the autograph, the last quarter note has a thick *staccato* stroke.) The piano takes over the theme, and by mm. 370ff., the entire *tutti* bursts jubilantly in with a phrase that, though related to the stormy motive (from mm. 30ff.), now sounds completely new in the major key. Here the piano practically ceases to be a solo instrument. It is part of the general rejoicing, and the pianist should play even in those measures where many editions prescribe rests instead of Mozart's *col basso* instruction (see chapter 10). In the *tutti* from mm. 370ff. and mm. 383ff. in which the texture aims at a complete blend of all the various tone colors, the main melodic line can well be doubled by the piano (not too loudly, of course); in particular, the oboes' upbeat quarter notes can be given support, since otherwise they will never be heard:

Ex. XII/21:

In mm. 372, 374, 384, and 386, the violins' high d³ should be deliberately accented, since it is the climax of the upper part. In mm. 379 and 391, the flute and bassoon can take over the melody from the oboe and horn, making an expressive continuation of it. A completely new motive is added in mm. 400ff., an *ostinato* of the wind instruments that, starting in m. 409, is very artistically interwoven with the remainder of the texture, so effortlessly that one does not notice the artistry with which it is done. The string chords in mm. 412–413 and 416–417 can well be supported by the piano's *basso continuo* playing.

This whole coda should be played with a sense of quiet urgency, particularly from m. 395 onward, as a major key *stretto* that brings release; but this mood should not be exaggerated. The canonic *stretto* of the *ostinato* figure (mm. 418ff.) should not be drowned out by the piano. The piano's figurations should be played in a translucent *non-legato*, with almost no *crescendo*, so that the violins' final run can be felt as a last triumphant enrichment of the texture.

Concerto in A Major, K. 488

- Best editions
  - *NMA* (ed. by Hermann Beck)
  - Eulenburg score (ed. by Friedrich Blume)
  - Peters edition (ed. by Edwin Fischer and Kurt Soldan)
- Cadenza
  Mozart's original cadenza is written into the score and reprinted in all the recommended editions.
- Suggested tempi
  - First movement, *Allegro*, ¢ ♩ *c.* 132
  - Second movement, *Adagio* 6/8 ♪ *c.* 96–102
  - Third movement, *Allegro assai* ¢ ♩ = *c.* 138–144

This concerto is famous for its wealth of themes and musical ideas. It is also more subtly and introspectively intimate than almost any other Mozart concerto, so its interpretation will depend to an unusual degree on the performer's personality.

The performer should avoid any trace of harshness or hardness in the first movement, which is "the most cantabile of all cantabile" *Allegro* movements. The orchestral *forte* in the opening *tutti* must be full and noble, never forced. A good way of judging the quality of the orchestra is to listen for the flute part in mm. 19–20: It is a counterpoint to the violins and ought to be clearly audible. In mm. 50, 57, 59, and 60, the first and second violins should accent the d³ and detach the following b² (in the autograph the slur clearly ends on the B).

We have already discussed the way in which Mozart's themes sometimes create a varying flow of tension by playing off metric against melodic accents in chapter 3 and chapter 8. Both the first and second subjects of this concerto show similar features. First subject:

Ex. XII/22:

Here the melody must aim, above all, at a true *cantabile*, which is best achieved by strong pressure. The left-hand accompaniment must be played very softly. Second subject:

Ex. XII/23:

The sixteenth after the dotted notes in mm. 99, 101, 103 in Ex. XII/23 should be clearly audible. Here the natural melodic accents are in mm. 2, 4, and 6. Of course, our suggestions for slight *crescendo*s and *diminuendo*s for the sake of tension should on no account be exaggerated. This theme contains an extremely attractive free motivic diminution; mm. 103 and 104 correspond exactly to mm. 99–102. Whereas in mm. 99–102 the tension runs in periods of one measure at a time, in mm. 103 and 104 it runs in half bars; this can also be seen from the articulation. The decrease in the number of notes is compensated by the greater melodic tension (sixth instead of fourth); mm. 105 and 106 return to the full-bar scheme and round off the theme, which is a miracle of musical creativeness, all the more since the harmonic tension also overlaps to some degree with the melodic tension:

Ex. XII/24:

The greatest degree of harmonic tension is in m. 3 of the example (m. 101): dominant of the dominant.

Mozart's passage work never completely lacks an expressive purpose, but in this work it is more than ever necessary to treat sixteenth-note passages so *cantabile* that their melodic content emerges clearly. Measures 87–88 should be played in such a way:

Ex. XII/25:

(As we have already said a number of times, *non-legato* is by no means incompatible with markedly melodic interpretation, and here we would again point out that in Mozart's passages, a *non-legato* should be the principal type of touch.)

Measures 93–94 should probably be played *p* and *leggiero*, mm. 95–96 (left-hand octaves) at a powerful *forte*, so that the woodwind instruments must play at least *mf* in order to be heard. The piano's off-beat groups of sixteenth notes should not be rushed; this can best be avoided by giving the second note of each group a slight accent.

Mozart's slurs are not always clear, but in the second subject at mm. 100 and 102, the reading in the Peters edition is certainly preferable, with the slurs beginning on the first eighth note. In the autograph, the slurs clearly start over the first note of mm. 100 and 102, but at the corresponding points later (mm. 230 and 232), they begin over the second note. (Compare the slurs in the orchestra at mm. 31, 33, 40, 42, 108, 110, etc.) The leaps of a fourth in the lowest bass part of the piano, mm. 103–104, must be clearly separated, whereas the middle part should be played *legato*. This passage is obviously more exactly notated in its previous appearance (*tutti*, mm. 35–36), with quarter notes and rests for the string basses. The contrast of major and minor (mm. 114ff., 117) should be underlined by nuances of *p* and *f*, as in the introductory *tutti*. In m. 120, it is advisable for the orchestra to play *pp subito*, by analogy with the subtle dynamic gradations in mm. 50 and 52. In the next few bars a motive suggesting supplication is repeated three times, and this passage must be handled very expressively by the soloist (but *p* and with the accent not on the A but on the succeeding G-sharp, to avoid giving the impression of a triplet).

It is rare to find a third subject introduced, as happens in m. 143. It is true that in his earlier works Mozart often replaced a real development by a play of virtuoso passage work around a new motive, and in this way he achieved a very personal synthesis of sonata form and three-part Lied form (A–B–A), but even he rarely succeeded in making a wholly new theme arise so organically out of what had gone before; it is such a natural necessity, it feels so integral that it hardly seems new at all. This theme has a particular significance of its own, as compared with the motives that are its counterparts in earlier works, since in this movement it returns at the end in a canon between the piano and clarinet. (The only parallel instance we know of occurs in the first movement of the E-flat major Violin Sonata K. 481.) Here the preceding general pause does not have any disrupting effect—it is a link, and more effective than any transition.

When the piano takes up a variant of this new theme in m. 149, we reach one of the climaxes of this concerto. Only by relaxing completely can one play this passage adequately; the sixteenths must seem to flow of their own accord (but not to run away!), and the long notes have to be slightly accented. But one must not *appear* to be trying to play the passage effectively or correctly.

The development that now follows tends toward the minor keys and is of elegiac character throughout. All of Mozart's works of his Viennese period are intermittently clouded by minor keys. These minor passages symbolize the inner distress that comes to disturb all enjoyment and all gaiety. The slurs at this point in the autograph are inconsistent, thus failing to clearly indicate what Mozart wanted. But, since both the first bassoon and the second clarinet have a slur starting at the second quarter note in m. 157, it seems that the reading in the Peters edition is probably a preferable version to that of the older Eulenburg score edited by Friedrich Blume (out of print). In other words, when the upbeat to the phrase rises, it is played detached and the rest of the phrase is *legato*; when it descends (the fifths in mm. 164–169), there should be a *legato* and, accordingly, in the next m. 170, the sixteenth note should be separated from the preceding dotted eighth:

Ex. XII/26:

In the bars after m. 170 the piano should maintain a crystalline, vital feeling in the decorative lines it spins round the theme, and the bass octaves must be played firmly enough to support the whole polyphonic texture. Figures such as these should always be grouped as follows:

(mm. 170ff.)

Ex. XII/27:

(see, however, m. 168):

In this way, with every second and tenth note played slightly accented, and every first and ninth unaccented, the bar line can be prevented from becoming unnecessarily audible, as is too often the case.

There should be a *crescendo* toward the end of the development. In mm. 198–199, the scoring is full, and in addition there is the interval F–D-sharp, with its sharpened leading note, and in this context the piano should certainly play loudly (*ff*). Mozart's ensuing lead-in is long and should have a degree of pathos. The dominant key has finally been reached after the disturbances of the development, and this gives a certain feeling of strength; the tension does not ebb until m. 197, with the return to the basic mood of gentleness associated with the opening. According to the autograph, this last measure should be played *legato*.

The next solo entry can, of course, be rather more bright and forceful than at the opening of the movement. The ensuing recapitulation brings nothing new until m. 259, when the piano takes over the violins' motive. The rest at m. 261 must be an open one, an effect to be achieved by playing m. 260 with a *crescendo* right up to the last note, so that the next bar seems to be deliberately thrown away. (This measure may be prolonged if its inner tension demands.) The chord on the third beat of m. 261 must in any event sound completely calm and relaxed, coming from another world (in the Peters edition, a tie is missing in the bass at mm. 262–263). And here the articulation of the theme must be exactly the same as on its first appearance in the strings (mm. 143ff.).

Mozart's cadenza that follows the opening motive, which stems from the development and uses a kind of *tremolando*, should not be played too forcefully; as it descends sequentially, one should aim to make the tone darker. Only Mozart could have dared to introduce yet another motive into a movement so rich in themes, peculiar to the cadenza and of an anxiously questioning character; its existence is justified, so to speak, by its rhythmic connection with the closing idea of the *tutti* (m. 63 onward).[4] These questioning phrases are answered by a clap of thunder in the bass, which sounds especially effective on a Mozart piano. Mozart surely used his knee lever as well as his pedal board (fortepiano pedal; see chapter 1) for this passage and added the lowest octave; the same can very well be done on the modern piano, with its greater compass:

Ex. XII/28:

The passage between the high D and the beginning of the trill, two bars later, only makes sense if the pedal (or the knee lever) is kept down—then the effect is magical!

The close of the ensuing *tutti* is problematic since the flute usually sounds too weak in m. 310, and one always has the impression that the *forte* begins only in the second half of the measure. We recommend doubling the initial A on the second clarinet (which is free to do so) or else

---

[4] There is a trill written very illegibly over the first sixteenth note of the thirteenth and fifteenth measures of the cadenza; this trill sign has been omitted by most editors but appears in the Peters edition and the latest Eulenburg score.

rescoring this passage so that the flute plays a middle part and a clarinet has the melody. A third solution, perhaps the most plausible, is to exploit the greater compass of the modern flute and rewrite the parts to correspond with the succeeding measure:

Ex. XII/29:

The texture accompanying the piano passage in the penultimate measure of the movement is very full; therefore, the entire orchestra must take care to play a soft *p* if the movement is not to end in a dull, lukewarm *mezzo forte*.

Second Movement, Adagio 6/8

This slow movement is of indescribable sadness. It is marked *Adagio* in the autograph, changed to Andante in most later editions (though not in the *NMA*). Mozart might have chosen the *Adagio* indication in order to ensure that the movement was not played too lightly and flowingly, as if it were a real Neapolitan style *siciliano*. If he had known that later generations would tend to let his slow movements drag sentimentally, he certainly would have agreed to an Andante marking.

Whereas at the opening of the solo (especially m. 2) each of the six eighth notes counts for something, most of the movement is based on a rhythm that runs in half bars, with two beats to one measure. For this reason, a slightly more flowing tempo may be adopted as from the first *tutti* (andante ♪ = *c.* 100–106), though perceptible changes of tempo in Mozart are usually not advisable. This will make the transition from six to a very peaceful two per measure. If one were to insist on adhering exactly to the tempo of the opening tempo (♪ = *c.* 96–104), the innocent ear would experience a decrease in tempo, since in the *tutti* the quarter notes have far less expressive density than in the solo.

Note that the first three notes of the first subject are *not* slurred. Played in this way, it sounds far more sad and hesitant than if slurred like a *bel canto* motive. The low E-sharp in the second measure is not merely a bass note—here the melody seems to sink into the underworld:

Ex. XII/30:

If Mozart had felt this passage differently, he would probably have written this low E-sharp as a quarter note, like the other bass notes that come on the beat. The eighth rests must on no account be obscured by overpedaling. The third and fourth eighth beat of m. 4 must be the merest breaths—no easy matter. This movement is in every way such a personal document that its interpretation depends to an unusual extent on intuition. How can one find words to describe the deep emotion of m. 7, the pallid dreariness of the Neapolitan sixths in m. 9, or the expressive eighth notes in m. 10 (which should be very gently separated, conjuring up a vision of slowly falling tears)?

The second solo, beginning at m. 20, has to make three attempts before it can get beyond the beginning of its song. The first brief comfort comes with the A major theme from m. 35 onward related to the main theme of the first movement. The triplet accompaniment in mm. 39–40 must suggest woodwind tone (compare the second clarinet in mm. 37–38) and should be played without pedal, *non-legato* and not too softly, since it is accompanying not merely the RH of the piano but the entire wind section of the orchestra.

Measures 51–52 present a brief return to the opening mood in two ways: a modulation from A major to F-sharp minor and a transition from two beats to six eighths to a measure through the introduction of upbeat thirty-second notes in the flutes, and the way the clarinet parts are written in m. 52. As the individual eighths thus take on added weight, a slight *ritardando* will occur almost automatically, as will a corresponding slight *decrescendo*.

The Neapolitan sixth chords are made more of in the reprise of the first solo than at the beginning. Measure 61 should be played absolutely **pp**, with a *crescendo* in m. 63 leading to the interrupted cadence in m. 64, which should be clearly accented. The wind instruments should join the piano in playing a slight **fp** at this point to emphasize the unexpected harmony. In the next two bars, the melody takes on an almost painfully grotesque character. The low G in the RH automatically suggests the open G string of the violin, and the ensuing isolated high D is like a despairing cry of pain. One should pay special attention to the length of the notes in this m. 66. It is best to let the left hand take over the G (silently) and hold it a fraction too long, so that the melodic continuity is made clear. The bass chord must, however, stop exactly on the third eighth note and should not be prolonged, even with the pedal. We are also opposed to the idea of filling in this wide melodic leap with a broken chord; however, a quick G major scale would be quite appropriate. In the last bar of this solo, the tension finally relaxes, and the leap of a third in the melody (instead of the enormous leap that occurred before) gives the impression of complete exhaustion after extreme excitement.

When the orchestra now takes up the sad tale, it should do so very gently. In m. 76, the piano takes over the superb tune that has previously only appeared in the orchestra. The little slurs in m. 77 should not break up the line; i.e., the second notes of these slurs are not to be cut off but joined *legato* to the following note as follows:

Ex. XII/31:

The short slurs can be quite adequately expressed by slightly deemphasizing the first, third, and fifth notes, etc.

We have already mentioned (p. 238) that from m. 80 on, some embellishment is necessary. In these bars, the left hand should alternate (*non-legato*) with the first bassoon, as if this were chamber music. From m. 84 on, the *NMA* edition gives the correct reading: first and second violins should play *arco* and not *pizzicato*. (In m. 84, the first note in the RH is, naturally, F-sharp—the D in the old Eulenburg edition is a printer's error.) Mozart's autograph has the *pizzicato* markings only for viola, 'cello, and bass, but not for the first and second violins—the autograph is quite clear on this point.

The close (mm. 92ff.) brings a final dying glow of the plaintive orchestral theme, heard three times, and each time with more intense instrumentation and harmony; here the solo adds a part whose childlike simplicity is most moving.

Third Movement

After this movement, the entry of the sparkling finale is like a change of scene in an opera, as if one were set down in the middle of some exciting celebration, and there is no doubt that this movement was influenced by *The Marriage of Figaro*, the opera that was in Mozart's mind night and day at the time. The leap to high A in the second measure tells of confident strength. The next bar should be articulated as in the succeeding *tutti*:

Ex. XII/32:

Mozart indicates this articulation by a slur over the first two eighths in m. 3 and two small slurs in m. 7. Thus, the only element missing, as compared with the *tutti*, is the second slur in m. 3. The accompaniment in these first bars must also take part in the rejoicing and must sparkle. We feel that the solo subject should be ever more effervescent with each repetition. This view is suggested by the last measure of the solo, which is more energetic each time it recurs. In the ensuing *tutti*, continuo playing is strongly recommended.

In mm. 16–20 and 24–28, there is something about the string parts that suggests a swaying dance; this should be underlined by slightly accenting the upbeat slurred quarter notes. The interrupted cadence on to F-sharp minor in m. 52 is naturally a reference back to the F-sharp minor Adagio and at the same time an energetic repudiation of the mood of the slow movement. In the next solo (mm. 62ff.), the E-sharp must be slightly accented, so that the listener feels it is a link to the next. In m. 74, the high E should be given a cheeky accent and the remaining eighths played *staccato*. In mm. 98ff., and later in mm. 129ff., and 150ff., the short upbeat notes should be sharply accented. This can best be done by scattering these notes elastically with the forearm.

With the second subject, in E minor, the mood darkens slightly. The center of gravity is, of course, the third measure of the subject (m. 100). The sixteenth-note figure in this measure as well as the triplets later on, from m. 158 on, show that Mozart did not want this movement played too quickly, since they are unplayable at the "presto" given in many editions for this movement. (In mm. 113, a *legato* slur should be added, by analogy with the slurs in the autograph at m. 337 during the recapitulation.) The high pathos of the modulation to the key of C major at m. 121 recalls an opera seria aria and can be emphasized by appropriate dynamics. The passage that follows (from m. 129 onward) seems to gloat over the E major that has at last been reached, with festive harmonies over a confidently descending bass. The strings and wind instruments should realize from m. 151 on that they are part of a play of powerful harmonies; above all, the wind instruments should not play too softly here, particularly when they have the secondary parts (mm. 157ff.). In mm. 135 and 157, the soloist should play *subito **p***, not only to let the woodwind come slightly into the foreground, but to leave room for a further *crescendo*. In bass figures such as occur in these bars, the weaker beats should always be accented:

Ex. XII/33:

In the figures from m. 163 onward the second of each pair of slurred notes should be similarly emphasized, so that the feeling of playful energy is further enhanced:

Ex. XII/34:

But the rejoicing reaches its bubbling climax in the codetta theme, which is introduced in the canon between the piano and the wind instruments. Mozart, unlike many of his editors, did not provide a single slur for this theme (the old Eulenburg edition wrongly allows a *legato* slur to remain in m. 177), and this makes it sound much more fiery and full of life (played throughout *non-legato*):

Ex. XII/35:

It is also useful to make a slight *diminuendo* from m. 189 on, or else to play *subito p* in m. 196, so that there is room for a *crescendo* as the piano surges up to the reentry of the first subject in m. 202. Now comes a powerful *crescendo* by the orchestra (whose modulations can be supported by a few chords on the piano). According to the autograph, at this point (m. 230 and also sixteen measures later) the right hand should play not the three-part chord, wrongly printed in all editions, but a four-part chord: C-sharp–F-sharp–A–C-sharp. Here the music moves to a very energetic, almost wild F-sharp minor, with occasional plaintive interjections from the woodwind instruments. Then Mozart introduces yet another theme (in D major) into this movement that is already so uniquely rich in melody.

In mm. 254–255, the left hand should play *legato*, like the orchestral basses, whose articulation should consequently be adopted by the pianist in mm. 267–268 and 429–430. The half-bar slurs in m. 288 and the slurs over each quarter note in m. 291 should be carefully observed. The surge up to the high C in m. 298, being a distant reference to the first subject, should be as powerful as possible.

As so often in Mozart's rondos, the recapitulation does not begin with the first subject but goes straight into the solo theme, saving the triumphal reentry of the first subject for the coda. Making allowances for a different plan of modulation, the recapitulation follows a course similar to that of the exposition, though with a few important deviations. Thus, the second subject surprisingly enters in the major key (m. 330) and does not appear in the minor until taken over by the piano eight bars later. The original modulation from A minor through F major to A major is extended when compared to the corresponding passage in the exposition: This is a stroke of genius, suddenly opening up terrifying depths of emotion unexpected in a concerto so full of social and socially pleasing music.

We suggest playing the passage from m. 346 on as follows:

Ex. XII/36:

After the codetta, a superb *crescendo* (mm. 437 and 444) leads to the return of the first subject. The swaying motive from the opening (mm. 17ff.) now returns for the first time, and this time the piano also takes part. Here the upbeat notes should be a little louder than the ensuing longer ones. In mm. 468–471, the left hand amusingly imitates the bassoon solo (originally mm. 28ff.) and the humor can be underlined by playing *staccato*, to suggest a bassoon.

The final *crescendo* is now due, but by a brilliant manipulation of the form it is further post-poned—as if Mozart wanted to play a practical joke on his audience, who were already on the verge of applauding; instead of the expected cadence, the cheerful third subject returns once more. At the same time, the progression to the subdominant (D major) makes it clear that this will only be a short delay and that the concerto is nearly over. And, in fact, the long-delayed final cadence, all the more eagerly awaited, now appears with virtuoso piano figurations woven around it. It is hardly likely that Mozart meant the soloist "to have done with the concerto" five bars before the orchestra concludes, and his notation of the *basso continuo* also supports such a view. Therefore, during the two closing *tutti* passages, the pianist should play powerful chords, and the last three notes in unison with the strings.

Concerto in C minor, K. 491

- Best editions
  - Eulenburg score (ed. by Friedrich Blume)
  - *NMA* (ed. by Hermann Beck)
  - Peters edition (ed. by Edwin Fischer and Kurt Soldan
  - Steingräber edition (ed. by Hans Bischoff; out of print); reprinted by Schirmer, New York.
- Cadenzas
  No original cadenzas or lead-ins extant. The cadenzas by Saint-Saens and Brahms are too foreign in style to be recommended. Relatively speaking, the best old cadenza is still that by J. N. Hummel, Mozart's favorite pupil. It was reprinted in the Stein-gräeber (Schirmer) edition. One cadenza by Paul Badura-Skoda has been printed by Doblinger, Vienna (1956, a new version 2003), another slightly altered one by Bärenreiter-Verlag. A new, daring one is forthcoming (Doblinger, 2007).
- Suggested tempos
  - First movement, Allegro 3/4 ♩= *c.* 144 (*c.* 152 in solo passages, such as mm. 165–199 and the excited passage in mm. 330–61)
  - Second movement, Larghetto ₵ ♩= *c.* 54–56
  - Third movement, Allegretto ₵ ♩= *c.* 80–84, intermittently a little slower (*c.* 76)

It is natural to want to compare Mozart's two piano concertos in minor keys. Although only thirteen and a half months separated their composition, they are worlds apart. In the D minor Concerto (K. 466), Mozart still faces suffering firmly; he is ready to fight, and the work's triumphant D major close is a quite Beethovenian victory over tragedy. The C minor concerto K. 491 is quite different. Although the work contains episodes of passionate rebellion and of gentle consolation, its ending is not triumphant—it is a macabre dance of death and despair. No wonder that to this day the C minor Concerto has not attained the same popularity as the one in D minor. It is too complicated, too oppressive to appeal to the average listener, who prefers a happy end in music, as in the cinema.

The difference between the two works is evident even in their smallest details. The D minor Concerto's self-possession is apparent in its clearly diatonic harmony; its principal themes, for all their tragic quality, are based on the cadential progression between tonic and dominant. This gives them a certain inner strength and firmness. There is little trace of this in the C minor Concerto. The opening theme has an inclination to sink toward bottomless depths[5] after its brief initial upsurge, and this effect is intensified by boldly chromatic harmony:

---

[5] See the discussion, particularly of this main theme and its possible sequence, in Eva Badura-Skoda, "W. A. Mozart. Klavierkonzert c-moll KV 491," pp. 15–16.

Ex. XII/37:

There is an obvious kinship with the first subject of the C minor Fantasia K. 475. There, too, we find a chromatic movement around the fifth (F-sharp–G–A-flat) and descending sequences with very bold chromaticisms.

The first movement of K. 491 is not wholly lacking in assertive, recurring energetic figures that pull in the opposite direction, and these constantly recur, but the music is definitely dominated, particularly toward the end of the development and at the end of the first movement, by the dark, somber forces in it. Whereas the first movement of the Concerto in D minor was in a march-like 4/4, with frequent rests for the whole orchestra, the first Allegro movement of K. 491 is in a flowing 3/4, time that tends to bind everything together. Whereas the first solo subject of the D minor Concerto settles firmly on the tonic in the very first measure and the subdominant in the third, here the solo subject slips from the tonic to the seventh in its fourth bar. Hearing a sequence, one expects that the tonic will at least be confirmed in the fifth measure of the theme (m. 104):

Ex. XII/38:

Instead, the second phrase runs down still lower than the first. The tonic is only reached in the ensuing four bars, then immediately afterwards the theme lingers indecisively on an unstable chord, an inversion of the supertonic seventh. After these four measures of lingering on D, the final cadence of the theme seems like a powerful effort to pull oneself together.

Comparing the two slow movements, that of the Concerto in D minor is again the more forceful and brighter one. The intimate Larghetto theme of the C minor Concerto is more melancholy than the Romance, and instead of a stormy middle section, there are two wonderful lyrical episodes, a plaintive elegiac oboe melody in C minor and a blissfully ecstatic A-flat section dominated by the clarinets. But the distinction is clearest in the two final movements: Instead of the D minor Concerto's pyrotechnic rondo theme, we find an apathetically drooping melody that serves as a basis for a set of variations:

Ex. XII/39:

The chromatic descent found in the first movement reappears here in mm. 10–12.

In its form, the first movement of this concerto is one of the greatest masterpieces in all music. The dominating power of the first subject is immediately apparent. Not only does it return in the codetta of the orchestral and solo expositions, but also its constituent motives appear in the most varied forms, in sequences now of two measures, now of one, these motives pervade the movement to such a degree that all the subsidiary themes seem like brief, moving interludes, never able to break the spell of this fateful principal theme. Its importance can be gauged by the fact that whereas the typical Mozart theme confines itself to one particular register, this one appears everywhere—now in the bass, now in the topmost register of the melodic instruments; it is all-pervasive, like some uncanny supernatural force or a premonition of death, lying in wait even in the few passages where there seem to be motives not dominated by the main theme.

The technique of composition displayed by Mozart in this movement is astonishingly reminiscent of J. S. Bach's handling of concerto form in such a work as the D minor Concerto BWV. 1052, where the principal theme returns in various keys in the course of the movement, like the *ritornello* of a rondo. It may return complete or only its opening, and the accompanying parts are formed by sequences built from its constituent motives; this is symphonic thought of a kind quite unknown to most of Bach's contemporaries. The construction of Mozart's first subject also recalls Bach; it is not symmetrical like most classical themes but is of the continuous development (*Fortspinnungs*) type, with a distinct, clearly shaped opening and sequential continuation. These relationships are all the more striking since in all probability Mozart did not know Sebastian Bach's concertos and thus seems to have created this form, unique in his music, on his own.

Starting from his first subject, which has a structure unprecedented in its complexity despite its apparent simplicity and self-contained quality, Mozart derives a wealth of rhythmic and melodic figures on which the entire movement is built:

Ex. XII/40:

Mozart often uses the two halves of motive (b) separately during the movement; (c) is an augmentation of the second half of (a); (d) is an inversion and diminution of (c); (f) is related melodically to the first half of (b). Mozart later freely alters these constituent motives' melodic steps and leaps, as well as their articulation, but it is always clear that they are derived from the first subject. Its opening often appears *forte* with the notes separated and not slurred, and motive b_1 often appears later *non-legato* or *staccato*.

Formal analysis cannot teach one how to perceive this entire movement of 523 measures as a single unit; this can only be achieved intuitively. For us this movement is a permanent wonder, before which we can only stand in awe.

This movement is built on a tense inner conflict between solo and *tutti*. The first *tutti* theme seems to symbolize an impersonal destiny that man, the soloist, must face—suffering, complaining, now in angry revolt, and then exhausted, resigned. Thus, it seems quite natural that the first four crucial bars of the first subject are never given to the solo piano part, just as the solo subject (mm. 100ff.), with its personal quality, is reserved for the piano throughout the movement. Yet such a metaphor is too schematic. *Fate*, as represented by the orchestra, also has human traits, while *Man* (piano) is not a helpless subject but enters in dialogue with it. Especially during the friendly subsidiary themes in a major key, an intimate dialogue is reached with single instruments or whole groups, an interaction not present elsewhere in Mozart's concertos. Only toward the end of the development section of the first movement is a real conflict reached, when the excited *arpeggios* of the piano alternate with the *tutti* and produce an astonishing intensity of sound (even on a period piano). But resignation follows: In the recapitulation all themes are played in the minor key.

A further division is discernible throughout this concerto, and it is found within the orchestra; there is often a contrast between the strings, which have many players to a part and are therefore in a sense impersonal, and the subjective, solo wind instruments; the latter thus occupy a middle position between the solo and *tutti*. Particularly in the second and third movements, the woodwind instruments become so independent that one could speak of a concertino, a second competitive group, as in *concerto grosso* form.

The opening *tutti* of the concerto should conjure up a fatalistic, gloomy mood. Here it would be a mistake to play with warmth. The first three measures should be played very *legato*, and the change of bow between mm. 2 and 3 should be as imperceptible as possible. It may even be advisable to divide the strings and make half of them change bows after the first measure:

Ex. XII/41:

Dynamic nuances should be kept to a minimum to ensure an impersonal quality; for example, the two quarter notes in m. 4 should be played quite indifferently. There should be a slight *crescendo* up to the third bar to emphasize the *legato*. The third quarter note G on beat three of m. 3 should not sound too short. Many interpreters take the first twelve measures of this movement a shade slower than the basic tempo, at ♩= *c.* 138 or even slower; this enhances the uncanny feeling of calm before the storm that pervades the opening (see p. 290 for a discussion of the dynamic course of the first solo subject). They retain great regard for rhythm in the phrases with short upbeats and great inner tension. The passionate outburst at m. 13 is then all the more powerful.

In m. 27, the trumpets should play *marcato*. The original articulation of the string parts in the ensuing mm. 23–33 should be scrupulously observed. In m. 34 the three horn notes are still *forte*. In the ensuing tender *piano* passage, the upbeats must not be played as eighth notes. In m. 40, the flute should play at least *mf*, since this is a continuation of the oboe part; there must not be the feeling of a *diminuendo*. In mm. 59ff., it is appropriate for the flute and the bassoon to make a slight *crescendo* up to the third quarter note of each bar. From bar 74 on, the first violins should play very expressively and *cantabile* (within the limits of piano dynamics, of course), and the important passing eighths e¹ and f-sharp¹ (second violins, mm. 77 and 79) must be clearly accented. From m. 89 on, the first violins' sixteenths should be played very rhythmically. Figures such as these (like those of the second violins, mm. 271ff.) and thematic figures such as the first theme of the second subject group (mm. 147ff.) show why we recommend not too fast an *Allegro* tempo for this movement. The sudden *p* in mm. 97–98 must be clearly distinguished from the preceding *f*; a breathing pause is recommended.

The first solo subject should be played strictly in time. In a movement such as this, sentimental variations of tempo are to be avoided. All too often the first note is not held long enough, and the eighths in the second measure are played unevenly and too quickly. Even this eloquent subjective solo subject must fit into the general scheme. Although this is a long movement, there is scarcely a single place where one need alter the tempo. The form can only be properly brought out by some degree of rhythmic severity.

In mm. 123ff., as throughout the movement, the upbeat sixteenths should be played incisive and *staccato*. The three slurred quarter notes, on the other hand, should sound very expressive, the leaps separated (without pedal) but with no shortening of the upper notes. The second violins' counterpoint in m. 134 should be slightly emphasized (*espressivo*), as should the viola part in the next measures. The piano's runs in mm. 135ff. must have a markedly melodic effect (while played *non-legato*), and here the dynamics must exactly follow the rise and fall of the line. The new theme in mm. 146–147 arises organically out of the preceding flow in a way so characteristic of Mozart. Here one may make a slight unforced *ritardando* and take the ensuing second subject a shade slower than the basic tempo. (This exception should be regarded as merely proving the rule that this movement, as with most of Mozart's concerto movements, is to be played strictly in time.) It is typical of Mozart (and a fact whose importance is not yet sufficiently appreciated) that in such passages that flow into a new theme, he writes *legato* slurs in the last measure and only there; e.g., K. 488/I (m. 197 in the Peters edition); K. 491/I, m. 38; K. 482/I, m. 246. Obviously, this use of *legato* loses its point if one also plays the preceding notes *legato*. The eighths in mm. 143–145 should therefore be separated, if possible with pedal vibrato (that is, from three to six changes of pedal per measure).

The string accompaniment of the ensuing second subject cannot be played too softly; only the quarter notes in mm. 149 and 151 may be played slightly more *espressivo*. The soloist must realize that the first measure of the melody should be felt as an upbeat, so that he can make a slight *crescendo* up to the high B-flat. The B in m. 153 should probably be slurred over to the next bar. Only a slight echo effect can be made in m. 154, with a return to a louder dynamic level at the cadence in the next bar. The next solo should be played in the basic tempo; here the first bassoon has a very fine subsidiary part, which is unfortunately usually nearly inaudible (the minor ninth as an accented passing note in mm. 165 and 167) because the piano's figurations steal the limelight. Therefore, this bassoon part should be played *forte*, perhaps also doubled if necessary. In m. 170 there are again difficulties, this time for the flute and oboe, which alternate with a singing line; they should not play too quietly. In mm. 175–157, a *forte* should be played, and then *piano* in the next bar, so that there is room to make a suitable *crescendo* in the two ensuing sequences. The strings' counterpoint should be clearly articulated:

Ex. XII/42:

The imitation between the piano and the double basses in mm. 190ff., with its octave motive, must be well brought out:

Ex. XII/43:

In m. 201 the second theme of the second subject group enters, distributed among the various woodwind instruments. Although this consolatory theme seems to fall (literally) prey to the dominating pull of the lower regions, there is a counterpoint in the oboe and horn that soars upwards and provides one of the few rays of light in this gloomy movement:

Ex. XII/44:

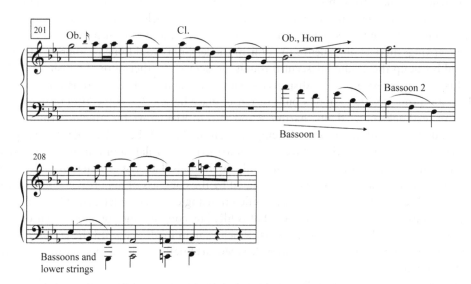

The theme is taken up by the strings, with accompanying figurations on the piano. As in so many of Mozart's *cantabile* themes, the first measure should be felt as an upbeat to the second (although from the structural point of view it is a strong measure). This is made admirably clear by the rhythmic scheme of this passage and the position occupied within it by the beginning of the theme:

Ex. XII/45:

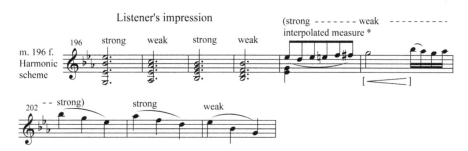

The interpolation at * means that two strong bars follow each other, but the listener does not notice this until later.

The piano's melodic figurations are best given life by a slight *crescendo* up to the third beat of each measure. At this point, the mildness of E-flat major is broken by a recurrence of the demonic first subject in the key of E-flat minor (tonic minor of the relative major of C minor). It is very unusual for Mozart to choose such a distant key. But he goes farther: In the middle of this thematic entry he surprisingly comes to rest for four bars on F-sharp (G-flat) major, using the first inversion of the F-sharp major triad (mm. 228ff.). Interestingly the strings are notated in F-sharp major, the piano and the wind instruments (with the exception of the flute) in G-flat—which was done probably out of the well-known convenience reasons for the string players. But it seems to prove convincingly that Mozart favored a well-tempered tuning system and apparently expected his orchestra musicians to play as well-tempered as they were able to hear. (In the C minor Fantasy K. 475, m. 10, Mozart wrote a B major harmony that also demands tempered tuning—it sounds horrible if the piano is tuned in the system of Kirnberger 2 or 3!)

The whole passage from mm. 220 to 238 makes up one unit, in that the bass gradually descends an entire octave from bass clef E-flat to the E-flat below the stave. One can hardly speak of a modulation to F-sharp major here, since the harmony is transitional and the result of part-writing; there is no cadence to confirm the key, nor would one be appropriate, since it would break up the gradual descent through the octave. Furthermore, the F-sharp (G-flat) chord is in first inversion—an indispensable choice if the overall structure is not to be disturbed, for a root position chord would be out of place here. (This is the kind of point overlooked in textbooks of academic harmony and also in Riemann's functional harmony.) The octave is divided naturally into two by emphasis on the fifth of the scale, B-flat (A-sharp). To make clear the division of the octave into a fourth (E-flat–B-flat) and a fifth (B-flat–E-flat), both of them filled in stepwise, Mozart not only dwells on B-flat (A-sharp) in mm. 228–232 but elects to make the change of octave necessitated by the compass of his instruments just after this B-flat. (The fourth in mm. 220–222 is filled in using every chromatic step; the fifth, mm. 232–238, omits one semitone, A-natural, but is filled by conjunct motion.) This clear division is also furthered by the piano's figurations, which remain unaltered until the end of the bass octave and only change from m. 239 onward, as Mozart finally reaches a cadence in the parallel key of E-flat major.[6]

The score gives no dynamic indication for this entry of the first subject (mm. 220ff.). Because the piano texture is fairly full here, the flute must play *forte* and expressively, while the excited string chords should be **mp**. From m. 228 onward, the first bassoon must stand out slightly. The piano's two F-sharp major scales can be played with slight differences between them (alternating *legato* with *staccato*, or an echo effect, or a combination of the two). The series of string and wind chords from mm. 232ff. has a definitely thematic character and should not be played too softly, despite the marking **p**. Not until m. 239 is there the cadence in E-flat major, after which the relative major is free to unfold with no further hindrance. The question of whether the two dotted notes should be embellished or not has long been a matter of discussion. After years of playing them as written, Paul Badura-Skoda has lately decided to play them in one of the following ways:

---

[6] We are grateful to Professor Hellmut Federhofer for pointing out this passage and for a harmonic analysis along the lines of Schenker.

Ex. XII/46:

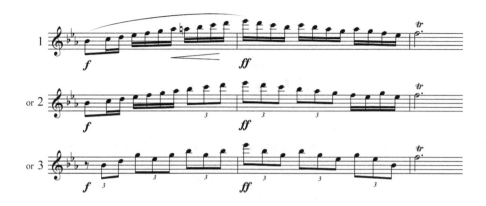

He changed his mind for two reasons: (1) In the E-flat major Concerto K. 449, which Mozart wrote not for himself but for his pupil Barbara Ployer, the trills in m. 169 and m. 319 are preceded by quick runs. (2) Even in the E-flat major Concerto K. 482, with its many abbreviated notations in the solo part, the horn passage before the cadential trill has simultaneous piano figurations that resemble mm. 261–262 of K. 491. See also the discussion of mm. 467–470 on pp. 235–236 (Ex. VI/25).

The horn solo in mm. 261–262 should sound triumphant, as should the *tutti* starting at m. 265; here the dynamic level of the low notes of the first violins is a problem that can only be solved if the winds play their sustained notes rather softer than their quarter notes. There can well be a slight broadening at the last two quarter notes and the dramatic rest before the *p* in m. 280. (This also applies to mm. 96 and 506.)

With the ensuing solo entry there is an abrupt change of mood. E-flat major, which in the preceding *tutti* had had a triumphant quality, takes on a regretful, melancholy character in this solo; but it should still be played *cantabile*. Melancholy is not the same as lachrymose. In particular, the first note of the melody must sound full and firm. It is not easy to play the three chords in m. 289 evenly, with a slight break between each as if on a woodwind instrument. The simple melodic step from G-flat to B-flat is extremely expressive—the previous feeling of a definite major key disappears at one stroke. The woodwind interpolations (mm. 291–292) should be expressive and not hurried. The right hand's counterpoint in mm. 295 and 299 must sound as independent of the theme in the left hand as possible: the RH is played *legato* with a slight *crescendo*, the LH slightly *staccato* (without pedal) and *diminuendo*. In m. 300, the E-natural in the middle part should be more accented than the C in the top part; otherwise, the latter note will sound like the start of the ensuing melody. This measure has to be practiced very thoroughly. There is an apparently innocuous new motive:

Ex. XII/47:

which is the nucleus of the stormiest outburst in any of Mozart's piano concertos—the passionate and powerful measures from mm. 330ff. In m. 300, this motive should therefore be played as if it had some hidden significance and articulated as it appears later on the strings:

Ex. XII/48:

The first subject appears *forte* at the beginning of the development and then continues sequentially, *piano* and *legato*, with a counterpoint that seems wholly new but in fact originates in mm. 59–62 of the opening *tutti*. There follows a ghostly play of various motivic figures; these motives at times combine to produce acrid false relations; for instance, it is hard to find any other passage in Mozart like the Brahmsian sixth of mm. 319–320, where the part-writing produces quite extraordinary clashes:

Ex. XII/49:

Throughout this section (mm. 302–329), the piano simply weaves a web of passage work, which should be performed expressively but not obtrusively. The play of motives dies away in the orchestra, and after five bars' solo, which should probably be played *crescendo*, there follows the stormy outburst already mentioned. The pianist who does not instinctively make a slight *accelerando* in this passionate section is a rare individual, indeed. This is only natural, for it has always been customary to express intense emotion in music by an *accelerando* (though only a slight one) that corresponds to the quickening of the pulse when one's emotions are aroused. Naturally, if one makes an *accelerando* here, the tempo must not become excessively quick—but not more than ♩ = *c*. 152. A feeling for the right degree of an agogic change is indeed something that cannot be taught. Although the whole sound builds up in this passage, the pianist should not force his tone. The piano's figures must not be played as if they were Brahms's heaviest outbursts—this would make them sound convulsive instead of powerful. (The *arpeggios* in this passage obviously need some pedaling. Measures 337, 341, and 345 are slightly easier technically if one plays the top note with the left hand.)

The excitement of this passage leaves its mark on the ensuing measures after m. 345 and takes some time to die away completely. The way Mozart notated the piano part in mm. 346–353 very much suggests a *forte*. In these bars, the left-hand phrases, which are a free diminution of the first subject:

Ex. XII/50:

derived from:

should be articulated like the bassoon part (mm. 346–347 *legato*, mm. 348–349 *staccato*, etc.).

The motivic interplay of the woodwind over a pedal point in mm. 354–361 should have biting clarity; the upbeat sixteenth notes, in particular, need the utmost plasticity. In Mozart's autograph, the notation of the piano's scales is not entirely clear at this point, but we find the reading in the *NMA*, the Eulenburg score, and the Peters editions most convincing. In m. 355, Mozart probably meant A-flat, even though the sharp sign is also missing before the fourth sixteenth. In m. 360, the only possible reading is the one given in the three editions just mentioned:

Ex. XII/51:

The two outer notes of the scale from A-flat to B-natural both function as leading notes to C minor. If the top note were A-natural, not only would there be an ugly diminished fifth (tritone A–E-flat) within the scale but also the outer notes would give a quite impossible interval:

Ex. XII/52:

Thus, the piano's A-flat like the orchestra's A-flat (part of the rising fourth G–A–B–C), is a logical result of part-writing. (We cannot accept the reading suggested by the editor of the Boosey & Hawkes edition, since he pays too little respect to the melodic independence of these scales in relation to the harmonic scheme. For instance, he questions the F-sharp in m. 354, which is definitely authentic.)

This use of notes foreign to the harmony in order to avoid tritones is something Mozart learned from Haydn and frequently used in other works; e.g., the first movement of the Concerto in E-flat Major, K. 449, m. 308:

Ex. XII/53:

In this passage, the pedal note should, of course, be played with a gradual *diminuendo* (and no *crescendo* in the last bar before the *tutti*). In m. 362, the first subject should break in with a sudden *forte* and summarily dispel the haze that has accumulated during the measures leading in to it.

In m. 390, one can underline the feeling of transition by a slight *ritardando*. The tempo should broaden unnoticeably at the third quarter note of m. 400. This bar is all the weightier since it contains two main harmonies, whereas throughout the remainder of the movement there is only one harmony to a bar. The violins must play a real *p* in m. 401, since otherwise the piano will not penetrate.

The other main theme of the second subject group follows immediately. Mozart rejected all three possible versions:

Ex. XII/54:

in favor of:

Ex. XII/55:

which clearly brings out the feeling of a minor key and also exploits the contraction of the octave leap to a sixth, in keeping with the oppressive character of the recapitulation. Instead of the consolation brought by this theme in the exposition, all has turned to heartrending lamentation. Even the cheerful triplet accompaniment of the clarinet (mm. 156–160) here turns into earnest *legato* eighths in the first bassoon. Because of its expressive content, this passage (mm. 410ff.) should be played still more softly than on its first appearance. When playing the final bars of this theme, the effect should be the opposite of that in the exposition; m. 417 not softer but louder, though the final bar should fall back as if exhausted.

The unexpected diminished seventh in m. 428 has something sharp and cutting about it; the lamentation of the preceding bars is brusquely cut off by the return of the first subject. If the second subject has been played a little slower, then it is best to return to the basic tempo at this point. Here again the wind syncopations are thematic and should therefore be slightly accented. The circle is now closed by the return of other thematic figures heard in the exposition. This time, of course, the triumphant horn call is missing before the final trill—not simply because of the limitations of the natural horn, for Mozart could quite well have given the figure to the bassoons, as in so many of his other works. Instead, in the immediately preceding mm. 463–468, the oboes and flute have yet another new complaining figure. (We already mentioned that the piano's figurations must be maintained through mm. 467–468 and also in mm. 469–470, where an energetic run is necessary; see discussion above.) This figure inevitably runs into the first subject, which breaks off dramatically on the customary 6/4 chord before a cadenza. The horn solo in bars 480–486 should emerge clearly, and the 6/4 chord should be prepared by a *crescendo* and *ritardando*.

It is only a small surprise that nobody has been able to write a satisfactory cadenza for this movement, which is unique even in Mozart's works. What possible form could it take? Every theme, every mood, has already been exploited to the utmost, and to recapitulate moods and emotions already experienced would only weaken the effect. This makes it not improbable that when Mozart played this concerto he introduced a wholly new theme and developed it dramatically (as in many of his earlier concertos). A further argument in favor of this idea is provided by the first three bars of the ensuing *tutti*, which are new and have no relation to any motive from the rest of the movement. Perhaps they are linked to some motive from Mozart's own cadenza.

TRACK 56 On Track 56 one can hear a cadenza which Paul Badura-Skoda played quite often; it is published by Doblinger.

But who else besides Mozart would dare to invent a new theme for this movement? One can, however, take two things for granted:

1. That Mozart did not modulate to the sharp keys in his cadenza. This follows from the fact that in the entire concerto he does not abandon the flat keys a single time. (The F-sharp major of mm. 228ff. must be regarded as an enharmonic notation of G-flat major, in view of the surrounding tonality—E-flat minor in m. 221, D-flat major in m. 233.) Mozart's feeling for the gravitational field of his basic tonality would certainly have prevented his overstepping the bounds of the dark minor keys anywhere in this work, even in the cadenza.
2. That the cadenza must have been highly dramatic but not too long. Too extended a cadenza would only disturb the balance of the movement, which for all its spaciousness is very concentrated.

Hummel's cadenza—despite surpassing the extension of Mozart's keyboard range by one octave—satisfies both these conditions. The first measures, for instance, are good indeed, and so is the increase in excitement in the middle part, where his rising sequential treatment of one of the motives from the first subject throws new light on it, and the later diminution of the first subject:

Ex. XII/56:

The sequence from m. 18 on, and the long chain of trills in the middle of the cadenza, however, are less satisfying; the trills make a rather superficial effect. They are better omitted, as can easily be done if the preceding measure is altered:

Ex. XII/57:

Another slightly disturbing feature of the Hummel cadenza is the fact that toward its end the cadenza lingers in the topmost register of the piano (a register that did not exist in Mozart's day), which disturbs, especially on modern pianos. This reduces the effect of the highest melodic notes in the rest of the concerto, without adding anything of its own to the composition. Here we recommend playing the RH an octave lower than written while keeping the LH as it is, also shortening the chain of trills by two measures.

Ex. XII/58:

Edwin Fischer, unlike Malcolm Bilson, used to play the coda after the cadenza (mm. 509ff.) softly, glassily, without pedal; this made the passage sound very uncanny. He also played the left hand an octave lower than written and, of course, *pp*, like a very soft, low note on the organ. There would certainly be no objection to this, were it not for the fact that the closing three measures of passage work oblige one to leave this low note—Mozart was here more fortunate since he had a pedal board. He could play the end as follows:

Ex. XII/59:

and probably did. (As discussed in chapter 1, the piano pedal board was a separate instrument that hardly anybody other than Mozart owned; therefore, he had a reason to refrain from writing down a part for it.)

After the cadenza, a lonely, lamenting flute hovers above the gloomy waves of the coda. It should certainly be treated as a solo part. The end of the movement dies away in a resigned *pp*. It must be played strictly in time, with no trace of a *ritardando*—as if the music moved inaudibly on to infinity, beyond the final cadence. For all its gloom, it is an inconceivably beautiful ending.

Second Movement

To speak of an error of Mozart may seem an act of great boldness; but he must have made a mistake when he marked the Larghetto of this concerto *alla breve* (𝄵). This opinion, expressed fifty years ago, has been contested by several eminent Mozart interpreters, such as Max Rudolf or George Szell. By now we agree that the opening theme could well be interpreted *alla breve*; yet the two episodes in C minor (mm. 20–38) and A-flat major (mm. 43–62) as well as the coda are definitely in 4/4 and not *alla breve*. More than once in this book, we have insisted that Mozart's *alla breve* markings in slow movements should be observed and acted on. But just by comparing this movement with the other—in our opinion—genuine *alla breve* movements in the concertos K. 466, K. 537, and K. 595, we had to conclude that this Larghetto should better be felt and played in common time.

There are various reasons for this conviction. At the beginning, an *alla breve* movement is indeed imaginable. But then the encounter with the smallest unit of movement in this Larghetto, the thirty-seconds, creates difficulties with the *alla breve* time. No such figuration as that in mm. 24–25:

Ex. XII/60:

ever occurs in the slow movements of the aforementioned concerto movements, nor can one imagine them with a 𝄵 time signature. The note values in this movement correspond to notes twice as long in *alla breve* movements, as can be seen if one compares these two identical syncopated rhythms:

Ex. XII/61:

Larghetto mvt. of the Concerto K. 491, m. 48:   *Larghetto mvt. of the Concerto K. 595, m. 71:*

For this same reason, the opening solo is only four bars long, not eight as in the second movement of the "Coronation" Concerto. Finally, in no other *alla breve* movement would one find a harmonic rhythm like that in the second (and even more the sixth) measure of the Larghetto of K. 491, where each eighth note takes on importance because of the change of harmony; this is in fact not found elsewhere in Mozart.

It is easy to imagine how Mozart might have made this mistake. Mozart probably marked the movement *alla breve* because of mm. 9–12, which do in fact only contain two strong beats in each bar, and because of the numerous repeated notes in the main theme. When beginning to compose this movement he had a different idea, then started with the thirty-second-note motive—and forgot to alter the meter. A composer who left behind such an enormous body of music certainly had little time for subtle notational distinctions when writing out his music. The surprising thing is rather that he so seldom went wrong in his markings for tempo and time signature. And the autograph of this concerto shows more corrections than any other work— Mozart must have been under special pressure.

The opposite happened in the final movement of the "'Haffner" Symphony, a common time *presto*, which certainly demands to be taken *alla breve*, because it resembles, for instance, the overture to *Figaro*, whose rhythmic structure is exactly alike. Mozart also referred to this in a letter of 7 August 1782 when he said: "The last [Allegro] [must be played] as fast as possible." Perfectionists who insist at all costs that Mozart was infallible should note that Mozart marked the first version of the first movement of this symphony ¢ and the second, more fully instrumented version ¢. Although it is not practical to play the whole movement of the "Haffner" Symphony *alla breve*, one can feel it in this way, so that the intimate opening motive, built out of four single-measure cells, does not disintegrate. (This single-measure cellular structure would in fact be impossible in a true *alla breve* movement.)

In the utterly simple but eloquent theme of the Larghetto in E-flat major from K. 491, every note must speak. The sixteenths after the dotted eighth notes must not be made too short.

Ex. XII/62:

All five notes in the fourth bar should be played quite evenly and calmly, without any *crescendo* or *diminuendo*.

If played from the heart, this simple theme can move the listener to tears. And what trouble Mozart took in handling it! Every repetition shows some harmonic and rhythmic variation, which taxes the interpreter's memory quite severely. In the second part of the melody, particular care must be devoted to the eighth notes in each measure: They must not be hammered out, but played with an even, sustained tone; the whole expressiveness of this passage depends on them. The measure before the pause should be a little softer than those preceding it, with a fairly considerable *crescendo* up to the pause (the clarinet and bassoon joining in the *crescendo*). The pause should be held by the strings only, not by the wind instruments; this is often overlooked.

After the pause, there should obviously be a short lead-in; it would be grossly unstylistic to leave the melody hanging on the dominant seventh (as unfortunately sometimes occurs). Here we can recommend Hummel's very tasteful lead-in:

Ex. XII/63:

though it is still better to simply use the lead-in from a similar passage in the D minor Concerto K. 466/II, m. 67, in a suitable transposition:

Ex. XII/64:

or possibly the following (inspired by the "Coronation" Concerto K. 537/II):

Ex. XII/65:

On the other hand, for the corresponding passage in m. 73 of K. 491/II, we are decidedly against Hummel's lead-in, whose virtuoso character is quite out of keeping with the movement's lyrical nature. There are so many possible ways to effect the simple melodic transition back to the theme; for example:

Ex. XII/66:

or:

Edwin Fischer once played the following lead-in, as a continuation of the bassoon part:

Ex. XII/67:

Mozart's choice of a five-section Lied form (A B A' C A" + coda) for this movement shows once again his unique feeling for the importance of moods. A single middle section in C minor would have overly emphasized the dark side of the Larghetto movement, so that there would have been too little contrast with the outer two movements. A single middle section in a major key, on the other hand, would have made it too innocuous and thus lack the weight to balance the first movement.

The woodwind phrases in mm. 20–23 must be played with great expression. The thirty-second-note figures for flute and bassoon are usually too disturbed, too heavy and too uneven in their rhythm. It helps if one can persuade the players not to be nervous about these exposed solo phrases. We recommend playing m. 20 as follows:

Ex. XII/68:

The marked d-flat[1] (x) should be very expressive, since it marks the inversion of the oboe's motive.

In m. 23, the piano should grow out of the *tutti* in a slight *crescendo*. In mm. 24ff., the strings should play expressively but softly, avoiding too full a tone. Here again it is better to use only two or three desks, playing *p* and with vibrato (see p. 350). If the string parts are played here by sixteen first violins and fourteen second violins (as often happens), these can only avoid drowning the piano sound by playing so softly as to preclude almost all expressiveness. It goes without saying that here the piano must sing, even in those phrases in very short note values. The rising *arpeggio* up to A-flat in m. 24 should be played very expressively. In m. 25 of the autograph, the turn is written as follows:

Ex. XII/69:

and not as given in the AMA and many other old editions, with two sixteenth notes at the end:

Ex. XII/70:

In this theme, again, every single note matters. For example, how difficult it is to give the right weight to the upbeat sixteenth notes before m. 26, and to make the thirty-seconds in this measure light and delicate without robbing them of their effect as part of the melody! The F-sharp in the next measure must be slightly separated from the preceding D. In the second part of this solo (mm. 32ff.), the accompanying G in the first violins is higher by a third than the beginning of the piano part; therefore, it must be played quite softly, but should still sing.

There is now a brief retransition (lead-back) to the first reprise of the main theme. The thirty-seconds in m. 37 must again be particularly even and *cantabile*. It is important to feel the rest at the beginning of this measure correctly. The first A♭ should be played as an upbeat to the high C, without any accent; otherwise, the listener is given a confused impression of the entire measure. The first half of m. 38 should be played *non-legato*, with a slight *crescendo* up to the middle of this measure, after which the remaining notes can build up a little tension with a slight *ritardando* as they flow into the main theme. Only four bars of the latter are quoted at this point. (We have already mentioned Mozart's obvious oversight in writing two simultaneous harmonizations of the theme; see p. 330, Ex. IX/11.)

The second episode in A-flat major follows immediately. Mozart rarely uses this key; when he does so, it always carries a feeling of some secret ecstasy (as in the slow movement of the E-flat String Quartet K. 428). The first bassoon progression F–F-flat–E-flat in m. 43 should not be overlooked. The mellow sound of the clarinets contrasts wonderfully with the rough, pastoral quality of the oboe tone in the preceding episode. The two clarinets interweave in m. 45, and in the next measure all the instruments blend in a warm glow of sound.

At the solo entry in m. 46, the strings' accompaniment should be *pp*, the merest breath. Two bars later, however, when the first and second violins alternate (as the clarinets had a few bars earlier), they should take over the melody from the piano. The syncopations are more effective if they are played all with the same finger, using the pedal, since this obliges the performer to make use of the arm, thus achieving a quite unusual bell-like tone.

This time it is the turn of the wind instruments to lead back to the theme. In m. 59, the lower strings should feel that their motive from the episode theme is a melodic line but should not make too much of a break between the pairs of slurred notes:

Ex. XII/71:

In many editions of the orchestral parts, the flat is missing before the C in the cello and double-bass part. In m. 62, all the players must make a marked *diminuendo* down to *pp*, together with a slight *ritardando* to ease the transition to the main theme.

When Edwin Fischer would play the ensuing solo, it was even more quiet and simple than at the opening of the movement, probably because he realized that the version occurring here is the simplest of all: no dotted rhythm on the second beat of mm. 1 and 3, no woodwind sounds added in mm. 2 and 4. He played the sixteenth notes in m. 64 particularly peacefully and began the second half of the melody very quietly and reflectively. Not until just before the pause would there be a *crescendo* leading to an *f*. The last melodic refrain, where the woodwinds join in approvingly, does indeed require a full, round tone from the pianist.

The coda stays throughout in the blissful E-flat major key. The scales in the piano and the flute must of course be *non-legato*. It is not a bad idea if everybody plays the entire repetition of the first four bars softer to achieve an echo effect. It is not easy to accomplish a sufficiently transparent sound in the closing bars (mm. 85ff.); the best way is to treat the passage as a duet between the piano and the first bassoon, accompanied by the remaining instruments. There is an unusually bold harmonic clash in mm. 86–87, between the piano and the clarinets:

Ex. XII/72:

Like the first movement, this one also ends softly, dies away, rather than ending normally (therefore, a *ritardando* at the end would be out of place)—only this time with a dream-like feeling of light and contentment.

Third Movement

With the third Allegretto movement we are back in the C minor mood of the work's opening. But the harmonic color is richer than in the previous movement because for the first time in this concerto Mozart makes use of the Neapolitan sixth (with its root D-flat in C minor and A-flat in the dominant key G minor); he seems to have kept the Neapolitan sixth chord in reserve for this movement, and he uses it not in its usual form (first inversion):

Ex. XII/73:

but in the even more poignant second inversion:

Ex. XII/74:

This gives an especially somber quality to the entire movement.

The choice of variation form for the last movement of a concerto is also unusual. Unlike most of Mozart's other variation movements, these variations have nothing playful about them; the movement is caught up in an inexorable march rhythm. Each variation is linked to the next without a break, and the customary Adagio variation is missing. The relentless succession of eight-bar periods gives the impression of hopelessness in a never ending circle. To catch the basic rhythm that binds these variations together, despite their great differences in character, is a very tricky problem. It will be impossible without perceptible and disturbing changes of tempo unless one captures exactly the right tempo in the very first measure.

The whole movement seems overlaid with a veil that only parts twice—in the *forte* variation, starting at m. 73, and in the last three measures. It is therefore not a good idea to play the theme too expressively at the outset. The motive in mm. 5–8, repeated time after time during the movement, is like a melancholy refrain, suggesting a similar mood as in Schubert's song "Der Leiermann." It would be a mistake to play this theme with the *crescendos* and other expressive devices appropriate in a Romantic sonata. The only place where a slight expressive accentuation is needed is at the chromatic harmonies in m. 11, where the upbeat note should be emphasized. But the remainder of the theme can be played almost without conscious expression, though every articulation marking must be most exactly followed. The wind instruments and the timpani must establish an ironclad march rhythm in the first two measures and must make the quarter notes not a fraction of a second too short or too long. The repeats in the first two variations may be played more softly, but this is not essential.

Even nowadays, many editions place a mysterious turn over the first note of the piano part in m. 16, but this ornament has no business being there and is the result of a misreading of the text, as is rightly explained by Bischoff in the Steingräeber edition. This bar's way of circling chromatically around G is another reminder of the first movement's first subject. There is a hovering, weightless quality about this first variation, and one can understand why it is often played noticeably faster than the theme. But Mozart's intentions are probably better served if the movement contains no audible alterations of tempo. (If the change is limited to one or, at most, two degrees of the metronomic scale, $\quarternote$ = *c*. 80–4, this can certainly be regarded as an imperceptible quickening, and there could be no possible objection.) The fine subsidiary part for the first violins at m. 22 deserves attention, as does the rhythm

Ex. XII/75:

of the violas in m. 21. The piano's scale up to top D in m. 26 should ripple, as should the next piano variation (starting at m. 41); this is dovetailed with one for woodwind instruments, making Variation II a double variation. But these runs must not be inexpressive, and here it is important to ensure that the rise and fall of the piano's figurations is matched by the scheme of dynamics. In m. 59, the middle part (G–F-sharp–F, played with the thumb) should be slightly emphasized, as should the top part in the next bar (E–E-flat). Variation III (starting at m. 65) must be played *subito forte* and with the utmost energy. It is important to play the sixteenth after the dotted eighths *marcato*, particularly in mm. 70 and 71. The last five notes in m. 72 are best taken by the right hand, so that they sound with greater power.

The ensuing orchestral entry must also be very energetic—it is a truly demonic outburst— but the second violins' scales, like tongues of flame, must not be obscured. After this *tutti* outburst, the piano's entry at m. 80 must be suitably powerful. In m. 84, there should be considerable dynamic gradation during the LH figures. The last eighth note of this measure should be *meno forte*, so that one can start another big *crescendo* up to the end of the variation.

The next Variation IV in A-flat major (mm. 97ff.) should follow straight in at the same tempo. In those measures with an accented half note, it is important to cut off the final note and to let the piano's rhythm emerge clearly:

Ex. XII/76:

(There is a mistake in the Breitkopf & Härtel orchestral parts at m. 125: the first note of the second violin and cello/bass parts should be D, not d-flat.)

In the course of this variation, which is scored for exactly the same instruments as the A-flat major section of the *Larghetto*, one can gradually get a little slower. But this must seem to happen quite unintentionally and should not be noticed by the listener. This gradual slowing down is in order because it is hardly possible to play the expressive polyphonic variation V, beginning at m. 129, in the same tempo as the stormy one ($\downharpoonleft$ = *c.* 78–82). This variation V has a delicate network of parts, and its frequent chromatic *melismata* will sound clear and beautiful at only a slightly slower tempo. However, on no account should one go down below $\downharpoonleft$ = *c.* 72–76. There should still be the feeling of a prevailing basic tempo. One could draw a comparison with a group of people who walk along deeply engrossed in a conversation. If the discussion gets livelier, they automatically start to walk a little faster, and vice versa, but without being aware of it. Variation V must be very carefully practiced, and the first thing is to choose the best fingering. Here are some suggestions for fingering and for other points of performance:

Ex. XII/77:

It is another double variation. Whereas the first (polyphonic) section definitely must be played *p* and *cantabile*, it is difficult to choose the right dynamics for the second section (mm. 137–146, 155–164). This kind of energetic rhythm and the scales in the bass usually denote a *forte* in Mozart's music. On the other hand, the section's very similarity to the earlier variation beginning at m. 65 should make one stop and think twice: Mozart can scarcely have meant to repeat this *forte* outburst with less powerful resources, for this would only weaken the formal structure of the movement. Moreover, as far as we know, Mozart never accompanies his *forte* passages with sustained chords in the strings, as he does here; on the other hand, this is just the kind of accompaniment one constantly finds in typical soft passages (e.g., the concerto's first movement, mm. 147ff.). So we feel it is not unreasonable to regard this section as a somber reminiscence of the previous passionate outburst. The introductory measures 136 and 154 also support the inclination to consider a *p*: Without contrast they grow out of what has preceded.

If, instead of writing a phrase analogous to m. 128:

Ex. XII/78:

Mozart had written an insistent upbeat:

Ex. XII/79:

then the case for a *forte* would be much stronger. As it is, we recommend that this variation should be played in a ghostly, rhythmic *mezza voce*, with a slight *crescendo* in the last four bars. It is interesting that the second half period of this section is extended from four to six measures.

And now we come to the last and brightest ray of light in this great concerto—the wonderful C major variation. This lasting C major appears for the first and only time in the work: an economy raised to the level of genius. We shall not try to settle the question of whether this is a very freely created variation or a new episode. One could perhaps call this section an anti-variation, for—although the modulation scheme is the same as that of the theme—everything else is different; and this is in itself enough to link them very closely. Instead of the drooping first motive of the theme, there is a wonderful phrase that rises through more than an octave:

Ex. XII/80:

This is related to the very similar melodic phrase at m. 205 of the first movement:

Ex. XII/81:

Perhaps there is more than coincidence here. Instead of the march-like quarter-note rhythm of the theme, here we find a filigree eighth- and sixteenth-note figuration; the close of each half (originally mm. 8, 16) becomes a feminine ending, the chromaticism in m. 11 is replaced by diatonicism, etc.

If this last variation is played at the right speed (not too slowly, and most definitely not slower than ♩ = 74), there is something ethereal—unreal—about it. The entire variation must therefore be played with great sensibility. The first quarter note of m. 170 should not be played *staccato* but rather with sustained tones. In mm. 173–176, the strings should be very soft, but from m. 176 on they should come to the fore. The pianist must now play the theme gently and expressively, with a switch to glittering passage work in mm. 176–179. The last four bars are repeated, the string parts being replaced and intensified (transposition an octave higher) by the wind instruments, and the piano can also stand out a little more here.

At this point, C minor makes its somber reappearance in a variation that has such close relations with the theme that it sounds like a recapitulation. In case the C major variation has been played a shade slower than the basic tempo, the initial tempo must, of course, return here, but there should be no feeling of an abrupt tempo change. It is probably better to make a very slight *accelerando* in the first four bars than to quicken up suddenly at m. 201.

There are no particular interpretative problems in this variation. After a short buildup of four bars, there is at last a moment of rest, on the poignant augmented sixth chord in m. 219. In these bars, the woodwind instruments have multiple leading notes that create some acute dissonances, such as the clash of B-flat, B, and C in m. 217, or the Brahmsian harmony in m. 218, an enormously bold stroke that must have been a shock in Mozart's day:

Ex. XII/82:

The fermatas in mm. 219 and 220 indicate lead-ins. Hummel's *Eingang* for m. 219 is excellent, but there is no reason to begin on the topmost e-flat⁴ of the modern piano (an octave higher than Mozart's top note); we would recommend simply omitting the top octave of Hummel's lead-in:

Ex. XII/83:

However, Hummel's rather empty passage work in m. 220 is less satisfactory. After the complex run in m. 219, a simple *arpeggio* would probably be better:

Ex. XII/84:

The player must use his judgment as to whether he goes straight into the closing section after this or plays another short lead-in in m. 220.

The ensuing final section, whose mood is unusually somber, begins with a 6/8 variation of the theme, in which the Neapolitan sixth is further enriched by an enharmonic alteration (only in the *NMA* is the articulation correctly printed):

Ex. XII/85:

As we have said, the piano can only resort to an accent on the f-sharp as a substitute for the difference in intonation between G-flat and F-sharp, which on a stringed instrument was perhaps not inconsiderable in Mozart's time.

From the second half of m. 236 on, one could also opt for playing an echo effect. As said above, the whole of this closing Allegro (for it is an Allegro more than an Allegretto, though Mozart left no tempo indication for the movement) must be played extremely rhythmically and particular care must be taken over the figure:

Ex. XII/86:

The first dotted note must be held long enough, and the short sixteenth note should be played rather clearly *staccato*; otherwise, it will be swallowed up.

The coda from m. 241 on is marked by a mood of somber chromaticism. Whereas the first subject of the first movement moved chromatically around the dominant tone, here there is chromatic movement around the tonic. It is very difficult to decide whether this coda should be played *forte* or *piano*. The latter seems more in keeping with its macabre, dance-of-death quality, but one could also find convincing reasons for playing it *forte*: the searing upward scale in m. 240, the LH tremolos, and the wide *arpeggio* in m. 250 would justify a *forte*. Whether one decides on *p* or *f*, the chromatic melody (mm. 241ff.) must in all events be played with the maximum expressiveness and excitement.

Toward the end of the coda, it begins to look as if the music is going to settle on the Neapolitan sixth for good (mm. 253–255, 270–276). The bass octaves (A-flat) should be louder each time this harmony reappears. The passage work at the end from m. 278 on should certainly be played without any *crescendo*—a final descent into the depths, with a final gesture of dismissal from the full orchestra, a clap of thunder that brings to an end this uniquely tragic masterpiece.

Piano Sonata in A Minor, K. 310

Among Mozart's symphonies, piano concertos, and piano sonatas, there are only two in each group that are in the minor key, and each reflects an intense personal expression. For this reason, they soon received wide recognition. With the advent of the Romantic era, they came to be favored over many of Mozart's works in major keys and were more frequently performed.

Long before Mozart, the equations "major key = serene, happy" and "minor key = sad, tragic" had generally been established (with exceptions, of course).

The predominance of the major key in works up to Beethoven's time was founded in the aesthetics of the eighteenth century, when it was thought that one of the principal tasks of music was to delight the soul of the listener and to enliven the spirit. Besides, the major key, thought of as being based on the natural overtones, was considered to be more natural. Thus, it is not surprising that, in keeping with the aesthetics of the time as well as deriving from his own *joie de vivre* and fundamentally optimistic nature, Mozart wrote the bulk of his works in a major key. It is fascinating, though, to observe that among his sketches, fragments, and unfinished works, the minor key appears more frequently than in his finished compositions. And his works in major keys, even the most serene ones, are rarely devoid of dark, melancholic interludes that distinguish them from the less profound compositions of his contemporaries and throw light on the unfathomable depth of his personality.

A direct connection between a serious, life-threatening experience and the creation of a work with tragic content cannot necessarily and automatically be established. It might take years before a composer or a poet is able to pour his tragic experience into a work of art. But in the case of this A minor Sonata, there can hardly be any doubt that its composition in the summer of 1778 came under the impact of the sudden death of Mozart's mother while the two of them were in Paris, far from his father and sister in Salzburg. His deeply moving letter to Abbé Bullinger of 3 July 1778, the day his mother died, bears witness to how deeply Mozart was shaken by this tragic event: "Mourn with me, dear friend!—it was the saddest day of my life [Trauern Sie mit mir, mein freund!—es war der traurigste Tag meines Lebens]."

The inexorable march rhythm of the first movement with its indication *Allegro maestoso* tempo may symbolize Death's solemn majesty. The intimate song and gracefulness of the second movement—Andante cantabile con espressione—suggest solace and respite from the anguish of the Allegro maestoso. A violent passage in the middle of this second movement rudely dissipates this tranquil atmosphere, however, and recalls the first movement's development with its equally poignant dissonances. The storm at last subsides and the Andante ends in a peaceful resignation. What a contrast, then, is the ensuing Presto third movement, a haunting piece of music, of a kind Mozart never wrote again (although Schubert was to do so repeatedly). Like a mirage, a blissful dream, a delicate A major episode suddenly appears—the only time in the whole sonata that this variant key appears—but it is a dream soon to be shattered by a merciless reality, and the dark mood of the opening theme returns as the sonata goes to its finish with a violent gesture of defiance.

All modern editions follow the text of Mozart's autograph. It was stolen shortly after World War II from the Deutsche Staatsbibliothek, Berlin, but luckily found eventually its way to the Pierpont–Morgan Library in New York. A facsimile of this beautiful autograph has been published in the "Faksimile und Urtext" series of the UE—Wiener Urtext Edition (UT 51010). Of much less importance is the first contemporary edition by Heina (Paris, ca. 1782). Despite several blatant errors, it does contain a few dynamic marks missing in the autograph, namely an *f* in the middle of m. 46 and two *f* indications in mm. 49 and 133 (all in the first movement). There is a possibility that Mozart might have added them when a copy was being prepared for the French publisher. The only major discrepancy between modern editions concerns the first note in m. 76 of the first movement, which was not written out by Mozart. The *NMA* and the Wiener Urtext edition print the g-sharp[1] from m. 78 as the logical continuation of the previous a[1], whereas Henle takes a literal repeat from m. 74 with e[2] as the first note. We have tried both versions and find g-sharp[1] more convincing.

First Movement

(Suggested tempo *Allegro maestoso* ♩= 126–130)

The very first *appoggiatura* d-sharp[2] has been the subject of numerous discussions. Being at the very beginning of a piece (and before a series of repeated notes) it has to be very short and unaccented. We prefer to play it before the beat, similar to the written-out d-sharp[2] at the end of m. 79. However, the *appoggiatura* a[1] in the second measure should be played as an eighth note and not very short or gypsy-like (see the discussion in chapter 5). Being on the dominant and containing dissonances, this second measure should have more weight than the first one.

The opening theme starts with Mozart's favorite march rhythm. While it ought to be firm and precise, any harshness of sound should be avoided; the sixteenth note on the second beat should be light and detached. The accompanying chords in the LH should be played less loudly, of course, with firm fingers. Edwin Fischer and Vladimir Horowitz recommended a discreet use of the pedal. The first note of the accompanying chords (mm. 1–5) should have an emphasis; namely, a slight accent, thus underlining the relentless march rhythm of the theme.

TRACK
64

In the sixth measure, there are staggered sighs in the right and left hands. This means that the soft resolution of the thirds in the RH coincides with the dissonant (accented) entry of the thirds in the LH, which resolve into consonances on the third beat.[7]

Ex. XII/87:

---

[7] Mozart wrote only one slur for the left hand, yet it is fairly obvious that all four voices ought to be connected and that a tie on the highest voice D–D (m. 7 C–C) was intended. (In this sonata, on various occasions Mozart forgot to notate necessary ties; e.g., first mvt., mm. 67, 69 upper voice; second mvt., m. 6, left hand D–D, m. 14 C–C, m. 31 C–C, m. 67 C–C, etc.)

In m. 8, Mozart's articulation is often ignored. Many times one hears the wrong rendering:

Ex. XII/88:

Correct interpretation:

Ex. XII/89:

The return of the opening motive is intensified by the new harmonies in mm. 10 and 12. Here the LH should bring out the new notes F (tenor) and G (bass), respectively. In m. 16, the RH finishes its phrase softly while the LH starts already *forte*. This needs independent control of both hands! Measure 18 contains one of the very few echo effects in Mozart's writings. (But do not dare to invent an echo later in mm. 76–77!)

Measure 22 brings a total change of scenery, a *coup de théatre*, from anguish to (apparent) serenity. Certainly a short breath has to be taken between the last bass note G and the three upbeat notes in the RH. Only those few pianists incapable of understanding the musical language and the dialectical principle of contrasting themes in sonatas will continue without a break—as if nothing had happened.

The lightness of the following subsidiary theme evokes a feeling of weightlessness, of a momentary freedom from suffering. There is a feeling of unreality in this continuing flow of sixteenth notes that ends only with the very end of the exposition. Normally, the second subsidiary subject brings a singing (*cantabile*) contrast to the stern opening theme. But there is nothing like that in this sonata. It is unique in a sonata movement to have both the second subject and the epilogue present themselves as a perpetuum mobile. This has a deeper meaning, of course: In this tragedy there is no place for lyricism, for relaxing into a beautiful tune. Despite its nearly ebullient C major character, this second part of the exposition evokes a feeling of restlessness, of bustle and agitation while trying to ignore the presence of doom. But it would not be Mozart if this theme did not have its hidden *cantabile* quality. Here is the tune nestled within the sixteenths, for which we suggest the following articulation (only *staccato* strokes for the three upbeat notes are Mozart's):

Ex. XII/90:

It is no coincidence that *legato* slurs appear only in mm. 28–29 (and are probably to be continued thereafter): note that nearly every fourth sixteenth note contains a dissonance, i.e., a small emphasis. Obviously the previous five measures were meant to be played *non-legato*. In this respect, the nineteenth century completely misunderstood Mozart and his contemporaries.

Editors of that century simply decreed that every passage in sixteenth notes had to be *legato*. What is even more amazing is that this *legato* obsession is still around today!

Attention has to be drawn to the notation in mm. 36, 41 (also 117, 122). By this notation Mozart indicates a *Luftpause*, a breathing space between the first and second sixteenth note.

Ex. XII/91:

It is simply wrong to continue strictly in time here.

Unlike most of the Mozart sonatas, there are no dynamic indications for thirty-one measures between m. 23 and m. 54. When one considers the subtle dynamics of the first page, this is amazing, especially remarkable. But Mozart had simply left the task of supplying dynamic ups and downs to the enlightened performer. We do not want to impose our personal interpretation of dynamics. Suffice it to say that a *crescendo* was probably intended in mm. 38 and 42 and that the increasing of parts toward the end of the exposition (and the end of the first movement) imply a substantial *crescendo* over the last three or even five measures.

But where we are pretty certain is that—as in the very beginning—the reappearance of the demonic first theme at the outset of the second part (m. 50) must be *f* and not *p* as found in some nineteenth-century editions. The reason is simple: Whenever a theme reappears at the start of a new section in a sonata or in a symphony, it assumes its original character. Thus, in the C minor Sonata K. 457 it will be strong; in the B-flat major Sonata K. 333, it will be sweet. Here the theme in m. 50 is very strong, indeed. The *f p* indications in mm. 54, 55 do not contradict this statement. They indicate an extra accent on each first beat followed by weaker notes, perhaps even later than the second beat. Without the extra *f* sign, one could play a *p* too soon by mistake. And it leads to the strongest outburst found in any Mozart sonata; namely, to the *fortissimo* in m. 58.

This is a shattering climax, indeed, unsurpassed even by Mozart himself, one that is enhanced and dramatized by the equally unique insertion of two *pianissimo* measures. This nearly unbearable dynamic contrast is reminiscent of some of Petrarch's sonnets, where the great Italian poet speaks of "fire and ice" or of "war and peace" (see, for example, Sonnetto No. 104). For the correct rendering of this climax, two observations seem to be important: First, every time the initial march motive appears, it is the second measure, with its poignant dissonance of a semitone, that needs to be more intense, more heavily accented than the first one. Thus, m. 59 should be even stronger than m. 58. Second, with regard to the tied notes of the upper voice in nearly every measure, it is simply wrong to replace these ties by rests on the third beat.

Ex. XII/92:

The immense dynamic contrast between *ff* and *pp* (foreshadowing Beethoven) poses a considerable technical challenge for the pianist. Before the sudden *pianissimo*, a very short break is necessary to dampen the previous loudness. The best way to achieve a controlled *pianissimo* is to play with firm, steel-like fingers, but let them sink only two to three millimeters into the keyboard. In this way, the hammers receive only a weak initial impulse. Obviously, the LH has to play softer than the RH throughout; otherwise, it would kill the discourse. The agitated character continues after m. 70 but probably a little less loudly than before. (Paul Badura-Skoda plays the trills in both hands with a main note start because the trilled note in the upper voice is a dissonance, and the LH trills carry the fundamental bass.) In these places, the sixteenth notes should be played a shade lighter than the thematic quarter notes.

We recommend starting the chromatic scale in m. 79 a little softer (approx. *mp*) and to make a *crescendo* toward the beginning of the recapitulation in the following measure. In the recapitulation, Mozart did not write out the initial eight measures 80–87 but wrote "Da capo 8 mesur[es]" instead. (The last two letters were probably cut off at the binding.) We agree with the majority of editors that this repeat does not include the first *appoggiatura* d-sharp[1] because this note appears already as the last note of the preceding run. The novelty in this recapitulation is the expressive entry of the main theme in the LH (mm. 88–94) while the RH plays a sort of violin *tremolo*, also expressive, in which the highest notes form a melodic descent in mm. 89–96, with dissonances on the first beat that need to be accented.

It is simply astonishing how the bustling secondary subject has now changed its character from serenity to tragedy, simply by being transposed from C major into the basic minor key. No doubt the ascent in m. 119 requires a substantial *crescendo* toward the highest note E in the following measure, followed by a decrease of intensity. (The trill in m. 120 should start with the main note b[1], which resolves the preceding harmony on the 6/4 chord.) The three dramatic measures 126–128 are entirely new and should be played, like sudden lightning in a thunderstorm, *forte* or even *fortissimo*.

This is one of the densest sonata movements ever written.

Second Movement, Andante cantabile con espressione

(Suggested tempo ♩ = 44–48)

"Singing and with expression": A singing touch does not only involve sensitive dynamic inflections but also the rendering of continuing phrases of four or more measures as if in one breath; hence, a rather fluent and yet calm pace.[8] As said before, the expression is that of a dream of peace, of redemption from suffering, like the soft touch of a mother's hand bringing comfort to a despairing soul.

Unlike the first movement, this Andante movement (also in sonata form) abounds with dynamic indications. It is as if Mozart wanted to help us to understand and render well those singing inflections mentioned earlier. It is useful to remember that the frequent *fp* indications have to be treated according to the context: Within a *piano* texture, *fp* often means a moderate accent or emphasis but not a real *forte* followed by an immediate *piano*. We repeat what we said earlier about the opening motive: It is a vocalization (still used today in singing lessons or exercises). The soprano voice starts on the note f[1] and gradually rises by semitones until a-flat and even higher starting notes are reached culminating in high c as the fifth note.

---

[8] With our historical perspective we dare to compare this pacing with Debussy's *Les Danseuses de Delphe*, which Debussy played much more fluently than his own metronomic indication suggests.

In modern notation, the opening figure might be sung this way:

Ex. XII/93:

We omit the *appoggiatura* c² here on purpose because its role is harmonic, and it would hardly be included in a vocal rendering. The *fp* accent in the first measure notwithstanding, the emphasis of the longer line is placed on the first notes in the second and in the fourth measures. These are subtleties that sometimes defy verbal explanations. But even the third and the fifth measures of the theme need a slight accent because they start on a dissonance. The small note preceding the trill in the seventh measure is an eighth note and should be treated as a long, accented *appoggiatura*:

Ex. XII/94:

From the eighth measure on, the texture becomes lighter. The trill symbol on the first sixteenth note in m. 8 indicates a *gruppetto*, a four-note turn starting with g¹. The thirty-second *appoggiatura*s in mm. 9, 13, and 25 are accented passing notes and should be played on the beat. Even though no *crescendo* is marked in mm. 8 and 10, the rising figuration calls for a voice-like increase in volume, although less than in mm. 9, 12, or 13. The off-beat accents in m. 11—often inadvertently ignored—probably intend a slight prolongation in *rubato*:

Ex. XII/95:

The second and third trills in m. 12 are to be played as very short *appoggiatura*s. An identical passage at the end of the Andante of the Duet Sonata in C major, K. 521, was notated in just this way; that is, with small notes instead of trills.

The second subject in this movement has to be played in a graceful way. The repeated sixteenth notes have (round) *staccato* dots in m. 15 (and none in the following measure), while at the recapitulation, namely, in mm. 68, 69, the obviously needed *staccato* signs are missing in the autograph.

It is a frequent mistake to play such repeated notes with the wrist instead of the finger(s): They become too heavy. And we consider it also important to recommend that these repeated notes should be played with only one (second or index) finger while caressing the key, stroking rather than striking it. It might be instructive to know that a similar motive is played by the muted first violins at the beginning of the Andante of the A major Symphony K. 201 (mm. 5–6).

Ex. XII/96:

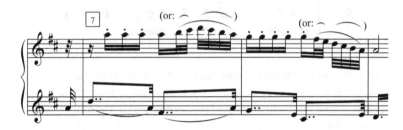

For the accompanying eighth notes, Mozart wrote short strokes, his normal *staccato* notation. This does not at all imply, however, that these notes should be played louder or more *marcato* than the upper voice. As a matter of rule, an eighth note is twice as long as a sixteenth; and since *staccato* usually means "half as long," the current rendering would be something like this:

Ex. XII/97:

The *fp* signs in mm, 22, 23, and 25 mark off-beat accents that must not be exaggerated. Despite these accents, the high notes following these accents also need a certain weight, being the highest note(s) of each group.

The notation of the chord in m. 27 almost certainly means a fast *arpeggio* execution, thus creating a natural accent on the highest note g². For the trills in the following m. 28, we recommend an execution à la Chopin.

Ex. XII/98:

Mozart probably forgot to write a *forte* there (found in the parallel passage in m. 83). For the ambiguous sign in m. 30 we recommend the execution as a *pralltriller* starting with f¹.

The eventful development section starts with a free variation of the opening motive accompanied by solemn chords in the low register that sound better on the fortepiano than on the modern grand because of its thinner strings and soundboard.

TRACK 69

Gradually the serene atmosphere is overshadowed by harmonies in the minor key that lead to an outburst of agitation and anguish (mm. 43–49) reminiscent of the climax in the middle of the first movement. In the sense of an oncoming storm, the three *f* signs in mm. 38, 40, and 42 should gradually increase in intensity, the first one being rather like an *mf* only. In m. 39, the trilled note should be e-flat¹ (and not e¹), as the minor sixth of the accompanying G minor harmony. However, in the following measures, the prevailing harmony is already D minor (sixth step, respectively submediant with augmented sixth) with E-natural. With the possible exception of the first trill in m. 41, all trills should have a closing suffix (c-sharp¹–d¹) because of the D minor harmony. Edwin Fischer played a gradual *accelerando* from m. 37 to m. 43 leading to a *più mosso* at the climax (mm. 43ff.) until the entrance of the *calando* in m. 50, which he interpreted in the modern sense as *diminuendo* plus *rallentando*; it was very convincing. During this climax, the dissonant minor and major seconds express pain and need to be accented, and the following upper octave notes, which evoke lightning, should also be accentuated. The hermeneutics, the emotional meaning of this agitated passage, is fairly obvious: The comfort, the attempt to find comfort and peace after the upheaval of the opening movement, has not quite succeeded, and the tragic background of the whole work comes to the fore even in the middle of an otherwise serene lyrical movement.

The delicate reentry of the opening theme has a redeeming effect after all that turmoil. The recapitulation follows the line and the content of the exposition with only a few changes in detail and brings this great movement to a peaceful close.

Third Movement, Presto

(Suggested tempo ♩ = 96–104)

It is an uncanny piece of music; Edwin Fischer spoke of its "breathless anxiety." In order to express this feeling of being haunted, it is recommended that the slurs of the theme be treated as articulation slurs with a detached second note:

Ex. XII/99:

TRACK 70

In this movement, we find a frequent juxtaposition of *piano* and *forte*, "cold and hot," reminiscent of the first movement, mostly with three intermediate eighth notes that form a short bridge passage; for example, in mm. 16–17 and 20–21. Suggested execution:

Ex. XII/100:

In other places there is no such transition (mm. 37, 72, 199, 211, 233, 237, 239, 243). This poses a technical challenge similar to the dynamic changes in the first movement discussed earlier.

When the dotted main motive appears in *forte* passages (RH in mm. 37, 45, et alia; LH in mm. 72, 80, et alia) it has no *legato* slurs, certainly by intention. To make sure of the separation, Mozart wrote short *staccato* strokes on each note at the first *forte* entry in m. 17. We recommend that the first (dotted) note be played as a quarter note, with an eighth rest being played instead of the prolongation dot. (Pay attention to the grouping of notes in mm. 43–44!)

Ex. XII/101:

Execution:

and not:

Ex. XII/102:

(This way of indicating articulation by separating the note beams is frequently found in the works of Beethoven and Schubert; it is often overlooked by students.)

In mm. 64–71, Mozart did not notate *legato* slurs for the LH. In view of the parallel passage in mm. 203–210, however, *legato* execution here was almost certainly intended.

The enormous leaps in the RH in mm. 72–75 and elsewhere present the greatest technical difficulty in the whole sonata. They are considerably harder to play than the similar leaps in the LH that appear earlier in mm. 37–40, 45–48, and elsewhere. For practicing, one should concentrate on the leaps downward between the bar lines, mostly by an octave plus a fifth (= twelfth or duodecima).

The long notes in the upper voice (mm. 87–93) should be played *tenuto* and probably connected, with more pressure of course on the fifth finger than the lower voices. The *forte* should continue until m. 105. It is, however, also possible to start a *diminuendo* six measures earlier. But the real challenge for the interpreter comes in the contrasting A major episode, mm. 143–174. This is the only time in the whole sonata that the parallel major key of the tonic A minor is heard. This wonderful episode creates the impression of a blissful dream in the midst of a dark and desolate night. It is a typical aspect of tragedy that, before the final scene with its inevitable outcome arrives, there often is a flurry of hope for a happy ending—alas, in vain. (If it had not been for that tragic misunderstanding, Romeo and Juliet might have married and lived happily ever after.) This A major dream has to be played with the greatest delicacy and tenderness. At the same time, one must resist the temptation to play it slower than the rest, for that would damage its dream-like lightness. The most likely phrasing is this one:

Ex. XII/103:

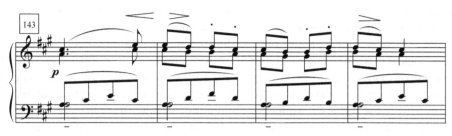

Some pianists play every pair of thirds *legato*—well, why not? It is a legitimate alternative.

For the execution of the trill in m. 157 we suggest:

Ex. XII/104:

thus connecting the dissonance e² with its resolution d-sharp².

One should give attention to the two-part accompaniment: The notes A must not be shortened, for they are meant to create the impression of a Musette, a merry hurdy-gurdy. In m. 163, one should be aware of the second note c-sharp², for it easily becomes inaudible. The *pralltriller* over the first note can be played in two ways:

Ex. XII/105:

And then, as unexpectedly as it came, the dream-like A major episode evaporates and the unremitting atmosphere of sheer despair reasserts itself, only to climax in an energetic gesture of defiance. (When played on modern pianos, the octaves of the LH in the mm. 249–250 tend to become disproportionately loud—be aware of this!).

The movement must end in a way that befits its inexorably tragic nature. That means: it should be played up to the very last note without any *ritardando*, not even the slightest!

Sonata in A Major, K. 331

Together with the *Sonata facile* K. 545, this is probably the best known and most liked of Mozart's piano sonatas. Children anywhere from 6 to 96 play it. It is technically not too difficult; its serene content is as evident as its humor. And yet, beneath the smooth surface there linger hidden mysteries: Why can the same notes produce pure pleasure under one pianist's hands and sound dull on other occasions? We cannot provide a definite answer; yet we believe that if this sonata is played with a sense of beauty and *con amore*, it will not fail to have an enchanting effect on both the player and his listeners. One of the keys to achieving such a magical interpretation is the intuitive understanding of the music's meaning. Most children have this genuine understanding; adults may have to use the powers of the intellect. But woe to the pianist who buries authentic feelings behind a screen of intellectuality!

Being adults—alas!—we cannot dismiss our rational approach. The A major Sonata K. 331 is most unusual insofar as it is the only one that contains no movement in sonata form and because all three movements are based on the same tonality of A major or A minor. Thus, it rather resembles a Baroque suite or a *divertimento*. But the apparent lack of a conventional sonata form and logic is more than made up by an unusual amount of motivic and psychological links between the three movements. To name but a few: The last two measures of the opening theme are melodically identical with the close of the menuetto; the hand-crossing of Variation IV finds its counterpart in the trio of the menuetto. The A minor sections in the first and second movements prepare the opening of the "Turkish March." And the triumphant military section of this march is prefigured in Variation VI of the opening movement.

The key of A major, relatively rare in Mozart's output, represents an elevated state of mind. In opera it may represent seduction ("La ci darem la mano" from *Don Giovanni* or "Un'aura amorosa" from *Cosi fan tutte*). The very rare tempo indication Andante grazioso of the first movement points in the same direction: *grazioso* means more than "with grace," for it is also a state of grace. But here it rather expresses an enamored feeling of affection not unlike the Andante amoroso of the earlier Sonata K. 281. This is one of the hidden mysteries mentioned above: It is not enough to play in the right tempo and with correct articulation—body and mind should jointly express serene affection, so that a gracious smile is better than a deadly earnest face.

With the exception of the last page, the original manuscript of this sonata is lost. For this reason, modern editors have to rely on the first edition, which was probably supervised by Mozart but nevertheless contains a number of obvious errors (we shall deal with them in due course). The fortuitous survival of the last autograph page is of immense value to us: Examination of watermarks, the origin of the paper, and of Mozart's writing style by the eminent scholars Alan Tyson and Wolfgang Plath has made it possible to ascertain the most probable date of the composition: 1783—much later than previously thought. This date is exactly one hundred years after the last siege of Vienna by the Turkish army, ending with its defeat thanks to the help of a liberation army (*Entsatzheer*); this defeat initiated a gradual collapse of the Turkish empire. Anniversary celebrations were not less common than nowadays; it had become fashionable already some years prior to write librettos on Turkish subjects (inter alia by Gluck, Haydn, and Mozart) and peaceful visits of colorful Turkish delegations established the custom to promote military bands with Turkish musicians and instruments in nearly all European countries. Therefore, it cannot be excluded that this centenary date inspired Mozart to compose the Turkish March as final movement of this sonata, which certainly contributed to its popularity. The inciting effect of the march music by the Turkish Janissary bands with their numerous percussion instruments was probably also the source of the so-called Turkish music stop on pianos.

Regarding the number of variations, Mozart followed the general convention of six including an *Adagio* variation; here is a description from Milchmeyer's *Klavierschule* (p. 69):

In pieces with variations, the main theme should be an Arietta which is known to listeners and generally liked. One must allow the public the pleasure to softly join in singing them. Altogether one should avoid to make too many variations because too great a number of them would be boring for the listeners. Six variations for an Ariettas with a length of three or four lines, of which both parts are repeated, I consider sufficient. ... In these pieces with variations one immediately can discover the musician who can keep a steady tempo and does neither makes the mistake of hurrying or slowing down.

[Stücke mit Veränderungen sollen beständig solche Arietten seyn, die den Zuhörern bekannt und allgemein beliebt sind. Man muß bei solchen Stücken dem Publikum das Vergnügen gönnen, sie sachte mitsingen zu können. Im ganzen soll man Stücke mit zu vielen Veränderungen vermeiden, da die zu große Anzahl derselben den Zuhörern nur lange Weile macht. Bei Arietten von drei bis vier Linien, in denen beide Theile wiederholet werden, halte ich sechs Veränderungen für hinlänglich. ... In diesen Stücken mit Veränderungen kann man zugleich den Taktfesten Musikus erkennen, denn der Spieler muß nicht das geringste Eilen oder Nachlassen des Taktes [Tempos] sich zu Schulden kommen lassen.]

While slight fluctuations of tempo for the different variations are tolerable, the frequent habit of playing each variation in an audible different tempo is certainly not correct; and to separate the variations by pauses has also no historical justification and seems wrong to us.

First Movement: Theme with Six Variations, Andante grazioso

(Suggested tempo ♪ = 144)

Theme: The very first chord of the theme breathes beauty if the upper note is played with emphasis, not as an end in itself but aiming at the fourth note e^2; the bass note(s) softer, the middle voice filling in, hardly audible (one can tell already after hearing this first chord whether a sensitive or an unmusical person is playing). Be sure not to play the last note of each bar as an accented upbeat! Even good musicians sometimes commit the error of connecting the measures by adding slurs over the bar line, thus creating artificial upbeats:

Ex. XII/106:

The correct declamation of the tune requires, however, that the last eighth notes should be unaccented because they repeat (and belong to) the previous heavy note.

Mozart's melodies need to be sung, not only with the fingers but with the voice as well. Of course, real singing requires a text. In many such cases we invented, for our own purpose, underlying texts that helped us to play (and to sing) phrases in one breath. Later we found out that this method proved to be useful for teaching students of all nations: A poem creates an elevated state of mind similar to music.

In this theme, the *grazioso* feeling of serene affection might be evoked by a corresponding text. As mentioned earlier we invented the following text:

"Let us play who cares who hears us, Mozart's music always cheers us.
It brings happiness and pleasure, it can heal a wounded heart."

The reader might invent another text, more poetic than ours; it might help the inventor even better to play *cantabile*.

In the second part of the theme, the light *fp* accents and the reverence in the twelfth measure will continue to evoke the enamored feeling. A stroke of genius is the affirmation of the concluding two final bars, meaning "Yes, I say you are my love!"

The repeats in the theme (and elsewhere) may be played for a change somewhat softer; however, a stereotype mumbling of repeats seems to be counterproductive to the fresh, spontaneous

TRACK 72

TRACK 73

expression. Why should one not play a repeat louder for a change? And, as a matter of course, some players might even decide to play the theme without repeats, which, however, seems to us a regrettable shortening.

Variation I.   Here and in the ensuing two variations, the first part is subdivided into a *piano* and a *forte* section of four measures each, solo and *tutti*, with different motivic material, as it were. In the first variation, the *piano* section splits the tune into small fragments, giving it a more speaking character, while the LH answers with just one eighth note as if saying "Yes," "Oh," "What?" One should take care that those separated speaking phrases are not further broken up into hiccups; these very short slurs need not to be taken literally. In the *forte* sections, the penultimate chords are certainly wrong in the original first edition; doubtlessly they should be identical with the respective chords of the theme. Do not miss the capricious offbeat accents on e^2 in the second part of this variation!

Variation II.   It is strange to say, but the short trills on the third beat are a source of anxiety even to experienced pianists. There is a tendency to start them a fraction too early and to play them too quickly, thus interrupting the even flow of the accompanying triplets. More attention to the left hand might help to correct such shortcomings. As for the trills, it is acceptable to start either with the upper note or with the main note, six or five notes being sufficient. In the *forte* sections, the upper notes in the RH part need to be emphasized, eventually slightly prolonged, while the rising *appoggiaturas* in the LH certainly ought to be short and unaccented. In the second part of this variation, the melody should be played with a gracious singing *staccato*, not too short and starting on the key notes. The *pralltriller* should be played as lightly as possible; they may be substituted by upbeat *appoggiaturas*. In m. 12, the dotted low eighth note E regrettably is missing in the original edition. Modern editors timidly print it as an alternative; but it must be surely considered a necessity!

Variation III.   It is a bad habit (alas, widespread) to play minor key variations considerably slower than the rest, and not only in Mozart's works. This is totally unfounded. To our knowledge, Mozart never prescribed *meno mosso* at the head of a minor key variations. A slight hesitation in m. 12 is justified in order to avoid a rushed execution of the ornament, but only there. The octave passages pose certain difficulties, particularly for small hands. A relaxed wrist and emphasis on the slurred higher notes might help to facilitate the problem. Do not neglect the up and down motion of the thumb!

Variation IV.   As in Variation II, the upper notes in the RH figures should have a singing character while accompanying the *cantabile* high notes of the LH. The RH takes the melodic lead only in the second part of m. 7. Quick change of position of the left arm is required in order to avoid unwanted wrong accents. The bass notes should be touched only lightly! The use of pedal (or knee levers on Mozart pianos) is strongly recommended. It will help to enhance the sensual beauty of this variation. In m. 5, some editors suggest a *forte*, but this is not necessary since this variation is the only one in which—as in the theme—the same figuration is maintained throughout the first eight measures. A strange dissonance (c-sharp¹–d-sharp¹) rarely found elsewhere in Mozart, appears in m. 12. While it may be regarded as an unusual inversion of the normal chord from m. 12 of the first variation, it makes a strange effect of interrupting the sweet flow of consonances found elsewhere in this variation. We have a suspicion that it could be a hitherto undetected engraver's error, similar to the error in the third measure of the menuetto (see below). By placing the a–c-sharp¹ a third lower, perfect harmony would be achieved, similar to the corresponding harmony in the theme and the second variation:

TRACK
74

TRACK
75

Ex. XII/107:

Variation V. This Adagio variation is one of the emotional highlights of the entire sonata. Loving tenderness should prevail with a singing touch and the soft murmur of the accompaniment. As in other variation cycles by Mozart, the most appropriate tempo is half the tempo of the theme, ♪ = 72: Sixteenth notes assume the speed of the former eighth notes; the pulse remains the same. The *staccato* wedge on the first note (missing in some editions) indicates not only a slight separation from the following *legato* phrase but also an emphasis, comparable to the down-bow of a violin. Here the subdivision of the *legato* into shorter slurs (right and left), typical of the eighteenth-century writing or printing, does not mean a separation between slurs. No singer in his right mind would take a new breath in between. Just think of the possibility of underlying words; i.e., "Du mein Geliebter!" (You, my beloved one!). The thirty-second-note scales in mm. 5 and 6 (95, 96) require a very light finger *staccato* (without wrist motion), but in m. 7 (97) the repeated notes a² most likely should be played *non-staccato* as in m. 15.

In the second part of this variation we find inconsistent articulation in mm. 11–12 (101–102), probably due to carelessness or reading problems of the engraver:

Ex. XII/108:

The choice of the proper articulation, the one meant by Mozart, is left to the player. If he or she goes by democratic majority, all five groups should be played *legato*. We prefer, however, the minority articulation of the first group of four thirty-seconds. Of course, a literal execution with different articulation is not to be excluded as a possibility. The ornaments in mm. 13–14 (81–82) have been explained in chapter 5.

Variation VI. Lively and spirited, ♩ = 144 with the eighth note twice as fast as in the theme. The march-like character and the percussion-like *forte* entry in the fifth measure are somehow foreshadowing the later *Alla Turca* (which, however, is marked in a slightly slower tempo). Two measures before the end, the old André edition (André bought many of Mozart's manuscripts from his widow) notates an alternation between *piano* (sixteenth notes) and *forte* (full chords). This distinction, missing in the first print, could possibly have been derived from the lost autograph: It sounds quite Mozartean and can be compared to the end of the Sonata in B-flat Major, K. 333.

Second Movement Menuetto

(Proposed tempo ♩ = 132.)

Be aware of two misprints: In the third measure, the last note of the right hand had been a third too low (a² instead of c-sharp³), a typical engraver's error. Later prints corrected it according to m. 33 but prolonged the slur between the first two beats up to the bar line, thus eliminating the *staccato* on the c-sharp³, creating another mistake that survived for over one hundred years. Another error from the earliest edition consisted of the missing natural signs before c-sharps in mm. 24 to 26. All modern editors concur that Mozart must have meant A minor from m. 24 until the first note of m. 30 as a consequence of the previous B minor (mm. 19–22).

The metric construction of this menuetto is more complex than in minuets written for dancing: The first period consists of two groups of five measures each, followed by a regular period of 4 + 4. In the second part of the menuetto, m. 23 is a variation of m. 19 with a double function: respective (as the conclusion of the previous B minor passage) and anticipatory (looking ahead to the following A minor section). For interpretation, it is important to maintain the graceful, lilting character of a minuet with emphasis on the first beat while being aware of the complex rhythmic situation. The opening bars have an orchestral character: The *arpeggio* of the first violins should not come before the entrance of the horns.

The *legato* slurs in mm. 4–5 and 9–10 should extend over the bar line. Suggested execution:

Ex. XII/109:

In mm. 15 and 44, we propose a *non-legato* execution of the sixteenth notes. The *appoggiatura* in m. 17 should be played on the beat. Measure 40 offers some technical difficulties. We recommend the following execution:

Ex. XII/110:

As mentioned above, the last two measures repeat the final notes of the Andante theme of the first movement in a different rhythm, thus underlying the unity of this sonata. The trill in m. 47 sounds best when played very short (*pralltriller* recommended).

The trio with its echo repeats of the overlapping LH represents a *dolce* contrast to the rather energetic menuetto part. There can be little doubt that the first measures should be played in a continuing *legato* and that the upper voice should be performed in *legato* quarter notes similar to m. 8 of the Adagio movement of the C minor Sonata K. 457.

TRACK
78

Ex. XII/111:

In the second part (m. 65), the unexpected harmonic surprise with the bass octave note B–b requires a delicate rendering, a sort of standstill on the dominant released by the *forte* outbreak of the tonic of E minor. From the entrance of C major (mm. 73ff.), the dynamics are incomplete. We suggest a *crescendo* in m. 75 leading to a *(poco) forte* in m. 79 or m. 81 and a return to the *piano* in m. 85. It is a common mistake to slur the last notes in mm. 73–78 over the bar line—they ought to be detached.

Third Movement, Alla Turca, Allegretto

(Suggested tempo ♩ = 126.)

As mentioned before, this special piece of music, loved by old and young, might have been inspired by the Viennese celebrations for the centenary of the victory over the Turks.

Naturally, one cannot expect authentic Turkish folk music from Mozart, but what he did in a masterly way was to convey the impression of the exotic. He achieved this by two means: by a liberal use of the minor keys on one hand and by a superb imitation of the Turkish military band in the A major *ritornello* to suggest the sound of drums and cymbals. Many Viennese pianos from around 1800 had a special pedal, called a *Turkish music* or *Janissary stop*, that imitated the sound of a military percussion band with remarkable effect. Though no Turkish register could be documented yet on pianofortes prior to 1796, it cannot be excluded that such a device existed earlier and was invented in the course of the celebrations around 1783 because approximately only 1 percent of eighteenth-century fortepianos have survived (how can we claim that this stop did not exist in 1783?). Many pianos in Mozart's Viennese years had a bassoon stop, however, which also created a percussive effect, though to a lesser degree.

Fortunately, the interpretation itself of this movement does not offer many problems if only two principles are observed; namely, a strict military observation of the march rhythm and a moderate tempo: These Turkish soldiers (or puppet soldiers) march steadily and not slowly, but they do not run. It is amazing that the frequent use of harmonies in the minor key never produces the effect of pain or suffering usually associated with minor keys but rather creates the feeling of an exotic serenity. But it is the military band of the A major section and its repeats that are simply irresistible. While in general Mozart's *forte* need not be exaggerated, here a certain noisiness is welcome. In the opening phrase, the high c^3 in m. 4 should be treated as a climax, followed by a subtle decrease toward the C minor half close in m. 8. (It is possible that the lost autograph had an *fp* there, similar to the *fp* in m. 20.)

The concluding coda brings this unique and great sonata to a jubilant end, imitating even the sound of flutes and triangles. The *Alberti* figuration during the none-too-soft piano interlude should be played with a rather light *staccato* touch. One hardly notes the fact that groups of five or six measures, respectively, are not strictly military but rather reminiscent of those irregular periods in the menuetto. The final chords are fuller in texture in the original edition than in the surviving one-page manuscript, and we firmly believe that what was printed here was Mozart's final intention.

Appendix 1: Mozart's Reported Tempo for Pamina's G-minor Aria

An interesting tempo indication is given by Nissen, Constanze Mozart's second husband, for Pamina's famous G-minor aria from *The Magic Flute*, "Ach, ich fühl's, es ist verschwunden":

In his biography of Mozart Nissen (who came to Vienna in 1793) reports that at that time the tempo of this aria was "6 to 7 Rhein. Zoll," according to the tradition inherited from Mozart. (*Rheinisch Zoll* was a pendulum measure that can be regarded as a primitive forerunner of the metronome.) Although the time gap of more than a year means that we cannot be sure of the correctness of the tradition, this single concrete tempo indication still deserves close attention. Whether one takes it literally or only roughly, it means an Andante, which to our way of thinking is unbelievably fast: Converted into a metronome marking it is ♪ = 138–148.[1] At first sight this seems such a fast tempo that one would dismiss it as impossible.

But it is very important to know that almost all those later composers who left exact metronome markings for their andante movements also held the view that Andante is not meant to be a slow tempo. Chopin's Andante in the D-flat major Nocturne, op. 27, no. 2 (♩ = 50) is just as fast. Beethoven's original marking for the second movement of the second symphony, ♪ = 92, also shows that he regarded this tempo as a flowing one, as did Schumann, if we look, for instance, at the Andante ♩ = 100 that he demanded for his *Träumerei*. Brahms, who usually refused to give metronome markings, made an exception in the Second Piano Concerto in B-flat major for the third movement; but we have never heard a single performance where his Andante indication ♩ = 84 was observed. One can trace this view that composers thought of Andante as a flowing tempo marking down to Hindemith, who has marked the third movement of his Third Sonata (a typical Andante) as *Mässig schnell* — "moderately fast," ♩ = ca. 84.

In considering this vital problem of tempi, one should bear in mind that a full tone tends to stretch the tempo, whereas the more slender the tone, the more mobile it is. This is a decisive factor in Mozart's music. If one takes the trouble to secure a tone that is free from thickness, it is astonishing how much room there is even in a flowing *Andante* for expression. The individual notes may perhaps lose a little, but the coherence of complete phrases more than makes up for this.

There is still another early piece of evidence for a more flowing Andante tempo in Mozart.[1] As early as 1815, Gottfried Weber published an article under the heading "*Ein Zweifel*" ("A Doubt") in the *Allgemeine Musikalische Zeitung,* Leipzig, 1815 (pp. 207–215), and in this he warned against too slow a tempo in the Pamina aria from *The Magic Flute*, cited above, and called attention to the dramatic events of the aria, where a very young woman tearfully

---

[1] The authors are indebted to a valuable article by Max Rudolf: "Pamina's Aria, Questions of Tempo" in *Max Rudolf. A Musical Life. Writings and Letters* (Hillsdale, NY: Pendragon Press, 2001), 207–10.

expresses her passion and threatens to take her own life. The aria's unconventional, syncopated instrumental postlude expresses a sorrowful passion, according to Weber. He ends his article by saying that it would be interesting to hear first-hand evidence from anyone who may have performed under Mozart's baton. Four months later there appeared in the same magazine (pp. 247–249) an article by a Viennese correspondent who confirmed Weber's remarks on the tempo and character of Pamina's aria. He had questioned numerous orchestral musicians who participated in the premiere of *The Magic Flute*. Every one of them confirmed that Mozart took a lively tempo, "the genuine expression of passionate pain."

The contemporary Viennese musicians' answer to this article from 1815 reads as follows:

In the 15th issue of this year's publication [Allgemeine Musikalische Zeitung, Leipzig] *Mr. Gottfried Weber, to whom we are indebted for various knowledgeable contributions, expressed doubt as to the tempo of the aria "Ach ich fühl's, es ist verschwunden" from* The Magic Flute. *This writer not only recalls precisely Mozart's conducting, but in addition has discussed the matter with several members of the theater orchestra who played under the baton of the late maestro, and I can confirm Mr. Weber's opinion entirely. Indeed, Mozart took precisely a tempo for this aria which no person sensitive to genuine expression and understanding of Pamina's sorrowful passion could find boring. On this occasion I would like to add a few remarks about the Terzett "Soll ich dich, Theurer, nicht mehr sehn?" in this opera. This piece too Mozart took nearly twice as fast as is nowadays the custom. Most conductors remember the word* Andante *and forget that Mozart prescribed* alla breve. *If one thinks of Allegro moderato in common time (4/4) everything takes on a new life. The individual motion of the celli and bassoons, whereby Mozart requested the first of the three eighths always be emphasized, characterize exactly Pamina's feelings of anxious unrest, the joy with which she could speak to her beloved, and the pain to have to leave him.*

It is unfortunate that even today we hear this aria sung extremely slowly. This is just the sort of piece where the tempo often drags wrongly in the interests of expression.

What is astonishing is that, on the other hand, Papageno's aria "Nun wohlan, es bleibt dabei," also an Andante, is generally sung properly in a relatively quick, flowing tempo. Thus, this aria can be fully enjoyed.

Appendix 2: A List of the Best Presently Available Editions of Mozart's Piano Music

Piano Concertos

1: K. 37, F major	*NMA (Neue Mozart Ausgabe)*
2: K. 39, B-flat major	*NMA*
3: K. 40, D major	*NMA*
4: K. 41, G major	*NMA*
[4a]: K. 107, D major, G major and E-flat major	*NMA*
5: K. 175 + 382, Rondo D major	*NMA*, Eulenburg Nr. 1270
6: K. 238, B-flat major	*NMA*, Eulenburg Nr. 1266
7: K. 242, für 3 Klaviere, F major	*NMA*, Eulenburg Nr. 10050
8: K. 246, C major	*NMA*, Eulenburg Nr. 1269
9: K. 271, E-flat major [Jenamy]	Breitkopf & Härtel; also Peters (Fischer-Soldan)
10: KV. 365, Concerto for Two Pianos, E-flat major	Eulenburg Nr. 741; also *NMA*
11: KV. 413, F major	*NMA*
12: KV. 414, A major	*NMA*, Eulenburg Nr. 800
13: KV. 415, C major	*NMA*
14: KV. 449, E-flat major	*NMA*
15: KV. 450, B-flat major	*NMA*; also Eulenburg Nr. 743
16: KV. 451, D major	*NMA*
17: KV. 453, G major	*NMA*
18: K. 456, B-flat major	*NMA*
19: K. 459, F major	*NMA*
20: K. 466, D minor	Eulenburg Nr. 721, *NMA*, Peters (Fischer-Soldan)
21: K. 467, C major	*NMA*, Peters (Fischer-Soldan)
22: K. 482, E-flat major	*NMA*, Peters (Fischer-Soldan)
23: K. 488, A major	*NMA*, Peters (Fischer-Soldan)
24: K. 491, C minor	Eulenburg Nr. 740, Peters (Fischer-Soldan)
25: K. 503, C major	*NMA*, Eulenburg Nr. 774
26: K. 537, D major ("Coronation-Concerto")	Schirmer Nr. 2045, *NMA*
27: K. 595, B-flat major	*NMA*
[28]: K. 386 , Rondo A major	Schott ED 12357

Piano Solo Works

Sonatas	*NMA*, Henle

Note: C minor Sonata K 457, first mvt., mm. 68, 70, left hand, fourth beat: Several editions print wrongly B-flat as the lowest note. Correct is E-flat.

Piano Pieces ("Klavierstücke")	*NMA*, Henle, Peters

Fantasy in D minor	Leduc, Paris
Piano Variations	Henle
Variations on a Theme by Duport K. 573	Alfred Edition (California)

> Note: A probable writing slip by Mozart in the variations on "*Ah, vous dirai-je maman*" K. 265 has so far gone unnoticed: All the known versions of this song, e.g., "Twinkle, Twinkle, Little Star," have a half note g (and not two quarter notes) in m. 4 (and 20, which Mozart did not write out but indicated by a *da capo* abbreviation for mm. 17–24). Most of the trills in these variations probably are to be played as *pralltriller* or turns; e.g., the first trill in Var. 2.

Chamber Music with Piano

I. Piano Four Hands
   - Wiener Urtext
   - Henle

II. Works for Two Pianos
   - *NMA*
   - Henle

III. Sonatas and Variations for Piano and Violin
   - Henle
   - Wiener Urtext
   - *NMA*

> Note: Sonata in G Major, K. 379 (373a), first mvt., m. 48, violin: Several editions omit the sixteenth-note *appoggiatura* C-natural before the second note, found in the first print. The same is true of the A major Sonata K. 526, second mvt., mm. 28 and 76, where the first edition has *appoggiaturas* similar to mm. 23 and 71 of the piano part. They are most probably authentic.

IV. Piano Trios
   - *NMA*
   - Henle
   - Wiener Urtext

V. Piano Quartets
   - Henle
   - *NMA*

VI. Quintet for Piano and Winds K. 452
   - Henle
   - *NMA*

> Note: The fermata at the end of the introduction to the first movement does not need any embellishment.

Appendix 3: An Example for *basso continuo* Realisation (K. 449/I)

As an example of *basso continuo* playing we suggest the following for the opening (mm. 1–64) of the Piano Concerto in A major, K. 414:

Selected Bibliography

Abert, Hermann. *W. A. Mozart*, 2 vols. Leipzig: VEB Breitkopf & Härtel, 1955.

Ahrens, Christian. *Hammerklaviere mit Wiener Mechanik*. Frankfurt: Bochinsky, 1996.

Albrecht, Otto. *A Census of Autograph Music Manuscripts of European Composers in American Libraries*. Philadelphia: University of Pennsylvania Press, 1953.

Albrechtsberger, Johann Georg. *Anfangsgründe der Klavierkunst*. Archiv der Gesellschaft der Musikfreunde Wien, n.d.

Allgemeine Musikalische Zeitung. Vols. I and XVI. Leipzig: Breitkopf & Härtel, 1798 and 1813.

Anderson, Emily. *Letters of Mozart and His Family*. Complete ed., 3 vols. London: Macmillan, 1938.

Angermüller, Rudolph. "Eine neue Quelle zu Mozarts Klavierkonzert D-Dur KV 175." *Mozart-Studien* 13 (2004): 197–209.

Armbruster, Richard. "Joseph Sardi—Autor der Klaviervariationen KV 460 (454a). Zum Schaffen eines unbekannt gebliebenen Komponisten in Wien zur Zeit Mozarts." *Mozart-Jahrbuch* (1997): 225–248.

Badura-Skoda, Eva. "Über die Anbringung von Auszierungen in den Klavierwerken Mozarts." *Mozart-Jahrbuch 1957* (1958): 186–198.

———. "Textual Problems in Masterpieces of the 18th and 19th Centuries." *The Musical Quarterly* 51 (1965): 301–317.

———. "W. A. Mozart. Klavierkonzert c-moll KV 491." *Meisterwerke der Musik* 10 (1972).

———. "Haydn, Mozart and Their Contemporaries." In *Keyboard Music*, edited by Denis Matthews, 108–165. London: Penguin, 1972.

———. "Prolegomena to a History of the Viennese Fortepiano." In *Israel Studies in Musicology*. Vol. II, 77–99. Kassel: Bärenreiter, 1980.

———. "Dittersdorf über Mozarts und Haydns Quartette." In *Collectanea Mozartiana*, edited by Mozartgemeinde Wien, 41–50. Tutzing: Schneider, 1988.

———. "Aspects of Performance Practice." In *Eighteenth-Century Keyboard Music*, edited by R. Marshall, 33–67. New York: Schirmer, 1994.

———. "Mozart and the Compound Pianoforte." In *Musicologia Humana (Kirkendale Festschrift)*, 473–484. Firenze: Olschki Editore, 1994.

———. "On Improvised Embellishments and Cadenzas in Mozart's Piano Concertos." In *Mozart's Piano Concertos*, edited by Neal Zaslaw, 365–371. Ann Arbor: University of Michigan Press, 1995.

———. "The Anton Walter Fortepiano—Mozart's Beloved Concert Instrument." *Early Music* 28, no. 3 (2000): 469–473.

Badura-Skoda, Paul. "Über das Generalbaß-Spiel in den Klavierkonzerten Mozarts." *Mozart-Jahrbuch 1957* (1958): 96–107.

———. "Missing Bars and Corrupted Passages in Classical Masterpieces." *Music Review* 22, no. 2 (1961): 94–107. First published in *Neue Zeitschrift für Musik* 2 (1958).

———. *Kadenzen, Eingänge und Auszierungen zu den Klavierkonzerten von W. A. Mozart*. Kassel: Bärenreiter BA, 1967.

———. "Ein authentischer Eingang zum Klavierkonzert in B Dur KV 595?" In *Mozart Jahrbuch 1971/72* (1973): 76–80.

———. "Mozart's Rondo in A Minor." *Piano Quarterly* 35 (1976): 29–32.

———. "Mozart's Trill." In *Perspectives on Mozart Performance*, edited by R. Larry Todd and Peter Williams, Cambridge (University Press) 1991: 1–26.

———. "Problematische Textstellen in Mozarts Klavierwerken und ihre fragwürdige Übertragung in die Neue Mozart Ausgabe, W. A. Mozart." In *Symposiums Bericht*, 122–144. Leipzig: Gewandhaus, 1991.

———. "Mozart without 'Pedal?'" *Galpin Society Journal* 15 (2003): 332–350.

Badura-Skoda, Paul and Eva Badura-Skoda. "Zur Echtheit von Mozarts Variationen K.460." *Mozart-Jahrbuch 1959* (1960): 127–140.

Banowetz, Joseph. *The Pianist's Guide to Pedaling.* Bloomington: Indiana University Press, 1985.

Becking, Gustav. *Der musikalische Rhythmus als Erkenntnisquelle.* Augsburg: 1928.

Berke, Dietrich. "Mozart-Forschung und Mozart-Edition. Zur Erinnerung an Wolfgang Plath," *Bericht über das Mozart-Symposium zum Gedenken an Wolfgang Plath (1930–1995), Augsburg 2000,* published as *Mozart-Jahrbuch 2001,* Salzburg 2003.

Bernet-Kempers, Karel Ph. *Hemiolenbildungen bei Mozart.* Kassel: Festschrift Osthoff, 1961.

Beyschlag, Adolf. *Die Ornamentik der Musik.* Leipzig: VEB Breitkopf & Härtel, 1953.

Biba, Otto. "Grundzüge des Konzertwesens in Wien zu Mozarts Zeit." *Mozart-Jahrbuch 1978/1979* (1979): 132–143.

Bilson, Malcolm. "The Mozart Concertos Rediscovered." *Mozart-Jahrbuch 1986* (1987): 58–61.

_____. "Execution and Expression in Mozart's Sonata in E-flat, K 282." *Early Music* 20/2 (1992): 237–243.

_____. "Do we know how to read Urtext Editions?" *Piano and Keyboard Magazine* (August 1995): 24–30.

_____. "The Myth of the Authentic Pianoforte." *International Piano* (July 2002): 46–52.

Blume, Friedrich. "Fortspinnung und Entwicklung." *Peters-Jahrbuch* 36 (1930): 51–70.

Boyden, David D. "Dynamics in Seventeenth- and Eighteenth-Century Music." *Essays in Honor of Archibald Thompson Davidson,* 185–193. Cambridge, MA: Harvard University Press, 1957.

Broder, Nathan. "Mozart and the 'Clavier.'" In *The Creative World of Mozart,* edited by P. H. Lang. New York: Norton, 1963.

Brown, A. Peter. "On the Opening Phrase of Mozart's K. 271: A Singular, Yet Logical, Event." *Mozart-Jahrbuch 1980–1983* (1983): 310–318.

Brown, Clive. "Dots and Strokes in Late 18th- and 19th Century Music." *Early Music* 21 (1993): 593–610.

_____. *Classical & Romantic Performing Practice 1750–1900.* Oxford: 1999.

_____. Busby, Thomas. *A Musical Manual or Technical Directory: Containing Full and Perspicuous Explanations of All the Terms, Ancient and Modern.* 1828. Reprint, London, 1976.

Busby, Thomas. *A Musical Manual, or Technical Directory, Containing Full and Perspicuous Explanations of All the Terms, Ancient and Modern.* New York: Da Capo Press, 1976 reprint.

Busoni, Frederico. *Entwurf einer neuen Ästhetik der Tonkunst.* Trieste 1907. Reprint, Wiesbaden, 1954. English translation: *Sketch of a New Aesthetic of Music.* New York: Schirmer, 1911.

Clementi, Muzio. *Introduction to the Art of Playing on the Piano Forte.* London: 1801.

Croll, Gerhard. "Das Andantino für Klavier KV 236 (588b)–eine Gluck-Bearbeitung als Variationen-Thema. Bemerkungen zur autographen Überlieferung, zu Zweckbestimmung und Datierung." In *Bericht über das Mozart-Symposion zum Gedenken an Wolfgang Plath (1930–1995), Augsburg, 13. bis 16. Juni 2000,* published as *Mozart-Jahrbuch 2001* (2003): 245–256.

Czerny, Carl. *Vollständige theoretisch-praktische Pianoforte-Schule…,* op. 500. 3 vols. Vienna: Diabelli, n.d.

_____. "Memoirs." In *On the Proper Performance of all Beethoven's Works for the Piano,* edited by Paul Badura-Skoda. Vienna: 1970.

Danckwardt, Marianne. "'muß accurat mit den gusto, forte and piano, wie es steht, gspiellt werden.' Funktionen der Dynamik bei Mozart." *Mozart-Jahrbuch 1997* (1997): 293–316.

Davidson, Michael. *Mozart and the Pianist.* London: Kahn and Averill, 1998.

Dechant, Hermann. "Dirigieren: Zur Theorie und Praxis der Musikinterpretation." Vienna Wien: Herder, 1985.

Dee, James H. "Mozart's Trills, Some Eighteenth Century Evidence." *The Piano Quarterly* no. 146 (summer 1989).

Derr, Ellwood. "Mozart's Transfer of the Vocal 'fermata sospesa' to his Piano-Concerto First Movements." *Mozart-Jahrbuch 1991* 1 (1992): 155–163.

_____. "Composition with Modules. Intersections of Musical Parlance in Works of Mozart and J. C. Bach." *Mozart-Jahrbuch 1997* (1997): 249–292.

Deutsch, O. E. "Dänische Schaupieler zu Besuch bei Mozart," *Österreichische Musikzeitschrift, 11,* (1956): 406–410.

_____. *A Documentary Biography of Mozart.* Kassel: Bärenreiter, 1961.

_____. *Addenda und Corrigenda zur Documentary Biography*, collected by Joseph H. Eibl. Kassel: Bärenreiter, 1978.

Deutsch, O. E. and C. B. Oldman. "Mozart-Drucke." *Zeitschrift für Musikwissenschaft* 13 (1931–32).

Dietrich, Marie-Agnes. "Die Klaviermusik." In *Mozart Handbuch*, 482–560. Kassel: Bärenreiter, 2005.

Dittersdorf, Karl v. *Autobiography.* 1896. Reprint, translated by A. D. Coleridge. London: Bentley, 1970.

Einstein, Alfred. *Greatness in Music.* London: Oxford University Press, 1945.

_____. Foreword to *The 10 Celebrated String Quartets by Mozart, First Authentic Edition.* London: Novello, 1945.

_____. *Mozart, His Character and Work.* Translated by Arthur Mendel and Nathan Broder. London: Cassell, 1946.

Eisen, Cliff. "The Mozarts' Salzburg Copyists: Aspects of Attribution, Chronology, Text, Style, and Performance Practice." In *Mozart Studies*, edited by C. Eisen, 253–308. Oxford: Clarendon Press, 1991.

_____. *New Mozart Documents: A Supplement to O. E. Deutsch's Documentary Biography.* London: Stanford University Press, 1991.

_____. "Mozart's Salzburg Orchestras." *Early Music* 20 (1992): 89–103.

_____. "The Mozarts' Salzburg Music Library." In *Mozart Studies 2*, 85–138. Oxford: Clarendon Press, 1997.

Eisen, Cliff and Keefe, Simon P. *Cambridge Mozart Encyclopedia.* Cambridge: Cambridge University Press, 2006.

Engel, H. *Die Entwicklung des Deutschen Klavierkonzerts von Mozart bis Liszt.* Leipzig: 1927.

_____. "Probleme der Aufführungspraxis." *Mozart Jahrbuch 1955* (1956): 56–65.

Fadini, Emilia. "Indicazioni di movimento e velocità di esecuzione nelle sonate per pianoforte di W. A. Mozart." *Mozart-Jahrbuch 1991* 1 (1992): 327–333.

Fellerer, K. G. "Mozarts Bearbeitung eigener Werke." *Mozart-Jahrbuch 1952* (1953): 70–76.

Ferguson, Faye. "Mozart's Keyboard Concertos: Tutti Notations and Performance Models." *Mozart-Jahrbuch 1984/85* (1986): 32–38.

Fischer, Edwin. *Reflections on Music.* London: 1951. Originally published as *Musikalische Betrachtungen* (Leipzig: 1949).

Fischer, Kurt von. "Come un' Agnello-Aria del Sigr. SARTI con Variazioni." *Mozart-Jahrbuch 1978/79* (1979): 112–121.

Fischer, Wilhelm. "Zur Entwicklungsgeschichte des Wiener klassischen Stils." In *Studien zur Musikwissenschaft, Beihefte der Denkmäler der Tonkunst in Österreich*, Vol. III, 25–85. Wien: Artaria, 1915.

_____. "Der, welcher wandelt diese Strasse voll Beschwerden." *Mozart-Jahrbuch 1950* (1951): 41–48.

_____. "Zu W. A. Mozarts Tonartenwahl und Harmonik." *Mozart-Jahrbuch 1952* (1953): 9–16.

_____. "Selbstzeugnisse Mozarts für die Aufführung seiner Werke." *Mozart-Jahrbuch 1955* (1956): 7–16.

Flothuis, Marius. *Mozart.* S Gravenhage: 1938.

_____. "Über einige metrische Probleme bei Mozart." *Mozart-Jahrbuch 1978/79* (1979): 47–51.

_____. "Mozart bearbeitet und variiert, parodiert und zitiert." *Mozart-Jahrbuch 1980–1983* (1983): 196–207.

_____. "Bühne und Konzert." *Mozart-Jahrbuch 1986* (1987).

_____. "Autograph–Abschrift–Erstdruck. Eine kritische Bewertung." In *Bericht über das Mozart-Symposion zum Gedenken an Wolfgang Plath (1930–1995), Augsburg, 13. bis 16.* Juni 2000, published as *Mozart-Jahrbuch 2001* (2003): 13–18.

_____. "Lernen aus Mozarts Autographen." In *Bericht über das Mozart-Symposion zum Gedenken an Wolfgang Plath (1930–1995), Augsburg, 13. bis 16.* Juni 2000, published as *Mozart-Jahrbuch 2001* (2003): 295–304.

Franz, G. von. "Mozarts Klavierbauer Anton Walter." *Neues Mozart-Jahrbuch* 1 (1941): 211–217.

Freeman, Daniel E. "Josef Mysliveček and Mozart's Piano Sonatas K. 309 (284b) and 311 (284c)." *Mozart-Jahrbuch 1995* (1995): 95–110.

Fuchs, Ingrid. "Nachrichten zu Anton Walter in der Korrespondenz einer seiner Kunden." *Mitteilungen der Internat. Stiftung Mozarteum* 48 (2000): 107.

_____. "W. A.Mozart in Wien. Mozarts Klavierkonzert in d-moll KV 466 - Bemerkungen zum Autograph und zum Instrument der Uraufführung." In *Mozartiana. Festschrift for the 70th Birthday of Professor Ebisawa Bin*, 543–554. Tokyo: 2001.

_____. "W. A.Mozart in Wien. Unbekannte Nachrichten in einer zeitgenössischen Korrespondenz aus seinem persönlichen Umfeld." In *Festschrift Otto Biba zum 60*, 187–208. Tutzin: Schneider, 2006.

Furtwängler, Wilhelm. *Concerning Music*. Translated by L. J. Lawrence. London: 1953. Originally published in Wilhelm Furtwängler, *Gespräche über Musik* (Vienna: 1948).

_____. *Ton und Wort*. Wiesbaden: Brockhaus, 1955.

Gerstenberg, Walter. "Zum Autograph des Klavierkonzerts KV 503 (C-Dur)." *Mozart-Jahrbuch 1953* (1954): 38–46.

_____. "Die Krise der Barockmusik." *Archiv für Musikwissenschaft* (1953/2): 81–94.

Gesellschaft f. Musikforschung, *Die Bedeutung der Zeichen Keil, Strich und Punkt bei Mozart. Fünf Lösungen einer Preisfrage*. Kassel: Bärenreiter, 1957.

Gieseking, Walter. *Mozart mit oder ohne Pedal?* In *Melos*. Mainz: 1949.

Girdlestone, G. M. *Mozart and His Piano Concertos*. London: 1948.

Gottron, Adam. "Wie spielte Mozart die Adagios seiner Klavierkonzerte?" *Die Musikforschung* 13 (1960): 334.

Haas, Robert. "Aufführungspraxis der Musik." In *Handbuch der Musikwissenschaft*, edited by Ernst Bücken. Wildpark-Potsdam: 1931.

Harich-Schneider, Eta. *Die Kunst des Cembalospiels*. Kassel: Bärenreiter, 1939.

Harrison, Bernard. *Haydn's Keyboard Music. Studies in Performance Practice*. Oxford: Clarendon Press, 1997.

Heartz, Daniel. *Haydn, Mozart and the Viennese School 1740–1780*. New York: Norton, 1995.

Herttrich, Ernst. "Studien zum Ausdruck des Melancholischen und seiner kompositions-technischen Mittel in der Musik von Mozart." Dissertation Würzburg, 1969.

Hindemith, Paul. *A Composer's World*. Cambridge: 1952.

Huber, Alfons and Rudolf Hopfner. "Instrumentenkundlicher Befund des Mozart-Flügels." *Mitteilungen der Internat. Stiftung Mozarteum* 48: 146–159.

Hudson, Richard. *Stolen Time: The History of Tempo Rubato*. Oxford: Claredon Press, 1994.

Hummel, J. N. *Ausführliche theoretisch-praktische Anweisung zum Pianoforte-Spiel*. Vienna: 1828.

Huneker, Josef. *Franz Liszt*. Munich: 1922.

Irving, John. *Mozart's Piano Sonatas, Contexts, Sources, Style*. Cambridge: Cambridge University Press, 1997.

Keefe, Simon P., ed. *The Cambridge Companion to Mozart*. Cambridge: Cambridge University Press, 2003.

_____. "Mozart's Late Piano Sonatas (K. 457, 533, 545, 570, 576): Aesthetic and Stylistic Parallels with His Piano Concertos." In *Words about Mozart, Essays in Honour of Stanley Sadie*, edited by D. Link and J. Nagley, 59–76. Woodbridge: The Boydell Press, 2005.

Keller, Hermann. *Phrasierung und Artikulation*. Kassel: Bärenreiter, 1955.

King, A. Hyatt, "A Census of Mozart Musical Autographs in England." *Musical Quarterly* (1952).

_____. *Mozart in Retrospect*. Oxford: Oxford University Press, 1955.

Kirkendale, Ursula. "Bach's 'Musical Offering': The *Institutio Oratoria* of Quintilian." *Jams* 33 (1980): 88–141.

Kirkendale, Warren. *Fuge und Fugato in der Kammermusik des Rokoko und der Klassik*. Tutzing: Schneider, 1966.

Klaus, Sabine Katharina and Scheibner, Sabine. "Ein 'ausserordentlicher Flügel von Herrn Tschudy' und die Sonate KV 19d." In *Mozart Studien 15*, edited by M. H. Schmid. Tutzing: Schneider, 2006.

Köhler, Karl- Heinz. „Zur Bewertung der Korrekturen und Provenienznachweise im Autograph zum Klavierkonzert KV 450. Ein Beitrag zu Mozarts Kompositionsweise 1784." *Mozart-Jahrbuch 1984/85* (1986): 52–60.

Komlós, Katalin. "'Ich praeludirte und spielte Variationen': Mozart the fortepianist." In *Perspectives on Mozart Performance*, edited by Larry Todd and Peter Williams, Cambridge Studies in Performance Practice, 127–154. Cambridge: Cambridge University Press, 1991.

_____. "Mozart the Performer." In *The Cambridge Companion to Mozart*, 215–226. Cambridge: Cambridge University Press, 2003.

Konrad, Ulrich. *Mozarts Schaffensweise*. Göttingen: Vandenhoeck & Ruprecht, 1992.

_____. "'In seinem Kopfe lag das Werk immer schon vollendet [...]' Bemerkungen zu Mozarts Schaffensweise am Beispiel des Klaviertrios B-Dur KV 502." *Mozart-Jahrbuch 1991* 1 (1992): 540–551.

_____. "Was ist interpretatorische Gewalt? Zum aufgefundenen Zettel von Mozart." *Mozart-Jahrbuch 1993* (1994): 77–82.

_____. "Neuentdecktes und wiedergefundenes Werkstattmaterial Wolfgang Amadeus Mozarts. Erster Nachtrag zum Katalog der Skizzen und Entwürfe." *Mozart-Jahrbuch 1995* (1995): 1–28.

Kottick, Edward. *A History of the Harpsichord*. Bloomington: Indiana University Press, 2003.

Küster, Konrad. *Mozart und seine Zeit*. Laaber: Laaber-Verlag, 2001.

Landon, H. C. Robbins. *1791 Mozart's Last Year*. London: Thames & Hudson, 1988.

_____. *The Mozart Compendium*. London: Thames & Hudson, 1990.

_____. *Mozart and Vienna*. New York: Schirmer, 1991.

Lang, Paul Henry, ed. *The Creative World of Mozart*. New York: W. W. Norton, 1963.

Latcham, Michael. "Mozart and the Pianos of Anton Gabriel Walter." *Early Music* 25, no. 3 (1997): 382–402.

_____. *The Combination of the Harpsichord and the Piano in the Eighteenth Century*. In *Instruments à claviers–expressivité et flexibilité sonore / Keyboard Instruments–Flexibility of Sound and Expression*. Proceedings of the *harmoniques* Congress, 113–152. Lausanne: Peter Lang, 2002.

Lechleitner, Gerda. "Mozarts Klaviersonate KV 331/300i im Lichte moderner Interpretationsanalyse." *Mozart-Jahrbuch 1991* 1 (1992): 353–363.

Leeson, Daniel N. "On the Authenticity of K. Anh. C 14.01 (297b), a Symphonia Concertante for Four Winds and Orchestra." *Mozart-Jahrbuch 1976/77* (1978).

Levin, Robert D. *"[Mozart's] Konzerte."* In *Das Mozart Kompendium*, edited by H. C. R. Landon. Droemer-Knaur, 1991. 63-71.

_____. "Mozart's Solo Keyboard Music and Mozarts Keyboard Concertos." In *Eighteenth-Century Keyboard Music*, 308–349. Schrimer Books: New York: 1994.

_____. "The Devil's in the Details: Neglected Aspects of Mozart's Piano Concertos." In *Mozart's Piano Concertos: Text, Context, Interpretation*, edited by Neal Zaslaw, 29–50. Ann Arbor: University of Michigan Press, 1996.

_____. "Performance Practice in the Music of Mozart." In *The Cambridge Companion to Mozart*, 227–245. Cambridge: 2003.

Löhlein, Georg Simon. *Clavier-Schule*. Leipzig and Zülichau, 1765.

Luithlen, V. "Der Eisenstädter Walterflügel." *Mozart-Jahrbuch 1954* (1955): 206–209.

Mandyczewsky, E. Vorwort zur Faksimile-Ausgabe neu aufgefundener Kadenzen, issued by the Mozarteum, Salzburg, 1921.

Mann, Alfred. *Theory and Practice. The Great Composers as Teachers and Students*. New York: Norton, 1987.

Marguerre, Karl. "Forte und Piano bei Mozart." *Neue Zeitschrift für Musik* (1967): 153–160.

Marpurg, W. Fr. *Anleitung zum Klavierspielen*. Berlin: 1755.

Marshall, Robert L. *Mozart Speaks: Views on Music, Musicians, and the World*. New York: Schirmer, 1991.

_____. "Mozart's Unfinished: Some Lessons of the Fragments." *Mozart-Jahrbuch 1991* 2 (1992): 900–921.

Marty, Jean-Pierre. *The Tempo Indications of Mozart*. New Haven, CT: Yale University Press, 1988.

_____. "Mozart's Tempo Indications and the Problems of Interpretation." In *Perspectives on Mozart Performance*, edited by Larry Todd and Peter Williams, Cambridge Studies in Peformance Practice, 55–73. Cambridge: Cambridge University Press, 1991.

Mies, Paul. "Die Artikulationszeichen Strich und Punkt bei Mozart." *Die Musikforschung* 11 (1958): 428–455.

Milchmeyer, J. P. *Die wahre Art das Pianoforte zu spielen*. Dresden: 1797.

Moser, Hans Joachim. "Über Mozarts Chromatik." *Mozart-Jahrbuch 1956* (1957): 167–199.

Mueller von Asow, Erich H. *Briefe W. A. Mozarts*. 2 vols. 1942.

———. "Mozartiana." *Musikforschung* 8, no. 1 (1955): 74–83.

Münster, Robert. "Zur Mozart-Pflege im Münchener Konzertleben bis 1800." *Mozart-Jahrbuch 1978/79* (1979): 159–163.

———. "Vorschlag und Appoggiatur in Mozarts Rezitativ." *Mozart-Jahrbuch 1980–83* (1983): 363–384.

Neumann, Frederick. *Ornamentation and Improvisation in Mozart.* Princeton, NJ: Princeton University Press, 1986.

———. "Eine Klauselfamilie bei Mozart." *Mozart-Jahrbuch 1984/85* (1986): 75–79.

———. *New Essays on Performance Practice.* Ann Arbor, MI: UMI Research Press, 1989.

———. "A New Look at Mozart's Prosodic Appoggiatura." In *Perspectives on Mozart Performance*, edited by Larry Todd and Peter Williams, Cambridge Studies in Peformance Practice, 92–116. Cambridge: Cambridge University Press, 1991.

———. "Dots and Strokes in Mozart." *Early Music* (1993): 429–436.

Niemetschek, F. *Leben des k.k. Kapellmeisters W. G. Mozart, nach Originalquellen beschrieben.* Prague: 1798. Translated by H. Mouther (London: Hyman, 1956).

Orel, Alfred. "Gräfin Wilhelmine Thun (Mäzenatentum in Wiens klassischer Zeit)." *Mozart-Jahrbuch 1954* (1955): 89–101.

Patier, Dominique. "La dynamique musicale au XVIIIème siècle." Dissertation 1978. Atelier National de Reproduction des Thèses, Université de Lille, 1983.

Paumgartner, Bernhard. "Von der sogenannten Appoggiatur in der älteren Gesangsmusik." *Musikerziehung* 5 (1953): 34.

Pestelli, Giorgio. *The Age of Mozart and Beethoven.* Cambridge: Cambridge University Press, 1984.

Petri, Johann Samuel. *Anleitung zur praktischen Musik.* 2nd ed. Leipzig: 1782.

Plath, Wolfgang. "Beiträge zur Mozart-Autographie I: Die Handschrift Leopold Mozarts." *Mozart-Jahrbuch 1960/61* (1961): 82–117.

———. "Beiträge zur Mozart—Autographie II. Schriftchronologie 1770–1780." *Mozart-Jahrbuch 1976/77* (1978): 131–173.

Pleyel, Ignaz. *Klavierschule.* 3rd ed. Leipzig: Kühnel und Hoffmeister, 1804.

Reeser, Eduard. *Ein Augsburger Musiker in Paris: Johann Gottfried Eckard 1735–1809.* Augsburg: Deutsche Mozart-Gesellschaft e. V., 1984.

Reijen, Paul van. "Die Temporelationen in der Aufführung von Mozarts Variationszyklus 'Ah, vous dirai-je Maman' KV 265/300e." *Mozart-Jahrbuch 1991* 1 (1992): 334–352.

Reinecke, Carl. *Zur Wiederbelebung der Mozart'schen Clavier-Concerte.* Leipzig: 1891.

Rellstab, J. C. Friedrich. *Anleitung für Clavierspieler.* Berlin: 1790.

Restle, Konstantin. "Mozarts Hammerflügel." *Mozart-Jahrbuch 1991* 1 (1992): 313–318.

Rosen, Charles. *The Classical Style: Haydn, Mozart, Beethoven.* London: Faber & Faber, 1971.

Rosenberg, Richard. *Die Klaviersonaten Mozarts.* Hofheim a.T. , Friedrich Hofmeister Verlag, 1972.

Rosenblum, Sandra P. *Performance Practices in Classic Piano Music.* Bloomington: Indiana University Press, 1988.

Rosenthal, Albi. "Leopold Mozart's Violinschule Annotated by the Author." In *Mozart Studies,* edited by Cliff Eisen. Oxford: Clarendon Press, 1991.

Rowland, David. *A History of Pianoforte Pedalling.* Cambridge: Cambridge University Press, 1993.

Rück, U. "Mozarts Hammerflügel erbaute Anton Walter." *Mozart-Jahrbuch 1955* (1956): 246–262.

Rudolf, Max. "Ein Beitrag zur Geschichte der Temponahme bei Mozart." *Mozart-Jahrbuch 1976/77* (1978): 204–224.

———. "Pamina's Aria, Questions of Tempo." In *A Musical Life: Writings and Letters*, 207–210. Hillsdale, NY: Pendragon Press, 2001.

Schenk, Erich. "Zur Tonsymbolik in Mozarts Figaro." *Neues Mozart-Jahrbuch* (1941): 114–134.

Schenker, Heinrich. *Ein Beitrag zur Ornamentik.* Vienna: 1908.

———. "Weg mit den Phrasierungs-Bögen." In *Das Meisterwerk der Musik*, Jb. I, Vienna: 1925.

Schering, A. "Vom musikalischen Vortrage." *Peters Jahrbuch for 1930* (1931): 9–23.

Schiedermair, Ludwig. *Mozart. Sein Leben und seine Werke.* Munich: 1922.

Schmid, Ernst Fritz. "Ein neues Autograph zu KV 265." *Mozart-Jahrbuch 1950* (1951): 10–13.

Schmid, Manfred Hermann. "Klaviermusik in Salzburg um 1770." *Mozart-Jahrbuch 1978/79* (1979): 102–112.

_____. "Zur Mitwirkung des Solisten am Orchester-Tutti bei Mozarts Konzerten." *Basler Jahrbuch für historische Musikpraxis* 17 (1993): 89–112.

_____. "Orchester und Solist in den Konzerten von W. A. Mozart." In *Mozart-Studien Bd. 9.* Tutzing: Schneider, 1999.

Schmitz, G. M. *Die Kunst der Verzierung im 18.* Jahrhundert. Kassel: Bärenreiter, 1995.

Schubart, Christian Friedrich Daniel. *Ideen zu einer Ästhetik der Tonkunst.* Vienna: 1806.

Schünemann, Georg. *Musikerhandschriften von J. S. Bach bis Schumann.* Berlin: 1936.

Seiffert, Wolf-Dieter. "Punkt und Strich bei Mozart." In *Musik als Text, Bericht über den internationalen Kongress der Gesellschaft für Musikforschung,* 133–143. Kassel: Bärenreiter, 1994.

Staehelin, Martin. "Giuseppe Tartini über seine künstlerische Entwicklung." *Archiv für Musikwissenschaft* 35 (1978): 251–274.

Starke, Joseph. Klavierschule: Unpublish Manusript, *Wiener Piano-Forte Schule* in III Abtheilungen, op. 108, Archiv der Gesellschaft der Musikfreunde Wein, ca 1810? Printed version as Part 1: Starke; Part 2: D. Sprenger; Part 3: Starke / J. Bermann). Vienna 1819–1829.

Steglich, Rudolf. *Die elementare Dynamik des musikalischen Rhythmus.* Leipzig: 1930.

_____. "Studien an Mozarts Hammerflügel." *Neues Mozart-Jahrbuch* 1 (1941): 181–210.

_____. "Über den Mozart-Klang." *Mozart-Jahrbuch 1950* (1951): 62–75.

_____. "Über Mozarts Adagio-Takt." *Mozart-Jahrbuch 1951* (1953): 90–111.

_____. "Über Mozarts Melodik." *Mozart-Jahrbuch 1952* (1953): 47–58.

_____. "Über das melodische Motiv in der Musik Mozarts." *Mozart-Jahrbuch 1953* (1955): 128–142.

_____. "Das Auszierungswesen in der Musik W. A. Mozarts." *Mozart-Jahrbuch 1955* (1956): 181–237.

Strasser, Stefan. "Mozarts Orchesterdynamik." *Mozart-Jahrbuch 1997* (1997): 38–40.

Strauss, R. *Recollections and Reflections.* Translated by L. J. Lawrence. London: Boosey & Hawkes, 1953. Originally published in *Betrachtungen und Erinnerungen* (Zürich: 1949).

Stravinsky, I. *Poetics of Music.* Translated by Arthur Knodel and Ingolf Dahl. Cambridge: Harvard University Press, 1947.

Sulzer, Johann Georg. "Allgemeine Theorie der Schönen Künste." In *Einzelnen nach alphabetischer Ordnung der Kunstwörter aufeinanderfolgenden Artikeln abgehandelt,* 4 vols. Berlin: 1792. Reprint, Hildesheim, 1967.

Sutcliffe, Dean W. "The Keyboard Music." In *The Cambridge Companion to Mozart,* edited by Simon P. Keefe. Cambridge: Cambridge University Press, 2003.

_____. "Change and Constancy in Mozart's Keyboard Varations K. 180, K. 354 and K. 455." *Mozart-Jahrbuch 2003/04* (2005): 73–94.

Tosi. P. F. *Opinioni di cantori antichi e moderni o sieno Osservazioni sopro il canto figurato.* Bologna: 1723.

Tyson, Alan. *Mozart: Studies of the Autograph Scores.* Cambridge: Harvard University Press, 1987.

_____. "Proposed New Dates for Many Works and Fragments Written by Mozart from March 1781 to December 1791." In *Mozart Studies,* edited by Cliff Eisen. Oxford: Clarendon Press, 1991.

Virneisel, W. "Mozartiana (Berichtigung)." *Musikforschung* 8 (1955): 345.

Weinmann, A. *Verzeichnis der Verlagswerke des Musikalischen Magazins in Wien, 1784–1802.* Vienna: 1950.

_____. *Vollständiges Verlagsverzeichnis Artaria & Co.* Vienna: 1952.

Whitmore, Philip. "Unpremeditated Art: The Cadenza in the Classical Keyboard Concerto." *Oxford Monographs on Music.* Oxford: Clarendon Press, 1991.

Wichmann, Kurt. *Der Ziergesang und die Ausführung der Appoggiatura.* Leipzig: VEB Deutscher Verlag für Musik, 1966.

Wittmayer, Kurt. "Der Flügel Mozarts. Versuch einer instrumentenbaugeschichtlichen Einordnung." *Mozart-Jahrbuch 1991* 1 (1992): 301–312.

Wolf, Georg Friedrich. *Unterricht im Klavierspielen.* 2nd ed. Halle, 1784. Later edition, *Gründliche Clavierschule* (Vienna: 1801).

Wolff, Christoph. "Zur Chronologie der Klavierkonzert-Kadenzen Mozarts." *Mozart-Jahrbuch 1978/79* (1979): 235–246.

_____. "Über kompositionsgeschichtlichen Ort und Aufführungspraxis der Klavierkonzerte Mozarts." *Mozart-Jahrbuch 1986* (1987): 90–92.

Zaslaw, Neal. *Mozart's Symphonies: Context, Performance Practice, Reception*. Oxford: Clarendon Press, 1989.

———, ed. *The Classical Era*. Englewood Cliffs, NJ: Prentice Hall, 1989.

———, ed. *Mozart's Piano Concertos: Text, Context, Interpretation*. Ann Arbor: University of Michigan Press, 1996.

Zimmermann, Ewald. "Das Mozart-Preisausschreiben der Ges. für Musikforschung." In *Festschrift für Joseph Schmidt-Görg*, 400–408. Bonn: 1957.

Subject Index

A

Abbellimenti (embellishments), 214

"*Abbruttimenti,*" (lit. "uglification"/"en- ugliments") 215, 216

Abduction from the Seraglio, 52, 59, 72, 307

Accelerando, 86, 87, 88, 90, 95, 262, 414, 430, 439

Accent signs, 53–59, 103, 127, 128, 296

Accented passing notes, 133, 138, 139, 161, 268, 274, 295, 347, 410, 437

Accented single *appoggiaturas,* 139

Acciaccatura, 174, 339

Additions of notes
out of style, 243–250
taste, 233–242

Ad libitum, 213, s363

Adriano in Siria K. 293e, 233

Affect, 11, 58, 92, 127, 220, 249, 290, 315, 367

Affekt, 11, 290, 298

Affektenlehre, 290

Afternote (*Nachschlag*), 173, 203

Agogics, 84–88, 92

Alberti bass (Alberti figures), 17, 28, 44, 131, 271, 303–306, 447

Albrechtsberger, J. G., 189–190, 203, 455

Alla breve sign, 78, 82–83

Alla breve time, 71, 82, 419–420

Alla Turca, 9, 175, 445, 447

Anacruses, 94, 195

Anderson, Emily, ix, 455

Anschlag, 170

A piacere, 86

Appoggiaturas, 28, 109, 132, 133, 135–173, 188, 189, 197–198, 206–207, 250, 323, 324, 338, 341, 387, 390, 433, 436, 437, 444, 446, 452, 460, 461; *See also* Compound *appoggiaturas,* Single *appoggiaturas,* Vocal *appoggituras*

Arco, 403

Arens, Matthias, xv, 34

Arpeggiando, 62

Arpeggios, 23, 25–26, 28, 30, 62, 63, 138, 174–176, 256, 257, 270, 331, 339, 373, 378, 379, 380, 381, 391, 409, 414, 423, 431, 432, 438, 446
vs. broken chords, 30

Articulation, 61, 65, 75–76, 82, 103–134, 295, 305, 324, 326, 340, 346, 379, 380, 391, 392, 397, 400, 404, 408, 409, 434, 439, 442, 445
expression, 295–300
signs, 46, 61, 75, 103–105, 117, 124, 129, 130, 131, 216, 219, 227, 230, 249, 320, 337, 344, 345, 379, 387, 403, 425, 431, 434, 440, 445
slurs, 107–120, 439
theme clarification, 296

B

Bach, C. P. E., 1, 16, 21, 44, 85, 92, 133, 135, 136, 143, 150, 176, 204, 205, 207, 213, 220, 244, 255, 367
quotation about "linking notes," 248–249

Bach, Johann Christian, 21, 151, 160

Bach, Johann Sebastian, 21
Brandenburg Concerto, 44
Chromatic Fantasy BWV 903 (mm. 18-31), 25–26
Clavier-Übung, 44
dynamics, 43–44
embellishments, 219
Italian Concerto BWV 971, 44, 91, 219

Backhaus, Wilhelm, 88

Balance, 69, 311–312

Bärenreiter edition, 320, 346, 395, 406, 455, 456, 457, 458, 461

Barrel organ, 191

Baroque period style features, 289, 442
basso continuo, 213, 359, 367
dynamics, 44, 50
echo, 68
embellishments, 219
instruments, 34, 44
notation, 308
ornaments, 174, 192
rhythm, 4, 88, 93, 94, 97
tempo rubato, 88

Basso continuo, 213, 359, 361–362, 366–367

Basso continuo obbligato, 359

Basso continuo realisation for K. 449/I, 453–454

Bassoon stop, 8, 23, 447

Beethoven, Ludwig van, 3, 9, 10, 15, 24, 39, 44, 47, 48, 51, 69, 75, 88, 105, 129, 174, 181, 203, 214, 238, 244, 254, 260, 269, 274, 319, 321, 323, 339, 346, 353, 355, 360, 378, 384, 388, 395, 432, 436, 440, 449, 456, 460
    Broadwood piano, 23
    contemporary pianos, 39
    "Emperor" Concerto, 243, 252, 293, 383
    "Moonlight Sonata," 66, 214
    pedals, 24, 33, 36, 105
Bel canto, 118, 401
Beyschlag, Adolf, 153, 189, 190, 456
Bilson, Malcolm, xii, 8, 124, 219, 359, 381, 419, 456
Bischoff, Hans, 332, 406, 426
Böhm, Karl, 279
Bösendorfer, 19, 377
Boyden, David, 52, 456
Brahms, Johannes, 47, 75, 88, 89, 203, 254, 323, 368, 406, 449
    Piano Concerto No. 1 in D minor, Op. 15, 368
    Piano Concerto No. 2 in B-flat major, Op. 83, 368
"Breathing space," 300, 435
Brendel, Alfred, ix, 384
Broadwood piano, 23
Broder, Nathan, 322, 456, 457
Broken chords, 23, 25, 62, 105, 288
    vs. arpeggios, 30
Broken octaves, 62, 155, 306, 375–376
Brown, Clive, 125, 456
Busby, Thomas, 59, 456
Busoni, Frederico, 1, 214, 456

C

Cadenza, 251–288
    closing sections of, 269–274
    improvisations *vs.* premeditated compositions, 252
    length, 256
    middle sections of, 264–285
    opening sections, 257–258
    virtuoso opening, 259–264
Caesura, 86, 300–301
Calando, 51, 52, 86, 439
Campianu, Eva, 80
Cannabich, Christian, 59
Cannabich, Rosa, 59
Cantilena, 42, 173, 350, 369, 386, 389
Capriccio, 216, 251, 286
Celeste stop, 23
Cembalo, 15, 383, 458

    meaning fortepiano, 15
Chamber music with piano, 322
    best available editions, 452
Chopin, Frédéric, 12, 47, 77, 88, 97, 103, 115, 176, 190, 271, 338, 368, 438, 449
    Allegro in A major, op. 46, 345
    Nocturne in D-flat major, Op. 27, No. 2, 449
Cimbalo con martellini (cimbalo di martellato), 15
Clarke, Bruce Cooper, xii
Clavecin, 15–18
    meaning fortepiano, 15
Clavichord, 10, 11, 12, 14, 16, 18, 19, 21, 34, 44, 136
Clementi, Muzio, 15, 19, 82, 171, 205, 214, 248, 291–292, 317, 369, 456
    ornaments, 137
    Pianoforte School, 136–137
    trills, 190
Col basso, 36, 216, 339, 352, 354, 355, 367, 396
Compound *appoggiaturas*, 138, 170–171, 172, 341
Compound harpsichords, 8, 11, 12, 44
Compulsory repeats, 315–317
Concertante, 281, 362, 364
Continuo chord, 364, 367
Continuo playing, 352
"Continuous development" (*Fortspinnung*), 265, 408, 456
Cooke, Deryck, 309
Cornet stop, 12
Cortot, Alfred, 9, 370
Così fan tutte, 162, 165, 307, 442
"Crescendo-forte," 391
Crescendo hairpins, 52–53
Czerny, Carl, 80, 129, 190, 456

D

Da Capo, 160, 216, 220, 221, 287, 288, 309, 316, 452, 456; *See also* Repeats
    "Da Capo 8 mesures" (writing abbreviation), 154, 436
    Da Capo symbol, 316
Damper-lifting device, 8, 24–32
    Damper-lifting knee lever (= pedal), 8, 9, 21–27, 42, 105, 400, 444
    technical problems, 378–382
Dittersdorf, 214, 244, 248–249, 291–292, 310, 455, 457
Ditzel, Constance, xii
Dolce indications, 43, 48, 49–50, 446
Don Giovanni, 32, 52, 73, 79, 95, 100, 164, 254, 310, 312, 442
Doppelschlag, see Turn
Dorfmusikanten-Sextett, K. 522, 50

Double forte (ff), *see Fortissimo*

Dreiklangs-Zerlegungen (vs. *arpeggios*), 30

Dürnitz Sonata, 46

Dynamics, Rococo expression *vs.* register dynamics (terrace dynamics/*Terrassen-Dynamik*), 50

    gradually increasing and decreasing, 11

    signs, 43–44, 69

    vs. flat performance, 43

E

Echo, 65–69, 316, 370, 410, 412 424 431, 434, 446

Eckard, Johann Gottfried, 4, 16–17, 460

Eine kleine Nachtmusik, K. 525, 168, 198, 288, 311

Eingänge, 62, 215, 216, 230, 242, 251–288, 321, 341, 386, 390, 394, 395, 400, 406, 421, 422, 430, 431, 455; *See also* Lead-ins

Einstein, Alfred, 74, 217, 221, 384, 388, 457

Embellishments, 135, 161, 213–243; *See also* Ornamentation

Engführung, 273

Entführung aus dem Serail, see Abduction from the Seraglio

Epilogue, 64, 221, 254, 301, 434

Eulenburg edition, 37, 66, 95, 96, 160, 208, 235, 322, 328, 338, 384, 387, 392, 396, 399, 400, 403, 404, 406, 415, 451

F

Facial control, 314

Federhofer, Hellmut, ix, 279, 281, 412

Ferguson, Faye, 353, 457

"Ferma nell' Andante," 78

Fermata embellishments, 215, 216, 254, 275–285, 329

    no lead-ins, 284

    proper places, 279–284

    questionable, 284–285

Fermata (meanings), 285–288

ff, *see* Fortissimo

Finger action, 370–372

Fingering, 194, 320, 337, 338, 342, 374, 375, 386, 387, 391, 427

Finger pedaling, 105

Fischer, Edwin, ix, 5, 9, 88, 127, 172, 236, 313, 317, 346, 368, 381, 384, 389, 391, 395, 396, 406, 419, 422, 424, 433, 439, 451, 457

Fischer, Wilhelm, ix, 265, 457

Flothuis, Marius, 252, 256, 286, 335, 457

Flügel (harpsichord), 12, 14, 15, 18, 377, 458, 461

fp Fortepiano (dynamic sign), xv, 7, 14, 52, 53, 54, 55, 56–57, 58, 59, 63, 110, 127, 388, 402, 436, 437, 438, 443, 447

Fortepiano (instrument), 7, l9, 10, 12, 14-22, 28, 29, 40–42

    changes, 10

    pedal instrument, 33–34

    Piano Sonatas K. 279 - 284, 16

    Piano Sonatas K. 6-8, 17

    range, 35–39

    sound, 10, 19–21

    una corda stop, 9

    Wilhelm Rück's copy, 34

"Forte-piano-clavecins", 17

Forte stop, 8, 378

Forte trill, 375

Fortissimo, 10, 11, 19, 43, 46, 47, 48, 61, 80, 350, 387, 400, 435, 436

Fortspinnung, 265, 408, 456

fp, *see* Fortepiano

Frantz, Albert, xii

Free improvisations 253

Friderici (Friederici), Christian Ernst, 11, 12

Friderici Two-manual harpsichord, 11, 12, 13, 14

Friedlaender, Max, 166

Fuchs, Aloys, 243

Fuchs, Ingrid, 23, 33, 457

Fugato, 269, 272, 273, 458

Fugato stretto, 272, 273

Fugue for Two Pianos, K. 426, 194

Fugue, 21, 37, 43, 81, 436

    Prelude and Fugue, K. 394, 299

Fugue of Sonata for A major, K. 402 for Violin and Piano: 93–94

Fugue of "Hammerklavier" Sonata, 129

Furtwängler, Wilhelm, 83, 85, 458

G

Gardiner, John Eliot, 359

Gerstenberg, Walter, 68, 226, 333, 458

Gieseking, Walter, 378, 458

Giulini, Fernanda, 23

Glinka Museum Moscow, xv

Glissando, 377

Gottsched, Johann Christoph, 290

Goût, 289; *See also* "Mannheim goût"

Grassi, Anton, xv

Grassi, Joseph, xv

Guénin, M. Alexandre, 151

Gusto, 68, 289–318, 456

H

Haffner, Elisabeth, 18
Haffner Serenade, K. 250, 18
Haffner Symphony, 66, 72, 81, 82, 237, 420
    Minuet, 164
Hagenauer, Lorenz, 12, 14
Hairpins, 52, 53, 110; *See also* Crescendo
Halbtriller, 178
Half-shake, 205, 206
Hamburger, Paul, ix
Hammerflügel, 9, 15, 460, 461
Hammer-harpsichord, 15
Hammerklavier Sonata, 269
Hand crossing, 9, 31, 442
Harmonic expression, 301–302
Harmonic tension, 274, 397, 398
Harpsichord, 8, 11, 12, 14, 15, 16, 17, 38, 44, 65,
    105, 206, 294, 354, 355, 459
    Friderici, 11, 12
    Friderici two-manual, 13
    meaning pianoforte, 11, 15
Haydn, Joseph, xv, 9, 44, 45, 68, 69, 78, 80, 127,
    138, 170, 174, 178, 179, 190, 207, 214, 219,
    209, 310, 312, 339, 343, 344, 347, 353, 355,
    381, 415, 442, 455, 458, 460
Hemiolas, 98–101
Henle edition, 46, 47, 124, 125, 228, 316, 322, 324,
    326, 337, 338, 433, 451, 452
Hiccup effect, 107, 444
Hoffmann, P. C., 243, 244, 248
Honauer, Leontzi, 17
Horns in B-flat alto or basso?, 347
Hüllmandel, Nicolas-Joseph, 316
Hummel, Johann Nepomuk, 24, 78, 80, 190, 224,
    230, 243–249, 406, 417, 418, 421, 430,
    431, 458
    embellishments, 244–247
"Hunt" Quartet, K. 458, 54, 148, 154
Hypermeasure, 98

I

Idomeneo, 52, 307
Il filo, 59
    conduttore, 286
Improvised embellishments, 213–259
    models by Mozart, 227–233
    old placing rules, 215
Improvisation, 3, 33, 135, 161, 188, 213, 214, 251,
    252, 253, 460
Incomplete dynamics, 60–65
Inverted turn, 173

J

Janissary music stop, 9, 442, 447
Jeu perlé, 369
Jonas, Oswald, ix
"Jupiter" Symphony, K. 551, 65, 83, 115, 128, 202

K

Kempff, Wilhelm, 9, 88, 346
Keyboard instruments
    Mozart's time, vii–ix
    Mozart's training, 10–19
Kielflügel, 15, 16, 25–26
Klavierschulen, 136
Knee levers, 8–9, 21, 42, 105, 400, 444
    lifting, 22–24
    necessary use of, 24–33
    technical problems, 378–383
Koch, Heinrich Christoph, 316
Köchel numbers, xvi
Krause, Martin, 317

L

La Clemenza di Tito, 51, 354
Landon, Christa, ix
Landon, H. C. Robbins, ix, 347, 459
Landowska, Wanda, 174, 339
Lange, Aloysia, xv; *See also* Weber, Aloysia
Lange, Joseph, xv, 35
La Roche, Renee, ix
Latcham, Michael, 22, 459
Lead-ins *(Eingänge),* 62, 215, 216, 230, 242,
    251–288, 321, 341, 386, 390, 394, 395,
    400, 406, 421, 422, 430, 431
Leather hammers, 10, 41
Legatissimo, 105, 303, 305
Legato octaves, 376
Legato scales, 370
Legato slurs, 103, 105, 107–108, 107–120, 120, 242
Leggiero, 398
Le Nozze di Figaro, 52, 79, 117, 118, 161, 163, 206,
    300, 309, 312, 403, 420, 460
Lento, 74, 77
Levin, Robert, 30, 49–50, 54, 62, 85, 124, 218, 219,
    237, 256, 260, 273, 275, 322, 327, 331, 332,
    334, 338, 339, 341, 342, 359, 381, 459
"Linz" Symphony, K. 425, 285
Lipatti, Dinu, 296
Liszt, Franz, 2, 4, 10, 85, 214, 311, 317, 368, 457, 458
Lombardian rhythm, 143–144, 169, 213
Luftpause, 286, 395, 435; *See also* "Breathing
    space"

Lute stop, 12

M

Maestoso, 81, 255, 432, 433
Magic Flute, 52, 74, 94, 118, 240, 249, 299, 308, 317,
    354, 449–450
    Overture, 308
Mahler, Gustav, 214, 279
Main-note trills, 136, 137, 189–193, 195–199, 207,
    209, 436, 444
Mancando, 51
Manieren, 213, 215
"Mannheim goût," 51, 59
Marcato, 43, 409, 426, 438
Marguerre, Karl, 50, 459
Marriage of Figaro, 52, 79, 117–118, 161, 163, 206,
    300, 309, 312, 403, 420, 460
Martellato, 388
Marty, Jean-Pierre, 77, 82, 83, 459
Masonic Funeral Music (*Maurische Trauermusik*),
    K. 477, 52, 120
Mass in C minor, K. 427, 94, 273
Mattheson, Johann, 289
"Meistersinger chord," 333
Menuetti ballabile, 80
Messa di voce (mezza voce), 48, 52
Meter, 72, 82, 98, 138, 153, 180, 300, 420
    2/4, 100, 256
    3/4, 74, 100
    4/4, 256
    5/8, 287
    6/8, 83, 255
Metronome, 84, 85, 87, 449
    markings, 71, 74, 75, 77, 80, 83, 84, 449
Mezzo-forte (mf), 24, 47–50, 58, 61, 306, 350, 351,
    385, 387, 390, 391, 398, 409, 439
Mezzo-fortepiano (mfp), 53, 54
Mezzo piano (mp), 48, 61, 378, 385, 387, 412, 436
Milchmeyer, Johann Peter, 8–9, 136, 140, 150, 157,
    170, 172, 175, 178, 181, 183, 190, 205,
    306, 459
Missing dynamics (supplementing), 60–65
Mixed articulation, 121–123
Moderato stop, 8, 9, 23
Mozart, Constanze, xv, 22, 35, 449
Mozart, Leopold, 12, 14, 16, 17, 233, 253, 289, 290,
    324, 351, 390, 460
    accents, 55, 58, 128, 294
    affect, 367
    appoggiaturas, 109, 133, 139, 143, 149–152, 170,
        171

articulation, 130
cadenzas, 253
cantabile playing, 11, 31
compound *appoggiaturas,* 171
embellishment, 215, 231, 232, 243, 248
fermata, 288
figured bass, 352, 353
forte, 367
grace notes, 339
il filo, 59, 61, 85
instruments, 11–14, 33
legato slurs, 106
"Mannheim goût," 51
Nachschlag, 173
ornaments, 178, 184, 230, 248
out of style additions, 243
overdotting, 93
playing in time, 84
portato, 109, 123
repeat sign, 219
rubatos, 88, 92, 292
shortening notes, 25–26
singing, 313
staccato strokes, 125, 128
teacher, 11, 136
tempo, 72–73, 82–83
trilletto, 206, 208, 209
trills, 190, 210
Violinschule, 1, 48, 52, 53, 55, 58, 71, 84, 88, 92,
    93, 106–107, 109, 123, 128, 130, 133, 136,
    149, 150, 173, 178, 184, 190, 206, 215,
    232, 243, 248, 288, 292, 294, 313, 367,
    460
Mozart, Wolfgang,
    accent signs, 53–60
    anniversary of 1956, 8
    autographs, xi
    damper-lifting device or pedal, 24–33
    dynamic signs, 45–48
    fortepiano, xv, 20, 33, 34
    fortepiano pedal instrument, 33–35
    fortepiano range, 35–40
    keyboard instruments, vii–ix
    knee levers lifting, 22–23
    Pamina's G-minor Aria, contemporary tempo,
        449–450
    piano, Wilhelm Rück's copy, 34
    pianos *vs.* modern pianos, 10
    presently available editions, 451–452
    reported tempo, 449–450
    unfinished oil portrait, xv
    world of sound, 7–42

Mozart family, 12, 13, 14, 18, 78, 217
  portrait, xv
Müller, A. E., 243
Müller, Otto Werner, 331
Mutation of sound, 8, 18
Mutation-stop, 8, 18

N

Nachschlag, see Afternote
Nägeli, Hans-Georg, 310–311
Neapolitan sixth, 388, 402, 425, 431, 432
Neapolitan style siciliano, 401
Neue Mozart Ausgabe (NMA), xi, 320–321
  successors, 337–338
Neumann, Frederick, 80, 125, 135, 161, 163, 188,
  198, 460
NMA, *see Neue Mozart Ausgabe (NMA)*
Non-legato, 129, 304, 370, 387, 388, 424

O

Off-beat accents, 55, 57, 297, 437
Open pedal, 381
Orchestra,
  playing with 343–368
  continuo playing, 352–366
  final chords, 367–368
  pianists studying piano concertos, 343–349
  sizes and ripieno parts, 350–351
Orel, Alfred, ix, 460
Organ, 12, 14, 18, 33, 37, 42, 193, 313, 355, 419
Ostinato, 396
Overdotting, 93–97

P

Page turning, 342
Pamina's G-minor Aria, 74, 240, 449–450, 460
"Pandaleons-Clavecins," 18
Pantaleon, 17
Parlando, 118
Pedals, 8–9, 22, 24–33
  fortepiano, 33
  piano, 33–34
  Fantasy in C major, K. 394, 27
Pendulum tempo measure, 449
Perpetuum mobile, 395, 434
Peters edition, 235, 248, 329, 338, 345, 352, 384,
  387, 396, 398, 399, 400, 406, 410, 415,
  451, 456, 460
Phrasing, 69, 103, 117, 301, 346, 369, 390, 440
Phrygian cadence, 308
Pianos,
  Walter *vs.* Stein, 23–24

Pitch
  identification problems, xiii
Pizzicato, 9, 403
Playing "in time," 84–85
Pleyel, Ignaz, 207, 460
Ployer, Barbara, 38, 344, 413
Portato, 29, 104, 109, 123–127, 340
Posthorn Serenade, K. 320, 51
"Prague" Symphony, K. 504, 285
Pralltriller, 137, 138, 205–210, 217, 325, 439, 441,
  444, 446, 452
Preisler, Joachim Daniel, 35
Primus inter pares (first among equals), 445

Q

Quantz, J. J., 11, 55, 61, 66, 71, 103, 147, 289–290,
  294
Qui tollis of C minor Mass, 94, 308

R

Raaff, 243–244
Rallentando, 439
Raphael, Ignaz Werner, 35
Raupach, Hermann Friedrich, 17
Ravel, Maurice, 2, 214
Recitative, 75, 78, 86, 161, 163, 164, 307–308, 386
Recommendable editions, 322
Register dynamics (*Terrassen-Dynamik*)
  vs. expression dynamics, 50
Rellstab, J. C. F., 136, 152, 170, 460
Repeats, 66, 126, 219–223, 233, 315–317, 327, 426,
  443–447
Requiem, K. 626, 96, 100, 354, 359, 384
Rex tremendae majestatis of Requiem, 96, 308
rf, see Rinforzando
Rheinisch Zoll, 449
Rhythmic notation peculiarities, 93–97
Richter, Georg Friedrich, 291, 314
Richter, Sviatoslav, 314
Rinforzando (rf), 54, 59–60, 325
Ritardando, 63, 74, 77, 86–88, 301, 388, 391, 402,
  410, 416, 417, 419, 424, 425, 441
Ritornellos, 9, 46, 159, 220, 221, 345, 351, 354, 360,
  408, 447
Rosen, Charles, 353, 460
Rosenblum, Sandra, 88, 135, 136, 152, 188, 190,
  316, 460
Rosing, Michael, 35
Rousseau, Jean-Jacques, 44, 68, 289
Rubato, 84–85, 88–93, 133, 153, 170, 191, 213, 292,
  437, 458
Rück, Wilhelm, xv, 34

Rück, Ulrich, 460

S

Sarti, Giuseppe, 21, 253–254, 310, 457
Scarlatti, Domenico, 12, 38, 43
Schiff, András, 9
Schnabel, Artur, 88, 346
Schobert, Johann, 16
Schubart, Christian Friedrich Daniel, 255, 313, 382, 461
Schubert, Franz, 44, 78, 80, 97, 166, 203, 244, 263, 319, 395, 425, 432, 440
Schumann, Clara, 4
Schumann, Robert, 4, 84, 99, 226, 310, 311, 449, 461
    Concert sans Orchestre, op. 14, 345
    Piano Concerto in A minor, Op. 54, 252
"Scottish snap," 143–144, 169, 213, 387
Seiffert, Wolf-Dieter, 125, 127, 338, 461
Serenade, 317
    "Eine kleine Nachtmusik," 49, 168–169, 288
    Haffner Serenade, K. 250, 18
    Posthorn Serenade, K. 320, 51
    Serenade for String Quintet, K. 406, 49
    Wind Serenade in B-flat major, K. 361, 32, 285, 347
    Wind Serenade in C minor, K. 388, 49
Serenata Notturna K. 239, 146
Serkin, Rudolf, 346
sf Sforzato, 53, 54, 58, 59, 64, 127, 305, 324, 324, 325, 390
Sforzato-piano (sfp), 54, 55, 59, 63, 329
Shortening notes, 24–25, 63, 84, 90, 95, 104, 109, 410
Short shakes, 137
Siciliano, 401
Siciliano rhythm, 172, 210, 238
Silbermann, Gottfried, 12, 15, 16, 17, 23, 44
Sillem, Maurits, ix
Sims, Robert, xii
Single appoggiaturas, 138–139, 145
Slurs,
    articulation, 107–120
    legato, 106, 107–120
Smith, Amand Wilhelm, 33
Soldan, Kurt, 338, 345, 384, 396, 406, 451
Sordino, 8, 9, 42
Sotto voce, 42, 43, 48–50, 378
Sound
    Mozart's fortepiano, 19–21
    mutation, 8, 18
Späth, Franz Jakob, 8, 12, 17, 18

Späth, Franz Xaver Anton, 18
Späth piano, 14, 16, 17, 18, 22
Spiccato, 348
Spiegel, Fritz, ix
Spieß, Pater Meinrad, 11
Square pianos, 8, 18
"Static and dynamic markings," 50
Starke, Friedrich von, 78, 140
Stein, Johann Andreas, 12, 14, 16, 18, 19, 22, 23, 84, 370
Stein, Nannette, 72, 84, 312, 369–370
Stein piano, 11, 16, 19, 22
    action, 40
    vs. Walter piano, 23–24
Steinway, 10, 19
Sterkel, F.X., 72
Stradivari, 8
Strasser, Stefan, 52, 53, 461
Strauss, Richard, 83, 355, 461
Stravinsky, Igor, 2, 461
Stretto, 272–273, 396
Strinasacchi, Regina, 63, 216, 291
"Sündendecker," 24
Super-legato, 105–106
Sustained high notes, 31–32
Syncopation, 55, 89, 90, 92, 100, 213, 294, 360, 385, 390, 391, 416, 424
Szell, George, ix, 333, 419

T

Tafelklaviere, 18
Tangentenflügel, 17
Tartini, Giuseppe, 189, 214, 461
Tasto solo, 352, 364, 366
Tchaikovsky, Pyotr Ilyich
    First Piano Concerto, 355
    Symphonie Pathétique, 44
Tek, Denny, xii
Tempo markings, 77–82
Tempo rubato, 88, 458
Tenuto, 29, 127, 285, 349, 380, 388, 440
Terzetto of Così fan tutte, 162
Thematic opening of cadenzas, 257–259
Thern, Viola, ix
Tone
    clusters, 310
    color, 9, 19, 21, 41, 42, 238, 355, 396
Torricella, 45, 46, 47, 106, 168, 253, 319, 322, 323
Trattner, Therese von, 46
Tremolando, 332, 400
Tremolo, 61, 62, 288, 387–388, 432, 436
Triadic fanfares, 309

Trills, 188–211
   bass, 193–194
   chains, 196
   dissonant notes, 193
   endings, 203–204
   end of rising and descending scales, 194–195
   preceded by same note, 195
   preceded by three rising or falling notes,
      192–193
   special cases, 196
   upper auxiliary, 199–200
Trilletto, 206, 208, 209
Tripletization, 97
"Tristan harmony," 310
Tuning, 21, 39, 354, 356, 412
Türk, Daniel Gottlob, 62, 77, 81, 104, 105, 107, 109,
      116, 123, 124, 129, 136, 150, 152, 170, 171,
      173, 174, 175, 176, 178,184, 203, 205,206,
      215, 256, 285, 287, 288, 305, 315
"Turkish March," K. 331, 9, 66, 313, 442
Turkish music stop, 9, 442
Turn (Doppelschlag), 176–188
   after dotted note, 182–183
   immediately over note, 176–177
   between two notes, 182–183
"Twinkle, Twinkle, Little Star," 452

U

"Übergangsdynamik," 11
"Überwurf," 170
Unaccented, anticipatory appoggiaturas, 152–154
Unaccented single appoggiaturas, 145–150, 170
Una corda pedal, 8, 9, 41, 42, 378
Una corda stop (fortepiano), 9, 42
Unmarked passages, 46, 51, 129–134
"Urtext editions," 319–320, 456
Urtext editors, 107

V

Vienna Tonkünstlersozietät, 343
Viennese minuet, 80
Vocal appoggiaturas, 138, 161–168
   in instrumental compositions, 164–165
Vogl, Michael, 166
Vogler, Abbé, 72, 219, 231, 250
"Vorklassik," 68
Vorschlag, see Appoggiaturas

W

Wagenseil, Georg Christoph, 8, 263
Walter, Anton, xv, 7, 23, 457
Walter piano, 7, 19, 20, 22, 23, 24, 38, 39, 350, 455,
      459, 460
   bassoon stop, 23
   knee lever, 22, 23, 378
   pedal piano, 33, 34
   vs. Stein piano, 23–24
   weight, 10
Weber, Aloysia, 72, 232–233, 252, 306–307, 313,
      384
Weber, Gottfried, 449–450
Wesentliche Manieren (essential ornaments), 213,
      215
Westminister Recording Company, 7
Wiener Urtext Edition, 47, 322, 324, 327, 433, 452
Willkürliche Manieren, 213
Wolff, Ernst Wilhelm, 290

Z

Zaslaw, Neal, 52, 343, 354, 455, 459, 462
Zwischenschläge, 136, 138

Index of Works Cited

K. 107
Piano Concerto in D major, 160, 451
K. 175
Piano Concerto in D major, 16, 252, 344, 383, 451, 455
K. 179
Variations on a Minuet by Fischer, 155
K. 183
Symphony in G minor, 53, 311
K. 186
Divertimento for Wind instruments in B-flat major, 288
K. 201
Symphony in A major, 95, 141, 151, 152, 197, 438
K. 216
Violin Concerto in G major, 154, 164, 169, 275, 301
K. 219
Violin Concerto in A major, 69, 80, 160, 221, 283
K. 238
Piano Concerto in B-flat major, 16, 78, 159, 197, 203, 256, 258, 264, 275, 352, 364, 451
K. 239
Serenata Notturna, 146
K. 242
Concerto for Three Pianos in F major, 40, 77, 80, 148, 200, 201, 209, 286, 304, 451
K. 246
Piano Concerto in C major, 16, 81, 147, 150, 152, 169, 197, 250, 251, 252, 256, 352, 353, 366, 367, 451
K. 264
Variations, 170, 377, 452
K. 265
Piano Variations *"Ah vous dirai-je maman",* 108, 184, 288, 452, 460
K. 271
Piano Concerto in E-flat major, 16, 17, 28, 47, 68, 75, 78, 82, 96, 138, 141, 173, 184, 210, 216, 244, 252, 257, 259, 261, 264, 265, 269, 275-276, 277, 304, 338-341, 344, 352, 364, 367, 451, 456

K. 279
Piano Sonata in C major, 16, 17, 21, 45, 46, 131, 145, 152, 158, 174, 303
K. 279-284
Piano Sonatas, 16, 17, 21, 45, 46, 131
K. 280
Sonata in F major, 150, 210
K. 281
Piano Sonata in B-flat major, 16, 17, 21, 45, 46, 52, 99, 131, 199, 210, 281, 344, 369, 442
K. 282
Piano Sonata in E-flat major, 16, 17, 21, 45, 46, 104, 131, 287, 456
K. 283
Piano Sonata in G major, 16, 17, 21, 45, 46, 80, 131, 270, 379
K. 284
Piano Sonata in D major, 16, 17, 21, 22, 45, 46, 75, 131, 168, 220, 228, 229, 322-324, 328
K. 293e (KV 6) Gesangskadenzen:
Adriano in Siria, 233, 252
K. 294
Recitative and Aria, "Non sò, d'onde viene," 232
K. 296
Violin Sonata, 78, 98, 149
K. 301
Violin Sonata in G major, 168
K. 304
Violin Sonata in E minor, 49, 139, 203
K. 305
Violin Sonata in A major, 179, 198
K. 306
Violin Sonata in D major, 47
K. 309
Piano Sonata in C major, 51, 55, 59, 74, 75, 78, 144, 220, 231, 324-325, 457
K. 310
Piano Sonata in A minor, 28, 29, 45, 47, 48, 52, 55, 56, 57, 58, 62, 63, 68, 74, 78, 81, 82, 108, 114, 126, 131, 142, 154, 168, 207, 211, 220, 303, 305, 377, 432-440, 456
K. 311
Piano Sonata in D major, 24, 25, 31, 52, 63, 75, 78, 109, 110, 187, 457

K. 319
Symphony in B-flat major, 53
K. 320
Posthorn Serenade, 51
K. 330
Piano Sonata in C major, 46, 47, 48, 50, 52, 63,
67, 111, 143, 146, 184, 204, 209, 221, 249
K. 330–332
46, 63
K. 331
Piano Sonata in A major, 9, 31, 46, 47, 63, 74,
78, 85, 114, 131, 145, 147, 175, 187, 198,
296–297, 306, 376, 441–448, 459
K. 332
Piano Sonata in F major, 46, 47, 63, 77, 90, 100,
105, 118, 144, 147, 167, 183, 187, 207, 216,
220, 221, 228, 231, 305, 328
K. 333
Piano Sonata in B-flat major, 45, 46, 59, 60,
63–65, 64–65, 106, 110, 122, 185, 192,
220, 263–264, 269, 322, 325–326, 435,
445
K. 339
"Laudate Dominum" from the *Vesperae
Solemnes de Confessore,* 165
K. 352
Variations for Piano, 31
K. 355
Piano Minuet in D major, 51
K. 359
Variations for Violin and Piano, 141
K. 361
Wind Serenade, 32, 285, 247
K. 364
Sinfonia Concertante, 51, 198
K. 365
Concerto for Two Pianos in E-flat major, 51, 69,
94–95, 98, 142, 180, 183, 191, 194–195,
196, 199, 201, 225, 261, 272, 286,
324–325, 328–329, 339, 451
K. 366
Idomeneo, 52
K. 37
Piano Concerto in F Major, 352, 383, 451
K. 375b
Sonata for Two Pianos, 77
K. 377
Violin Sonata in F major, 59, 87, 148, 223
K. 378
Piano and Violin Sonata in B-flat major Sonata,
176

K. 379
Sonata for Piano and Violin in G major, 73, 96,
125, 175, 177, 203, 452
K. 381
Sonata for Four Hands in D major, 75
K. 382
Concert Rondo in D major, 81, 121, 126, 225,
226, 257–258, 261, 299, 311, 365, 381, 383,
451
K. 385
"Haffner" Symphony, 66, 72, 81, 82, 164, 237
K. 386
Piano and Orchestra Rondo in A Major, 221,
451
K. 387
String Quartet in G major, 80
K. 388
Wind Serenade in C minor, 49
K. 39
Piano Concerto in B-flat major, 352, 451
K. 394
Piano Fantasia and Fugue in C major, 27, 37, 77,
78, 81, 274, 299, 380
K. 397
Piano Fantasia in D minor, 26, 45, 48, 123, 218,
254, 286, 337, 394
K. 398
Variations on "Salve tu Domine," 191, 194, 369
K. 40
Piano Concerto in D major, 17, 352, 451
K. 402
Violin and Piano Sonata for A major, 93
K. 406
Serenade for String Quintet, 49
K. 413
Piano Concerto in F major, 73, 256, 261, 344,
349, 352, 451
K. 414
Piano Concerto in A major, 73, 128, 144, 211,
251, 256, 258, 261, 264, 277, 281, 283,
286, 329, 344, 349, 352, 356, 359, 363,
365, 367, 369, 383, 451
K. 415
Piano Concerto in C major, 73, 225, 258, 264,
275, 277, 344, 349, 352, 353, 451
K. 421
String Quartet in D minor, 52–53
K. 425
"Linz" Symphony, 285
K. 426
Fugue for Two Pianos, 194
K. 427
Mass in C minor, 94, 273

K. 428
String Quartet in E-flat major, 424
K. 448
Sonata for Two Pianos in D major, 38, 39, 49,
75, 81, 173, 204, 206, 309
K. 449
Piano Concerto in E-flat major, 52, 76–77,
78, 100, 112, 130, 178, 186, 195, 205,
206, 256, 258, 261, 264, 265, 266, 339,
344, 345, 349, 358, 361, 362, 363, 364,
366–367, 381, 383, 386, 413, 415, 451,
453–454
K. 450
Piano Concerto in B-flat major, 31, 98, 171, 179,
193, 258, 260–261, 264, 271, 275, 277,
339, 344, 357, 358, 383, 386, 451, 458
K. 451
Piano Concerto in D major, 54, 114, 130, 167,
183, 185, 231, 216, 248, 250, 271, 272,
309, 329, 339, 344, 353, 354, 383, 451
K. 452
Quintet for Piano and Winds, 49, 50, 205, 273,
284, 364, 368, 452
K. 453
Piano Concerto in G major, 40, 93, 127, 131,
169, 170–171, 200, 202, 208, 209, 237,
251, 256, 257, 258, 260, 264, 265, 267,
269, 281, 282, 294, 301, 302, 344, 377,
383, 386, 451
K. 454
Piano and Violin Sonata in B-flat major, 47, 63,
64, 74, 77, 140, 143, 157, 175, 210, 216,
225, 284, 322
K. 455
„Unser dummer Pöbel meint," 31, 141, 157, 210,
253, 337, 461
K. 456
Piano Concerto in B-flat major, 122, 201, 205,
251, 259, 264, 265, 268, 270, 297, 325,
356, 362, 364, 367, 383, 386, 451
K. 457
Piano Sonata in C minor, 50, 51, 56, 68, 77,
81, 82, 83, 86, 89, 90, 131, 132, 133, 155,
184–185, 187, 195, 198, 216, 220, 221, 231,
238, 249, 284, 288, 328, 377, 378, 380,
390, 435, 446, 451, 458
K. 458
String Quartet in B-flat major, 54, 148, 154
K. 459
Piano Concerto in F major, 81, 82, 115, 149,
195, 235, 248, 251, 256, 253, 258, 259,
261, 262, 263, 265, 271, 279, 283, 294,
361, 362, 383, 451

K. 460
Sarti Variations, 31, 192, 197, 253–254, 455, 456
K. 465
String Quartet in C major, 21, 310
K. 466
Piano Concerto in D minor, 30, 31, 33, 34, 36,
37, 54, 55, 77, 82, 139–140, 153, 156, 167,
177–178, 186, 218, 233, 244, 245, 252,
253, 295, 298, 345, 346, 347, 348, 349,
350, 351, 353, 354, 360, 363, 384–395,
406, 419, 421, 451, 458
K. 467
Piano Concerto in C major, 51, 77, 81, 110, 113,
141, 183, 195, 201, 237–239, 248, 252, 253,
294, 337, 353, 383, 386, 451
Andante of the, 82, 237
K. 475
Piano Fantasia in C minor, 57, 62, 77, 112, 116,
119, 159, 177, 183, 254, 255, 288, 297, 307,
308, 316, 378, 380
K. 477
Masonic Funeral Music, 52, 120
K. 478
Piano Quartet in G minor, 62, 200, 221, 281,
285, 368
K. 481
Violin Sonata in E-flat major, 111, 399
K. 482
Piano Concerto in E-flat major, 37, 62, 66, 80,
83, 87, 97, 99, 130, 146, 174, 179, 180, 182,
193, 194, 196, 199, 204, 207, 215, 222,
223, 225, 226, 235, 241, 252, 253, 274,
294, 295, 297, 300, 309, 337, 347, 350,
362, 365, 374, 383, 386, 410, 413, 451, 459
K. 485
Piano Rondo in D major, 73, 131, 143, 150–151,
192, 293, 298
K. 488
Piano Concerto in A major, 38, 81, 82, 112, 116,
126, 199, 206, 216, 238–239, 252, 256,
257, 259, 260, 264, 297, 303, 330, 350,
357, 360, 361, 362, 365, 370, 374, 375, 381,
386, 396–405, 410, 451
K. 491
Piano Concerto in C minor, 15, 32, 62, 75, 112,
124, 155, 223, 225, 226, 234–237, 246,
248, 252, 253, 257, 273, 274, 292, 298,
302, 309, 310, 311, 327, 330–333, 360,
362, 368, 380, 381, 386, 406–432, 451,
455
K. 493
Piano Quartet, 368

K. 494
Piano Rondo in F major, 12, 73, 92, 149, 159, 175, 185, 186, 220, 269, 272, 381–382

K. 496
Piano Trio in G major, 63, 81, 180, 285

K. 497
Piano Sonata in F major for Four Hands, 46, 47, 95, 173, 284, 327–328

K. 498
Trio, 32

K. 501
Variations for Piano-Four Hands in G major, 9, 96, 184

K. 502
Piano Trio in B-flat major, 63, 295, 459

K. 503
Piano Concerto in C major, 51, 53, 62, 74, 81, 145–146, 185, 226, 233, 240–242, 248, 252, 256, 257, 274, 309, 333, 334, 335, 350, 383, 386, 451, 458

K. 511
Piano Rondo in A minor, 46, 51, 52, 61, 108, 123, 131, 171, 220, 232, 296, 344

K. 515
String Quintet in C major, 49, 50, 204

K. 521
Piano Sonata for Four Hands in C major, 94, 111, 113, 180, 207, 221, 285, 437

K. 522
Dorfmusikanten-Sextett, 50

K. 525
"Eine kleine Nachtmusik," 168, 198, 288, 311

K. 526
Violin Sonata in A major, 133, 452

K. 533
Piano Sonata in F major, 62, 73, 78, 82, 92, 115, 149, 171, 196, 204, 269, 272, 314, 369, 381, 458

K. 537
Piano Concerto in D major, 75, 121, 128, 215, 218, 221, 222, 225, 247, 248, 252, 256, 257, 298, 337, 354, 383, 419, 421, 451

K. 540
Piano Adagio in B minor, 58, 59, 77, 131, 146, 249, 274

K. 542
Piano Trio in E major, 21, 74, 205

K. 543
Symphony in E-flat major, 80, 221

K. 545
Sonata facile in C major, 145, 152, 303, 305, 441, 458

K. 548
Piano Trio in C major, 145, 299

K. 550
Symphony in G minor, 80, 83, 100, 110, 211, 310, 311, 391

K. 551
Jupiter Symphony, 65, 80, 83, 115, 128, 202

K. 570
Piano Sonata in B-flat major, 25, 115, 119, 131, 249, 299, 326, 327, 458

K. 573
Duport Variations, 29, 191, 206, 207, 253, 254, 380, 452

K. 576
Piano Sonata in D major, 51, 62, 65, 68, 77, 81, 83, 85, 120, 123, 182, 199, 249, 317, 458

K. 590
String Quartet Menuetto, 85

K. 593
String Quintet in D major, 49

K. 595
Piano Concerto in B-flat major, 32, 39, 63, 69, 75, 78, 82, 92, 96, 114, 115, 131, 145, 148, 175, 181, 191–192, 206, 218, 226, 242, 243, 251, 252, 253, 256, 258, 259, 262, 264, 265, 268, 270, 275, 276, 277, 284, 305, 314, 335–342, 344, 345, 348, 349, 350, 354, 355, 362, 372, 373, 383, 386, 419, 420, 451, 455

K. 589
String Quartet in B-flat major, 50

K. 613
Piano Variations, 181, 254, 277

K. 622
Clarinet Concerto, 32